MICHELIN
CHARMING PLACES TO STAY

1 000 hotels
and guesthouses
in France
for less than € 80

MICHELIN

Travel Publications

SUMMARY

INTRODUCTION

The guide

This first edition of **Michelin Charming Places to Stay** features a selection of 1 000 establishments at reasonable prices throughout France. Having travelled the length and breadth of France, our incognito inspectors were left free to make their own choices. From a tiny rustic inn to a prestigious medieval castle, from clifftop villages and historic market towns to Paris itself, the following represents their all-time favourites for authenticity, character, warmth and setting. All the establishments in this guide have one thing in common - that special something which makes a memorable holiday.

All offer double rooms for two people at under € 80 a night, half are under € 55 and 113 establishments offer double rooms at a top price of € 40, indicated by the €€€ sign. The prices for meals and half board, when appropriate, are, however, per person. A few lines at the top of each description, indicated by our familiar 🙂, aim to highlight the little extra that we particularly liked and want to share with you, whether it be "Waking up to the enticing aroma of fresh bread", "Your hosts' friendly welcome" or simply a few words to set the scene. The guide is divided into 21 French regions and the establishments are listed by département and place within each region.

Maps

The map of France at the beginning of the guide shows the 21 regions and their départements. At the beginning of each chapter is a regional map with the hotels marked in blue and the maisons d'hôte in red; each has a number which corresponds to the number at the top of the establishment's description. The maps and directions in this guide use the metric system for reasons of practicality; as a reminder 1km = about 0.6miles. Always allow plenty of time for your journey and make sure you have the latest edition of the Michelin Atlas France or the new Local maps.

Gîtes, maisons d'hôte, chambres d'hôte and tables d'hôte

A gîte is a self-catering cottage or flat. Maisons and chambres d'hôte are, loosely speaking, bed & breakfast establishments and generally have fewer rooms than a conventional hotel. Often converted mills, country houses or farms, they are also the private homes of the people who will welcome you and endeavour to make your stay as

pleasant as possible. We definitely recommend booking ahead, particularly during the summer or the long spring weekends. You should also call if you think you may arrive late in the evening. Some offer dining facilities (table d'hôte), others don't and this also should be booked. This home-cooked set menu at a fixed price is usually served only to residents: you may be invited to sit down with the family and other guests at a large communal table or the dining room may have a number of small tables. There is no rule, or rather the only rule is to treat your hosts as if they were friends who had invited you down for a weekend, which is often what your stay will feel like.

Hotels

Many of our hotels are in converted castles, mansions,

convents, abbeys and the like. As with the chambres d'hôte, all have been selected for their character, tranquillity and hospitality. The rooms are pleasant, ranging from simple to luxurious, many are personalised and all are warm and welcoming. Each has its own distinctive and often indefinable charm.

Indexes

All the establishments in the guide are listed in alphabetical order in the index.
The general index is supplemented by three themed indexes:
- **Low price:** this index lists all the €€ establishments which offer double rooms for two at under € 40 a night.

- **Wining and dining breaks:** this index lists all the gastronomic establishments whose cooking we found particularly worthy of mention.
- **Activity breaks:** this includes all the establishments which have a swimming pool and also offer at least one other sport (fishing, riding, tennis, golf, etc.).

Exploring France

Staying in hotels and chambres d'hôte like these is an opportunity to discover an area off the beaten track or an aspect of France that you perhaps weren't aware of. With this in mind, we point out opportunities to explore your hosts' region, whether it be on foot, by bicycle, by boat or on horseback. You might also want to delve into the Michelin Green Guide of the region you are visiting for further historic or cultural information.

We have endeavoured to make this guide practical and readable and trust that it will accompany you on family holidays and romantic weekends. We have included a questionnaire at the back of the guide: all your comments and suggestions for new addresses are most welcome. They will help us make the next edition even better than the first.

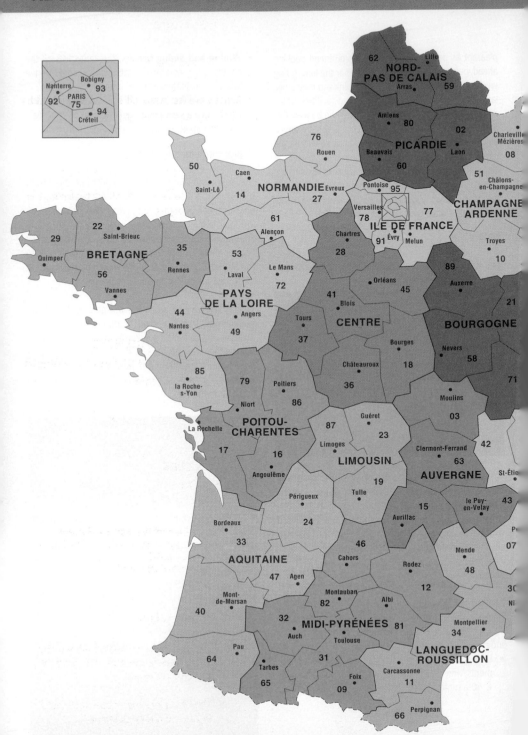

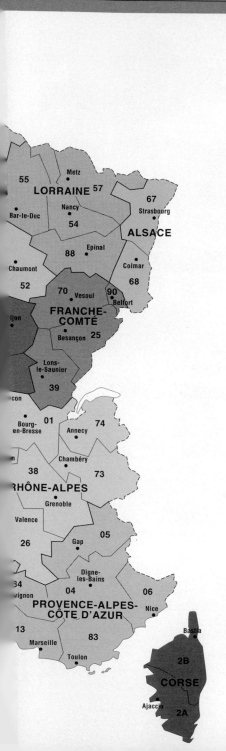

- ALSACE
- AQUITAINE
- AUVERGNE
- BURGUNDY
- BRITTANY
- CENTRE AND UPPER LOIRE VALLEY
- CHAMPAGNE-ARDENNE
- CORSICA
- FRANCHE-COMTÉ
- ÎLE-DE-FRANCE AND PARIS
- LANGUEDOC-ROUSSILLON
- LIMOUSIN
- LORRAINE
- MIDI-PYRÉNÉES
- NORD-PAS-DE-CALAIS
- NORMANDY
- PAYS-DE-LA-LOIRE
- PICARDY
- POITOU-CHARENTES
- PROVENCE-ALPS - FRENCH RIVIERA
- RHÔNE-ALPES

Symbols used in the guide

 Number of the establishment in the guide and on the regional map: blue for hotels red for maisons d'hôte

 Hotel

 Maison d'hôte

 Hotel or maison d'hôte offering rooms at a maximum price of € 40 per night for a double room

 The little extra that makes the hotel or maison d'hôte different

ALSACE

Alsace is perhaps the most romantic of France's regions, a place of fairy-tale castles guarding the foothills of the mountains, gentle vine-clad slopes and picturesque dolls' house villages perched on rocky outcrops or nestling in lush green valleys. From Colmar's Little Venice with its flower-decked balconies and famous storks to Strasbourg's Christmas market whose multicoloured lights illuminate the magnificent cathedral or the half-timbered houses of Little France reflected in the meanders of the River Ill, an inner warmth radiates from Alsace that even the cold winter winds cannot chill. So make a beeline for the boisterous atmosphere of a brasserie and sample a real Alsace beer or head for a picturesque *winstub* – wine bar – and tuck into a steaming dish of choucroute – sauerkraut with smoked pork – and a huge slice of *kugelhof* cake, all washed down with a glass of fruity Sylvaner or Riesling wine.

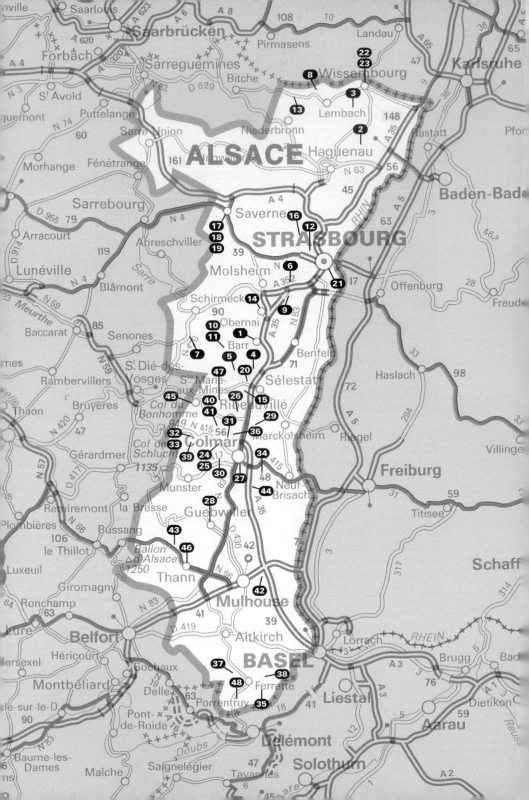

BARR - 67140

BETSCHDORF - 67660

 1 CHÂTEAU D'ANDLAU
Mr Boulard

 113 allée St-Ulrich
67140 Barr
Tel. : 03 88 08 96 78
Fax : 03 88 08 00 93
hotel.château-andlau @ wanadoo.fr

Closed in Jan • 23 rooms, 6 of which have bath/WC,
16 have shower/WC and 10 have television • €42 to €61;
breakfast €7 • Closed lunchtime during the week, Sun
evening and Mon; menus €20 to €39, children's menu
€8 • Private car park, garage, no dogs allowed in rooms

2 KRUMEICH
Mr Krumeich

 23 rue des Potiers
67660 Betschdorf
Tel. : 03 88 54 40 56
Fax : 03 88 54 47 67

Open all year • 3 rooms • €53, breakfast included • No
table d'hôte • Garden, car park. No dogs allowed
• Pottery courses

We most liked
The well-preserved rustic character.

We most liked
**The warm welcome of the owner, who
is also a potter.**

This long, half-timbered inn surrounded by woodland
stands on the banks of the Kirneck, making a pretty rural
picture just off the road to one of Alsace's most
important pilgrimage sites, Mont Sainte Odile. The inn's
new restaurant boasts an extravagant selection of over
1 000 appellation wines, with a house preference for
champagne. The lovely gardens and the guarantee of
a good night's sleep make it a haven for pollution-weary
urbanites!

Situated in the heart of a village renowned for its
stoneware pottery, this large property provides clean,
quiet rooms decorated with elegant period furniture
– including beautiful wardrobes – and a lovely shaded
flower garden. The owner, the proud descendant of a
long line of potters, organises introductory pottery
courses all year long.

Access : Drive westbound for 2km on the Mont
Ste-Odile road (D 854)

Access : 15 km north-east of Haguenau, towards
Wissembourg on the D 263 then the D 243

 3 **KLEIN**
Mrs Klein

59 rue Principale
67160 Cleebourg
Tel. : 03 88 94 50 95
annejp.kleinlaposte.net

Open all year • 3 rooms • €38, breakfast included • Table
d'hôte €12 • Garden, car park. Credit cards not accepted

 4 **LE VIGNOBLE**
Mr Boulanger

1 rue de l'Église
67650 Dambach-la-Ville
Tel. : 03 88 92 43 75
Fax : 03 88 92 62 21

Closed from 22 Jun to 4 Jul, from 24 Dec to 9 Mar, and
Sun out of season • 7 rooms, one of which has disabled
access, most have bath/WC, all have television • €45 to
€50; breakfast €6 • No restaurant • Private car park. No
dogs allowed

 **The lovingly preserved, authentic
Alsatian décor.**

This 18C-19C Alsatian house in the heart of an
acclaimed wine-growing village could well prove
irresistible: there's no mistaking the true Alsatian style.
The peaceful rooms, all on the ground floor, are
decorated with pristine antique furniture; wood is the
predominant feature of the dining room which serves
typical regional cuisine. Guests can relax in the pretty
garden to the rear.

 **Walking along the Dambach wine
path.**

This hotel's architecture is characteristic of the modest
wine-growers houses dotted along the Wine Route. A
narrow façade facing onto the street, only the upper
residential storey of which has the traditional half-
timbering, and a ground floor devoted to grape pressing
equipment and the cellar. The peaceful rooms have
retained their oak beams and the bells of the
neighbouring church remain considerably silent during
the night. Family breakfast room.

Access : 7km south-west of Wissembourg on the
D 7, in the centre of the village

Access : In the centre of the village

 5 LA ROMANCE
Mr Geiger

17 route de Neuve-Église
67220 Dieffenbach-au-Val
Tel. : 03 88 85 67 09
Fax : 03 88 57 61 58
corinne @ la-romance.net
www.la-romance.net

Open all year • 4 rooms, one of which is split-level, two have sitting rooms • €70, breakfast included • No table d'hôte • Garden, car park. No dogs allowed • Sauna and spa

 6 PÈRE BENOIT
Mr Massé

34 route de Strasbourg
67960 Entzheim
Tel. : 03 88 68 98 00
Fax : 03 88 68 64 56
hotel.perebenoit @ wanadoo.fr
www.hotel-pere-benoit.com

Closed from 4 to 25 Aug and from 23 Dec to 6 Jan • 60 rooms on 2 floors, 4 of which have disabled access, all have bath/WC and television • €51 to €72; breakfast €7 • Air-conditioned restaurant; menu €17 • Terrace, garden. Private car park. No dogs allowed in restaurant • Fitness room, sun deck

We most liked **The modern comfort of this pretty regional residence.**

Although rather difficult to find, this snug house is so comfortable that, once over the threshold, you may not want to leave! Warm welcome and spotless interior. The well-appointed, tastefully decorated rooms are named after flowers and trees and two of them overlook the valley. Add to this a warm welcome, spotless housekeeping and a garden on the edge of the forest which is the perfect spot for breakfasts in the summertime.

We most liked **A farmhouse full of character near Strasbourg airport.**

Behind the half-timbered, red façade of this genuine 18C Alsatian farmhouse, a range of dining choices reveals a real love of good food. Take your pick from a family dining room, the adorable balcony-cum-terrace installed under a wooden gallery, a snug "winstub" – literally a "wine room" with paintings, wood panelling and earthenware stove – or a vaulted cellar serving local tartes flambées. Snug rooms, most overlooking a peaceful flowered courtyard.

Access : 12km north-west of Sélestat on the N 59 and the D 424, towards Villé

Access : 12km from Strasbourg on the A 35 (exit no 8), then take the D 400 and D 392

  7 **JULIEN**
Mr Goetz

 12 route Nationale
67130 Fouday
Tel. : 03 88 97 30 09
Fax : 03 88 97 36 73
hoteljulien@wanadoo.com
www.hoteljulien.com

Closed from 3 to 20 Jan and for several days in Oct
• 45 rooms, 8 of which are split-level, all have bath/WC
or shower/WC and television • €52 to €79, breakfast
€8 • Air-conditioned restaurant, closed Tue; menus
€10.50 (lunchtime) to €34 • Terrace, garden, indoor
swimming pool. Car park • Indoor pool, sauna, jacuzzi.
Tours of Alsace

   8 **GIMBELHOF**
Mr Gunder

 67510 Gimbelhof
Tel. : 03 88 94 43 58
Fax : 03 88 94 23 30

Closed 20 Nov to 26 Nov and during the February
holidays • 7 rooms, most of which have shower/WC
• €32 to €38; breakfast €5; half board €32 to €37 • Restaurant closed Mon and Tue; menus €11 (in the week)
to €26 • Car park

We most liked **The scenic valley view with the hotel's footbridge in the foreground.**

We most liked **The ruins and caves of Fleckenstein Castle.**

Even though the street façade with its copper-roofed
overhang may strike visitors as unusual, it is nothing
in comparison to the breathtaking sight of the garden
side simply overflowing with flowers. In just a few years
this family-run establishment has evolved immensely
and the rooms reflect this renovation, ranging from
comfortable to luxurious. Another of the establishment's
appeals is its delicious regional cuisine.

A narrow forest road leads to this unassuming family
inn hidden away in the dense woodland of Northern
Vosges. The countrified rooms and dining room are
simply furnished but there is no better starting point for
nature lovers, walkers and history enthusiasts to explore
the surrounding countryside. A fir tree-lined footpath
winds its way past four ancient fortresses, along the
edge of the Franco-German border affording superb
views over the Palatinate countryside.

Access : On leaving the village drive towards
Schirmeck

Access : Leave Lembach on the D 3, after 3.5km
take a right onto the D 925, then the forest road on
the right

 9 AU CEP DE VIGNE
Mr Schall

5 route de Barr
67880 Innenheim
Tel. : 03 88 95 75 45
Fax : 03 88 95 79 73

Closed from 15 to 28 Feb, Mon (except the hotel) and Sun evening • 36 rooms, one of which has disabled access, all have bath/WC or shower/WC and television • €46 to €61; breakfast €7; half board €51 • Menus €15 (evenings in the week) to €38 • Garden, car park

 10 CHAMBRE D'HÔTE TILLY'S INN
Mr and Mrs Hazemann

28 rue Principale
67140 Le Hohwald
Tel. : 03 88 08 30 17
Fax : 03 88 08 30 17

Open all year • 3 rooms • €49; breakfast €8 • Table d'hôte €16 • Car park. Credit cards not accepted, no dogs allowed

 Hospitality in the old French tradition.

The steep eaves, impressive half-timbered façades and wooden balconies are in keeping with the consistently high hotel standards and attention to detail shown by the Schall family, owners of this traditional establishment since 1902. The rooms vary from functional and light to rustic and a little dark; ask for one of the quieter ones overlooking the garden. Cosy dining room with dark wood panelling and carved ceiling.

 The conspicuous, brightly coloured decoration.

The bright red façade decorated with naive paintings makes it impossible to miss this guesthouse. The interior decoration is just as colourful, beginning with the breakfast room, painted in vivid hues and further embellished by a 19C piano and a wooden horse from a merry-go-round. The rooms, some of which are lined in wood, are less ostentatious and the two suites are extremely spacious. Warm, friendly welcome.

Access : Between Strasbourg and Obernai, in the village

Access : In the village

11 CLOS ERMITAGE
Mr Heguenauer

34 rue du Wittertalhof
67140 Le Hohwald
Tel. : 03 88 08 31 31
Fax : 03 88 08 34 99

Closed from 2 Jan to 9 Feb, from 4 Nov to 15 Dec and Tue • 12 rooms, one of which has disabled access and 7 are studios with kitchenettes. All the rooms have bath/WC and television • €68 (€53 low season) studios €57 to €73; breakfast €9 • No restaurant, but it is possible to have meals at the nearby La Petite Auberge • Park, car park • Indoor swimming pool, fitness room with sauna and jacuzzi

We most liked **The Hohwald region, popular with pilgrims and tourists alike.**

This former 19C hermitage lies in the heart of the lush, green meadows of the Hohwald on the edge of a pine forest. The ancient walls and beams have been well preserved and the interior has recently been restored. The range of accommodation is such, from rooms, studios with kitchenettes, split two- and three-level suites to lakeside cabins, that something can be found for everyone, whether they be families, couples or single travellers. In this country setting, peace and quiet are guaranteed.

Access : On the outskirts of the village, 1.5km on a minor road

12 AU TILLEUL
Mrs Lorentz

5 route de Strasbourg
67206 Mittelhausbergen
Tel. : 03 88 56 18 31
Fax : 03 88 56 07 23
autilleul @ wanadoo.fr
www.autilleul.com

Closed from 15 Feb to 5 Mar and from 29 Jul to 16 Aug • 12 rooms, one of which has disabled access, 3 are non-smoking and all have bath/WC and television • €50; breakfast €8; half board €45 to €48 • Restaurant closed Tue and Wed; menus €15 (lunchtime in the week) to €55 • Car park

We most liked **A cooking lesson in the family atmosphere of this inn close to Strasbourg.**

Within easy reach of France's "Capital of Europe", this unpretentious country inn dates from 1888. Its spotless, modern rooms are enlivened by painted furniture and some of the attic rooms have sloped skylight windows. The family dining room has recently been redone and treated to new tableware. In the kitchen, the accent is on fresh local produce with a subtle southern influence. Cooking lessons given all year round.

Access : 5km north-west of Strasbourg on the D 31

NIEDERSTEINBACH - 67510 **OBERNAI - 67210**

13 **AU CHEVAL BLANC**
Mr Zinck

11 rue Principale
67510 Niedersteinbach
Tel. : 03 88 09 55 31
Fax : 03 88 09 50 24
contact @ hotel-cheval-blanc.fr
www.hotel-cheval-blanc.fr

Closed 28 Jan to 7 Mar, late Jun to early Jul and late Nov to early Dec • 25 rooms, 3 of which are suites, with bath/WC or shower/WC and television • €48 to €53; breakfast €8; half board €49 • Menus €16 (in the week) to €50 • Terrace, garden. No dogs allowed in restaurant • Outdoor swimming pool, tennis, children's play area

14 **LA CLOCHE**
Mrs Drendel and Mr Friedrich

90 rue du Général Gouraud
67210 Obernai
Tel. : 03 88 95 52 89
Fax : 03 88 95 07 63
hotel.lacloche @ wanadoo.fr

Closed from 4 to 19 Jan • 20 rooms with bath/WC or shower/WC, all have television • €43 to €49; breakfast €6; half board €42 to €45 • Part of the restaurant is air-conditioned; closed Sun evenings from mid-Nov to Mar; menus €23 to €36

We most liked
The owners' gracious welcome.

We most liked
Opening the shutters onto a delightful market square.

An impressive traditional country inn set in the midst of a land of medieval fortresses dating from the Holy Roman Empire. Most of the slightly old-fashioned, but comfortable and well-kept rooms overlook wooded vales; ask for one which doesn't overlook the street. Tuck into generously served regional dishes served in cosy, regional dining rooms, modelled after the "winstub" wine-bar. Half-timbered reading room. Former German leader and keen gastronome, Helmut Kohl, is said to be a regular!

This historic house, located in the heart of Obernai, stands on 14C foundations. A 16C well with six pails stands proudly in front of the hotel. The recently renovated rooms are not immense but are well appointed and very reasonably priced. Don't miss the hotel's pride and joy in one of the dining rooms: a sumptuous décor of marquetry and frescoes signed by a master craftsman, Spindler.

Access : 8 km north-west of Lembach on the D 3, towards Bitche

Access : On the main square, opposite the town hall

 15 LE FIEF DU CHÂTEAU
Mr and Mrs Fretz

 20 Grand'Rue
67600 Orschwiller
Tel. : 03 88 82 56 25
Fax : 03 88 82 26 24
info@fief-château.com
www.fieff-château.com

Closed from 7 to 21 Jan, from 25 to 30 Jun, from 12 to 20 Nov and Wed • 8 rooms, most have bath/WC, all have a television • €45; breakfast €7; half board €43 • Menus €17 to €32 • Car park

 16 LA MAISON DU CHARRON
Mrs Gass

 15 rue Principale
67370 Pfettisheim
Tel. : 03 88 69 60 35
Fax : 03 88 69 85 45

Open all year • 5 rooms, 2 are split-level and 2 are gîtes • €48, breakfast included • No table d'hôte • Garden. Credit cards not accepted

We most liked **The delightful welcome and family atmosphere.**

The simply decorated façade of this late-19C house, brightened up by summer window boxes of geraniums, hides a warm, friendly interior. Spotless family-sized rooms. Traditional dishes with a local flavour are served in a bright, beamed dining room, accompanied by some of the region's famous vintages: this is on the famous Wine Route after all!

We most liked **The personalised decoration of each room.**

The owners of these two 1858 houses enthusiastically took a hand in their renovation. The master-carpenter husband undertook the individual decoration of the rooms, each of which is devoted to a different essence: birch, maple, larch, etc, while his wife, a gifted seamstress, decorated the house with her patchworks. The small garden is very pleasant in the summer and the horses are always popular with children.

Access : Between Ribeauvillé and Sélestat; at Saint-Hippolyte take the road to Haut-Koenigsbourg

Access : 13km north-west of Strasbourg on the D 31

17 LE CLOS DE LA GARENNE
Mr Schmitt

88 route du Haut Barr
67700 Saverne
Tel. : 03 88 7120 41
Fax : 03 88 02 08 86

Closed for the first fortnight in Jul • 12 rooms with bath/WC or shower/WC and television • €61 to €84, breakfast €7 • Restaurant closed Tue evening, Sat lunchtime and Wed; menus €12.20 (lunchtime) to €58.50 • Car park, park

The landscaped gardens.

This early-20C family residence is peacefully located on the edge of a forest of fir trees. It is impossible to resist the temptation to snuggle up in the individually decorated rooms furnished in a tasteful period or country style. The all-wood, snug dining room is reminiscent of an old mountain-pasture inn. The terrace overlooks a landscaped park on a hillside.

18 EUROPE
Mr Kuhry

7 rue de la Gare
67700 Saverne
Tel. : 03 88 71 12 07
Fax : 03 88 71 11 43
info @ hotel-europe-fr.com
www.hotel-europe-fr.com

Open all year • 28 rooms, 20 of which have shower/WC, 8 have bath/WC, all have television • €58 to €81, breakfast €9 • No restaurant • Garage, public car park nearby • Visits to the nearby Château des Rohans

The individual decoration of each room.

Within easy reach of the station and the castle on the banks of the canal which links the Marne to the Rhine, this family-owned business has recently been partly refurbished. In keeping with the hotel's namesake, each spacious room features a different European style: the choice includes "Scandinavian", "French", "English" and "contemporary". A delightful sitting room decorated with frescoes and an Art Nouveau-style breakfast room. Private garage and car park opposite.

Access : From place des Dragons take the road to Haut Barr Castle

Access : Near the railway station

19 CHEZ JEAN
Mr Harter

3 rue de la Gare
67700 Saverne
Tel. : 03 88 91 10 19
Fax : 03 88 91 27 45
chez-jean@wanadoo.fr
www.chez-jean.com

Closed from 20 Dec to 10 Jan; restaurant closed Mon (open Mon evening in the summer) and Sun evening • 25 rooms with bath/WC or shower/WC, all have television • €56 to €74; breakfast €9; half board €66 to €69 • Restaurant: menus €23 to €37; Winstub S'Rosestiebel: à la carte for around €30 • No dogs allowed • Sauna, sunbed

 Saverne's rose garden on the banks of the Zorn with over 7 500 roses and 550 varieties.

Midway between the station and the city centre, with Rohan Castle and its old wood-framed houses, the well-groomed 17C façade is said to have once housed a convent. Some of the snug, inviting rooms are appointed with painted Alsatian furniture. For dinner, there's a choice to be made: the elegant, panelled Louis XIII-style room with a traditional menu to match, or S'Rosestiebel, based on the traditional "winstub" (wine bar) and serving wholesome country dishes.

Access : In the town centre

20 AUBERGE RAMSTEIN
Mr and Mrs Ramstein

1 rue du Riesling
67750 Scherwiller
Tel. : 03 88 82 17 00
Fax : 03 88 82 17 02

Closed from 15 Feb to 2 Mar, Sun evening and Wed • 15 rooms, one of which has disabled access, with bath/WC or shower/WC, all have television • €42 to €52; breakfast €7; half board €49 • Menus €23 to €40 • Terrace, car park • Mountain bike rental

 The walks through the vineyards.

Good country cooking, gargantuan breakfasts with cooked meats and home-made jams, spacious, pristine rooms, all thoughtfully equipped, superb views overlooking the vineyards, a warm Franco-Austrian welcome and attentive staff. Recently built along traditional lines, the Auberge may lack the charm of Alsace's older residences, but its desire to please more than compensates for this shortcoming.

Access : North-west of Sélestat on the N 59, at Châtenois turn right onto the D 35

  21 **DIANA-DAUPHINE**
Mr Baly

30 rue de la 1ʳᵉ Armée
67000 Strasbourg
Tel. : 03 88 36 26 61
Fax : 03 88 35 50 07
hotel.dianadauphine@wanadoo.fr
www.hotel-diana-dauphine.com

Closed from 22 Dec to 1 Jan • 45 rooms, 41 have bath/WC, 4 have shower/WC and all have television • €76 to €84, breakfast €9 • No restaurant • Garage

 Comfortable bedrooms and sitting rooms.

Within walking distance of the Place de l'Étoile, this hotel provides impeccable rooms whose decoration is loosely based on Louis XV and Louis XVI styles. A distinctly contemporary style has been adopted for the sitting room which overlooks a pleasant breakfast room and leads into the lobby. Excellent soundproofing means that the traffic in the busy street and the nearby trams do not spoil the establishment's calm. Useful private garage.

Access : Near the town centre, towards Place du Marechal De Lattre-de-Tassigny

  22 **HOSTELLERIE DU CYGNE**
Mr and Mrs Eberhardt

3 rue du Sel
67160 Wissembourg
Tel. : 03 88 94 00 16
Fax : 03 88 54 38 28
hostellerie-cygne@wanadoo.fr

Closed from 12 to 28 Feb, from 26 Jun to 12 Jul, from 13 to 28 Nov and Wed • 16 rooms in two adjacent houses, with bath/WC or shower/WC, all have television • €50 to €65; breakfast €7; half board €49 to €58 • Restaurant closed on Thu lunchtime and Sun evening; menus €25 (in the week) to €52 • Terrace. No dogs allowed in rooms

 The Salt House (1448) and its amazing roof.

This inn's two buildings, one of which was built in the late 14C and the other in 1535, typify the style of this well-preserved small town, where over 70 of the houses date from before 1700. The bedrooms, somewhat old-fashioned but still comfortable, are ideal for an overnight halt. The restaurant's two dining rooms are lit by stained-glass windows; the cosiest has recently been embellished with a lovely marquetry ceiling. A terrace in the courtyard overlooks a handsome half-timbered façade.

Access : In the town centre, next to the town hall

ALSACE

WISSEMBOURG - 67160 | AMMERSCHWIHR - 68770

23 AU MOULIN DE LA WALK
Mr Schmitt

2 rue de la Walk
67160 Wissembourg
Tel. : 03 88 94 06 44
Fax : 03 88 54 38 03
hotel.moulin.la.walk @ wanadoo.fr
www.moulin-walk.com

Closed from 7 to 28 Jan and from 18 Jun to 4 Jul • 25 rooms, one of which has disabled access, with bath/WC or shower/WC and television • €48 to €54; breakfast €6; half board €52 to €55 • Restaurant closed Sun evening, Mon and Fri lunchtime; menus €29 to €37 • Terrace, garden, car park. No dogs allowed in rooms

 A slice or two of raisin cake – the famous "kugelhof" – at breakfast time.

This cluster of buildings built on the foundations of an old mill, whose well-preserved wheel is still in working order, stands on the banks of the Lauter on the outskirts of the town. Most of the rooms have been refurbished. Tasty, traditional fare is served in a cosy, wainscoted dining room and a pretty flowered terrace.

Access : Out of the town centre, on the banks of the Lauter

24 AUX ARMES DE FRANCE
Mr Gaertner

1 Grand' Rue
68770 Ammerschwihr
Tel. : 03 89 47 10 12
Fax : 03 89 47 38 12
aux.armes.de.France @ wanadoo.fr
www.aux-armes-de-france.com

Closed from 17 to 27 Feb, Wed and Thu • 10 rooms with bath/WC and television • €66 to €81; breakfast €11.50 • Menus €43 to €87, children's menu €18.50 • Private car park • Located in the heart of the Alsace vineyards. Golf 1km away

 Good taste abounds in this warm Alsatian inn.

Numerous famous chefs have learnt their craft in this handsome house rebuilt after the air raids of the Second World War. Its long culinary tradition dates back to the Thirties, when the grandmother of the present chef ruled the kitchen. Spacious rooms and a bourgeois-style dining room where mouth-watering dishes are served under the watchful eye of ancestors' portraits. Definitely worth tasting!

Access : At the entrance to the town centre

25 MAISON THOMAS
Thomas family

41 Grand'Rue
68770 Ammerschwihr
Tel. : 03 89 78 23 90
Fax : 03 89 47 18 90
thomas.guy@free.fr
www.thomas.guy.free.fr

Open all year • 4 rooms with a kitchenette • €44, breakfast included • No table d'hôte • Garden, car park. Credit cards not accepted • Sauna

26 CHEZ NORBERT
Mr Moeller

9 Grand'Rue
68750 Bergheim
Tel. : 03 89 73 31 15
Fax : 03 89 73 60 65

Closed from mid-Feb to mid-Mar, Wed lunchtime and Thu • 12 rooms, some split-level, most have bath/WC, all have television • €68; breakfast €9; half board €84 • Menus €27 (lunchtime in the week) to €48 • Terrace, courtyard, private car park

Extremely well-appointed rooms.

Home-made cakes and jams for breakfast.

This former wine-grower's house – painted an unmissable turquoise – stands in the most picturesque part of the village. Each of the spacious, well-equipped rooms carries a name and all have kitchenettes. The well thought-out garden has something for everyone: a shaded corner for afternoon naps, bower, barbecue, swings, table-tennis and boules, not forgetting the view over the vineyards. The house also boasts a sauna and keep-fit equipment.

The cachet of this group of wine-growers' farms is undeniable. The colourful, half-timbered façades (14C) vie for pride of place with the other picturesque houses of this town on the Alsace Wine Route. Some of the contemporary, practical rooms are located under the eaves; ask for one overlooking the courtyard. Good country fare served in a typically Alsatian restaurant or on a pleasant terrace, bedecked with geraniums in the summer.

Access : In the village

Access : On the main street in the centre of the village

27 **TURENNE**
Mr Glé

10 route de Bâle
68000 Colmar
Tel. : 03 89 21 58 58
Fax : 03 89 41 27 64
turennecol @ aol.com
www.turenne.com

Open all year • 83 rooms, 42 of which are non-smoking, all have bath/WC or shower/WC and television • €41 to €63; breakfast €7.50 • No restaurant • Garage

28 **CHÂTEAU DE LA PRAIRIE**
Mr Hetzel

Allée des Marronniers
68500 Guebwiller
Tel. : 03 89 74 28 57
Fax : 03 89 74 71 88
prairie @ chateauxhotels.com
www.chateau-prairie.com

Open all year • 18 rooms, 4 of which are non-smoking, most have bath/WC, all have television • €59 to €89; breakfast €8 • No restaurant • Park, private car park

 A convenient distance from the old town.

Conveniently located two minutes away from the picturesque Little Venice district, you can't miss the distinctive pink and yellow façade of this large house. Spacious, refurbished double rooms some of which have traditional regional furniture. Smaller, single rooms, equally well-kept and soundproofed, are also available. Breakfasts are served in a typically Alsatian dining room. Wainscoted sitting room and bar, heaven-sent private garage and friendly family welcome.

 The five-acre private grounds, parts of which are virtually wilderness!

This small manor house, built in 1858 for a local industrialist, had long been threatened with ruin, but it has recently been rescued and restored. The spacious bedrooms, some with terrace, still seem a little bare but, refurbished in a rural style, they have recovered a little of their former glory; delicate ceiling moulding and original parquet floors add to the period charm. Settle down with a book in of the many wainscoted sitting rooms, warmed by open fires.

Access : Coming from the railway station, head for the A 35 motorway and turn left at the Elf petrol station

Access : To the north-west of Mulhouse on the D430

 29 LES HIRONDELLES
Mr and Mrs Muller

33 rue du 25 Janvier
68970 Illhaeusern
Tel. : 03 89 71 83 76
Fax : 03 89 71 86 40
hotelleshirondelles@wanadoo.fr
www.hotelleshirondelles.com

Hotel closed in Feb and from 20 to 27 Dec • 19 rooms, most have shower/WC, all have television • €51 to €55, breakfast €7, half board €53 • The "Restaurant à la Truite" nearby • Garden, private car park, No dogs allowed in restaurant • Outdoor swimming pool

 The swallows, which really do make the summer.

Rustic painted furniture and oak beams set the tone of the relatively soberly-decorated rooms which overlook a flowered inner courtyard or a picture-book landscape of kitchen gardens. The recent swimming pool, complete with teak sun-deck and air-conditioning in the adjacent accommodation building makes the hotel very pleasant during the hot summer months. The dining room is tastefully decorated with wood panelling and traditional Alsatian ornaments.

Access : In the centre of the village

 30 À L' AGNEAU
Mr and Mrs Mann

16 Grand'Rue
68230 Katzenthal
Tel. : 03 89 80 90 25
Fax : 03 89 27 59 58
hotel-restaurant.agneau@wanadoo.fr
www.hotelrestaurantagneau.fr

Closed from 6 Jan to 5 Feb, early Jul and from 12 to 20 Nov • 10 rooms, 2 of which are in a separate wing, with shower/WC and some with television • €51 to €55, breakfast €7, half board €43 to €54 • Restaurant closed Mon and Tue but open in the evenings in season; menus €15 (in the week) to €43 • Private car park. No dogs allowed in rooms • Wine tasting

 The tour of the family's wine business.

The creamy façade and blue shutters of this house in the heart of a wine-growing town catch the eye of all who pass. The almost monastical rooms are spotlessly kept and some enjoy a view over the vineyard. Two newer annexe rooms, added in 1998, are a touch more spacious and up-to-date. The menu features excellent Alsatian dishes, complete with wine from the estate. The young husband and wife team are known for their warm welcome.

Access : In the centre of the village

ALSACE

 31 **HOSTELLERIE SCHWENDI**
Mr and Mrs Schillé

2 place Schwendi
68240 Kientzheim
Tel. : 03 89 47 30 50
Fax : 03 89 49 04 49

Hotel closed from 2 Jan to 15 Mar, and Wed. Restaurant closed 23 Dec to 15 Mar, Thu lunchtime and Wed • 17 rooms all with bath/WC and television • €67; breakfast €7 • Menus €19 to €51 • Terrace, private car park

 32 **LES ALISIERS**
Mr and Mrs Degouy

68650 Lapoutroie
Tel. : 03 89 47 52 82
Fax : 03 89 47 22 38
jacques.degouy@wanadoo.fr
www.alisiers.com

Closed 3 Jan to 3 Feb, 20 to 26 Dec, Mon evening and Tue (except the hotel in season) • 18 rooms, one of which has disabled access and 5 are non-smoking. Rooms have bath/WC or shower/WC • €60 to €92; breakfast €9; half board €55 to €84 • Non-smoking restaurant; menus €14 to €36 • Terrace, garden, car park. No dogs allowed

 The delightful welcome of the hotel owners-cum-wine-growers.

 The kindness of the staff and the owners.

An old well, around which the terrace is laid in the summer, stands in the paved courtyard of this 17C inn. Guests are accommodated in rooms with old oak-beamed ceilings; it's worth asking for one of the renovated rooms. A likeable blend of the rustic and the classical – Louis XIII chairs and bare stone walls – adds a cosy feel to the dining room, where wholesome country cooking is served with glasses of home-made wine.

All the windows of this extended farmhouse built in 1819 overlook the pleasant, rolling countryside of the Béhine Valley, whether it be from the snug and countrified or more contemporary rooms; you can choose your favourite on the hotel's web-site. The veranda restaurant shares the same great view; generous helpings of regional cooking, with an accent on local produce, are served in the non-smoking dining room. Pleasant garden overlooking the village of Lapoutroie.

Access : 3km to the east of Kaysersberg on the D 28

Access : In the upper reaches of the village, 3km to the south-west on a minor road

 33 **DU FAUDÉ**
Mr and Mrs Baldinger

28 rue du Général Dufieux
68650 Lapoutroie
Tel. : 03 89 47 50 35
Fax : 03 89 47 24 82
info @ faude.com
www.faude.com

Closed from 27 Feb to 16 Mar and from 4 to 29 Nov
• 31 rooms, 2 of which are suites, with bath/WC or shower/WC, all have television • €61 to €80; breakfast €9; half board €55 to €73 • Menus €15 to €65, children's menu €10 • Garden, terrace, private car park • Indoor swimming pool, fitness room, hammam, jacuzzi, skiing

 34 **À LA VIGNE**
Mr Bauer

5 Grande-Rue
68280 Logelheim
Tel. : 03 89 20 99 60
Fax : 03 89 20 99 69

Closed from 24 Jun to 11 Jul and from 23 Dec to 9 Jan
• 9 rooms with bath/WC or shower/WC and television
• €49 to €67; breakfast €6; half board €44 • Restaurant closed Sat lunchtime, Sun evening and Mon; menus €10 (lunchtime in the week) to €23 • A few parking spaces. No dogs allowed in rooms

 A riverside country garden.

The Baldinger family has run this traditional country inn for over 40 years and have certainly learnt a thing or two about making their guests feel at home. Well-soundproofed bedrooms are spacious and comfortable. The restaurant staff, dressed in traditional Alsatian costume, serves tasty, locally sourced food whose continued popularity is due to the chef's ability to move with the times, introducing lighter dishes and vegetarian meals. Attractive indoor swimming pool and a fitness room.

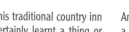 **The simple, friendly atmosphere.**

An attractive village house with a redbrick façade and a totally renovated interior. Only 10min from Colmar, this tranquil hotel is an excellent choice for an overnight stop. The tastefully decorated rooms are pleasant and spotless. Wood is the predominant feature of the family dining room which offers a menu of French classics, while the bar serves the region's famous tartes flambées – light pizzas on an extra-thin crust – by the warmth of an earthenware stove.

Access : In the centre of the village

Access : To the south-east of Colmar, on the D 13 then the D 45

 35 **AUBERGE ET HOSTELLERIE PAYSANNE**
Mrs Litzler

24 rue Principale
68480 Lutter
Tel. : 03 89 40 71 67
Fax : 03 89 07 33 38

Closed from 1 to 15 Jul, 2 weeks in winter and Mon
• 7 rooms at the Auberge and 9 in the separate wing
(L'Hostellerie) 200m away. Rooms have bath/WC or
shower/WC, all have television • €47 to €68, breakfast
€6, half board €45 to €52 • Restaurant closed Tue
lunchtime out of season and Mon; menus €21 to
€51 • Terrace, garden, car park • Hiking, cycling and
horse-riding 2km away

 36 **DOMAINE BOUXHOF**
Mr and Mrs Edel

Rue du Bouxhof
68630 Mittelwihr
Tel. : 03 89 47 93 67
Fax : 03 89 47 84 82

Open all year • 3 rooms and 3 gîtes • €44, breakfast
included • No table d'hôte • Garden, car park

**The picturesque, unspoilt landscapes
of the Sundgau.**

**Staying in a wine-growing property
and trying a glass – it would be
impolite to refuse!**

This establishment does offer its own modern accommodation, but most people prefer the annexe, 150m
away: a 1618 farmhouse typical of the Sundgau region,
which was actually taken apart brick by brick and rebuilt
here, a short distance from the Swiss border. Some of
the rooms, of varying quality it must be said, have oak
beamed ceilings, and a pretty flowered garden leads out
towards the fields. Check-in at the main inn and sample
the regional specialities and seasonal game in its dining
room.

This 17C castle flanked with square towers seems to rise
out of a sea of vines. Guests can choose between two
types of accommodation: modern, spotless rooms or very
well-equipped cottages; those with a balcony overlooking the vineyards are the most attractive. The superb
breakfast room is housed in a 15C chapel. Don't pass
up a chance to visit the cellar and its oak vats where
the estate's wine is made, finishing with a wine-tasting
session.

Access : Leave Ferrette south-east bound on the
D 23, at Sondersdorf take the D 21B, then at
Raedersdorf go back onto the D 23

Access : In the upper part of the village, in the
wine-growing estate

37 AUX DEUX CLEFS
Mrs Enderlin

 68480 Moernach
Tel. : 03 89 40 80 56
Fax : 03 89 08 10 47

Closed for two weeks in February and from 26 Oct to 9 Nov • 7 rooms with shower/WC, almost all have television • €40 to €46; breakfast €6; half board €46 to €52 • Restaurant closed Wed evening and Thu; menus €15 (in the week) to €40 • Garden, car park, garage

38 MOULIN DE HUTTINGUE
Mr Thomas Antoine

 68480 Oltingue
Tel. : 03 89 40 72 91
Fax : 03 89 07 31 01

Closed in Jan and Feb • 4 rooms • €54, breakfast included • Table d'hôte €13 to €23 • Car park, garden, terrace. Credit cards not accepted, no dogs allowed

 An afternoon nap in the pretty tree-lined garden.

A handsome half-timbered and gabled country house, characteristic of the Sundgau; look for its attractive wrought-iron sign of two crossed keys. Taste the local delicacy, fried carp, in the welcoming wood-panelled dining room, tastefully decorated with paintings. Comfortable, inviting rooms, which are being progressively renovated, occupy a wing which dates from the Sixties.

 The decorative features which bear witness to the mill's long history.

The Franco-Swiss border is only a short distance from this 17C wheat mill on the banks of the Ill, which is little more than a stream here. The rooms, all upstairs, are quite simply appointed on the whole. The superb loft under the eaves has been fitted with a useful kitchenette. Breakfast is served in a dining room complete with magnificent wooden pillars or on the terrace when the weather permits.

Access : At Vieux-Ferrette leave the D432 for the D 473 which goes through Koestlach and Moernach

Access : 1.5km south of Oltingue on the D 21e

 39 FERME DU BUSSET
Mrs Batôt

 33 rue du Busset
68370 Orbey
Tel. : 03 89 71 22 17
Fax : 03 89 71 22 17

Open all year • 6 rooms • €45, breakfast included • No table d'hôte • Garden, car park. Credit cards not accepted, no dogs allowed

 40 L' ORIEL
Mrs Wendel

 3 rue des Écuries-Seigneuriales
68340 Riquewihr
Tel. : 03 89 49 03 13
Fax : 03 89 47 92 87
oriel @ club-internet.fr

Open all year • 19 rooms, 3 of which are split-level, with shower/WC or bath/WC, all have television • €67 to €78; breakfast €9 • No restaurant • Shaded terrace

 The panoramic view over the Orbey Valley.

A steep road winds its way up to this farmhouse, which still breeds its own poultry and sheep, high on a lush green plateau at an altitude of 600m. Choose from self-catering cottages or bed and breakfast rooms: the latter are lined in wood and while not enormous are very well-kept and quiet. Before leaving, make sure you stock up on cheese, cooked meats and home-made jams.

 Breakfast served in the inner courtyard in summertime.

The frontage of this 16C country home is adorned with a handsome two-storey oriel window and an amusing wrought-iron sign; the delightful maze of corridors and staircases bear witness to the house's old age. The rooms, in the progress of being renovated, are decorated in a variety of styles, ranging from rustic to more modern – families generally prefer one of the split-level rooms.

Access : 1km to the east of Orbey on a minor road

Access : From the town hall take Rue du Général de Gaulle then the first street on the right

41 LE SARMENT D'OR
Mr and Mrs Merckling

4 rue du Cerf
68340 Riquewihr
Tel. : 03 89 86 02 86
Fax : 03 89 47 99 23

Closed from 6 Jan to 12 Feb, from 1 to 9 Jul, Sun evening, Mon and Tue lunchtime • 9 rooms, 2 of which are split-level, most have bath/WC, all have television • €64 to €75; breakfast €8; half board €60 to €71 • Menus €20 to €52

The owners' attentive welcome.

The Sarment d'Or – or golden vine – has put down its roots in a quiet street lined with handsome 16C houses. A spiral staircase leads up to the cosy, modern bedrooms. The snug, warm dining rooms are characteristic of Alsatian interior decoration with pine panelling and dark beams lit up by the crackling flames of a welcoming log fire.

Access : From the town hall square, drive to the end of Rue du Général de Gaulle and turn left (pedestrian street)

42 LE CLOS DU MÛRIER
Mrs Volpatti

42 Grande-Rue
68170 Rixheim
Tel. : 03 89 54 14 81
Fax : 03 89 64 47 08

Open all year • 5 rooms with kitchenettes, bathrooms with separate WC • €56; breakfast €7 • No table d'hôte • Garden, car park. No dogs allowed

The spacious, comfortable rooms.

This venerable 16C Alsatian house has been tastefully renovated. Old beams blend well with a modern décor and each bedroom has its own kitchenette. On the leisure side, the house has a pleasant walled courtyard and the owners are happy to lend bicycles to guests.

Access : 6km eastbound from Mulhouse, drive towards Basle, in the centre of Rixheim

 43 AUBERGE DU MEHRBÄCHEL
Mr and Mrs Kornacker

Route de Geishouse
68290 Saint-Amarin
Tel. : 03 89 82 60 68
Fax : 03 89 82 66 05

Closed from 21 Feb to 8 Mar, from 25 Oct to 10 Nov, Thu evening and Fri • 23 rooms located in 2 buildings, with bath/WC or shower/WC • €45 to €49; breakfast €8; half board €45 • Air-conditioned restaurant; menus €16 (in the week) to €25 • Car park. No dogs allowed • Walking

 44 AU MOULIN
Mr and Mrs Woeffle

Route d'Herrlisheim
68127 Sainte-Croix-en-Plaine
Tel. : 03 89 49 31 20
Fax : 03 89 49 23 11

Open from 28 Mar to 3 Nov • 17 rooms with bath/WC, almost all have television • €52 to €80; breakfast €8 • No restaurant • Garden, car park • Small museum about Alsace in the inner courtyard

 Toasting your toes by the warm stove after a hard day's trekking.

This old farmhouse built on the edge of a forest of fir trees, so characteristic of the Vosges scenery, has been in the family since 1886. Half the simple but spacious and well-kept rooms have balconies and most of them overlook the wonderful Rossberg mountain range. Game and regional dishes are served in the air-conditioned dining room, its walls are adorned with hunting trophies. A hiking trail runs past the inn, ideal for walkers!

 Lingering over breakfast in the enchanting flowered courtyard.

With its flowered courtyard and half-timbered buildings, this former flour-mill, built in 1880, represents a haven of peace and quiet, just a short distance from an interchange on the A 35! The sizeable rooms are practical and tastefully decorated with cane furniture. Some overlook the peaks of the Vosges, while others look down on the plain; all are wonderfully quiet. Interesting mini-museum on the Alsace of yesteryear.

Access : Between Thann and Bussang, drive for 4km on the Mehrbächel road

Access : 10km southbound from Colmar on the D 201, then at Sainte-Croix-en-Plaine take the D 1

 45 AUX MINES D'ARGENT
Mrs Willmann

8 rue du Docteur Weisgerber
68160 Sainte-Marie-aux-Mines
Tel. : 03 89 58 55 75
Fax : 03 89 58 65 49

Open all year • 9 rooms with shower/WC and television • €39 to €43; breakfast €6; half board €43 • Menus €15 to €27 • Terrace

 46 MOSCHENROSS
Mr Geyer

42 rue du Général de Gaulle
68800 Thann
Tel. : 03 89 37 00 86
Fax : 03 89 37 52 81
info@le-moschenross.com
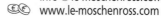 www.le-moschenross.com

Open all year • 23 rooms, one of which has disabled access, most have shower/WC, some have bath/WC, all have television • €38 to €49; breakfast €6; half board €35 to €42 • Restaurant closed Sat lunchtime and Sun evening; menus €15 to €45 • Terrace, private car park

 The busy atmosphere surrounding the famous Mineral, Gem And Fossil Show (June).

The mullioned windows of the façade testify to the old age of this house, said to have been built in 1596 by a miner who would appear to have struck it rich! The original spiral staircase leads up to the rooms, graced with large windows and furniture dating from 1900 or thereabouts. The family dining room, in the "winstub" style, is embellished with wood carvings which depict the miners' lives: the seam at Ste Marie was mined from the 9C to the 18C.

 The path winding through the vineyards up the Rangen.

Close to the post-office and opposite the station, this neat, ochre-red fronted 1839 hotel has been renovated from top to bottom. The small, modern rooms are practical and well soundproofed: ask for one commanding views over the steep slopes of the famous Rangen vineyards. The spacious dining room is decorated in a hybrid contemporary-bourgeois style. Charming service.

Access : In the centre, in the street parallel to the main road (where the town hall is)

Access : In the village

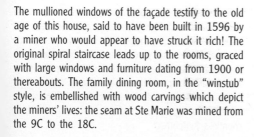

  47 **AUBERGE LA MEUNIÈRE**
Mr and Mrs Dumoulin

30 rue Sainte-Anne
68590 Thannenkirch
Tel. : 03 89 73 10 47
Fax : 03 89 73 12 31
info @ aubergelameuniere.com

Open from 25 Mar to 20 Dec • 23 rooms at the rear of the building. Rooms have bath/WC or shower/WC, all have television • €55 to €75; breakfast €6; half board €41 to €56 • Restaurant closed Mon and Tue lunchtime; menus €17 (in the week) to €30 • Terrace, car park, garage • Sauna, fitness room, table-tennis, billiards

  48 **AU CERF**
Mr Koller

76 rue Principale
68480 Winkel
Tel. : 03 89 40 85 05
Fax : 03 89 08 11 10

Closed from 4 to 25 Feb and 20 to 27 Aug • 6 rooms upstairs with bath/WC, some have television • €48; breakfast €6; half board €45 • Restaurant closed Mon and Thu; menu €23 • No dogs allowed • Hiking

We most liked **The restful view of the forest, from some of the bathrooms!**

We most liked **The family atmosphere behind these red walls.**

The imposing flowered façade of this inn conceals a host of attractions. Almost all the rooms are rear-facing – avoid those overlooking the street – with a view of the Bergenbach Valley and the towers of Haut-Koenigsbourg Castle, which film buffs may recognise as the location of Jean Renoir's anti-war masterpiece "La Grande Illusion". The restaurant is decorated in a delightful rustic style and the terrace opens out onto the splendid Vosges scenery.

The smart red frontage of this inn near the Swiss border cannot be missed. The rather bare rooms are tiled and furnished practically; nearly all have been recently renovated and the proverbial Swiss obsession with cleanliness has clearly made it over the border here. Family dining rooms in an up-to-date "winstub" style. Bring a rucksack and walking stick and explore the beautiful Sundgau region and the source of the Ill along countless footpaths.

Access : Between Ribeauvillé and Sélestat, in a village very near Haut-Koenisbourg

Access : In the centre of the village

AQUITAINE

F riendly Aquitaine has welcomed mankind since prehistoric times. Its varied mosaic of landscapes is as distinctive as its inhabitants' dedication to hospitality, invariably spiced with a generous sprinkling of forthright rural humour. Don't be surprised if your purchase of home-made foie gras or confit of goose leads to an invitation to look around the estate, finishing up with a few tips on how to fatten up your own poultry at home! No stay in Aquitaine would be complete without visiting at least one of Bordeaux' justly famous châteaux and vineyards. Afterwards head for the "Silver Coast", prized by surfers and rugby fans alike, and sample delicious Basque gâteau, have a drink in a tapas bar or even take ringside seats for a bullfight! This rugged yet sunny land between the Pyrenees and the Atlantic has always been fiercely proud of its identity and the inhabitants of the Basque country still celebrate their time-honoured traditions in truly vigorous style. If you spend a little time in one these sleepy Basque villages, all of which sport the region's colours, red and green, you will be astounded by the ease with which they suddenly burst into spirited song and games.

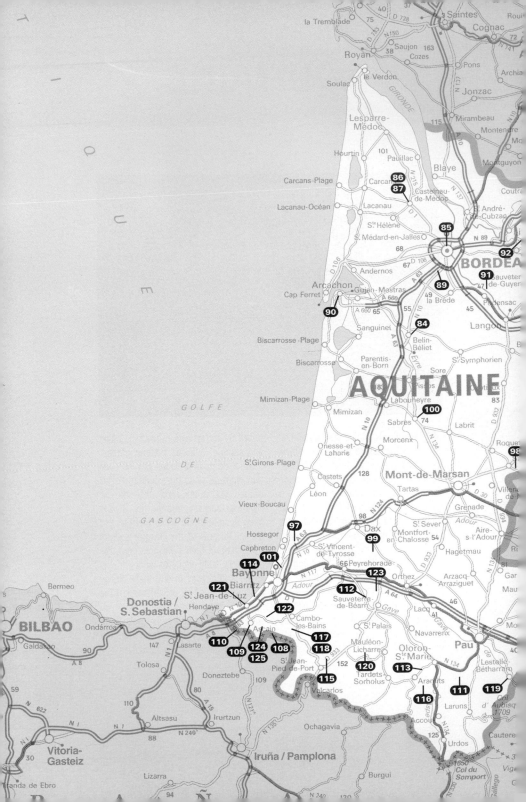

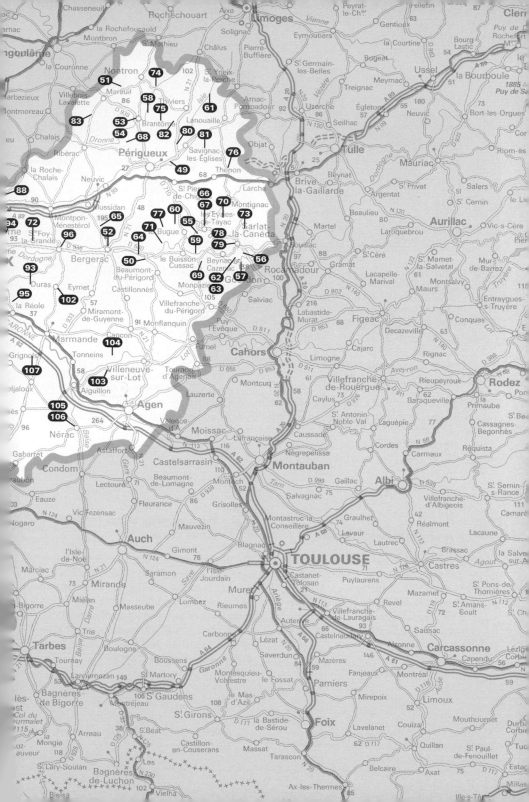

49 ▶ L' ÉCLUSE
Mr Pierunek

Route de Limoges
24420 Antonne-et-Trigonant
Tel. : 05 53 06 00 04
Fax : 05 53 06 06 39
contact@ecluse-perigord.com
www.ecluse-perigord.com

Open all year • 47 rooms on 3 floors, one of which has disabled access, all have bath/WC or shower/WC and television • €42 to €55; breakfast €8; half board €54 (€50 low season) • Menus €17 (in the week) to €29 • Terrace, park on the banks of the Isle, car park

50 ▶ LE RELAIS DE LAVERGNE
Mrs Pillebout

La Vergne
24150 Bayac
Tel. : 05 53 57 83 16
Fax : 05 53 57 83 16

Open all year • 4 rooms upstairs, one suite has disabled access, all have bathrooms • €55, breakfast included • Table d'hôte €20 • Park, terrace, car park. Credit cards not accepted • Outdoor swimming pool

 Five acres of landscaped park.

This impressive historic house stands on the banks of the Isle. Half the rooms, some of which have a balcony, enjoy a riverside view. Rustic furniture, bathrooms a mite outdated, a splendid buffet breakfast. Meals are served in the immense panoramic dining room and in the cane-furnished conservatory-sitting room. A haven of peace.

 The tranquillity of this handsome 17C manor house.

The peaceful appeal of this house is such that guests often wish they had planned to stay longer. The attentive welcome of the two hostesses, the tranquil atmosphere and mouth-watering smells wafting from the kitchen never fail to enchant. Light, airy bedrooms combine the charm of yesteryear with modern-day comforts. The spacious restaurant and inner courtyard provide a perfect setting for elegant dining.

Access : Leave Périgueux on the N 21 towards Thiviers, after 11km the hotel is set back from the road on the banks of the Isle

Access : 10km to the south-east of Lanquais, on the Beaumont road

 51 L' ANCIENNE BOULANGERIE
Mr Chapelle

Le Bourg
24340 Beaussac
Tel. : 05 53 56 56 51
Fax : 05 53 56 56 59
katerine.chapelle-welffens @ wanadoo.fr

Open all year • 4 rooms with shower/WC • €41,
breakfast included • No table d'hôte • Garden, car park.
Credit cards not accepted • Swimming pool, fishing and
hiking nearby

 52 LA FLAMBÉE
Mr Dupouts

153 avenue Pasteur
24100 Bergerac
Tel. : 05 53 57 52 33
Fax : 05 53 61 07 57
www.laflambee.com

Open all year. Restaurant closed Sat lunchtime, Sun
evening and Mon (from mid-Sep to mid-Jun) • 21 rooms,
7 of which are in a separate wing. Rooms have bath/WC,
some have shower/WC, all have television • €54 to €77;
breakfast €8; half board €70 (€66 low season) • Menus
€16 to €31 • Terrace, park, car park • Swimming pool,
tennis

Wake up to the enticing smell of freshly baked bread.

A tennis match and swim in the pool, or a quiet glass of Bergerac for the less energetic!

As the name suggests, this large square townhouse in
the upper part of the town used to be a bakers' shop;
the old bread oven can still be seen in the dining room.
White-wood furniture, beautiful wardrobes and old
photos adorn the tranquil rooms. A wealth of information
about the region can be gleaned from the sitting room's
bookshelves and guests can relax in the pretty little
garden.

This pleasant old country home on the doorsteps of the
tobacco capital of France has been recently renovated.
The rooms, practical and spacious with a personal touch,
are named after one of the surrounding vineyards; those
in the annexe are more simply decorated but have
private terraces overlooking the flowered grounds. The
stylish dining rooms feature cosy armchairs, wrought-
iron furniture, oak beams, log fires and a veranda.

Access : Between Mareuil and Nontron, a few
kilometres north of the D 708

Access : Leave Bergerac on the N 21 towards
Périgueux: after 3km, the hotel is on the right

 53 **LES HABRANS**
Mr Falcoz

 24310 Brantôme
Tel. : 05 53 05 58 84
Fax : 05 53 35 00 56

Closed from Nov 1 to May • 5 rooms, 4 of which are on the first floor • €52, breakfast included • No table d'hôte • Terrace, garden. Credit cards not accepted

 54 **LA MAISON FLEURIE**
Mr and Mrs Robinson

 54 rue Gambetta
24310 Brantôme
Tel. : 05 53 35 17 04
Fax : 05 53 05 16 58
holsfrance @ aol.com

Closed in Feb • 5 non-smoking rooms • €79, breakfast included • No table d'hôte • Credit cards not accepted, no dogs allowed • Outdoor swimming pool

 Boating down the Dronne.

The riverside setting of this unpretentious little house is without question its main asset. The simple rooms are tastefully decorated; those on the first floor under the eaves have sloped ceilings and windows overlooking the river. When the weather is fine, guests can tuck into breakfast on the delightful terrace.

 Staying in the heart of the hometown of the 16C court chronicler Brantôme.

This 19C property, in the shadow of the elegant Romanesque belfry of the abbey, boasts a number of attractions: a convenient town centre location, exemplary welcome, excellent value for money and above all, its charming, comfortable rooms. Whenever the weather permits, generous breakfasts are served in the flowered courtyard and the small swimming pool is always appreciated during the hot weather.

Access : In the lane opposite the gendarmerie (police station)

Access : In the town centre

 55 HÔTEL DU CHÂTEAU
Mr Petit

 24260 Le Bugue
Tel. : 05 53 07 23 50
Fax : 05 53 03 93 69

Open from 24 Mar to 15 Oct • 12 rooms with bath/WC, some have shower/WC, all have television • €54; breakfast €6; half board €45 (€42 low season) • Menus €19 to €39 • Terrace, car park. No dogs allowed in rooms

 56 DOMAINE LACOSTE
Mr Augustin

 "Lacoste"
24200 Carsac-Aillac
Tel. : 05 53 59 58 81
Fax : 05 53 59 51 87
domaine.lacoste @ wanadoo.fr

Open all year. Only half board in Jul and Aug • 4 rooms upstairs, all have bathrooms • €52, breakfast included • Table d'hôte €17 • Terrace, garden, car park. Credit cards not accepted, no dogs allowed • Outdoor swimming pool

The simple authenticity of this family home.

A handsome country house in the midst of an enchanting Périgordian hamlet. The charming, old-fashioned rooms are spacious, comfortable and well looked-after, kept cool even in the height of summer by thick stone walls. From the windows of the dining room, diners can see Campagne Castle while they sample the chef's carefully prepared regional cooking. Pleasant, shaded terrace, decked in flowers in the summer.

The owners' warm hospitality and welcome.

Located in the upper part of town, this traditional old Périgordian townhouse, renovated and extended, enjoys a sumptuous view over the Dordogne and Montfort Castle. A tasteful colour scheme of blue, beige and yellow adorns the bedrooms, all of which have new bathrooms. The ground floor suite opens directly onto the swimming pool. Your hosts make it a point of honour to use local produce.

Access : Leave Le Bugue south-east bound on the D 703 and drive for 4km

Access : In the upper part of the village

 57 LA GUÉRINIÈRE
Mr and Mrs Demassougne

 "Baccas"
24250 Cénac-et-Saint-Julien
Tel. : 05 53 29 91 97
Fax : 05 53 30 23 89
contact@la-gueriniere-dordogne.com
www.la-gueriniere-dordogne.com

Closed from Nov 1 to Easter • 6 rooms upstairs and 2 gîtes • €80, breakfast included • Terrace, park, car park. No dogs allowed • Outdoor swimming pool, tennis, bicycles, golf

 58 CHÂTEAU DE LA BORIE-SAULNIER
Mr and Mrs Duseau

 24530 Champagnac-de-belair
Tel. : 05 53 54 22 99
Fax : 05 53 08 53 78
château-de-la-borie-saulnier@wanadoo.fr

Closed in Jan • 5 rooms • €74, breakfast included • No table d'hôte • Park, car park. Credit cards not accepted, no dogs allowed • Outdoor swimming pool

 We most liked
Sampling the tasty meals made with fresh farm produce.

This 18C manor farm, extensively remodelled over the centuries, is reminiscent of a charterhouse. Each of the extremely spacious rooms with bare stone walls, period furniture and tasteful fabrics is named after a flower. Cats, dogs and farmyard animals enjoy the run of the extensive grounds, to the invariable delight of children.

 We most liked
The tennis courts, free for guests.

The owners of this fortified medieval château have been lovingly renovating their property, which once ruled the whole Dronne Valley, for some twenty years. The towers and crenellated walls complete with firing positions, are carefully preserved and the interior has been sensitively redecorated. Each room features a different colour – turquoise, yellow, green, grey and blue – and commands a lovely view over the park. The breakfast room is simply beautiful.

Access : On the D 46 road to Gourdon

Access : 6km to the north-east of Brantôme on the D 75 and then the D 83

 59 MANOIR DE LA BRUNIE
Mr Orefice

 La Brunie
24220 Coux-et-Bigaroque
Tel. : 05 53 29 61 42
marc.orefice @ wanadoo.fr
www.abscisse.com

Open all year • 5 rooms upstairs with bathrooms • €69, breakfast included • No table d'hôte • Terrace, park, car park

 60 LES LANDETTES
Mr Stocklouser

 24260 Journiac
Tel. : 05 53 54 35 19

Open all year • 3 rooms on garden level, with bathrooms • €45, breakfast included • No table d'hôte • Credit cards not accepted, no dogs allowed • Outdoor swimming pool

 We most liked
The romantic charm of the parkland.

 We most liked
The scenery of the Vézère Valley.

Every aspect of this beautifully renovated 18C manor house seems more appealing than the last, starting with the refined decoration of the dining room and sitting room on the ground floor. The bedrooms upstairs are well-dimensioned and most of the antique furniture has been in the family for generations; bathrooms are all very well appointed. Breakfast is served in the lush, green garden in the summertime.

The setting of this wonderfully renovated 1850 Périgordian farmhouse couldn't be more rural. The bedrooms, fitted-out in the outhouses, make up in charm what they lack in dimensions, with pastel shades, white tiled floors, colourful fabrics and old furniture; all overlook the swimming pool. The shade of a giant lime-tree makes the inner courtyard very pleasant in the summer.

Access : 15km from Bugue towards Villeneuve-sur-Lot

Access : 13km westbound from La Madeleine

 LES VIGNES DE CHALUSSET
Mrs Chedeville

 24630 Jumilhac-le-Grand
Tel. : 05 53 52 38 25
nsenee @ free.fr
 www.multimania.com/vigneschalusset

Closed from Nov to Easter • 5 air-conditioned rooms, one of which has disabled access • €40, breakfast included • Table d'hôte €14 • Terrace, park, car park. Credit cards not accepted • Outdoor swimming pool

 LA BELLE ÉTOILE
Ongaro family

 24250 La Roque Gageac
Tel. : 05 53 29 51 44
Fax : 05 53 29 45 63
hotel.belle-etoile @ wanadoo.fr

Open from late Mar to late Oct • 16 rooms with bath/WC and television • €69; breakfast €7; half board €57 to €68 • Restaurant closed Wed lunchtime and Mon; menus €20 to €32, children's menu €10 • Terrace, garage • Canoeing, swimming, fishing

 Riders and horses can be sure of a warm welcome.

This old barn turned into a bed and breakfast is a successful blend of old and new. Oak beams and bare stone walls add character to the spacious, air-conditioned rooms and those on the ground floor have been adapted for disabled guests. The delicious home cooking, an excellent opportunity to try a local Périgordian recipe, is served on the communal table in the dining room or in the inner courtyard during the summer.

Floating down the Dordogne in a "gabarre".

This fine old creamy-coloured stone house perched on the cliff commands a wonderful view over the peaceful meanders of the Dordogne. The bedrooms have been painted white and most are furnished in a period style. The typical Périgordian repertoire, served in two pleasant dining rooms, or in the summer, under a trellis, will tempt even the most refined of palates. Numerous nearby leisure activities, including canoeing, swimming and fishing.

Access : 4km from Jumilhac-le-Grand, towards St-Yrieix

Access : On the D 703, between the cliff and the river

63 AUBERGE LA PLUME D'OIE
Mr and Mrs Walker

24250 La Roque-Gageac
Tel. : 05 53 29 57 05
Fax : 05 53 31 04 81

Closed from 10 Jan to early Mar and from late Nov to 20 Dec • 4 rooms upstairs, reserved mainly for the restaurant clients, with bath/WC and television • €70 to €76; breakfast €11 • Open evenings only in the summer, closed Tue lunchtime and Mon out of season; menus €34 to €49

64 DOMAINE DE LA MARMETTE
Mrs Ossedat

"La Crabe"
24150 Lanquais
Tel. : 05 53 24 99 13
Fax : 05 53 24 11 48
george.ossedat@wanadoo.fr

Open all year • 5 rooms on garden level • €52, breakfast included • Table d'hôte by reservation • Garden, terrace, car park. Credit cards not accepted, no dogs allowed • Outdoor swimming pool

The picturesque site of La Roque-Gageac.

This old residence, built on the flanks of the cliff, stands in the heart of the idyllic medieval town. A spiral staircase leads up to a few refreshingly cool bedrooms decorated with pastel fabrics. The pretty dining room features light wooden beams, painted straw-bottomed chairs and bare stone walls. Diners can enjoy a view of the picturesque "gabarres" and canoes floating down the Dordogne. Imaginative menu.

Back to basics in a land of open fields.

This 16C farm and outbuildings dotted with lawns and countless clumps of flowers could almost be called a hamlet. The former loose-boxes have been turned into bedrooms on the ground floor and each one is decorated with a personalised fabric, chest of drawers and a wrought-iron bed. A sitting room, library and dining room-conservatory are located in the main house. A kitchen is also available for use by guests.

Access : In the village, on the banks of the Dordogne

Access : Take the Faux road then turn left for Bournaz after leaving town and continue for 200m

65 **MAISON DE LA FORÊT**
Mr Swainson

Pas de l'Eyraud
24130 Laveyssière
Tel. : 05 53 82 84 50
Fax : 05 53 82 84 51
info @ aubergerac.com

Open all year • 5 rooms with bathrooms • €57, breakfast included • No table d'hôte • Park, garden, car park. Credit cards not accepted, no dogs allowed • Outdoor swimming pool

66 **HOSTELLERIE DU PASSEUR**
Mr Brun

Place de la Mairie
24620 Les Eyzies-de-Tayac
Tel. : 05 53 06 97 13
Fax : 05 53 06 91 63
hostellerie-du-passeur @ perigord.com
www.hostellerie-du-passeur.com

Open from early Feb to early Nov; restaurant closed Mon and Tue except from Jul to Sep • 19 rooms on 3 floors, most have shower/WC, some have bath/WC, all have television • €60 to €85; breakfast €7; half board €58 to €68 • Menus €19 to €42 • Terrace, car park • A short distance from the Prehistory Museum

 Staying just 10min away from Bergerac without suffering the hordes of tourists.

This welcoming white house stands in its own extensive grounds, surrounded by forest. Run by a delightful English couple, the establishment offers colourful rooms under the eaves, on the small side but all with views of the countryside. The prettiest rooms are to the rear of the house. Breakfast is served on the terrace in fine weather.

 The home-made foie gras which can be bought in the hotel or from its web-site.

This handsome stone house covered in Virginia creeper stands in the heart of the Périgord, known for its prehistoric heritage. The stylish, recently redecorated rooms are very colourful and some overlook the cliffs dotted with oak trees. Diners can choose from a traditional dining room complete with an attractive stone fireplace, a bright conservatory or a country terrace under lime-trees facing the Vézère in which to savour the hotel's renowned regional dishes.

Access : 14km northbound from Bergerac on the D 709, then take a minor road

Access : In the town centre, not far from the Vézère

AQUITAINE

LES EYZIES-DE-TAYAC - 24620   LISLE - 24350

67 LE MOULIN DE LA BEUNE
Mr Soulié

24620 Les Eyzies-de-Tayac
Tel. : 05 53 06 94 33
Fax : 05 53 06 98 06

Open from Apr to Oct; restaurant closed on Tue, Wed and Sat lunchtime • 20 rooms with bath/WC or shower/WC, all have television • €46 to €60; breakfast €7; half board €61 to €66 • Au Vieux Moulin restaurant: menus €21 to €61 • Terrace, garden, car park. No dogs allowed in restaurant

68 LE PIGEONNIER DE PICANDINE
Mr Lacourt

24350 Lisle
Tel. : 05 53 03 41 93
Fax : 05 53 03 28 43
picandine @ aol.com
www.picandine.com

Closed Dec and Jan • 5 rooms with shower or bath • €45 • Table d'hôte €16 • Terrace, car park. Credit cards not accepted, no dogs allowed • Outdoor swimming pool

 Talking into the early hours of the morning on the riverside terrace.

The attractive stone walls of this former seed and sawmill now house a charming hotel-restaurant. All the pleasant, tastefully decorated rooms enjoy peace and quiet and the stylish wood-panelled dining room commands views of the wonderfully preserved paddle wheel and the garden and river. The setting, on the banks of the Beune, is quite idyllic in fine weather.

 The sweeping view over the Périgord countryside.

This lovely 17C farmhouse is graced with two-hundred-year-old chestnut trees in the inner courtyard. Stone walls and wood beams set the tone for the bedrooms in the main wing, while two suites in the renovated barn are well suited to families. It's an ideal place to unwind: snuggle up with a good book in the cosy sitting room-library or treat yourself to a game of billiards.

Access : In the town centre, off the road on the banks of the Beune

Access : In the town

 69 LA GRANDE MARQUE
Mrs Cockcroft

24440 Marnac
Tel. : 05 53 31 61 63
grande.marque@perigord.com

Open all year • 5 rooms with bathrooms • €60, breakfast included • No table d'hôte • Terrace, park, car park. Credit cards not accepted, no dogs allowed • Outdoor swimming pool

 70 HÔTEL DES BORIES
Mr and Mrs Dalbavie

24620 Marquay
Tel. : 05 53 29 67 02
 Fax : 05 53 29 64 15

Open from 1 Apr to 2 Nov • 30 rooms, 20 of which are in a separate wing, 5 have private terraces, all have bath/WC or shower/WC and television • €38 to €61; breakfast €6 • No restaurant, but half board can be arranged with L'Esterel • Terrace, garden, car park • 2 outdoor swimming pools

 Strolling round the magnificent ten-acre parkland.

This wonderful 17C Périgord estate commands a sumptuous view of the Dordogne Valley and the quaint, riverside village of Siorac-en-Périgord. The rooms under the eaves have recently been treated to a simple, tasteful facelift. The estate boasts a wide range of leisure activities including a fitness room, sauna and tennis court.

Peace and quiet guaranteed.

Despite the name, you won't have to sleep in a "borie", one of the somewhat Spartan dry-stone huts that abound in the region. The accommodation in this family home may not be luxurious, but it is well equipped with modern comforts. Some rooms also have a terrace where you can take breakfast, and the most stylish of all has a superb stone fireplace and wooden beams. Relax in the swimming pool overlooking the countryside.

Access : 9km to the north-east on the D 703, take the road to Sarlat and then turn right

Access : On leaving Sarlat-la-Canéda, drive towards Les Eyzies-de-Tayac and follow the D 6 on the right

  71 LA CHÊNAIE
Mr Pons

Les combes Sud
24150 Mauzac-et-Grand-Castang
Tel. : 05 53 74 33 30
Fax : 05 53 74 33 30

Closed from mid-Oct to Easter • 4 rooms • €51, breakfast included • No table d'hôte • Terrace, park, car park. Credit cards not accepted, no dogs allowed • Outdoor swimming pool

  72 CHÂTEAU DAME DE FONROQUE
Mrs Fried

Fonroque
24230 Montcaret
Tel. : 05 53 58 65 83
Fax : 05 53 58 60 04
brigittefried@wanadoo.fr
www.pays-de-bergerac.com

Closed from Dec to 15 Feb • 5 rooms with bathrooms and 2 gîtes • €58, breakfast included • Table d'hôte €17.50 • Terrace, park, car park. Credit cards not accepted, no dogs allowed • Outdoor swimming pool

 A dip in the salt-water swimming pool.

This attractive country home, surrounded by oaks, overlooks the Dordogne and one of its most famous meanders at Trémolat. Wooden floors, beams, carpentry work and family furniture take pride of place in the bedrooms upstairs. On the ground floor are the dining room, sitting room and vast terrace where breakfast is served. The nearby Mauzac nautical leisure base offers sailing and trips in the local "gabarre" boats.

 Visiting the Gallo-Roman ruins at Montcaret.

The talented proprietor of this 16C fortified manor house successfully runs both a wine business and a bed and breakfast establishment. The comfortable, often spacious rooms are decorated with stylish, old furniture and all overlook the parkland and its hundred-year-old trees. You will adore the wholesome, country cooking.

Access : 5km westbound from Trémolat

Access : In the Fonroque Park

 73 LES GRANGES HAUTES
Mr Querre

 Le Poujol
24590 Saint-Crépin-et-Carlucet
Tel. : 05 53 29 35 60
Fax : 05 53 28 81 17
jquerre @ aol.com

Closed from 7 Oct to 28 Mar • 5 non-smoking rooms, all have baths or showers • €79, breakfast included • No table d'hôte • Garden, car park. No dogs allowed

74 L' FOMPEYRINIÈRE
Mr and Mrs Vandamme

 Lapeyronnie
24470 Saint-Pardoux-la-Rivière
Tel. : 05 53 60 53 30
 Fax : 05 53 56 75 16

Open all year • 4 rooms with bath/WC • €37, breakfast included • Table d'hôte €16 • Sitting room, garden, car park. Credit cards not accepted, no dogs allowed • Swimming, fishing

 The sophisticated charm of a French country house.

It is hard to resist the charm of this 18C-19C Périgord country house, surrounded by superb gardens and a salt-water swimming pool. The stylish rooms feature oak beams, warm, sunny colours and immaculate bathrooms. The sitting room, whose central feature is a large fireplace, is the perfect place to relax and read. The charming owners are delighted to recommend interesting places to visit in the region.

 All the jams are home-made.

Located in the heart of the town, this former farmhouse boasts a pleasant garden and a scenic view of the countryside. Inside, colourful fabrics and rugs set off a tasteful blend of antique and contemporary furniture; modest-sized rooms are stylish and immaculately kept. The master of the house, a former pork butcher, whips up delicious dishes in the kitchen.

Access : 12km to the north-east of Sarlat towards Brive then Salignac

Access : In the centre of the village

75 DOUMARIAS
Mr and Mrs Fargeot

24800 Saint-Pierre-de-Côle
Tel. : 05 53 62 34 37
Fax : 05 53 62 34 37
doumarias@aol.com

Closed from 15 Oct to 1 Apr • 6 rooms • €44, breakfast included • Table d'hôte €14 • Garden, car park. Credit cards not accepted, no dogs allowed • Outdoor swimming pool

76 VILLA DES COURTISSOUS
Mr Dalibard

24210 Saint-Rabier
Tel. : 05 53 51 02 26
villa.courtissous@libertysurf.

Closed from Nov to Mar • 4 rooms with bathrooms • €72, breakfast included • No table d'hôte • Terrace, garden, car park. Credit cards not accepted, no dogs allowed • Outdoor swimming pool

 Hooking a fish in the River Côle just a step away.

The leaves and branches of a great lime-tree throw a welcome shadow over the courtyard of this pleasant country property curtained in Virginia creeper, at the foot of the crumbling towers of Bruzac Castle; the charm of the Périgord at its best. The stylish, peaceful rooms are lavishly adorned with period furniture, ornaments and paintings. The swimming pool and garden are most appreciated, as is the staff's friendly welcome.

 Visiting nearby Hautefort Castle.

This dignified villa was built in 1800 in the middle of a landscaped garden. The recently renovated, well-proportioned rooms are painted white, adorned with the occasional photo, carefully chosen fabrics and lovingly restored old furniture. The bathrooms are faultless, with all mod-cons to hand. Depending on the season, breakfast is served at the large kitchen table in front of the open fire or on the terrace next to the swimming pool.

Access : 12km eastbound from Brantôme on the D 78

Access : 12km southbound from Saint-Rabier on the D 704

 77 **LE MOULIN NEUF**
Mrs Chappeu

 Paunat
24510 Sainte-Alvère
Tel. : 05 53 63 30 18
Fax : 05 53 63 30 55
moulin-neuf @ usa.net
www.francedirect.net

Closed from 1 to 8 Apr and from 15 to 31 Oct • 6 rooms
with bathrooms • €74, breakfast included • No table
d'hôte • Terrace, garden. Credit cards not accepted, no
dogs allowed

 78 **HÔTEL DE LA MADELEINE**
Mr Mélot

 1 place de la Petite Rigaudie
24200 Sarlat-la-Canéda
Tel. : 05 53 59 10 41
Fax : 05 53 31 03 62
hotel.madeleine @ wanadoo.fr
www.hoteldelamadeleine-sarlat.com

Hotel closed from 2 Jan to 8 Feb; restaurant closed from
15 Nov to 15 Mar • 39 rooms, 2 of which have disabled
access, with bath/WC or shower/WC, all have air-
conditioning and television • €71 to €81; breakfast €9;
half board €71 (€62 low season) • Restaurant closed
Mon and Tue lunchtime out of season; menus from
€22 to €39 • Terrace

 The laughter of children playing in the estate's pond.

This attractive old mill house is hidden in the heart of
a country estate complete with pond. The cosy interior
features light colours, roomy sofas and floral print
fabrics. The modest-sized rooms are tastefully decorated
and located in a beautifully restored old barn. In the
summer months, breakfast is served under an arbour
and by the fireside in the sitting room in the winter.

 Ideally located a step from the centre of historic Sarlat.

Freshly painted sky-blue shutters, restored frontage,
stylishly renovated rooms with modern amenities, a
brand-new dining room in shades of red and orange and
a spacious sitting room decorated with prints and green
plants. This fine hotel, said to be the oldest in town,
dating from 1840, has just been renovated from top to
bottom. Extremely practical garage (at an extra cost).

Access : Take the D 2 southbound

Access : On a main square at the entrance to the
medieval town

  79 **LE MAS DE CASTEL**
Mrs Castalian

Sudalissant
24200 Sarlat-la-Caneda
Tel. : 05 53 59 02 59
Fax : 05 53 28 25 62

Open from 30 Mar to 11 Nov • 13 rooms, half of which are on garden level and one has disabled access. Rooms have bath/WC or shower/WC and television • €53; breakfast €6 • No restaurant • Garden, car park. No dogs allowed • Outdoor swimming pool

  80 **CHAMBRE D'HÔTE AU VILLAGE**
Mr Valentini

Le Bourg
24420 Sorges
Tel. : 05 53 05 05 08

Closed in Oct • 3 rooms • €34, breakfast €5 • No table d'hôte • Terrace, garden. Credit cards not accepted

 We most liked
The enchanting countryside feel of this authentic farmhouse.

Located in the heart of an unspoilt countryside, this farmhouse has been turned into a welcoming hostelry with rustic rooms upstairs or level with the garden (our favourites). A cockerel, the last remaining survivor of the hen house, joyfully serenades guests with a not-too-early morning call. Enjoy the relaxed pace of a traditional Périgord home and take a dip in the swimming pool before breakfast. The nights are so peaceful that you'll even be philosophical about the rooster's morning chorus.

 We most liked
Sampling the "black diamond" that has made Sorges famous.

This tiny village house, probably built in the 15C, is just next door to the Truffle Museum and the Tourist Office. Bedrooms in a charming rural style feature wooden floorboards, stone walls, wooden ceilings and antique furniture. In the summer, breakfast is served in the lovely inner courtyard under the welcome shade of an enormous lime-tree.

Access : 3km from Sarlat-la-Canéda on the D 704 towards Gourdon, right onto the route de la Canéda, then take a minor road

Access : In the village

81 L' ENCLOS
Mr and Mrs Ornsteen

Pragelier
24390 Tourtoirac
Tel. : 05 53 51 11 40
Fax : 05 53 50 37 21
rornsteen @ yahoo.com

Closed from Oct to Apr • 5 rooms • €61 to €90, breakfast
included • Table d'hôte €15 to €20 • Park, car park.
Credit cards not accepted • Outdoor swimming pool

82 FERME DES GUEZOUX
Mr Fouquet

24800 Vaunac
Tel. : 05 53 62 06 39
Fax : 05 53 62 88 74

Open all year • 3 rooms and one gîte • €38, breakfast
included • No table d'hôte • Garden, car park

We most liked
The unusual complex of seven independent cottages.

You too will fall under the charm of this unusual hamlet
of cottages, also prized by a number of American film
stars! The luxuriously decorated, personalised rooms are
dotted around the garden in various outhouses, such as
the former chapel, bakery and estate manager's house.
Definitively rustic in character, all feature beautiful
Provençal fabrics. Walnut and fruit trees abound in the
beautiful parkland which is well worth a ramble.

We most liked
Delicious home-made walnut cake served at breakfast time.

Hidden by dense woodland, this stone farmhouse was
restored in 1990 and makes a wonderfully peaceful
retreat for anyone hoping to get away from it all.
Whitewashed walls, tiled floors and pine furniture paint
the picture of the simple, but impeccably kept bedrooms.
The genial proprietor loves showing his guests his very
own snail farm.

Access : 5km westbound from Hautefort on the
D 62, then the D 67

Access : 9km northbound on the RN 21, then take
the lane on the right

 83 HOSTELLERIE LES AIGUILLONS
Mr Beeuwsaert

 Le Beuil
24320 Saint-Martial-Viveyrols
Tel. : 05 53 91 07 55
Fax : 05 53 91 00 43
lesaiguillons @ aaol.com
www.hostellerielesaiguillons.com

Open from 28 Mar to 1 Nov; closed Sun evening and Mon out of season • 7 rooms, one of which has disabled access, all have bath/WC and television • €61 to €77; breakfast €8; half board €77 to €91 • Restaurant closed lunchtime (except for Sun and reservations); menus €25 to €54 • Terrace, park, car park • Outdoor swimming pool

 Woods, hills and open fields for as far as the eye can see.

Here you will find total peace and quiet and a place in the sun, disturbed only by the twittering of birds and the occasional distant murmur of country life. Built on the ruins of an old farmhouse, this hotel offers fresh, spacious rooms, a restaurant in hacienda style and a terrace overlooking the grounds, surrounded by countryside. If you find yourself suffering withdrawal symptoms, the traffic jams, pollution and stress of Paris are a mere 500km stone's throw away!

Access : 5km to the north-west of Verteillac on the D 1, then right on the D 101, the C 201 and finally a minor road

  84 CHAMBRE D'HÔTE M. CLÉMENT
Mr and Mrs Clément

1 rue du Stade
33830 Belin-Béliet
Tel. : 05 56 88 13 17

Open all year • 5 rooms • €46, breakfast €6 • No table d'hôte • Park, car park. Credit cards not accepted, no dogs allowed

 The refined decoration of this 16C manor house.

This handsome manor house is encircled by grounds, planted with immemorial oaks and many rarer varieties. The interior decoration is sophisticated down to the tiniest details, from the elegant wainscoting in the lobby and the thick oak doors with wrought-iron locks to the parquet floors and marble fireplace in each sitting and dining room. The light, airy bedrooms are equally elegant and most overlook the beautiful parkland. Discreet staff.

Access : In the park

85 **CONTINENTAL**
Mr Landereethe

10 rue Montesquieu
33000 Bordeaux
Tel. : 05 56 52 66 00
Fax : 05 56 52 77 97
continental @ hotel-le-continental.com

Open all year • 50 rooms, 22 of which are air-conditioned, all have bath/WC or shower/WC and television • €56 to €90; breakfast €6.50 • No restaurant • Car park nearby

86 **CHÂTEAU LE FOULON**
Mrs de Baritault

33480 Castelnau-de-Médoc
Tel. : 05 56 58 20 18
Fax : 05 56 58 23 43

Closed from 15 Dec to 2 Jan • 4 rooms and 4 suites • €77, breakfast included • No table d'hôte • Park, car park. Credit cards not accepted, no dogs allowed

Ideally located to explore Bordeaux on foot.

This 18C town mansion is located on a semi-pedestrian, shopping street in historic Bordeaux. The entrance hall, staircase and glass-ceilinged breakfast room testify to the establishment's stylish history, and though the bedrooms cannot compete for character, a hospitable master of the house makes it a point of pride to see that they are comfortable and well kept. Snug sitting room.

The ear-shattering silence.

This 1840 castle makes an excellent base to explore the region and is ideally tucked-in between Médoc vineyards and the sprawling pine forests of the Landes region. The handsome proportions of the rooms provide a pleasant backdrop for the old furniture. All the rooms overlook the peaceful grounds and the river, home to a number of graceful swans. The well-appointed apartments are ideal for longer stays.

Access : In the pedestrian area

Access : On leaving Castelnau towards Bordeaux, turn right at the gendarmerie (police station)

 87 DOMAINE DE CARRAT
Mr and Mrs Péry

Route de Sainte-Hélène
33480 Castelnau-de-Médoc
Tel. : 05 56 58 24 80
Fax : 05 56 58 24 80

Closed at Christmas • 4 rooms • €54, breakfast included
• No table d'hôte • Park, car park. Credit cards not
accepted

 88 HENRI IV
Mr Chalvet de Recy

Place du 8-Mai-1945
33230 Coutras
Tel. : 05 57 49 34 34
Fax : 05 57 49 20 72
hotel-henryIV.gironde @ wanadoo.fr

Open all year • 14 rooms on 2 floors with bath/WC or
shower/WC and television • €42 to €56; breakfast
€6 • No restaurant • Garden, car park

Romance pervades this country estate.

This red-shuttered country seat, built in 1885, nestles
in its own grounds, surrounded by 50 acres of woodland.
Formerly the stables of the neighbouring castle, it now
houses comfortable, quiet bedrooms, graced with family
heirlooms. The most pleasant, on the ground floor, open
directly onto the lawn. A roaring open fire welcomes
guests in the winter, while the summer months ring to
the voices of children swimming in the Jalette. Extremely
attentive staff.

The hotel's polished service.

Coutras rose to fame following a battle fought here in
1587 by Henry of Navarre, the future Henry IV. The 19C
mansion with a graceful courtyard-garden to the front
now houses a well-kept hotel with pine furnished rooms.
Double-glazing efficiently blocks out the rumble of the
nearby railway and the attic rooms on the top floor are
air-conditioned.

Access : 1km to the south-west of
Castelnau-de-Médoc

Access : In the town centre, opposite the railway
station

 89 LE CHALET LYRIQUE
Mr Goichon

 169 cours du Général de Gaulle
33170 Gradignan
Tel. : 05 56 89 11 59
Fax : 05 56 89 53 37
lechaletlyrique @ chaletlyrique.com
www.chalet-lyrique.fr

Hotel open all year; restaurant closed from 5 Aug to 1 Sep • 44 rooms, 2 of which have disabled access, with bath/WC and television • €65 to €76; breakfast €9 • À la carte €28 to €35 • Patio used as a terrace in the summer, car park

 90 LES BUISSONNETS
Mr Garrigue

 12, rue Louis Garros
33120 Arcachon
Tel. : 05 56 54 00 83
Fax : 05 56 22 55 13

Closed in Oct • 13 rooms with bath/WC or shower/WC and television • €72; breakfast €8 • No restaurant • Garden, shaded terrace, car park

 The Provençal-style patio, complete with olive and palm trees and a huge earthenware vase.

The village church, post office and café have all undergone the same lyrical renovation. In fact, Le Chalet started out as a ballroom, and the former owner was a talented drummer in his day. The renovation has created an eclectic, almost bohemian mix, combining a country bistro and patio with rooms which range from simple to more luxurious – the most recent are furnished in a modish style and creatively decorated.

 The delightful winter town and its eccentric follies.

Despite its position on the outskirts of Archachon, Le Moulleau is the centre of the town's busy night-life. It dates from the 1920s, just a few years before this villa was built in 1925. Most of the practical and soberly-decorated rooms overlook a garden full of flowers and palm trees, where you will be able to breakfast in fine weather.

Access : South of Bordeaux, on the bypass (exit no 16) or on the N 10, by the main road near the church

Access : Southbound from Arcachon on the Biscarrosse road (3km on the D 218)

91   **CHÂTEAU DU BROUSTARET**
Mr Brunet

 La Greche
33410 Rions
Tel. : 05 56 62 96 97
Fax : 05 56 76 96 97

Closed from Nov to the Easter holidays • 5 rooms with bath/WC • €45, breakfast included • No table d'hôte • Park, car park. Credit cards not accepted, no dogs allowed

92   **CHÂTEAU MEYLET**
Mme Favard

33330 Saint-Émilion
Tel. : 05 57 24 68 85

Open all year • 5 rooms with bathrooms • €51, breakfast included • No table d'hôte • Sitting room, garden, car park. Credit cards not accepted

 Soaking up the atmosphere of a Bordeaux vineyard.

This stately late-19C manor house on a wine-growing estate enjoys a wonderful position in the heart of the acclaimed Côtes de Bordeaux vineyards. Well-proportioned, tranquil rooms command views over the hills, vineyards and woodland. Guests can prepare their own breakfast in a fitted kitchen. Wine-tasting and visits of the cellars organised on request.

 The rustic charm of the rooms.

A five-acre vineyard surrounds this elegant 1789 property. The rooms boast polished parquet floors and lovely 18C furniture inherited by the family or unearthed in the local flea markets. Some bedrooms enjoy a view of the vineyard, while others overlook the garden's magnificent Indian bean tree. Breakfast is served in the conservatory in the winter and under the arbour in the summer.

Access : 6km northbound from Cadillac on the D 11 towards Targon, then take the D 120

Access : 1.5km eastbound from Saint-Émilion on the Libourne road (D 243)

 93 LE MANOIR DE JAMES
Mr and Mrs Bubois

Route de Sainte-Colombe
33580 Saint-Ferme
Tel. : 05 56 61 69 75
Fax : 05 56 61 89 78
midubois@wanadoo.fr

Closed from 15 Dec to 15 Jan • 3 rooms, one is on the ground floor, the other 2 are on the first floor, all have bath/WC • €55, breakfast included • No table d'hôte • Car park. Credit cards not accepted • Barbecue. Outdoor swimming pool, bicycles, table-tennis, boules, board games

 94 CHÂTEAU MONLOT CAPET
Mr Rivals

33330 Saint-Hippolyte
Tel. : 05 57 74 49 47
Fax : 05 57 24 62 33
mussetrivals@belair-monlot.com
www.belair-monlot.com

Open all year • 5 rooms with bathrooms • €61 to €84, breakfast included • No table d'hôte • Garden, car park

 We most liked
The manor's unbeatable position in the heart of a sought-after tourist region.

 We most liked
The personalised decoration of the rooms.

Set in ancient woodland and meadows, this 18C manor makes an ideal base camp for touring the hilly vineyards of the legendary Entre-Deux-Mers region. Period furniture adorns the well-proportioned, quiet rooms, all of which offer wonderful views of the surrounding countryside. The lady of the house, a former tourist guide, is happy to share her valuable insights into the region. Excellent welcome.

This château, with its chalk façade and lovely tiled roof is typical of the many stately homes of the region. Each room, stylishly furnished with antiques, paintings and old photos, is named after a variety of grape: Merlot, Cabernet, Sauvignon and so on. The vine theme is also prominent in the pleasant breakfast room. The lovely shaded garden is at its most idyllic in summer.

Access : 15km eastbound from Sauveterre-de-Guyenne on the D 230 and then the D 139

Access : 3km eastbound from St-Émilion, towards Castillon on the D 245

95 LA LÉZARDIÈRE
Mr and Mrs Mattei

Boimier-Gabouriaud
33540 Saint-Martin-de-Lerm
Tel. : 05 56 71 30 12
Fax : 05 56 71 30 12

Closed from 13 Nov to 22 Mar • 4 rooms and one gîte with shower/WC or bath/WC • €48, breakfast included • Table d'hôte €16 • Garden, car park. Credit cards not accepted • Outdoor swimming pool

 Lazing by the swimming pool in the immense garden.

A beautifully restored 17C farmhouse enjoying a stunning view over the Dropt Valley. Stone and wood add warmth to the welcoming rooms in the renovated cowsheds. The exposed beams, terracotta tiled floor, huge table and fireplace and original mangers lend the breakfast room a real country character. Ask to see the owner's fine collection of works on the local wines and produce.

Access : 8km to the south-east of Sauveterre-de-Guyenne on the D 670, the D 230 and then the D 129

96 L' ESCAPADE
Mr Peyroche

Route des Chaumes, La Grace
33220 Port-Sainte-Foy
Tel. : 05 53 24 22 79
Fax : 05 53 57 45 05
info @ escapade-dordogne.com
www.escapade-dordogne

Open from Feb to early Nov; closed Sun evening and Fri out of season • 12 rooms with bath/WC or shower/WC and television • €45; breakfast €6; half board €47 • Restaurant only open in the evening; menus €15 to €30 (booking necessary) • Terrace, car park. No dogs allowed • Outdoor swimming pool, fitness room, sauna, squash

 An active country-break in an unspoilt setting.

This 17C tobacco farm, run by a Franco-English team, boasts impressive leisure installations including a swimming pool, fitness room, squash court and sauna. The countrified rooms all look out over the peaceful, unspoilt countryside. Some also have a view of the foals, mares and stallions of the nearby riding stables. Rustic-style restaurant.

Access : Westbound from Sainte-Foy-la-Grande on the D 936, then a minor road

97 TYBONI

Mr and Mrs Boniface

1831 route de Capbreton
40150 Angresse
Tel. : 05 58 43 98 75

Open all year • 3 rooms • €58, breakfast included • No table d'hôte • Park, car park. Credit cards not accepted, no dogs allowed • Outdoor swimming pool

98 LE DOMAINE DE PAGUY

Mr and Mrs Darzacq

40240 Betbezer-d'Armagnac
Tel. : 05 58 44 81 57
Fax : 05 58 44 68 09

Open all year; table d'hôte closed on Sun, except for Easter lunchtime, in Jun and Wed in the summer • 4 rooms • €46, breakfast included • Table d'hôte €29 • Park, terrace, car park. Credit cards not accepted • Outdoor swimming pool. Guided tours of the Armagnac cellars

 The owners' warm, generous welcome.

Only the chirping of birds and gentle breezes rustling through the pine trees interrupt the peace and quiet of this contemporary house in regional style. The soberly decorated rooms are very pleasant. Guests can cook their own meals in a guest kitchen. The park and swimming pool next to the pond are highly appreciated during the summer months. An ideal situation within easy reach of the beach and the lively seaside village of Hossegor.

 The tour and commentary of the Armagnac cellars.

This 16C manor house stands in the centre of a vast wine-growing estate overlooking the Douze Valley. Spacious, attractive rooms open onto the landscaped park and the vineyards, where hens and ducks roam free. Fine local Landes cuisine takes pride of place in the kitchen of this handsome property.

Access : 3km eastbound from Hossegor on the D 33

Access : 5km to the north-east of Labastide-d'Armagnac on the D 11 then the D 35

99 CAPCAZAL DE PACHIOU
Mrs Dufourcet

606 route de Pachiou
40350 Mimbaste
Tel. : 05 58 55 30 54
Fax : 05 58 55 30 54

Open all year • 4 rooms • €57, breakfast included • Table d'hôte €17 • Car park. Credit cards not accepted

100 LES ARBOUSIERS
Mrs Labri

Le Gaille
40630 Sabres
Tel. : 05 58 07 52 52
Fax : 05 58 07 52 52

Open all year • 6 rooms • €43, breakfast included • Table d'hôte €14 • Park, car park. Credit cards not accepted, no dogs allowed

The authenticity of the house and the welcome.

This wonderful old house has been in the same family since it was built in the 17C. Its loving restoration has preserved countless traces of its illustrious past, such as a dovecote, bird cage, original panelling and parquet floors. The house exudes history, as the canopied beds, carved fireplaces and old prints illustrate, and this same proud commitment to tradition is in evidence in the kitchen, where duck and goose feature prominently in mouth-watering local dishes.

The enchanting picture of this half-timbered house.

Set in a clearing in a pine forest, this half-timbered home, typical of the region, never fails to attract admiring glances. The comfortable new rooms are bright and airy. The large bay windows of the restaurant also flood the dining room with light, while diners can enjoy the view of a park which makes no secret of the owner's passion for wildlife and ornithology. What's more, the owner's simple, unaffected welcome is quite irresistible.

Access : 12km to the south-east of Dax on the N 947 then the D 16

Access : 7.5km westbound from Sabres on the D 44

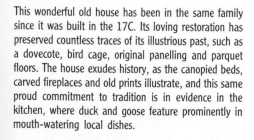

101 CHAMBRE D'HÔTE M. LADEUIX
Mr and Mrs Ladeuix

26 avenue Salvador-Allende
40220 Tarnos
Tel. : 05 59 64 13 95
Fax : 05 59 64 13 95

Open all year • 5 rooms and one gîte • €46, breakfast
included • No table d'hôte • Park, car park. Credit cards
not accepted • Outdoor swimming pool

102 HOSTELLERIE DES DUCS
Mr Blanchet

Boulevard Jean Brisseau
47120 Duras
Tel. : 05 53 83 74 58
Fax : 05 53 83 75 03
hostellerie.de.ducs@wanadoo.fr
www.hostellerieducs-duras.com

Closed Sat lunchtime, Sun evening in winter and Mon
(apart from the evenings in summer) • 16 rooms with
bath/WC or shower/WC and television, some are air-
conditioned • €51 to €81; breakfast €7; half board
€55 to €70 • Menus €25 to €38 • Terrace, garden,
garage, private car park. No dogs allowed in rooms
• Outdoor swimming pool

 **The pleasant surprise of the woodland
to the rear of the house.**

From the road, it is impossible to imagine that this house
covered in wisteria opens onto such a sumptuous park
of oak, chestnut, maple, mimosa, banana and pear
trees. Most of the rooms are relatively simply decorated,
except one which has a distinctly Basque accent. Guests
have the use of a laundry room and a kitchen. Children
will love the sheep pen, as well as the nearby rabbit
and poultry cages.

 **Lucky guests claim to have glimpsed
the castle's ghosts!**

The superb, well-tended garden of this old 17C
presbytery regularly wins flower awards. The modest but
practical bedrooms are named after the local vineyards.
Comfortable Louis XIII dining room and a terrace with
wrought-iron furniture commands a splendid view of the
Castle of the Dukes of Duras.

Access : 5km northbound from Bayonne on the
N 10

Access : In the upper part of Duras, on the road
near the castle

103 LES RIVES DU PLANTIÉ
Mr Chamel and Mr Mora

Route de Castelmoron
47110 Le Temple-sur-Lot
Tel. : 05 53 79 86 86
Fax : 05 53 79 86 85
lesrivesduplantie @ wanadoo.fr
www.perso.libertysurf

Closed in Jan and from 20 Oct to 8 Nov • 10 rooms, one of which has disabled access, all have bath/WC and television • €57 to €63; breakfast €9; half board €91 • Restaurant closed Sat lunchtime, Sun evening and Mon; menus €20 to €29 • Terrace, garden, car park • Outdoor swimming pool, landing stage on the Lot

104 CHÂTEAU DE SEIGLAL
Mr and Mrs Decourty

47380 Monclar
Tel. : 05 53 41 81 30
Fax : 05 53 41 85 10
decourty-chambres-hotes @ wordline.fr

Open all year • 5 rooms • €55, breakfast included • Table d'hôte €16 • Park, car park. Credit cards not accepted, no dogs allowed • Outdoor swimming pool, table-tennis, table football, football field, fishing, walking, cycling

We most liked
A boat trip down the Lot.

This secluded, early-19C farmhouse is bounded by a pleasant shaded garden complete with well. The recently renovated rooms are well equipped and proportioned and the inspired decision to turn the stables into a dining room provides a perfect backdrop to the tasty cooking, in which local produce and recipes figure prominently. A floating landing stage has recently been built on the banks of the Lot.

We most liked
The friendly atmosphere of this 19C castle.

Hidden by a park planted with ancient trees, this small château built in 1820 is a haven of peace and quiet. The well-proportioned, comfortable rooms, named after the owner's five sisters, overlook the park and the surrounding meadows. The dining room is a real treasure chest of period furniture, carved hunting scenes and a superb marble and earthenware fireplace. Local produce and delicious home-made pastries are the mainstay of the menu.

Access : From Le Temple-sur-Lot drive towards Castelmoron-sur-Lot

Access : 6km northbound from Fongrave on the D 238 then the D 667, at the no 25 kilometre marker

105 LE DOMAINE DU CAUZE
Mrs Pope

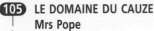

47600 Nérac
Tel. : 05 53 65 54 44
Fax : 05 53 65 54 44
cauze.pope @ wanadoo.fr

Closed from 1 Nov to 28 Feb • 4 rooms • €52, breakfast included • Table d'hôte €19 • Car park. No dogs allowed • Outdoor swimming pool

106 HÔTEL DU CHÂTEAU
Mr Cellié

7 avenue de Mondenard
47600 Nérac
Tel. : 05 53 65 09 05
Fax : 05 53 65 89 78

Closed from 2 to 18 Jan • 16 rooms on 3 floors with bath/WC or shower/WC, some have television • €39; breakfast €5; half board €35 • Restaurant closed Fri eve, Sat lunch and Sun eve from Oct to May; menus €11 (in the week) to €38

The tranquillity of this hundred-year-old establishment.

Wandering around the old town.

This superbly restored old farmhouse has it all. First and foremost, an idyllic situation on a hillside with sweeping views of the dense forests of the Landes and the Gers on fine days. Add to this the tranquillity of the tastefully decorated rooms and last, but not least, the meals, served under the arbour in the summer and whipped up with rare enthusiasm by the imaginative owner-chef. Friendly, hospitable hosts.

The setting of this imposing solid-stone establishment would be hard to beat: in the heart of the capital of the Albret region, just a stone's throw from the castle and the River Baïse. Uncluttered and well-kept bedrooms are spread over three floors. Tasty cooking with a rich local character is served in the impeccable dining room.

Access : 2.5km eastbound from Nérac towards Agen (D 656)

Access : In the town centre

107 CHÂTEAU CONTET
Mr and Mrs Raitrie

47250 Samazan
Tel. : 05 53 20 60 60

Open all year • 3 rooms with bath or shower and separate WC • €58, breakfast included • Table d'hôte €19 • Park, car park. Credit cards not accepted, no dogs allowed • Outdoor swimming pool. Children's games room

108 OPPOCA
Mr and Mrs Massonde

Face au fronton
64250 Aïnhoa
Tel. : 05 59 29 90 72
Fax : 05 59 29 81 03
oppoca @ wanadoo.fr

Closed from 15 Nov to 15 Dec, Sun evening and Mon except in Aug • 12 rooms, most of which have bath/WC • €36 to €49; breakfast €6; half board €40 to €44 • Menus €15 to €28 • Terrace, courtyard, car park. No dogs allowed

The wide range of leisure activities.

An elegant 16C manor house set in well-tended grounds in the heart of the countryside. The bright colour scheme of the rooms sets off a smart but homely interior, with a hint of rustic style. Meals are served in the Louis XIII-style dining room or under the arbour around the pool. The choice of leisure activities is vast: play room, bicycles, lawn croquet, billiards, table-tennis, basketball, pétanque and only 10km away, a golf course and tennis courts.

Watching an energetic game of "pelota" – squash played with baskets instead of rackets!

Among the main attractions of this small family home are its simple, country-style rooms, compact and smartly kept, the dining room furnished with regional antiques, exposed beams and a courtyard terrace full of flowers in season. This mostly 17C family house with traditional whitewashed walls and red-painted timbers and shutters is right in the heart of a picturesque Basque country village, opposite the high wall of the pelota court!

Access : 10km southbound from Marmande towards Casteljaloux

Access : To the south-east of Cambo-les-Bains on the D918 then the D 20, 3km from the border

 109 **CHAMBRE D'HÔTE ARRAYOA**
Mrs Ibarburu

64310 Ascain
Tel. : 05 59 54 06 18

Open all year • 4 rooms with bathrooms • €46, breakfast included • No table d'hôte • Living room with a kitchen and library

 110 **LES JARDINS DE BAKÉA**
Mr and Mrs Duval

64700 Biriatou
Tel. : 05 59 20 02 01
Fax : 05 59 20 58 21
bakea @ fr.st
www.bakea.fr.st/

Open from Easter to late Sep; closed Sun and Mon except in Jul, Aug and Sep • 23 rooms, 2 of which have disabled access, all have bath/WC or shower/WC and television • €43 to €61; breakfast €8; half board €62 to €67 • Meals served at the Bakéa • Terrace, garden, car park. No dogs allowed

We most liked **Getting away from it all without entirely forgoing the social whirl of the Basque coast.**

We most liked **Sauntering around this quaint picture-postcard Basque hamlet.**

This lovely house seems to have been designed with the good life in mind, from the charming countrified rooms to the tempting home-made foie gras and other delicacies served in the former cowshed. If your waistband feels a little tight, you can try your hand on the establishment's private pelota court or don your walking boots and hike up the Rhune. The superb view is more than worth the effort, but those with fewer calories to burn may prefer to catch the little train from the Col de St Ignace.

This rambling regional-style house at the entrance to a hamlet is reached by a tiny mountain road. Some of the practical, unostenatious bedrooms overlook the neighbouring Bidassoa Valley. Next door is a restaurant with all the charm of a mountain chalet: exposed stonework and beams and a fireplace. In fine weather, sample the tasty, traditional flavour of local cooking under the pleasant shade of the plane trees on the terrace.

Access : 800m from the pelota court

Access : To the south-east of Hendaye, drive for 4km on the D 258

  111 **CHEZ ROLANDE AUGAREILS**
Mrs Augareils

6 place Cazenave
64260 Buzy
Tel. : 05 59 21 01 01
rolande.augareils @ wanadoo.fr

Closed from Oct to Easter • 5 rooms • €46, breakfast included • Table d'hôte €16 to €25 • Car park. Credit cards not accepted, no dogs allowed

  112 **LA BELLE AUBERGE**
Mr and Mrs Vicassiau

64270 Castagnède
Tel. : 05 59 38 15 28
Fax : 05 59 65 03 57

Closed from mid-Dec to mid-Jan • 12 rooms with bath/WC or shower/WC, all have television • €39 to €43; breakfast €5 • Restaurant closed Sun and Mon evening; menus €10 to €20 • Terrace, garden, car park. No dogs allowed • Outdoor swimming pool

 The warm welcome extended by the lady of the house, Rolande, and her staff.

This attractive Béarn farmhouse with its wrought-iron gate, flowered window boxes and courtyard, lies in the heart of the village. Don't stand on ceremony, just sit down with the other guests and Rolande's family at the huge open-air table, which can seat up to 25, and enjoy a wonderful meal, invariably accompanied by a song or two. The rooms are lovingly decorated with old lace and family heirlooms, but, beware, none are heated. 100% authentic Béarn cooking.

Access : 4km northbound from Arudy on the D 920

 Killing time around the swimming pool.

Nothing could be more welcoming than this family-run establishment nestling in a picturesque hamlet on the fast-flowing Gave d'Oloron river. The bar and two country-style dining rooms, serving generous helpings of hearty, local dishes, are located in the main wing of the old house. The bedrooms, in a later wing, are not luxurious but they are well looked-after and all overlook the spacious garden and unusually-shaped swimming pool.

Access : Leave Salies-de-Béarn on the D 17 (towards Peyrehorade), then left onto the D 27 and right onto the D 384

 113 LE CHÂTEAU DE BOUES
Mrs Dornon

64570 Féas
Tel. : 05 59 39 95 49
Fax : 05 59 39 95 49

Closed from late Sep to Apr • 4 rooms • €57, breakfast included • No table d'hôte • Garden, car park. Credit cards not accepted, no dogs allowed • Outdoor swimming pool

 114 BRIKÉTÉNIA
Mr and Mrs Ibarboure

142 rue de l'Église
64210 Guéthary
Tel. : 05 59 26 51 34
Fax : 05 59 54 71 55

Open from 15 Mar to 15 Nov • 28 rooms, 12 of which are in a separate wing (some have balconies), one has disabled access, all have bath/WC and television • €69 to €84; breakfast €8 • No restaurant • Car park. No dogs allowed

We most liked **The kindness of the hospitable owners.**

On the doorstep of Baretous Valley, the pristine walls of this lofty 18C castle dominate the surrounding Béarn countryside. The bedrooms, located in the central wing – the owners occupy the towers – enjoy views of the garden, swimming pool and superb kitchen garden. Breakfast is a lively, friendly affair and guests are made to feel like friends of the family.

We most liked **Grab a "makhila" – a traditional Basque walking stick – and explore this seaside resort.**

The coaching inn, built in 1680 on the heights of Guéthary, is a fine example of traditional Basque architecture: steep tiled roof, balcony, whitewashed walls, timber frames and red shutters. Perhaps it was the ocean view from some of the rooms that appealed to one Napoleon Bonaparte, an illustrious former guest? Be that as it may, the energetic proprietors are not the sort to rest on their laurels and the inn has recently been renovated from top to toe.

Access : 8km to the south-west of Oloron-Ste-Marie on the D 919

Access : Near the church

115 **FERME ETXEBERRIA**
Mr Mourguy

64220 Ispoure
Tel. : 05 59 37 06 23

Closed in Dec and Jan • 4 rooms • €39, breakfast included • No table d'hôte • Car park

116 **LA FERME AUX SANGLIERS**
Mr Delhay-Cazaurang

Micalet
64570 Issor
Tel. : 05 59 34 43 96
Fax : 05 59 34 49 56

Open all year • 5 rooms with bathrooms • €49, breakfast included • Table d'hôte €14 • Car park. Credit cards not accepted, no dogs allowed • Tasting and selling of home-made "charcuterie"

Donkey rides through Irouleguy's vineyards.

What better way to really get to know the Basque country than by staying in this attractive farmhouse surrounded by vineyards? The converted barn houses modern, soberly decorated and very pleasant rooms. Guests have the use of a kitchenette, an attractive breakfast room and a conservatory which overlooks the vines. The owners, who also produce wine and raise donkeys, are happy to help guests organise hikes throughout the region.

The stunning view from all the bedrooms.

A narrow road winds its way up to this lovingly restored Béarn farmhouse. You can be sure of a warm, generous welcome, together with comfortable rooms, all of which command sweeping views of the valley and the Pyrenean peaks. The focus is on healthy, local produce and the owner, who breeds animals, adores taking visitors round his boar parks, to the delight of children.

Access : 0.8km to the north-east of Saint-Jean-Pied-de-Port on the D 933

Access : 10km westbound from St-Christau on the D 918 as far as Asasp, then the N 134 and the D 918 towards Arette

 117 HÔTEL DU CHÊNE
Mrs Salaberry

 64250 Itxassou
Tel. : 05 59 29 75 01
Fax : 05 59 29 27 39

Closed in Jan and Feb, on Tue from Oct to Jun, and on Mon in Jul, Aug and Sep • 16 rooms with bath/WC, some have television • €38; breakfast €6; half board €42 • Menus €14 to €29 • Terrace, garden, car park. No dogs allowed in restaurant

 118 SOUBELETA
Mrs Régérat

 64250 Itxassou
Tel. : 05 59 29 78 64

Open all year • 5 rooms • €49, breakfast included • No table d'hôte • Garden, car park. Credit cards not accepted, no dogs allowed

 We most liked **The superb Villa Arnaga, nearby, onetime home to Edmond Rostand, creator of Cyrano de Bergerac.**

The doors of this hospitable country inn have been open since 1696. The bedrooms, some of which are graced with marble fireplaces and old Basque furniture, overlook the cherry trees of Itxassou – a sight to behold in the spring! Make sure you sample the famous blackcherry jam under the colourful blue beams of the dining room or in the shade of the sweet-scented wisteria.

 We most liked **The tranquil mood of this peaceful 17C mansion.**

This imposing mansion, built in 1675, enjoys a lovely spot in the upper part of the village. The generously proportioned rooms, graced with gleaming family antiques, look over meadows and the orchard; two have marble fireplaces. The light, airy sitting room is very pleasant and children will love visiting the cows in the neighbouring dairy farm.

Access : Near the church

Access : In the village, stay on the D 918 until the Nive bridge, then turn right

LESTELLE-BÉTHARRAM - 64800   **PAGOLLE - 64120**

 119 LE VIEUX LOGIS
Mr Gaye

Route des Grottes
64800 Lestelle-Bétharram
Tel. : 05 59 71 94 87
Fax : 05 59 71 96 75
hotel.levieuxlogis @ wanadoo.fr
www.perso.wanadoo.fr/vieuxlogis/

Closed in Feb, from 25 Oct to 8 Nov, and on Sun evening
and Mon out of season • 40 rooms, 2 of which have
disabled access, with bath/WC or shower/WC and
television • €50; breakfast €8; half board €44 to
€51 • Menus €20 to €38 • Terrace, park, car park. No
dogs allowed in rooms • Outdoor swimming pool

 120 MAISON EILICHONDOA
Mr and Mrs Walther

64120 Pagolle
Tel. : 05 59 65 65 34
Fax : 05 59 65 72 15
jeanwalter @ online.fr

Open all year • 4 rooms • €45, breakfast included • Table
d'hôte €16 • Garden, car park. No dogs allowed

 The spectacular caves of Bétharram,
two minutes' walk from the hotel.

This "old abode" in fact turns out to be quite modern.
The old farm, which houses the rustic restaurant, is
somewhat overshadowed by a more recent guest wing
with practical rooms, all with balconies overlooking the
mountains. Alternatively, treat yourself to one of the five
little chalets lined in wood which are dotted around the
50-acre wood and parkland; a perfect setting for the
ultimate game of hide-and-seek!

 The pastoral charm of this remote
spot.

Those in need of a serious break should head for this
17C farm, set among open fields, on one of the old
pilgrim roads to St James of Compostela. The bedrooms,
recently fitted-out with all the modern comforts,
overlook the surrounding hillsides. Meals are taken in
the vast dining room where the exposed stone work and
timbers cannot fail to catch the eye. Friendly service.

Access : 2km from Lestelle-Bétharram, towards the
caves

Access : 13km westbound from Mauléon-Licharre on
the D 918 then the D 302

  121 VILLA ARGI-EDER
Mr Basset

Avenue Napoléon III
64500 Saint-Jean-de-Luz
Tel. : 05 59 54 81 65
villa-argi-eder @ wanadoo.fr

Open all year • 4 rooms • €46, breakfast €4.50 • No table
d'hôte • Terrace, garden, car park. Credit cards not
accepted

  122 L' AUBERGE BASQUE
Mrs Bastres

Vieille route de Saint-Jean-de-Luz
64310 Saint-Pée-sur-Nivelle
Tel. : 05 59 54 10 15

Open from Easter to Oct • 16 rooms located in
2 buildings with shower/WC • €49 to €53; breakfast
€6 • No restaurant • Garden, car park

 **Admire the reckless surfers braving
the giant waves.**

This handsome Basque villa, recently spruced up with
a new coat of paint, has something for everyone:
tranquillity, a well-tended lawn lined in flowers and a
superb location just 100m from the surfing beach. The
brand-new spacious bedrooms are an invitation to
meditation and those overlooking the garden have
private terraces. The bathrooms are neat and well
appointed. One of the resort's most pleasant hotels.

 **Buying a souvenir pelota basket from
one of the village's renowned
craftsmen.**

This traditional three-hundred-year-old timber-framed
Basque homestead enjoys a lovely view of the Nieville
Valley. Accommodation is immaculate and splendidly
peaceful, if a little on the old-fashioned side; rooms in
the main wing have most character. In summer, make
a beeline for the garden and the shade of the trees.

Access : 5km to the north-east of Saint-Jean-de-Luz
on the N 10 towards Biarritz, then take a minor road

Access : Westbound from Saint-Pée-sur-Nivelle, on
the old St-Jean-de-Luz road

123 LA CLOSERIE DU GUILHAT
Mrs Potiron

Le Guilhat
64270 Salies-de-Béarn
Tel. : 05 59 38 08 80
Fax : 05 59 38 08 80

Open all year • 4 rooms and one gîte • €52, breakfast
included • Table d'hôte €16 • Park, car park. Credit cards
not accepted, no dogs allowed

124 ARRAYA
Mr Fagoaga

64310 Sare
Tel. : 05 59 54 20 46
Fax : 05 59 54 27 04
hotel @ arraya.com
www.arraya.com

Open from late Mar to early Nov • 20 rooms, most have
bath/WC, some have shower/WC, all have television
• €68 (€61 low season); breakfast €8; half board €67 to
€76 (€60 to €68 low season) • Restaurant closed Sun
evening and Mon lunchtime out of season; menus €21 to
€30 • Terrace, garden. No dogs allowed in rooms • Shop
with Basque linen and local produce

 **Whiling away the evenings on the
terrace facing the Pyrenees.**

It is difficult to find a fault with such a lovely old country
house, especially one with a sumptuous landscaped park
and an exquisite terrace overlooking the valley, set
against a backdrop of Pyrenean peaks. A bold colour
scheme distinguishes the quiet, well-dimensioned
rooms, each of which is named after a flower. The
mistress of the house makes guests feel truly welcome
and dining on the winter veranda or summer terrace is
an unforgettable experience.

 **Chugging up the Rhune in an old train
(1924).**

This village, nestling at the foot of the Rhune, is a
treasure chest of Basque heritage. In keeping with its
historic past, the 17C coaching inn, which formerly
welcomed pilgrims of St James, is a fine example of
regional interior design with dark timbers, old furniture
and colourful fabrics. The surrounding countryside, a
former "smugglers' paradise" is now heaven on earth:
footpaths criss-cross the region, winding through
meadows where the local ponies and sheep graze
peacefully.

Access : 4km northbound from Salies towards
Puyoo, in the upper reaches of Salies

Access : In the heart of the village, near the main
square, next to the pelota court

125 **OLHABIDEA**
Mr and Mrs Fagoaga

64310 Sare
Tel. : 05 59 54 21 85
Fax : 04 59 47 50 41

Closed from Dec to Feb • 4 rooms • €60, breakfast
included • No table d'hôte • Park, car park. Credit cards
not accepted, no dogs allowed

**The impeccable decoration of this
typical Basque farmhouse.**

The sight of this 17C-18C farmhouse nestling among
roses and wisteria is already a delight for the eyes:
carefully restored for over 20 years by local craftsmen,
it's something of a local success story. The sunlit rooms
are exquisitely decorated with embroidered bed linen,
old prints, feathered quilts and lovingly polished
furniture. Breakfast on the terrace overlooking the
garden is a wonderful start to the day.

Access : 13km to the south-west of Saint-Jean-de-Luz
on the D 918 and then the D 4

AUVERGNE

Shh! Auvergne's volcanoes are dormant and have been for many millennia, forming a natural rampart against the inroads of man and ensuring that this beautiful wilderness will never be entirely tamed. If you listen very carefully, you may just make out a distant rumble from Vulcania, where spectacular theme park attractions celebrate the sleeping giants. The region's windswept domes and peaks, sculpted by long-extinguished fires, are now the source of countless mountain springs that cascade down the steep slopes into brooks, rivers and crystal-clear lakes. Renowned for the therapeutic virtues of its waters, the region has long played host to countless well-heeled *curistes*, come to take the waters in its elegant spa resorts. It has to be said that many find it impossible to follow doctor's orders when faced with the enticing aroma of a country stew or a full-bodied Cantal cheese.

50 ESTABLISHMENTS

126 to **175**

 126 **G. H. MONTESPAN-TALLEYRAND**
Mr Livertout

Place des Thermes
03160 Bourbon-L-Archambault
Tel. : 04 70 67 00 24
Fax : 04 70 67 12 00
hotelmontespan@wanadoo.fr
www.hotel-montespan.com

Open from 1 Apr to 20 Oct • 45 rooms, 4 of which have kitchenettes, all have bath/WC or shower/WC and television • €50 to €75; breakfast €9; half board €49 to €66 • Menus €15 (in the week) to €34 • Garage. No dogs allowed in restaurant • Outdoor swimming pool, fitness room

 127 **LE CHALET**
Mr Schweizer

03000 Coulandon
Tel. : 04 70 46 00 66
Fax : 04 70 44 07 09
hotel-chalet@cs3i.fr
www.hotel-lechalet.com

Closed from Dec to Jan • 28 rooms, 19 of which are in a separate wing, one has disabled access. Rooms have bath/WC or shower/WC and television • €54 to €74; breakfast €8; half board €55 to €65 • Restaurant "Le Montégut": menus €18 (in the week) to €39 • Terrace, park, car park • Outdoor swimming pool

The attractive flowered garden at the foot of a medieval tower.

These historic houses stand next door to the spa centre with the Castle of the Dukes of Bourbon in the background. Practically all the ceilings feature traditional dark-timbered beams, while simple white-stone walls, adorned with elegant fireplaces, light up the cosy, personalised rooms. Talleyrand, and a number of noble ladies, including Mme de Montespan and Mme de Sévigné resided here while taking the waters. A grand old establishment which is definitely a cut above your average spa hotel.

Generous breakfasts with a distinctly Alpine flavour; the landlord is Swiss.

A cluster of three buildings make up this 10-acre country estate, complete with a large pond for fishing, hundred-year-old parkland and a swimming pool. The rooms are situated in the "chalet", which also houses the reception and in the former stables, while the restaurant is in a more recent building. Savour the pleasure of waking up in the heart of the peaceful Bourbon countryside.

Access : In the centre of the resort, next to the spa

Access : 7km to the south-west of Moulins on the D 945 (towards Souvigny), then right on a minor road

 128 DEMEURE D'HAUTERIVE
Mrs Lefebvre

03340 La Ferté-Hauterive
Tel. : 04 70 43 04 85
Fax : 04 70 43 00 62
www.wraaf.com/hauterive.fr

Open all year • 5 rooms, one of which is on the ground floor • €65, breakfast included • Table d'hôte €16 • Park, car park. Credit cards not accepted

 129 LES BOURBONS
Mr and Mrs Bujard

47 avenue Marx Dormoy
03100 Montluçon
Tel. : 04 70 05 28 93
Fax : 04 70 05 16 92

Hotel open all year, restaurant closed from 29 Jul to 12 Aug • 43 rooms with bath/WC or shower/WC and television, some have air-conditioning, 5 are non-smoking • €43 to €48; breakfast €6; half board €37 to €42 • Aux Ducs de Bourbon (air-conditioned): menus €19 (in the week) to €32. Brasserie Pub 47: €13 to €16 • Garage

 Strolling through the park bedecked in autumn colours.

It would be difficult to find a more gracious establishment than this opulent mansion, built in 1850 in the heart of an eight-acre park. The exquisitely decorated rooms, particularly those on the ground floor, are spacious. The house also provides its guests with a wide range of leisure activities, including billiards, badminton and table-tennis, but the most pleasant of all is a stroll through parkland dotted with ornamental pools and follies. Highly friendly atmosphere.

 The Folk Music Museum in the Castle of the Dukes of Bourbon, just 500m from the hotel.

The imposing stone façade of this hotel next door to the railway station dates from 1895. Its practical rooms have been recently refurbished in warm colours; the somewhat bleak bathrooms are nonetheless quite acceptable. Guests can choose to dine in the traditional Ducs de Bourbon restaurant or in Pub 47.

Access : 12km northbound from St-Pourçain-sur-Sioule on the N 9 then the D 32

Access : On the square near the railway station

130 LE CHALET DE LA NEVERDIÈRE
Mr and Mrs Vrel

Les Ferrons
03160 Ygrande
Tel. : 04 70 66 31 67
Fax : 04 70 66 32 64

Open all year • 4 rooms located in a small house 100m away • €40, breakfast included • Table d'hôte €11 to €16 • Garden, car park. Credit cards not accepted, no dogs allowed

131 BEAUSÉJOUR
Mr Puech

15340 Calvinet
Tel. : 04 71 49 91 68
Fax : 04 71 49 98 63
beausejour-puech @ wanadoo.fr

Closed from 6 Jan to 14 Feb, and on Mon and Tue except for the evenings in Jul and Aug. Closed Wed out of season • 12 rooms with bath/WC or shower/WC, all have television • €46; breakfast €7; half board €55 • Menus €16 (in the week) to €50 (booking advised) • Private car park

The gargantuan breakfasts.

An unforgettable dining experience.

This early 20C house with its ochre edged façade and steep roof nestling in the heart of the Bourbon countryside, looks nothing like the chalets the region abounds in, but who cares? Its well-proportioned and well thought-out rooms overlook lush, green countryside. Tronçais Forest, 12km away, is perfect to walk off the extremely generous breakfasts. Very friendly staff.

A larger than life genius reigns over the kitchens of this traditional Auvergne house in the middle of nowhere. The master chef whips up imaginative recipes based on wholesome local produce in which mushrooms, chestnuts and pork figure prominently. Guests feast on his inspired creations in an elegant brick-coloured dining room-veranda. The rooms, practical rather than charming, are amply compensated for by the quality of the cooking.

Access : 10km to the south-west of Bourbon-l'Archambault on the D 953, then a minor road

Access : On the Figeac road to Aurillac, leave the N 22 at Maurs for the D 19. In the centre of the village

 132 **AUBERGE DU VIEUX CHÊNE**
Mrs Moins

34 route des Lacs
15270 Champs-sur-Tarentaine
Tel. : 04 71 78 71 64
Fax : 04 71 78 70 88
danielle.moins@wanadoo.fr

Open from Apr to Oct, closed Sun evenings and Mon except from 15 Jun to 15 Sep • 15 rooms on 2 floors with bathrooms, some have television • €60 to €78; breakfast €9; half board €52 to €63 • Restaurant open only in the evenings; menus €21 to €29 • Terrace, garden, car park

 133 **AUBERGE DE L'ASPRE**
Mr Landau

15140 Fontanges
Tel. : 04 71 40 75 76
Fax : 04 71 40 75 27
auberge.aspre@wordonline.fr
www.auberge-aspre.com

Closed from Dec to Jan, Sun and Wed evenings and Mon from Oct to May • 8 rooms, one of which has disabled access. All have unusual split-level bathrooms and television • €46; breakfast €7; half board €48 • Menus €15 to €30 • Terrace, garden, car park • Outdoor swimming pool

 The picturesque Artense region, somewhat reminiscent of Scandinavia.

The frontage of this historic 19C farmhouse is almost hidden by Virginia creeper and flowers. The pretty, cosy rooms overlook a pleasant, peaceful garden. Exposed beams, thick stone walls and a huge fireplace add character to the dining room in the converted barn. Relax on the shaded terrace and admire the beautiful countryside of hills and meadows where the owners' horses graze.

 The tinkling of the cow-bells.

This old farmhouse with its beautiful stone-shingled roof lies in a secluded hamlet of the Aspre Valley not far from the village of Salers. The modern, brightly-coloured bedrooms, each of which has an unusual split-level bathroom, are situated in the old barn. Savour the traditional, tasty Auvergne menu in the rustic-style dining room, the veranda or on the pleasant terrace overlooking the garden.

Access : Not far from the centre of the village

Access : 5km southbound from Salers on the D 35

134 DE BARATHE
Mr and Mrs Breton

15130 Giou-de-Mamou
Tel. : 04 71 64 61 72
Fax : 04 71 64 85 10
barathe @ wanadoo.fr

Open all year • 5 rooms • €38, breakfast included • Table d'hôte €12 • Garden, car park. Credit cards not accepted, no dogs allowed

 The authentic character of this country setting.

If you like the idea of waking to the sound of the cow-bells from the Salers cattle grazing in the lush, green meadows, then make a beeline for this place! Simple, yet comfortable rooms, ideal for families. Exposed stonework, old furniture, a fireplace, wood benches and a sink set the scene of the authentic dining room. Meals are, of course, prepared using produce grown and reared on the farm.

Access : 7km eastbound from Aurillac on the N 122 then the D 58

135 AUBERGE DU PONT DE LANAU
Mr and Mrs Kergoat

Lanau
15260 Neuvéglise
Tel. : 04 71 23 57 76
Fax : 04 71 23 53 84
aubergedupontde lanau @ wanadoo.fr

Closed in Jan • 8 rooms on 2 floors, all have bath/WC or shower/WC • €50 to €60; breakfast €8 • Restaurant closed on Mon and Tue from 1 Nov to 1 Apr; menus €22 to €45 • Terrace, garden, car park

 The endless meanders of the River Truyère.

This former coaching house, built in 1821, spans one of the rare crossing-places over the Truyère. Good, solid furniture adorns the well-maintained rooms. The typical, Auvergne-style decoration of the dining room with its well-worn panelling, exposed beams and huge stone fireplaces, has been preserved by successive owners over the years. Guests have the run of a small garden and a pleasant, shaded terrace.

Access : 4.5km from Chaudes-Aigues on the D 921 (Saint-Flour road)

 136 **HOSTELLERIE LES BREUILS**
Mr and Mrs Rochès

 15300 Murat
Tel. : 04 71 20 01 25
Fax : 04 71 20 33 20
www.cantal-hotel.com/murat/hoteldesbreuils

Open from 1 May to 11 Nov and during the school winter holidays • 10 rooms, most have bath/WC, some have television • €65 to €76 (€63 to €74 low season); breakfast €7 • No restaurant • Garden, private car park • Indoor swimming pool, sauna, leisure area

We most liked
The friendly, personalised welcome.

All the rooms of this small 19C mansion backing onto the historic town, have recently been treated to a facelift of bright, bold colours and some have retained their Louis XVI furniture. The roomy bathrooms are well fitted-out. Attractive reading room with fireplace and piano. A building to the rear of the garden houses an indoor swimming pool.

Access : Outside the ramparts, by the main road

---

 137 **AUBERGE DES MONTAGNES**
Mr and Mrs Combourieu

 15800 Vic-sur-Cère
Tel. : 04 71 47 57 01
Fax : 04 71 49 63 83
aubdesmont @ aol.com
www.auberge-des-montagnes.com

Closed from 10 Oct to 20 Dec • 22 rooms, 10 of which are in a separate wing and one has disabled access. Rooms have bath/WC or shower/WC, some have television • €42 to €46; breakfast €6; half board €37 to €45 • Restaurant closed Tue out of season; menus €13 (except Sun lunch) to €21 • Terrace, car park, garage • 2 swimming pools (out and in), mountain biking, fishing, horse-drawn rides, cross-country skiing

We most liked
Visiting the farm where the film "With a friend like Harry" was shot.

The still waters of a pond reflect this picture-book hotel comprised of a handsome old farmstead with a stone-shingled roof, a more recent house flanked by a tower and a spacious stone terrace. The vast rooms are decorated in a rustic or a contemporary style. Swimming pool, mountain bikes, hiking, horse-drawn carts, fishing, skiing: the extensive range of activities illustrates the owners' get-up-and-go personality. Delicious feasts of Auvergne cooking.

Access : At Vic-sur-Cère leave the N 122 (Aurillac-Murat road) and take the D 54 for Pailherols

 138 LE BAILLIAGE
Mr and Mrs Gouzon

Rue Notre-Dame
15140 Salers
Tel. : 04 71 40 71 95
Fax : 04 71 40 74 90
info @ salers-hotel-bailliage.com
www.salers-hotel-bailliage.com

Closed from 15 Nov to 1 Feb • 30 rooms, 4 in a separate wing (La Demeure Jarriges, 300m away), all have bath/WC and television • €40 to €76; breakfast €7; half board €54 • Menus €11 to €30 • Terrace, garden, garage, car park • Outdoor swimming pool

 139 CHAMBRE D'HÔTE M. PRUDENT
Mr and Mrs Prudent

Rue des Nobles
15140 Salers
Tel. : 04 71 40 75 36
Fax : 04 71 40 75 36

Open all year • 6 rooms with separate entrances • €40, breakfast included • No table d'hôte • Garden

 Strolling past the historic buildings of Salers.

 Contemplating the exceptional panorama of the volcanic peaks of the Cantal.

The stone walls of this 1960s farmstead stand in one of the region's most enchanting medieval villages. The spacious, comfortable rooms overlook either the garden, the town or the slopes of the nearby Puy Violent. Soft lighting, cane furniture and red and orange drapes adorn the stylish redecorated restaurant. Gourmets come from miles around to enjoy the cuisine in which the region's famous Salers beef naturally takes pride of place, as does its namesake cheese. Pleasant garden-terrace.

This 17C house is idyllically situated in the heart of the picturesque medieval village of Salers. All the simply decorated yet comfortable rooms have their own private entrance and some command a fine view over the volcanoes. Treat yourself to breakfast in bed or venture downstairs and admire the attractive Auvergne dining room or the wonderful view from the terrace in fine weather. Souvenir shop in the hotel.

Access : At the entrance to the village next to the large car park

Access : In the town centre

 CHÂTEAU DE LA BASTIDE
Mrs Ichard

Esplanade Barrouze
15410 Salers
Tel. : 04 71 40 74 14
Fax : 04 71 40 75 94

Closed from Jan to Mar and from 6 Nov to 20 Dec
• 13 rooms with bath/WC or shower/WC and television
• €54; breakfast €6 • No restaurant • Terrace garden

 AUBERGE DE TOURNEMIRE
Mrs Louisfert

15310 Tournemire
Tel. : 04 71 47 61 28
Fax : 04 71 47 68 76
louisfert @ wanadoo.fr

Closed from 10 Jan to 6 Feb. Booking essential out of season • 6 rooms • €58, breakfast included • Menus €15 to €25 • Terrace, garden. No dogs allowed

 Feast your eyes on the head-spinning peaks and gorges of the Cantal mountains.

This 17C castle flanked with a tower was remodelled in the 19C. A modern flavour and good soundproofing characterise the rooms, some of which have sloping ceilings. Bare woodwork adds an extra splash of authenticity. The small dining room somewhat lacks character in comparison and most guests prefer the terrace overlooking the fields where the famous Salers cattle peacefully munch on the grass as they contemplate the distant Cantal peaks.

 The sheer magic of this lovely spot.

It is well-nigh impossible to resist the charm of this small hotel and its location, more than worth a trip in its own right. The enchanting, lavishly cared-for rooms make up in appeal what they may lack in space. On the ground floor, a pleasant bistro, lit by a roaring log fire in winter, opens onto a panoramic terrace. The restaurant is in the basement, also with a terrace. The menu offers a choice of tasty, local dishes and succulent sweet and savoury pancakes.

Access : In the medieval village

Access : In the centre of the village

 142 LES CÈDRES BLEUS
Mr and Mrs Duverney

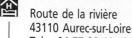 Route de la rivière
43110 Aurec-sur-Loire
Tel. : 04 77 35 48 48
Fax : 04 77 35 37 04

Closed from 26 Aug to 8 Sep, from 26 Dec to 22 Jan, Sun evening and Mon lunchtime • 15 rooms, one has disabled access, most have bath/WC, some have shower/WC, all have television • €54; breakfast €7; half board €51 to €54 • Menus €15 (in the week) to €58 • Terrace, garden, car park. No dogs allowed in rooms

 143 LA BOUGNATE
Mr and Mrs Klein

 Place du Vallat
43450 Blesle
Tel. : 04 71 76 29 30
Fax : 04 71 76 29 39
www.labougnate.com

Closed from 2 Jan to late Feb and Mon, Tue, Wed from early Oct to late Mar • 12 rooms, 3 of which are in a round tower, one has disabled access. Rooms have bath/WC or shower/WC, all have television • €61; breakfast €6 • Menu €25 • Terrace

 Trying your hand at water-skiing on Lake Grangent.

Even though the site may lack the giant redwood trees, grizzly bears and log cabins of America's national parks, the same spirit reigns in this lakeside spot. The reception and restaurant are installed in the old family house, while three modern "chalets" house functional rooms, all of which overlook the garden and cedars. A well cared-for flowered terrace adds the final touch to this pastoral picture of unspoilt countryside.

 Salers beef – straight from Mr Klein's farm!

Mrs Klein, a local lass, has entirely restored this 18C home. The eye is immediately drawn to the exquisite furniture, made out of rare ebony and rosewood, in the charming rooms, each of which is lovingly and tastefully decorated; three are in the circular tower. Attractive rustic-style restaurant, dusty pink beams in the inviting reading room and a pleasant terrace. What more could you want?

Access : To the south-west of Saint-Étienne on the D 46, then at Aurec-sur-Loire towards Bas-en-Basset

Access : In the centre of the village, between Lempdes-sur-Allagnon and Massiac (D 909)

 144 LA PARAVENT
Mr Jourde

 43700 Chaspinhac
Tel. : 04 71 03 54 75
Fax : 04 71 03 54 75

Open all year • 4 rooms • €42, breakfast included • Table d'hôte €14 for 2 people • Garden. Credit cards not accepted, no dogs allowed

 145 HÔTEL DE L'ÉCHO ET DE L'ABBAYE
Mr and Mrs Degreze

 Place de l'Écho
43160 La Chaise-Dieu
Tel. : 04 71 00 00 45
Fax : 04 71 00 00 22

Open from 29 Mar to 3 Nov; closed Wed (except in Jul and Aug) • 10 rooms with bath/WC or shower/WC and television • €48 to €58; breakfast €8; half board €52 to €55 • Menus €17 (in the week) to €58 • Terrace. No dogs allowed

The warm atmosphere of this handsome early-20C house.

The sterling welcome, constant attention to detail and eagerness to please immediately strike the visitor to this country house, just a few minutes' drive from Le Puy-en-Velay. The rustic-style interior decoration is full of character. Some of the cosy rooms have their own small sitting room and all have a private entrance. In the winter the lady of the house runs patchwork courses.

The amazing VIP feel to the hotel during the annual Music Festival.

The walls of this hotel formerly housed the kitchens which cooked for the 300 or so members of the monastery. The somewhat old-fashioned rooms have recently been treated to new beds. Some rooms overlook the roofs of La Chaise-Dieu, but the most popular peep into the cloister of St Robert. Pleasant dining room and terrace opening onto the main square. Come festival time – late August to early September – the hotel is crammed with tenors, politicians and prima donnas of all sorts.

Access : 10km to the north-east of Le Puy on the D 103 towards Retournac, then take the D 71

Access : Near the abbey, in front of the large square used as a visitors' car park

LA CHAISE-DIEU - 43160

LE PUY-EN-VELAY - 43000

 146 LA JACQUERELLE
Mrs Chailly

 Rue Marchédial
43160 La Chaise-Dieu
Tel. : 04 71 00 07 52

Open all year • 5 rooms • €49, breakfast included • Table d'hôte €19 • Car park. Credit cards not accepted, no dogs allowed

 147 RÉGINA
Mr Venosino

 34 boulevard du Maréchal Fayolle
43000 Le Puy-en-Velay
Tel. : 04 71 09 14 71
Fax : 04 71 09 18 57
www.hotelrestregina.com

Open all year • 24 rooms, one of which has disabled access and 3 are non-smoking. Rooms have bath/WC (3 have showers) and television. 3 suites • €54 to €58; breakfast €9 • Air-conditioned restaurant; menus €20 to €30 • Garage

 Going mushrooming for cèps in the surrounding forest.

Entirely built out of local stone, this characterful house stands in the lower part of town. Countless family heirlooms, including a beautiful Louis-Philippe wardrobe and elegant looking mirrors grace the tastefully decorated, predominantly wood interior. A roaring log fire, lit in the dining room's magnificent stone fireplace, takes the chill off the short autumn and winter days.

 The awe-inspiring site of Le Puy-en-Velay.

Standing on a street corner, this stone building, topped with a dome, was built in the early 20C by the architect responsible for Nice's opulent Negresco Hotel. The rooms combine modern furniture with Italian-style hand-painted walls and bright, bold fabrics. The bathrooms of the three suites peep out from behind a thick glass wall. Stylish restaurant embellished with Murano lights.

Access : In the lower part of town

Access : In the centre, on the main road through the town

148 LES REVERS
Mr and Mrs Chevalier

43130 Retournac
Tel. : 04 71 59 42 81
Fax : 04 71 59 42 81
 jean-pierre.chevalier6 @ libertysurf.fr

Closed from Sep to Mar • 4 rooms • €37, breakfast included • No table d'hôte • Garden, car park

149 L' HERMINETTE
Mr Mathieu

Bigorre – Les Maziaux
43550 Saint-Front
Tel. : 04 71 59 57 58
Fax : 04 71 56 34 91
lherminette @ wanadoo.fr

Open all year, bookings necessary out of season
• 6 rooms with bathrooms • €37, breakfast included
• Menus €10 to €15 • Garden, car park. No dogs allowed
• Museum nearby

 The unspoilt countryside of this rural hideaway.

Those on a quest for silence, nature and authenticity will swoon at the sight of this extraordinarily secluded spot, wedged in between field and forest. The capacious, well appointed rooms are furnished with comfortable bedding and all overlook the unspoilt countryside. Two rooms are on split-levels. The owner breeds horses and can organise rides for guests. A perfect hideaway for a relaxed, peaceful break.

 The change of scenery offered by this hamlet.

An enchanting hamlet of stone farmsteads topped with well-combed thatched roofs forms the backdrop to this typical Auvergne inn. Large, airy bedrooms, two on split-levels, regional-style dining rooms and delicious country cooking at unbeatable prices. If you're interested in finding out more about daily life in years gone by and how thatched roofs are made, stop by the Ecomuseum, and all will be revealed.

Access : 8km to the south-east of Retournac on the D 103, then follow the signs

Access : 5km to the north-west of Saint-Front on the D 39, then take the lane on the right

AUVERGNE

150 AUBERGE DE LA VALLÉE
Mr and Mrs Merle

43340 Saint-Haon
Tel. : 04 71 08 20 73
Fax : 04 71 08 29 21
aubergevallee43@aol.com

 www.auberge-de-la-vallee.fr

Closed from 1 Jan to 15 Mar, Sun evening and Mon from Oct to Apr • 10 rooms with bath/WC or shower/WC • €32 to €40; breakfast €6; half board €39 • Menus €13 to €32 • Terrace • Hiking, river water sports

151 LES GABALES
Mr Gauthier

Route du Puy-en-Velay
43170 Saugues
Tel. : 04 71 77 86 92
Fax : 04 71 77 86 92
pierrelesgabales@wanadoo.fr
www.lesgabales.com

Open all year, reservation necessary • 5 non-smoking rooms • €68, breakfast included • Table d'hôte €15 • Sitting room, park, car park. Credit cards not accepted, no dogs allowed

 Diving into the crystal-clear waters of Bouchet Lake at the bottom of a crater.

The legend of the "Beast of Gévaudan" continues to echo around the narrow gorges of the Allier, although today's walkers and nature-lovers are more enamoured of its peaceful setting than its "gory" past. Rustic furniture and roughcast walls set the tone for the small, beautifully kept rooms of this unpretentious inn. Recently spruced up, the dining room now boasts new light fittings, a stylish wooden ceiling and a bold colour scheme.

 Finding out more about the legendary "Beast of Gévaudan".

The legend of the "Beast of Gévaudan" is far from dead as you will find out when you listen to the tales related by the owner of this good-sized 1930s house. His other passion is walking and he is happy to share tips. Once safely back inside the hotel's walls, relax in the cosy sitting room-library; the wood panelling in the dining room is original. In the morning, after a well-earned night's sleep in one of the charmingly "retro" personalised rooms, guests can also enjoy a walk in the park.

Access : Between Le Puy-en-Velay and Pradelles, 10km from the N 88 (west of La Sauvetat)

Access : On the road from Le Puy-en-Velay

 152 LE MOULIN DES VERNIÈRES
Mrs Hansen

63120 Aubusson d'Auvergne
Tel. : 04 73 53 53 01
Fax : 04 73 53 53 01
www.lemoulindesvernieres.com

Closed from Nov to Feb • 5 non-smoking rooms • €55 to €64, breakfast included • Table d'hôte €17 • Sitting room, park, car park. No dogs allowed • Outdoor swimming pool

 153 CHAMBRE D'HÔTE MME BEAUJEARD
Mrs Beaujeard

8 rue de la Limagne à Chaptes
63460 Beauregard-Vendon
Tel. : 04 73 63 35 62

Closed from Nov to 1 Mar except by reservation • 3 non-smoking rooms • €58, breakfast included • No table d'hôte • Garden. Credit cards not accepted, no dogs allowed

 The chef's inventive recipes using delicious local produce.

It is easy to see why the owner fell in love with this old mill and the artistically laid out garden and cascading stream. The scent of rose and jasmine fills the pretty rooms, named after cottage garden flowers (English rose, Forget-me-not, Poppy). Inside the owner has given free rein to her decorative flair with polished antique furniture, classic black and white photos by Doisneau and naive paintings. The cooking is just as inventive and your host loves rustling up mouth-watering dishes.

 The enchanting, old-fashioned decoration.

This handsome late-18C country seat is the epitome of charm and tranquillity. The tastefully furnished rooms, all non-smoking, are perfect for winding down at the end of the day. The cosy sitting room with its fireplace, lavishly flowered garden in the summer, generous breakfasts, excellent welcome and moderate prices all add to the appeal.

Access : 7km eastbound from Coupière on the D 7 and the D 311

Access : 9km northbound from Riom on the N 144 then the D 122

154 HOSTELLERIE DU BEFFROY
Mr Legros

26 rue Abbé Blot
63610 Besse-en-Chandesse
Tel. : 04 73 79 50 08
Fax : 04 73 79 57 87

Closed from 18 to 26 Apr, from 9 to 26 Dec and on Mon and Tue (except in Feb, Jul and Aug) • 11 rooms with bath/WC or shower/WC and television • €54 to €84; breakfast €8; half board €61 • Menus from €22 to €54 • Garage. No dogs allowed in restaurant

155 RÉGENCE
Mr and Mrs Porte

31 avenue des États-Unis
63140 Chatelguyon
Tel. : 04 73 86 02 60
Fax : 04 73 86 02 49
hotel-regence3 @ wanadoo.fr

Closed from 20 Oct to 20 Nov and on Sun evening and Mon from 21 Nov to 30 Apr • 26 rooms with bath/WC or shower/WC, some have television • €44; breakfast €7; half board €43 (€34 in low season) • Menus from €16 to €22 • Garden, private car park. No dogs allowed • Free shuttle bus to the spa

The contrast between the medieval city of Besse and the mountain resort of Super-Besse.

This 15C house beside the belfry at the entrance to the town is thought to have housed the old town guards. A few old pieces of furniture add style to the rooms' slightly faded air. In the dining room, the rugs strewn here and there, dark timbered beams, heavy fabrics and straw-bottomed chairs covered in tasteful cream hemp further accentuate the house's historic character.

The architecture of this quaint old resort.

A splendid carved wooden fireplace, well-worn, polished antique furniture and an upright piano contribute to maintaining the delicious 1900s atmosphere of the Régence. The ground floor has however been entirely renovated with a fresh coat of paint, double-glazing and a smart red and gold facelift for the sitting and dining rooms; the bedrooms are next in line. Lush green garden.

Access : In the centre of the medieval village

Access : At the entrance to the resort, on the main road

 156 **CHÂTEAU DE COLLANGES**
Mr and Mrs Félus

 63340 Collanges
Tel. : 04 73 96 47 30
Fax : 04 73 96 58 72
château.de.collanges@wanadoo.fr
www.château.de.collanges.free.fr

Open all year • 4 rooms and a suite • €79, breakfast included • Table d'hôte €30 • Park, car park

 157 **AUBERGE DE LA FORGE**
Mr and Mrs Zuk

 Place de l'Église
63160 Glaine-Montaigut
Tel. : 04 73 73 41 80
Fax : 04 73 73 33 83
a.delaforge@wanadoo.fr
www.aubergedelaforge.com

Closed from 1 to 20 Sep • 4 rooms with showers/WC • €49; breakfast €6; half board €58 • Restaurant closed Sun evening and Tue; menus €14 to €25 • Terrace

We most liked **Strolling leisurely back in time.**

Guests are treated like royalty in this castle surrounded by seven acres of parkland. The vaulted ceilings, original parquet floors and superb antique furniture will take you on a voyage through time from the Renaissance to the 18C. Imagine what it was like to be lord or lady of the house as you wake up in a canopied bed draped with rich fabrics, then draw back the curtains on a view of the park. A genuine Gaveau piano and a marquetry-inlaid billiard table add to the castle's sophistication.

We most liked **Wholesome country snacks served all day long.**

Situated opposite a beautiful Romanesque 11C-12C church, the village café and forge have been successfully converted into a pleasant country inn. A smart façade with pale blue shutters, traditional old walls, simple yet appealing rooms and a restaurant, with a reconstruction of the former blacksmith's workshop complete with hearth, bellows and anvil, serving yummy country cooking. A renovation which marries authenticity with intelligence.

Access : 12km southbound from Issoire, on the A 75, exit Saint-Germain-Lembron

Access : Around 5km to the north-east of Billom, towards Thiers on the D 229 and the D 212

 158 **AUBERGE DE FONDAIN**
Mrs Demossier

Lieu-dit Fondain
63820 Laqueuille
Tel. : 04 73 22 01 35
Fax : 04 73 22 06 13
auberge.de.fondain @ wanadoo.fr
www.auberge-fondain.com

Closed early Mar, for a fortnight in early Nov, Sun evening and Mon in low season • 6 rooms with bath/WC or shower/WC • €58; breakfast €6; half board €46 (€43 low season) • Menus €10 (lunchtime in the week) to €21 • Terrace, garden, car park • Fitness room with sauna, hiking, mountain biking, themed walks

 159 **LA CLOSERIE DE MANOU**
Mrs Larcher

Genestoux
63240 Le Mont-Dore
Tel. : 04 73 65 26 81
Fax : 04 73 81 11 72

Closed from 15 Oct to 28 Feb • 5 non-smoking rooms • €69, breakfast included • No table d'hôte • Garden, car park. No dogs allowed

 Signposted footpaths on themes such as fauna, flora and crater lakes.

This elegant 19C country house lost among fields and meadows is said to have belonged to the inventor of a local blue cheese: Laqueuille. The recently renovated rooms, named after flowers, combine a light, airy colour scheme with contrasting dark timbers, discreetly modern fittings and in some cases, a view of the Banne d'Ordanche. A fitness room, sauna and a dozen or so mountain bikes will make sure you work up an appetite for the tasty Auvergne cooking served in a welcoming rustic dining room.

 The wealth of information about the region.

Nestling in the countryside, this traditional 18C Auvergne house with its stone walls and white shutters is quite enchanting. The decoration of the spacious rooms wavers between modern-uncluttered and snug; all are non-smoking. The sitting and dining rooms, furnished with antiques, provide a wonderful backdrop to the delicious breakfasts. The charm and attention of your hostess will be another reason why you won't want to leave.

Access : 2km to the north-east of Laqueuille, on the D 922 then a minor road

Access : 3km westbound from Mont-Dore on the D 996

160 CHÂTEAU DE GRANGE FORT
Mr and Mrs Van Bronkhorst

63500 Les Pradeaux
Tel. : 04 73 71 02 43
Fax : 04 73 71 07 69
château@grangefort.com
www.grangefort.com

Closed from Dec to Mar • 5 rooms • €68, breakfast included • Table d'hôte €19 • Park, car park. No dogs allowed • Outdoor swimming pool, guided tour of castle

161 AUBERGE DE MAZAYES
Mr Michy

Mazayes-Basses
63230 Mazaye
Tel. : 04 73 88 93 30
Fax : 04 73 88 93 80

Closed from 15 Dec to 15 Jan, Fri lunchtime and Mon and Tue lunchtime out of season • 15 rooms, one of which has disabled access, with shower/WC, all have television • €44 to €50; breakfast €7; half board €43 to €46 • Menus €13 (in the week) to €32 • Terrace, car park

The atmosphere steeped in history.

The magnificent crenellated towers of this 17C castle look proudly down over extensive parkland surrounded by mountains. Each of the rooms has been decorated individually, some with a canopied bed, others with carved doors or paintings depicting the royal former owners of the castle. Meals are served under a superb vaulted ceiling. For those who prefer roughing it, the owners also run a campsite nearby!

The farm's ideal situation for exploring the Monts Dôme.

This attractive Auvergne farmhouse built out of solid basalt stone is located just near the popular tourist site of the Puy de Dôme (1 465m). Bold colours, carefully chosen fabrics and a few old pieces of furniture adorn the rooms which are a stylish blend of rustic and modern. The stables have been converted into a dining room full of character with a lava stone floor and a low ceiling supported by dark timber rafters. Wholesome regional cooking.

Access : 7km south-east of Issoire on the A 75, exit no 13 towards Parentignat, then to Auzat-sur-Allier on the D 34

Access : South of Pontgibaud, 6km on the D 986, cross the Sioule at St Pierre-le-Chastel and drive to Mazayes

 162 CHAMBRE D'HÔTE M. ASTRUC
Mr and Mrs Astruc

Rue du Donjon
63114 Montpeyroux
Tel. : 04 73 96 69 42

Open all year • 5 non-smoking rooms • €55, breakfast included • No table d'hôte • Car park. Credit cards not accepted

 163 CHEZ MADAME GAUTHIER
Mrs Gauthier

Recoleine
63210 Nébouzat
Tel. : 04 73 87 10 34
Fax : 04 73 87 10 34
jocelyne.gauthier@wanadoo.fr

Closed in Jan • 3 rooms • €40, breakfast included • No table d'hôte • Sitting room. Credit cards not accepted, no dogs allowed

 Exploring this historic village overlooking the Allier River.

Set at the foot of a 13C keep, this pretty sandstone house is well worth the short climb up the hill from the town car park; there are a few parking spaces in front of the house if needed. Each of the bedrooms boasts its own little extra bonus: terrace, fireplace, canopied bed or jacuzzi bath. After taking refreshments in the vaulted dining room, set off round the narrow lanes and meet the painters and potters who have replaced the wine-growers of yesteryear.

 The pastoral scene just two minutes from the Dôme mountain range.

A warm welcome awaits visitors inside this old barn, beautifully renovated by a farming couple. The comfortable, tasteful rooms all overlook the surrounding countryside. The immense living-sitting room and the spacious sofa are most appreciated. Guests have the use of a fitted kitchen. The charming, talkative hostess will be more than happy to point out walks and hikes. Ideal for nature lovers.

Access : 8km to the south-west of Vic-le-Comte on the A 75, exit no 7

Access : 3km from Randanne on the N 89

 164 DOMAINE DE TERNANT
Mrs Piollet

 Ternant
63870 Orcines
Tel. : 04 73 62 11 20
Fax : 04 73 62 29 96
domaine.ternant @ free.fr
www.domaine.ternant.free.fr

Closed from 15 Nov to 15 Mar • 5 non-smoking rooms
• €80, breakfast included • No table d'hôte • Sitting
room, park, car park. Credit cards not accepted, no dogs
allowed • Tennis, billiard room

165 HOSTELLERIE LES HIRONDELLES
Mr Amblard

 Route de Limoges
63870 Orcines
Tel. : 04 73 62 22 43
Fax : 04 73 62 19 12

Closed from 3 Feb to 3 Mar, from 23 to 31 Dec, Sun
evening and Mon from Oct to Apr • 18 rooms, one of
which has disabled access. Rooms have bath/WC or
shower/WC, all have television • €52; breakfast €7; half
board €40 to €45 • Menus €15 (in the week) to
€32 • Terrace, car park

 **The sheltered environment of this old
building.**

This elegant 19C property stands in 25 acres of grounds
at the foot of the Dôme mountain range. A profusion
of family heirlooms scattered throughout the bedrooms,
sitting room, library and games room creates a warm,
lived-in feel. The personal touch and taste of the lady
of the house, a patchwork artist, can be felt everywhere.
Tennis court in the grounds and other sports facilities
nearby, including Vulcania, the Regional Volcano Park.

 The fascinating Monts Dôme.

This old grey-stone family farmstead, recently converted
into an inn, nestles at the foot of the Monts Dôme. The
rooms situated in the converted barn are practical before
all else; those overlooking the street are larger and
lighter. The vaulted dining room located in the former
cow-shed offers more character; the swallows' nests,
from which the inn takes its name, complete the rural
picture.

Access : 11km north-west of Clermont-Ferrand on
the D 941A and the D 90

Access : Westbound from Clermont-Ferrand, take the
D 941A then the D 941B (Limoges road) to Orcines

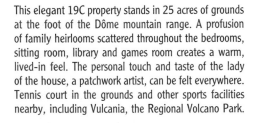

 166 CHAMBRE D'HÔTE PAUL GEBRILLAT
Mr Gebrillat and Mrs de Saint-Aubin

Chemin de Siorac
63500 Perrier
Tel. : 04 73 89 15 02
Fax : 04 73 55 08 85
quota @ infonie.fr

Open all year • 3 rooms and one suite • €52, breakfast included • No table d'hôte • Garden, car park. Credit cards not accepted, no dogs allowed

 Strolling in the park bounded by the Couze de Pavin River.

This handsome 18C country house is perfect for those wishing to get to know the Dore Mountains a little better. The tastefully decorated rooms marry charm and comfort. As soon as the first rays of sun appear, the breakfast table is laid outdoors under a heated awning which overlooks a delightful inner courtyard; warm sweaters advisable. Your host, Paul, is cordial and a gold mine of useful tourist tips.

Access : 3km westbound from Issoire on the D 996

 167 CHÂTEAU DE VOISSIEUX
Mr and Mrs Phillips

Saint-Bonnet- près-Orcival
63210 Rochefort-Montagne
Tel. : 04 73 65 81 02
Fax : 04 73 65 81 27

Closed from Nov to Jan • 3 rooms with bathrooms • €52, breakfast included • No table d'hôte • Terrace, park, car park. Credit cards not accepted • Mountain biking, horse-riding, swimming, golf, paragliding, hot-air ballooning and skiing nearby

 Being treated like the lord or lady of the manor in the heart of the Auvergne Regional Park.

Volcanic stone was of course used to build this 13C castle, it was also used to restore it to its present-day state. In the park a 400-year-old lime tree keeps watch over the estate's quiet solitude. You have a choice between two soberly furnished rooms or a more exuberant rococo style in the third. Breakfasts are served in the kitchen by the fireside or on the flowered terrace overlooking the park. It isn't possible to lunch or dine in the castle, but restaurants are hardly in short supply.

Access : 4km to the north-east of Orcival on the D 27

 168 **CHÂTEAU DE CHARADE**
Mr and Mrs Gaba

63130 Royat
Tel. : 04 73 35 91 67
Fax : 04 73 29 92 09

Closed from 1 Nov to Easter • 6 rooms with bathrooms • €75, breakfast included • No table d'hôte • Park, car park. Credit cards not accepted, no dogs allowed

 169 **AU PONT DE RAFFINY**
Mr and Mrs Beaudoux

Raffiny
63660 Saint-Romain
Tel. : 04 73 95 49 10
Fax : 04 73 95 80 21

Closed from 1 Jan to 15 Feb, Sun evening and Mon (in March only open at the weekends) • 12 rooms, 2 of which are small wooden chalets with private gardens. All rooms have bath/WC or shower/WC, some have television • €30 to €40; breakfast €6; half board €36 • Menus €14 to €27 • Car park • Games room with billiards, hiking, mountain bike rental

 We most liked **The country house feel of this whimsical castle just two minutes from the regional capital.**

This castle which borders the Royat golf course extends a majestic welcome. High ceilings, a stone staircase and the antique furniture in the bedrooms and bathrooms all bear witness to an illustrious past. As for the present, guests are invariably charmed by the appeal of the lady of the house's gracious welcome, the tinkling of the piano playing in the sitting room or the click of billiard balls. If you don't feel like visiting the town, head for the nearby Dôme mountains.

 We most liked **A ride in the panoramic "Livradois-Forez" train.**

Two chalets designed for families, complete with kitchenette and private gardens, have recently been added to the hotel's amenities. The bedrooms in the main wing – a former village café – are more simply furnished, even if those on the second floor, lined in wood, do have a certain alpine charm. A rockery fountain affords an amusing touch to the rustic dining room. All in all, we were quite won over by the charm of this country hotel.

Access : 6km to the south-west of Royat on the D 941C and the D 5, towards the racing track and golf course

Access : Leave Saint-Anthème southbound on the D 261 and drive for 5.5km

 170 **CASTEL HÔTEL 1904**
Mr Mouty

 63390 Saint-Gervais-d'Auvergne
Tel. : 04 73 85 70 42
Fax : 04 73 85 84 39
castel.hotel.1904@wanadoo.fr

Open from Mar to Nov; restaurant closed Wed lunchtime, Mon and Tue • 17 rooms with bath/WC or shower/WC, all have television • €56 to €61; breakfast €8; half board €48 • Menus €32 to €49; Comptoir à Moustaches (closed in Dec and Feb, Sun evening and Wed) €13 to €30 • Garden, car park. No dogs allowed

171 **MONTARLET**
Mr and Mrs Pelletier

 63390 Saint-Gervais-d'Auvergne
Tel. : 04 73 85 87 10
Fax : 04 73 85 75 79
montarlet@libertysurf.fr

Open all year • 3 rooms with bathrooms • €40, breakfast included • No table d'hôte • Park, car park. Credit cards not accepted

 The rather quaint old-fashioned atmosphere.

The carved "1616" over the fireplace bears witness to the age of these walls. This private residence, built for the Marquis of Maintenon, passed into the hands of a religious community in the 19C before it became a coaching inn in 1904. Beams, creaky floorboards, well-worn furniture, gleaming silver and 1900 statuettes and lights bestow an almost nostalgic feel to this "castel". Sample the excellent home cooking of the Comptoir à Moustaches, a nearby country bistro.

 The enchanting natural site of this farmhouse.

Guests are often in raptures over the charm and tranquillity of this renovated farmhouse in the middle of the countryside. The rooms illustrate how much the owners have their guests' welfare at heart, from the sponge-painted walls and antique furniture gleaned in local flea markets to the matching bed-linen and curtains and roomy bathrooms. The sitting room is graced with a fireplace and floor made out of Volvic stone and the landscaped parkland commands a fine view over the Auvergne mountains.

Access : In the centre of the village

Access : 3km westbound from St-Gervais-d'Auvergne on the D 90 towards Espinasse and take the lane on the left

AUVERGNE

172 RÉGINA
Mr and Mrs Valla

63710 Saint-Nectaire
Tel. : 04 73 88 54 55
Fax : 04 73 88 50 56
regina.st-nectaire @ wanadoo

Closed from Nov to Dec • 24 rooms, 6 are in a separate wing, most have shower/WC, some have bath/WC, all have television • €42 to €52; breakfast €6; half board €46 (€43 in low season) • Menus €15 to €20 • Car park • Heated outdoor swimming pool with sun deck

173 LE VIEUX LOGIS
Mr and Mrs Mantelet

Route de Palladuc
63550 Saint-Rémy-sur-Durolle
Tel. : 04 73 94 30 78
Fax : 04 73 94 04 70

Closed Jan and Feb, from 1 to 15 Oct, Sun evening and Mon • 4 rooms, 2 have bath/WC, 2 have shower/WC • €29; breakfast €5 • Menus €13 (in the week) to €26 • Terrace, garden, car park. No dogs allowed

Cheese-making and tasting!

The tower of this 1904 building makes it easily recognisable in this small spa-resort. The well-soundproofed and recently freshened-up small bedrooms are soberly furnished; we recommend avoiding those in the annex. Exposed beams and period wood panelling add character to the dining room. The attractive swimming pool and the vast sun deck are also extremely popular.

The nautical leisure centre two minutes' walk from the hotel.

This ivy-covered establishment lies on the edge of a narrow, very quiet mountain road. The simply furnished rooms command beautiful views of the Bois Noirs massif. Two former cutlery workshops and an old barn complete with manger and a variety of old tools, have been turned into three rustic dining rooms full of character. A wooden lean-to provides welcome shade on the terrace.

Access : In the lower part of Saint-Nectaire, on the main road

Access : 3.5km northbound on the D 201 towards Palladuc

 174 LE PARC DE GEOFFROY
Mr Brugere

49 avenue du Général de Gaulle
63300 Thiers
Tel. : 04 73 80 87 00
Fax : 04 73 80 87 01
reservation @ parc-de-geoffroy.com
www.parc-de-geoffroy.com

Open all year • 31 rooms on 3 floors. Rooms have
bath/WC and television • €68; breakfast €8; half board
€48 • Menus €14 to €36 • Terrace, garden, car park

 175 LES BAUDARTS
Mrs Verdier

63500 Varennes-sur-Usson
Tel. : 04 73 89 05 51
Fax : 04 73 89 05 51

Closed from Oct to 1 May • 3 rooms • €66, breakfast
included • No table d'hôte • Garden, car park. Credit
cards not accepted, no dogs allowed

 **Enjoying a cutting-edge visit to the
House of Cutlery-makers.**

A luxurious walled garden protects the residence from
the bustle of the nearby busy shopping centre. The
comfortable reception and dining rooms decorated with
frescoes are housed in a former cutlery workshop. The
rooms, located in a quiet, modern wing, are light, airy
and practical. The well-provisioned breakfast table
provides guests with the energy necessary to embark on
the "ascent" of the upper town.

 **The unadulterated sophistication of
every room.**

Tucked away in the countryside, this establishment may
not be easy to find, but it is well worth persevering
because its dusty pink walls contain a marvel of
sophistication, calm and comfort. The superb, spacious
rooms are exquisitely decorated in light, warm tones.
The sitting room, lit in the winter by a roaring log fire,
is crammed with books. Who could resist Mrs Baudart's
delightful welcome?

Access : 5km along the N 89 towards
Clermont-Ferrand

Access : On leaving Varennes take the first right
(D 123), then turn into the wooded lane at the first
bend

BURGUNDY

A visit to Burgundy takes travellers back through time to an era when its mighty Dukes rivalled even the kings of France. Born of an uncompromising desire for perfection, their stately castles and rich abbeys bear witness to a golden age of ostentation and prestige. As we look back now, it is difficult to reproach them for the flamboyance which has made Dijon a world-renowned city of art. And who would dispute Burgundy's claim to the "best wines in Christendom" when one sees how the hordes of today continue to lay siege to the region's cellars, where cool and canny wine-growers guard the secret of their finest vintages? This dedication to time-honoured traditions also rules the region's steadfast homage to the culinary arts, from strong-smelling époisses cheese to gingerbread dripping with honey. After sinning so extravagantly, you may be tempted to make amends and take a barge trip down the region's canals and rivers to digest in peace amidst the unspoilt countryside.

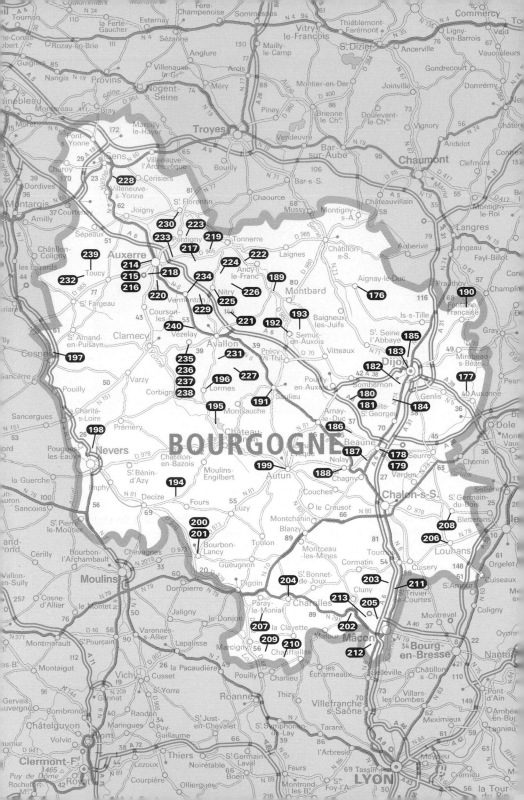

 176 MANOIR DE TARPERON
Mr de Champsavin

 Route de Saint-Marc
21510 Aignay-le-Duc
Tel. : 03 80 93 83 74
Fax : 03 80 93 83 74
manoir.de.tarperon @ wanadoo.fr

Closed from Nov to Mar • 5 rooms with bathrooms
• €60, breakfast included • Table d'hôte €22 • Sitting
room, terrace, garden. Credit cards not accepted, no
dogs allowed • Stabling, concerts, exhibitions

 177 LES LAURENTIDES
Mrs Royer-Cotti

 27 rue du Centre
21130 Athée
Tel. : 03 80 31 00 25

Open all year • 4 rooms, 2 of which open onto the garden
• €42, breakfast included • Table d'hôte €17, only from
Fri to Sun and on national holidays by reservation
• Garden, car park. Credit cards not accepted

 The beautiful "Wind in the Willows" feel to this location.

 The personalised decoration of the bedrooms.

A unique charm emanates from this manor and its superb riverside setting on the banks of the Coquille. The bedrooms, of varying sizes, are colourfully and tastefully furnished. The sitting room, complete with library, leads onto a pleasant veranda overlooking the garden. Fly fishing enthusiasts are in for a treat with a private stream all of their own. Those otherwise inclined will enjoy boat trips and an excursion to the source of the Seine.

This attractive flower-decked farmhouse, built in the heart of the village in 1870, is a perfect marriage of charm and comfort. The rooms in the converted attic reveal the lady of the house's exquisite taste and painting talents; the most pleasant have a view of the magnificent garden. Meals are only served at weekends or on national holidays and bookings are essential. An establishment that has made gracious living its byword.

Access : Take the small road in the direction of Saint-Marc

Access : 6km northbound from Auxonne on the D 24

  178 GRILLON
Mr and Mrs Grillon

 21 route de Seurre
21200 Beaune
Tel. : 03 80 22 44 25
Fax : 03 80 24 94 89
joel.grillon@wanadoo.fr
www.hotel-grillon.fr

Closed from 1 Feb to 3 Mar • 18 upstairs rooms, most of which have bath/WC and television. Several are non-smoking • €46 to €60; breakfast €6 • No restaurant • Garden, terrace, private car park

  179 VILLA FLEURIE
Mrs Chartier

 19 place Colbert
21200 Beaune
Tel. : 03 80 22 66 00
Fax : 03 80 22 45 46
la.villa.fleurie@wanadoo.fr

Open from Mar to Nov • 10 rooms, most have bath/WC, all have television • €62 to €70; breakfast €8 • No restaurant • Garden, private car park

We most liked **A haven of greenery close to the Hospices de Beaune.**

This spruce pink house with light-green shutters is almost hidden in the summer by a thick curtain of chestnut trees, but we highly recommend venturing past the wrought-iron gate and inside the comfortable 19C mansion. The rooms vary between light and airy or cosy and some feature interesting old pieces of furniture picked up in local antique shops. The vaulted cellar has been turned into a sitting room and bar. Breakfast is served on a pretty flowered terrace.

We most liked **The friendly, family atmosphere.**

This small 1900 villa is entwined in the sweet-scented branches of an old wisteria bush. It offers three styles of room: contemporary, bourgeois and split-level family on the top floor. Chintz curtains, a fireplace and mouldings give the breakfast room a distinctly English feel, while the deck-chairs on the garden-terrace invite guests to relax and unwind.

Access : At the entrance to Beaune, from Seurre (D 973, Dôle road)

Access : Set back from the lane, on a small square near the swimming pool

180 CHAMBRE D'HÔTE MME BAGATELLE
Mrs Bagatelle

Rue des Moutons
21320 Châteauneuf
Tel. : 03 80 49 21 00
jean-michel.bagatelle @ wanadoo.fr

Closed during the February holidays • 4 rooms with shower/WC • €58, breakfast included • No table d'hôte • Garden, car park. Credit cards not accepted, no dogs allowed

181 HOSTELLERIE DU CHÂTEAU
Mr Hartmann

21320 Châteauneuf
Tel. : 03 80 49 22 00
Fax : 03 80 49 21 27
hostellerie-du-château @ hostellerie-chateauneuf.com

Closed from 30 Nov to 10 Feb, Mon and Tue except in Jul and Aug • 17 rooms, 8 of which are in a separate wing (4 are split-level for families) and one has disabled access. Rooms have bath/WC or shower/WC • €61 to €70; breakfast €8; half board €52 to €64 • Menus €23 to €40 • Terrace, garden

 Wandering through the narrow streets of this lovely fortified village.

This old stone sheepfold stands in the centre of the medieval village on the banks of the Burgundy Canal. Stone and wood take pride of place in this tastefully decorated house. Guests immediately feel at home in the welcoming bedrooms, one of which has a fireplace, while the split-level rooms are perfectly suited to families.

 Contemplating the medieval castle over a refreshing kir.

The fortified town, perched high above France's "motorway to the south", formerly controlled the entire plain below. Today its heavy doors swing open to reveal a pleasant stopping place. The hostelry is just an arrow's distance from the majestic medieval castle which can be seen from the garden. The main building and annex, a 17C house, are home to a few rooms decorated with original old beams and stonework. Warm medieval-style sitting room.

Access : In the village

Access : In the centre of the village, next to the castle

182 CHAMBRE D'HÔTE LES BRUGÈRES
Mr and Mrs Brugère

7 rue Jean-Jaurès
21160 Couchey
Tel. : 03 80 52 13 05
Fax : 03 80 52 93 20
brugere @ aol.com
www.francoisbrugere.com

Closed from Dec to Mar • 4 rooms with shower/WC
• €52, breakfast included • No table d'hôte • Car park

183 WILSON
Bonnouvrier Family

Place Wilson
21000 Dijon
Tel. : 03 80 66 82 50
Fax : 03 80 36 41 54
hotelwilson @ wanadoo.fr

Open all year • 27 rooms, 18 of which have bath/WC,
9 have shower/WC, all have television • €64 to €81;
breakfast €9 • No restaurant • Garage

 Soak up the atmosphere of a wine estate.

This charming 16C establishment, the property of a Marsannay wine-grower, provides a perfect opportunity to get to know more about the region's wine. The attractively restored rooms are decorated with exposed beams and old furniture; one of them has a piano. In the winter, roaring log fires light up the breakfast room, hung with tapestries. The cellar is open for visits and wine-tastings.

 Snug as a bug in this house of character.

Lovingly and tastefully restored, this 17C coaching inn has now added the bonus of modern comforts to its beautifully preserved Burgundian architecture. The exposed beams and cosy, lived-in feel of the well-soundproofed rooms, laid out round an inner courtyard, never fail to win over guests. Breakfast is served by an open fire in winter.

Access : 2km southbound from Marsannay on the D 122

Access : From the town centre, drive to Place du Théâtre and then along Rue Chabot-Charny

184 LES GRANDS CRUS
Mrs Farnier

Rue de Lavaux
21220 Gevrey-Chambertin
Tel. : 03 80 34 34 15
Fax : 03 80 51 89 07
hotel.lesgrandscrus@ipac.fr
www.hoteldesgrandscrus.com

Open from 1 Mar to 1 Dec • 24 rooms on 2 floors, all have bath/WC and television • €75; breakfast €8 • No restaurant • Garden, private car park. No dogs allowed

185 LA MUSARDE
Mr and Mrs Ogé

7 rue des Riottes
21121 Hauteville-lès-Dijon
Tel. : 03 80 56 22 82
Fax : 03 80 56 64 40
hotel.rest.lamusarde@wanadoo.fr
www.logisdefrance.fr

Closed from 22 Dec to 8 Jan • 12 rooms with bath/WC or shower/WC and television • €43 to €54; breakfast €8; half board €54 to €61 • Restaurant closed Sun evening, Mon and Tue lunchtime; menus €19 (in the week) to €62 • Terrace, garden, car park

 Burgundy's amply justified pride in its wine.

Treat yourself to a night in this village, also known as the kingdom of wine and celebrated by hosts of writers and wine-lovers alike. The bourgeois or rustic-style rooms command fine views over the vineyards which turn a beautiful shade of ruddy gold in autumn. In wintertime, snuggle up in the deep armchairs next to a log fire and wax lyrical over the merits of this or that vintage year. Pleasant flowered garden.

 Unspoilt countryside on the doorstep of Dijon.

Follow the suggestion on the sign – literally the "idler" – and put off a visit to the capital of the Dukes of Burgundy in favour of dawdling in the local countryside. Relax in the welcome shade of the thick branches of cypress, hazelnut and oak trees on the terrace and enjoy the tranquillity of this charming village on the heights of Dijon. A rustic style has been adopted for the family-sized, simply furnished rooms, which all look out over the peaceful garden.

Access : On the corner of Route des Grand Crus and Rue de Lavaux

Access : 6km to the north-west of Dijon, on the N 71 (towards Troyes), then take the D 107 on the right

 186 **LA SAURA**
Mr and Mrs Berthaud

Rue de Beaune
21360 Lusigny-sur-Ouche
Tel. : 03 80 20 17 46
Fax : 03 80 20 07 73
la-saura@wanadoo.fr

Open all year • 6 rooms with shower/WC • €75,
breakfast included • No table d'hôte • Garden, car park.
Credit cards not accepted • Outdoor swimming pool.
Horse-riding, tennis, golf and boating on the canal
nearby

 187 **DOMAINE DU MOULIN AUX MOINES**
Mr Hanique

Auxey-Duresses
21190 Meursault
Tel. : 03 80 21 60 79
Fax : 03 80 21 60 79
contact@laterrasse
www.laterrasse.fr

Open all year • 1 room and 1 suite at the mill, 3 rooms
500m away at Meursault, all have bathrooms • €55 to
€87, breakfast included • No table d'hôte • Garden, car
park

 We most liked **The fine collection of contemporary art.**

The owner, a painter in his spare time, has acquired
a wonderful collection of contemporary works, including
several abstract works which blend in beautifully with
the original fireplace, beams and stone floors. The rooms
are decorated in a variety of eclectic styles, marrying
parquet floor and antiques in one and a wrought-iron
bed, terracotta tiles and painted furniture in another; all
overlook the terraced garden. An art gallery and a
swimming pool have recently been built in the
outbuildings.

 We most liked **The unique location in the heart of the prestigious Meursault vineyard.**

This handsome property surrounded by vineyards was
once part of the Abbey of Cluny. Stone walls, beams,
tiled floors and a fireplace add a great deal of cachet
to the tastefully-appointed rooms; ask for one in the mill.
The inner courtyard, right on a riverbank, is also very
pleasant. A wealth of activities awaits guests, including
tastings of the estate's wine and visits to the dovecote
and to the small wine-growing museum with its
interesting 15C wine press.

Access : 2km southbound from Bligny-sur-Ouche on
the D 970

Access : In the middle of the vineyards

 188 AU TEMPS D'AUTREFOIS
Mr Pocheron

 Place Monge
21340 Nolay
Tel. : 03 80 21 76 37
Fax : 03 80 21 76 37

Open all year • 4 rooms, one of which is a suite • €54, breakfast included • No table d'hôte • Credit cards not accepted

 189 CHAMBRE D'HÔTE M. BACCHIERI
Mr and Mrs Bacchieri

La Forge, bord du canal de Bourgogne
21500 Rougemont
Tel. : 03 80 92 35 99
Fax : 03 80 92 35 99

Closed at Christmas • 3 rooms with bath/WC • €42, breakfast included • No table d'hôte • Car park. Credit cards not accepted • Boating

 The well-preserved charm of yesteryear.

 Boating on the peaceful waters of the Burgundy Canal.

A deliciously faded atmosphere emanates from this attractive 14C half-timbered house, standing on a little square opposite a fountain. The warm, welcoming interior features exposed beams, antique furniture, chequered curtains and tiled floors. The quiet, pretty rooms are adorned with old black and white photos of Nolay. In the summer, breakfast is served on the terrace of the inn, on the opposite side of the square.

This charming small house on the banks of the Burgundy Canal in the Armançon Valley lives up to its promise of peace and quiet. The welcoming, well-kept rooms are full of character and above all very peaceful; all have a fireplace. The manicured garden near the lock and the bicycle towpath along the banks of the canal further enhance its charm. Gracious welcome.

Access : In the heart of the village

Access : 10km to the north-west of Montbard on the D 905

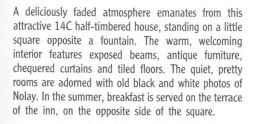

190 LA COMMANDERIE DE LA ROMAGNE
Mr and Mrs Quenot

Hameau de la Romagne
21610 Saint-Maurice-sur-Vingeanne
Tel. : 03 80 75 90 40

Open all year • 3 rooms • €65, breakfast included • No table d'hôte • Garden, car park. No dogs allowed

The chivalric service in keeping with the fortress' knightly past.

The foundations of this historic former fortress of the Knights Templar date back to 1144. The 15C drawbridge tower is home to generously sized rooms embellished with terracotta tiled floors, old beams and antique furniture; all the rooms overlook the river. The splendid breakfasts and courteous service add the finishing touches to an exceptional establishment.

Access : 9km northbound from Fontaine-Française on the D 27J and the D 30

191 HOSTELLERIE DE LA TOUR D'AUXOIS
Mr Prevost

Square Alexandre Dumaine
21210 Saulieu
Tel. : 03 80 64 36 19
Fax : 03 80 64 93 10
jlprevost @ tourdauxois.com
www.tourdauxois.com

Open all year • 35 air-conditioned rooms, 6 of which are split-level and 2 have disabled access. Rooms have bath/WC or shower/WC and television • €65 to €90; breakfast €8; half board €82 (€79 low season) • Menus €15 (in the week) to €34 • Terrace, landscaped garden, garage, private car park • Heated outdoor swimming pool, piano bar

The split-level room in the old presbytery.

Formerly very popular, this famous town and stopping point has declined in favour since the motorway diverted much of the traffic off the traditional holiday road. This 17C hostelry nonetheless remains true to its tradition of service and hospitality. The building has been renovated from top to bottom with whitewashed walls, tiled floors, painted furniture and exposed beams in some rooms. The circular dining room overlooks a landscaped garden with a view of the ruins of an old 14C tower.

Access : On the road through the town, next to the 14C tower

192 LES CYMAISES
Mr and Mrs Faidide

7 rue Renaudot
21140 Semur-en-Auxois
Tel. : 03 80 97 21 44
Fax : 03 80 97 18 23
hotel.cymaises@libertysurf.fr
www.proveis.com/lescymaises

Closed from 10 Feb to 3 Mar and from 4 to 24 Nov
• 18 rooms, one of which has disabled access, most have
bath/WC, some have shower/WC, all have television
• €50 to €55; breakfast €6 • No restaurant • Garden,
private car park

 A leisurely stroll on the ramparts of Semur.

The small capital of Auxois is within "cannonball"
distance of some of the most noted jewels of Burgundy,
including the Abbey of Fontenay, the fortified village of
Flavigny and the excavations at Alésia. A street near the
Porte Sauvigny leads to this imposing 18C townhouse.
The rooms are well soundproofed and furnished in a
practical country style, while a comfortable sitting room
plus conservatory makes a perfect setting for breakfast.
Pleasant, peaceful garden to the rear.

Access : On a side street in the medieval city

193 LES LANGRONS
Mrs Collins

21140 Villars-et-Villenotte
Tel. : 03 80 96 65 11
Fax : 03 80 97 32 28

Closed in Dec • 3 rooms upstairs • €50, breakfast
included • No table d'hôte • Garden, car park. Credit
cards not accepted, no dogs allowed

 The welcoming warmth of the old stove after a hard day's exploring.

This entirely restored farmhouse, situated very close to
the picturesque medieval town of Villars, can hardly be
said to lack character. A handsome staircase leads up
to the whitewashed walls, exposed beams, rugs and
matching curtains and bedspreads in the rooms. Lavish
breakfasts are served in a rustic dining room with
flagstones, heated in the winter by the welcoming
embers of an old stove. Mountain bikes can be rented.

Access : 5.5km to the north-west of Semur-en-Auxois
on the D 954 then the D 9A

 194 LE VAL D'ARON
Mr and Mrs Terrier

 5 rue des Écoles
58340 Cercy-la-Tour
Tel. : 03 86 50 59 66
Fax : 03 86 50 04 24
terrierje @ wanadoo.fr
www.pageszoom.com/val-aron

Closed from 23 to 31 Dec and Fri evening, Sat, Sun and Mon lunchtime in winter • 12 rooms with bath/WC and television; the 4 rooms overlooking the garden have a balcony • €61 to €69; breakfast €8; half board €49 to €54 • Menus €16 to €43 • Terrace, garden, car park • Outdoor swimming pool

 195 LE CHÂTEAU
Mr Vaissette

58120 Chaumard
Tel. : 03 86 78 03 33
Fax : 03 86 78 04 94

Closed from Dec to Feb, Thu and Sun evening • 6 rooms • €44, breakfast included • Table d'hôte €15 to €23 • Terrace, garden, park, car park. Credit cards not accepted

 Whiling away a few hours on the Nivernais Canal.

This 19C mansion formerly housed the local police station before it was turned into a hotel. The attic rooms feature exposed beams and timbers, while those on the ground floor open onto the garden: take your pick when you book – all are spacious and cool. In the winter, meals are served in the rustic dining room with fireplace, and in the summer on a "terrace" under the rafters of a reconstructed farmhouse.

 The location just two minutes from the largest lake in the region.

This large 18C square manor house is pleasantly situated in a five-acre park opposite Lake Pannesière-Chaumard on a woody hillside. Antique furniture graces all the attractive rooms, four of which overlook the lake. Breakfast is served on the terrace in the summer. An especially warm welcome is extended to riders.

Access : Midway between Decize and Saint-Honoré-les-Bains

Access : In the château grounds

 196 PERREAU
Mr and Mrs Girbal

 8 route d'Avallon
58140 Lormes
Tel. : 03 86 22 53 21
Fax : 03 86 22 82 15

Closed from 10 Jan to 20 Feb, Sun evening and Mon from Oct to Apr • 17 rooms, 9 of which are in a separate wing, have bath/WC or shower/WC, all have television • €43 to €46; breakfast €5; half board €41 to €43 • Menus €14 to €34 • Private car park. No dogs allowed • Hiking, horse-riding and mountain biking

 197 CHAMBRE D'HÔTE CROQUANT
Mrs Kandin

 L'Orée des Vignes Croquant
58200 Saint-Père
Tel. : 03 86 28 12 50
Fax : 03 86 28 12 50
loreedesvignes@wanadoo.fr

Open all year • 5 non-smoking rooms • €45, breakfast included • Table d'hôte €20 • Terrace, garden, car park. Credit cards not accepted, no dogs allowed

 The fine views of the Morvan from Lormes and the Mount of Justice.

This traditional hostelry stands on the road through a picturesque Morvan town. Behind its recently spruced up façade lie pleasant bedrooms, while those in the other wing are quieter and more modern. The exposed stone, dark timbers and stained-glass lights make the dining room most inviting.

 The well-stocked information corner in the hall.

This pretty stone-walled farmhouse topped with a traditional tiled roof has a number of assets. First and foremost, its spacious, tastefully decorated rooms with sloping ceilings. Next, the pleasure of eating in the handsome dining room complete with Burgundy and Spanish Renaissance furniture. Finally the sitting room with its old bread oven and the terrace where you can sit back and contemplate the beautiful garden.

Access : In the centre of the village, 29km southbound from Avallon on the D 944

Access : 3.2km eastbound from Cosne-sur-Loire on the D 33 and the D 168

BURGUNDY

198 LA ROCHERIE
Mr and Mrs Reparet

N 7
58640 Varennes-Vauzelles
Tel. : 03 86 38 07 21
Fax : 03 86 38 23 01

Closed from 5 to 19 Aug, Sat afternoon and Sun (except national holidays) • 12 rooms with bath/WC or shower/WC and television • €48 to €64; breakfast €7 • Menus €19 to €42 • Terrace, park, car park

199 HOSTELLERIE DU VIEUX MOULIN
Mr and Mrs Tarel

Porte d'Arroux – Route de Saulieu
71400 Autun
Tel. : 03 85 52 10 90
Fax : 03 85 86 32 15

Open from Mar to Dec; closed Sun evening and Mon out of season • 16 rooms, most have bath/WC, all have television • €39 to €58; breakfast €8 • Menus €23 to €39 • Terrace, garden, car park

 The restful view over the parkland from the rooms.

 The chef frequently plunders the vegetable garden for his fresh produce.

The park of this elegant Napoleonic château has unfortunately been reduced by half following the construction of the motorway round Nevers. But let's look on the bright side of things: the superb two-hundred-year-old cedar of Lebanon has withstood the onslaught of the earth movers and the hotel is now much easier to get to thanks to a slip-road off the A77! The well-worn rustic flavour of the place lends the rooms and the comfortable dining room a certain "je ne sais quoi".

Two of the turbines of this former flour mill built in 1878 just a stone's throw from the Gallo-Roman Arroux Gate are still in working order and even generate the hotel's electricity. The slightly faded rooms enjoy a peaceful setting and a pleasing view over the flowered garden and pool. In the country-style dining room, the accent is on rustic furniture and exposed beams and stonework. The terrace on the banks of the Arroux is shaded by tall trees.

Access : 5km from Nevers, on the N 7 towards Orléans, or on the A 77 towards Pignelin exit no 33, then take the private lane

Access : Near the Porte d'Arroux, at the northbound exit (towards Saulieu) out of town

200 LE GRAND HOTEL
Mr Poncet

Parc Thermal
71140 Bourbon-Lancy
Tel. : 03 85 89 08 87
Fax : 03 85 89 32 23
bourbon.thermal @ wanadoo.fr
www.grand-hotel-thermal.com

Open from 3 Apr to 25 Oct • 29 rooms with bath/WC or shower/WC, all have television and 8 have a kitchenette • €52 to €74; breakfast €6; half board €46 to €49 • Menus €12 to €22 • Terrace, inner courtyard, park, car park. No dogs allowed in the restaurant

201 VILLA DU VIEUX PUITS
Mr and Mrs Perraudin

7 rue de Bel Air
71140 Bourbon-Lancy
Tel. : 03 85 89 04 04
Fax : 03 85 89 13 87

Closed from mid-Feb to mid-Mar, Sun evening and Mon • 7 rooms upstairs with bath/WC or shower/WC, all have television • €40 to €48; breakfast €8; half board €39 to €46 • Menus €16 to €40 • Terrace, garden, car park

A leisurely stroll along the ramparts of this spa town.

This hotel, a former convent, lies on the edge of the spa centre's woody park. The gradually renovated and spacious rooms feature a variety of functional or more old-fashioned furniture and all benefit from the pervading restful atmosphere. Light floods in through the dining room's large bay windows but on fine days many guests prefer the terrace in the cloisters.

The landscaped garden complete with pond.

The walls of a former tannery now house this smart country inn. The rooms of variable size are both cosy and modern; those on the garden side are quieter and enjoy a better view. A countrified dining room, pleasant outdoor terrace and a slightly threadbare sitting room, its piano still in good tone, complete the picture of this unpretentious, excellent family establishment where guests can always be sure of a warm welcome.

Access : In the town centre, next to the spa and park

Access : Near to Place d'Aligre and the spa

 202 LE MOULIN DES ARBILLONS
Mr and Mrs Dubois-Favre

 71520 Bourgvilain
Tel. : 03 85 50 82 83
Fax : 03 85 50 86 32
arbillon @ club-internet.fr

Open in Jul and Aug • 5 rooms • €72, breakfast included
• No table d'hôte • Sitting room, terrace, garden, park.
Credit cards not accepted, no dogs allowed • Wine cellar,
tasting and sales

 203 MANOIR DE CHAMPVENT
Mrs Rullière

 Lieu-dit Champvent
71700 Chardonnay
Tel. : 03 85 40 50 23
Fax : 03 85 40 50 18

Closed from Nov to Feb • 5 rooms • €46, breakfast
included • No table d'hôte • Garden, park, car park
• Performing arts room

We most liked 🙂 **The rural setting of this group of 18C, 19C and 20C buildings.**

The 18C mill is flanked by a handsome 19C country house and set in a park which boasts a river and a pond. Beautiful period wardrobes grace the generally well-proportioned rooms, all of which overlook the valley and village. A bold blue and white colour scheme and vaulted ceiling make the smallest room our favourite. Breakfast is served in the 20C orangery which features frescoes, iron furniture and a porcelain stove.

Access : 8km southbound from Cluny on the D 980 then the D 22

We most liked 🙂 **The regular drama performances.**

Venture past the porch and you will discover a lovely stone manor house. The rooms are in the outbuildings and furnished with antiques, still-lifes and abstract works by a family ancestor. A room is set aside for regular drama performances and exhibitions of sculpture. The gardens are equally attractive and children generally love romping through the meadow. Flowered courtyard.

Access : 11km to the south-west of Tournus on the D 56 then the D 463

BURGUNDY

204 LA POSTE
Mr and Mrs Doucet

2 avenue de la Libération
71120 Charolles
Tel. : 03 85 24 11 32
Fax : 03 85 24 05 74
hotel-de-la-liberation-doucet @ wanadoo.fr
www.la-poste-hotel.com

Closed from 15 Nov to 2 Dec, Sun evening and Mon
• 11 rooms, 3 of which have a terrace. Rooms have
bath/WC and television • €57 to €63; breakfast €8; half
board €60 • Menus €21 (in the week) to €55 • Terrace,
garage

205 CHÂTEAU DE SALORNAY
Mr Guérin

71870 Hurigny
Tel. : 03 85 34 25 73
Fax : 03 85 20 11 43

Open all year • 4 rooms • €50, breakfast included • No
table d'hôte • Garden, car park. Credit cards not
accepted

 The festive atmosphere of the cattle markets.

 The sweeping view over Mâcon from the castle terrace.

The comfortable bedrooms of this traditional well-kept Burgundian house are equally classical with their "chocolate-box" patterns. Alcove statues, ornaments, period furniture and Charolles porcelain tableware abound in the refined bourgeois décor of the dining room. Burgundy's legendary generosity and hospitality are done full justice in the delicious menu, where the local Charolais beef, of course, has pride of place. Meals are served in the flowered courtyard in fine weather.

The towers, thick walls and guard posts of this 11C and 15C castle, on the doorstep of Mâcon, cannot fail to attract admiring glances. The antique furnished rooms were built along the same grand lines and overlook the fields. The room in the keep has retained its original terracotta flooring and mullioned windows. Not to be outdone, the dining room boasts beams, flagstones and a fireplace. Children are always welcome to visit the barnyard animals in the nearby farm.

Access : On a street corner, opposite the church in the town centre

Access : 6km westbound from Mâcon on the D 82 then a minor road

 206 MOULIN DE BOURGCHÂTEAU
Mr Donatelli

 Rue du Guidon
71500 Louhans
Tel. : 03 85 75 37 12
Fax : 03 85 75 45 11
bourgchateau@netcourrier.com
www.bourgchateau.cc

Closed from 20 Dec to 20 Jan and Sun from 15 Sep to Easter • 18 rooms with bath/WC or shower/WC, all have television • €43 to €85; breakfast €8 • Dinner only, menus €25 to €29 • Park, car park • 2 pedalos available, local wines sold in an outbuilding

 207 CHAMBRE D'HÔTE M. MATHIEU
Mrs Mathieu

 Sermaize
71600 Poisson
Tel. : 03 85 81 06 10
Fax : 03 85 81 06 10

Closed from 11 Nov to 15 Mar • 5 rooms with shower/WC • €54, breakfast included • Table d'hôte €16 • Garden, parking. Credit cards not accepted

 Relaxing amidst the cogs and gears of the old mill's machinery.

This enchanting 1778 mill spanning the Seille River was in use up until 1973. The modern, immaculate rooms on the upper floors enjoy a wonderful view of the woodland and river. A millstone and its hopper, leftovers from the mill's working days, lend the dining room a great deal of character. Local wines are on sale in an outbuilding. Two pedalos are available for the use of guests who fancy a spin on the river.

 The library's excellent collection of works about the region.

This former 14C hunting lodge with its impressive circular tower and flowered courtyard forms a very pleasing picture. An original spiral staircase winds up to a few personalised rooms, two of them have bathrooms in the tower. The suite boasts immense beams, cosy armchairs and walls lined with prints of 19C paintings and old photos by Doisneau. The garden overlooking the open countryside is very pleasant in the summer.

Access : Leave Louhans towards Chalon on Rue du 11-Nov-1918, then Rue du Guidon, turn right into the lane towards Bourgchâteau

Access : 12.5km south-east of Paray-le-Monial on the D 34 then the D 458, towards Saint-Julien-de-Civry

208 HOSTELLERIE BRESSANE
Mr and Mrs Picardat

2 route de Sens
71330 Saint-Germain-du-Bois
Tel. : 03 85 72 04 69

 Fax : 03 85 72 07 75

Closed from 17 to 30 Jun, from 23 Dec to 7 Jan, Sun evening and Mon • 8 rooms upstairs, with bath/WC or shower/WC • €22 to €39; breakfast €5; half board €30 to €35 • Menus €9 to €27 • Private car park

209 PONT
Mr and Mrs Pont

71110 Saint-Julien-de-Jonzy
Tel. : 03 85 84 01 95
Fax : 03 85 84 14 61

Closed during the February holidays • 7 rooms, most of which have shower/WC, all have television • €47; breakfast €6; half board €38 to €43 • Restaurant closed Mon and Sun evening; menus €13 to €28 • Terrace, private car park • Outdoor swimming pool

 The ecomuseum about the Bresse region in the castle of Pierre-en-Bresse.

This manor house built in the 18C for the Marquis of Scorailles has been an inn since 1815. The somewhat faded allure of the bedrooms is compensated for by the generous sprinkling of well-polished regional furniture. Polished oak floors, dark timber beams and a fireplace adorn the rustic dining room while attractive frescoes lighten the more urban 1900 room. Classic French dishes, plus some local Bresse delicacies, like the famously tender chicken.

 The charming views of the Brionnais region from the hillside village.

A country inn in the heart of a small Brionnais village. The practical rooms feature colourful fabrics and rustic or cane furniture. A sitting room, next to the dark panelled dining room, is reserved for meals ordered in advance. The chef cooks up good wholesome country dishes and can always be sure of the best ingredients: he owns the butcher's shop and charcuterie next door! Guests have exclusive use of an indoor heated swimming pool 250yds away.

Access : In the centre of the village

Access : Midway between Marcigny and Châteauneuf, on the D 8

210 LA VIOLETTERIE
Mrs Chartier

71740 Saint-Maurice-lès-Châteauneuf
Tel. : 03 85 26 26 60
Fax : 03 85 26 26 60

Closed from 11 Nov to Easter • 3 rooms, one of which is in the attic, all have bath/WC • €46, breakfast included • No table d'hôte • Garden, car park. Credit cards not accepted, no dogs allowed

211 LA CHAUMIÈRE
Mr and Mrs Vulcain

71260 Saint-Oyen-Montbellet
Tel. : 03 85 33 10 41
Fax : 03 85 33 12 99

Closed Thu lunchtime and Wed • 9 rooms upstairs with bath/WC or shower/WC, all have television • €44 to €60; breakfast €7 • Menus €29 (in the week) to €42 • Terrace, garden, 2 car parks, one is private • River fishing

The sophisticated 19C ambience.

A wrought-iron gate takes you into the courtyard and garden and a flight of steps leads into this 19C mansion. The former holiday home of architect Roux-Spitz, it is now a hotel with light, airy rooms. Those in the attic with painted furniture have retained their original tiled floors and beams. The elegant wood panelling and the fireplace in the sitting and dining room further add to the establishment's appeal.

The banks of the Saône – heaven on earth for anglers!

On your travels through this region, don't pass up the chance to spend a night within the gold-coloured stone walls of this farmhouse. You will fall in love with the charmingly simple rooms – ask for one with a balcony overlooking the immense garden – and the country-style dining room complete with well-polished, dark timbered beams. Friendly and hospitable.

Access : 10km to the north-east of Charlieu on the D 487, then the D 987 towards La-Clayette

Access : On the N 6, between Tournus and Mâcon

  212 **AUBERGE DU SAINT-VÉRAN**
Mrs Leguet

 La Roche
71570 Saint-Vérand
Tel. : 03 85 23 90 90
Fax : 03 85 23 90 91

Closed 3 weeks in Jan, and on Mon and Tue out of season
• 11 rooms with shower/WC and television • €51 to €60;
breakfast €7; half board €52 to €75 • Menus €20 (in the
week) to €41 • Terrace, garden, private car park

 213 **LE CHÂTEAU D'ESCOLLES**
Mr and Mrs De Potter

 71960 Verzé
Tel. : 03 85 33 44 52
Fax : 03 85 33 44 80

Open all year • 5 rooms with bathrooms • €60, breakfast
included • No table d'hôte • Park, car park. No dogs
allowed

**Tune your ears to the delightful music
of French country life.**

The creaking of the millstone and the gears of this old
flour mill have given way to the funky beat of dinner
concerts in the evening. The magnificent piano, which
graces the rustic dining room, bears witness to the lady
of the house's passion for music. The dawn chorus is
however sung by a company of ducks. As the water
gently laps the banks of the Pétry, catch a quick forty
winks, before being awakened by the joyful laughter of
the village children playing in the nearby river.

**The faultless decoration of this
elegant house.**

Guests are always welcomed warmly to this outbuilding
of a 17C castle, standing on the edge of a 12-acre park
with pond and surrounded by vineyards and woodland.
The sloping ceilings of the bedrooms add a cosy touch,
further enhanced by thick carpets, beams and old
furniture. Breakfasts, a chance to feast on home-made
jams and fresh fruit juice, are served in a beautiful room
graced with a dresser, old kneading machine and
wrought-iron light. Delightful terrace.

Access : Leave the N 6 at Crêches-sur-Saône for the
D 31 to Saint-Vérand

Access : 4km to the north-east of Berzé-la-Ville on
the D 17 then the D 85

BURGUNDY

214 MAXIME
Mrs Lenfant

2 quai de la Marine
89000 Auxerre
Tel. : 03 86 52 14 19
Fax : 03 86 52 21 70
hotel-maxime@ipoint.fr

Closed from 23 Dec to 15 Jan • 26 rooms with bath/WC and television • €60 to €72; breakfast €9 • Air-conditioned restaurant (30m away): menus €33 to €48; Bistrot du Terroir: menus €15 to €17 • Terrace, private car park

215 NORMANDIE
Mrs Ramisse

41 boulevard Vauban
89000 Auxerre
Tel. : 03 86 52 57 80
Fax : 03 86 51 54 33
normandie@acom.fr
www.acom.jr/normandie

Open all year • 47 rooms, most at the rear of the building. All rooms have bath/WC or shower/WC and television, 4 are non-smoking • €53 to €73; breakfast €7 • No restaurant • Terrace, garage • Billiards

We most liked Trying to learn how to pronounce "Ausserre" like the locals.

This hotel is in the midst of Auxerre's riverside district, surrounded by the barge owners half-timbered houses and the Horse-Drawn Barge Museum. The rooms facing the quay with a view of the Yonne are being gradually renovated, but those to the rear are quieter. The typically Burgundian restaurant and the vaulted bistro have, over the years, become the haunt of Auxerre's successful football team. The sounds of liberally washed-down post match celebrations still echo round the walls.

We most liked Endless discussions over a game of billiards.

Virginia creeper has covered the pretty redbrick and white stone façade of this comfortable 19C townhouse with a pleasant gravel forecourt where breakfasts are served in the summer. Most of the rooms, which are in the process of being renovated, are situated in a more recent, quieter wing. The rooms are comfortable and some have power showers. Room service possible. Guests' welfare is the prime concern of this pleasant establishment.

Access : On the road on the left bank of the Yonne

Access : On the ringroad round town, right at the roundabout coming from the A 6 (Paris) and the N 6 (Sens)

216 **LE PARC DES MARÉCHAUX**
Mr and Mrs Royer

6 avenue Foch
89000 Auxerre
Tel. : 03 86 51 43 77
Fax : 03 86 51 30 72
contact@hotel-parcmarechaux.com
www.hotel-parcmarechaux.com

Open all year • 25 rooms on 2 floors, all have bath/WC
and television • €60 to €90; breakfast €9 • No restaurant
• Terrace, park, car park • Swimming pool

217 **HOSTELLERIE DES CLOS**
Mr and Mrs Vignaud

Rue Jules Rathier
89800 Chablis
Tel. : 03 86 42 10 63
Fax : 03 86 42 17 11
host.clos@wanadoo.fr
www.hostellerie-des-clos.fr

Closed from 23 Dec to 17 Jan • 26 rooms with bath/WC
and television • €66 to €84; breakfast €9; half board
€81 to €103 • Menus €33 to €69 • Garden, car park

 **The recently sunk swimming pool
which blends into the abundant
foliage.**

A Parisian judge had this elegant mansion built in
1854 in a style favoured by Napoleon III. When it was
converted into a hotel in 1980, the owners were astute
enough to retain as much of its original character as
possible. The Empire bedrooms are named after
Marshals of the French army, while the sitting rooms
and breakfast room are reminiscent of Victorian parlours.
The superb park and its hundred-year-old trees add a
certain hint of romanticism to the mansion.

 **Savouring a Havana cigar in the
smoking room instead of being
banished to the garden.**

This former hospital, which still has its original 14C
chapel, used to own numerous vineyards. The beautiful
vaulted cellar bears witness to the house's wine-growing
heritage and has a choice of over 30 Chablis. Rich
fabrics and modern comforts adorn the recently
renovated rooms. The bow windows of the restaurant
open onto a patio where drinks are served in the
evenings and breakfast in the morning, the cooking is
generous and full of flavour and the wine-list is quite
simply out of this world!

Access : From the A 6 or N 6 turn right at the
Boulevard Vauban roundabout, then right past the
Natural History museum

Access : In the centre of the village

 218 CHÂTEAU DE RIBOURDIN
Mr and Mrs Brodard

 89240 Chevannes
Tel. : 03 86 41 23 16
Fax : 03 86 41 23 16

Open all year • 5 rooms, one of which is on the ground floor and has disabled access • €65, breakfast included • No table d'hôte • Garden. Credit cards not accepted, no dogs allowed • Outdoor swimming pool

 219 LA MARMOTTE
Mr and Mrs Lecolle

 2 rue de l'École
89700 Collan
Tel. : 03 86 55 26 44
Fax : 03 86 55 26 44

Open all year • 3 non-smoking rooms with bathrooms • €42, breakfast included • No table d'hôte • Garden, car park. Credit cards not accepted, no dogs allowed • Horse-drawn carriage rides, boating on the Burgundy canal and fishing nearby

We most liked **The select atmosphere of this wonderful little castle.**

The 16C dovecote and castle stand at the foot of the village in the midst of wheat fields. Patience and care lavished over the years have resulted in the beautiful restoration visible today. The 18C barn now houses the bedrooms, each of which is named after a local castle and the spacious breakfast room has a fireplace. The overall look is rustic, mirroring the countryside views from the windows.

We most liked **The footpaths through the Chablis vineyards.**

This beautiful old stone house lies in the heart of one of the Yonne's picturesque little villages. All the personalised rooms are named after a colour chosen for the interior decoration. The "Blue" room has cane furniture, while open beams and a wrought-iron four-poster bed grace the "Pink" room. Breakfast is served in the winter garden to the tinkling sound of the fountain.

Access : 9km to the south-west of Auxerre on the N 151 then the D 1, then a minor road

Access : 7.5km to the north-east of Chablis on the D 150 then the D 35

ESCOLIVES-SAINTE-CAMILLE - 89290

L'ISLE-SUR-SEREIN - 89440

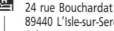

220 DOMAINE BORGNAT LE COLOMBIER
Mrs Borgnat

1 rue de l'Église
89290 Escolives-Sainte-Camille
Tel. : 03 86 53 35 28
Fax : 03 86 53 65 00
domaineborgnat @ wanadoo.fr

Closed from mid-Nov to Feb • 5 rooms, 3 of which have shower/WC, the other 2 have bath/WC • €46, breakfast included • Table d'hôte €20 to €34 • Garden, car park • Outdoor swimming pool, tours of the wine cellars

221 AUBERGE LE POT D'ÉTAIN
Mr and Mrs Pechery

24 rue Bouchardat
89440 L'Isle-sur-Serein
Tel. : 03 86 33 88 10
Fax : 03 86 33 90 93
potdetain @ ipoint.fr
http://www.potdetain.com

Closed in Feb, the last week of Oct, Sun evening and Mon out of season • 9 rooms, the most spacious has a fireplace. All rooms have bath/WC or shower/WC and television • €43 to €73; breakfast €7; half board €57 to €68 • Menus €18 (in the week) to €49 • Terrace, garage

We most liked

Visiting the superb cellars.

This fortified 17C farmhouse presides over a superb wine-growing estate. On the accommodation side, guests can choose between the simple comfort of B&B rooms or the self-catering cottage in the former dovecote. Bistro tables, a piano and a terrace around the swimming pool set the scene for breakfasts. Meals are invariably served with a choice of "home-grown" wines. Don't miss the chance to visit the splendid 12C and 17C cellars for further tasting sessions.

We most liked

Meals are served in the flowered inner courtyard in the summer.

Who could possibly want to remain stuck to the boiling tarmac of the A6 when the enchanting valley of Serein is so close at hand? Particularly as we've found "the" place that will capture your heart for ever. Nothing quite matches the unparalleled desire to please as that of this 18C coaching inn. Choose your room from the inn's web-site. All display the same faultless style and character as that present in the tasty Burgundian dishes and the fine selection of Chablis vintages.

Access : 9.5km southbound from Auxerre on the D 239

Access : In the village, on the D 86: leave Avallon north-east bound on the D 957 then left 2km after Montréal

 222 **CHAMBRE D'HÔTE M. PIEDALLU**
Mr and Mrs Piedallu

 5 avenue de la Gare
89160 Lézinnes
 Tel. : 03 86 75 68 23

Open all year • 3 rooms • €40, breakfast included • No
table d'hôte • Sitting room, garden, car park. Credit cards
not accepted, no dogs allowed

 223 **LE RELAIS SAINT VINCENT**
Mrs Vuillemin

 14 Grande rue
89144 Ligny-le-Chatel
Tel. : 03 86 47 53 38
Fax : 03 86 47 54 16
relais-saint-vincent @ libertysurf.fr

Closed from 21 Dec to 6 Jan • 15 rooms in 2 buildings,
one room has disabled access, all have bath/WC and
television • €47 to €63; breakfast €7; half board €38 to
€50 • Menus €13 to €26 • Terrace, inner courtyard,
private car park • Ideally located to visit the vineyards and
abbeys

We most liked
**The immaculate upkeep of this
contemporary house.**

We most liked
The Chablis white wines.

This brand-new house has been built in keeping with
local styles and even has a square stone tower. The
interior is equally pleasing and the spacious, well-
appointed rooms with sloping ceilings are furnished with
antiques. The breakfast room leads onto a pleasant
veranda and guests have the run of a private sitting
room for a quiet read.

Precious historic clues narrate the illustrious past of
these 17C walls, formerly the home of the bailiffs of
Ligny. The slightly faded rooms are spacious and calm.
The Renaissance era of the restaurant is apparent in the
monumental fireplace, open beams and old tapestries.
When the weather is fine, meals are served in the inner
courtyard surrounded by stone walls or traditional timber
frames. The magnificent Abbey of Pontigny is 4km
away.

Access : 11km to the south-east of Tonnerre on the
D 905

Access : Leave Auxerre on the N 77 towards
St-Florentin, turn right between Montigny-la-Resle and
Pontigny (D 8)

MOLAY - 89310

NITRY - 89310

224 LE CALOUNIER
Mr and Mrs Collin

5 rue de la Fontaine. Hameau de Arton
89310 Molay
Tel. : 03 86 82 67 81
info @ lecalounier
www.lecalounier.fr

Open all year • 5 non-smoking rooms, 2 of which are on the ground floor and have disabled access. All rooms have bathrooms with WC • €51, breakfast included • Table d'hôte €19 • Sitting room, library, garden, car park. Credit cards not accepted, no dogs allowed

 The cookery courses run by the owner, a cordon-bleu chef.

It is impossible to resist the charm of this lavishly restored Burgundian farm, named after the walnut trees on the estate. The rooms are situated in two wings and are decorated in a hybrid mixture of "colonial" and rustic styles, with bold colour schemes, old furniture picked up in local antique shops and works by local artists. The barn, graced with two large windows, is home to the dining and sitting rooms. Local produce has pride of place on the dining table.

Access : 8km northbound from Noyers on the D 86, and then a minor road

225 AUBERGE LA BEURSAUDIÈRE
Mr and Mrs Lenoble

chemin de Ronde
89310 Nitry
Tel. : 03 86 33 69 69
Fax : 03 86 33 69 60
auberge.beursaudiere @ wanadoo.fr
www.beursaudiere.com

Closed from 6 to 19 Jan • 8 rooms located in several buildings around the courtyard, all have television, bath/WC • €70 to €99; breakfast €8 • Menus €21 to €37, served in regional costume • Terrace, 2 car parks, one of which is private • Visits to vineyards, wine cellars and wine tastings

Visiting the hotel's medieval 15m-high dovecote with 650 nesting places.

This old farmhouse steeped in charm stands just 500m from a junction of the A6 motorway, midway between Auxerre and Avallon. The stylish brand new rooms, named after old trades, can be chosen on its excellent web-site. Ornaments gleaned from flea markets add character to the pleasant restaurant, delicious breakfasts are served in a vaulted cellar and an exquisite courtyard terrace. However if you are really determined to taste one of France's legendary motorway sandwiches, that's fine by us!

Access : A short distance from the A 6 motorway no 21 exit

226 CHÂTEAU D'ARCHAMBAULT
Mr Marie

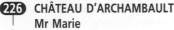

Cours
89310 Noyers
Tel. : 03 86 82 67 55
Fax : 03 86 82 67 87
château-archambault.com

Open all year • 5 rooms with bathrooms • €69, breakfast included • Table d'hôte €14 to €20 • Sitting room, garden, park, car park

227 AUBERGE DES BRIZARDS
Mr Besancenot

89630 Quarré-les-Tombes
Tel. : 03 86 32 20 12
Fax : 03 86 32 27 40
www.aubergedesbrizards.com

Closed from 6 Jan to 15 Feb and on Mon and Tue • 20 rooms, 7 of which are split-level, most have bath/WC, some have television • €54 to €84; breakfast €9; half board €52 to €79 • Menus €23 to €45 • Terrace, garden, park, car park • Tennis, ponds

The panoramic view of the Serein Valley from the elegant dining room.

This handsome 19C mansion was once the property of Napoleon III's chef. Restored with taste and flair, it now offers light, airy rooms and bathrooms complete with portholes. Parquet floors, painted ceilings, fireplace, cane furniture and wrought-iron candlesticks set the scene for the pleasant sitting and dining rooms. Enjoy a stroll around the terraced garden, parkland and cottage garden.

The forest path leading to the Abbey of Pierre-qui-Vire.

The position of this inn in the heart of the Morvan region would be hard to beat, surrounded by lakes, ponds, forests, unspoilt countryside and utter peace and quiet. A group of outbuildings, including two dolls' houses hidden in the park, make up the hotel; most of the snug rooms have been freshly renovated. The sophisticated restaurant, overlooking the flowered garden, serves generous country cooking. Ideal for nature lovers who enjoy the good things in life. Fishing possible.

Access : 2km southbound from Noyers on the D 86

Access : South-east of Quarré-les-Tombes, 10km on the D 55 and the D 355, after Moulin Colas and Trinquelin

 228 AUBERGE DE L'HÉLIX
Mr Eimery

 52 Route Nationale 6
89100 Rosoy
Tel. : 03 86 97 92 10
Fax : 03 86 97 19 00

Closed from 10 to 24 Feb, from 5 to 26 Aug, and on Sun evening and Mon • 10 rooms with bath/WC or shower/WC and television • €31 to €37; breakfast €5; half board €40 • Menus €15 to €33 • Car park

 229 LES VIEILLES FONTAINES
Mr and Mrs Moine

89270 Sacy
Tel. : 03 86 81 51 62
Fax : 03 86 81 51 62

Closed in Jan and Feb • 4 rooms • €44, breakfast included • Table d'hôte €23 • Garden, car park

Ever fancied a spot of snail hunting!

The sign outside this former boatman's inn wedged between the Yonne River and the N 6 highway testifies to the region's famous gastronomic mascot, the snail. Double-glazing protects guests from the bustle of the road, but the rooms at the rear are even quieter; all have been renovated. Immense beams and a handsome fireplace with a carved wooden mantelpiece take pride of place in the dining room.

Putting your feet up with a good book in the magnificent vaulted cellar-sitting room.

This delightful stone house in the heart of an old Burgundian village used to belong to a local wine-grower. The simple, comfortable rooms have parquet floors. The sitting room and kitchen, fitted out in the old vaulted wine cellar, are definitely worth a look. Meals are served in the owners' dining room, graced with a fireplace and a beautiful wrought-iron light.

Access : 3km southbound from Sens on the N 6 (towards Joigny)

Access : 10km eastbound from Vermenton on the D 11

BURGUNDY

 **230 LES TILLEULS**
Mr and Mrs Hubert

3 rue Decourtive
89600 Saint-Florentin
Tel. : 03 86 35 09 09
Fax : 03 86 35 36 90
alliances.tilleuls @ wanadoo.fr

Closed from 10 Feb to 10 Mar, from 26 Dec to 6 Jan and
Sun evening from Sep to May • 9 rooms, all have
bath/WC or shower/WC and television • €40 to €51;
breakfast €8 • Restaurant closed Sun evening and Mon
out of season; menus €17 (in the week) to €39 • Shaded
terrace, garden, private car park

231 LE HARAS DE KENMARE
Mrs O'Sullivan

19 route du Morvan. Le Meix
89630 Saint-Germain-des-Champs
Tel. : 03 86 34 27 63
Fax : 03 86 34 24 91
kenmare89 @ aol.com

Open all year • 5 rooms with bathrooms • €50, breakfast
included • Table d'hôte €18 to €25 • Sitting room,
terrace, garden, car park. Credit cards not accepted

 The peace and quiet reigning in this village.

The walls of this former Capuchin convent (1635) are
home to a peaceful hotel whose charm is further
enhanced by a pretty flowered garden. Book your room
on the garden side to get the full benefit of the ambient
serenity. The dining room, redone in a Provençal style,
and the terrace shaded by a linden tree, are an invitation
to take things easy. Relax and treat yourself to a few
of the region's succulent cheeses, like the famous
St-Florentin and Soumaintrain.

Access : In the centre of the village near the church,
take Rue St-Martin then Rue du Faubourg St-Martin
(towards Troyes) and turn left

 The easy-going, lived-in feel of this family estate.

The pride and joy of this 19C home is the tapestry
adorning the entrance, a copy of a medieval piece
entitled "Offering of the heart". The establishment which
endeavours to make guests feel totally at home more
than lives up to the tapestry's message. Each of the
personalised bedrooms is named after one of the
region's illustrious sons and daughters (Vauban, Colette,
Lamartine, Vincenot and the story-teller Marie Noël) and
decorated appropriately. The family's stud farm is just
next door.

Access : 10km southbound from Avallon on the
D 944, the D 10 then the D 75

TANNERRE-EN-PUISAYE - 89350   **VENOY - 89290**

 232 LE MOULIN DE LA FORGE
Mr and Mrs Gagnot

 89350 Tannerre-en-Puisaye
Tel. : 03 86 45 40 25

Open all year • 5 rooms, 3 of which are on the ground floor, all have bath/WC • €50, breakfast included • No table d'hôte • Terrace, garden, car park. Credit cards not accepted • Outdoor swimming pool

 233 LE MOULIN DE LA COUDRE
Mr and Mrs Vaury

La Coudre
89290 Venoy
Tel. : 03 86 40 23 79
Fax : 03 86 40 23 55
lemoulin89 @ wanadoo.fr
www.moulin-de-la-coudre.com

Closed from 6 to 29 Jan, from 1 to 15 Jul, Sun evening, Tue lunchtime and Mon • 7 rooms, 5 of which are in a house at the other side of the garden. Rooms have bath/WC or shower/WC and television • €57 to €70; breakfast €8; half board €61 • Menus €17 (in the week) to €46 • Terrace, garden, car park

 Fishing in the estate's river.

It is impossible not to admire the careful restoration of this 14C mill. The wheel has been rebuilt and the old sawmill turned into a pleasing rustic room with a kitchenette for the sole use of guests. Bare beams and 1930s furniture grace the comfortable rooms. Venture out into the landscaped parkland and explore the river, waterfall and pond teeming with fish.

 The peace and quiet just a giant's step from a slip-road off the A6 motorway.

The gardener-handyman clearly has his work cut out here amid the pools full of croaking frogs, borders of primroses and pansies and well-tended paths. This 19C mill on the banks of the Sinotte is perfect for a relaxing night's sleep on your journey southwards. The countrified rooms are a haven of peace and quiet and, in the summer, meals are served in the shade of dense foliage. Staff will happily give the lovingly restored millwheel a spin if so requested, to the delight of young and old alike.

Access : 11km to the north-east of Saint-Fargeau on the D 18 then the D 160

Access : Leave Auxerre on the N 65 towards Chablis, turn left past the A 6 (Auxerre-Sud interchange)

 234 LE MOULINOT
Mrs Tavasoff

 Route d'Auxerre
89270 Vermenton
Tel. : 03 86 81 60 42
Fax : 03 86 81 62 25
lemoulinot @ aol.com

Open all year • 6 rooms with bathrooms • €68, breakfast included • No table d'hôte • Garden, park, car park. Credit cards not accepted • Outdoor swimming pool

 235 LES AQUARELLES
Mrs Basseporte

 Fontette
89450 Vézelay
Tel. : 03 86 33 34 35
Fax : 03 86 33 29 82

Closed from 29 Dec to 15 Mar, Tue evening, and Wed in Nov and Dec • 10 rooms, one of which has disabled access, most have bath/WC • €45 to €48; breakfast €5; half board €48 • Menu €10, à la carte €20 to €30 • Terrace, car park. No dogs allowed

 The wealth of water activities.

Guests have to cross a narrow bridge over the rapid waters of the Cure to reach the idyllic site of this 18C mill. A fine wood staircase leads up to pretty, spacious rooms each of which is individually decorated. Cane furniture, beams, fireplaces and reproduction Impressionist paintings adorn the dining and sitting rooms overlooking the pond. Swimming, fishing, canoeing and mountain biking are just a few of the countless outdoor activities close at hand and the port is just five minutes away.

 The path winding its way through the fields to Vézelay.

When this old farmstead was turned into a hotel, the owners were determined to preserve its original character and cachet. The stables now house a sitting room, while the oak furnished bedrooms have been installed in the former hayloft. Meals are served on two enormous farm tables. In the summertime, Mrs Basseporte insists that dinner be taken outside to benefit from the warmth of the beautiful old limestone walls.

Access : Take the small private bridge spanning the Cure

Access : 5km eastbound from Vézelay on the D 957 (Avallon road)

BURGUNDY

236 **CHAMBRE D'HÔTE CABALUS**
Cabalus Sarl

Rue Saint-Pierre
89450 Vézelay
Tel. : 03 86 33 20 66
Fax : 03 86 33 38 03
contac@cabalus.com

Closed Tue and Mon out of season • 6 rooms • €50, breakfast €8 • Table d'hôte €15 • Terrace

237 **CRISPOL**
Mrs Schori

Fontette
89450 Saint-Père-sous-Vézelay
Tel. : 03 86 33 26 25
Fax : 03 86 33 33 10

Hotel and restaurant closed from 10 Jan to late Feb, Tue lunchtime and Mon (except hotel from May to Sep) • 12 rooms in a separate wing, one of which has disabled access. All rooms have bath/WC and television • €67 to €72; breakfast €9; half board €66 • Menus €20 to €46 • Terrace, garden, car park. No dogs allowed

We most liked **The art gallery exhibiting contemporary pottery, sculpture and paintings.**

The magic of this inn and its amazing location just 100yds from the basilica lend it a quite unique charm. It was built as the hostelry of the Abbey of Vézelay and its magnificent 12C vaulted room is now home to a tea-room and an art gallery. The extremely well-proportioned and comfortable rooms are imaginatively decorated. Generous breakfasts are served on an enchanting terrace shaded by a scent-laden wisteria.

We most liked **The impeccable upkeep of this establishment.**

A number of surprises await visitors inside the thick stone walls of this building in the heart of a hamlet. Firstly, the unexpected contemporary style of the rooms' decoration with sharp corners, lacquered ceilings and works by the owner-artist. Next, the peaceful garden sheltered from the hairpin bend in the road. Finally, the elegant restaurant which surveys the Cure Valley, with the hilltop basilica in the background.

Access : Near the abbey

Access : Leave Vézelay on the D 957 towards Avallon and drive 5.5km; the hotel is on the roadside

 238 **LA PALOMBIÈRE**
Mr Danguy

 Place du Champ-de-Foire
89450 Vézelay
Tel. : 03 86 33 28 50
Fax : 03 86 32 35 61

Closed in Jan • 9 rooms with bathrooms • €77, breakfast included • No table d'hôte • Garden, car park

 239 **LE RELAIS SAINT BENOÎT**
Mr and Mrs Roche

 89130 Villiers-Saint-Benoît
Tel. : 03 86 45 73 42
Fax : 03 86 45 77 90
micheline.roche @ wanadoo.fr
www.relais-saintbenoit.fr

Closed from 3 to 16 Feb, from 25 to 30 Dec and on Sun evening and Mon • 6 rooms with shower/WC and television • Double room €43 to €54; breakfast €7; half board €78 to €94 • Menus €17 to €32 • Terrace, garden • Second-hand-antique "shop" at the bottom of the garden

We most liked **The pleasant blend of styles and periods.**

Situated in the lower part of town, this elegant 18C mansion swamped in Virginia creeper is not lacking in character. The spacious, snug rooms feature an eclectic mixture of styles and periods ranging from Louis XIII, Louis XIV and Empire to satin bedspreads and "retro" bathrooms. Breakfasts, which are lavishly accompanied with home-made jams, are served on the veranda which opens onto the surrounding countryside. The flowered garden is at its best in full bloom in early summer.

We most liked **Picking up bargains in the back room of this hotel-cum-restaurant-cum-antique shop.**

Those who have read Colette, a local author born in the nearby town of St Sauveur, will immediately recognise Claudine's surroundings. Indeed the village even boasts an Art and History Museum just a step from the hotel to further steep yourself in local traditions. The hotel features renovated rooms, a sandstone collection from the region in the restaurant and a tiny shaded terrace. A country inn which lives up to the best local traditions.

Access : In the lower part of town

Access : Leave the Auxerre-Saint-Fargeau road (N 965) at Toucy to take the D 950 for 8.5km

 AUBERGE LE VOUTENAY
Mr and Mrs Poirier

 89270 Voutenay-sur-Cure
Tel. : 03 86 33 51 92
Fax : 03 86 33 51 91
auberge.voutenay @ wanadoo.fr

Closed from 2 to 25 Jan, from 17 to 25 Jun, from 18 to 26 Nov and on Mon and Tue • 6 rooms with bath/WC, and a suite opening onto the garden • €45 to €55; breakfast €7; half board €48 • Menus €18 to €40 (limited seating so it is necessary to book) • Garden, car park

 The mountain bikes and canoes available for use by guests.

The inn's canine mascot, Lafayette, happily does the honours of this handsome 18C mansion which is little by little undergoing a facelift. The bedrooms are being renovated, a spacious 45m² flat has just been installed and the restaurant boasts a handsome fireplace with a carved wooden mantelpiece. The slightly unruly walled garden planted with hundred-year-old trees and extending down as far as the River Cure, is sheer bliss. A hiking path runs alongside the establishment.

Access : On the N 6 from Auxerre to Avallon

BRITTANY

B rittany – Breizh to its inhabitants – is a region of harsh granite coastlines, dense, mysterious forests and pretty ports tightly packed with brightly painted fishing boats. Its charm lies in its brisk sea breeze, its incredibly varied landscapes, its countless legends and the people themselves, born, so they say, with a drop of salt water in their blood. Proud of the customs and language handed down from distant Celtic ancestors, today's Bretons nurture their identity throughout the year with a calendar of events, in which modern-day bards and minstrels exalt their folklore and traditions. Of course, such devotion to culture requires plenty of good, wholesome nourishment: sweet and savoury pancakes, thick slices of *kouign-aman* (pronounced "queen-aman") dripping in caramelised sugar and salted butter and mugs of cold cider. However, Brittany's gastronomic reputation extends far beyond such tasty titbits and gourmets can feast on the oysters, lobster, crab and other seafood delicacies for which this rocky peninsula is renowned.

52 ESTABLISHMENTS
241 to **292**

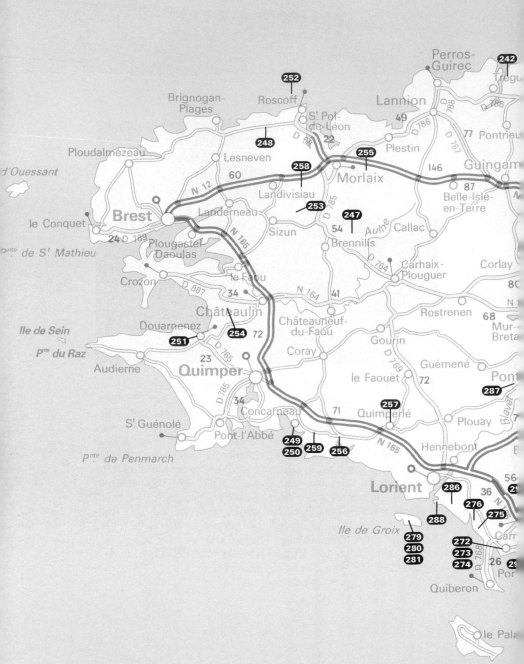

Perros-
Guirec
242
Tregu

Brignogan-
Plages
Roscoff **252**
Lannion
St Pol
de Léon
49
248
22
Pontrieu
77
Lesneven
258
255
Plestin
146
Guingam
d'Ouessant
60
Morlaix
87
Belle-Isle-
en-Terre
Ploudalmézeau
Landivisiau
253
247
le Conquet
Brest
Landerneau
54
Callac
Aulne
24 D 789
Sizun
Brennilis
Corlay
P^{nte} de St Mathieu
Plougastel-
Daoulas
N 164
41
Carhaix-
Plouguer
80
Crozon
le Faou
N 1
D 887
34
Rostrenen
68
Mur-
Breta
Ile de Sein
254 72
Châteaulin
Châteauneuf-
du-Faou
Douarnenez
Gourin
P^{nte} du Raz
251
Coray
Guémené
Pon
Audierne
23
Quimper
le Faouët
72
287
34
Concarneau
71
Quimperlé
257
St Guénolé
249
259 **256**
Plouay
Pont-l'Abbé
250
N 165
Hennebont
P^{nte} de Penmarch
Lorient
286
36
56
2
288
276
275
Ile de Groix
279
Carr
272
280
273
26
2
281
274
Po
Quiberon
le Pala
BELLE-ILE

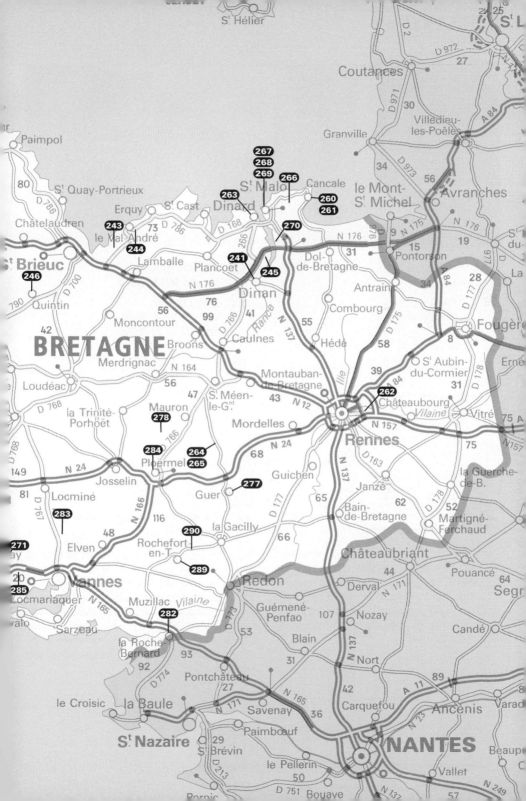

241 **ARVOR**
Mr Pierre

5 rue A. Pavie
22100 Dinan
Tel. : 02 96 39 21 22
Fax : 02 96 39 83 09

Closed from 5 Jan to 1 Feb • 23 rooms, one of which has disabled access, all have bath/WC or shower/WC and television • €46 to €61; breakfast €6 • No restaurant • Private car park

242 **TROÉZEL VRAS**
Mr and Mrs Maynier

22610 Kerbors
Tel. : 02 96 22 89 68
Fax : 02 96 22 90 56

Closed early Nov to early Apr • 5 rooms • €52, breakfast included • Table d'hôte €16 • Garden, car park. Credit cards not accepted, no dogs allowed

 Dinan's streets lined with lovely old half-timbered houses.

Guests are often struck by the amazing contrast between the old 18C walls of this former convent and the distinctly modern flavour of the bedrooms. A handsome Renaissance porchway leads into the reception and functional, well-equipped identical rooms. A few parking spaces near a ruined chapel are most welcome in the heart of the old town.

 The numerous walking and biking opportunities.

This pretty 17C manor house surrounded by rambling peaceful countryside has everything the travel-weary visitor could wish. Terracotta tiled floors, apricot painted walls, antique wardrobes and prints of local landscapes adorn the bedrooms. The equally agreeable dining room features white-painted beams and a stone fireplace. Depending on the season, meals are served in the garden or near a log fire: seafood is a speciality all year round.

Access : In the old town almost opposite the theatre

Access : 9km to the north-east of Tréguier on the Paimpol road towards Pleumeur-Gautier, then Kerbors

243 **LE MANOIR DE LA VILLE GOURIO**
Mr and Mrs Guihot

22400 Morieux
Tel. : 02 96 32 72 60
Fax : 02 96 32 75 68

Closed in winter • 4 rooms with bath/WC and television • €58 to €84; breakfast €8 • Table d'hôte €11 to €17 • Sitting room, terrace, garden, park, car park. No dogs allowed

244 **GRAND HOTEL DU VAL ANDRE**
Mr Crété

80 rue Amiral Charner
22370 Pléneuf-Val-André
Tel. : 02 96 72 20 56
Fax : 02 96 63 00 24
accueil @ grand-hotel-val-andre.fr
www.grand-hotel-val-andre.fr

Closed in Jan • 39 rooms, 2 of which have disabled access, 36 have bath/WC and 3 have shower/WC • €73 to €82; breakfast €8; half board €67 to €76 • Restaurant closed Sun eve and Mon, except in summer. Menus €20 to €40, dinner only in the week • Private car park • Tennis, horse-riding and water sports nearby

Taking a golf lesson with a pro.

This 17C Brittany manor house overlooks a 9-hole golf course surrounded by trees which are almost as old as the house. The rustic rooms upstairs all overlook the garden, fairways and ponds. On the ground floor, guests have the run of a reading room, a billiards table and a breakfast room where a fire takes the chill out of those brisk autumn mornings. The former stables house a bar, restaurant, night-club and the clubhouse – ask here for expert tips and private coaching.

The idyllic situation on the edge of a white sandy beach.

The faded charm of yesteryear's grand seaside hotels can still be felt in this stone and brick edifice built in 1895. Rest assured however, most of the rooms have been recently renovated with cane furniture and brand new bathrooms, while light coloured walls contrast beautifully with navy blue carpets and bedspreads. Those overlooking the sea are well-nigh perfect. Panoramic dining room and a terrace planted with hundred-year-old pine trees.

Access : 11km southbound from Val-André on the D 786 and the D 34

Access : Along the seafront

245 MANOIR DE RIGOURDAINE
Mr Van Valenberg

Route de Langrolay
22490 Plouër-sur-Rance
Tel. : 02 96 86 89 96
Fax : 02 96 86 92 46
hotel.rigourdaine@wanadoo.fr
www.hotel-rigourdaine.fr

Open from 29 Mar to 11 Nov • 19 rooms, 5 of which are split-level, 2 have disabled access. Rooms have bath/WC or shower/WC and television • €67 to €72; breakfast €7 • No restaurant • Park, private car park • Games room with billiards, private fishing

The countless paths around the Rance estuary.

A narrow lane leads up to this picturesque farmstead, which is almost as old as the River Rance itself. Its secluded position overlooking the estuary ensures guests a peaceful night's sleep, awakened only by the calls of the seagulls overhead. Good old country furniture and brightly coloured fabrics grace the bedrooms, while beams, bare stone walls and a gigantic family table adorn the breakfast room. Full of character.

Access : 3km northbound from Plouer-sur-Rance on the D 12 towards Langrolay, then right at a private road

246 COMMERCE
Mr Gourdin

2 rue Rochonen
22800 Quintin
Tel. : 02 96 74 94 67
Fax : 02 96 74 00 94

Closed from 24 Aug to 1 Sep, from 23 Dec to 5 Jan and on Sun evening and Mon • 11 rooms, all have shower/WC and television • €48 to €55; breakfast €6; half board €45 to €49 • Menus €12 (in the week) to €34

Walking along the banks of the Gouët.

The origins of this impressive granite house covered in Virginia creeper have been traced back to the 18C. The modern, personalised rooms have been recently renovated and each is named after an appetising spice or condiment, such as Fleur de sel, paprika or cinnamon. A beautiful period fireplace with a carved wooden mantelpiece is the centrepiece of the rustic wainscoted dining room.

Access : In the centre of the village, on the D 790 between Saint-Brieuc and Rostrenen

247 LA FERME DE PORZ KLOZ
Mr and Mrs Berthou

Trédudon-le-Moine
29690 Berrien
Tel. : 02 98 99 61 65
Fax : 02 98 99 67 36
porzkloz @ wanadoo.fr

Closed late Nov to Easter and on Tue. Bookings only
• 7 rooms with bath/WC • €61; breakfast €7 • Restaurant reserved for guests • Car park. No dogs allowed
• Horse-riding, swimming pool, tennis and golf nearby

248 COZ-MILIN
Mrs Moysan

29233 Cléder
Tel. : 02 98 69 42 16
Fax : 02 98 69 42 16

Open all year • 3 non-smoking rooms, all have bathrooms
• €43, breakfast included • No table d'hôte • Sitting room, garden, car park. Credit cards not accepted, no dogs allowed

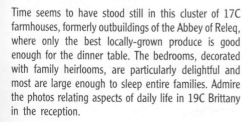

Finding out more about Brittany's less well-known hinterland.

Time seems to have stood still in this cluster of 17C farmhouses, formerly outbuildings of the Abbey of Releq, where only the best locally-grown produce is good enough for the dinner table. The bedrooms, decorated with family heirlooms, are particularly delightful and most are large enough to sleep entire families. Admire the photos relating aspects of daily life in 19C Brittany in the reception.

Traditional Breton fare at breakfast.

The seaside and coastal footpaths are not far from this stone-built house with slate roof. Individually decorated bedrooms combine old and new in an imaginative blend and, on the ground floor, the elegant sitting and breakfast rooms are furnished in the same eclectic style. Tuck into a delicious spread of pancakes, "far", a local rum and raisin flan and other traditional Breton fare at breakfast, before relaxing on a deck chair in the flowered garden.

Access : 11km to north-west of Huelgoat on the D 14, take the Berrien road and the D 42 on the left

Access : 3km northbound from Saint-Pol-de-Léon

BRITTANY

 249 **KER MOOR**
Mr Violant

Plage des Sables-Blancs
29900 Concarneau
Tel. : 02 98 97 02 96
Fax : 02 98 97 84 04
kermoor @ lespiedsdansleau.com

Closed on Tue from Sep to Jun (open in the evenings from Apr to Jun and from Sep to Nov), and Mon • 12 rooms • €74; breakfast €7 • No restaurant • Car park. No dogs allowed

250 **LE MANOIR DE COAT CANTON**
Mr and Mrs Simon

Grandbois
29140 Rosporden
Tel. : 02 98 66 31 24

Open all year • 4 rooms, 2 of which are on the ground floor, all have bathrooms • €45, breakfast included • No table d'hôte • Sitting room, car park. Credit cards not accepted, no dogs allowed • Horse-riding in the grounds

 A sweeping view of the ocean.

This delightfully situated 1900 villa is located right on the white sandy beach overlooking the ocean. The distinctly maritime décor of the interior decoration features white-painted wood lined walls, nautical prints and photos and model boats. All the rooms overlook the sea and three have a terrace. Totally unforgettable!

 Going hacking around the lush, green Breton countryside.

The construction of this pleasing manor house full of character took place from the 13C to the 17C. The rooms, located in a converted farmhouse, are decorated in a variety of styles, including medieval, Breton and English. The antique furnished breakfast room is very pleasant. The owners, who also run a riding stable nearby, will be only too happy to introduce you to the joys of riding.

Access : Northbound, towards the Forêt-Fouesnant

Access : 13km north-east of Concarneau on the Pont-l'Abbé road (D 783), and right on the Rosporden road (D 70)

 251 **AUBERGE DE KERVEOC'H**
Mr and Mrs Chacun

 42 route de Kerveoc'h
29100 Douarnenez
Tel. : 02 98 92 07 58
Fax : 02 98 92 03 58
auberge.de-kerveoch @ worldonline.fr
www.auberge-kerveoch.com

Open all year • 14 rooms, 10 of which are in a separate wing, all have bath/WC or shower/WC and television • €45 to €60; breakfast €9; half board €46 to €52 • Menus €15 to €19 • Terrace, car park. No dogs allowed in restaurant

 252 **TI VA ZADOU**
Mr and Mrs Prigent

 Le bourg
29253 Île-de-Batz
Tel. : 02 98 61 76 91
Fax : 02 98 61 76 91

Closed from 15 Nov to 1 Mar • 4 rooms on 2 floors, all have bathrooms, except for one family room with a bathroom on the landing • €49, breakfast included • No table d'hôte • Sitting room. Credit cards not accepted, no dogs allowed

We most liked **The owners' warm welcome.**

The inn of Kerveoc'h was a farm and a riding stables before becoming a hotel; guests can now enjoy the peace and quiet of the Breton countryside whilst being on the doorstep of a host of local sights. These include the Museum Port of Douarnenez, Locronan's medieval square and the breathtaking view of the sharp rocks battered by the waves. The simple, yet spacious rooms are located in a spruce white house and all have been treated to new bedding. Dining in the former stables is not to be missed.

We most liked **Cycling around on the lanes of this tiny island village.**

A sense of humour and a love of life set the tone in this blue-shuttered residence, whose name means "house of my fathers" in Breton. Old and new mingle happily in the cosy, welcoming bedrooms and all have a splendid view of the port, the cluster of islets and the mainland. Family heirlooms take pride of place in the sitting and breakfast rooms, both with fireplace. Bicycles can be rented nearby.

Access : 4km from Douarnenez on the Quimper road

Access : Near the harbour

 253 TY-DREUX
Mrs Martin

29410 Loc-Eguiner-Saint-Thégonnec
Tel. : 02 98 78 08 21
Fax : 02 98 78 01 69
ty-dreux@club.internet.fr

Open all year • 3 rooms with shower/WC • €43, breakfast included • Table d'hôte €17 • Garden. Credit cards not accepted, no dogs allowed

 254 PORZ-MORVAN
Mr Nicolas

29550 Plomodiern
Tel. : 02 98 81 53 23
Fax : 02 98 81 28 61

Open weekends (except Jan and Feb), school holidays and from 1 Apr to 30 Sep • 12 rooms, 4 upstairs, 8 are in a separate wing. All have bath/WC or shower/WC and television • €46 to €49; breakfast €6 • Crêperie in an old barn • Terrace, garden with pond, car park. No dogs allowed • Tennis

We most liked **It is worthwhile remembering that home-grown cider is pretty potent!**

The name of this dairy farm, more than worth a trip, in the heart of the countryside means "weaver's house" in testimony to its textile heritage. Period furniture, a huge 18C granite fireplace and a permanent exhibition of costumes belonging to former generations set the scene for this establishment which upholds local traditions. Modern canopied beds add character to the renovated rooms. Meals are a chance to sample the succulently prepared farm-grown produce.

 We most liked **Feasting on pancakes!**

Those in search of peace and quiet will adore this delightful stone farmhouse built in 1830 just next door – as the seagull flies – from the famous viewpoint of Ménez-Hom (330 m), which overlooks the region. Most of the gradually-renovated rooms are on the garden level in the former cow-shed. The barn has been converted into a friendly crêperie where the old rafters and timbers have been preserved. Large garden with pond and warm welcome guaranteed.

Access : 3.5km to the south-east of Guimiliau on the Plouneour-Menez road (D 111)

Access : 3km eastbound from Plomodiern on a minor road

 255 **MANOIR DE LANLEYA**
Mr Marrec

Au bourg de Lanleya
29610 Plouigneau
Tel. : 02 98 79 94 15
Fax : 02 98 79 94 15
manoir.lanleya @ libertysurf

Open all year • 5 non-smoking rooms with shower/WC
• €63, breakfast included • No table d'hôte • Garden,
car park. Credit cards not accepted, no dogs allowed

 256 **LE MOULIN DE ROSMADEC**
Mr and Mrs Sébilleau

29930 Pont-Aven
Tel. : 02 98 06 00 22
Fax : 02 98 06 18 00

Closed during the February holidays, from 14 to 30 Oct,
Sun evening out of season and Wed • 5 rooms in a
separate wing with bath/WC and television • €74 to €77;
breakfast €8 • Menus €27 to €48, à la carte €55 to €75;
limited seating so book in advance

 **The manor's legend, related by the
lord of the house.**

The quality of the restoration is such that it is difficult
to believe that this 16C manor house and its adjoining
18C malouinière were saved from ruin in the nick of
time. The stunning interior features Breton furniture, old
beams, schist floors, exposed stone walls, beautiful spiral
staircase, pink granite fireplace and rich fabrics. The
Louis XV room is particularly splendid, but the others,
which are smaller, display the same exquisite taste.
Lovely riverside garden.

 **Breakfasting on the delightful veranda
overlooking the river.**

This bucolic mill was built in 1456. According to a local
proverb, "Pont Aven, a town of standing, boasts fourteen
mills and fifteen houses". The town no doubt owes at
least part of its celebrity to the millers who settled by
its fast-flowing river, but the town's renowned pancakes
and the painters who endowed it with worldwide
posterity, also played their part. The traditional Breton
restaurant is decorated with artwork from the local
school. Spacious, modern bedrooms.

Access : 5km to the south-east of Morlaix on the
D 712, then take the D 64 towards Lanmeur

Access : In the town centre, near the bridge

257 CHÂTEAU DE KERLAVEC
Mr and Mrs Bellen

29300 Quimperlé
Tel. : 02 98 71 75 06
Fax : 02 98 71 74 55

Open all year • 6 rooms • €60 to €84, breakfast included • No table d'hôte • Sitting room, park, car park. Credit cards not accepted • Outdoor swimming pool, tennis, exhibitions. 18-hole golf course and horse-riding nearby

258 AR PRESBITAL KOZ
Mrs Prigent

18 rue Lividic
29410 Saint-Thégonnec
Tel. : 02 98 79 45 62
Fax : 02 98 79 48 47
andre.prigent @ wanadoo.fr

Open all year • 6 rooms on 2 floors, 4 of which have bath/WC, the other 2 have shower/WC • €45, breakfast included • Table d'hôte €15 • Garden, car park. Credit cards not accepted, no dogs allowed

We most liked **The well-preserved Second Empire style.**

It is easy to see why the current owners fell in love with this 1830 mansion set in a park complete with ornamental pool. The Second Empire rules undisputed amid the period frescoes, antique furniture and objets d'art gleaned from local antique shops and flea markets or brought back from voyages overseas. Relax in the peace and quiet of the spacious, individually decorated bedrooms. Don't leave without a look at the Jeanne d'Arc room.

We most liked **The nearby "enclos paroissiaux".**

This former 18C presbytery, hidden by a curtain of cypress trees, is home to comfortable, well-dimensioned rooms, each of which is decorated in a different colour and furnished with antiques. The largest has a fireplace. Admire the collection of ducks from all over the world in the smoking and sitting rooms. In the summer, wander round the garden and vegetable plot or rent a bicycle (from the hotel) and venture further afield.

Access : 6km eastbound from Quimperlé on the D 765 Lorient road, and left onto the Arzano road (D 22)

Access : Near the Saint Bernadette Retirement Home

 259 AUBERGE LES GRANDES ROCHES
Mr Raday

Les Grandes Roches
29910 Trégunc
Tel. : 02 98 97 62 97
Fax : 02 98 50 29 19

Open from late Mar to early Nov • 21 rooms located in several houses and cottages, all have bath/WC or shower/WC • €52 to €96; breakfast €8; half board €48 to €81 • Restaurant open evenings only, closed all day Mon; menus €16 to €40 • Park, car park

 260 LE CHATELLIER
Mrs Lescarmure

Route de Saint-Malo
35260 Cancale
Tel. : 02 99 89 81 84
Fax : 02 99 89 61 69

Open all year • 13 rooms, one of which has disabled access, with bath/WC or shower/WC and television • €50 to €55; breakfast €7 • No restaurant • Garden, car park

 The 100% "Breizh" (Breton) character of this establishment.

This delightful hamlet of old farms and two-hundred-year-old cottages nestles in the semi wilderness of five acres of parkland where a giant dolmen and sacred menhir still stand. The stylish, tastefully decorated and regularly refurbished rooms resound to the immense silence all around. The restaurant proudly has all the authentic character of traditional Breton houses with huge fireplaces and thick stone walls.

 The untamed landscape of the rocky Pointe du Grouin just a stone's throw away.

This comfortable stone house, a former farm, makes an ideal base camp to explore the region and get away from the bustling seaside resort. The relatively generously sized rooms are decorated in a rustic style and spotlessly clean. A log fire heats the sitting room during the cold winter nights.

Access : 0.6km to the north-east of Trégunc on a minor road

Access : 2km westbound on the D 355 towards Saint-Malo

 261 **LA POINTE DU GROUIN**
Mrs Simon

La Pointe du Grouin
35260 Cancale
Tel. : 02 99 89 60 55
Fax : 02 99 89 92 22
hotel-pointe-du-grouin @ wanadoo.fr
www.hotelpointedugrouin.com

Open from 25 Mar to 30 Sep • 16 rooms on 2 floors with
bath/WC or shower/WC, all have television • €74 to €84;
breakfast €8; half board €65 to €73 • Restaurant closed
Thu lunchtime and Tue out of season; menus €19 to
€54 • Car park. No dogs allowed • 400m from the beach

 262 **GERMINAL**
Mr and Mrs Goualin

9 cours de la Vilaine
35510 Cesson-Sévigné
Tel. : 02 99 83 11 01
Fax : 02 99 83 45 16

Closed during the Christmas school holidays • 20 rooms
on 3 floors, all have bath/WC and television • €61 to €80;
breakfast €10 • Restaurant closed Sun; menus
€19 (lunchtime, except weekends and holidays) to
€50 • Terrace, car park. No dogs allowed in restaurant

 Venturing onto the outcrop at sunset.

 The terrace overlooking the river.

In the summer, things can get a bit frantic here. What's
more, the iconic landmark of the Pointe du Grouin is
the starting point of the famous Route du Rhum sailing
race which takes place every four years (2006). Come
sunset, however, the view from this stone house perched
on a cliff is totally breathtaking. The cosy rooms have
been recently renovated and the panoramic restaurant
commands a splendid vista over the Island of Landes,
sanctuary to countless seabirds, and the St Michel Bay.
Words fail!

An unusual spot, to say the least: this 19C mill stands
on an islet of the River Vilaine. Another little island has
a car park and guests reach the hotel over a footbridge.
The new owners have set about renovating both the
restaurant and the rooms, some of which have canopied
beds. The tranquillity and idyllic location in the middle
of the river make this establishment quite unforgettable.

Access : 5km northbound from Cancale on the
D 201

Access : 6km eastbound from Rennes, on a small
island in the Vilaine

 263 MANOIR DE LA DUCHÉE
Mr Stenou

 35800 Dinard
Tel. : 02 99 88 00 02
http://perso.wanadoo.fr/manoir.duchee

Open all year • 5 rooms • €77, breakfast included • No table d'hôte • Park. Credit cards not accepted, no dogs allowed

 264 LA CORNE DE CERF
Mrs Morvan

 35380 Paimpont
Tel. : 02 99 07 84 19

Closed in Jan • 3 rooms, one of which is on the ground floor, with bathroom • €46, breakfast included • No table d'hôte • Sitting room, library, garden. Credit cards not accepted, no dogs allowed

 We most liked **Admiring the horses as they canter in the fields.**

Elegance and good taste abound in this perfectly restored 16C manor house in the heart of the countryside. The rooms, decorated with eye-catching period furniture, overlook the trees and flowers of the park. Breakfasts are served in a winter garden. The "antique" room is often used for exhibitions of paintings and sculpture and the carriage collection in the old barn is well worth a look. Genuinely warm welcome.

 We most liked **The epitome of sophistication.**

This lovely old home is hidden deep in the heart of the forest of Brocéliande, a land steeped in legends of wizards and magic. A profusion of paintings, tapestries and painted furniture set the tone for the tasteful, elegant interior decoration. The light, airy rooms open onto a delightful, well cared-for garden. There is absolutely no shortage of leisure activities in the vicinity including many footpaths and water sports on the village lake.

Access : 3km to the south-east of Saint-Briac on the D 3

Access : 2km southbound from Paimpont on the D 733

 265 LE MANOIR DE LA RUISSELÉE
Mrs Herminier

Lieu-dit La Ruisselée
35380 Paimpont
Tel. : 02 99 06 85 94

Open all year • 3 rooms • €46, breakfast included • No table d'hôte • Sitting room, garden, car park. Credit cards not accepted

 266 AUBERGE DE LA MOTTE JEAN
Mrs Simon

35350 Saint-Coulomb
Tel. : 02 99 89 41 99
Fax : 02 99 89 92 22
HOTEL.POINTE.DU.GROUIN @ wanadoo.fr
www.hotelpointedugrouin.com

Open all year • 9 rooms located in 2 modern buildings. Rooms have bath/WC or shower/WC, all have television • €74; breakfast €7 • No restaurant in the hotel but the owners have a restaurant at La Pointe du Grouin • Garden, duck pond, car park. No dogs allowed

 Merlin gathered his herbs in these forests and moors.

This attractive 1769 manor house lies next to the ruins of an abandoned farmhouse and is on the doorstep of the forest of Brocéliande, birthplace of Merlin, whom everyone knows was Breton and not Cornish at all! The rooms are comfortable and tastefully decorated; some have original parquet floors. Breakfasts are served in front of a roaring log fire in the winter and in the garden during the summer months.

 Breakfasts are served by the fireside in winter and opposite the garden in summer.

The headlands, bluffs and capes carved by the ocean and the island of Guesclin, whose fort belongs to singer-songwriter Léo Ferré, are just two minutes away from this secluded farmhouse which dates from 1707. The good taste of the lady of the house can be seen in the cosy style and old furniture in the rooms, particularly those in the former stables. Gardeners will adore the rose bushes in the beautiful garden "à la française".

Access : A short distance from Brocéliande forest

Access : On leaving Cancale, take the D 355 towards Saint-Malo

  267 LES CROIX GIBOUINS
Mrs Baslé

35400 Saint-Malo
Tel. : 02 99 81 12 41
Fax : 02 99 81 12 41

Open all year • 4 rooms with bathrooms • €46, breakfast included • No table d'hôte • Terrace, garden, car park. Credit cards not accepted

  268 JEAN BART
Mrs Moreau

12 rue de Chartres
35400 Saint-Malo
Tel. : 02 99 40 33 88
Fax : 02 99 56 98 89
hoteljeanbart@wanadoo.fr

Open from 15 Mar to 15 Nov and from 26 Dec to 6 Jan
• 18 rooms on 4 levels, all have bath/WC and television
• €59 (€45 low season); breakfast €6 • No restaurant

 Taking the time to relax in the garden overlooking the orchard.

It is difficult to believe that behind these heavy stone walls hides a delightful, fully restored 16C manor house. A wonderful wooden staircase, the work of talented cabinetmakers, leads up to snug rooms with excellent soundproofing thanks to the thickness of the walls. Granite benches and a fireplace add style to the inviting breakfast room. Don't miss the garden and orchard.

 The unforgettable walk round the ramparts.

This is the place to discover the unique atmosphere that reigns in the walled city of St Malo, beautifully restored after the Second World War. The sign outside depicts a Dunkirk corsair ship in honour of Jean Bart, Louis XIV's daredevil sea captain, and the hotel stands in the heart of France's proud capital of pirates and privateers. The labyrinth-like interior and the narrow rooms, are typical of St Malo. Practical bedrooms; some command a view of the port and its forest of bobbing masts.

Access : 6km eastbound from Saint-Malo on the D 301, Saint-Méloir-des-Ondes road

Access : In the old town, the road runs alongside the Bassin Vauban between la Grande Porte and the Porte Saint-Louis

 269 QUIC-EN-GROIGNE
Mr Roualec

8 rue d'Estrées
35400 Saint-Malo
Tel. : 02 99 20 22 20
Fax : 02 99 20 22 30
rozenn.roualec @ wanadoo.fr
www.quic-en-groigne.com

Open all year • 15 rooms on 2 levels, all have bath/WC
or shower/WC and television • €55 to €61; breakfast
€6 • No restaurant • Garage. No dogs allowed

 270 LES MOUETTES
Mrs Rouvrais

17 Grande-Rue
35430 Saint-Suliac
Tel. : 02 99 58 30 41
Fax : 02 99 58 39 41

Open all year • 5 rooms, one of which has disabled
access, all have bathrooms • €45, breakfast included
• No table d'hôte • Garden

 We most liked
**The peace and quiet of this hotel
located in the heart of St Malo.**

 We most liked
The sincerity of the warm welcome.

The name, taken from the tower next to the castle, is
a reminder of Anne of Brittany's haughty reply to the
townspeople of St Malo who took a very poor view of
the ramparts erected round their town. The duchess
dismissed them with the words: "Grumble as you will
('qui qu'en groigne'), so I decide." The hotel is in an
old stone house near the beaches. The rooms are
modern and gradually being redone. Breakfasts can be
taken in the cane-furnished veranda or the pleasant
garden.

Formerly the village grocery store and pork butchers,
this stone house built in 1870 stands on the main road
leading to the banks of the River Rance. Today it
features snug rooms painted in pastel colours and
decorated with old paintings and furniture picked up in
second-hand antique shops. One of the rooms is
equipped for disabled guests. The breakfast room,
complete with library, as well as the small garden in
the rear, are both very pleasant.

Access : In the old town, take Rue de Toulouse from
Porte Saint-Louis, at the end turn right twice

Access : In the heart of the village

271 LES CHAUMIÈRES DE CAHIRE
Mr Trochery

Hameau de Cahire
56400 Auray
Tel. : 02 97 57 91 18
trochery @ leschaumieres.com
www.leschaumieres.com

Closed in Jan and a fortnight in Mar • 4 rooms with shower/WC • €58, breakfast included • No table d'hôte • Garden, car park. Credit cards not accepted, no dogs allowed • Tennis and horse-riding nearby

272 L' ALCYONE
Mrs Balsan

Impasse de Beaumer
56340 Carnac
Tel. : 02 97 52 78 11

Open all year • 5 rooms with bathrooms • €54, breakfast included • No table d'hôte • Sitting room, garden, car park. Credit cards not accepted

The manicured lawns and flowerbeds.

Three instantly likeable 17C cottages stand clustered together in a listed hamlet. Beautiful antiques and contemporary works of art adorn the sophisticated, well-dimensioned rooms. Two are in the converted press-house, another is in the old bakery and the last is in the main wing. Fortifying breakfasts are served in the wonderful kitchen before an open fire.

Scrumptious breakfasts.

Whitewashed walls, parquet floors and tasteful fabrics await behind the creeper-clad façade of this 1870 farmhouse. The soft, inviting sofas in the sitting room and the deck chairs in the garden overlooking the fields make it impossible not to take things easy. The sea and menhirs are within easy reach, as is one of the most beautiful beaches of the bay of Carnac.

Access : 7km on the Vannes road, Plougoumelen exit, then drive towards Cahire

Access : On leaving Carnac Plage drive towards Trinité-sur-Mer

BRITTANY

 273 AUBERGE LE RÂTELIER
Mr and Mrs Bouvart

4 chemin du Douet
56340 Carnac
Tel. : 02 97 52 05 04
Fax : 02 97 52 76 11

Hotel open all year; restaurant closed from mid-Jan to mid-Feb • 9 rooms, some have shower/WC and television • €49; breakfast €6; half board €51 to €53 • Restaurant closed Sun evening and Mon from Oct to Mar; menus €15 (in the week) to €39 • Courtyard, car park, No dogs allowed

 274 TY ME MAMM
Mrs Daniel

56340 Carnac
Tel. : 02 97 52 45 87

Open all year • 4 rooms, one of which is on the ground floor • €42, breakfast included • No table d'hôte • Garden, car park. Credit cards not accepted

 The superb view of Carnac's famous menhirs without risking wrack and ruin!

This stone farmhouse on a quiet side street of the old village was built by a soldier home from the Napoleonic Wars, or so the story goes. Its granite façade, swamped by Virginia creeper, hides a welcoming, country interior: the unfussy rustic charm of the bedrooms makes up for their small size. The beams and manger in the former cow-shed, converted into a dining room, are original and the pretty flowered fabrics add a cheerful touch.

Your hosts' hospitality and spontaneity.

Off the beaten track, this handsome farmhouse, built in 1900 and entirely restored, stands in a large garden, bordered by a pond on one side. Each of the immaculate rooms, named after one of Carnac's beaches, is decorated in a mixture of rustic and modern styles. Breakfast time by the side of the huge granite fireplace is always pleasant. Guests have the use of a fridge and a microwave.

Access : In the old village, a short distance from the church

Access : 5km northbound from Carnac on the D 768 and then the Quelvezin road (C 202)

ERDEVEN - 56400

ÉTEL - 56410

 275 CHAMBRE D'HÔTE M. MALHERBE
Mr and Mrs Malherbe

Kerimel
56400 Erdeven
Tel. : 02 97 56 84 72
elisabeth.malherbe @ wanadoo.fr

Open all year • 4 non-smoking rooms, with bathrooms and television • €68, breakfast included • No table d'hôte • Garden, car park Credit cards not accepted, no dogs allowed

276 LE TRIANON
Mrs Guezel

14 rue du Général Leclerc
56410 Étel
Tel. : 02 97 55 32 41
Fax : 02 97 55 44 71

Closed in Jan • 24 rooms, 7 of which are in a villa in the garden. Rooms have bath/WC or shower/WC and television • €48 to €60; breakfast €8; half board €61 (€51 low season) • Restaurant closed Sun evening and Mon lunchtime from Nov to Mar; menus €14 to €35 • Garden, car park

 The enveloping warmth of the wood stove after a day in the open air.

This cluster of 17C cottages laid out around a large lawn complete with flower-beds is definitely worth a photo or two. Inside, the stylish renovation of the attic rooms with period furniture, comfortable bedding and well-fitted bathrooms leaves nothing to be desired. Tuck into the profusion of Breton delicacies at breakfast time (croissants, "far", pancakes, home-made jams), served in front of the huge granite fireplace in winter. Guests also have the run of a pleasant sitting room and library.

 The awe-inspiring sight of the Barre d'Étel during bad weather.

Don't be put off by the somewhat ordinary façade of this building in the heart of the little fishing port, the interior has a few surprises up its sleeve. The bedrooms, decorated in a chocolate-box style, vary in size and comfort; some still have original hip baths – ask for one in the villa at the end of the peaceful garden. Attractive rustic and homely dining room and very warm welcome.

Access : 8km northbound from Carnac on the D 119

Access : In the centre of the village, near the church

277 FERME DE SÉJOUR DE LA BILIAIS
Mr and Mrs Chotard

56380 Guer
Tel. : 02 97 75 74 84
Fax : 02 97 75 81 22

Closed for 10 days in winter • 5 rooms with bathrooms • €46, breakfast included • Table d'hôte €15, only in the evening and by reservation • Sitting room, garden, car park. Credit cards not accepted, no dogs allowed

278 RELAIS DU PORHOËT
Mr and Mrs Courtel

11 place de l'Église
56490 Guilliers
Tel. : 02 97 74 40 17
Fax : 02 97 74 45 65

Closed from 1 to 21 Jan, from 1 to 8 Oct, Sun evening and Mon (open in the evening in season) • 12 rooms with bath/WC or shower/WC and television • €39 to €44; breakfast €6; half board €35 to €37 • Menus €13 (in the week) to €26 • Garden, private car park. No dogs allowed

The carriage rides.

This hamlet of houses covered by ivy is as idyllic a country hideaway as you could wish to find. The uncluttered bedrooms are modern in flavour; the one on the ground floor is adapted to disabled guests. It is easy to slip into the gentle pace of this farm and read or play games on the veranda, "think with your eyes closed" in the comfortable leather armchairs in the sitting room, go on a carriage ride or visit the tractor collection. Excellent home-grown produce and delightful prices.

The delightful young owners so in love with their region.

Let's not beat about the bush, this handsome country inn adorned with flowers in the summer is a very special place. Peaceful nights of refreshing sleep in rustic-style bedrooms more than large enough to swing a cat and delicious, generous helpings of good local recipes served in a pretty dining room complete with a huge fireplace. Children can romp to their heart's content in the garden.

Access : 16km southbound from Paimpont

Access : In the centre of the village, opposite the church

 279 **LA GREK**
Mr and Mrs Le Touze Pascalle

3 place du Leurhé
56590 Île de Groix
Tel. : 02 97 86 89 85
Fax : 02 97 86 58 28
groe @ infonie.fr
www.groix.com

Open all year • 4 non-smoking rooms, with bath/WC • €46, breakfast included • No table d'hôte • Sitting room, garden, car park. Credit cards not accepted, no dogs allowed

 280 **LA MARINE**
Mrs Hubert

7 rue du Général de Gaulle
56590 Île de Groix
Tel. : 02 97 86 80 05
Fax : 02 97 86 56 37
hotel.dela.marine @ wanadoo.fr
www.hoteldelamarine.com

Closed in Jan, and Sun evening and Mon out of season except in the school holidays • 21 rooms with bath/WC or shower with or without WC • €41 to €75; breakfast €8; half board €43 to €63 (€40 to €54 low season) • Menus €14 to €25 • Terrace, garden

 Hoping a storm would blow up and cut us off for days.

The name of this Art Deco-style property, formerly the home of a tuna boat owner, is the nickname given to the inhabitants of this windswept island. Restored in 1993 and 1997, the hotel has retained its appealing insular charm. One of the best things about the elegant, comfortable bedrooms is the enormous bathrooms. Antique furniture adorns the sitting rooms, one of which has a fine collection of old coffee pots. Laze about in the large walled garden.

 Sailing round the island on an old pirate ship.

The short walk from the landing stage to the main town is enough to work up a healthy appetite and ensure you do full justice to the hearty, varied dishes rustled up in the kitchen of this plush bourgeois 19C home. Don't worry about the calories, the best way to explore the Island of Groix is on foot or by bicycle! Simple, spotless rooms, a terrace shaded by tall pine trees and a walled garden will make you wish you had planned to stay longer...

Access : In the village

Access : In the town, 5min walk from the port

281 LA JETÉE
Mrs Tonnerre

1 quai Port-Tudy à Port-Tudy
56590 Île-de-Groix
Tel. : 02 97 86 80 82
Fax : 02 97 86 56 11

Closed from 5 Jan to 15 Feb • 8 rooms with bathrooms • €49 to €65; breakfast €7 • No restaurant • Terrace. No dogs allowed

282 LECOLIBRI
Mrs Loyer

1 rue du Four
56130 La Roche-Bernard
Tel. : 02 99 90 66 01
Fax : 02 99 90 75 94

Closed from 24 Jan to 9 Feb • 11 rooms, one has disabled access and 3 are non-smoking, all have bath/WC or shower/WC and television • €28 to €50; breakfast €5.50 • No restaurant • Private car park • Tennis, swimming pool, hiking and canoeing nearby

 We most liked
The picture-postcard view of the sea.

Heaven on earth for lovers of Brittany! From the front, boats can be seen bobbing up and down near the pier, while the view from the rear reveals isolated creeks of white sand buffeted by crashing waves. Fresh, spring colours adorn the wax-scented bedrooms which offer one or other of the above scenes; immaculate bathrooms. Salt air pervades the marine bar with terrace and an Irish-style bar serves excellent oysters.

 We most liked
Pretend you're French and treat yourself to breakfast with the morning paper!

This rather ordinary façade hides an establishment that will make you want to stay forever. First of all the rooms, which are peaceful, next the modern, impeccable bathrooms and last but not least, the warmth and charm of the staff who bend over backwards to satisfy any little whim. As parking places cannot be had for love nor money in the busy season, remember to book one in the hotel.

Access : To the north of Groix

Access : In the town centre

LOCQUELTAS - 56390

PLOËRMEL - 56800

283 LA CHAUMIÈRE DE KERISAC
Mrs Cheilletz

56390 Locqueltas
Tel. : 02 97 66 60 13
Fax : 02 97 66 67 57
chaumierekerisac @ minitel.net

Closed from Jan to 5 Feb • 3 rooms, 2 of which are attic rooms, the third is in a small cottage • €61, breakfast included • No table d'hôte • Sitting room, garden, car park. Credit cards not accepted, no dogs allowed • Swimming pool, tennis and horse-riding nearby

284 LE THY
Mr and Mrs Dinael

19 rue de la Gare
56800 Ploërmel
Tel. : 02 97 74 05 21
Fax : 02 97 74 02 97
hotel @ le-thy.com
www.le-thy.com

Open all year • 7 rooms with bath/WC or shower/WC and television • €50 to €55; breakfast €5 • No restaurant but the bar serves sandwiches • Small car park. No dogs allowed • Concerts and theatre at weekends

Winding down in this utterly relaxed atmosphere.

If you dream of waking up to a vision of sprawling fields and meadows, then this charming 1750 cottage in the heart of Brittany's lush green countryside is just the place for you. The rustic interior perfectly echoes the scenery outside. The slightly faded aura of the enormous bedrooms adds a further hint of charm. If even a pin dropping awakens you, ask for one of the rooms in the cottage, next to the lady of the house's bookbinding workshop. Delicious breakfasts served amid family heirlooms.

The 3km-long path lined with 220 species of hydrangea on the banks of the lac au Duc.

This unusual hotel has absolutely nothing in common with your run-of-the-mill establishments. As the web-site proudly proclaims, the imaginative rooms are named after and decorated in the style of artists from all periods: "Tapies", "Hopper", "Bonnard", "Hugo Pratt", "Klimt", "Van Gogh" and a "Flemish artist's studio". A cabaret room, decorated with three hundred drawers, stages "rock" concerts at the weekends. Trendy, personalised and immaculate – definitely worth a visit!

Access : 13km northbound from Vannes on the D 767 Pontivy road

Access : In the town centre

  285 GUERLAN
Mr Le Douaran

Guerlan
56400 Plougoumelen
Tel. : 02 97 57 65 50
Fax : 02 97 57 65 50
ledouaran @ aol.com

Closed from Jan to Mar • 5 rooms, one of which is a family room and one has disabled access • €42, breakfast included • No table d'hôte • Sitting room, garden, car park. Credit cards not accepted

 The rapturous smiles of toddlers visiting the farm.

This impressive 18C country seat makes an ideal base for exploring the Gulf of Morbihan. The spotless rooms are a happy marriage of old and new. One is designed for families and another for disabled guests. A fireplace graces the enormous dining room and guests have the use of a kitchen and a shaded garden. The owners are very happy to show you round the farm.

Access : 12km westbound from Vannes on the N 165, then take a minor road towards Plougoumelen

  286 HÔTEL DE KERLON
Mr and Mrs Coeggec

56680 Plouhinec
Tel. : 02 97 36 77 03
Fax : 02 97 85 81 14
hotel-de-kerlon @ wanadoo.fr
www.auberge-de-kerlon.com

Hotel open from mid-Mar to 4 Nov, restaurant from Easter to 4 Nov • 16 rooms, some of which have bath/WC, the others have shower/WC, all have television • €45 to €54; breakfast €8; half board €47 to €52 • Restaurant open in the evening only; menus €13 to €25 • Garden, car park. No dogs allowed

 The spectacle of the sea crashing against the Ria d'Étel.

This stone-built 19C farmstead, cradled in a peaceful Morbihan hamlet, commands a wonderful view of the Ria d'Étel. The bedrooms are somewhat outdated and hardly enormous but very well cared for and at delightfully reasonable prices. All overlook the peaceful, flowered garden. Traces of the establishment's farming past can be seen in the restaurant, which serves home-reared poultry and lamb. The sea is just 10min away.

Access : 1.5km to the north-east of Plouhinec, on the D 158 then a minor road

287 AUBERGE DE QUELVEN
Mr and Mrs Bolé

La Chapelle
56310 Quelven
Tel. : 02 97 27 77 50
Fax : 02 97 27 77 50

Open all year, closed on Wed • 7 rooms have shower/WC and television • €43 to €48; breakfast €6 • No restaurant, but there is a crêperie: prices are around €10 to €20 • Car park. No dogs allowed

288 LA CHAUMIÈRE DE KERVASSAL
Mr and Mrs Watine

Lieu-dit Kervassal
56670 Riantec
Tel. : 02 97 33 58 66
Fax : 02 97 33 49 47
gonzague.watine@wanadoo.fr
http://perso.wanadoo.fr/chaumiere.kervassal/

Closed from Nov to Feb • 3 non-smoking attic rooms with modern bathrooms • €49, breakfast included • No table d'hôte • Sitting room, garden, car park. Credit cards not accepted, no dogs allowed • Beach nearby

"Napoléonville" or Pontivy: a geometric town laid out by the Emperor himself.

The long granite façade of this inn is in the heart of this secluded hamlet in the Morbihan countryside. Practical, spotless bedrooms, some of which overlook the pretty 16C chapel and a traditional-style crêperie full of character with stone walls and a beautiful old fireplace. A very pleasant establishment noted for its warm welcome.

The faultless taste of this delightful home.

It is difficult not to fall head over heels in love with this beautifully restored 17C cottage. It has everything from an impeccable thatched roof, exposed beams and stone walls, period furniture and tasteful fabrics down to abundant bouquets of flowers. Inside and out it is a delight for the eyes. The tranquil bedrooms have high ceilings and ultra-modern bathrooms. Exquisite breakfasts are served in the garden in the summer.

Access : 10km to the south-west of Pontivy on the Plouay road. Opposite the chapel

Access : 8km eastbound from Port-Louis on the D 781, then the D 33, Merlevenez road

289 LE PÉLICAN
Mr Nays

Place des Halles
56220 Rochefort-en-Terre
Tel. : 02 97 43 38 48
Fax : 02 97 43 42 01

Closed from 13 Jan to 11 Feb, Sun evening (restaurant) and Mon • 7 rooms with bath/WC or shower/WC and television • €43 to €46; breakfast €6; half board €42 • Menus €12 (lunchtime in the week) to €25 • No dogs allowed

290 CHÂTEAU DE CASTELLAN
Mr and Mrs Cossé

56200 Saint-Martin
Tel. : 02 99 91 51 69
Fax : 02 99 91 57 41
auberge @ club-internet.fr
www.castellan.fr.st

Open all year • 5 non-smoking rooms with bathrooms • €77 to €84, breakfast included • Table d'hôte €23 • Park, car park. No dogs allowed • Walking, horse-riding and mountain biking nearby

We most liked **A picturesque site worthy of a watercolour or, for the less artistic among us, a photo!**

A charming Breton town is home to this delightful 16C-18C house whose window-boxes are adorned with brightly coloured geraniums in the summer. The spruce, modern rooms are decorated with modern furniture, with one exception, which boasts an old wardrobe and bed. The high rafters of the dining room add a rustic air, further enhanced by a handsome fireplace.

We most liked **The immaculate upkeep of this estate.**

Every nook and cranny of this 18C castle, a hideout for the Chouans counter-revolutionaries, oozes with history and character. The elegant bedrooms overlook a graceful park and open fields. The superb parquet floor, wood panelling and painting in the "Médaillons" bedroom are totally original. The stables have been converted into a beautifully decorated rustic dining room where you can sample delicious local delicacies, including home-made crêpes, jams and gingerbread at breakfast time.

Access : On the main square, next to the town hall and tourist office

Access : 13km north-east of Rochefort-en-Terre on the Gacilly road (D 777) and the Saint-Congard road (D 149)

 291 CHAMBRE D'HÔTE MADAME GOUZER

 17 route de Quéhan (C 203)
56470 Saint-Philibert
Tel. : 02 97 55 17 78
Fax : 02 97 30 04 11

Open all year • 3 rooms • €54, breakfast included • No table d'hôte • Garden, car park. Credit cards not accepted

292 L' AUBERGE
Mr and Mrs Larvoir

 56 route de Vannes
56400 Sainte-Anne d'Auray
Tel. : 02 97 57 61 55
Fax : 02 97 57 69 10
auberge-jl-larvor @ wanadoo.fr

Closed from 24 Feb to 13 Mar, from mid-Nov to mid-Dec, Tues (except Jul and Aug) and Wed • 6 rooms with bath/WC or shower/WC, all have television • €44; breakfast €6; half board €50 to €52 • Air-conditioned restaurant; menus from €23 (in the week) to €62 • Car park

 The sweeping view over the River Crach and the oyster beds.

Lovers of seafood, oysters in particular, and Brittany in general will adore this place. This charming oyster farmhouse enjoys an exceptional situation, in the midst of pine trees, overlooking the River Crach and opposite the busy port of Trinité sur Mer. Guests are always welcomed warmly. The light, airy rooms all command a view of this fascinating coastal scenery. Two rooms are equipped with a kitchenette and the largest also boasts a balcony.

The pilgrimages or "pardons" of Saint Ann are a sight to behold.

The impressive basilica, the house of Nicolazic and the pilgrimages in honour of Saint Anne, the patron saint of Brittany, offer an authentic insight into Breton tradition at its most fervent and picturesque. This spruce, flower-decked inn offers modern rooms in bright fabrics, decorated with regional or Art Deco-style furniture. Admire the elegant Quimper tableware as you eat in the traditionally-furnished Breton dining room, which is clearly (and justifiably) proud of its local produce.

Access : 2km on the Auray road, turn left at the first set of traffic lights (after the Kérisper bridge)

Access : At the entrance to the village, on the main street

IOSEPH: SOMINIAT

CENTRE
AND UPPER LOIRE VALLEY

S leeping Beauty is said to slumber still within the thick walls of one of the Loire's fairy-tale castles, like Chambord, Azay-le-Rideau or Chenonceau. A list of the region's architectural wonders and glorious gardens would be endless; but its treasures are shown to full effect in a season of 'son et lumière' shows depicting the fabled deeds of brave and courtly knights and the thwarted love of fair demoiselles. The landscape has inspired any number of writers, from Pierre de Ronsard, "the Prince of Poets", to Balzac and Georges Sand. All succumbed to the charm of this valley of kings, without forgetting to give the game-rich woodlands their due. To savour the region's two-fold talent for storytelling and culinary arts, first tuck into a delicious chicken stew, then curl up by the fireside to hear your hosts' age-old local legends.

58 ESTABLISHMENTS

293 to **350**

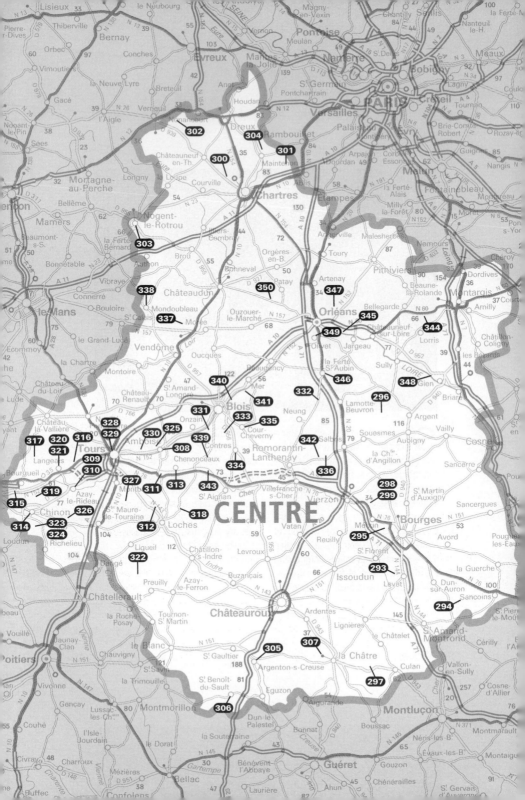

  293 CHÂTEAU DE BEL AIR
Mr and Mrs Maginiau

Lieu-dit le Grand-Chemin
18340 Arcay
Tel. : 02 48 25 36 72
Fax : 02 48 25 36 72

Open all year • 6 rooms with bath/WC • €39, breakfast
included • No table d'hôte • Park, car park. Credit cards
not accepted

  294 LE MOULIN DE CHAMÉRON
Messers Rommel and Mérilleau

18210 Bannegon
Tel. : 02 48 61 83 80
Fax : 02 48 61 84 92
moulindechameron @ wanadoo.fr
www.moulindechameron.frce.fr

Open from 1 Mar to 15 Nov; closed Mon except for the
evening in season, and Tues lunchtime • 13 rooms
located in 2 small buildings, with bath/WC or
shower/WC, all have television • €60 to €83; breakfast
€9 • Menus €21 to €32 • Terrace, garden, car park
• Swimming pool, small museum of milling

 Unbeatable value for money.

This 19C castle stands in a 10-acre parkland whose
trees and grounds afford calm and comfort. Most of the
large rooms are furnished in a Louis XVI style. One also
features a private sitting room with fireplace, while
another connects with a room which can accommodate
two child-sized beds. The stately dining room, complete
with monumental fireplace, is equally characterful.
Bicycle rentals and golf practice in the grounds.

 **You might not believe us but paying
your bill amid the machinery of the
old mill is a pleasure!**

Nature lovers are in for a real treat! For starters, there
is the monastical peace and quiet that emanates from
the two cottages in which the somewhat antiquated
bourgeois rooms are located. Then there's the mill lost
in the midst of fields and which is now a pleasant rustic
restaurant, with a wheel in working order. And finally,
the utterly rural setting of the terrace and the sound of
webbed feet splashing about in the duck pond.

Access : 11km northbound from Châteauneuf on the
D 73

Access : Leave Bannegon on the D 76, then drive
along a minor road, 3km in all

295 DOMAINE DE L'ERMITAGE
Mr and Mrs De La Farge

L'Ermitage
18500 Berry-Bouy
Tel. : 02 48 26 87 46
Fax : 02 48 26 03 28

Open all year • 5 rooms with bathrooms • €52, breakfast included • No table d'hôte • Car park. Credit cards not accepted, no dogs allowed

296 LA SOLOGNOTE
Mr and Mrs Girard

Au centre du village
18410 Brinon-sur-Sauldre
Tel. : 02 48 58 50 29
Fax : 02 48 58 56 00

Closed from 15 Feb to 20 Mar, 21 to 30 May, 11 to 20 Sept and Tue and Wed from Oct to Jun • 13 rooms with bath/WC or shower/WC and television • €56 to €74; breakfast €10; half board €73 to €80 • Air-conditioned restaurant; menus €26 to €55 (from Jul to Sep, open Tue and Wed at dinner time) • Garden, car park. No dogs allowed in rooms

We most liked **The tranquillity of the park disturbed only by the twittering of birds.**

This handsome property, formerly the priory of the Abbey of Saint Sulpice of Bourges, owes its name to a hermit who stayed here for a while. The nearby paper mill dates back to 1495. Nowadays, the quite large, tastefully decorated rooms are situated in two buildings, each as quiet as the next. Take a pleasant stroll through the grounds and admire the ancient trees.

We most liked **A glimpse of village life in France.**

Anyone who has read Alain-Fournier will instantly recognise the inimitable soul of this old country village full of French character and charm. The unpretentious hotel stands in the main street where it blends in perfectly with the other redbrick houses. Cosy or more contemporary rooms are laid out around a delightful courtyard-garden. The red floor tiles, stained-glass and period furniture are all synonymous with local styles and the fine porcelain bears the hallmark of Gien.

Access : 6km to the north-west of Bourges on the D 60

Access : Leave the N 20 at Lamotte-Beuvron onto the D 923

297 AUBERGE DU PIET À TERRE
Mr and Mrs Finet

21 rue du Château
18370 Châteaumeillant
Tel. : 02 48 61 41 74
Fax : 02 48 61 41 88
tfinet @ wanadoo.fr

Open from Mar to Oct and closed Tue lunchtime, Sun evening and Mon • 7 rooms with bath/WC or shower/WC, all have television • €43 to €60; breakfast €8; half board €50 to €58 • Air-conditioned restaurant; menus €20 (in the week) to €70; limited seating, booking necessary • No dogs allowed

298 VILLEMENARD
Mr and Mrs Gréaud

18500 Vignoux-sur-Barangeon
Tel. : 02 48 51 53 40
Fax : 02 48 51 58 77

Open all year • 6 rooms • €44, breakfast included • No table d'hôte • Park, terrace, car park. Credit cards not accepted, no dogs allowed • River and pond on the property. Billiards room

We most liked **The parents' suite with a proper child's room.**

Hear ye, hear ye, good folk! Here is a pleasant inn where every weary traveller should rest awhile! Entrust your faithful steed to the groom, have no fear, the stables, sorry the car park, is next door to the mounted constabulary, and rest your tired feet in this country haven. The rooms are as pretty as a picture and the tavern replete with good victuals to tickle even the finest palate. The chef's devotion has won the establishment a well-earned Michelin star.

We most liked **An afternoon stroll through ancient woodland.**

The lane, lined with ponds, crosses a river before entering this wonderful 19C country house which is still the hub of a thriving agricultural business. The interior decoration is particularly worthy of note: beautiful azulejos tiles grace the entrance and dining room, weapons and prints adorn the staircase and a superb varnished wooden bar stands in the billiards room. All the well-dimensioned, quiet rooms overlook the peaceful Berry countryside.

Access : Next to the gendarmerie (police station)

Access : 6km northbound from Méhun on the D 79 towards Vouzeron

299 LE PRIEURÉ
Mr Manfred and Mr Manuel Ribail

2 route de Saint-Laurent
18500 Vignoux-sur-Barangeon
Tel. : 02 48 51 58 80
Fax : 02 48 51 56 01
prieurehotel @ wanadoo.fr
www.leprieurehotel.com

Closed Tue and Wed, except for the hotel from Jun to Sep • 7 rooms upstairs with shower/WC and television • €49 to €60; breakfast €6; half board €54 to €57 • Menus €16 (lunchtime in the week) to €61 • Terrace, garden, car park. No dogs allowed • Outdoor swimming pool

Devotion to guests' welfare.

Built in 1860 for the village priest, the ogival windows immediately evoke this priory's religious roots. The establishment's former spiritual vocation has given way to a more down to earth, but equally committed desire for hospitality. The intimate, bright rooms are named after flowers. Traditional dishes and flavourful Berry wines are consumed with gusto on the pleasant terrace. Connoisseurs will immediately recognise the beautiful tableware as Foëcy porcelain!

Access : Set back from the lane, on the D 30 (towards Neuvy-sur-Barangeon), near the church

300 LA FERME DU CHÂTEAU
Mr and Mrs Vasseur

Lévesville
28300 Bailleau-l'Évêque
Tel. : 02 37 22 97 02
Fax : 02 37 22 97 02

Open all year • 3 rooms • €55, breakfast included • Table d'hôte by reservation, €15 • Garden, car park. Credit cards not accepted, no dogs allowed

The overwhelming peace and quiet of this country spot.

A pretty manor farm laid out around a spacious inner courtyard next door to a small castle. The good-sized rooms are cheerful, well equipped and all are peaceful. The simple, unaffected welcome, reasonable prices, pretty garden and its location only 15km from Chartres are among the most noteworthy of this establishment's many charms.

Access : 8km to the north-west of Chartres on the N 154 then the D 134

301 CHÂTEAU DE JONVILLIERS
Mr and Mrs Thompson

17 rue d'Épernon
28320 Écrosnes
Tel. : 02 37 31 41 26
Fax : 02 37 31 56 74
www.chateaudejonvilliers.com

Closed from Nov to Feb • 5 rooms with shower/WC • €65, breakfast included • No table d'hôte • Garden, car park. No dogs allowed

302 LE MOULIN DES PLANCHES
Mrs Maï

28270 Montigny-sur-Avre
Tel. : 02 37 48 25 97
Fax : 02 37 48 35 63
moulin.des.planches @ wanadoo.fr
www.moulin-des-planches.fr

Closed in Jan, Sun evening and Mon • 18 rooms, most have bath/WC, all have television • €45 to €78; breakfast €8; half board €53 to €78 • Menus €19 (in the week) to €48 • Terrace, park, car park. No dogs allowed in rooms • Board games, billiards

 The sheer elegance of this majestic property.

A pleasant drive leads up to this elegant 18C castle which stands in private grounds next to thick woodland. Peace and quiet reign in all the spacious, tastefully decorated rooms. Delicious and generous helpings of breakfast fare are served in a huge antique furnished dining room. Note that the establishment is entirely non-smoking.

 The total seclusion of this riverside mill.

However hard you listen, the only sounds you will hear are those of the countryside, but those who know the embattled history of the borderlands between France and Normandy may think they can still make out the distant echo of battle cries over the river. Nowadays the mill is a perfect haven of tranquillity, to which is added the pleasure of rooms decorated in period furniture and overlooking the river or the park. Beams, red floor tiles and open brickwork further enhance the rustic ambience.

Access : 4km to the north-east of Gallardon on the D 32

Access : 1km to the north-east on the D 102 (towards Tillières-sur-Avre)

303 L' AULNAYE
Mr and Mrs Dumas

28400 Nogent-le-Rotrou
Tel. : 02 37 52 02 11

Open all year • 3 rooms • €54, breakfast included • No table d'hôte • Park, car park. Credit cards not accepted, no dogs allowed

304 LES CHANDELLES
Mr and Mrs Simon

19 rue des Sablons, village les Chandelles
28130 Villiers-le-Morhier
Tel. : 02 37 82 71 59
Fax : 02 37 82 71 59
info @ chandelles-golf.com
www.chandelles-golf.com

Open all year • 5 non-smoking rooms with bath/WC and television • €58, breakfast included • No table d'hôte • Garden, car park. No dogs or cats allowed

 The tranquillity of the park so close to the town centre.

The main appeal of this almost Victorian-looking 19C mansion is its priceless position in the heart of a park full of countless species of trees and plants. The plush interior decoration is also worthy of note: a handsome wooden staircase leads up to the rooms, all of which boast parquet floors, period furniture and marble fireplaces. Delicious breakfasts are served in the wainscoted dining room in winter and in the delightful wrought-iron conservatory in the summer.

 A wealth of leisure activities so close at hand.

An impressive wooden porch leads into this renovated 1840 farmhouse set in grounds where horses graze peacefully. The barn has been converted into a guest wing which features bold colour schemes and excellent bathrooms. Interesting old furniture picked up from antique dealers and flea markets adds character to the breakfast room. On the leisure side, you can choose between golf and horse-riding (the owner's twin passions – he is a golf pro) or try your hand at fishing.

Access : 3.5km westbound from Nogent-le Rotrou towards Alençon

Access : 8km northbound from Maintenon on the D 116, towards Coulomb

305 MANOIR DE BOISVILLERS
Mr and Mrs Brea

11 rue du Moulin-de-Bord
36200 Argenton-sur-Creuse
Tel. : 02 54 24 13 88
Fax : 02 54 24 27 83
manoir.de.boisvillers@wanadoo.fr
www.manoir-de-boisvillers.com

Closed from 15 Dec to 10 Jan • 15 rooms located in 2 buildings, all have bath/WC or shower/WC and television • €57 to €89; breakfast €7 • No restaurant • Garden, private car park • Outdoor swimming pool

306 LE PORTAIL
Mrs Boyer

Rue Émile-Surun
36170 Saint-Benoît-du-Sault
Tel. : 02 54 47 57 20
Fax : 02 54 47 57 20

Open all year • 3 rooms, one of which is a studio • €46, breakfast included • No table d'hôte • Credit cards not accepted, no dogs allowed

Diving into the pool after a hot day's sight-seeing.

Wandering around the historic medieval city.

The Boisvilliers went into exile during the Revolution, but their manor house in old Argenton continues to honour their memory. Cheerful Jouy tapestries and antique furniture set the tone in the main wing which overlooks the valley, while the other wing is more modern. All the hotel's bedrooms have been lovingly renovated by the current owners, but the sitting room is resolutely modern with luxurious designer sofas, high-tech TV and striking modern works of art. Delightful garden.

A fortified gate, carved stone cross and spiral staircase bear witness to the venerable age of this beautiful 14C-15C former property of the Knights Templar. Character and authenticity emanate from the old beams and medieval or Renaissance inspired furniture in the bedrooms and apartment. The breakfast room is equally appealing and the lady of the house's gracious welcome is quite faultless.

Access : In the town centre, drive towards Gargilesse, turn right at Rue Paul Bert, left at Rue d'Orion then a sharp right

Access : In the medieval city

 307 **MONTGARNI**
Mr and Mrs Labaurie

36230 Sarzay
Tel. : 02 54 31 31 05
Fax : 02 54 31 30 10

Open all year • 3 rooms • €38, breakfast included • Table d'hôte €12 to €24 • Park, car park. No dogs allowed • Outdoor swimming pool. Farm-grown produce

 308 **LE BLASON**
Mr Béjarano

11 place Richelieu
37400 Amboise
Tel. : 02 47 23 22 41
Fax : 02 47 57 56 18
leblason @ wanadoo.fr

Closed from 15 Jan to 1 Feb, Wed and Sat lunchtime and Tue • 28 rooms, 2 of which have disabled access, all have shower/WC and television • €49; breakfast €6; half board €39 • Air-conditioned restaurant; menus €12 to €37 • Terrace

 The gourmet owner-chef's inspired culinary talents.

This farming couple have been extending their friendly hospitality to guests in search of tranquillity and the good things in life for over 15 years. The rooms in the 19C mansion, half-hidden by greenery, are extremely comfortable. Only 100% local produce crosses the threshold of the kitchen to become healthy, mouth-watering dishes. If you feel like some gentle exercise, the immense parkland which extends into the unspoilt Berry countryside offers some great walks.

The easy-going atmosphere.

Leonardo da Vinci ended his days in this town, now home to a family inn offering appealing attic rooms with a dash of local character. If you're feeling downhearted, ask for one of the rooms facing the street, which overlook "Rue Joyeuse". A discreetly rustic atmosphere reigns in the dining room and the terrace-veranda in the rear courtyard, where good home cooking can be savoured.

Access : 1.5km southbound from Sarzay on the D 41 towards Chassignolles

Access : On a square in the town centre

309 **LE CLOS PHILLIPA**
Mrs de Drezigue

10-12 rue de Pineau
37190 Azay-le-Rideau
Tel. : 02 47 45 26 49
Fax : 02 47 45 31 46

Open all year • 5 rooms with bathrooms • €69, breakfast included • No table d'hôte • Sitting room, garden, car park

310 **DE BIENCOURT**
Mrs Marioton

7 rue Balzac
37190 Azay-le-Rideau
Tel. : 02 47 45 20 75
Fax : 02 47 45 91 73
biencourt @ infonie.fr

Open from 1 Mar to 15 Nov • 17 rooms located in the main building and the old school, with bath/WC or shower/WC, some have television • €52 to €60; breakfast €7 • No restaurant • Inner courtyard. No dogs allowed

The exceptional situation of this pleasant mansion.

The priceless location, in the heart of the town two minutes walk from the castle, explains much of the appeal of this pleasant 18C mansion. Spacious, well laid-out rooms are embellished with interesting antique pieces. The large sitting room is very friendly. The delightful garden, where breakfast is served in fine weather, is just next door to the castle grounds. Ask about wine tastings of local vintages.

Being on the doorstep of a famous castle and parkland.

This elegant 18C property is tucked away in a semi-pedestrian street which leads to one of France's most beautiful Renaissance castles. Space and rustic furniture characterise the rooms, which have sloping ceilings on the top floor. A number of rooms decorated in Directoire style are also available in a building in the rear of the courtyard. Attractive cane-furnished sitting room, comfortable 19C-style dining room with a winter garden conservatory where breakfast is served.

Access : In the town centre

Access : In the town centre (near the post office), on the semi-pedestrian street leading to the castle

 LE CHEVAL BLANC
Mr and Mrs Blériot

Place de l'Église
37150 Bléré
Tel. : 02 47 30 30 14
Fax : 02 47 23 52 80

Closed from Jan to mid-Feb; restaurant closed Sun evening, Mon and Fri lunchtime out of season • 12 rooms with bath/WC or shower/WC and television • €56 to €72; breakfast €8; half board €69 to €73 • Air-conditioned restaurant; menus €17 (in the week) to €38 • Terrace, garden, private car park • Outdoor swimming pool

 LE CLOS DU PETIT MARRAY
Mr and Mrs Plantin

37310 Chambourg-sur-Indre
Tel. : 02 47 92 50 67
Fax : 02 47 92 50 67

Open all year • 4 spacious rooms with bathrooms • €62, breakfast included • Table d'hôte €10 to €21 • Garden, car park. Credit cards not accepted • Play area and fishing for children

 Wine and dine among the lush foliage of the inner courtyard.

Built in the 17C opposite the parish church, this townhouse was converted into an inn in the 19C. The view from the rooms of the restful inner garden compensates for their rather outdated appearance. Meals are served in two elegant dining rooms – the one with the fireplace has most character – or on the delightful flowered courtyard-terrace. The chef has made it a point of honour to uphold French culinary traditions.

 Cycling round the splendid countryside.

Children can fish in the pond in the grounds of this handsome 19C farmhouse in the heart of the countryside. Names evocative of well-being and freedom have been given to each of the generously-sized and tastefully decorated rooms. Guests have the run of a kitchen. A library, bicycle rentals and the nearby forest will keep you busy throughout your stay.

Access : In the town centre, in the pedestrian quarter near the church

Access : 5km northbound from Loches on the N 143, towards Tours

 313 HOSTELLERIE DE LA RENAUDIÈRE
Mr and Mrs Camus

24 rue du Dr Bretonneau
37150 Chenonceaux
Tel. : 02 47 23 90 04
Fax : 02 47 23 90 51
gerhotel @ club-internet.fr

Closed from 9 Dec to 6 Feb; restaurant closed Wed and lunchtime except Sat and Sun • 16 rooms, 5 of which are in a separate wing, all have bath/WC or shower/WC and television • €47 to €70; breakfast €7; half board €46 to €61 (€41 to €54 low season) • Menus €19 to €39 • Terrace, park, car park. No dogs allowed in the restaurant • Outdoor swimming pool, fitness room

 314 DIDEROT
Mr and Mrs Kazamias

4 rue Buffon
37500 Chinon
Tel. : 02 47 93 18 87
Fax : 02 47 93 37 10
hoteldiderot @ wanadoo.fr

Closed from mid-Jan to mid-Feb and from 22 to 28 Dec • 28 rooms, 4 of which are in a separate wing, all have bath/WC or shower/WC, some have television • €50 to €69; breakfast €6 • No restaurant • Inner courtyard, private car park. No dogs allowed

We most liked
The cockerel's morning call.

We most liked
Home-made lavender jam made with home-grown lavender!

This attractive manor house dating from 1802 once belonged to Pierre Bretonneau, a famous local doctor. It boasts spacious rooms which are gradually being personalised. Those in the other wing are smaller but delightful and calm, opening directly onto the garden. The dining room-veranda and the terrace both enjoy a view of the magnificent two-hundred-year-old redwoods and cedars of Lebanon.

Olive, banana, lemon, mandarin and medlar trees form a spectacularly exotic curtain of greenery to this 18C hotel acquired in the 1970s by the Cypriot owner. A classical accent is being given to the gradually renovated rooms, the quietest overlooking the courtyard. Home-made jams figure prominently on the breakfast table, served next to a crackling log fire in winter or out on the terrace whenever the weather permits.

Access : Leave the town on the Chissay-de-Touraine road

Access : A short distance from the town centre, on a quiet street between Place Jeanne d'Arc and Rue Diderot

315 LE COTTAGE DU CHÂTEAU DES RÉAUX
Mr and Mrs Goupil de Bouillé

37140 Chouzé-sur-Loire
Tel. : 02 47 95 14 40
Fax : 02 47 95 18 34
reaux @ club-internet.fr

Closed from 15 Nov to 1 Mar • 5 non-smoking rooms, 2 of which are on the ground floor, all have bath/WC and telephone • €54; breakfast €11 • Table d'hôte €46 • Park, car park. No dogs allowed • Tennis, boating on the moat. Ice rink, swimming pool and golf nearby

316 LA MEULIÈRE
Mr Voisin

10 rue de la Gare
37130 Cinq-Mars-la-Pile
Tel. : 02 47 96 53 63

Open all year • 3 rooms with bathrooms • €40, breakfast included • No table d'hôte • Garden, car park. Credit cards not accepted, no dogs allowed

We most liked **Rowing round the castle moat.**

This impressive 15C castle, whose foundations date back to the 13C, is fully worth a detour, if only for the two crenellated towers adorned with a magnificent patchwork of brick and stone and the sumptuous parkland. The freshly redecorated rooms are simply stunning, in particular the "Petite Provence" room which commands a sweeping view of the gardens, as do the "Bon-papa" and "Bonne maman" suites. And another thing, the breakfasts are out of this world!

We most liked **The tranquillity of this establishment within walking distance of the station.**

The uncontested bonus of this handsome 19C mansion is its situation close to the station without any of the noise or fuss you might expect. A fine wooden staircase takes you up to colourful, well-soundproofed rooms furnished with antiques. A comfortable dining room provides the backdrop to breakfasts. In the summer, deck chairs can be found in the garden for a quiet afternoon nap.

Access : 4km southbound from Bourgueil on the D 749, towards Port-Boulet

Access : Near the railway station

CONTINVOIR - 37340

GENILLÉ - 37460

317 LA BUTTE DE L'ÉPINE
Mr Bodet

37340 Continvoir
Tel. : 02 47 96 62 25
Fax : 02 47 96 07 36

Closed from 24 Dec to 5 Jan • 3 rooms, one of which is upstairs • €54, breakfast included • No table d'hôte • Park. Credit cards not accepted, no dogs allowed

318 LE MOULIN DE LA ROCHE
Mrs Mieville

37460 Genillé
Tel. : 02 47 59 56 58
Fax : 02 47 59 59 62
clive.mieville @ wanadoo.fr
www.moulin-de-la-roche.com

Closed in winter • 4 non-smoking rooms • €58, breakfast included • No table d'hôte • Garden, parking. Credit cards not accepted, no dogs allowed

The amazing care taken to restore this period house to its former glory.

A lazy afternoon's fishing or "déjeuner sur l'herbe" in a beautiful rural setting.

The owners have spent years faithfully restoring this delightful residence of 16C-17C origins using only authentic materials. The sitting-breakfast room is imaginatively strewn with period furniture and features a huge fireplace. The spotless rooms are genuine boudoirs, the most romantic of which is upstairs. Well-tended flower-beds grace the park behind the house.

Feast your eyes on this picture of paradise! The old water mill smothered in Virginia creeper stands on the banks of the somewhat fickle River Indrois. The oldest sections date from the 17C and 18C as can be seen from the original beams and terracotta floor tiles. The rooms are endowed with the charm of an English cottage, down to the ubiquitous tea and coffee making facilities; all overlook the garden and river. A snug sitting room is lined with books, antiques and lit by a log fire in winter.

Access : 2km eastbound from Gizeux on the D 15

Access : 10km to the north-east of Loches on the D 31 and the D 764, Montrichard road

319 LA PILLETERIE
Mrs Prunier

37420 Huismes
Tel. : 02 47 95 58 07

Open all year • 4 rooms • €54, breakfast included • No table d'hôte • Garden, car park. Credit cards not accepted, no dogs allowed • Nearby: Châteaux of Azay le Rideau, Villandry, etc

320 DOMAINE DE CHÂTEAUFORT
Mr Grosos

37130 Langeais
Tel. : 02 47 96 85 75
Fax : 02 47 96 86 03

Closed from Nov to Mar • 5 rooms with bathrooms • €66 to €88, breakfast included • Table d'hôte €23 • Terrace, park, car park. Credit cards not accepted, no dogs allowed • Outdoor swimming pool

The convenient situation near the castles of Azay and Villandry.

If in dire need of a break from the stress of urban life, this 19C farm in the middle of the countryside is just what the doctor ordered. Original red floor tiles add character to the rustic rooms, the quietest of which are located in an independent cottage. Young children adore the sheep, geese and other farmyard animals all of whom happily cohabit in a single pen. Relaxed and friendly hosts will make you feel at home the moment you arrive.

The sheer beauty of the place.

An elegant drive leads up to this graceful manor house built in the middle of immense grounds, just two minutes from the castle of Langeais. The stark austerity of the interior is softened by a few welcome feminine touches; peaceful rooms have large beds and all enjoy wonderful landscape views, although the best are from the second floor. The graceful welcome is worthy of the setting: only the moderate prices seem out of place.

Access : 6km northbound from Chinon on the D 16

Access : 800m from the centre of Langeais

 321 **ERRARD-HOSTEN**
Mr and Mrs Errard

 2 rue Gambetta
37130 Langeais
Tel. : 02 47 96 82 12
Fax : 02 47 96 56 72
info @ errard.com
www.errard.com

Closed from 18 Feb to 26 Mar, Sun evening, Mon and Tue lunchtime out of season • 10 rooms with bath/WC and television • €56 to €84; breakfast €14 • Menus €24 to €39 • Terrace, garage

 322 **AUBERGE SAVOIE-VILLARS**
Mr and Mrs Hauchecorne

 10 place Savoie-Villars
37350 Le Grand Pressigny
Tel. : 02 47 94 96 86
 Fax : 02 47 91 07 81

Closed during February holidays, early Nov, Sun evening (except in Jul and Aug) and Mon • 10 rooms, one of which has disabled access. Rooms have shower/WC and some have television • €36 to €39; breakfast €6; half board €30 • Menus €16 to €24 • Terrace. No dogs allowed

 The gargantuan hospitality of this provincial inn.

This hostelry is surrounded by some of Touraine's most beautiful castles and within walking distance of Langeais. Guests can choose between plush 19C or contemporary rooms, but those overlooking the street are noisier, even though the traffic can hardly be called "busy" after nightfall. Any doubts you may still have that you are in the birthplace of Rabelais' Gargantua, epic trencherman, will immediately vanish at the sight of the Brobdingnagian dishes liberally washed down with light Loire wines.

Your hosts' kindness and warm welcome.

You can recognise this welcoming inn in front of the church by its smart local stone façade. Rustic or Louis Philippe-style furniture graces the well-equipped rooms of varying sizes. The carefully decorated dining room is discreetly rural. In the summer, mealtimes are a joy on the pleasant terrace and the walled garden is an open invitation to some serious lounging. Make sure you pay your respects to the house's illustrious next door neighbour in the person of the Regional Museum of Prehistory.

Access : In the town centre, opposite the tourist office

Access : On the market square

 323 **LE CLOS DE LIGRÉ**
Mrs Descamps

37500 Ligré
Tel. : 02 47 93 95 59
Fax : 02 47 93 06 31
martinedescamps@hotmail.com

Open all year • 3 rooms with bathrooms • €75, breakfast included • No table d'hôte • Garden, car park. Credit cards not accepted, no dogs allowed • Outdoor swimming pool

 324 **LA MILAUDIÈRE**
Mr and Mrs Marolleau

37500 Ligré
Tel. : 02 47 98 37 53
Fax : 02 47 93 36 74

Open all year • 4 rooms, one of which is on the ground floor and 3 are upstairs • €52, breakfast included • No table d'hôte • Car park. Credit cards not accepted, no dogs allowed

Ideally located on the border of Touraine and Poitou.

This elegant 19C Touraine property was formerly part of a wine-growing estate. Indeed one of the rooms has been installed in the old press-house; the others are spacious, colourful, tastefully furnished and boast super bathrooms. In the winter, meals are served in the huge dining room covered in knick-knacks and in the summer on the terrace overlooking the garden. Friendly and welcoming.

The owners' exquisite charm and hospitality.

The walls of this original old 18C house are built out of "tuffeau", a soft local chalk. The owners dug in and undertook the majority of the restoration work themselves and can rightly be proud of the result. The rooms under the eaves are extremely pleasant and those on the ground floor with their old tiled floors, net curtains and rustic furniture are full of character. The breakfast room which boasts an old bread oven is also something of an eye-opener.

Access : 9km to the south-east of Chinon towards Richelieu, then take the D 115 and a minor road

Access : 8km to the south-east of Chinon, towards Île-Bouchard on the D 749, then take the D 29

 CHÂTEAU DE NAZELLES
Mr and Mrs Fructus

16 rue Tue-la-Soif (derrière la poste)
37530 Nazelles-Négron
Tel. : 02 47 30 53 79
Fax : 02 47 30 53 79

Open all year • 3 rooms • €72 to €89, breakfast included
• Table d'hôte (by reservation in summer) €23 • Garden,
car park • Outdoor swimming pool

 DOMAINE DE BEAUSÉJOUR
Mr and Mrs Chauveau

37220 Panzoult
Tel. : 02 47 58 64 64
Fax : 02 47 95 27 13
dom.beausejour@wanadoo.fr
www.domainedebeausejour.com

Open all year • 3 rooms • €77, breakfast included • No
table d'hôte • Car park. No dogs allowed • Outdoor
swimming pool

 Taking a well-earned rest in the
sitting room complete with billiards
table and fireplace.

There's no point in attempting to withstand the charm
of this 16C castle built on a hillside by the architect of
Chenonceau. The rooms on the first floor are a fine
example of how well old can be married with new; all
overlook the valley and Amboise Castle. Those in the
independent wing with old floor tiles, beams and
terracotta tiled showers, never fail to charm even the
most discerning traveller. The highlight has however got
to be the swimming pool, sunk into the rock and the
terraced garden.

 Relaxing on a genuine wine-growing
estate in Gargantua's homeland:
in vino veritas!

This delightful house was built in 1978 from old
materials gleaned in the region, some said to be three
centuries old! The slate floors of the carefully decorated
rooms contrast beautifully with the choice antique
furniture. The superb view over Rabelais' beloved
Chinon vineyards bodes well for a pleasant stay; those
who so desire can taste some of the estate's best
vintages in the company of the proprietress.

Access : 3km northbound from Négron on the D 5

Access : 5km to north-west of Bouchard on the
D 757, then drive towards Chinon on the D 21

327 LE LOGIS DE LA PAQUERAIE
Mr and Mrs Binet

La Paqueraie
37320 Saint-Branchs
Tel. : 02 47 26 31 51
Fax : 02 47 26 39 15
http://wanadoo.fr/lapaqueraie

Open all year • 4 rooms with bathrooms and one gîte • €73, breakfast included • Table d'hôte €23 • Garden, car park. Credit cards not accepted • Outdoor swimming pool. Fishing, hiking, tennis, 18-hole golf course and riding nearby

328 CHÂTEAUX DE LA LOIRE
Mr and Mrs Dutertre

12 rue Gambetta
37000 Tours
Tel. : 02 47 05 10 05
Fax : 02 47 20 20 14
hoteldeschateaux.tours @ wanadoo.fr

www.perso.wanadoo.fr

Open from Mar to Nov • 30 rooms with bath/WC or shower/WC, all have television • €37 to €48; breakfast €6.50 • No restaurant • Private car park

 The delightful landscaped garden and swimming pool.

You may well find it hard to believe this house was only built in the 1970s, but it is difficult to say if that's because of the regional architectural style, its rampant curtain of Virginia creeper or the venerable old oaks in the park. The rooms display an excellent blend of practicality, comfort and sophistication. Mirrors, antiques and an original fireplace grace the sitting room. If you're still not convinced, the peace and quiet of the wooded gardens are bound to win you over.

 The lively personality and kindness of the owners and staff.

This traditional establishment makes an ideal base camp to embark on a tour of the Loire châteaux and guests are immediately made to feel they are in expert hands. The hotel is located in a narrow side street near the town hall and the old city that Balzac would have known. The rooms are well kept and very comfortable, even if those on the upper floors are less spacious. All are being progressively renovated.

Access : On leaving Cormery (coming from Tours) take the D 32 and turn right after the level-crossing

Access : Near the town hall and the law court

 329 MIRABEAU
Mrs Boissel

89 bis boulevard Heurteloup
37000 Tours
Tel. : 02 47 05 24 60
Fax : 02 47 05 31 09
www.hotel-mirabeau.fr

Closed from 24 Dec to 2 Jan • 25 rooms, 3 of which are in the attic, most have bath/WC, some have shower/WC, all have television • €43 to €51; breakfast €6 • No restaurant • Small garden courtyard

 330 LES PERCE-NEIGE
Mrs Chemin and Mr Laguette

13 rue Anatole France
37210 Vernou-sur-Brenne
Tel. : 02 47 52 10 04
Fax : 02 47 52 19 08
brigitte @ perceneige.com
www.perceneige.com

Closed from 1 to 8 Mar, from 18 to 28 Nov, Wed and Thu (except from 16 Jun to 14 Sep) • 15 rooms, mainly with bath/WC or shower/WC and television • €31 to €46; breakfast €6; half board €31 to €42 • Menus €15 (except Sun lunchtime) to €37 • Terrace, shaded garden, private car park

 Dedication, friendliness and old-world hospitality.

 The peaceful village encircled by the vineyards of Vouvray.

This excellent old establishment stands on one of the main streets of Tours and is just a few minutes from the station and the international conference centre. Discreetly personalised and often with antique furniture, most of the rooms overlook the small rear courtyard-garden. This is where breakfast is taken whenever the sun shows its face. The rest of the year, steaming coffee and fresh croissants are served in a light, airy room which shows its turn-of-the-century (20C!) origins.

This modest 19C mansion formerly served as the offices of the solicitor of Vernou. An "old France" aura still pervades the rooms, which vary in comfort: book one which overlooks the spacious gardens and the old well. Local Loire dishes and wines are served in two elegant dining rooms and on the terrace to a backdrop of greenery and flowers.

Access : On the main road, near the railway station

Access : In the centre of the village, 4km eastbound from Vouvray (D 46)

 331 **LE LION D'OR**
Mr Pillault

 1 route de Blois
41120 Candé-sur-Beuvron
Tel. : 02 54 44 04 66
Fax : 02 54 44 06 19

Closed from 5 to 30 Jan, Mon out of season and Tue
• 9 rooms with bath/WC or shower/WC and television
• €31 to €40; breakfast €6; half board €28 to
€39 • Menus €15 (except Sun lunchtime) to €37 • Terrace, garden, car park

 332 **LA FARGE**
Mr de Grangeneuve

 41600 Chaumont-sur-Tharonne
Tel. : 02 54 88 52 06
sylvie.lansier @ wanadoo.fr

• 4 rooms with bath/WC • €77, breakfast included • No
table d'hôte • Swimming pool

 **Being pampered from morning to
night!**

This long-established village inn offers rooms that may
not feature all the latest gadgets, but which are spacious
and well looked after. Book one of those in the rear
with a view through the trees to the hotel's cottage
garden, the owner's pride and joy and a source of choice
ingredients for the dinner table. Beautiful old beams and
a friendly family atmosphere set the scene for the
country-style dining room.

 **The surrounding forest, full of
surprises and adventure.**

This 16C and 19C traditional farmhouse hidden deep
in the forest makes a fine picture with its half-timbered
brick walls and turret. The rooms are located in three
buildings. The most pleasant boasts old beams and
fabric lined walls, the others' main claim to fame is their
size and all are decorated with sturdy country furniture.
The swimming pool, shaded garden and nearby riding
stables also make this farm a perfect place from which
to explore the secrets of the Sologne.

Access : In the centre of the village, located on the
D 751 between Blois and Amboise

Access : 4km to the north-east of Chaumont
towards Vouzon on a minor road

CHITENAY - 41120

333 LE CLOS BIGOT
Mr and Mrs Bravo

41120 Chitenay
Tel. : 02 54 44 21 28

Closed from 16 Nov to 28 Feb • 3 rooms and one suite • €65, breakfast included • No table d'hôte • Garden, car park. Credit cards not accepted, no dogs allowed

We most liked **The place's tranquil invitation to take things easy.**

A deafening calm reigns throughout this 17C Sologne farmstead surrounded by forest and fields. The attic rooms are very pleasant and a suite has been built next to the dovecote, which is now a bathroom. Comfy old furniture and a warm, welcoming stove in the sitting room are all the invitation you'll need to while away an hour or two. An 18-hole golf course, tennis court, riding stables, and, of course, the world-famous Loire châteaux are all within easy reach.

Access : 2km to the south-east of Chitenay towards Contres, then a lane

CONTRES - 41700

334 LA RABOULLIÈRE
Mrs Thimonnier

Chemin de Marçon
41700 Contres
Tel. : 02 54 79 05 14
Fax : 02 54 79 59 39

Open all year • 5 rooms, one of which is upstairs • €46, breakfast included • No table d'hôte • Sitting room, park, car park. Credit cards not accepted, no dogs allowed

We most liked **The sophisticated decorative flair.**

The half-timbered walls of this Sologne farmhouse look so authentic it is hard to believe they were entirely built from materials found in neighbouring farms. The sumptuously furnished rooms all have exposed beams. Breakfasts are served by the fireside in winter and in the garden in summer. The gentle countryside is perfect for long country rambles.

Access : 10km southbound from Cheverny on the D 102, then a minor road

 335 LE BÉGUINAGE
Mr and Mrs Deloison

41700 Cour-Cheverny
Tel. : 02 54 79 29 92
Fax : 02 54 79 94 59
le.beguinage @ wanadoo.fr

Open all year • 6 rooms, 4 of which are in a separate wing • €60, breakfast included • No table d'hôte • Park, car park. Credit cards not accepted • Hot-air ballooning, golf, hiking

 336 AUBERGE À LA TÊTE DE LARD
Mr Benni

13 place des Tilleuls
41300 La Ferté-Imbault
Tel. : 02 54 96 22 32
Fax : 02 54 96 06 22
www.aubergealatetedelard.com

Closed from 23 Jan to 13 Feb, 6 to 20 Sep, Sun evening, Tue lunchtime and Mon except for holidays • 11 rooms with bath/WC or shower/WC, all have television • €45 to €72; breakfast €7; half board €45 to €60 • Air-conditioned restaurant; menus €20 (in the week) to €46 • Terrace, car park. No dogs allowed in rooms

 Flying over the Loire châteaux in a hot-air balloon.

 The typically local activities.

The manicured park and pond are not the only treasures of this stone property covered in Virginia creeper. Parquet or tiled floors, exposed beams, fireplaces, king-size beds and generous dimensions all grace the sophisticated bedrooms. With the smallest room measuring 20sq m, this is truly "the great indoors". For a quite matchless view of some of France's architectural gems, forget the cost and treat yourself to a flight over the Loire châteaux in a hot-air balloon piloted by the proprietor.

A private fishing domain on the banks of the Sauldre and a boat at your disposal, miles of mountain-bike trails and cycles to rent from the hotel, not to mention the regular hunting days (kennels available): surely something takes your fancy? After a day in the open air, this Sologne inn offers modern rooms with good bedding and recently refitted bathrooms, a pleasant countrified dining room and a shaded terrace.

Access : In a park

Access : On the village square

 337 LE MANOIR DE LA FORÊT
Mr and Mrs Redon

Fort Girard
41160 La Ville-aux-Clercs
Tel. : 02 54 80 62 83
Fax : 02 54 80 66 03
www.manoirdelaforet.fr

Open all year; restaurant closed Sun evening and Mon from Oct to Easter • 18 rooms on 2 floors, all have bath/WC or shower/WC and television • €58 to €63; breakfast €8; half board €75 to €85 • Menus €26 to €46 • Terrace, park, car park. No dogs allowed

 338 CHAMBRE D'HÔTE PEYRON-GAUBERT
Mr and Mrs Peyron-Gaubert

Carrefour de l'Ormeau
41170 Mondoubleau
Tel. : 02 54 80 93 76
Fax : 02 54 80 88 85

Closed from Nov to Mar • 5 rooms with bathrooms • €47, breakfast included • Table d'hôte €20 • Garden, car park. Credit cards not accepted, no dogs allowed • Exhibition and concert room

 The suite with a terrace overlooking the park (sadly the most expensive!).

This redbrick and stone hunting lodge was built in the heart of the countryside on the edge of the forest of Fréteval. The slightly faded rooms are furnished with antiques and all overlook the immense eight-acre park. The tall French windows of the stately dining room are thrown open to the terrace and flowered garden. Two sitting rooms, also furnished with antiques, are perfect for a quiet after-dinner drink or coffee.

 This one-off address, also a cabinetmaker's workshop.

The least you can say about this 17C redbrick house is that it is unusual, home to both a B&B establishment and exhibition hall for the cabinetmaker-owner's imaginative furniture. The rooms, of varying sizes, house some of the finished articles; simple, elegant waxed furniture made out of elm, ash and acacia wood. Concerts are sometimes held on the top floor. The garden to the rear is also very pleasant.

Access : 1.5km eastbound on a minor road

Access : In the town

339 HÔTEL DE L'ÉCOLE
Mr and Mrs Preteseille

12 route de Montrichard
41400 Pontlevoy
Tel. : 02 54 32 50 30
Fax : 02 54 32 33 58

Closed from 16 Feb to 14 Mar, from 19 Nov to 12 Dec, Sun evening and Mon except in Jul and Aug • 11 rooms with bath/WC or shower/WC, some have television • €45 to €63; breakfast €8; half board €55 • Menus €16 to €43 • Terrace, garden, private car park. No dogs allowed

340 LA VILLA MÉDICIS
Mr and Mrs Cabin-Saint-Marc

1 rue Médicis, Macé
41000 Saint-Denis-sur-Loire
Tel. : 02 54 74 46 38
Fax : 02 54 78 20 27

Open all year • 5 rooms and one suite • €66, breakfast included • Table d'hôte €16 to €31 • Park, car park. No dogs allowed

We most liked
The delightful flowered garden and murmuring fountain.

Your hand will immediately reach for your camera when you catch sight of this adorable house covered in variegated vine and surrounded by masses of brightly coloured geraniums. A distinctly old-fashioned feel in the rooms is compensated for by their size and spotless upkeep. Tables are prettily laid-out in one of two rustic dining rooms or on the pleasing shaded terrace. What better invitation to enjoy finely judged dishes which make the most of local produce!

We most liked
The exuberant foliage all around.

Once a spa hotel, this 1852 building is named after Marie de Médici who used to take the waters in the park. Some of the beautifully laid-out rooms command a view of the park. Tea and coffee making facilities can be used by guests in the pretty sitting room. If the sun is shining, take breakfast outside, then set out on a stroll or try your hand at kayaking, golf or riding nearby.

Access : In the town centre, on the D 764 between Montrichard and Blois

Access : 4km to the north-east of Blois on the N 152, towards Orléans

 MANOIR DE BEL AIR
Mr Abel

1 route d'Orléans
41500 Saint-Dyé-sur-Loire
Tel. : 02 54 81 60 10
Fax : 02 54 81 65 34
manoirbelair @ free.fr
www.manoirdebelair.com

Closed in Feb • 42 rooms located in 3 wings, with bath/WC (3 shower/WC) and television • €55 to €88; breakfast €6; half board €64 • Menus €21 to €40 • Inner courtyard, park, private car park. No dogs allowed in rooms

 LA FERME DES ATELLERIES
Mr and Mrs Quintin

41300 Selles-Saint-Denis
Tel. : 02 54 96 13 84
Fax : 02 54 96 13 78
caroline.quintin @ wanadoo.fr
www.perso.wanadoo.fr/caroline.quintin

Closed from 1 to 18 Feb • 3 rooms with bath/WC • €46, breakfast included • No table d'hôte • Sitting room, park. Credit cards not accepted, dog kennels

 Ambling down the old towpath which skirts the hotel.

 The beautiful Sologne countryside surrounding this farm.

A wine merchant and governor of Guadeloupe was among the proprietors of this elegant 17C manor house made out of "tuffeau", the chalky local stone. Most of the rooms have been renovated as has the restaurant which features a fine stone fireplace and regional furniture. All command fine views of the Loire. Pleasant leafy park.

Set in a 150-acre estate of woodland, moors and ponds, this old Sologne farm is sure to appeal to small-game hunters. Dog kennels are available and guests can go out hunting for the day with locals who know all the best coverts. As for the accommodation, the rooms are soberly decorated and well kept, two are installed in the former bakery where the old bread oven is still visible. Bicycles can be rented from the estate.

Access : 15km from Blois towards Orléans, on the D 951 bordering the Loire

Access : 16km to the north-east of Romorantin-Lanthenay on the D 60

 343 LE MOULIN DE LA RENNE
Mr Suraud

15 impasse de Varennes
41140 Thésée
Tel. : 02 54 71 41 56
Fax : 02 54 71 75 09
contact@moulindelarenne.com

 www.moulindelarenne.com

Closed from 1 Jan to 15 Mar, Sun evening and Mon from 15 Sep to 30 Apr • 15 rooms on 2 floors, almost all have bath/WC or shower/WC • €24 to €48; breakfast €7; half board €43 • Menus €15 (in the week) to €35 • Terrace, garden, car park • Children's play area

 344 LA FERME DU GRAND CHESNOY
Mr and Mrs Chevalier

45260 Chailly-en-Gâtinais
Tel. : 02 38 96 27 67

Open all year (by reservation from 1 Nov to 31 Mar) • 4 non-smoking rooms with bathrooms • €53, breakfast included • No table d'hôte • Sitting room, garden, car park. Credit cards not accepted, no dogs allowed • Tennis

 Walking next to the peaceful river as far as the first of the ponds of Sologne.

Once upon a time, there lived an old mill surrounded by a shaded garden through which passed the River Renne (Queen). Nearly all the simply decorated rooms have been renovated mirroring the dining room's bright, bold colours. An aquarium, a fireplace and children's games are most appreciated in the spacious sitting room, while the terrace on the banks of the millpond adds the finishing touch.

 The country spirit of the decoration.

This two-hundred-acre estate of woodland, fields and ponds surrounds an immense property built on the banks of the Orléans Canal. Luckily, the owners retained the original parquet floors, family heirlooms, antiques and tapestries in the rooms installed in the 1896 tower. The extremely generously-sized bathrooms are very well fitted-out. A charming dovecote, tennis courts and countless footpaths into the immense forest complete the picture.

Access : Between Montrichard and Noyers-sur-Cher on the D 176, on the banks of the Renne

Access : 8.5km northbound from Lorris on the D 44, take the Bellegarde road and then the minor road on the right

 LES COURTILS
Mrs Meunier

Rue de l'Ave
45430 Chécy
Tel. : 02 38 91 32 02
Fax : 02 38 91 48 20
les.courtils @ wanadoo.fr

Open all year • 4 rooms with bathrooms • €49, breakfast included • No table d'hôte • Garden. Credit cards not accepted, no dogs allowed

 LA VIEILLE FORÊT
Mrs Ravenel

Route de Jouy-le-Potier
45240 La Ferté-Saint-Aubin
Tel. : 02 38 76 57 20
Fax : 02 38 64 82 80

Closed during the February school holidays • 4 rooms, 3 of which are on the ground floor • €42, breakfast included • No table d'hôte • Sitting room, garden, car park. Credit cards not accepted, no dogs allowed

 The owners' loving care and attention is visible in every tiniest detail.

All you have to do is put your foot over the threshold to begin to feel at home! The view of the Loire is quite exceptional and the interior decoration rises to the challenge. Flowered fabrics, a tasteful blend of beiges and creams, antique and modern furniture, tiled floors. Each room is named after a local plant – let's see whether you can match the English to the French: "Bitter Apple", "Morning Glory", "Honeysuckle" and "Nasturtium". The friezes in the bathrooms were hand-stencilled.

 The beautiful Sologne scenery surrounding this handsome 20-acre property.

This brick farmhouse, which stands at the end of a forest path much frequented by deer, is equally popular with families, walkers and those who've had enough of towns in general. The converted stables are now home to mainly modern looking rooms, with one exception, which has a beautiful tiled floor and fireplace. The split-level rooms command a good view of the fishing pond.

Access : 10km eastbound from Orléans on the N 460

Access : 5.5km to the north-west of Ferté-Saint-Aubin on the D 18, and take the lane on the right

 LES USSES
Mr Marin

145 rue du Courtasaule
45760 Marigny-les-Usages
Tel. : 02 38 75 14 77
Fax : 02 38 75 90 65
kris.marin @ wanadoo.fr

Open all year • 3 rooms with bath/WC, television and telephone • €50, breakfast included • No table d'hôte • Garden, car park. Credit cards not accepted, no dogs allowed • Children's play area, badminton court, mountain biking

348 LE DOMAINE DE SAINTE-BARBE
Mrs Le Lay

45500 Nevoy
Tel. : 02 38 67 59 53
Fax : 02 38 67 28 96
www.France-bonjour.com/sainte-barbe

Closed from 20 Dec to 6 Jan • 4 rooms, 3 of which have bathrooms, and one gîte 25m from the house • €58, breakfast included • No table d'hôte • Garden, car park. Credit cards not accepted, no dogs allowed • Outdoor swimming pool, jacuzzi, tennis

 The encroaching silence of the Forest of Orléans.

After two years of titanic work, this modest 1850 farmhouse has been brought back to life. The beautiful stone walls are inviting and the interior makes you want to stay forever. Period furniture graces the bedrooms, equipped with excellent bathrooms. Breakfast is served in the old stables, complete with manger. The silence of the vast garden is interrupted only by the leaves rustling in the dense forest.

 The easy-going personality of the hospitable lady of the house.

This house is imbued with the charm of homes which have belonged to the same family for generations. A few decorative touches from the lady of the house have lent the interior chintz fabrics, tiled floors, ornaments and old furniture. The rooms, some of which have a canopied bed, overlook the garden. Breakfast is served on the terrace overlooking fields and woods in the summer. For those who can't tear themselves away, there's also an independent self-catering holiday cottage.

Access : 12km to the north-east of Orléans, towards Pithiviers on the N 152

Access : 4km north-east of Gien towards Lorris, after the level-crossing take the second road on the left and follow the signs

 349 LE RIVAGE
Mr and Mrs Bereaud

635 rue de la Reine Blanche
45160 Olivet
Tel. : 02 38 66 02 93
Fax : 02 38 56 31 11
hotel-le-rivage.jpb @ wanadoo.fr
http://site.wanadoo.fr/le.rivage.olivet

Closed from 26 Dec to 26 Jan • 17 rooms, most have bath/WC and television, all are air-conditioned • €77 to €80; breakfast €11; half board €84 to €92 • Restaurant closed on Sun evening from Nov to Mar, and Sat lunchtime; menus €26 to €54 • Terrace, garden, private car park. No dogs allowed • Tennis, fishing, canoeing

 350 LE RELAIS SAINT-JACQUES
Mr Pinsard

35 rue de la Mairie
45310 Tournoisis
Tel. : 02 38 80 87 03
Fax : 02 38 80 81 46

Closed during the February holidays, Sun evening and Mon • 5 rooms upstairs with bath/WC or just bath, and television • €37; breakfast €5; half board €33 to €55 • Menus €12 (in the week) to €32 • Private car park

The footpath spanning the stream full of paddling ducks.

From the outside this house may not look like anything worth writing home about, but once inside, all that changes. An elegant, modern dining room whose bow windows let in floods of light and an exquisite terrace on the riverbank worthy of the most idyllic "Wind in the Willows" scene. Book one of the practical rooms overlooking the river. Picturesque walks in the area will reveal Olivet's enchanting villas and old mills hidden by greenery.

An unostentatious yet authentic interior.

This ancient coaching inn has been a stopping point for St James pilgrims and less devoted travellers since the 16C. The magnificent fretwork of original old oak beams in some of the rooms adds the touch of character so distinctive of old houses. The exposed brick or stone walls, tiled floors or flagstones, fireplace and bread oven of the sitting and dining rooms are equally warm and welcoming. The former "coaching room" is now a banquet hall.

Access : On the right bank of the Loiret

Access : In the village, between Orléans and Châteaudun

CHAMPAGNE-ARDENNE

It is easy to spot visitors bound for Champagne-Ardenne by the sparkle in their eyes and a sudden, irrepressible delight when they finally come face to face with mile upon mile of vineyards: in their minds' eye, they are already uncorking a bottle of the famous delicacy which was known as "devil's wine" before a monk discovered the secret of Champagne's divine bubbles. As they continue their voyage, the beautiful cathedral of Reims rises up before them and they remember the delicious taste of its sweet pink biscuits delicately dipped in a glass of demi-sec. At Troyes, their eyes drink in the sight of tiny lanes lined with half-timbered houses while their palate thrills to the flavour of andouillettes, the local chitterling sausages. After such indulgence, our pilgrims welcome the sanctuary of the dense Ardennes forests, bordered by the meandering Meuse. But far from fasting and penitence, this woodland retreat offers a host of undreamt-of delights: the graceful flight of the crane over an unruffled lake or the prospect of sampling the famous Ardennes wild boar.

22 ESTABLISHMENTS

351 to **372**

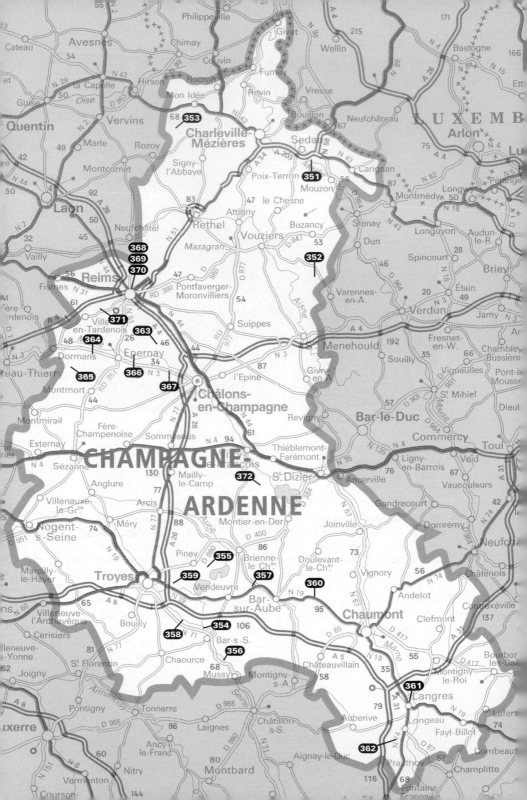

351 CHÂTEAU DE BAZEILLES
Mr Guilhas

Château de Bazeilles
08140 Bazeilles
Tel. : 03 24 27 09 68
Fax : 03 24 27 64 20
www.chateaubazeilles.com

Open all year • 20 rooms with bath/WC or shower/WC and television • €66 to €76; breakfast €8 • Menus €19 (in the week) to €43 • Terrace, park, car park

352 CHÂTEAU DE CHÂTEL
Mr and Mrs Huet

08250 Châtel-Chéhéry
Tel. : 03 24 30 78 54
Fax : 03 24 30 25 51

Open all year • 3 rooms • €69, breakfast included • Table d'hôte €16 to €23 • Park, car park. Credit cards not accepted, no dogs allowed • Outdoor swimming pool

 The park which borders on wilderness in parts!

The establishment is made up of two pavilions on either side of the castle, built in 1750 by Louis Labauche, a rich draper. The stables now house the hotel and the guest rooms, whose functional look is somewhat compensated for by the view of the peaceful garden "à la française". The restaurant is located in an orangery whose curious roof is in the shape of an overturned ship; the original rafters and stone walls are still visible.

 A glass of champagne is offered to guests on the "Gastronomic" package.

This 18C hillside castle and park dominating the Aire Valley has charm in abundance. Despite major renovation work, numerous traces of the apartments' former glorious days are still visible, including a superb staircase, huge fireplaces and period furniture. All the well-dimensioned rooms have excellent bathrooms. A wide choice of leisure activities is also available with swimming pool, tennis courts on request and walking or cycling trails.

Access : 3km eastbound from Sedan, in the outbuildings of Château de Bazeilles

Access : 9km to the north-west of Varennes-en-Argonne on the D 38A and then the D 42

 353 LA COUR DES PRÉS
Mrs Avril

 08290 Rumigny
Tel. : 03 24 35 52 66
Fax : 03 24 35 52 66

Closed from Nov to Mar and Tue in Jul and Aug • 2 rooms
• €65, breakfast included • No table d'hôte • Park, car
park. Credit cards not accepted, no dogs allowed • Castle
visits, dinner-concerts in the summer

 354 CAPITAINERIE DE SAINT-VALLIER
Mr and Mrs Gradelet

 Rue du Pont
10110 Bourguignons
Tel. : 03 25 29 84 43

Closed from 1 Jan to 15 Apr • 4 rooms • €54, breakfast
included • No table d'hôte • Garden, terrace, car park.
Credit cards not accepted

We most liked **The lady of the house's spontaneity
and warmth.**

We most liked **The artistic salon atmosphere around
the breakfast table.**

It would be difficult to find somewhere more authentic
than this moated stronghold, built in 1546 by the
provost of Rumigny. The present owner, a direct
descendant, is clearly proud of her roots and only too
happy to relate her family's history. The wood panelling
and period furniture in the rooms are original, as is the
magnificent dining room in what was formerly the guard
room. Stroll round the park and admire the ancestral
beeches.

Once seen, it is impossible to forget this old lock house.
The current lady of the house, a keen art and culture
enthusiast, adores receiving artists and scholars of all
sorts and regularly organises exhibitions and concerts.
The personalised rooms overlook the Seine. Old
porcelain adorns the breakfast room, while the
bread-oven room is now the home of the master of the
house's egg-painting workshop! The large, well-tended
garden masks the noise of the nearby road.

Access : At the entrance to the village

Access : 3km northbound from Bar-sur-Seine on the
N 71

355 **LE VIEUX LOGIS**
Mr and Mrs Baudesson

1 rue de Piney
10220 Brévonnes
Tel. : 03 25 46 30 17
Fax : 03 25 46 37 20
logisbrevonnes @ wanadoo.fr
www.pnrfo.org/partenaires/vieuxlogis/fr/

Closed from 1 to 24 Mar, Sun and Mon out of season, Mon lunchtime in season • 5 rooms with shower/WC and television • €34 to €40; breakfast €6; half board €38 • Menus €13 (in the week) to €32 • Terrace, garden, private car park • At the edge of the regional park of Forêt d'Orient

356 **FERME DE LA GLOIRE DIEU**
Mr Ruelle

10250 Courteron
Tel. : 03 25 38 21 77
Fax : 03 25 38 22 78

Closed from 1 Jan to 15 Feb • 3 rooms • €34, breakfast included • Table d'hôte €16 • Park, terrace, car park. Credit cards not accepted

 We most liked **140km of signposted footpaths through the Forêt d'Orient.**

Fishing, water sports, or just walking along the beaches: the lakes of Orient and Temple, names which recall the medieval religious orders who once owned the land, offer a wide range of activities. Right on the doorstep stands this recently spruced up "old abode", whose delightfully old-fashioned interior preserves the charm of times past. Country furniture, ornaments and flowered paper set the scene for this unostentatious and unpretentious establishment with a singularly friendly atmosphere.

We most liked **The delicious farm-grown produce which can be tasted there and/or taken home.**

The sign "Farm to the Glory of God" rather gives the game away, even before you've had a chance to glimpse the fascinating architectural remains of the 13C monastery. This immense 16C fortified farm nestles at the foot of a valley; its pretty, well-kept rooms still have their original exposed stone walls. The profusion of patés, cooked meats and poultry, fresh from the farm, will entice even the most delicate of palates. Warm, friendly and very reasonably priced.

Access : To the north-east of Troyes, drive 25km on the D 960, then at Piney take the D11

Access : 10km eastbound from Riceys on the D 70 then the N 71

 357 LE MOULIN DU LANDION
Mr and Mrs Bajolle

Rue Saint-Léger
10200 Dolancourt
Tel. : 03 25 27 92 17
Fax : 03 25 27 94 44

Closed from 15 Nov to 15 Feb • 16 rooms, all have bath/WC and television • €65 to €74; breakfast €8; half board €67 to €74 • Menus €18 (in the week) to €52 • Terrace, park, car park. No dogs allowed in restaurant • Outdoor swimming pool

 We most liked **The swimming pool hidden by a curtain of foliage.**

Whether it be sports or nature in the Regional Park of the Forêt d'Orient, fun for the children at Nigloland or meditation and culture at Colombey-les-Deux-Églises, this hotel is the ideal base camp for anyone wishing to explore the region. The rooms are more practical than they are charming but have balconies overlooking the beautiful parkland. The old millwheel is the centrepiece of the restaurant and there is a pleasant terrace on the banks of the millpond.

Access : 9km to the north-west of Bar-sur-Aube on the N 19 Troyes road

 358 LE PRIEURÉ
Mr and Mrs Berthelin

1 place de l'Église
10260 Fouchères
Tel. : 03 25 40 98 09
Fax : 03 25 40 98 09

Open all year • 5 rooms in one of the priory towers, all have bathrooms • €45, breakfast included • No table d'hôte • Garden, car park. Credit cards not accepted

 We most liked **Canadian-style breakfasts.**

This former priory now manages a thriving farming business from the top of its haughty 11C towers and Renaissance-style wings. Patience and love were lavished on the building to restore it to its current splendid state. The substantial, quiet rooms are decorated with 18C and 19C regional furniture and two boast fireplaces typical of the region. Children are most welcome: one room can sleep up to four. The exuberant hosts, formerly residents of Quebec, make guests feel totally at home.

Access : 10km to the north-west of Bar-sur-Seine on the N 71

359 LES COLOMBAGES CHAMPENOIS
Mrs Jeanne

33 rue du Haut
10270 Laubressel
Tel. : 03 25 80 27 37
Fax : 03 25 80 80 67

Open all year • 6 rooms with shower/WC • €37, breakfast included • No table d'hôte • Garden, car park. Credit cards not accepted • Outdoor swimming pool

360 AUBERGE DE LA MONTAGNE
Mr Natali

17 rue Argentolles
52330 Colombey-les-Deux-Églises
Tel. : 03 25 01 51 69
Fax : 03 25 01 53 20

Closed from 12 to 26 Jan, one week in Mar, from 22 to 28 Dec, Mon and Tue • 8 rooms with bath/WC or shower/WC and television • €46 to €57; breakfast €8 • Menus €20 (in the week) to €75 • Garden with orchard, car park. No dogs allowed in rooms

Gazing over the meadows stretching over the horizon.

Although built only 10 years ago from old materials gleaned from neighbouring ruins, these two enchanting half-timbered houses look as if they've always been here. The ingenious owner has even managed to rebuild a dovecote! The stylish rooms are a tasteful mixture of old beams and modern furniture. The kitchen serves mainly farm-grown produce.

The happy marriage of history and gastronomy.

You would never believe that Charles de Gaulle thought Champagne's landscapes were "sad and mournful"! In fact, we defy you not to succumb to the charm of the Natali family and their peaceful inn. Who could resist the pleasure of throwing one's windows wide open onto the orchard garden and countryside? If the soft autumn colours only leave you downcast, trip downstairs to the elegant country dining room and the creative blend of classical and imaginative recipes will soon lift your spirits.

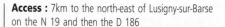

Access : 7km to the north-east of Lusigny-sur-Barse on the N 19 and then the D 186

Access : On the outskirts of the village

 361 CHEVAL BLANC
Mr and Mrs Chevalier

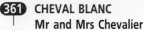
4 rue de l'Estres
52200 Langres
Tel. : 03 25 87 07 00
Fax : 03 25 87 23 13
info @ hotel-langres.com
www.hotel-langres.com

Closed from 15 to 30 Nov • 22 rooms, 11 of which are in a separate wing and one has disabled access. All have bath/WC or shower/WC and television • €55 to €77; breakfast €9; half board €67 to €105 • Restaurant closed Wed lunchtime; menus €23 to €61 • Garage. No dogs allowed in restaurant

 362 L' ORANGERIE
Mr and Mrs Trinquesse

Place de l'Église
52190 Prangey
Tel. : 03 25 87 54 85
Fax : 03 25 88 01 21

Open all year • 3 rooms • €55, breakfast included • No table d'hôte • Credit cards not accepted, no dogs allowed

 A past which dates back to 834.

First an abbey, then a parish church, the White Horse became an inn during the Revolution and its walls could date from anything between the 9C to the 16C. One thing is sure though, they provide excellent natural soundproofing! The rooms in the "Diderot pavilion", a stone house opposite the main hotel, have been recently renovated and their vaulted ceilings and arches are full of character. Paintings and contemporary light fittings set the scene for the restaurant.

 The graceful feminine touch.

Gentility and the romantic reign supreme in this ivy-covered house, next door to the castle and church in a pleasantly secluded village, set in Champagne's unspoilt countryside. Charm fills the bright, cosy rooms, one of which, decorated in shades of blue, commands a view of the stately abode and its 12C tower. Best of all, though, is the lady of the house's exquisite welcome.

Access : In the town centre

Access : 16km southbound from Langres on the N 74 and then the D 26

 363 AUBERGE SAINT-VINCENT
Mr and Mrs Pelletier

1 rue Saint-Vincent
51150 Ambonnay
Tel. : 03 26 57 01 98
Fax : 03 26 57 81 48
asv51150 @ aol.com
www.auberge-st-vincent.com

Closed in Feb, Sun evening and Mon • 10 rooms with bath/WC or shower/WC, all have television • €49 to €60; breakfast €9; half board €69 to €72 • Menus €23 to €55 • Garage. No dogs allowed in rooms • In the heart of Champagne's vineyards

 364 LA BOURSAULTIÈRE
Mrs De Coninck

44 rue de la Duchesse-d'Uzès
51480 Boursault
Tel. : 03 26 58 47 76
Fax : 03 26 58 47 76

Closed in Feb • 4 rooms • €48, breakfast included • No table d'hôte • Garden, car park. Credit cards not accepted, no dogs allowed

 We most liked
Walking along the GR14 footpath through vineyards and fern-filled forests.

This smart Champagne inn stands in the heart of a village encircled by wine-growing estates and within close reach of the Montagne de Reims National Park. The house offers practical rooms and a modern dining room complete with a huge fireplace adorned with old kitchen utensils. The delicious dishes cooked up by the chef do full justice to the delicious local produce.

 We most liked
The mammoth breakfasts, liberally served with smiles.

Bordered by Champagne vineyards on all sides, this attractive stone house provides enchanting rooms lined with medieval or Renaissance-style printed fabrics. The luxurious bathrooms are lightened by beautiful Italian tiles. As soon as the sun shines, you will appreciate the refreshing cool of the paved courtyard, strewn with succulent green plants. Exemplary welcome.

Access : Take the D 1 from Épernay to Châlons-en-Champagne as far as Condé-sur-Marne, then take the D 37

Access : 9km westbound from Épernay on the N 3 and then the D 222

365 CHÂTEAU DU RU JACQUIER
Mr Granger

51700 Igny-Comblizy
Tel. : 03 26 57 10 84
Fax : 03 26 57 82 80

Open all year • 6 rooms • €76 to €92, breakfast included • Table d'hôte €23 • Sitting room, terrace, park, car park. Credit cards not accepted, no dogs allowed • Swimming pool uncovered in summer, trout fishing, forest walks. 18-hole golf course nearby

366 LA FAMILLE GUY CHARBAUT
Mr and Mrs Charbaut

12 rue du Pont
51160 Mareuil-sur-Ay
Tel. : 03 26 52 60 59
Fax : 03 26 51 91 49
www.champagne-guy-charbaut.com

Open all year • 6 rooms with bath/WC • €61, breakfast included • Table d'hôte €30 to €46 • Car park • Visits to the family's vineyards and the wine cellars

Walking round the animal park.

The rambling park around this 18C château is full of surprises. Young and old are amazed by the park's truly cosmopolitan fauna of kangaroos, fallow deer, llamas and stags, to name but a few. There is an aura of inviting elegance about the rooms, installed in the main stately wing or in the outbuildings. Dinners are served in a beautiful dining room with fireplace. Those who still have itchy feet can go bicycling, fish for trout or play a round on the nearby 18-hole golf course.

Access : 9km to the south-east of Dormans on the D 18

The tour of the family estate's vineyard, cellars and grape presses.

Wine growers from father to son since 1930, the Charbauts bend over backwards to make your stay as pleasant as possible in their beautiful old house. They relish taking guests round the grape presses and cellars and introducing them to some of the best white and rosé vintage champagnes. All the airy, spacious rooms have their own sitting room and are decorated with period furniture. In the evenings, dinner is served in the superb wine cellar where the champagne, of course, flows freely!

Access : In the wine estate

 367 **LA GROSSE HAIE**
Mr and Mrs Songy

51510 Matouges
Tel. : 03 26 70 97 12
Fax : 03 26 70 12 42
songy.chambre@wanadoo.fr

Open all year • 3 non-smoking rooms upstairs • €45, breakfast included • Table d'hôte €18 to €27 • Garden, park, car park. Credit cards not accepted, no dogs allowed • Farm visits

 368 **CRYSTAL**
Mrs Jantet

86 place Drouet d'Erlon
51100 Reims
Tel. : 03 26 88 44 14
Fax : 03 26 47 49 28
hotelcrystal@wanadoo.fr
www.hotel-crystal.fr

Open all year • 31 rooms, 23 of which have shower/WC, 8 have bath/WC, all have television • €48 to €61; breakfast €6.50 • No restaurant • Garden

We most liked
Breathing in the rich, evocative scents of the orchard.

A stone's throw from a farm which rears splendid Charolais cattle, this hospitable house knows how to tempt its guests into the out-of-doors. The children can romp unfettered in the orchard and the strawberries, artichokes and other cottage-garden delights are just waiting to be plucked, and, it comes as no surprise to discover, figure prominently on the menu. Pink, white and blue adorn the simply decorated rooms and the traffic on the nearby road will have almost disappeared by nightfall.

We most liked
The fully original lift shaft.

This 1920s house provides a welcome and unexpected haven of greenery and calm in the heart of busy Reims, sheltered from the bustle of Place Drouet-d'Erlon by a curtain of buildings. The rooms have recently been treated to good quality furniture and new bedding and the bathrooms are spruce and practical. In the summer, breakfast is served in the charming flowered courtyard-garden.

Access : 12km westbound from Châlons-en-Champagne on the D 3, towards Épernay

Access : In the town centre

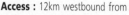

CHAMPAGNE ARDENNE

 369 GRAND HÔTEL CONTINENTAL
Mr Delvaux

 93 place Drouet d' Erlon
51100 Reims
Tel. : 03 26 40 39 35
Fax : 03 26 47 51 12
grand-hotel-continental @ wanadoo.fr vb
www.grandhotelcontinental.com

Closed from 20 Dec to 6 Jan • 50 rooms with bath/WC
or shower/WC and television • €65 to €85; breakfast
€9 • No restaurant • Public car park nearby

 **The sheer luxury of this Belle Époque
establishment.**

The late-19C walls of the Grand Hotel Continental stand
on a pedestrian square right in the heart of the town.
A variety of styles can be found in the rooms, which
are being renovated little by little; those on the top floor
with sloping ceilings are more modern in character. The
quietest rooms overlook Boulevard du Général-Leclerc.
Plush, stylish sitting room with moulded ceilings, period
light fixtures and wrought-iron banisters.

Access : In the town centre

 370 UNIVERS
Mr Bombaron

 41 boulevard Foch
51100 Reims
Tel. : 03 26 88 68 08
Fax : 03 26 40 95 61
hotel-univers @ ebc.net
www.ebc.fr/hotel-univers

Open all year • 42 rooms, 36 of which have bath/WC,
6 have shower/WC, all have television • €68 to €76;
breakfast €9 • Restaurant closed Sun evening; menus
€15 to €30, children's set menu €9 • Public car park
nearby

 **Sipping a glass of champagne at the
hotel bar.**

The Art Deco origins of this corner building built in
1932 opposite Colbert Square are betrayed by a number
of architectural features. Most of the bedrooms have
been redone with good soundproofing, king size beds,
gleaming burr walnut furniture and beautiful bathrooms.
The stylish lounge-bar is snug and cosy and there are
plans to panel the restaurant in dark wood.

Access : Near the railway station, opposite the
Colbert Gardens

371 CHAMBRE D'HÔTE DELONG
Mr and Mrs Delong

24 rue des Tilleuls
51390 Saint-Euphraise-et-Clairizet
Tel. : 03 26 49 20 86
Fax : 03 26 49 24 90
jdf.com @ wanadoo.fr

Open all year • 4 rooms, with baths and separate WC
• €52, breakfast included • No table d'hôte • Sitting
room, car park. No dogs allowed • Visits to the wine
cellar and press. Hiking, mountain biking

372 AU BROCHET DU LAC
Mr Gringuillard

15 Grande-Rue
51290 Saint-Rémy-en-Bouzemont
Tel. : 03 26 72 51 06
Fax : 03 26 73 06 95
aubrochetdulac @ libertysurf.fr

Closed from 24 Dec to 3 Jan • 5 rooms • €40, breakfast
included • Table d'hôte €16 • Sitting room, terrace, car
park • Mountain bike rental and canoeing

 Opening a bottle of champagne after visiting the estate's cellars.

This former cowshed has stylishly been given a new
lease of life in the heart of a thriving family wine
business. Exposed stone walls, beams and rafters add
character while good quality bedding and furniture and
pleasant bathrooms add comfort to the rooms. The
equally attractive breakfast room boasts brick walls and
a huge country dining table. The owner, a descendant
of a long line of "vignerons", happily does the honours
of his cellar and grape press.

Access : In the heart of the village

 Awaiting the arrival of the migratory birds over the nearby Lake Der.

This enchanting wood-framed house is the ideal spot to
explore Lake Der-Chantecoq and try some of its
countless leisure activities – boating, water-skiing,
fishing, swimming. The house is very well-equipped and
rents out mountain bikes and canoes. Pristine bedrooms
are decorated with good country furnishings and wood
features prominently in the red-tiled living room where
a roaring fire is most welcome in winter.

Access : 6km westbound from Arrigny on the
D 57 and the D 58, in the centre of the village and
not far from the lake

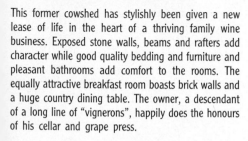

CORSICA

Corsica catches the eye like a jewel glinting in the bright Mediterranean sun. Its citadels perched up high on the island's rocky flanks will amply reward you for your perseverance and courage as you embark upon the twisting mountain roads. Enjoy spectacular views and breathe in the fragrance of wild rosemary as you slowly make your way up the rugged, maquis-covered mountains. The sudden sight of a secluded chapel, the discovery of a timeless village or an encounter with a herd of mountain sheep are just a few of the prizes that travellers to the Île de Beauté take home in their memories. Corsicans are as proud of their natural heritage as they are of their history and traditions. Years of experience have taught them how to revive the weary traveller with platters piled high with cooked meats, cheese and home-made pastries. After exploring the island's wild interior, you will probably be ready to plunge into the clear turquoise waters and recharge your solar batteries as you bask on the warm sand of a deserted bay.

14 ESTABLISHMENTS

373 to **386**

373 MARE E MONTI
Mr and Mrs Renucci

20225 Feliceto
Tel. : 04 95 63 02 00
Fax : 04 95 63 02 01

Open from 1 Apr to 15 Oct • 16 rooms with bath/WC or shower/WC • €74 to €80; breakfast €7 • No restaurant • Car park. No dogs allowed

374 A MARTINELLA
Mrs Corteggiani

Route du Port
20245 Galéria
Tel. : 04 95 62 00 44

Open all year • 5 rooms on the first floor with private terraces • €52, breakfast included • No table d'hôte • Garden, car park. Credit cards not accepted, no dogs allowed • Beach and the Scandola Nature Reserve nearby

The sweet scent of Corsica's wild flowers wafting over the sun-drenched terrace.

Exquisitely set between sea and mountain ("mare e monti" in Corsican), this is one of the rare "American palaces" of Balagne, of which there are many more around the coast of Cap Corse. After striking it rich in sugar cane, this family's ancestors returned from Puerto Rico in the 19C to build this elegant blue-shuttered white house. Character overflows from the slightly monastic rooms offset with brass beds, red floor tiles, fireplaces, etc. Delightful little chapel and exuberant garden.

Access : 20km southbound from Île-Rousse

Exploring the under-water treasures of the Nature Reserve of Scandola.

An unpretentious, excellently-kept place, to which you should add the priceless location just 150m from a large pebble beach and the nature reserve of Scandola. It is easy to see why the place is so popular. The simple rooms all have their own private terrace, while the tranquillity of the garden and the owner's genuinely warm welcome all contribute to its charm.

Access : 150m from the beach

375 FUNTANA MARINA
Mr and Mrs Khaudi

Route de Monticello
20220 L'Île-Rousse
Tel. : 04 95 60 16 12
Fax : 04 95 60 35 44

Closed in Feb • 29 rooms with bath or shower • €80; breakfast €8 • No restaurant • Car park. No dogs allowed • Outdoor swimming pool

376 LI FUNDALI
Mr and Mrs Gabelle-Crescioni

Spergane
20228 Luri
Tel. : 04 95 35 06 15

Closed from Nov to Mar • 5 rooms • €40, breakfast included • Table d'hôte €11 • Terrace, garden, car park. Credit cards not accepted, no dogs allowed

The site dominating the harbour of Île Rousse.

The narrow mountain lane that leads up to this recent house hidden by luxuriant vegetation is worth taking, if only to enjoy the super view of the sea and the harbour of Île Rousse. Comfortable renovated rooms all have matching bathrooms, but it's the panoramic swimming pool and your hosts' wonderful welcome that make this place so memorable.

The owners' boundless hospitality.

This charming house, drenched in sunshine and encircled by foliage, nestles in a hollow (fundali) of the lush green valley of Luri. After trekking along the countless paths around the estate, you will happily return to a simple, yet immaculate room for a well-earned rest. Afterwards you can sit down around the large communal table and sample the delicious family recipes, under your host's attentive eye.

Access : In the upper part of Île-Rousse, 1km drive

Access : In the valley

OLMETO - 20113

PIGNA - 20220

 377 SANTA MARIA
Mr and Mrs Ettori

 20113 Olmeto
Tel. : 04 95 74 65 59
Fax : 04 95 74 60 33
ettorinathalie @ aol.com
www.hotel-restaurant-santa-maria.com

Closed in Nov and Dec • 12 rooms with shower/WC and television • €52 (€41 low season); breakfast €6; half board (half board only in Aug) €40 to €52 • Set menus €12 (only lunchtime) to €23 • Terrace

 378 CASA MUSICALE
Mr and Mrs Casalonga

 20220 Pigna
Tel. : 04 95 61 77 31
Fax : 04 95 61 74 28
casa.musicale.pigna @ wanadoo.fr
casa-musicale.org

Closed from 7 Jan to 10 Feb and Mon from Nov to Mar • 7 rooms with bath/WC or shower/WC • €74 (€56 low season); breakfast €6 • À la carte €30 to €42 • No dogs allowed • Live music (Corsican polyphonic concerts)

 Realising how out of place the word "stress" seems on the Island of Beauty.

This old granite house which stands opposite the church has been gazing down on the Gulf of Valinco for over a century. A steep staircase leads up to practical, well-kept rooms, rather lacking in charm however. The vaulted dining room, the only remains of an old oil mill, is pleasant enough, but the highlight of the establishment has got to be the wonderful flowered terrace where you can sample Mimi's delicious cooking.

 The "Terza" room with its tiny sun terrace reached by a ladder!

Keep it under your hat! This priceless gem can only be reached on foot through the lanes of its delightful high-perched village laden with the scent of bougain-villaea. The frescoes on the walls of the rooms are a work of art in themselves and all overlook the sea or Corsica's mountainous slopes. The restaurant can be found in a converted olive oil press and the idyllic terrace and concert room are regularly the scene of lively traditional Corsican musical evenings.

Access : In the centre of the village, 8km northbound from Propriano on the N 196

Access : Drive from Île-Rousse towards Calvi on the N 197, after 2km turn left onto the D 151 (8km); park on the square (pedestrian village)

379 **A TRAMULA**
Mr Giovanetti

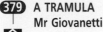

20259 Pioggiola
Tel. : 04 95 61 93 54

Closed from Oct to Apr • 6 rooms • €58; breakfast €7 • No restaurant • Park, car park. Credit cards not accepted

380 **PIAGGIOLA**
Mr and Mrs Paolini

20166 Porticcio
Tel. : 04 95 24 23 79

Closed from late Jan to 15 Apr • 6 rooms • €61, breakfast included • Table d'hôte €19 • Car park. Credit cards not accepted, no dogs allowed • Swimming pool

 The genuine sincerity of the 100% born and bred Corsican owner.

After months of labour, this stone built Corsican house is now ready to receive visitors in style. All the upper rooms display the same tasteful blend of salmon-coloured walls, terracotta floor tiles, new furniture and modern bathrooms. The bar and sitting room, heated by a stove and fireplace, are most welcoming. Pull on your walking boots and hike round the grounds on the slopes of the mountainside.

 The convenient location just a few minutes from the island's most beautiful beaches.

A warm welcome, innate sense of hospitality and tasty home-cooking are just a few of the many attractions of this neat granite house cradled in the heart of superb grounds. Admire the sweeping view of the Gulf of Valinco or the forest from the windows. The rooms are furnished with fine wardrobes. If you can tear yourself away from the beach, venture out into the grounds which are rich in surprises.

Access : 1.9km westbound from Olmi-Cappella towards Tartagine forest

Access : 13km to the south-east of Agosta beach on the D 255A (towards Pietrosella), then right on the D 255

381 U SANT'AGNELLU
Mr and Mrs Albertini

20247 Rogliano
Tel. : 04 95 35 40 59
Fax : 04 95 35 40 59

Closed from 10 Oct to Easter • 14 rooms with bath/WC or shower/WC • €55; breakfast €6 • Set menu €16 • Terrace, garden

382 CHÂTEAU CAGNINACCI
Cagninacci family

20200 San-Martino-di-Lota
Tel. : 04 95 31 69 30
Fax : 04 95 31 91 15

Closed from Oct to 14 May • 4 rooms • €78, breakfast included • No table d'hôte • Terrace. Credit cards not accepted, no dogs allowed

The generous table laden with local delicacies.

The salmon coloured walls and contrasting dark blue shutters make this old communal house a most appealing sight. The pleasantly sober rooms are immaculate and most overlook the mountain, while a few take in the deep blue waters between the islands of Elba and Capraglia. This unforgettable view can be savoured while you sample the typically Corsican food in the beautiful panoramic dining room or on the shaded terrace.

The utter peace and quiet of this spot hidden in greenery.

This lovely 17C Capuchin convent, remodelled in the 19C style of a Tuscan villa, is built on a steep mountain hillside. Tastefully renovated, it offers spacious rooms furnished with antiques, and immaculate bathrooms. Wherever you look, you are met with the superb view of the island of Elba and the sea. Taking breakfast on the terrace surrounded by greenery and warmed by the sun's first rays is a moment of sheer bliss.

Access : Almost at the tip of Cap Corse, to the west of Macinaggio

Access : 10km to the north-west of Bastia on the D 80 (towards Cap Corse), then the D 131 at Pietranera

 383 LA CORNICHE
Mr Anziani

20200 San-Martino-di-Lota
Tel. : 04 95 31 40 98
Fax : 04 95 32 37 69
info@hotellacorniche.com
www.hotel-lacorniche.com

Closed from 1 Jan to 15 Feb • 18 rooms with bath/WC
and television • €62 to €90 (€41 to €58 low season);
breakfast €8; half board €62 to €73 (€47 to €53 low
season) • Restaurant closed Tue and Wed lunchtime and
Mon; set menus €20 to €23 • Terrace, car park. No dogs
allowed in rooms • Outdoor swimming pool

 384 DOMAINE DE CROCCANO
Mr and Mrs Perrier

Route de Granace
20100 Sartène
Tel. : 04 95 77 11 37
Fax : 04 95 73 42 89
christian.perrier@wanadoo.fr

Closed in Dec • 4 rooms • €68, breakfast included • No
table d'hôte • Terrace, park, car park • Horse-riding in
the grounds

 **The swimming pool on the flanks of
the mountain, sheltered by a chestnut
grove.**

The shaded terrace of this establishment perched up
high above Bastia is a feast for the eyes. Look out and
savour the view of the two-storey bell tower and the
houses of the old village cut into the rock face in sharp
contrast with the deep blue water stretching out in the
background. The practical rooms are gradually being
individualised with terracotta tiles and hand-painted
walls; they too command a view of the sea. The
restaurant is known and appreciated for its excellent
Corsican menu.

 **Watching the horses cantering
through the maquis.**

Travellers in search of nature, silence and peace and
quiet will fall in love with this solid granite house
peeping out from behind a wilderness of cork oaks and
olive trees. Beautiful old stone walls and terracotta floor
tiles add style to the snug, cosy rooms. The simply
adorable owners will share their love of horses with you
as they take you out riding round the Corsican shrub
permeated by the scent of wild rosemary.

Access : 13km northbound from Bastia on the D 80,
then turn left on the D 131

Access : 3.5km to the north-east of Sartène on the
D 148

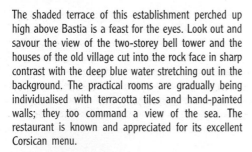

385 **A SPELUNCA**
Mrs Princivalle

202216 Speloncato
Tel. : 04 95 61 50 38
Fax : 04 95 61 53 14

Closed from 15 Oct to 15 Apr • 18 rooms • €60;
breakfast €5 • No restaurant • Terrace

386 **L' AIGLON**
Mr Quilichini

20124 Zonza
Tel. : 04 95 78 67 79
Fax : 04 95 78 63 52
aiglonhotel @ free.fr

Closed on Mon out of season • 10 rooms • €46;
breakfast €7 • Set menus €23 to €26 • Terrace, car park

The sweeping view of the region of upper Balagne.

The stately architectural masterpiece you see before you is none other than the former palace of Cardinal Savelli, Minister of Police to Pope Pius IX. The vast halls, sitting rooms rich in period furniture, old light fixtures and turret still remain from its glorious past. The discreetly luxurious bedrooms are bathed in an aura of gentility; three command an enchanting view of the valley and village. Highly recommended.

The regularly organised Corsican musical evenings.

This venerable granite house standing in the heart of the village has committed itself to upholding the soul of Corsica. Much love and time has been poured into the stylish interior decoration where collections of old objects such as coffee grinders and irons are proudly displayed. Each of the small but delightful rooms is decorated in a different colour and two have sloping ceilings. The restaurant takes you on a gastronomic tour of Corsica's many local specialities.

Access : In the heart of the village

Access : In the heart of the village

FRANCHE-COMTÉ

Once upon a time in a land called Franche-Comté... So begin many of France's tales and legends, inspired by the secret wilderness of this secluded region on the Swiss border. The Jura's peaks and dales are clad in a dark cloak of fragrant conifers, casting their magic charm over unwitting explorers of the range's grottoes and gorges. The spell is also woven by a multitude of torrents, waterfalls and deep, mysterious lakes, their dark blue waters reflecting the surrounding hills. The nimble fingers of local woodworkers transform its wood into clocks, toys and pipes which will delight anyone with a love of fine craftsmanship. Hungry travellers will be only too happy to give in to temptation and savour the rich hazelnut tang of Comté cheese, made to a recipe passed down through the generations. But beware, the delicate aroma of smoked and salted meats, in which you can almost taste the pine and juniper, together with the tempting bouquet of the region's subtle, fruity wines may well lure you back for more.

27 ESTABLISHMENTS
387 to **413**

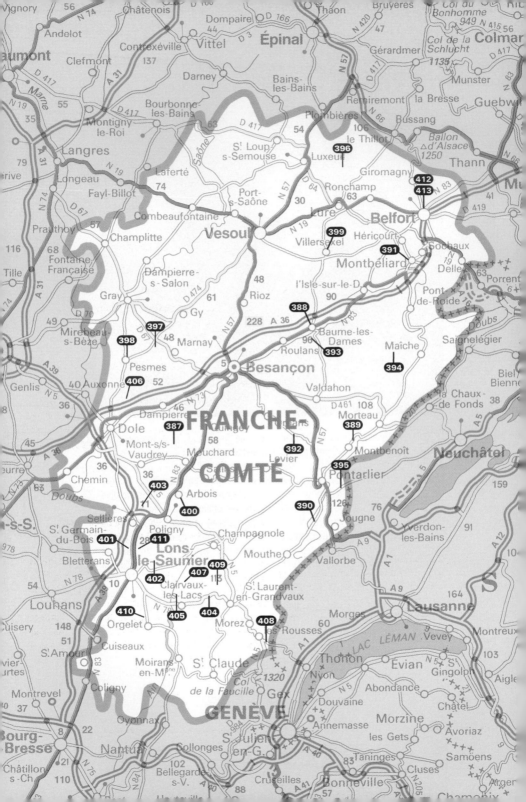

 387 DE HOOP
Mr De Hoop

 36 Grande-Rue
25610 Arc-et-Senans
Tel. : 03 81 57 44 80

Closed from 2 Apr to 1 May • 6 rooms • €54; breakfast
€7 • Menus €15 to €22 • Park, car park

 388 HOSTELLERIE DU CHÂTEAU D'AS
Mr Patrick and Mr Laurent Cachot

 24 rue du Château Gaillard
25110 Baume-les-Dames
Tel. : 03 81 84 00 66
Fax : 03 81 84 39 67
château.das@wanadoo.fr
www.château-das.fr

Closed from 27 Jan to 10 Feb, from 18 Nov to 9 Dec, Sun
evening and Mon • 7 rooms with bath/WC or
shower/WC and television • €55 to €65; breakfast €9;
half board €49 to €62 • Menus €23 to €57 • Terrace,
car park

 The ever-present friendliness.

**You either love or hate the local
cheese speciality: Cancoillotte!**

The windows of this elegant 18C edifice, a former
coaching post, command a view of the magnificent
architectural complex of the Saline royale, the Royal Salt
Works. The unpretentious rooms are calm and comfortable and most have a terrace overlooking the garden.
Choose the spacious restaurant, decorated with a nod
to the styles of yesteryear, or the smaller, more intimate
and no less charming dining room. Local Morteau
sausage and Dutch specialities feature high on the
menu.

This comfortable house, which would blend in perfectly
in any number of German or Swiss towns, was built on
the heights of this little town in the 1930s. The light,
airy and well-equipped rooms have recently been
treated to a facelift. The dining room has however
retained the grandeur of its bygone days with original
light fixtures and grandfather clock. Classic cuisine.

Access : In the village

Access : In the upper part of town, on the outskirts

 389 LE CRÊT L'AGNEAU
Mr and Mrs Jacquet-Pierroulet

25650 La Longeville
Tel. : 03 81 38 12 51
Fax : 03 81 38 16 58

Closed in Jul and Aug • 5 rooms • €69, breakfast included • Table d'hôte €19 to €22 • Car park. Credit cards not accepted, no dogs allowed • From Christmas to late March snowshoe trekking and cross-country skiing possible

 390 AU BON ACCUEIL
Mr and Mrs Faivre

Lac Saint-Point
25160 Malbuisson
Tel. : 03 81 69 30 58
Fax : 03 81 69 37 60
lebonaccueilfaivre @ wanadoo.fr

Closed 2 to 10 Apr, 21 to 29 Oct, 16 Dec to 16 Jan and Sun evening from Sept to Jun, Tue lunchtime and Mon • 12 rooms, most of which have shower/WC, some have bath/WC, all have television • €55 to €65; breakfast €8; half board €54 to €58 • Menus €26 to €44 • Garden, garage, car park. No dogs allowed

 The countless excursions organised by the owner, a cross-country ski instructor.

 The breakfast table laden with brioche, jams, home-made yoghurt and fresh fruit juice.

This superb 17C farmhouse, tucked in between fir trees and meadows has been offering accommodation and sustenance to all those "in the know" for over twenty years. Wood prevails in the cosy bedrooms. However the main reason for its lasting success is two-fold: first the generous helpings of locally-sourced food cooked by the lady of the house, and second the variety of outings on foot, snowshoes or skis organised by the owner. Theme weekends organised frequently and mushrooming in autumn.

On the edge of a forest of fir trees, this manicured, hospitable village inn is the sort of place you want to tell your friends about. Immaculate, modern, spacious rooms. Beautiful spruce wood rafters, brightly coloured blinds and large windows overlooking the forest set the scene for the recently extended dining room. The cherry on the cake is without doubt the deliciously inventive cooking.

Access : 5.5km northbound from Montbenoît on the D 131, until you reach La Longeville-Auberge

Access : In the village, on a bend by the side of the road

391 LA BALANCE
Mr and Mrs Receveur

40 rue de Belfort
25200 Montbéliard
Tel. : 03 81 96 77 41
Fax : 03 81 91 47 16
hotelbalance @ wa,adoo.fr

Closed from 23 to 28 Dec • 42 rooms with bath/WC and television. 2 rooms have disabled access and 5 are non-smoking • €58 to €80; breakfast €8; half board €54 • Restaurant closed Sat and Sun; menus €11 (lunchtime in the week) to €25 • Terrace, private car park

392 LA CASCADE
Mr and Mrs Savonet

4 route des Gorges-de-Noailles
25920 Mouthier-Haute-Pierre
Tel. : 03 81 60 95 30
Fax : 03 81 60 94 55

Open from 3 Mar to 11 Nov • 19 rooms, one of which has disabled access, most have bath/WC, some have shower/WC, all have television • €53 to €59; breakfast €7; half board €49 to €56 • Restaurant non-smoking only; menus €18 to €39 • Car park. No dogs allowed • Trout fishing and canoeing on the Loue

We most liked **The Peugeot Adventure Museum.**

At the foot of the castle, this 16C abode was the HQ of one of France's best-known Second World War generals, Marshal De Lattre de Tassigny. A beautiful old wooden staircase leads up to renovated, practical rooms of varying sizes. The warm old-fashioned style and light-wood panelling of the dining room is still visible. We loved the veranda where breakfast is served.

We most liked **Canoeing down the beautiful gorges of the River Loue.**

The valley of the Loue is what you will see when you throw open the windows of the recently spruced-up rooms of this traditional old hostelry. Excellent family cooking is served in a non-smoking atmosphere, while huge bay windows provide guests with a restful view of the green landscape.

Access : In the main shopping street, at the foot of the castle

Access : On the main road, in the centre of the village

393 L' AUBERGE DES MOULINS
Mr and Mrs Porru

Route de Pontarlier
25110 Pont-les-Moulins
Tel. : 03 81 84 09 97
Fax : 03 81 84 04 44
auberge.desmoulins@wanadoo.fr

Closed from 20 Dec to 28 Jan, Sun and Fri from Sep to Jun (except holidays) • 14 rooms with bath/WC or shower/WC, all have television • €47; breakfast €6; half board €45 • Menus €15 (in the week) to €25 • Park, car park. No dogs allowed in restaurant • Private fishing

394 LE MOULIN
Mr and Mrs Malavaux

Le Moulin du Milieu, route de Consolation
25380 Vaucluse
Tel. : 03 81 44 35 18

Closed from 15 Jan to 15 Feb and for one week in Oct • 6 rooms, all have bath/WC or shower/WC and television • €40 to €61; breakfast €6; half board €43 to €54 • Menus €17 to €26; for lunch it is best to book • Garden, car park. No dogs allowed in restaurant • Private fishing

 The wealth of magnificent natural sites: grottoes, nature reserves and unforgettable views.

Jura is renowned for its excellent trout and this place is bound to appeal to those bitten by the fishing bug: the country house stands in a park which boasts its very own private stream. Back at the hotel, relax in rooms of varying sizes and styles and dream of the one that got away. A cosy restaurant serves tasty regional dishes.

 The spectacular natural site of the Cirque de Consolation.

This unusual 1930s villa, complete with turret and a colonnaded terrace, was built by a miller from the valley. Subsequent owners have lovingly preserved the superb Art Deco decoration – including a Le Corbusier chaise longue in the hall which would be the envy of any collector. The windows of the dining room open onto a shaded garden which leads down to the banks of the Dessoubre.

Access : Southbound from Baume-les-Dames, drive for 6 km on the D 50

Access : From Montbéliard leave the D 437 at St-Hippolyte, take the D 39 and at Pont Neuf turn left towards Consolation

 395 AUBERGE LE TILLAU
Mr Parent

Le Mont-des-Verrières
25300 Verrières-de-Joux
Tel. : 03 81 69 46 72
Fax : 03 81 69 49 20
luc.parent @ wanadoo.fr

Closed from 2 to 10 Apr and from 12 Nov to 12 Dec • 12 rooms • €46; breakfast €6 • Menus €16 to €35 • Sitting room, terrace • Sauna, games room, hiking and mountain biking

 396 LA CHAMPAGNE
Mr and Mrs Bork

70270 Écromagny
Tel. : 03 84 20 04 72
Fax : 03 84 20 04 72

Open all year • 5 rooms with shower/WC • €39, breakfast included • Table d'hôte €13 to €19 • Terrace, garden, car park. No dogs allowed

🐤 We most liked
Toast your toes in front of a roaring log fire after a day in the open air.

This enchanting mountain inn, 1 200m up, is ideal to clear your lungs of urban pollution as you breathe in the crisp, fresh scent of meadows and fir trees. The rooms are appealingly decorated in a Jura mountain spirit and you can relax in the reading room or soothe your muscles in the sauna. The mountain air is guaranteed to work up a healthy appetite for the profusion of local delicacies, including cooked meats and cheeses, sometimes accompanied by more eclectic creations.

Access : 7km eastbound from La Cluse-et-Mijoux on the D 67bis and a minor road

🐤 We most liked
La Champagne is the region and le champagne is the drink!

This rambling old farm enjoys an exceptionally secluded location in the heart of the forest on the plateau of Mille Étangs. Light and calm fill every corner of the soberly decorated rooms. It is difficult to do justice to the size of the breakfasts, or the delicious evening meals, prepared in the French tradition or reflecting your hosts' German origins, whichever you prefer. In fine weather, you will want to linger on the flowered terrace overlooking the swimming pool. Loose-box for horses.

Access : 1.5km eastbound from Écromagny on the Melay road

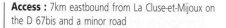

 397 LES PÉTUNIAS
Mr and Mrs Knab

 70150 Hugier
Tel. : 03 84 31 58 30

Closed in Sep • 3 rooms • €39, breakfast included • No table d'hôte • Terrace, car park. Credit cards not accepted, no dogs allowed

 398 LA MAISON ROYALE
Mr Hoyet

 70140 Pesmes
Tel. : 03 84 31 23 23
Fax : 03 84 31 23 23

Closed from 15 Oct to 15 Mar • 6 rooms • €69, breakfast included • No table d'hôte • Garden, car park. Credit cards not accepted, no dogs allowed • Library, billiards, organ, art exhibitions and cultural events

 Sipping a glass of Alsatian wine in the charming company of your hosts.

This impressive 18C farmstead, hidden by Virginia creeper, lies in the lower valley of the River Ognon, renowned for its fishing, canoeing and kayaking. The establishment's name betrays the current owners' lifelong passion for gardening. Family heirlooms adorn the comfortable, well-kept rooms. A pleasant swimming pool, a veranda strewn with plants and games and a barbecue in the garden will ensure that your stay is full of fun.

Access : 7km to the north-west of Marnay on the D 67, then the D 228, on the way out of the village

 Living like royalty without blowing the family fortune!

The quality of the restoration and the sheer beauty of this superb 15C stronghold always draw gasps of admiration. The hospitable owners have filled this aptly named establishment with objects from their countless trips around the world. Most of the highly individualised rooms enjoy an exceptional view over the village rooftops and the countryside. Relax in style with a game of billiards, play a few notes on the organ and if the weather is fine, take time to enjoy the pretty flowered garden.

Access : In the town centre, near a service station

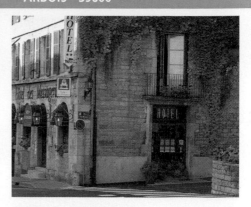

399 LA TERRASSE
Mrs Routhier

Route de Lure
70110 Villersexel
Tel. : 03 84 20 52 11
Fax : 03 84 20 56 90

Closed from 8 Dec to 3 Jan, Sun evening and Mon lunchtime out of season • 13 rooms with bath/WC or shower/WC, all have television • €36 to €46; breakfast €6; half board €38 to €42 • Menus €14 to €28 • Terrace, garden, car park • Bicycle rentals, table tennis, boules

400 MESSAGERIES
Mr and Mrs Ricoux

2 rue de Courcelles
39600 Arbois
Tel. : 03 84 66 15 45
Fax : 03 84 37 41 09
hotel.lesmessageries@wanadoo.fr

Closed in Dec and Jan • 26 rooms with bath or shower, 8 do not have WC in the room, most have television • €33 to €51; breakfast €6 • No restaurant • Arbois wine tasting and the Pasteur museum are nearby

 The old sand quarries now filled with water and the venue for many water sports.

Anglers hold this country inn on the banks of the Ognon, a stream renowned for its fishing, in high esteem. The rooms of varying sizes have recently been treated to a facelift, as has the dining room overlooking the garden. In the summer the dense foliage of the huge trees clothes the terrace in a welcome cool shade. Relaxing and restful.

 Tasting the local vintages in the numerous wine cellars dotted round the village.

Wine lovers should make a point of stopping at Arbois, highlight of Jura's vineyards, a delightful village off the beaten track simply bursting with treasures. This former ivy-covered coaching inn offers modest comfort, at equally modest prices, which is all the more appreciated if you are there during the Biou procession, a traditional "grape parade" that takes place in early September. Book one of the rooms at the back which have bathrooms.

Access : On leaving the village drive towards Lure

Access : In the town centre

401 LE JARDIN DE MISETTE
Mr and Mrs Petit

Rue Honoré-Chapuis
39140 Arlay
Tel. : 06 11 63 86 58

Open all year • 4 rooms with shower and separate WC
• €45, breakfast included • Table d'hôte €15 • Landscaped garden. Credit cards not accepted • Bread oven, regional library

402 GOTHIQUE CAFÉ
Mr Broulard

39210 Baume-les-Messieurs
Tel. : 03 84 44 64 47
Fax : 03 84 44 90 25

Open all year • 3 rooms with bath/WC • €60, breakfast included • Table d'hôte €15 to €19 • Car park • Regional produce

The delicious meals prepared by the gourmet couple.

A wine-grower's home on the banks of the Seille. The rooms are comfortable, well decorated and above all, as quiet as a mouse. The "Chabotte" room in the little house at the end of the garden has the most character. A piano, fireplace and well-lined bookshelves will make you want to linger in the sitting room, particularly if the owner, a very decent singer and musician, steps in and plays a few notes on his accordion.

The faultlessly restored medieval setting.

Located in one of the outbuildings of the prestigious abbey of Baume les Messieurs, every corner of this establishment seeps with charm and authenticity. You will be entranced by the architecture of the spacious, yet snug rooms, impeccably decorated and all enjoying a priceless view of the delightful village below. The restaurant serves tasty dishes with a local flavour.

Access : 12km westbound from Château-Chalon on the D 5 until Voiteur, then the D 120, in the heart of the village

Access : 15km eastbound from Lons-le-Saunier on the D 471 and then the D 70

 403 LA FERME DU CHÂTEAU
Association E. de Villeneuve-Bargemont

 Rue de la Poste
39800 Bersaillin
Tel. : 03 84 25 91 31
Fax : 03 84 25 93 62

Closed in Jan • 9 rooms, one of which has disabled access
• €52, breakfast included • Table d'hôte €10 • Car park
• Painting exhibitions, concerts in the summer

 404 L' ALPAGE
Mr Lerch

 1 chemin de la Madone
39130 Bonlieu
Tel. : 03 84 25 57 53
Fax : 03 84 25 50 74
reservation @ alpage-hotel.com

Closed from 15 Nov to 15 Dec and Wed except during
the school holidays • 9 rooms and 2 gîtes • €46;
breakfast €7 • Menus €17 to €30 • Terrace, car park

 **Just two minutes from Jura's
vineyards and the "Route du Comté".**

Many of the original features of this admirably restored
18C farmhouse have been preserved, including the
wonderful vaults and columns of the main chamber,
where exhibitions and concerts are held in the summer.
The sober, yet elegant bedrooms command a view of
the countryside and one has been specially equipped for
disabled guests. Guests also have the use of a
well-equipped kitchen.

 **The sweeping view over the entire
valley of lakes.**

A narrow road winds up to this delightful chalet built
in the upper reaches of Bonlieu. The valley of lakes and
its wooded hillsides are visible from almost all the
comfortable bedrooms. Plants and immense bay
windows bathe the dining room in dappled light and the
sheltered terrace also commands the same sweeping
view. Tasty local dishes.

Access : 9km westbound from Poligny on the
N 83 and then the D 22

Access : On the N 78 drive towards
Saint-Laurent-en-Grandvaux

 405 CHAMBRE D'HÔTE CHEZ MME DEVENAT
Mrs Devenat

 17 rue du Vieux-Lavoir
39130 Charezier
 Tel. : 03 84 48 35 79

Open all year • 4 rooms • €32, breakfast included • Table d'hôte €9.15 • Garden, car park. No dogs allowed

 406 LA THUILERIE DES FONTAINES
Mr and Mrs Meunier

 2 rue des Fontaines
39700 Châtenois
Tel. : 03 84 70 51 79
Fax : 03 84 70 57 79
michel.meunier2 @ wanadoo.fr

Open all year • 4 rooms • €41, breakfast included • No table d'hôte • Terrace, park, car park. Credit cards not accepted, no dogs allowed • Outdoor swimming pool

 The wide range of regional delicacies on offer.

Guests immediately feel at home in this large, welcoming family house cradled in a tiny village halfway between Clairvaux les Lacs and Lake Chalain. The rooms in the little house near the thicket are more independent and a handsome wooden staircase leads up to the others in the main house. The memory of the delicious local specialities, a different one each day, will have you planning your return trip the moment you arrive home.

 Pick your owners' brains about their beloved region.

Hospitality and attention to detail are the hallmarks of this 18C country house located between the extensive Serre forest and the lower Doubs valley. A flight of stone stairs leads up to well-cared for, very "comfy" and totally peaceful rooms. Stroll round the attractive park or laze on the deck chairs round the swimming pool near the old stables.

Access : 13km to the south-west of Lake Chalain on the D 27

Access : 7.5km to the north-east of Dole on the N 73 towards Besançon, then take the D 10 and the D 79 until you reach Châtenois

  **407** **LE COMTOIS**
Miss Roux and Mr Artières

39130 Doucier
Tel. : 03 84 25 71 21
Fax : 03 84 25 71 21
restaurant.comtois@wanadoo.fr

Closed from Dec to Feb, Tue evening, Sun evening and Wed from mid-Sep to mid-Jun • 9 rooms with showers, some have WC • €46, breakfast included; half board €37 to €42 • Menus €19 to €26 • Terrace

 We most liked
The wonderful footpath to Hérisson Falls just a few kilometres away.

Le Comtois offers an ideal introduction to this fascinating region. The heart of a remote Jura village is home to this spruce auberge offering a few rooms and above all a menu worthy of the most demanding traveller. A warm Neo-rustic setting provides the backdrop to delicious recipes with a modern slant prepared with a strong focus on local products. The owner, who is also President of Jura's Association of Wine Waiters, will wax lyrical about wine and food for as long as you'll listen...

Access : In the centre of the village, opposite the post office

---

  408 **ARBEZ FRANCO-SUISSE**
Mr Arbez

La Cure
39220 Les Rousses
Tel. : 03 84 60 02 20
Fax : 03 84 60 08 59
hotelarbez@infonie.fr

Closed in Nov, on Mon and Tue except during the school holidays • 10 rooms, half are in France and half are in Switzerland. Rooms have bath/WC or shower/WC, all have television • €50 to €57; breakfast €7; half board €55 • Menus €22 to €30; at the Brasserie: à la carte €16 to €24 • Car park

 We most liked
Testing your balance on the "commando" course at nearby Fort Rousses!

Make sure you take your passport when you go to the bathroom and also remember to decide which half of you will sleep in Switzerland and which in France! This Swiss-French inn, quite literally on the border, offers modern rooms lined in pine and has a choice of classic restaurant fare or quick brasserie snacks and dishes, all within easy reach of alpine ski slopes, cross-country ski trails, snowshoe paths and Rousses Lake. Is there anything else to declare?

Access : On the Swiss border, to the south-east of Rousses, drive 2.5km on the N 5 (towards Geneva)

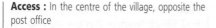

FRANCHE-COMTÉ

409 LES CINQ LACS
Mr and Mrs Colombato

66 route des Lacs
39130 Le Frasnois
Tel. : 03 84 25 51 32
Fax : 03 84 25 51 32
pcolombato @ club-internet.fr

Open all year • 5 non-smoking rooms, one of which has disabled access. 2 chalets have been converted into gîtes • €43, breakfast included • Table d'hôte €14 • Terrace. Credit cards not accepted, no dogs allowed • Excursions around the lakes

410 LA BARATTE
Mr and Mrs Chalet

39270 Présilly
Tel. : 03 84 35 55 18
Fax : 03 84 35 56 05

Open all year • 4 rooms • €52, breakfast included • Table d'hôte €17 • Car park. Credit cards not accepted, no dogs allowed

 The owners' useful tips about the area.

Hikers have held this old Jura farmstead in great esteem ever since it opened; it nestles in the heart of a lush green landscape of lakes, waterfalls and forest. The comfortable rooms were individually decorated by the lady of the house and each is named after one of the region's innumerable lakes. Don't miss the opportunity to taste the many local specialities on the dining table, served before a roaring fire in winter or on the sheltered terrace in the summer.

 The happy marriage of modern comfort and rustic charm.

This village house stands within a stone's throw of the impressive dam of Vouglans. The imaginative restoration has endowed it with all the modern comforts whilst preserving numerous traces of its old age, such as the fine flagstone floor in the dining room where you will savour tasty local dishes. The rustic flavour of the bedrooms contrasts admirably with a few modern touches. Stabling for horses.

Access : 3.5km northbound from Illay on the D 75

Access : 5km northbound from Orgelet on the D 52 then the D 175

 411 HOSTELLERIE SAINT-GERMAIN
Mr and Mrs Bertin

 39210 Saint-Germain-les-Arlay
Tel. : 03 84 44 60 91
Fax : 03 84 44 63 64

Closed from 15 to 30 November • 8 rooms, most have bath/WC, some have shower/WC, all have television • €61; breakfast €6; half board €46 • Menus €18 to €36 • Terrace, car park. No dogs allowed

 412 LES CAPUCINS
Mrs Girods

 20 Faubourg de Montbéliard
90000 Belfort
Tel. : 03 84 28 04 60
Fax : 03 84 55 00 92

Closed from 2 to 18 Aug and from 20 Dec to 6 Jan • 35 rooms on 3 floors with bath/WC or shower/WC and television • €48 to €55; breakfast €6; half board €47 to €49 • Restaurant closed Sat (except evenings from May to Sep) and Sun; menus €15 (in the week) to €30

 The mouth-watering "pâté en croute" a sort of porkpie!

Should you want to find out more about this region's rich store of traditions and legends, the Hostellerie St Germain, right in the heart of Jura's vineyards, is the ideal place to start. A refreshing night's sleep in the spotless rooms will leave you eager to begin exploring, and after a hard day's touring, you will be able to tuck into the delicious traditional recipes served in one of three vaulted dining rooms, complete with exposed beams and stonework.

The visit to the splendid camp of Belfort and its famous Lion.

Before you set off exploring the beautiful historic town of Belfort, set up camp in this hotel full of character two minutes from the banks of the Savoureuse and the pedestrian town centre. Small, but comfortable rooms are decorated with modern furniture and those on the second floor have sloping ceilings. Depending on your whim and appetite, you can choose between an elegant restaurant or the warm bustle of the brasserie. A very pleasant halt.

Access : At the crossroads in the centre of the village, opposite the church

Access : On the main road near the town centre, at the corner of Rue des Capucins, opposite the large public car park

 413 **VAUBAN**
Mr and Mrs Lorange

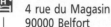 4 rue du Magasin
90000 Belfort
Tel. : 03 84 21 59 37
Fax : 03 84 21 41 67
hotel.vauban@wanadoo.fr
www-hotel-vauban.com

Closed from Christmas to 1 Jan, February holidays and
Sun • 14 rooms with bath/WC or shower/WC, all have
television • €56; breakfast €7 • No restaurant • Garden.
No dogs allowed

 We most liked

The easy-going family atmosphere.

You will feel more like a friend of the family than a
paying guest behind the colourful façade of this inviting
hotel where hundreds of paintings by the owner and his
artist friends adorn the walls. The rooms, gradually
being renovated, are pretty and well soundproofed; ask
for one in the rear from which you will enjoy a view
of the pretty flowered garden stretching down to the
banks of the Savoureuse.

Access : Near the tourist office, on the street
running alongside the Savoureuse

ÎLE-DE-FRANCE AND PARIS

Historic Paris, the City of Light, is the first name to spring to mind at the mention of the Île de France. The slender outline of the Eiffel Tower dominates France's chic and cosmopolitan capital, where former royal palaces are brazenly adorned with glass pyramids, railway stations become museums and close-set alleyways of bohemian houses lead off broad, plane-planted boulevards. Paris is a never-ending kaleidoscope of contrasts: the sleepy village side street decked in flowers and the bustle of the big department stores; the artists' studios of Montmartre and the crowded cafés where screen celebrities sit side by side with star-struck fans; a view of Paris by night from a bateau-mouche and the whirlwind glitz of a cabaret. But the fertile land along the Seine is not content to stay in the shadows of France's illustrious first city; the region is also home to secluded châteaux set in formal gardens, the magic of Disneyland and the turn-of-the-century gaiety of the summer cafés along the banks of the Marne. And who could forget the sheer splendour of Versailles, home to the 'most beautiful palace in the world'?

35 ESTABLISHMENTS

414 to **448**

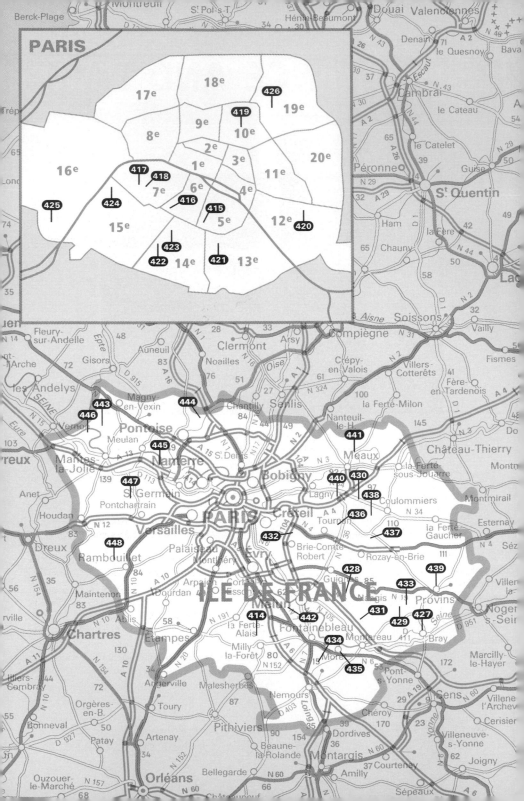

  414 **CHAMBRE D'HÔTE MONSIEUR LENOIR**
Mr Lenoir

9 rue du Souvenir
91490 Moigny-sur-École
Tel. : 01 64 98 47 84

Open all year • 3 rooms, one of which is on the ground floor • €49, breakfast included • No table d'hôte • Garden. Credit cards not accepted, no dogs allowed

 415 **PIERRE NICOLE**
Mr Dayot

39 rue Pierre-Nicole
75005 Paris
Tel. : 01 43 54 76 86
Fax : 01 43 54 22 45

Open all year • 33 rooms, most have bath/WC or shower/WC, all have television • €60 to €70; breakfast €6 • No dogs allowed

 The sheltered landscaped garden.

High walls protect this handsome stone house and its beautifully laid-out garden from prying eyes. The tastefully decorated rooms are totally tranquil and the one on split-levels is very practical for families. If you listen quietly you may still hear the clucking of the former inhabitants of the breakfast room, where the chicken roosts can still be seen. A pleasant stay and cordial welcome assured.

 Ambling round the deliciously romantic Jardin de Luxembourg.

This hotel in a handsome Haussmann building, pays homage to a controversial 17C theologian of Paris's Port-Royal Abbey. Many more recent celebrities, such as novelist Gabriel García Márquez and Patrick Modiano have stayed in these compact, practical and well-kept rooms, which maybe lack a little Parisian chic. The comparative calm of this side street, close to the busy restaurants of Boulevard Montparnasse, should ensure a good night's sleep.

Access : 3.5km northbound from Milly-la-Forêt

Access : Coming from Bd du Montparnasse, continue onto Bd de Port-Royal and take the third street on the left

416 SÈVRES-AZUR
Mr Baguès

22 rue de l'Abbé-Grégoire
75006 Paris
Tel. : 01 45 48 84 07
Fax : 01 42 84 01 55
sevres.azur @ wanadoo.fr
www.sevres-azur.com

85 Euros ✓

Open all year • 31 rooms with bath/WC or shower/WC
and television • €74 to €89; breakfast €7 • No restaurant

417 CHAMP DE MARS
Mr Gourdal

7 rue du Champ-de-Mars
75007 Paris
Tel. : 01 45 51 52 30
Fax : 01 45 51 64 36
stg @ club-internet.fr
www.hotel-du-champ-de-mars.com

Open all year • 25 rooms with bath/WC or shower/WC
and television • €72 to €76; breakfast €7 • No restaurant
• No dogs allowed

The unusual chapel of the Miraculous Medal on Rue du Bac.

A 19C stone building near the smart Bon Marché department store: well-soundproofed rooms, some of which have brass beds, are decked out with colourful fabrics. Plants adorn the light breakfast room. The preferential rates in the nearby car park for hotel guests are a definite bonus.

The lively quarter of Gros-Caillou, the closest the 7th arrondissement gets to "roughing it"!

The eye is drawn to the attractive green façade of this charming establishment, on the doorstep of the Champ de Mars and the Invalides. The cosy rooms within reveal the owners' attention to detail, with those on the ground floor overlooking a flowered courtyard. The imaginative interior decorator clearly has a liking for "Liberty" prints. The breakfast and sitting rooms are equally charming. Given the very reasonable prices, make sure you book well in advance.

Access : Go up Rue de Vaugirard and take the second left past Bd du Montparnasse

Access : At Place de l'École Militaire, go along Avenue Bosquet, then turn right

 418 L' EMPEREUR
Mr Garcia

2 rue Chevert
75007 Paris
Tel. : 01 45 55 88 02
Fax : 01 45 51 88 54
contact @ hotelempereur.com

Open all year • 38 rooms with bath/WC or shower/WC
and television • €75 to €85; breakfast €7 • No restaurant
• No dogs allowed

 419 HÔTEL FRANÇAIS
Mr and Mrs Bienvenu

13 rue du 8-Mai-1945
75010 Paris
Tel. : 01 40 35 94 14
Fax : 01 40 35 55 40
hotelfrancais @ wanadoo.fr
www.hotelfrancais.com

Open all year • 71 air-conditioned rooms, all have
bath/WC or shower/WC and television • €73 to €81;
breakfast €8 • No restaurant

 **The War Museum and the unusual
Relief Map Museum.**

Most of the bedroom windows command a view of the
magnificent gold dome of the Invalides Hotel built for
the soldiers wounded during the Napoleonic Wars and
Bonaparte's final resting place. Indeed, the stamp of the
Empire can be felt throughout the establishment in the
Imperial crown motif, shades of gold and green and
distinctively styled mahogany furniture and the hotel, in
the process of renovation, makes no secret of its
allegiance to "l'Empereur".

 **The picturesque Passage Brady which
places Pondichery on the doorstep of
Paris.**

A delightful carved wooden porch points to the entrance
of this hotel opposite Paris's busy Gare de l'Est railway
station. Air-conditioning, hairdryers, trouser press, iron,
safe and a mini-bar all come as standard in the
gradually renovated rooms of this comfortable but
unostentatious hotel which offers better mod-cons than
many pricier establishments. Spacious breakfast room in
contemporary style.

Access : From Place de l'École Militaire, turn into Av
de Tourville and take the first left

Access : Near the Gare de l'Est, between Bd
Magenta and Bd de Strasbourg

 420 NOUVEL HÔTEL
Mr and Mrs Marillier

 24 avenue du Bel-Air
75012 Paris
Tel. : 01 43 43 01 81
Fax : 01 43 44 64 13
nouvelhotel @ wanadoo.fr
www.nouvel-hotel-paris.com

Open all year • 28 rooms, 24 of which have shower/WC, 4 have bath/WC, all have television • €63 to €90; breakfast €7 • No restaurant

 421 RESIDENCE VERT GALANT
Mr and Mrs Laborde

 43 rue Croulebarbe
75013 Paris
Tel. : 01 44 08 83 50
Fax : 01 44 08 83 69

Open all year • 15 rooms, 11 of which have bath/WC, 4 have shower/WC, all have television • €80 to €87; breakfast €7 • No restaurant

 Within easy reach of the unusual Picpus cemetery.

This establishment has been in the hands of the same family since the 1930s and the pride and pleasure they take in receiving guests is clear for all to see. Snug, immaculate rooms, regularly spruced up, are tastefully decorated in a distinctly "Laura Ashley" style. Almost all overlook the Nouvel Hotel's pride and joy: its well-tended lush green patio garden. Breakfasts are served on the patio in the summer under the welcome shade of a medlar tree.

 The village ambience, just two minutes from the Place d'Italie.

This hotel in the Gobelins area is welcome proof that it is still possible to find quiet accommodation in the heart of Paris at a reasonable price. All the functional, neatly kept rooms are sheltered by a restful curtain of greenery. Depending on the weather, breakfast is served in the small garden lined by vines or in a winter-garden dining room. The owners of the Vert Galant also run the cheerful Basque restaurant next door.

Access : Between Place de la Nation and Avenue de Saint-Mandé

Access : From Place d'Italie, go along Avenue des Gobelins and turn left

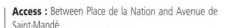

 422 **APOLLON MONTPARNASSE**
Mr Prigent

 91 rue de l'Ouest
75014 Paris
Tel. : 01 43 95 62 00
Fax : 01 43 95 62 10
apollonm @ club-internet.fr
www.oda.fr/aa/apollon

Open all year • 33 rooms, 22 of which have shower/WC, 11 have bath/WC, all have television • €65 to €78; breakfast €6 • No restaurant • Nearby car park • Near Montparnasse railway station

 423 **DAGUERRE**
Mrs Montagnon

 94 rue Daguerre
75014 Paris
Tel. : 01 43 22 43 54
Fax : 01 43 20 66 84
hotel.daguerre.paris.14 @ gofornet.com

Open all year • 30 rooms, 2 of which have disabled access, with bath/WC or shower/WC, all have television • €69 to €104; breakfast €8 • No restaurant • Hotel can book shows for you

 A pleasant welcome in the heart of Montparnasse.

This small hotel is ideally placed for those intending to spend a few days in the French capital, close to the Montparnasse railway station and Air France's shuttle buses, Rue de la Gaîté and cinemas for evenings out and Ricardo Bofill's amazing architectural feats. The bedrooms are more practical than charming, but look all the better for their recent makeover. Vaulted breakfast room.

 This lively street market symbolises everything we love about France.

The formal reception of the lobby with marble, classical paintings, crystal chandeliers and a fountain hardly leads you to expect such an easy-going and friendly welcome. Gleaming furniture adorns the small bedrooms, and the breakfast room, in the old cellar, features a fresco depicting Napoleon's court at the Louvre and its contemporary pyramid designed by Pei.

Access : From Place de Catalogne go along Rue du Château and turn right

Access : Near Gaîté métro station

 424 HÔTEL DE L'AVRE
Mr and Mrs Vialettes

 21 rue de l'Avre
75015 Paris
Tel. : 01 45 75 31 03
Fax : 01 45 75 63 26
www.hoteldelavre.com

Open all year • 26 rooms with bathrooms • €77, breakfast €7 • No restaurant • Garden. No dogs allowed

We most liked

The bold, bright colour scheme.

This modest little hotel just a stone's throw from the Motte Picquet is quite adorable. The delightful, snug rooms are decorated in blue, white or yellow with brightly coloured curtains and wood framed pictures. Depending on the weather, breakfast is served in a lovely shaded courtyard or in a light, airy cane-furnished breakfast room. Definitely worth writing home about.

Access : On Bd de Grenelle, coming from the Seine, turn right after La Motte-Picquet métro station

 425 BOILEAU
Mr and Mrs Mahé

 81 rue Boileau
75016 Paris
Tel. : 01 42 88 83 74
Fax : 01 45 27 62 98
boileau @ cybercable.fr
www.hotel-boileau.com

Open all year • 30 rooms with bath/WC or shower/WC and television • €68 to €85; breakfast €6 • No restaurant • No dogs allowed

We most liked

The cheerful welcome from Oscar, the hotel parrot.

Situated in a smart street of what used to be the "village of Auteuil" until 1860, a distinctly un-Parisian atmosphere continues to reign in this hotel. Paintings and ornaments picked up in antique shops relate tales from Brittany and North Africa, the owner's twin passions. The statues in alcoves and wainscoting in the lobby lend it a resolutely classical air. Ask for one of the renovated Eastern-styled rooms. Breakfast is served in a room flooded with sunlight overlooking a flowered patio.

Access : From Place de la Porte de Saint-Cloud take Rue Michel-Ange, then first right and second left

426 LE LAUMIÈRE
Mrs Desprat

4 rue Petit
75019 Paris
Tel. : 01 42 06 10 77
Fax : 01 42 06 72 50

Open all year • 54 rooms with bath/WC or shower/WC
and television • €53 to €63; breakfast €7 • No restaurant

 A (well-needed) breath of fresh air in the picturesque Buttes Chaumont Park.

This charming small hotel, run by the same family since 1931, makes up for its distance from Paris' main monuments with a whole host of other advantages: the attractive modern flavour of the renovated interior, a leafy corner where breakfast is served on sunny days and the nearby Laumière métro station. If you prefer more space and calm, book one of the rooms overlooking the cheerful garden.

Access : From Place de Stalingrad take Av J Jaurès, turn right into Rue A Carrel, take the second on the left and the second on the right

427 LA FERME DE TOUSSACQ
Mrs Colas

Hameau de Toussacq
77480 Bray-sur-Seine
Tel. : 01 64 01 82 90
Fax : 01 64 01 82 61

Open all year • 5 non-smoking rooms with bathrooms
• €45, breakfast included • Table d'hôte €12 (only by reservation) • Garden, park, car park. Credit cards not accepted • Chapel and dovecote visits

 The country atmosphere on the banks of the Seine.

Don't be put off by the somewhat forbidding aspect of this 17C farmhouse: you will, in any case, be sleeping in the castle outbuildings, whose loving restoration has taken more than 25 years. Bedrooms are simply styled with sloping ceilings and the breakfast room is a pleasant blend of rustic and modern. A fountain, chapel and dovecote together with a few sheep can be seen in the park. Appetising home cooking with a sprinkling of home-grown produce.

Access : 20km southbound from Provins on the Nogent-sur-Seine road (N 19), then the D 78 and the D 411

 428 LA FERME DU COUVENT
Mr and Mrs Legrand

77720 Bréau
Tel. : 01 64 38 75 15
Fax : 01 64 38 75 75
ferme.couvent @ wanadoo.fr
www.lafermeducouvent.com

Open all year • 9 rooms, 5 of which are attic rooms • €43, breakfast included • Table d'hôte €14 (in the week, by reservation only) and €17 (at the weekend) • Garden, park. Credit cards not accepted • Tennis, hot-air ballooning

 429 CLOS THIBAUD DE CHAMPAGNE
Mr and Mrs Dineur

1 rue du Souci
77520 Cessoy-en-Montois
Tel. : 01 60 67 32 10
Fax : 01 64 01 36 50

Open all year • 4 rooms • €70, breakfast included • Table d'hôte €25 to €80 • Terrace, garden. Credit cards not accepted

 Flying over the Brie region in a hot-air balloon.

What better place to relax than this handsome 18C farmhouse planted in the middle of nearly 20 acres of parkland in the countryside. Attractive modern furniture graces the bedrooms, freshly painted in shades of cream with sloping ceilings. If you fancy something different, climb aboard the experienced owners' multicoloured hot-air balloon for a proper bird's eye view of the Brie region.

 Relaxing in the garden surrounded by wheat fields.

The green fields stretching for as far as the eye can see invite you to take things easy in this 19C farmhouse. The restoration work has removed none of its former regional character, in fact, quite the opposite. The vast bedrooms on the first floor have appetising names such as Cinnamon and Vanilla. A log fire adds warmth to the dining room in winter and the sitting room boasts a billiards table, but the garden which merges into the rural landscape is the real highlight of this charming spot.

Access : 14.5km eastbound from Vaux-le-Vicomte on the Provins road (D 408) and then the D 227 on the left

Access : 16km to the south-west of Provins on the N 19 and the D 75

430 LA HÉRISSONIÈRE
Mr Bordessoule

4 rue du Barrois
77580 Crécy-la-Chapelle
Tel. : 01 64 63 98 57
Fax : 01 64 63 00 72

Open all year • 5 rooms • €60, breakfast included • Table d'hôte €20 (dinner only) • Garden. Credit cards not accepted, no dogs allowed

431 CHAMBRE D'HÔTE DE LA RECETTE
Dufour family

Au hameau d'Échou
77830 Échouboulains
Tel. : 01 64 31 81 09
Fax : 01 64 31 89 42

Closed during the February holidays; open Sat and Sun • 3 rooms with bath/WC and television • €42, breakfast included • Table d'hôte €20 to €25 • 17C dovecote. No dogs allowed

The riverside location.

This delightful 18C manor house enjoys a wonderful position on the banks of the Morin, two minutes from the birthplace of writer and philosopher, Albert Camus. Wood panelling, old oak beams and family heirlooms are lovingly maintained. The elegant, comfortable bedrooms all overlook the river and the one with the balcony is particularly appealing. Dining under the pergola in the summer is an enchanting experience.

The farmer-owner's friendly, genuine welcome.

The origins of this farm, formerly the property of the Cistercian abbey of Preuilly, have been traced back to the 12C. It now houses cosy rooms with snug, inviting duvets. Meals are served in a dining room where stone and wood feature prominently. Remember to reserve one of the tables near the windows so that you can enjoy the view of the pond, meadows and contented grazing cows.

Access : Near the church square

Access : 11km to the north of Montereau-Fault-Yonne on the N 105 Melun road then on the D 107 at Valence-en-Brie

432 LE RÉVEILLON
Mr Chassier

Ferme des Hyverneaux
77150 Lésigny
Tel. : 01 60 02 25 26
Fax : 01 60 02 03 84

Open all year • 48 rooms, 2 of which have disabled access, all have bath/WC and television • €65 to €71; breakfast €9 • Restaurant on the first floor: menus €23 to €29 (club house brasserie on the ground floor) • Private car park. No dogs allowed • 100ha golf course

433 CHAMBRE D'HÔTE M. DORMION
Mr and Mrs Dormion

2 rue des Glycines
77650 Lizines
Tel. : 01 60 67 32 56
Fax : 01 60 67 32 56

Open all year • 5 non-smoking rooms, all are in the attic with kitchenettes • €40, breakfast included • No table d'hôte • Garden, park. Credit cards not accepted

The excellent soundproofing which masks the noise of Paris' busy outer ring road.

The remains of a 12C abbey can still be seen in this hotel. The addition of huge skylights and glass walls add a light, modern touch. The practical rooms and timbered restaurant command a view of an 18-hole golf course of nearly 250 acres. The terrace of the clubhouse is practically on the green.

The immaculate bedrooms.

This three-century-old building, still a working farm, has offered accommodation and sustenance to visitors for over a decade. The spotless rooms with sloping ceilings are decorated with rustic furniture and each one has its own kitchenette. An old barn has been converted into a light, airy breakfast room with an enormous bay window. Venture out of doors and admire the lawn and orchard in the garden.

Access : Drive to Lésigny on the "Francilienne" or on the A 4 (exit no 19), then head for the golf course

Access : 15km to the south-west of Provins on the N 19 and the D 209

 434 **CHAMBRE D'HÔTE M. GICQUEL**
Mr and Mrs Gicquel

46 rue René-Montgermont
77690 Montigny-sur-Loing
Tel. : 01 64 45 87 92

Open all year • 3 rooms • €42, breakfast included • No table d'hôte • Credit cards not accepted

 435 **AUBERGE DE LA TERRASSE**
Mr Mignon

40 rue de la Pêcherie
77250 Moret-sur-Loing
Tel. : 01 60 70 51 03
Fax : 01 60 70 51 69
aubergedelaterrasse @ wanadoo.fr

Closed from 20 Oct to 4 Nov • 17 rooms with bath/WC or shower/WC • €62, breakfast included • Menu €35

 We most liked **Exploring the twisting lanes of this tiny picturesque village.**

A traditional paved courtyard stands in the foreground of these former stables converted into a B&B. Exposed beams and old wardrobes add character to the rooms under the eaves, all of which are wonderfully quiet. When you go down to breakfast, don't forget to look up and admire the ceiling hung with wicker baskets. Excellently situated to explore the Loing Valley.

 We most liked **An establishment with a genuine family spirit.**

Families are welcomed with open arms in this idyllically situated hotel on the banks of the Loing, which offers well-appointed and fully renovated rooms. Children under 10 stay at no cost and one child's menu is offered free with two adult meals. In the winter, a log fire warms the dining room whose bay windows overlook the river.

Access : 7km to the south-west of Moret-sur-Loing on the D 104

Access : At the town hall, go along Rue Grande and turn left alongside the ramparts

 436 **BELLEVUE**
Mr and Mrs Galpin

 77610 Neufmoutiers-en-Brie
Tel. : 01 64 07 11 05
Fax : 01 64 07 19 27
bellevue @ fr.st
www.bellevue.fr.st

Open all year • 7 rooms, 5 of which are in a separate wing, all have bath/WC and television • €63, breakfast included • Table d'hôte €10 to €15 • Garden, car park. Credit cards not accepted

 437 **LA FERME DU VIEUX CHÂTEAU**
Mrs Maegerlein

 77540 Ormeaux
Tel. : 01 64 25 78 30
Fax : 01 64 07 72 91
bandb77 @ wanadoo.fr
www.chambres-table-hotes.com

Open all year by reservation • 4 non-smoking rooms • €59, breakfast included • Table d'hôte €13 to €49 • Garden, car park. No dogs allowed

 The elegant setting of this 19C manor house.

Don't be put off by the sight of the surrounding residential suburbia, because the garden of this fine 19C manor house commands a view of open fields which stretch as far as the eye can see. All the split-level bedrooms have a few personal touches. Two lodges with private garden and deck chairs are the most pleasant. A superb dining room with beams, old flagstones and a beautiful wood table set an elegant tone for mealtimes.

 Guests and their horses are received warmly.

The "old castle" is no longer visible, but the exquisitely restored 18C farmhouse is guaranteed to satisfy even the most demanding visitor. The owners' decorative flair has combined rich materials and period furniture with collections of old tools and popular arts. The bathrooms of the cosy rooms are all fitted with power showers. The high ceilinged lounge is graced with a huge Louis XIII fireplace. You are welcome to try your hand at carriage riding in the company of the farm's mare, Ivoire.

Access : 10km south of Disneyland-Paris, on the A 4 take exit no 13, the D 231 then the D 96

Access : In the town

 438 LE MOULIN DE POMMEUSE
Mr and Mrs Thomas

 32 avenue du Gén.-Herme
77515 Pommeuse
Tel. : 01 64 75 29 45
Fax : 01 64 75 29 45
www.le-moulin-de-pommeuse.com

Open all year • 6 non-smoking rooms • €49, breakfast included • Table d'hôte €20 to €24 • Park, car park. No dogs allowed • Watermill

 439 FERME DU CHATEL
Mr Lebel

 5 rue de la Chapelle-Saint-Jean
77160 Provins
Tel. : 01 64 00 10 73
Fax : 01 64 00 10 99
fermeduchatel @ wanadoo.fr

Open all year • 5 non-smoking rooms, all have bathrooms • €45, breakfast included • No table d'hôte • Garden, car park. No dogs allowed

 As soon as you've crossed the threshold, you'll start to feel at home.

The lady of the house certainly knows how to receive her guests in style, offering them a drink on arrival, the traditional sprig of lily of the valley on May 1 and gifts at Christmas. The setting of the 14C water mill is quite delightful, as are the rooms, which have suitably agricultural names such as Sowing, Harvesting, Threshing. Relax in the small sitting room in the old machine room or in the park which hides its very own island!

 "Wasting" time in the orchard garden.

This old house, built and rebuilt from the 12C to the 18C, enjoys a superb position in the heart of the medieval town. The bedrooms, under exposed rafters, are peaceful and spotless with well-equipped bathrooms. Breakfast is served in a rustic dining room full of character; afterwards head for the huge garden and wander between the fruit trees.

Access : 5km westbound from Coulommiers on the N 34, then a minor road

Access : In the medieval city

 440 LES HAUTS DE MONTGUILLON
Mr and Mrs Legendre

22 rue de Saint-Quintin,
hameau de Montguillon
77860 Saint-Germain-sur-Morin
Tel. : 01 60 04 45 53
Fax : 01 60 42 28 59
chantal.legendre @ wanadoo.fr
http://perso.wanadoo.fr/les-hauts-de-montguillon

Open all year • 3 rooms, 2 of which are upstairs, all have
bathrooms • €54, breakfast included • Table d'hôte €21
(in the evening only by reservation) • Garden, car park.
Credit cards not accepted, no dogs allowed • Disneyland-
Paris nearby

 441 AUBERGE DU CHEVAL BLANC
Mrs Cousin

55 rue Clairet
77910 Varreddes
Tel. : 01 64 33 18 03
Fax : 01 60 23 29 68
auberge-cheval-blanc @ libertysurf.fr
www.auberge-cheval-blanc.fr

Closed from 1 to 24 Aug, Sun evening, Tue lunchtime
and Mon • 8 rooms with bath/WC and television • €76
to €95; breakfast €9 • Menus €34 to €49 • Garden,
private car park

 The cheerful decoration.

 **The terrace decked in flowers and
shaded by trees.**

This lovingly restored farmhouse is conveniently located
near Disneyland-Paris. A tasteful contrast of pastel
shades and dark timbered beams prevails in the
bedrooms which have large beds, old wardrobes and
chest of drawers picked up in second-hand shops and
brand new bathrooms. This creative mixture of old and
new continues in the rest of the establishment,
particularly in the hall with its old bread oven. The
shaded, well-manicured garden is the place to be on
sunny days.

This former staging inn houses recently redone
"chocolate-box" bedrooms featuring designer fabrics,
pine and wrought-iron furniture and teak-floored
bathrooms. In the plush dining room hung with still-lifes,
the accent is on creativity and healthy local produce.
Don't even think about leaving without tasting the
inimitable Brie de Meaux cheese!

Access : Southbound from St-Germain sur Morin, in
the upper part of Montguillon

Access : On the main road in the village

442 LA FERME DES VOSVES
Mrs Lemarchand

155 rue de Boissise
77190 Vosves
Tel. : 01 64 39 22 28
Fax : 01 64 79 17 26

Open all year • 3 rooms • €50, breakfast included • No table d'hôte • Garden, car park. Credit cards not accepted, no dogs allowed

443 CHAMBRE D'HÔTE LE SAINT-DENIS
Mrs Pernelle

1 rue des Cabarets
95510 Chérence
Tel. : 01 34 78 15 02

Closed from Oct to Mar • 5 rooms with bathrooms • €46; breakfast €5. Booking necessary • No table d'hôte • Garden, car park. Credit cards not accepted, no dogs allowed

The simple, unpretentious welcome and setting.

This green-shuttered old farmhouse is bordered by two attractive gardens full of fruit trees and flowers and complete with a well. The unostentatious, tranquil bedrooms, spread throughout the buildings and the warm, unaffected welcome from the lady of the house are reason enough to stay, but the sitting room with piano and dining room with fireplace and watercolours by the owner are also delightful.

The lavish breakfasts.

This appealing stone house in the lovely medieval village of Chérence was formerly a traditional hotel-restaurant. It was turned into a B&B establishment in 1996, offering simple, compact rooms in all shapes and sizes. The ground floor, full of nooks and crannies, houses the dining and sitting room complete with fireplace. Spending or wasting time in the delightful garden is definitely a high point. Faultless welcome.

Access : 10km northbound from Barbizon on the N 7 and the D 372, then take Rue de la Gare

Access : 4km to the north-east of Roche-Guyon on the D 100

444 CHAMBRE D'HÔTE MONSIEUR DELALEU
Mr Delaleu

131 rue du Maréchal-Foch
95620 Parmain
Tel. : 01 34 73 02 92
Fax : 01 34 08 80 76
ladelaleu @ minitel.fr

Open all year • 4 rooms • €48, breakfast included • No table d'hôte • Garden, car park. Credit cards not accepted, no dogs allowed

445 LES ROMANCIERS
Mrs Priou

Quai de Seine
78670 Médan
Tel. : 01 39 75 82 22
Fax : 01 39 75 44 88
www.lesromanciers.fr

Closed from late Dec to mid-Jan, and on Sun evening • 10 rooms with bath/WC and television • €61; breakfast €7 • Menus €24 to €28 • Car park

The unusual bathrooms.

By the time you have opened your suitcase, you will feel that you have come home. Each of the spacious, colourful rooms is named after a playing card; Spade, Heart, Diamond and Club. However the highly unusual bathrooms, all are different, are what guests always rave about. Children are in heaven over the vaulted cellar turned into a games room, the mini football pitch and the visit to the working farm.

Candlelit dining on the riverside terrace.

Romance and fiction set the scene for this pleasant spot between land and water, opposite the riverside beach of Médan-Villennes and close to the house where Zola, Maupassant, Huysmans and friends began their collection of short stories, "Evenings at Médan". All the spacious, well-appointed bedrooms overlook the Seine and are decorated with a distinctly zany 1970s colour scheme and cane furniture. The shaded riverside terrace is worth the trip in itself. Traditional cuisine.

Access : 1km westbound from Isle-Adam on the D 64

Access : 6km westbound from Poissy on the D 153 then the D 164

446 **CHAMBRE D'HÔTE M. LÉVI**
Mr and Mrs Lévi

4 allée du Jamburée
78840 Moisson
Tel. : 01 34 79 37 20
Fax : 01 34 79 37 58
blevi @ free.com
www.gitesdefrance.com

Open all year • 3 rooms with bathrooms • €55, breakfast included • Table d'hôte €18 (only by reservation) • Garden, car park. Credit cards not accepted • Outdoor swimming pool. Golf, horse-riding, tennis and leisure park nearby

447 **LA FAUCONNERIE DU ROY**
Mr and Mrs Oger

1 rue de l'Ormoir
78124 Montainville
Tel. : 01 34 75 17 24
www.lafauconnerie.com

Open all year • 2 rooms and one gîte • €74, breakfast included • No table d'hôte • Car park. No dogs allowed • Outdoor swimming pool

 We most liked **A spin in one of the owner's vintage cars.**

A former 16C priory is an excellent place to spend a night in the heart of this village so dear to Monet. Time and care have clearly been lavished on the interior and each room is a delight to behold. The "Boat" room contains an 18C model sailing boat, "Scheherazade" is steeped in mystery and "Provence" bathed in bright, cheerful colours. Antique furniture, ornaments and a collection of LPs add a personal touch to the sitting room and the flowered garden is perfect to relax in.

 We most liked **The history behind these beautifully preserved buildings.**

History and character meet your eye wherever you turn in this falconry built in 1680 for Louis XIV. Everything is authentic from the original wooden carved staircase and doors, tiled floors and period furniture down to the piano in the breakfast room. Excellent bedding, good quality bathrooms and canopied beds have been chosen for the bedrooms. Children's play area in the park and bicycle rental available.

Access : 3km to the south-east of Roche-Guyon

Access : 6km eastbound from Thoiry on the D 45, take the Maule road and turn right

 LE CHÂTEAU
Mr Le Bret

2 rue de l'Église
78125 Poigny-la-Forêt
Tel. : 01 34 84 73 42
Fax : 01 34 34 7438
lechateaudepoigny@wanadoo.fr

Open all year • 6 rooms, one of which is a family room
• €63, breakfast included • No table d'hôte • Garden,
car park. Credit cards not accepted, no dogs allowed

 We most liked

The exquisite decoration of this 19C abode.

Magical! Words fail us when describing this sumptuous
19C castle, laden with furniture and objects brought
back from all over the world. The resulting mixture of
styles and periods is both bewildering and enchanting.
Each of the rooms is styled on a different theme:
"Morocco", "Indonesia", "Louis XIII" and even "Coca-
Cola". The garden full of ducks, ganders, dogs and
horses has a distinctly Noah's Ark air about it. Definitely
worth making a beeline for!

Access : 8km to the north-west of Rambouillet on
the D 936 then the D 107

LANGUEDOC-ROUSSILLON

Languedoc-Roussillon is home to a diverse collage of landscape and culture: the feverish rhythm of its festivals, the dizzying beauty of the Tarn Gorges, the haughty splendour of the Pyrenees, the bewitching spell of its caves and stone statues, the seclusion of its clifftop Cathar citadels which witnessed one of the bloodiest chapters of France's history, the heady perfumes of its sunburnt garrigue, the nonchalance of the pink flamingos on its long salt flats, the splendour of Carcassonne's ramparts, the ornamental exuberance of Catalan altarpieces, the quietly flowing waters of the Midi Canal and the harsh majesty of the Cévennes mountains. Taking in so many contrasts is likely to exhaust more than a few explorers, but effective remedies are close at hand: a steaming plate of *aligot* – mashed potato, garlic and cheese – and a simmering cassoulet, the famously rich combination of duck, sausage, beans and herbs, followed by a delectable slice of Roquefort cheese, all washed down with a glass of ruby-red wine.

43 ESTABLISHMENTS
449 to **491**

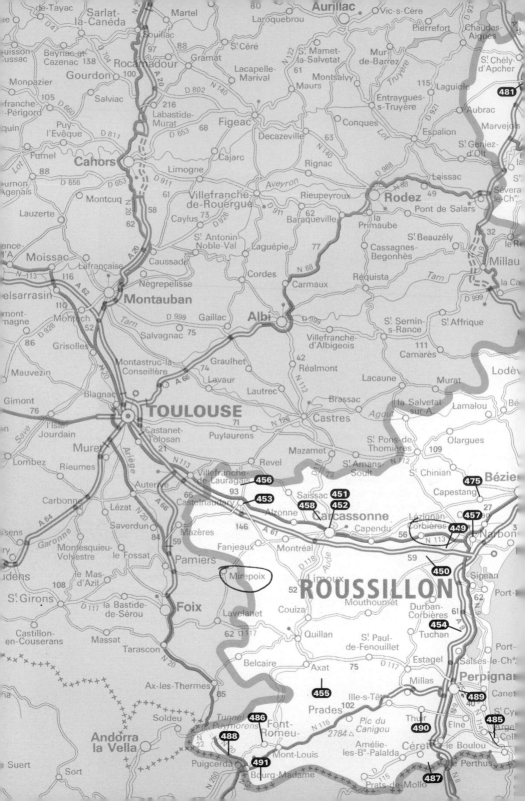

449 DOMAINE DE SAINT-JEAN
Mr and Mrs Delbourg

11200 Bizanet
Tel. : 04 68 45 17 31

Closed during the February holidays • 4 upstairs rooms, all have bathrooms • €62, breakfast included • No table d'hôte • Garden. Credit cards not accepted, no dogs allowed

450 LA BASTIDE DES CORBIÈRES
Mr and Mrs Camel

17 rue de la Révolution
11200 Boutenac
Tel. : 04 68 27 20 61
Fax : 04 68 27 62 7
bastide-corbières @ wanadoo.fr
www.perso.wanadoo.fr/bastide.corbieres

Closed in Feb and one week in Nov • 5 rooms with bath/WC • €65, breakfast included • Table d'hôte €23 • Terrace, garden. No dogs allowed • Reading room, table-tennis, mountain bike rental

 Whiling away time in the former wine cellar converted into a sitting room.

This rambling 19C wine-growing property stands amid vineyards and pine trees, ready to welcome travellers in search of quiet authenticity. Hand-stencilled furniture and walls adorn the accommodation in the converted vat house: each room is named after one of the family's ancestors; the one with a private terrace enjoys a particularly lovely view of the Fontfroide massif. The well-tended garden is Mr Delbourg's pride and joy.

 The apéritif offered to guests on arrival.

This late-19C mansion features a wonderful mixture of modern comforts and period atmosphere. The rooms, generously sized, brightly coloured and decorated with antiques are named after the grapes used to produce rich, full-bodied Corbières wines. The sweet scent of roses, irises, peonies and acacia fills the garden where meals are served.

Access : 2.5km to the north-west of the abbey on the D 613 towards Lagrasse, then on a minor road

Access : 7.5km southbound from Lézignan on the D 61 towards Luc-sur-Orbieu

451 LA MAISON SUR LA COLLINE
Mrs Galinier

Lieu-dit Sainte-Croix
11000 Carcassonne
Tel. : 04 68 47 57 94
Fax : 04 68 47 57 94
nicole.galinien @ wanadoo.fr

Closed from Nov to 15 Mar • 5 rooms and one small suite, with bathrooms and television • €77, breakfast included • Table d'hôte €23 • Garden, car park. Credit cards not accepted • Outdoor swimming pool

452 MONTSÉGUR
Mr Faugeras

27 allée d'Iéna
11000 Carcassonne
Tel. : 04 68 25 31 41
Fax : 04 68 47 13 22
reservation @ hotelmontsegur.com
www.hotelmontsegur.com

Closed from 22 Dec to 28 Jan • 21 rooms on 3 floors, all have air-conditioning, bath/WC or shower/WC and television • €64 to €84; breakfast €8 • No restaurant, but meals can be taken at the nearby "Languedoc" • Private car park. No dogs allowed

 As soon as you hear the chirping of the cicadas you know you're in the south.

 The unforgettable tour of the historic city ramparts.

Broom, cypress trees, thyme and wild mint lend a wonderfully relaxing atmosphere to this hillside farmstead overlooking the historic city of Carcassonne. Old red floor tiles, antiques and knick-knacks adorn the spacious rooms. Each has its own colour scheme, beige, blue, yellow – the "white" room has a private garden. Breakfast is served by the pool in the summer.

A late-19C mansion on the doorstep of the lower town. An undeniable faded charm emanates from these gradually spruced-up rooms filled with the scent of beeswax. Herringbone parquet floors, "retro" lights and a marble fireplace are among the features of the classic period sitting room. The breakfast room is graced with a beautiful old dresser.

Access : 1km southbound from the historic town on the Sainte-Croix road

Access : From Castelnaudary on the N 113 (Av du Prés F Roosevelt), turn right at Artigues Bridge

 453 DU CANAL
Mrs Geli

2 ter avenue Arnaut-Vidal
11400 Castelnaudary
Tel. : 04 68 94 05 05
Fax : 04 68 94 05 06

Open all year • 38 rooms, 2 have disabled access. All have bath/WC and television • €42 to €50; breakfast €6 • No restaurant • Garden, car park • Billiards room

 454 L' AUBERGE DE LA TOUR
Mr and Mrs Auber

Les Cabanes de Fitou
11510 Fitou
Tel. : 04 68 45 66 90
Fax : 04 68 45 65 97
daniel.auber @ wanadoo.fr

Closed from 2 Jan to 12 Feb, from 28 Oct to 8 Dec, Sun evening, Mon and Tue except in Jul and Aug • 6 rooms on 2 floors, with shower/WC and television • €60 to €64; breakfast €7 • Menus €25 to €38 • Car park

 Stepping out of the hotel onto the banks of the Canal du Midi.

These handsome ochre walls housed a quicklime factory back in the 19C. The quiet if ordinary rooms overlook the garden or the canal and in the summer, you will want to linger over breakfast for hours as you gaze at the canal's quietly flowing waters. It would be a crime to leave town without sampling its world-renowned cassoulet!

 Exploring Languedoc's distinctive salt marshes.

Visitors are often struck by the similarity between the medieval-style stone walls of this inn, which actually date from 1995, and the nearby Fort of Salses. The inn is, however, home to an 11C chapel, converted into a sitting room: an eclectic blend of rustic and classical 19C French furniture has been chosen for the reasonably priced rooms. A vaulted ceiling and exposed beams embellish the welcoming restaurant which serves good traditional fare, accompanied, of course, by the local Fitou wine.

Access : Towards Pamiers on the banks of the Midi canal

Access : On the N 9, midway between Sigean and Salses-le-Château

455 HOSTELLERIE DU GRAND DUC
Mr and Mrs Bruchet

2 route de Boucheville
11140 Gincla
Tel. : 04 68 20 55 02
Fax : 04 68 20 61 22
host-du-grand-duc @ ataraxie.fr

Open from 30 Mar to 5 Nov • 12 rooms, 3 of which are
in a separate wing, all have bath/WC or shower/WC and
television • €48 to €60; breakfast €7; half board €55 to
€59 • Restaurant closed on Wed lunchtime except in Jul
and Aug; menus €22 (in the week) to €42 • Terrace,
garden, garage, private car park • Ideal for exploring the
upper Aude Valley

 **Candle-lit dining overlooking the
garden and its ornamental pool.**

This grand old mansion built in 1780 stand proudly in
one of Cathar country's many remote villages, perfect
for long walks in the nearby forest. The accommodation
may be a tad old-fashioned, but certainly can't be
faulted for character; a second wing has just been
finished with three delightful rooms. Elegant rustic
dining room opening onto a terrace shaded by a thick
canopy of lime trees.

Access : At Lapradelle, leave the D 117 (Quillan to
Perpignan road) and take the D 22 alongside the
Bouizane

456 HOST. DU CHÂTEAU DE LA POMARÈDE
Mr Garcia

Place du Château
11400 La Pomarède
Tel. : 04 68 60 49 69
Fax : 04 68 60 40 71

Closed 12-25 Mar, 5-26 Nov, Tue except evenings in
season. Sun evening out of season and Mon • 7 rooms
with bath/WC and television • €64 to €79 (€49 to €64 in
low season); breakfast €9 • Menus €15 (lunchtime in the
week) to €48 • Terrace, car park

 **Wouldn't it be easy to get used to
living in luxury?**

An enthusiastic young couple are at the head of this
wonderful establishment tucked away in a hamlet of the
Montagne Noire. The outbuildings of a medieval fortress
have recently been converted into a likeable hostelry:
tastefully decorated rooms, an elegant dining room with
exposed timbers and wrought-iron furniture, a terrace
overlooking the valley and, above all, the mouth-
watering, confident and inventive cuisine, which earned
it a Michelin star, no less, in 2002.

Access : Set back from the D 624 from
Castelnaudary to Revel

457 **LA RÉSIDENCE**
Mr Aiguille

6 rue du 1ᵉʳ Mai
11100 Narbonne
Tel. : 04 68 32 19 41
Fax : 04 68 65 51 82

Closed from 15 Jan to 15 Feb • 25 rooms on 2 floors with bath/WC or shower/WC and television • €57 to €76; breakfast €7 • No restaurant • Small garage • Near the historic centre

458 **LE LIET**
Mr Meynier

11610 Pennautier
Tel. : 04 68 11 19 19
Fax : 04 68 47 05 22

Closed in Dec and Jan • 6 rooms with bath/WC • €61, breakfast included • No table d'hôte • Garden, park, car park. No dogs allowed • Outdoor swimming pool, tennis, mountain biking

Stepping back in time to the turn of the 20C.

This gracious late-19C residence was converted into a hotel in the 1950s: the atmosphere of old provincial France can still be felt in its lovingly preserved decoration. Some of the rooms overlook the Archbishops' Palace and the cathedral. The hotel has enjoyed the patronage of a whole host of famous politicians, sportsmen and artists, as a peep inside the Visitor's Book will reveal.

Lording it for a weekend.

The impressive stone walls and lofty turrets of this 19C castle are encircled by wood and parkland rich in flora and fauna, including peacocks, hares, pheasants and, to the delight of children, ponies. The immaculately decorated rooms and suites all enjoy views of this abundant countryside and some have a balcony. Magnificent breakfast room opening onto the grounds.

Access : Take the Narbonne-Sud exit and head for the town centre, cross the Robine canal, turn right at Rue J Jaurès and then the 2nd left

Access : 9km to the north-west of Carcassonne on the N 113 then the D 203

 459 LA SÉRÉNITÉ
Mrs L'Helgoualch

Place de la Mairie
30430 Barjac
Tel. : 04 66 24 54 63
Fax : 04 66 24 54 63

Open all year • 3 rooms with bath/WC or shower/WC
• €77, breakfast included • No table d'hôte • Terrace.
Credit cards not accepted, no dogs allowed

 460 LES DOCTRINAIRES
Mr Jusdado

Quai du Général de Gaulle
30300 Beaucaire
Tel. : 04 66 59 23 70
Fax : 04 66 59 22 26

Open all year • 32 rooms, one has disabled access. All
rooms have bath/WC and television • €51 to €59;
breakfast €9; half board €52 to €61 • Restaurant closed
on Sat lunchtime; menus €15 to €37 • Terrace, private
car park. No dogs allowed in restaurant

 Snuggling up in the book-lined bedroom or in front of the fire.

Fragrant lavender and beeswax greet you as you cross
the threshold of this 17C country home. Afterwards,
feast your eyes on the sophisticated good taste of the
ochre-coloured walls, hand-stencilled friezes, rich fabrics, antiques and ornaments picked up by the antique
dealer-owner and on the personalised rooms decorated
with fine linen and lace. Settle down and relax as you
savour the delicious breakfasts served by the fireside or
on the flowered terrace in the summer.

 Mr Jusdado's vivacious personality.

The austere cream-coloured stone walls of this 17C
religious seminary seem to have miraculously escaped
the passing of time, protected perhaps from the fierce
Provençal sun by the branches of a superb cedar tree.
The rather faded aspect of the rooms, those overlooking
the canal are more spacious and comfortable, is
compensated for by the restaurant and its beautiful
fretwork ceiling. A delightful, refreshing patio serves as
breakfast and also dining room.

Access : 6km westbound from Aven d'Orgnac on
the D 317 and then the D 176

Access : On the banks of the Rhone Canal at Sète,
on the corner of Rue Rabelais

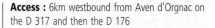

 461 VIC

Mr Vic

 Mas de Raffin
30210 Castillon-du-Gard
Tel. : 04 66 37 13 28
Fax : 04 66 37 62 55

Open all year • 5 rooms • €70 to €84, breakfast included
• No table d'hôte • Garden, car park. Credit cards not
accepted, no dogs allowed • Outdoor swimming pool

 462 LES CÉVENNES

Mr and Mrs Chomat

 14 route de Villefort
30530 Chamborigaud
Tel. : 04 66 61 47 27
 Fax : 04 66 61 51 01

Closed from 1 Jan to 16 Feb, from 23 Sep to 1 Oct and
Tue from 15 Sep to 15 Jun • 11 rooms with bath/WC
or shower/WC, all have television • €36 to €39; breakfast
€7; half board €35 to €37 • Menus €12 to €20 • Terrace,
private car park • Swimming in the river, hiking,
horse-riding, fishing

 The happy marriage of old and new.

It would be difficult to find a more idyllic spot for this
former wine-growing farm set amidst the unspoilt
landscape of fragrant scrub, vines and hundred-year-old
olive trees. Red and yellow features predominantly in
the bright rooms where modern amenities blend in
wonderfully with old stones and antique furniture; some
are vaulted while others are split-level. Savour breakfast
served under the refreshing shade of a mulberry tree.

 **Donkey-back – the only way to
explore Mount Lozère in style!**

This welcoming hostelry, a former coaching inn at the
foot of Mount Lozère, is home to rustically decorated,
well-kept rooms. Ravenous walkers dig into the
traditional fare served in a dining room whose lace
tablecloths, knick-knacks and family heirlooms are
clearly the work of somebody's sweet old grandmother.
The climbing vine over the terrace provides welcome
shade from the beating sun: time to sit back and read
Robert Louis Stevenson's "Travels With a Donkey in the
Cévennes".

Access : 4km to the north-east of Pont-du-Gard on
the D 19 and then the D 228

Access : Between Génolhac and Alès (D 906), in the
village

 463 **LA TONNELLE**
Mr and Mrs Rigaud

 Place des Marronniers
30200 La Roque-sur-Cèze
Tel. : 04 66 82 79 37
Fax : 04 66 82 79 37

Open all year • 6 rooms • €57, breakfast included • No table d'hôte • Credit cards not accepted, no dogs allowed

 464 **CHÂTEAU DU REY**
Mrs Cazalis de Fondouce

 Le Rey
30570 Pont-d'Hérault
Tel. : 04 67 82 40 06
Fax : 04 67 82 47 79
abeura @ club-internet.fr

Closed in Jan and Feb • 13 rooms, all have bath/WC and television • €73 to €88; breakfast €8; half board €59 to €73 • Restaurant closed on Sun evening and Mon except in Jul and Aug; menus €24 to €45 • Terrace, riverside park, car park • Outdoor swimming pool, private fishing

 We most liked **Row, row, row your boat, gently down the Cèze!**

Merrily, merrily, merrily, merrily, life is but a dream! The infectious good humour of the owner is impossible to resist as she guides you round her lovely country house that can't be missed on the way into the village. Each of the sober, immaculate rooms is named after a flower. In the summer, treat yourself to breakfast in the shade of an arbour while you gaze down on the village and its girdle of cypress trees.

 Ve most liked **Eight centuries of family history.**

This lovely 13C fortress, remodelled by the tireless Viollet-le-Duc, Napoleon's architect, has been in the same family for over eight centuries! The rooms, some with fireplace, are furnished with elegant period furniture. The former sheep pen is now the home of the dining room and its vaulted ceiling makes it pleasantly cool in summer. The view from the terrace extends over the immense parkland and river, much prized by anglers.

Access : 17km to the north-west of Bagnols-sur-Cèze on the N 86 then the D 298 towards Barjac, and the D 166

Access : 5km eastbound on the D 999 (towards Ganges), turn left just before Pont d'Hérault

 465 LA MAGNANERIE DE BERNAS
Mrs Keller

Le Hameau de Bernas
30630 Montclus
Tel. : 04 66 82 37 36
Fax : 04 66 82 37 41
lamagnanerie @ wanadoo.fr
http://avignon-et-provence.com/
magnanerie-de-bernas

Open from 14 Mar to 3 Nov • 10 rooms, one of which has disabled access, all have bath/WC and television • €60 to €95 (€45 to €85 low season); breakfast €9; half board €55 to €75 (€48 to €58 low season) • Restaurant closed on Mon lunchtime in season, Tue and Wed out of season; menus €15 to €44 • Terrace, garden, car park • Pool

 Treasure hunting in this 13C Knights Templar stronghold.

Patrick and Katrin, a young Swiss couple with energy to spare, have recently finished their patient, flawless restoration of this medieval former command post. Beautiful stone walls, exposed beams and rich, warm fabrics adorn the tasteful rooms, most of which look down over the Cèze valley. Character abounds in the vaulted dining room, but the highlight is perhaps the shaded courtyard-terrace and south-facing garden, designed by a professional landscape gardener, none other than Patrick himself.

Access : Between Barjac and Bagnols-sur-Cèze, then 2km eastbound from Monclus

 466 L' ARCEAU
Mr and Mrs Brunel

1 rue de l'Arceau
30210 Saint-Hilaire-d'Ozilhan
Tel. : 04 66 37 34 45
Fax : 04 66 37 33 90
patricia.brunel @ wanadoo.fr
www.multimania.com/arceau

Closed from 20 Nov to 15 Feb, Sun evening, Tue lunchtime, and Mon from 1 Oct to Easter • 25 rooms with bath/WC or shower/WC, all have television • €54 to €84; breakfast €6; half board €46 • Menus €20 (in the week) to €51 • Terrace, private car park

 The sweet-scented garrigue.

Before the sun has risen to its zenith, leave the sizzling A9 motorway and head straight for the shelter of this welcoming mas and its cool terrace just two minutes drive away. The fragrant odours of the scrub surrounding the village seep into every nook and cranny of its thick dry-stone walls. Even better, it is within easy reach of one of the marvels of French-Roman architecture, the Pont du Gard aqueduct. When you book, ask for one of the renovated rooms whose stone and beams are visible.

Access : 4.5km to the north-east of Remoulins on the D 792

 467 **LA MAZADE**
Mrs Couston

 Dans le village
30730 Saint-Mamert-du-Gard
Tel. : 04 66 81 17 56
Fax : 04 66 81 17 56
www.bbfrance.com/couston.html

Open all year • 3 rooms with bathrooms • €45, breakfast included • Table d'hôte €14 • Garden, car park. Credit cards not accepted, no dogs allowed

 468 **LE MAS DE CAROUBIER**
Mrs Charpentier

684 route de Vallabrix
30700 Saint-Quentin-la-Poterie
Tel. : 04 66 22 12 72
Fax : 04 66 22 12 72
contact @ mas-caroubier.com

Closed in Jan • 4 rooms • €61, breakfast included • Table d'hôte €20 to €23 • Garden. Credit cards not accepted, no dogs allowed • Outdoor swimming pool

 Mrs Couston's highly personal approach to interior decoration.

This beautiful country mas, set in the heart of a sleepy village, reveals the talents of its owner's flair for interior decoration. An almost staggering collection of antique and contemporary furniture, rugs and modern and folk art blends surprisingly well in the plant-filled rooms: the result is truly unique. All the rooms overlook the garden and arbour, where dinner is served in the long summer evenings.

 A secret hideaway.

The traditional ochre walls and sky-blue shutters of this 18C mas suddenly appear when you reach the end of a country lane. Inside, the guests' welfare is clearly the only thing that counts, from the gracious greeting and rooms filled with old furniture to the delicious home-made jams at breakfast time. Outside, the turquoise water of the swimming pool and quiet garden encourage you to idle away long summer afternoons, unless of course you would prefer to do a pottery, painting or cookery course.

Access : 17km westbound from Nîmes on the D 999 and then the D 1

Access : 5km to the north-east of Saint-Quentin-la-Poterie on the D 982 and then the D 5

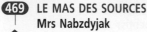

469 LE MAS DES SOURCES
Mrs Nabzdyjak

30140 Saint-Sébastien-d'Aigrefeuille
Tel. : 04 66 60 56 30

Open all year • 5 rooms • €51 to €57, breakfast included • Table d'hôte €19 • Terrace, park, car park. Credit cards not accepted • Second-hand antique "shop"

470 MAS FONTCLAIRE
Mrs Labbé

8 rue Émile-Jamais
30250 Sommières
Tel. : 04 66 77 78 69
Fax : 04 66 77 78 69

Open all year • 3 rooms • €67, breakfast included • No table d'hôte • Garden, car park. Credit cards not accepted, no dogs allowed • Outdoor swimming pool

Hotel or second-hand antique shop?

This 17C stronghold covered in wisteria and shaded by hundred-year-old chestnut trees may well entice you to stay longer than planned. The immaculate interior is a collage of old furniture, ornaments, knick-knacks and paintings patiently picked up by Madame, who runs an antiques shop on the ground floor. You could hear a pin drop within the quiet white walls of the rooms, lightened by brightly coloured curtains and bedspreads. In the summer, meals are served on a pleasant shaded terrace.

Speech may be silver, but silence is golden!

Imagine waking up to blue, cloudless skies and tucking into delicious home-made jams and freshly squeezed orange juice, served on the patio in the summer or by the fireside in winter. You only need to put one foot over the threshold of this former wine-grower's house to know you're in for a treat. The three rooms in the converted outbuildings are decorated in different styles: Provençal, modern and Louis XVI. The quality of the silence is such that you may even find yourself whispering!

Access : 5km northbound from Anduze on the D 50

Access : In the village

471 **LE PONT DU ROY**
Mr Sorgère

Route de Nîmes
30126 Tavel
Tel. : 04 66 50 22 03
Fax : 04 66 50 10 14
hotelpontduroy@wanadoo.fr
www.hotelpontduroy.fr

Open from 28 Mar to 13 Oct • 14 air-conditioned rooms with bath/WC or shower/WC and television • €70 to €89 (€58 to €76 low season); breakfast €7; half board €60 (€54 low season) • Menus €21 to €43, in the evening and only for guests • Terrace, garden, private car park • Outdoor swimming pool, pétanque, play area

  Never make the mistake of thinking that pétanque is "just a game"!

You can always dive into the swimming pool for a refreshing dip if things get too hot on the pétanque ground! Built in the style of a Provençal mas, this house was turned into a hotel in 1986. The pastel coloured rooms overlook either the shaded garden or the legendary vineyards of Tavel. A fresh country look prevails in the restaurant and in the summer tables are laid outside on the terrace. The self-taught owner-chef rustles up regional dishes depending on what he finds in the market.

Access : 3km to the south-east of Tavel, on the D 4 then the D 976 (Roquemaure-Remoulins road)

---

 472 **LA PASSIFLORE**
Mr and Mrs Booth

1 rue Neuve
30310 Vergèze
Tel. : 04 66 35 00 00
Fax : 04 66 35 09 21

Hotel open all year; restaurant from 14 Feb to 27 Oct • 11 rooms, all have bath/WC or shower/WC and television • €46 to €55; breakfast €6; half board €48 to €52 • Restaurant closed on Sun (except in Jul and Aug) and Mon; menus (dinner only) €23 to €26 • Terrace, private car park. No dogs allowed in restaurant

Treat yourself to one of Mr Mayle's tales of life in Provence as you relax in this picturesque mas.

At last you can find out if Peter Mayle's humorous accounts are true! This 18C mas in the heart of a pretty village is run by an English couple, Mr and Mrs Booth. They have clearly taken their adoptive land to heart as the Provençal decoration of the restaurant and breakfast room testifies, even though a snug sitting room is perfect for teas. Small, well-maintained, quiet rooms overlook a lush green inner courtyard or a small garden.

Access : Between Nîmes and Lunel, leave the N 113 for Codognan and follow the D 104 to Vergèze

473 LE GRAND LOGIS
Mr Léger and Mrs Lhopital

Place de la Madone
30210 Vers-Pont-du-Gard
Tel. : 04 66 22 92 12
Fax : 04 66 22 94 78

Closed mid-Nov to early Apr • 3 rooms • €69, breakfast
included • No table d'hôte • Garden, terrace. Credit
cards not accepted, no dogs allowed

474 L' ATELIER
Mr and Mrs Bermejo

5 rue de la Foire
30400 Villeneuve-lès-Avignon
Tel. : 04 90 25 01 84
Fax : 04 90 25 80 06
hotel-latelier @ libertysurf.fr

Closed in Nov • 23 rooms, all have bath/WC or
shower/WC and television • €60 to €90 (€52 to €84 low
season); breakfast €8 • No restaurant • Garden, garage
• Exhibition of painting and sculpture, tea room

Authenticity before all else.

As you push open the heavy wood door complete with
a "judas" spy hole, it is difficult to imagine that behind
it you will encounter such decorative opulence. Bright
Provençal colours adorn the well-dimensioned rooms.
The vaulted sitting and breakfast rooms have retained
their Directoire period frescoes. Climb upstairs to the
terrace on the top floor and toast yourself on the sun
deck. Others, perhaps more wisely, will prefer to nap
in the peaceful garden.

The view of Avignon from the patio and tiny terrace.

This 16C "workshop" in the heart of a picturesque town
has just been creatively redesigned by a film set
decorator. Tasteful ornaments, antique furniture, rush
matting, elegant bathrooms, exposed beams, fireplaces
and a lovely staircase are combined in this masterful
renovation which has retained the character of the
abode's ancestral walls. Mediterranean-style breakfast
room, exhibitions of painting and sculpture.

Access : 4km to the north-west of Pont-du-Gard on
the D 981

Access : In the old town

475 CHAMBRE D'HÔTE BERNARD FOUISSAC
Mr and Mrs Fouissac

La Bastide Vieille
34310 Capestang
Tel. : 04 67 93 46 23
Fax : 04 67 93 46 56

Closed from 1 Nov to 1 Mar • 3 rooms • €40, breakfast included • Table d'hôte €15 • Terrace, garden, car park. Credit cards not accepted, no dogs allowed

We most liked Whether by bicycle, carriage or barge (on request), the Canal du Midi is a joy to explore.

These old walls flanked by a 12C tower lie amid vineyards in a totally secluded spot, well off the beaten track. The spacious rooms installed in the former outbuildings are decorated with appealing Provençal prints and colours. The dining table is in the former bread-making room. On the leisure side, get to grips with a good book in the delightful sitting room-library or in the small garden.

Access : 13km westbound from Béziers, Castres road on the D 39

476 LE BARRY DU GRAND CHEMIN
Mr and Mrs Clarissac

88 faubourg Saint-Martin
34520 Le Caylar
Tel. : 04 67 44 50 19
Fax : 04 67 44 52 36

Open all year • 6 rooms • €46, breakfast included • Table d'hôte €17 • Car park. Credit cards not accepted, no dogs allowed

We most liked The secretive, silent countryside – the "causse" – surrounding this stone farmstead.

Built in 1850, the immaculate stone walls of this house stand at the foot of the strange, tormented Roc Castel in the heart of the unspoilt Larzac limestone plateau. The ground floor rooms are quiet and very well-maintained if not vast. Tuck into the delicious chargrilled fare cooked over an open fire in the delightful vaulted dining room, which remains refreshingly cool in the height of summer.

Access : In the village

LANGUEDOC-ROUSSILLON

 477 **CHAMBRE D'HÔTE MONSIEUR GENER**
Mr and Mrs Gener

34 avenue Pierre-Sirven
34530 Montagnac
Tel. : 04 67 24 03 21
Fax : 04 67 24 03 21

Open all year • 4 rooms with shower/WC • €42, breakfast included • No table d'hôte • Terrace, garden, car park. Credit cards not accepted

 478 **PARC**
Mrs Jacquin

8 rue Achille Bège
34000 Montpellier
Tel. : 04 67 41 16 49
Fax : 04 67 54 10 05
hotelduparc@ifrance.com
www.hotelduparc-montpellier.com

Open all year • 19 rooms, most have shower/WC, some have bath/WC or shower without WC, all have air-conditioning and television • €47 to €59; breakfast €7 • No restaurant • Car park. No dogs allowed

 We most liked
Pézenas and its wealth of craft stalls within easy reach.

In 1750, the buildings laid out around the well-sheltered, spacious inner courtyard belonged to the mounted constabulary. Nowadays, the stables have been converted into large, calm, well-appointed rooms, in some of which the old oak partitions between the loose-boxes can still be seen. In the summer, breakfast is served on a pleasant upstairs terrace.

 We most liked
Being treated like a regular guest.

Despite the fact that the park has been sold off, the noble walls of this 18C mansion are as smart as ever and the plush bourgeois rooms are being gradually and tastefully renovated. The regulars of this establishment, located in a quiet side street, appreciate its calm just two minutes away from the town centre and the nearest tram stop; they generally leave their cars in the private car park in the courtyard. In the summer, breakfast is sometimes served on the terrace.

Access : 6.5km to the north-west of Pézenas on the N 9 then the N 113

Access : Drive up Rue Proudhon (towards the zoo), and at the ECAT, take a left at Rue Turgot

479 DOMAINE DE SAINT-CLÉMENT
Mrs Bernabe Calista

34980 Saint-Clément-de-Rivière
Tel. : 04 67 66 70 89
Fax : 04 67 84 07 96
calista.bernabe@wanadoo.fr
www.ledomaine.fr

Closed from Dec to Feb • 5 rooms with bathrooms • €65 to €90, breakfast included • No table d'hôte • Sitting room, garden, car park. Credit cards not accepted, no dogs allowed • Outdoor swimming pool

480 OSTALARIA CARDABELA
Mr and Mrs Pugh

10 place de la Fontaine
34725 St-Saturnin-de-Lucian
Tel. : 04 67 88 62 62
Fax : 04 67 88 62 82
ostalaria.cardabela@free.fr

Closed from Nov to mid-Mar • 8 rooms on 2 floors with bath/WC • €70 to €80; breakfast €10 • No restaurant at the hotel, but the owners also run Le Mimosa at St-Guiraud • No dogs allowed

Faultlessly decorated and oozing with character.

This beautiful 18C mansion only 10min from the heart of busy Montpellier is a haven of peace and quiet. The immense rooms, furnished with antiques and paintings and equally enormous bathrooms, overlook the park or the swimming pool. A string of sitting rooms, decorated with red floor tiles and hung with eye-catching contemporary art, comprises the ground floor. Don't miss the library complete with fireplace and the hand-painted azulejos tiles in the patio.

Access : 10km northbound from Montpellier on the D 17 then the D 112

Ostalaria's authenticity.

The only clue that this delightful village house is a hotel is the tiny sign almost absentmindedly posted outside. The recently spruced up rooms have plenty of style with brightly coloured quilts, elegant lights and Provençal furniture blending in perfectly with the lovely exposed stone walls, polished floor tiles, well-worn beams and original fireplaces. Some overlook the quite exquisite little square of St Saturnin. Breakfast is served on a large friendly dining table. Delightful.

Access : On the village square, near the church

481 GRAND HÔTEL PROUHÈZE
Mr and Mrs Prouhèze

2 route du Languedoc
48130 Aumont-Aubrac
Tel. : 04 66 42 80 07
Fax : 04 66 42 87 78
prouheze @ prouheze.com
www.prouheze.com

Open 23 Mar to 1 Nov; closed Mon (except evenings Jul-Aug), Sun evening and Tue lunchtime • 26 rooms with bath/WC and television • €61 to €87; breakfast €13, half board €95 • Menus €29 (lunchtime in the week) to €89; at the Compostelle (bistro) €13 to €20 • Terrace, car park

482 LA LOZERETTE
Mrs Agulhon

48400 Cocurès
Tel. : 04 66 45 06 04
Fax : 04 66 45 12 93
lalozerette @ wanadoo.fr

Open from Easter to 1 Nov • 21 rooms, one of which has disabled access, all have bath/WC or shower/WC and television • €52 to €67; breakfast €7; half board €48 to €58 • Restaurant closed Wed lunchtime and Tue. In Jul and Aug closed Tue lunchtime. Menus €15 to €22 • Car park, garden. No dogs allowed in restaurant

 Mr and Mrs Prouhèze's spontaneity and warmth.

This traditional hostelry was founded in 1891 by the current owners' great-grandmother. Snug rooms are decorated with painted wood or Louis Philippe-style furniture. Brightly coloured fabrics are a recent addition to the main dining room which specialises in large helpings of good regional cooking. A country bistro caters to pilgrims on the way to St James of Compostela who pass by on the GR footpath through the village. Chinaware and home-made preserves on sale.

 Oleander bushes planted in the lovely glazed Anduze vases in the garden.

This inn is both a hamlet on the doorstep of the National Park of Cévennes and a genuine family home because the young owner was born here and the auberge was opened by her grandmother. Feast your eyes on the renovated rooms with matching bedspreads, lace curtains and flowered balconies overlooking the village and the countryside. Admire the carved ceiling in the "country chic" dining room. The extensive wine-list is further proof of the owner-sommelier's many talents.

Access : In the village, opposite the railway station

Access : 5.5km to the north-east of Florac on the N 106, then right onto the D 998

483 AUBERGE RÉGORDANE
Mr Nogier

48800 La Garde-Guérin
Tel. : 04 66 46 82 88
Fax : 04 66 46 90 29
www.demeures-de-lozere.com

Open from Apr to late Sep • 15 rooms with bath/WC or shower/WC, some have television • €55; breakfast €6; half board €45 to €50 • Restaurant closed Tue; menus €15 to €29 • Terrace in an inner courtyard

484 LE SAINT-SAUVEUR
Mr Bourguet

Place Jean Séquier
48150 Meyrueis
Tel. : 04 66 45 62 12
Fax : 04 66 45 65 94
saint-sauveur @ demeures-de-lozere.com
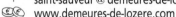 www.demeures-de-lozere.com

Open from 15 Mar to 15 Nov • 10 rooms, all have bath/WC and television • €37 to €40; breakfast €5; half board €36 to €40 (€34 to €38 low season) • Menus €15 to €28 • Terrace

 The head-spinning view of the gorges of Chassezac from the village.

This fortified village was founded by the bishops of Mende along the old Roman road linking Auvergne with the Languedoc in an effort to eradicate highway robbery. An order of knights from La Garde Guérin were entrusted with the task of escorting voyagers. The stronghold of one of these knights is now a characterful inn with small rooms and mullioned windows, a restaurant with vaulted ceiling and a beautiful terrace-courtyard of granite flagstones.

 The stone terrace shaded by a lovely old sycamore tree.

This elegant 18C mansion, full of character and very reasonably priced, stands in the heart of a region that abounds in magnificent natural sites: Aven Armand, Dargilan Cave and the Gorges de La Jonte. Well-appointed rooms are decorated with cherry wood furniture and well protected by double-glazing. The slightly faded feel of the comfortable bourgeois dining room is in fact quite appealing.

Access : In the heart of the village

Access : In the town centre

LANGUEDOC-ROUSSILLON

485 **ERMITAGE N. D. DE LA CONSOLATION**
Mr Mabit

66190 Collioure
Tel. : 04 68 82 17 66

Closed from 11 Nov to 31 Mar • 12 rooms • €31, breakfast included • No restaurant • Park, car park. Credit cards not accepted

486 **Y SEM BÉ**
Mr and Mrs Démelin

5 rue des Écureuils
66120 Font-Romeu
Tel. : 04 68 30 00 54
Fax : 04 68 30 25 42

Open from 15 Jun to 22 Sep, from 26 Oct to 3 Nov and from 14 Dec to 22 Apr • 22 rooms with bath/WC or shower/WC and television, 2 have kitchenettes • €56 to €70; breakfast €7; half board €41 to €60 (€39 to €45 low season) • Menus €15 at lunchtime, €18 in the evening • Terrace, small garden • Skiing and mountain walks, fishing

We most liked

A site fit for a pilgrimage.

There are so many delightful, even magnificent places to be discovered, such as the beautifully preserved arcades of this 15C pilgrimage site, swathed in a curtain of foliage and refreshed by the tinkling of three fountains. The airy, colourful rooms are immaculate and three are located in the former monks' cells. The chapel has a curious collection of sailors' ex-votos. Guests can picnic in the grounds in the evening and are free to organise barbecues.

We most liked

The south-facing aspect, to catch as many of the sun's warm rays as possible.

This 1950s wood and stone chalet lies in a quiet, residential quarter of the mountain resort. The modest rooms with balconies are gradually being renovated, while the dining room commands a lovely view over the Cerdagne. Above all, the establishment spares no effort to make guests feel at home, which is not surprising given its name – Y Sem Bé roughly translates as "At home" in Catalan!

Access : Take the Route des Crêtes (5km on the D 86)

Access : Take Avenue d'Espagne (towards Toulouse, Andora) and turn right on Rue des Écureuils

 HOSTAL DELS TRABUCAYRES
Mr Davesne

 66480 Las Illas
Tel. : 04 68 83 07 56

Closed from 1 Jan to 20 Mar, from 25 to 30 Oct, Tue and Wed out of season • 5 rooms upstairs, 3 of which have a terrace • €30; breakfast €5; half board €31 • Menus €11 (in the week) to €31 • Terrace, car park. No dogs allowed in the rooms • Walking

 AUBERGE CATALANE
Mrs Ernst

 10 avenue du Puymorens
66760 Latour-de-Carol
Tel. : 04 68 04 80 66
Fax : 04 68 04 95 25
carolee @ club-internet.fr
www.auberge-catalane.fr

Closed from 21 to 31 May, from 17 Nov to 17 Dec, Sun evening and Mon except during school holidays • 10 rooms with shower/WC and television • €48; breakfast €6; half board €38 • Menus €14 to €28 • Terrace, car park

 Long walks in the silent forest of cork oaks surrounding the hotel.

Don't give up! The winding hairpin bends of this tiny mountain road may seem endless but your efforts will be repaid tenfold. This tiny hamlet in the middle of nowhere is home to an old inn which provided accommodation to the exiled officers of Spain's Republican Army in 1936. Admire the view from the simple but pleasant rooms. The restaurant in a converted barn serves typically Catalan dishes.

 Taking a ride on the little yellow train through the picturesque Cerdagne region.

This inn, built in 1929, returned to the family when the original owner's grandchildren bought it back a few years ago and today the great-grandson, Benoît, presides over the kitchens. The rooms have been renovated and modernised, but the original Art Deco-inspired furniture has been retained; some bedrooms have balconies overlooking the village rooftops. Dining room-veranda.

Access : Take the D 618 between Céret and Le Boulou; at Maureillas take the D 13 and drive south-west for 11km

Access : On the main road of the village (N 20) between Bourg-Madame and the Puymorens Pass

 489 DOMAINE DU MAS BOLUIX
Mr and Mrs Ceilles

 Chemin du Pou de les Colobres
66100 Perpignan
Tel. : 04 68 08 17 70
Fax : 04 68 08 17 71

Closed from 1 to 20 Feb • 7 rooms with bath/WC • €57, breakfast included • Table d'hôte €20 • Terrace, garden, car park. Credit cards not accepted • Swimming pool and tennis nearby

490 CASA DEL ARTE
Mrs Fourment

 Mas Petit
66300 Thuir
Tel. : 04 68 53 44 78
Fax : 04 68 53 44 78
casadelarte @ wanadoo.fr

Open all year • 6 rooms • €61 to €99, breakfast included • No table d'hôte • Sitting room, garden, car park • Outdoor swimming pool, sun deck

 We most liked **The secluded situation on the doorstep of Perpignan.**

An easy-going atmosphere reigns throughout this 18C mas set in the midst of Cabestany's vineyards and orchards. Restored in 1998, the interior is comfortable, roomy and spotlessly clean. Each of the personalised rooms, whose immaculate walls are hung with bright regional fabrics, is named after a famous Catalan: Dali, Rigaud, Maillol, Picasso, Casals. The sweeping view over Roussillon, the coast and that emblem of Catalonia, the mighty Canigou mountain, is definitely worth a trip.

 We most liked **The arty feel to the individually decorated rooms.**

The owner-painter has converted this 11C and 14C mas into a real art gallery. The walls of the often well proportioned rooms and bathrooms are covered in colourful paintings; the one devoted to ancient Rome is particularly lovely. Works by local artists adorn the walls of the sitting room, whose centrepiece is a medieval fireplace. The sun deck overlooking the swimming pool, the hundred-year-old oaks in the park and the small bamboo grove invite guests to take life easy.

Access : 5km southbound from Perpignan towards Argelès

Access : 17km westbound from Perpignan, towards Thuir and Ille-sur-Têt

491 AUBERGE LES ÉCUREUILS
Mr and Mrs Laffitte

66340 Valcebollère
Tel. : 04 68 04 52 03
Fax : 04 68 04 52 34

Open from 20 May to 15 Oct and from 18 Dec to 9 May
• 15 rooms with bath/WC, some have television • €66 to
€80; breakfast €11; half board €54 to €68 • Menus
€24 to €45 • Terrace, fitness room • Cross-country skiing,
snowshoe trekking, hiking, mushrooming, fishing

 **Whether it be smuggler's footpaths or
secluded fishing spots, the owner is a
treasure-trove of tips.**

Only twenty-or-so souls still live in this half-abandoned
village, perched at an altitude of 1 500m on a dead-end
road in the remote Pyrenees. Should you decide to join
them for a day or so, you won't regret it! The genuine
warmth and solicitude of the owners of this former 18C
sheep-fold, full of character, are quite captivating.
Comfortable rooms, with bathrooms done out in Spanish
marble, and an elegant rustic dining room complete the
picture.

Access : 9km to the south-east of Bourg-Madame on
the D 70, then at Osséja take the D 30

LIMOUSIN

Life in Limousin is lived as it should be: tired Parisians in need of greenery flock here to taste the simple joys of country life, breathe in the bracing air of its high plateaux, stroll along the banks of rivers alive with fish and wander through its woodlands in search of mushrooms and chestnuts. The sight of peaceful cattle grazing in utter contentment or lambs frolicking in the meadows in spring is enough to rejuvenate even the most jaded city-dweller. By late October, the forests are swathed in a cloak of autumn colours and the ground becomes a soft carpet of russet leaves. A perfect backdrop to the granite walls and soft sandstone façades of sleepy hamlets and peaceful cities, where ancestral crafts, such as Limoges porcelain, St-Yrieix enamel and Aubusson tapestries, combine a love of tradition with a whole-hearted desire to embrace the best in contemporary art. The food is as wholesome as the region: savoury bacon soup, steaming Limousin stew and, as any proud local will tell you, the most tender, succulent beef in the world.

18 ESTABLISHMENTS

492 to **509**

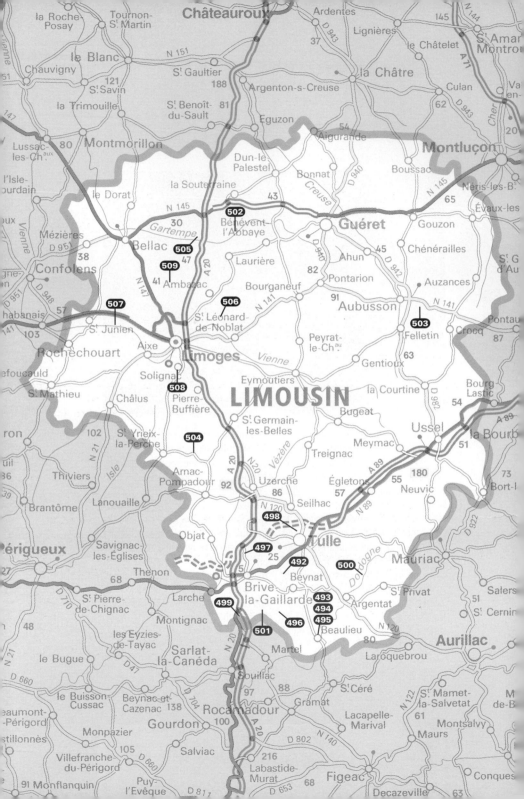

LIMOUSIN

 492 LA TOUR
Mr Lachaud

 19190 Aubazine
Tel. : 05 55 25 71 17
Fax : 05 55 84 61 83

Closed in Jan, Mon in winter and Sun evening • 20 rooms with bath/WC or shower/WC and television • €48; breakfast €6; half board €49 to €51 • Menus €15 (in the week) to €35

 493 LE TURENNE
Lefèvre family

1 boulevard St-Rodolphe-de-Turenne
19120 Beaulieu-sur-Dordogne
Tel. : 05 55 91 10 16
Fax : 05 55 91 22 42
turenne02@infonie.fr

Closed from mid-Nov to mid-Mar • 15 rooms with bath/WC or shower/WC, all have television • €42; breakfast €7; half board €60 • Restaurant closed Sun evening and Mon; menus €23 to €63 • Terrace

 Amble alongside the pretty Canal des Moines dug in the 12C.

On the village square, opposite the Cistercian Abbey stand two characterful houses, the older one flanked by the tower from which the hotel takes its name. Bright wallpaper livens up the bedrooms, while the main dining room and smaller rooms for families or business lunches feature a rustic flavour in keeping with the array of regional delicacies on the menu. Apéritifs and after-dinner coffee are served on the terrace.

 Beautifully located in the Dordogne Valley.

Lovers of Romanesque architecture will adore this establishment in the heart of the historic town. The prestigious walls of the old Benedictine Abbey now house this delightful medieval-style hotel. A lovely spiral sandstone staircase winds up to colourfully restyled bedrooms. Welcoming rustic lobby and elegant vaulted dining room with exposed beams and a superb stone fireplace: in summer, meals are also served amid the flowers outside.

Access : On the main square in the village, opposite the abbey

Access : In the town centre

494 **CENTRAL HÔTEL FOURNIÉ**
Mr and Mrs Bessière

4 place du Champ de Mars
19120 Beaulieu-sur-Dordogne
Tel. : 05 55 91 01 34
Fax : 05 55 91 23 57

Open from 1 Apr to 11 Nov and closed Tue from Oct to Jun • 23 rooms with bath/WC or shower/WC, some have television • €43 to €54; breakfast €6; half board €48 to €53 • Menus €16 (in the week) to €40 • Terrace, private car park

495 **LA MAISON**
Mr Henriet

11 rue de la Gendarmerie
19120 Beaulieu-sur-Dordogne
Tel. : 05 55 91 24 97
Fax : 05 55 91 51 27

Closed from Oct to Mar • 6 rooms, all have bath/WC • €57, breakfast included • No table d'hôte • Credit cards not accepted, no dogs allowed • Terraced garden, outdoor swimming pool

 Take a compass to explore the labyrinth of narrow lanes in the historic town.

The central location of this sturdy hotel, founded in 1912 by Amélie Fournié, does full justice to its name. When booking, ask for one of the renovated rooms. The house's excellent reputation is also due to the generous helpings of wholesome country cooking served in an agreeable rustic dining room or on the terrace where you can enjoy the warm breeze.

 More hacienda than country farmhouse.

The arcades, ruddy ochre walls and profusion of hydrangeas, rose bushes and lemon trees in the patio are more reminiscent of an exotic hacienda than a French country farmhouse: all becomes clear when you learn that this astonishing 19C house was built by one of Napoleon's generals, homesick for Mexico. The adorable, unusually named rooms – "The Bride", "The Indians", "The Caricatures" – are quite unique; two overlook the sumptuous hanging garden and swimming pool.

Access : On the main square in the centre of the village

Access : In the village

LIMOUSIN

 496 LA RAZE
Mrs Tatien

19500 Collonges-la-Rouge
Tel. : 05 55 25 48 16
Fax : 05 55 25 49 00

Open all year • 5 rooms • €42, breakfast included • No table d'hôte • Car park. Credit cards not accepted, no dogs allowed • Outdoor swimming pool

 497 LE RELAIS DU BAS LIMOUSIN
Mr and Mrs Bésanger

Sadroc
19270 Donzenac
Tel. : 05 55 84 52 06
Fax : 05 55 84 51 41
relais-du-bas-limousin @ wanadoo.fr

Closed for one week in November • 22 rooms with bath/WC or shower/WC and television • €42 to €61; breakfast €6; half board €40 to €54 • Restaurant closed Sun evening mid-Sep to mid-Jun and Mon lunchtime; menus €14 (in the week) to €43 • Terrace, garden, garage, car park. No dogs allowed • Outdoor swimming pool

 Throw open your windows and feast your eyes on the countryside.

This 18C farmstead lies just 800m outside the crimson sandstone village: serenity reigns, broken only by the high-pitched calls of the peacock in the mating season. The lady of the house's artistic talents can be admired in the hand-stencilled patterns on the walls of the comfortable bedrooms. The breakfast room, adorned with family furniture and heirlooms and the park "à l'anglaise" overflowing with fruit trees and roses, are magnificent.

 A visit to the disused slate quarries – if you're not afraid of heights!

This solid construction inspired by regional styles dates from the 1960s and was clearly built to last a few centuries. The stylish personalised rooms have matching fabrics, bedspreads and lampshades and those facing the rear look out over a peaceful Limousin landscape. Welcoming family dining rooms, a veranda flooded with light and a terrace opening onto the garden complete with swimming pool and play area.

Access : 5.5km to the south-west of Collonges on the D 38 and the D 19, then follow the La Raze signs

Access : 6km on the D 920 towards Uzerche

 498 CHEZ MONSIEUR ET MADAME PERROT
Mr and Mrs Perrot

 Gourdinot
19460 Naves
Tel. : 05 55 27 08 93

Open all year • 3 rooms upstairs, one of which has a loggia • €40, breakfast included • Table d'hôte €14 • Car park. Credit cards not accepted, no dogs allowed

499 À LA TABLE DE LA BERGÈRE
Mrs Verlhac

 Belveyre
19600 Nespouls
Tel. : 05 55 85 82 58

Open all year • 5 rooms • €33, breakfast included • Table d'hôte €12 • Garden, car park. Credit cards not accepted, no dogs allowed

 The sense of being right in the middle of nowhere.

This old Corrèze farmhouse built out of rough-hewn stone and nestling in a wooded valley is ideal for touring the region: Millevaches — literally "Thousand cows" plateau, Lake Seilhac and Uzerche. Soak up the peaceful atmosphere of the cosy bedrooms and relax by the fireside in the company of your lively young hosts. In the morning, you will awake to the enticing smell of fresh-baked bread, steaming coffee and a breakfast table piled high with a profusion of home-made gingerbreads and preserves.

 If this farm wins any more awards, it may well run out of space to display them.

This sturdily built farmstead in the midst of oaks, meadows and dry-stone huts is very well placed to explore the region's wealth of tourist sights. The rooms, furnished with family heirlooms, are very inviting, particularly those on the second floor, while the flavourful regional cooking, friendly atmosphere and Madame's ability to make you feel at home are unparalleled.

Access : 5km northbound from Naves on the N 20, then take a minor road

Access : 15km southbound from Brive towards Nespouls, then take the D 19 and the D 920

 500 LES VOYAGEURS
Mr and Mrs Chaumeil

 Place de la Mairie
19320 Saint-Martin-la-Méanne
Tel. : 05 55 29 11 53
Fax : 05 55 29 27 70

Open from mid-Feb to mid-Nov; closed Sun evening and Mon out of season • 8 rooms upstairs with bath/WC or shower/WC, some have television • €41 to €49; breakfast €5; half board €39 to €43 • Menus €15 to €31 • Terrace, garden, car park • Private pond for anglers

 501 LA MAISON DES CHANOINES
Mr and Mrs Cheyroux

 Chemin de l'Église
19500 Turenne
Tel. : 05 55 85 93 43

Open from 6 Apr to 26 Oct • 6 rooms located in 2 buildings, with bath/WC or shower/WC • €70 to €80; breakfast €8; half board €62 to €70 • Air-conditioned restaurant; closed Tue Wed Thu and Fri lunchtimes; menus €27 to €33 • Terrace. No dogs allowed

 The lady of the house's warm greeting.

This establishment, which has been run by the same family for five generations, is ideal to get away from it all and take things easy. Within its solid stone walls, built in 1853, you'll find simple, but well cared-for bedrooms. Admire the wood carving in the rustic dining room, if you can tear yourself away from the traditional cuisine prepared by the chef-owner for a minute. After lunch or dinner, venture out into the garden as far as the pond and watch the carp and pike.

 The terrace overlooking a manicured herb garden.

It is well worth venturing past the handsome late Gothic-style door and into this lovely 16C house built in the heart of a picturesque village. There is as much character inside as out, with the vaulted dining room, fireplace and spiral staircase climbing up to the rooms, which are furnished with the results of forays to local antiques dealers. At mealtimes, roll up your sleeves and dig into the chef's creative recipes prepared with the best local produce. Limited seating only.

Access : On a square in the centre of the village

Access : In the centre of the village, 16km south of Brive-la-Gaillarde

LIMOUSIN

 502 NOUGIER
Mr and Mrs Nougier

 2 place de l'Église
23290 Saint-Étienne-de-Fursac
Tel. : 05 55 63 60 56
Fax : 05 55 63 65 47

Closed from late Nov to early Mar, Sun evening and Mon from Sept to Jun • 12 rooms, all have bath/WC and television • €49 to €58; breakfast €7; half board €45 to €60 • Restaurant closed Mon lunchtime in Jul and Aug; menus €17 to €28 • Garden, private car park

503 CHAMBRE D'HÔTE M. DUMONTANT
Mr and Mrs Dumontant

 Les Vergnes
23200 Saint-Pardoux-le-Neuf
Tel. : 05 55 66 23 74
Fax : 05 55 67 74 16
sylvie.dumontant @ freesbee.fr

Closed from late Oct to early Apr • 6 rooms with bathrooms and separate WC • €74, breakfast included • Table d'hôte €17 • Terrace, car park. Credit cards not accepted • Fishing

 We most liked
Country charm and cosy comfort.

Cuddle up in the warm interior of the well-appointed old-fashioned bedrooms, appealing dining room and the sitting room with its fine rustic furniture, old fireplaces and a Pianola. This regional-style hostelry on the village square hides a wealth of creature comforts within its solid walls and the country appeal is further enhanced by a superb, well-tended garden.

 We most liked
Fishing in the nearby pond.

If in desperate need of a break from city life, your prayers will be answered in this 18C farmhouse, set in the heart of the countryside and surrounded by a prosperous working farm, only 7km from the tapestry capital of France. All the spacious, fully renovated rooms overlook the pond and nearby woodland. Original exposed stone walls and a huge fireplace add character to the dining room.

Access : 11km southbound from La Souterraine on the D 1

Access : 7km eastbound from Aubusson on the N 141

504 LE MOULIN DE MARSAGUET
Mr Gizardin

87500 Coussac-Bonneval
Tel. : 05 55 75 28 29

Fax : 05 55 75 28 29

Closed early Nov to mid-Mar • 3 rooms • €39, breakfast included • Table d'hôte €17 • Garden, terrace, car park. Credit cards not accepted, no dogs allowed • Cookery courses. Fishing, boating and swimming

505 MANOIR HENRI IV
Mr Broussac

D 220
87250 La Croix-du-Breuil
Tel. : 05 55 76 00 56
Fax : 05 55 76 14 14

Open all year; closed Sun evenings • 11 rooms on 2 floors, with bath/WC or shower/WC, all have television • €51; breakfast €6 • Menus €19 (in the week) to €41; one of the dining rooms is air-conditioned • Terrace, garden, car park. No dogs allowed

We most liked
Finding out how tasty farm delicacies are made.

The hospitality of this farming family will make you want to return to their rambling 18C farmstead and its immense 30-acre fishpond. Anglers will love catching pike while the others can go swimming or boating. The light, airy rooms are simply decorated and every evening brings an excellent opportunity to wine and dine on the succulent home-made delicacies in lively company.

We most liked
Walls steeped in history, a stone's throw from a motorway junction.

This fortified 16C farmstead, flanked by a pretty turret, does full honour to its namesake and former royal guest who used to hunt in the area. The rustic, well-kept rooms are smaller and less airy under the eaves. Countrified dining rooms with exposed beams and an interesting collection of farming implements on the walls; one has a lovely fireplace.

Access : 3.6km northbound from Coussac on the D 17 towards La Roche-l'Abeille, then take the D 57

Access : 3km northbound from Bessines-sur-Gartempe

LIMOUSIN

 506 LE RELAIS DU TAURION
Mr Roger

2 chemin des Contamines
87480 Saint-Priest-Taurion
Tel. : 05 55 39 70 14
Fax : 05 55 39 67 63

Closed from 15 Dec to 15 Jan, Sun evening and Mon
• 8 rooms with bath/WC or shower/WC, almost all have
television • €40 to €46; breakfast €6; half board €46 to
€49 • Menus €16 (in the week) to €31 • Terrace, garden,
car park • Swimming, fishing, canoeing nearby

 507 DOMAINE DU LOUBIER
Mr and Mrs Dauriac

Lieu-dit Le Petit-Loubier
87420 Saint-Victurnien
Tel. : 05 55 03 29 22

Open all year • 4 spacious rooms with bathrooms, one
room has disabled access • €42, breakfast included
• Table d'hôte €16 • Park, car park. Credit cards not
accepted, no dogs allowed • Fishing, canoeing, swimming, horse-riding and tennis nearby

 The delightful owners.

This grand hundred-year-old mansion covered in
Virginia creeper is home to immaculate little rooms,
some of which have old marble fireplaces. Old beams
and rustic furniture add charm to the sitting room. In
fine weather, tables are laid amid the luxuriant foliage
of the flowered garden. Traditional cuisine.

 **The allure of this estate will linger in
your memory for years.**

A park planted with lindens, oaks, chestnuts, giant
thujas and a superb monkey puzzle tree is the setting
for this gracious 18C-19C country residence. Well-
dimensioned rooms, tastefully decorated by the owner-
antique dealer. Sit down to meals with the family around
the immense guest table in winter or in the garden in
the summer. A feast for the eyes and the palate!

Access : 11km to the north-east of Limoges on the
D 29

Access : 5km southbound from Oradour-sur-Glane on
the D 9, take the D 3, then the dead-end road on the
right

SOLIGNAC - 87110

THOURON - 87140

 508 SAINT-ELOI
Mr Pagani

66 avenue Saint-Éloi
87110 Solignac
Tel. : 05 55 00 44 52
Fax : 05 55 00 55 56
lesaint.eloi@wanadoo.fr
www.lesainteloi.fr

Closed in Jan, from 10 to 20 Sep, Sat lunchtime, Sun evening and Mon • 15 rooms on 2 floors with bath/WC and television, one room has disabled access • €45 to €58; breakfast €7; half board €40 to €46 • Menus €14 (lunchtime in the week) to €38 • Terrace • Tea room with painting and sculpture exhibitions

 509 LA POMME DE PIN
Mr Mounier

Étang de Tricherie
87140 Thouron
Tel. : 05 55 53 43 43
Fax : 05 55 53 35 33

Closed during the February holidays, in Sep, Mon and Tue • 4 rooms with bath/WC and television • €54; breakfast €6 • Menus €21 to €30 • Terrace, garden. No dogs allowed in rooms

 The blessed union of medieval and modern.

Opposite the abbey founded by St Éloi, this half-timbered house in local stone welcomes guests in a spirit of peace and quiet. Spacious, well-soundproofed rooms are adorned with bright sunny fabrics and paintings. From his stained-glass window, good King Dagobert's treasurer, the patron saint of goldsmiths, gazes benignly down on diners as they savour the owner's flavourful cooking in a 12C dining room complete with granite fireplace.

 Feast your eyes on a landscape of ponds, lakes and forest.

All the quiet, spacious rooms in the former spinning mill enjoy a view of the river, while the old mill on the banks of the millpond houses two dining rooms. The first offers an authentically rustic setting with rough stone walls and a huge fireplace where meat is roasted; the second is airier and overlooks the wonderful Limousin countryside.

Access : 10km southbound from Limoges on the D 704 (towards St-Yrieix), then right on the D 32

Access : Northbound from Limoges on the A 20, drive until exit no 26, then take the D 5 towards Nantiat

LORRAINE

I f you are planning a trip to Lorraine and want to do justice to the region's wealth of wonderful sights, make sure you pack your walking boots. However, before you set off for the distant reaches of its lofty slopes, pause for a moment in Nancy and take in its splendid artistic heritage, without forgetting to admire the lights of Metz. You can then move on through a string of tiny spa-resorts, renowned for the slimming properties of their water, and the famous centres of craftsmanship which produce the legendary Baccarat crystal, enamels of Longwy and por-celain of Lunéville, before you reach the poignant silence of the dormant mines and quarries at Domrémy and Colombey. The deep lakes, thick forests and wild animals of the Vosges Regional Park will keep you entranced as you make your way down through the gentle hillsides, dotted with plum-laden orchards. Stop for a little "light" refreshment in a *marcairerie*, one of the region's old farm-inns, and sample the famous quiches, before finishing with a slab of pungent Munster cheese or a kirsch-flavoured dessert for the sweet-toothed among us.

20 ESTABLISHMENTS
510 to **529**

 510 CHÂTEAU DE LABESSIÈRE
Mr Eichenauer

 9 rue du Four
55320 Ancemont
Tel. : 03 29 85 70 21
Fax : 03 29 87 61 60
rene.eichenauer@wanadoo.fr

Closed at Christmas and 1 Jan • 3 rooms • €70, breakfast included • Table d'hôte €25 • Garden, car park • Outdoor swimming pool

 511 LES AGAPES-LA MAISON FORTE
Mr Joblot

6 place Henriot du Coudray
55800 Revigny-sur-Ornain
Tel. : 03 29 70 56 00
Fax : 03 29 70 59 30
lamaisonfortelesagapes@minitel.net

Closed for the first fortnight in Aug, Feb holidays, Sun evening and Mon • 7 rooms located in 2 buildings, one of which has disabled access, all have bath/WC and television • Double room €64 to €76; breakfast €9; half board €68 to €91 • Menus €27 to €51 • Terrace, garden, car park. No dogs allowed in rooms

We most liked　　**A mite outdated but full of charm.**

Midway between Argonne and the Côtes de Meuse, this unassuming 18C castle makes an ideal base camp to explore the region. Pastel wallpaper, canopied beds and old furniture all add to rather than detract from the rooms' appeal. The same pleasantly outmoded atmosphere prevails in the sitting room, remarkably well stocked with guides, brochures and works on the Meuse. The table d'hôte, open every evening, shaded garden and attractive outdoor swimming pool further enhance the establishment's allure.

We most liked　　**The rooms are full of little surprises.**

Part of the appeal of this 17C stone stronghold lies in its gilded French ceilings, tiled and parquet floors and its antiques; its rooms, spread over two wings, are not enormous but beautifully personalised. The dining rooms' medieval atmosphere makes a pleasant setting for tried-and-tested local favourites, in which local produce features prominently.

Access : 15km southbound from Verdun on the D 34 (Saint-Mihiel road)

Access : From Bar-le-Duc head for Sainte-Menehould, after 12km turn left, drive through Laimont and for 5km on the D 994

ARS-LAQUENEXY - 57530

GORZE - 57680

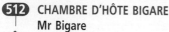 **CHAMBRE D'HÔTE BIGARE**
Mr Bigare

 23 rue Principale
57530 Ars-Laquenexy
Tel. : 03 87 38 13 88

Open all year • 3 rooms, all have bathrooms and separate WC • €39, breakfast included • No table d'hôte • Garden, car park. Credit cards not accepted

 HOSTELLERIE DU LION D'OR
Mr Erman

105 rue du Commerce
57680 Gorze
Tel. : 03 87 52 00 90
Fax : 03 87 52 09 62

Closed Sun evening and Mon • 15 rooms located in 2 buildings, with bath/WC or shower/WC, all have television • €43 to €51; breakfast €7; half board €46 • Menus €16 (lunchtime in the week) to €56 • Terrace, garden, car park • Children's play area

We most liked
Unaffected, genuine hospitality.

Hospitality and friendliness are the foundations of this village house within easy reach of Metz. The rooms are not luxurious and are furnished in a somewhat haphazard style but are certainly well-proportioned; the upstairs room is more akin to a small flat. The bathrooms are equally vast. At mealtimes, you will sit down in the company of your hosts in a plush 19C dining room, home to some beautiful old pieces of Lorraine furniture. Extremely good value for money.

We most liked
The dense foliage shading the terrace.

Run by the same family for over fifty years, this 19C coaching inn has moved with the times without losing sight of its roots. The rooms have been gradually updated and we recommend those opening onto the lovely patio with a trout aquarium and splendid rafters. Back in the restaurant, a huge stone fireplace, fine enough to grace any castle banquet hall, holds its own among the distinctly contemporary-style furniture.

Access : 9km eastbound from Metz towards Château-Salins, then take the D 999

Access : On the main road: to the south-west of Metz, on the D 6, then at Ancy-sur-Moselle turn right

514 AU RELAIS DU CHÂTEAU DE MENSBERG
Mr Schneider

15 rue du Château
57480 Manderen
Tel. : 03 82 83 73 16
Fax : 03 82 83 23 37

Closed from 1 to 20 Jan • 17 rooms, one of which has disabled access, almost all have shower/WC (2 have bath/WC), all have television • €46 to €58; breakfast €7; half board €51 • Restaurant closed Tue; menus €27 to €41 • Terrace, garden, car park

515 AUBERGE DES MÉSANGES
Mr and Mrs Walter

2 rue du Tiseur
57960 Meisenthal
Tel. : 03 87 96 92 28
Fax : 03 87 96 99 14
hotel-restaurant.auberge-mesanges @ wanadoo.fr
www.perso.wanadoo.fr/mesanges57/

Closed from 20 Feb to 11 Mar and from 23 to 27 Dec • 20 rooms with shower/WC, half of the rooms have television • €45; breakfast €6; half board €43 • Restaurant closed Sun evening and Mon; menus €13 to €20 • Terrace, car park

The castle forms a handsome backdrop to a wide variety of performances.

"Malbrouck" was the name the French soldiers gave to one of their worst enemies, the Duke of Marlborough. The duke set up his HQ here at Mensberg (also called Marlborough) Castle in 1705 but was unable to do battle, giving rise to a nursery rhyme still sung today. Three rooms overlook the beautifully restored castle. In addition to a rustic dining room graced by a huge stone fireplace, the inn has two split-level sitting rooms and a quiet terrace in the rear.

Need to get back in touch with the things that really matter?

This inn, on the edge of the Nature Reserve of the Northern Vosges, is ideally located in calm surroundings and close to a whole range of leisure pursuits, including walking, golf, museums and castles. Good-sized, practically-equipped rooms in excellent order. Meals are served in a dining room whose uncluttered rustic style perfectly complements the simple, regional fare.

Access : From Sierck-les-Bains take the N 153 northbound for 2km, then at Apach turn right on the D 64

Access : Near the centre of the village

 516 LA CATHÉDRALE
Mr Hocine

25 place de la Chambre
57000 Metz
Tel. : 03 87 75 00 02
Fax : 03 87 75 40 75
hotelcathedrale-metz@wanadoo.fr
www.hotelcathedrale-metz.fr

Closed from 1 to 15 Aug • 20 rooms on 3 floors, most
have bath/WC, some have shower/WC, all have television • €61 to €80; breakfast €10 • No restaurant

 517 LA BERGERIE
Mrs Keichinger

57640 Rugy
Tel. : 03 87 77 82 27
Fax : 03 87 77 87 07

Open all year • 48 rooms with bath/WC or shower/WC,
all have television • €66 to €69; breakfast €10; half board
€59 to €62 • Air-conditioned restaurant; menus €22 (in
the week) to €52 • Terrace, garden, car park

 **The splendid view of St Étienne
Cathedral from most of the rooms.**

The passing of time seems to have left no traces on the
fine façade of this former coaching inn, which first
opened its doors in 1627. Inside, however, the owners
have really gone to town: individually styled rooms are
adorned with wrought-iron furniture, bright fabrics or
old pieces of furniture picked up in auctions and antique
shops. The timber frames, fireplaces and parquet all bear
witness to the establishment's four-hundred-year commitment to hostelry.

 **Such character and calm so near Metz
and Smurf Village Theme Park!**

This sprawling stone farmstead complete with cottage
and chapel is a far cry from your average predictable
hotel chain. The feminine touch of the energetic lady
of the house can be seen all over the establishment,
particularly in the bedrooms' faultless decoration. Meals
are served in a pretty, rustic dining room which opens
onto a terrace; treat yourself to a chilled glass of Kir
in the garden before dinner.

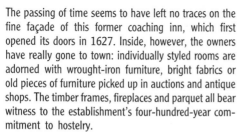

Access : In the town centre, near Saint-Étienne
Cathedral

Access : 12km northbound from Metz on the
D 1 leading to Thionville

518 LE RELAIS ROSE
Mr Loëffler

24 rue de Neufchâteau
88300 Autreville
Tel. : 03 83 52 04 98

Fax : 03 83 52 06 03

Open all year • 16 rooms located in 3 buildings, most have bath/WC or shower/WC, all have television, 2 are non-smoking • €37 to €64; breakfast €6; half board €43 to €57 (€40 to €54 low season) • Menus €11 (lunchtime in the week) to €20 • Terrace, garden, garage, car park

519 CHAMBRES D'HÔTES M. BENOÎT
Mr Breton

74 rue des Récollets
88140 Bulgnéville
Tel. : 03 29 09 21 72
Fax : 03 29 09 21 72
benoit.breton@wanadoo.fr

Closed for 2 weeks in January • 4 rooms • €65, breakfast included • No table d'hôte • Garden, car park

The whole family bends over backwards to please its guests.

A prayer-stool, a handsome wardrobe, a well-worn leather armchair, an unusual patchwork of wallpapers from every age and era, some adorned with wonderfully garish flowers: the list is endless and the result a higgledy-piggledy mixture which proudly refuses to toe the line to any theme or age, and will strike a chord with your secret nonconformist side! For all their casually eclectic style, the renovated rooms are most appealing and the restaurant tables are laid with elegant china from Limoges.

A faultlessly decorated country home.

This unostentatious country house dating from 1720 was entirely redecorated by the owner-antique dealer. The result invites the admiration of everyone who sees it: spacious, comfortable rooms decorated with a tasteful blend of period furniture and modern décor. The sandstone bathrooms are particularly lovely and the garden behind the house is also worthy of note.

Access : In the village, on the N 74 between Colombey-les-Belles and Neufchâteau

Access : 7.5km westbound from Contrexéville on the D 164

 520   **LA SOUVERAINE**
Mr Paris

Parc Thermal
88140 Contrexéville
Tel. : 03 29 08 09 59
Fax : 03 29 08 16 39
www.souveraine-hotel.com

Open all year • 31 rooms, half overlook the park, all have bath/WC or shower/WC and television • €60 (€57 low season); breakfast €7 • No restaurant • Car park

521   **LE CHALET DU LAC**
Mr Vallcaneras

97 chemin de la Droite du Lac
88400 Gérardmer
Tel. : 03 29 63 38 76
Fax : 03 29 60 91 63

Closed from 1 to 31 Oct • 11 rooms, 4 of which are in a separate chalet, with shower/WC and television • €66; breakfast €7; half board €51 • Menus €16 to €54 • Garden, car park • Table-tennis

 The branches laden with crows do have a slightly Hitchcockian air to them.

Contrexéville was "the" place to take the waters at the height of the Belle Époque. The glass awning and friezes which embellish the graceful pink and white façade of this elegant home, leave one in no doubt about its allegiance to a former illustrious guest, the Grand Duchess Vladimir, aunt of Czar Nicholas II. Marble fireplaces, moulded ceilings and brass beds continue to grace the recently renovated bedrooms, some of which overlook the resort park.

 Time seems to stand still on the shores of the lake.

This trim, traditional Vosgian chalet built in 1866 is one of the few holiday homes of this sort, so popular round Lake Gérardmer in the 19C, to have made it through to the present day. The sober, immaculate rooms are sometimes furnished with family heirlooms; ask for a renovated room. Alsace tableware and cut-crystal glasses adorn the tables in the "winstub" styled restaurant with a sweeping view. The garden tumbles down to the lake and it is a real pleasure to wander round its paths.

Access : In the spa-resort

Access : On the Épinal road, 1km to the west, opposite the lake

 522 JAMAGNE
Jeanselme family

2 boulevard Jamagne
88400 Géradmer
Tel. : 03 29 63 36 86
Fax : 03 29 60 05 87
hotel.jamagne@wanadoo.fr
www.jamagne.com

Closed in Mar and from 12 Nov to 20 Dec • 48 rooms with bath/WC or shower/WC, all have television • €70 to €80 (€64 to €70 low season); breakfast €9; half board €57 (€50 low season) • Menus €13 to €20, children's menu €8 • Terrace, private car park • Indoor swimming pool, fitness room, sauna, hammam, jacuzzi, hiking, water sports

 Upholding traditions since 1905.

It is impossible to miss this impressive building on a street corner. Its owners endeavour to cater to families, offering several partitioned rooms, and to those with fewer family worries, with a cosy bar and sitting rooms. Guests eager to sample the region's delicious recipes can head for two lovely dining rooms, while those who have come for the region's sporting pursuits will not be disappointed by the hotel's excellent keep-fit facilities, indoor swimming pool and the countless forest paths.

 523 AUBERGE DE LA VIGOTTE
Mr and Mrs Bouguerne

88340 Girmont-Val-d'Ajol
Tel. : 03 29 61 06 32
Fax : 03 29 61 07 88
courrier@lavigotte.com
www.lavigotte.com

Closed from 12 Nov to 20 Dec • 20 rooms, most have bath/WC, some have shower/WC • €43 to €65; breakfast €6; half board €39 to €54 • Restaurant closed Tue and Wed; menus €14 to €21 • Terrace, garden, car park • Tennis, fishing and swimming in private ponds, play area, hiking, cross-country skiing

 It is impossible to find a fault with this Vosgian inn.

A quick glimpse at the web site of the "via gotta" – "way of springs" – will give you an idea of the new owners' energetic, up-to-date approach since buying the inn in 2000. In no time at all, this old farmhouse, perched at a height of 700m in a forest of fir trees and ponds, has become a very pleasant and popular hostelry thanks to its delightful rooms and "country chic" restaurant. The chef's inventive recipes are a feast for the eyes as well as the mouth.

Access : In the town centre

Access : Between the Ajol Valley and Remiremont (D 23), at Faymon take the D 83 for 5km

 524 LES GRANDS PRÉS
Mrs Chassard

 9 les Grands-Prés
88240 La Chapelle-aux-Bois
Tel. : 03 29 36 31 00
Fax : 03 29 36 31 00

Open all year • 3 rooms and 2 gîtes • €38, breakfast included • Table d'hôte €13 • Sitting room, garden, car park. Credit cards not accepted

525 AUBERGE DU SPITZEMBERG
Mr and Mrs Duhem

 88490 La Petite Fosse
Tel. : 03 29 51 20 46
Fax : 03 29 51 10 12

Closed in Jan and on Tue • 10 rooms upstairs with bath/WC or shower/WC, some have television • €46; breakfast €7 • Menus €15 (in the week) to €23 • Garden, garage, car park • Mini-golf and walks in the forest

 Fishing in the garden.

This immense 19C house encircled by lush green countryside lies just a few minutes from the spa resort of Bains-les-Bains. Spotless, soberly styled rooms overlook a garden through which a fishing stream gurgles and babbles. Home-grown vegetables from the cottage garden and fresh poultry and rabbit reared on the premises are among the specialities on the dinner table.

 Swathed in a curtain of greenery.

Step inside this haven of tranquillity in the remote forest of the Vosges and forget your troubles for a while. The comfortable rooms are pleasantly homely and welcoming and the tasty, unfussy cooking, made with rigorously selected regional produce, is served in a rustic dining room. All you have to decide now is which direction to head off for your long walk in the country. No need to leave that trail of breadcrumbs, though; all the paths are well signposted.

Access : 3.5km to the south-east of Bains-les-Bains towards Saint-Loup, then take a minor road

Access : 3.5km from Provenchères-sur-Fave on the D 45, then take a forest road

LE VAL D'AJOL - 88340

LE VALTIN - 88230

 526 **LA RÉSIDENCE**
Mrs Bongeot

5 rue des Mousses
88340 Le Val d'Ajol
Tel. : 03 29 30 68 52
Fax : 03 29 66 53 00
contact @ la-residence.com
www.la-residence.com

Closed from 26 Nov to 26 Dec • 50 rooms located in 3 buildings with bath/WC or shower/WC and television • €48 to €76; breakfast €8; half board €66 to €90 • Restaurant closed Sun eve and Mon except national and school holidays; menus €15 (in the week) to €42 • Park, car park • Swimming pool with a retractable roof, tennis

 Waking up to a dawn chorus.

Contemporary and Louis XV rooms are spread over three buildings backing onto the forest which make up the Residence: a 19C country house, an "orangery" which can be reached by a glass-covered gallery, and a former coaching inn, 50m away. A fireplace is the centrepiece of a light, airy dining room. As for leisure, the hotel offers a swimming pool with removable roof, tennis courts and a mature wooded park for pre-dinner strolls.

Access : On leaving the village take the lane leading to Hamanxard

 527 **LE VAL JOLI**
Mr and Mrs Laruelle

12 bis Le Village
88230 Le Valtin
Tel. : 03 29 60 91 37
Fax : 03 29 60 81 73
le-val-joli @ wanadoo.fr

Closed from 10 to 18 Mar, from Oct to Nov, Sun evening and Mon evening except during school holidays • 16 rooms, one of which has disabled access, most have bath/WC, all have television • €44 to €70; breakfast €9; half board €30 to €56 • Restaurant closed Mon lunchtime all year; menus €14 (in the week) to €47 • Terrace, garden, car park • Tennis, hiking

 That sound, unlike anything else you have ever heard, is that of a rutting buck!

This appealing country inn almost on the doorstep of the superb Route des Crêtes (Peak Road) has a number of renovated rooms; and all the accommodation overlooks the dense pine forests and mountains. A strong emphasis is given to local produce on the menu and meals are served in the rustic dining room – yes, the 19C carved wooden ceiling is original – or in the more modern veranda. The owner-mayor is a mine of helpful tips about the "panoramic path" around the village, dotted with viewpoints.

Access : In the village, drive along the D 23 from Fraize to the Schlucht Pass

LORRAINE

528 BEAUSÉJOUR
Mr and Mrs Gall

 26 avenue Louis François
88370 Plombières-les-Bains
Tel. : 03 29 66 01 50
Fax : 03 29 66 09 45

Open all year • 23 rooms with bath/WC or shower/WC, all have television • €55; breakfast €7; half board €50 • Menus €13 (in the week) to €26

 A step back in time to the Roaring Twenties.

This spa hotel stands next door to a museum in honour of a local artist, Louis-Français, who was born in the village in 1814. The hotel has retained most of its original paintings, frescoes and furniture, lending it a discreetly old-fashioned charm in perfect keeping with the rest of the resort. The spacious, well-kept rooms are quietest to the rear. The huge dining room has a lovely homely feel to it.

Access : Between the thermal baths and the main shopping streets

529 LE COLLET
Mr and Mrs Lapôtre

 Le Collet
88400 Xonrupt-Longemer
Tel. : 03 29 60 09 57
Fax : 03 29 60 08 77
hotcollet @ aol.com

Closed from 7 to 21 Apr and from 11 Nov to 8 Dec • 21 rooms, all have bath/WC or shower/WC and television • €66; breakfast €9; half board €61 to €67 (€58 to €61 low season) • Restaurant closed Thu lunchtime and Wed; meals €15 (lunchtime in the week) to €26 • Terrace, car park. No dogs allowed in restaurant • Skiing and hiking trails nearby

 A perfect base camp to explore the breathtaking Route des Crêtes (Peak Route).

The walls of this hotel chalet, lost in a forest of fir trees, make it impossible to guess what is inside. For the hospitable owners, entertaining guests does not simply mean providing a cheerful mountain décor with pretty fabrics and painted furniture or a deliciously tempting regional menu: it is above all, a state of mind. Their attention to detail can be felt in the smell of warm brioche in the morning, the wealth of useful tips for walkers or the magic shows for children.

Access : 2km from the Schlucht Pass on the Gérardmer road, by the D 417

MIDI-PYRÉNÉES

Lourdes may be famous as the site of miracles, but some would say that the whole of the Midi-Pyrénées has been uniquely blessed. The region is home to a rich and varied plant and animal life, with the remoter parts of the Pyrenees still supporting a population of brown bears. A great rampart guarding the border with Spain, these breathtaking mountains are riven by spectacularly deep clefts and are drained by rushing torrents. At sunset, the towers of medieval cities and fortresses glow in the evening light; forbidding Cathar castles are stained a bloody red, Albi and its famous fortified cathedral turn crimson while Toulouse is veiled in dusty pink. Deep beneath the surface of the earth at Lascaux and elsewhere are equally extraordinary sights, the vivid cave-paintings of our gifted prehistoric ancestors. To this list of regional marvels must be added the bounteous lands along the River Garonne, a fertile garden famous for its cereal crops, vegetables, fruit and wine. This land of milk and honey has naturally given rise to a host of culinary traditions still practised today, and it would be a crime to leave without sampling a sumptuous cassoulet, confit de canard or foie gras.

87 ESTABLISHMENTS

530 to **616**

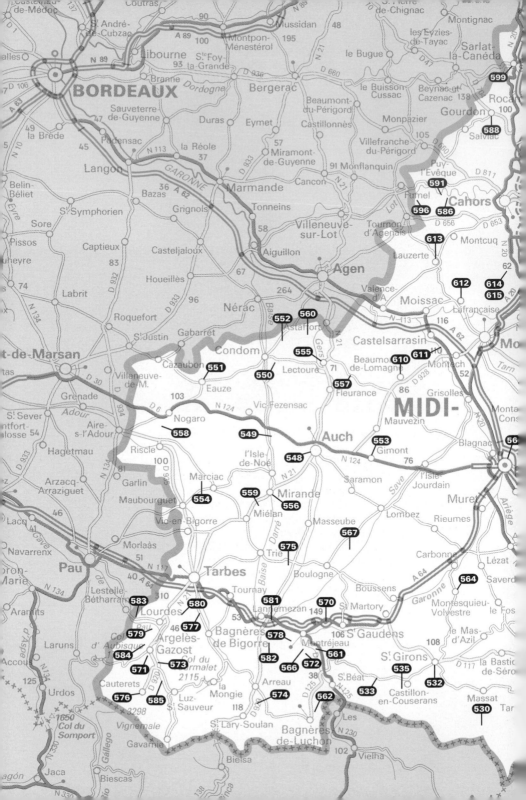

 530 LES OUSSAILLÈS
Mrs Charrue

09140 Aullus-les-Bains
Tel. : 05 61 96 03 68
Fax : 05 61 96 03 70

Open all year • 12 rooms on 2 levels with bath/WC or shower/WC and television • €42 to €49; breakfast €6; half board €43 to €45 (€40 to €43 low season) • Menus €15 to €21 • Terrace, garden, garage. No dogs allowed

 531 AUBERGE LES MYRTILLES
Mr and Mrs Blazy

Col des Marrous
09000 Foix
Tel. : 05 61 65 16 46
Fax : 05 61 65 16 46
aubergelesmyrtilles@wanadoo.fr

Closed from 4 Nov to 1 Feb • 7 rooms, 4 of which are in a separate chalet and 2 have a terrace. Rooms have shower/WC, 2 have bath/WC, all have television • €49 to €63 (€45 to €55 low season); breakfast €6; half board €44 to €51 (€42 to €47 low season) • Menus €14 (in the week) to €23 • Terrace, garden, car park. No dogs allowed in rooms • Indoor swimming pool, sauna, jacuzzi

So friendly, you'll think you're at home.

This 1920s stone house is flanked by a turret. The bedrooms overlooking the garden, by far the most pleasant, enjoy a lovely view of the flourishing green valley. Even better, you can ask for breakfast to be served on your own private balcony. In fine weather, the welcoming restaurant opens onto a shaded terrace.

The two rooms recently renovated in an alpine spirit.

Dig into a piece of blueberry pie, choose a vintage Bordeaux from the wine-list, dive into the swimming pool, walk along the signposted footpath through a beech forest, gaze down on Arget Valley from the terrace, listen to the bucks rutting or just soak up the priceless serenity. Shake them all up and voilà: a delicious "sport and leisure" cocktail! You can of course simply do absolutely nothing from dawn until dusk!

Access : In the heart of the village, 33km to the south-east of Saint-Girons

Access : 19km westbound from Foix on the D 17

 532 **EYCHENNE**
Bordeau family

 8 avenue Paul Laffont
09200 Saint-Girons
Tel. : 05 61 04 04 50
Fax : 05 61 96 07 20
eychen @ club-internet.fr
www.ariege.com/hotel-eychenne

Closed from 1 Dec to 31 Jan, Sun evening and Mon from Nov to Mar (except during holidays) • 41 rooms, all have bath/WC or shower/WC and television • €61 to €99; breakfast €8; half board €58 to €73 (€55 to €69 out of season) • Menus €22 to €50 • Private car park • Swimming pool

 We most liked **The banks of the Salat shaded by a long line of France's most characteristic tree, the plane.**

The Bordeau family has been running this coaching inn for seven generations. This lasting dedication probably explains the quality of the welcome and the deliciously old-fashioned atmosphere that reigns throughout the establishment. The stamp of a family business can be felt everywhere from the scent of beeswax in the bedrooms or the tad outdated wallpaper down to the lovely "retro" lamps. Classic cuisine and full-bodied wines from south-western France take pride of place on the table.

Access : Leave Bd du Général de Gaulle to take Av d'Aulot, then Rue F. Arnaud and turn right

  533 **AUBERGE DE L'ISARD**
Mr and Mrs Do Rosario

09800 Saint-Lary
Tel. : 05 61 96 72 83
Fax : 05 61 04 71 75
aubergeisard @ aol.com
 www.ariege.com/aubergeisard

Closed in Jan • 6 rooms located in 2 buildings, with bath/WC or shower/WC and television • €39 (€36 low season); breakfast €6; half board €41 (€39 low season) • Menus €15 to €24 • Terrace • Shop with local specialities; hiking, mountain biking

 We most liked **The boundless energy of Daniel and Florence, the young owners.**

Hemmed in by steep hillsides and dense forest, this village on the fringe of Ariège is surrounded by picturesque scenery. It is a region well worth exploring and this spanking new traditional hotel-restaurant, which also doubles as the village bar and grocery shop, makes an ideal base camp. Colourful, well-appointed rooms with practical bathrooms, a restaurant reached by a covered footpath spanning a mountain torrent and a wealth of local delicacies behind the counter.

Access : In the heart of the village, on the D 618, near the Portet-d'Aspet Pass

 534 CHAMBRE D'HÔTE M. SAVIGNOL
Mr and Mrs Savignol

 Chemin du Rec
09000 Saint-Paul-de-Jarrat
Tel. : 05 61 64 14 26

Closed from Oct to May • 3 rooms • €40, breakfast included • No table d'hôte • Garden, car park. Credit cards not accepted, no dogs allowed • Outdoor swimming pool

 535 LA GRANDE OURSE
Mrs Matulova

 09800 Salsein
Tel. : 05 61 96 16 51

Open weekends in winter • 3 rooms, one of which is independent. One room has a shower and 2 have a private sitting room and bathroom • €45, breakfast included • Table d'hôte €15 • Car park. Credit cards not accepted

 We most liked

Have you always dreamt of hang-gliding? Now's your chance!

This modern house set in the midst of meadows and woodland was built with materials brought back from Canada by the owner, who also designed the house himself. The interior decoration is just as pleasing as the outside: spacious, comfortable rooms lined in wood and furnished in a 1970s style. The large first floor terrace overlooking the garden is perfect for a quick nap or read.

 We most liked

The sophistication of this mountain dwelling.

This old village house has been beautifully restored. The rooms are tastefully decorated and the one under the eaves boasts a bathroom with a magnificent claw-footed bathtub and an enormous aquarium. Breakfast and meals are taken in the delightful flagstoned kitchen decorated with old furniture. Highly recommended.

Access : 7km to the south-east of Foix on the N 20 then the D 117

Access : 3km westbound from Castillon-en-Couserans

536 LA DÔMERIE
Mr David

12470 Aubrac
Tel. : 05 65 44 28 42
Fax : 05 65 44 21 47

Open from 28 Apr to 31 Oct • 23 rooms on 2 floors with bath/WC or shower/WC, some have television • €50 to €70; breakfast €8; half board €43 to €56 • Restaurant closed Wed lunchtime except in Aug; menus €17 to €35 • Garden, car park. No dogs allowed • Walking

537 HÔTEL DU VIEUX PONT
Mrs Fagegaltier

12390 Belcastel
Tel. : 05 65 64 52 29
Fax : 05 65 64 44 32
hotel-du-vieux-pont@wanadoo.fr
www.hotelbelcastel.com

Closed from 1 Jan to 15 Mar; hotel closed Sun and Mon except in Jul and Aug • 7 rooms in a converted barn, one of which has disabled access, all have bath/WC and television • €74 to €80; breakfast €10; half board €78 to €84 • Restaurant closed Sun evening (except in Jul and Aug), Tue lunchtime and Mon; menus €24 to €61 • Car park

Don't miss your chance to taste a real "aligot" – mashed potato with garlic and local cheese!

Aubrac is justly renowned for its exceptional wild flora, sprawling fields dotted with peacefully grazing light-brown cows and "burons", or cowherds' huts, its vast beech forests and its old Roman road. Countless footpaths criss-cross the region and the owner is more than happy to advise and point you in the right direction! His large house, built in 1870 out of local basalt, offers well-maintained rooms with sturdy farmhouse furniture and a timbered dining room in pale wood.

The village of Belcastel, voted one of the most beautiful in Aveyron.

Two old stone houses stand on either side of the beautiful 15C arched bridge which spans the River Aveyron. The hotel, on the left bank, is home to small rooms with parquet floors, most of which overlook the river. In the summer, breakfast is served in the garden. The restaurant, on the right bank, is an elegant blend of rustic and modern styles; its gourmet dishes do full justice to the excellent local produce and have earned the house "star" status in the Michelin Red Guide since 1991.

Access : In the centre of the village

Access : In the heart of the village, opposite the old bridge

538 LE RELAYS DU CHASTEAU
Mr and Mrs Senegas

12480 Brousse-le-Château
Tel. : 05 65 99 40 15
Fax : 05 65 99 21 25

Closed from 20 Dec to 20 Jan, Fri evening and Sat from Oct to May • 12 rooms with bath/WC or shower/WC • €39 to €41; breakfast €6; half board €34 to €37 • Air-conditioned restaurant; menus €14 to €27 • Car park

539 CHÂTEAU DE CASTELPERS
Mr de Saint-Palais

12170 Requista
Tel. : 05 65 69 22 61
Fax : 05 65 69 25 31

Open from 15 Apr to 15 Oct • 9 rooms, one of which is a suite, with bath/WC or shower/WC and television • €55 to €80; breakfast €8; half board €42 to €59 • Restaurant for guests only; menus €14 to €23, children's menu €10 • Park, car park. No dogs allowed in restaurant • Swimming pool, horse-riding and tennis nearby

The amusing treasure hunt visit around the castle.

Strolling around the shaded park.

St Sernin, birthplace of Victor, the "wild child" of Aveyron "captured" in the woods in 1797 by hunters, is just a few kilometres from this solid country house run by the same family for four generations. All the spotless, practical rooms overlook the fortified castle of Brousse. The dining room with its central fireplace is most welcoming in the winter.

This typical manor house with origins in the 17C was partly rebuilt in Gothic style following a fire in the early 20C. Don't miss the unusual sitting room in what was once the music room. The bedrooms, of varying comfort and a mite faded, are all wonderfully quiet and enjoy the same peaceful view of the park and its huge trees and gurgling stream. A fine fireplace and family portraits grace the restaurant.

Access : In the village, from St-Affrique on the D 999 towards St-Sernin-sur-Rance, then take a right on the D 902

Access : 12.5km to the south-east of Naucelle on the D 997, then the D 10

540 **GRAND HÔTEL AUGUY**
Muylaert-Auguy family

12210 Laguiole
Tel. : 05 65 44 31 11
Fax : 05 65 51 50 81
grand-hotel.auguy@wanadoo.fr

Open from 27 Mar to 11 Nov. Closed Sun evening, Tue lunchtime and Mon except evenings in the summer
• 20 rooms with bath/WC or shower/WC and television
• €70 to €80; breakfast €9; half board €61 to €71 • Menus €26 to €46, children's menu €14 • Garage
• Visits to the Laguiole cutlery workshops nearby

541 **CHÂTEAU DE CREISSELS**
Mr and Mrs Austruy

Route de Saint-Affrique-Creissels
12100 Millau
Tel. : 05 65 60 16 59
Fax : 05 65 61 24 63
www.château-de-creissels.com

Closed in Jan and Feb; hotel closed Sun out of season
• 30 rooms, 2 of which have disabled access, 12 are in the old castle. Most rooms have bath/WC, some have shower/WC, all have television • €53 to €71; breakfast €8; half board €46 to €60 • Restaurant closed Sun evening and Mon lunchtime out of season; menus €21 to €40 • Terrace, garden, car park

 Choosing a 100% authentic Laguiole folding knife in the workshop.

This traditional house is surprisingly dynamic and forward-looking. Book one of the renovated rooms which are smart and modern with balconies overlooking the countryside. The tables of the warm and comfortable wood-lined dining room are laid with Laguiole cutlery, all the better to dig into the sumptuous, well-judged cooking. This is the work of the granddaughter of the Grand Hotel's founder and has earned the restaurant a star in the Michelin Red Guide.

 View of the village and valley.

Chequered parquet floors, wainscoting, a marble fireplace and period furniture: the "Bishop's Room" in the medieval castle can hardly be said to lack character. The others, more everyday, are located in the 1970s wing and have balconies. A vaulted 12C hall houses the restaurant. On fine days, tables are laid outdoors under the arcades of a gallery overlooking the village rooftops.

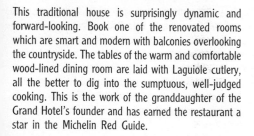

Access : In the town centre

Access : In a small village above Millau, on the road to Albi

542 **L' HERMITAGE SAINT-PIERRE**
Mr and Mrs Macq

Lieu-dit Saint-Pierre-de-Revens
12230 Nant
Tel. : 05 65 62 27 99

Open all year, table d'hôte closed in Jul and Aug
• 5 rooms • €70, breakfast included • Table d'hôte
€16 • Credit cards not accepted, no dogs allowed
• Swimming in the river

543 **HOSTELLERIE DE FONTANGES**
Mr Charrié

Route de Conques
12000 Rodez
Tel. : 05 65 77 76 00
Fax : 05 65 42 82 29
fontanges-hotel @ wanadoo.fr
www.hostellerie-fontanges.com

Open all year • 44 rooms, 4 of which are suites, most
have bath/WC, some have shower/WC, all have television • €60 to €69; breakfast €9; half board €61 to
€66 • Restaurant closed Sat lunch and Sun eve from
15 Oct to 31 Mar; menus €15 (in the week) to
€40 • Terrace, park, car park • Outdoor swimming pool,
tennis

We most liked **The laughter of the children swimming
in the crystal-clear waters of the
Dourbie.**

You can't blame the owners for falling head over heels
with this spot steeped in history which was originally
a chapel (10C and 11C), then a Knights Templar post
and a parish church. Now a B&B establishment, it offers
beautifully decorated rooms whose heritage can still be
seen in any number of details, such as the stone vaults,
period furniture, four-poster beds or a 17C altarpiece.
The garden at the foothills of the Causse Noir and on
the banks of the Dourbie is equally delightful.

We most liked **Authenticity oozes from every crack of
this castle.**

More of a castle than a house, it was built in the 16C
and 17C by a draper from Rodez. Parquet floors and
period furniture grace the bedrooms, most of which have
just been treated to a well-deserved facelift. A huge
fireplace and hunting trophies lend the breakfast room
a lordly air, while the exposed beams of the dining room
set the scene perfectly for traditional country fare. A
municipal golf course is just a few swings away.

Access : 11km to the north-west of Nant towards
Millau on the D 991

Access : 3.5km northbound from Rodez on the
D 901 (towards Marcillac-Vallon)

 544 **LES LANDES**
Mr and Mrs Esperse

 12620 Saint-Beauzely
Tel. : 05 65 62 03 14
domainedeslandes@fr.fm

Open all year • 4 rooms • €64, breakfast included • No table d'hôte • Sitting room, garden, car park. Credit cards not accepted • Outdoor swimming pool, jacuzzi

 545 **MIDI-PAPILLON**
Mr and Mrs Papillon

 12230 Saint-Jean-du-Bruel
Tel. : 05 65 62 26 04
 Fax : 05 65 62 12 97

Open from 23 Mar to 11 Nov • 18 rooms with bath/WC, some have shower/WC • €30 to €33; breakfast €4.50; half board €35 to €37 • Menus €12 (in the week) to €34 • Garden, car park, garage • Outdoor swimming pool

 Unusually decorated rooms.

The sprawling garden and orchard in the middle of nowhere are already a delight in themselves. However you will have to walk up the steps into this 17C and 19C farmhouse and cross the threshold if you want to see the result of the owners' desire to mix old stones with an unusual contemporary décor. The "Empire" and "Muse" rooms and the one with a Philippe Starck bathroom are out of this world. At breakfast, partake of or devour, depending on your appetite, the home-made patisseries and jams.

 A hotel committed to upholding country traditions.

Ten pigs fatted up each year by a local farmer, a full-time gardener supplying fresh fruit and vegetables to the kitchen table, a farmyard full of barn animals and mushrooms picked by shepherds: ever since 1850, the Papillon family has been a perfect illustration of the fierce local desire to remain close to its roots. Personalised bedrooms, without the modern distraction of television, and a restaurant which overlooks the Dourbie and its lovely 15C arched bridge.

Access : 5km from Castelnau towards Saint-Laurent

Access : In the village, on the D 999, next to the stone bridge

546 AU MOULIN D'ALEXANDRE
Mr and Mrs Alexandre

12130 Sainte-Eulalie-d'Olt
Tel. : 05 65 47 45 85
Fax : 05 65 52 73 78

Closed from 22 Apr to 5 May, from 30 Sep to 13 Oct and
Sun evening out of season • 9 rooms, most of which have
shower/WC • €46; breakfast €7; half board €49 • Menus
€10 (lunchtime in the week) to €23 • Terrace, garden

547 HOSTELLERIE DU LÉVEZOU
Mr Bouviala

12410 Salles-Curan
Tel. : 05 65 46 34 16
Fax : 05 65 46 01 19
info @ hostelleriedulevezou.com
www.hostelleriedulevezou.com

Open from Easter to Oct; closed Sun evening and Mon
except in Jul and Aug • 14 rooms with bath/WC or
shower/WC and television • €54 (€46 low season);
breakfast €7; half board €55 (€49 low season) • Menus
€21 to €42 • Terrace, garden • Water sports, swimming
and fishing in Lake Pareloup

**Visiting the cogs and wheels of this
mill-museum.**

The 16C mill in one of Aveyron's most characteristic
medieval villages now houses small and simply
furnished, but exceedingly quiet rooms. The lovely stone
walls and fireplace in the rustic, dark timbered dining
room explain much of its appeal. Whenever the sun is
warm enough, tables are laid outside on a little square.
Relax in the shade of the peaceful back garden.

**Within easy reach of Lake Pareloup
and its water sports and beaches.**

The pleasantly dilapidated air of the façade bears
witness to the age of the walls (14C) of what was once
the summer residence of the bishops of Rodez. The
former guardroom with its lovely stone vaults and dark
wainscoting is now an elegant restaurant: epicureans
can also sample the cooking in the shade of a pleasant
patio terrace. The rooms are due to receive a
well-deserved facelift in the near future.

Access : In the centre of the village, on the
D 6 from Saint-Geniès-d'Olt to Espalion

Access : On the banks of Lake Pareloup, on the
D 993 from Pont-de-Salars to Saint-Affrique

548 FRANCE
Mr Garaud

Place de la Libération
32000 Auch
Tel. : 05 62 61 71 71
Fax : 05 62 71 81
auchgarreau@intelcom.fr

Closed from 2 to 14 Jan • 29 rooms, 22 of which are air-conditioned, all have bath/WC or shower/WC and television • €73 to €104; breakfast €12 • Air-conditioned restaurant; menus €23 (lunchtime in the week) to €45

549 CHAMBRE D'HÔTE MADAME VOUTERS
Mrs Vouters

Engaron
32350 Biran
Tel. : 05 62 64 41 74
Fax : 05 62 64 41 74
www.gascogne.fr/engaron

Closed from Nov to Easter • 3 rooms • €46, breakfast included • No table d'hôte • Garden, car park. Credit cards not accepted, no dogs allowed

---

We most liked
Shopping for local produce in a vaulted cellar.

An old coaching inn with a classical façade houses spacious, more or less personalised rooms, which it is planned to spruce up in the near future, but you can bet your last euro that the room where the film "Le Bonheur est dans le pré" was shot will retain its rococo style. Tasty robust Gascony cuisine is served in a lovely old restaurant which is happy to let the latest fashions pass it by.

We most liked
The epitome of a French country house.

This 1840 farmstead surrounded by fields and swathed in silence enjoys a wonderful view of the Baïse Valley and the slopes of Biran. The colourful rooms upstairs are furnished with antique pieces. Countless leisure activities ranging from balneotherapy, carriage rides, fishing and walking. Leave the kids and pets – neither are admitted! – with mum and enjoy a well-earned break away from it all.

Access : In the town centre

Access : At St-Jean-Poutge, drive towards Brouilh-Mirande-Tarbes (D 939) then after 4km take a left

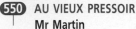

550 AU VIEUX PRESSOIR
Mr Martin

Saint-Fort
32100 Caussens
Tel. : 05 62 68 21 32
Fax : 05 62 68 21 32

Closed for a fortnight in February during the school holidays • 3 rooms • €47, breakfast included • Meals at l'Auberge: €15 to €24 • Terrace, garden, park, car park. No dogs allowed • Outdoor swimming pool, jacuzzi

The lively atmosphere at the weekends.

This lovely old 17C stone house commands a fine view over the vineyards, countryside and the flocks of ducks reared on the property. The rooms, furnished with old pieces, are comfortable and well looked after. The family suite in the attic has been thoughtfully equipped with a games room and a VHS recorder. Farm produce takes pride of place on the dinner table and connoisseurs in search of fine foie gras will not be disappointed.

Access : 11km from Caussens on the D 7 and take a lane on the right

551 CHAMBRE D'HÔTE HOURCAZET
Mr Lejeunne

Hourcazet
32800 Eauze
Tel. : 05 62 09 99 53
Fax : 05 62 09 99 53
claude.lejeunne @ mageos.com

Closed from 1 Nov to Easter. Open out of season by reservation • 4 rooms • €55, breakfast included • No table d'hôte • Terrace, park, car park. Credit cards not accepted

Soaking up the vineyard ambience.

An air of tranquillity reigns in these two houses standing side by side in the midst of Armagnac's vineyards. The rooms are tastefully decorated with beautiful fabrics and furniture and equipped with fine bathrooms. The largest are under the massive beams up in the converted attic, the other two open directly onto the garden. Meals are served in a traditionally decorated dining room or on one of two terraces. Forty winks can be had in the garden complete with pond.

Access : 7km westbound from Eauze on the D 926, then the Barbotan road and a lane on the right

552 DOMAINE DE POLIMON
Mr and Mrs Bolac

32480 Gazaupouy
Tel. : 05 62 28 82 66
Fax : 05 62 28 82 66
philippe.bolac@wanadoo.fr

Closed in Feb • 5 rooms • €60, breakfast included • Table d'hôte €18 • Terrace, garden, park. Credit cards not accepted, no dogs allowed • Outdoor swimming pool, tennis

 We most liked
The antique dealer-owner's impeccable flair and taste.

A long drive of plane trees leads up to this majestic Gascony property set in vast grounds and gardens. The dining room and kitchen are in the main house, but the enormous bedrooms are in the converted outbuildings: an orangery, a wine cellar and a dovecote. The owner, a former antique dealer, chose every single piece of furniture and item of decoration himself. Definitely worth staying a day or two, or three...

Access : 10km northbound from Condom on the D 931

553 AU SOULAN DE LAURANGE
Mr Crochet and Mr Petit

32200 Gimont
Tel. : 05 62 67 76 62
Fax : 05 62 67 76 62
www.canard-au-soulan.com

Closed for one week in January • 4 rooms with bath/WC • €75 to €83, breakfast included • No table d'hôte • Terrace, garden, car park. Credit cards not accepted, no dogs allowed • Outdoor swimming pool

 We most liked
A sweeping view over the Gers hills.

The regular lines and pink hues, the green shutters and the loggia supported by red columns lend this 18C manor house a definite Tuscan air. Perched on a hillside, it offers a superb view over Gascony and the Pyrenees on the horizon. Old furniture adorns the spacious rooms and equally roomy bathrooms which are modern and well equipped. Relaxing around the swimming pool in the garden is sheer bliss.

Access : 5km to the south-west of Gimont, Saramon road (D 12), then a lane on the right

 554 AU CHÂTEAU
Mr and Mrs de Rességuier

 32230 Juillac
Tel. : 05 62 09 37 93
deresseguier @ marciac.net

Closed for one week in October • 3 rooms with bathrooms • €46, breakfast included • Table d'hôte €16 • Terrace, garden, park, car park. Credit cards not accepted, no dogs allowed • Fishing

 555 DE BASTARD
Mr and Mrs Arnaud

 Rue Lagrange
32700 Lectoure
Tel. : 05 62 68 82 44
Fax : 05 62 68 76 81
hoteldebastard @ wanadoo.fr

Closed from 20 Dec to 1 Feb • 29 rooms on 2 floors, all have bath/WC or shower/WC and television • €42 to €61; breakfast €8; half board €49 to €65 • Menus €14 (lunchtime in the week) to €54 • Terrace, garden, garage • Outdoor swimming pool. Bar-lounge

 Lie on your back and gaze up into the branches of the hundred-year-old trees.

Fie, fair visitor! What you see is no castle, but an 18C charterhouse, now the headquarters of a thriving farming business. The rooms, in a separate wing, are vast and tastefully decorated and the bathrooms boast all the modern comforts. As you would expect, a generously spread table d'hôte showcases the wealth of produce grown and reared on the farm. Bicycling, walking and fishing feature among the possible leisure activities, and the owner and mayor of Juillac is a wonderful source of advice.

 One for all and all for one.

Your quest for a harbour in Gascony is over! Despite its name, the breeding of this 18C house is flawless. Elegance and opulence reign throughout. Progressively renovated rooms, a string of sophisticated sitting and dining rooms with parquet floors, moulded ceilings and fireplaces, a pleasant garden terrace, a cottage with a sitting room-bar for lovers of good cigars and Armagnac and succulent cooking worthy of the most demanding musketeers among you.

Access : 5km westbound from Marciac, towards Juillac on the D 255

Access : From Agen, follow Rue d'Alsace-Lorraine, turn left at the post office, then right on Rue Subervie, then left again

556 AU PRÉSIDENT
Mr Piquemil

32300 Mirande
Tel. : 05 62 66 64 06
Fax : 05 62 66 64 06
jacques.piquemil@wanadoo.fr
www.chez.com/aupresident

Open all year • 4 rooms, 2 of which are on garden level, with bathrooms • €46, breakfast included • No table d'hôte • Terrace, garden, car park. Credit cards not accepted, no dogs allowed • Billiards, play area

557 LA GARLANDE
Mr Cournot

Place de la Mairie
32380 Saint-Clar
Tel. : 05 62 66 47 31
Fax : 05 62 66 47 70
nicole.cournot@wanadoo.fr

Closed from 1 Nov to Easter • 3 rooms with bathrooms • €55, breakfast included • Table d'hôte €16 • Garden. Credit cards not accepted, no dogs allowed

Trying your luck on the billiards table in the elegant sitting room.

This lovely abode flanked with turrets belonged to the president of Mirande's law courts during the first half of the 20C, hence its name. The bedrooms with sloping ceilings all have brand new bathrooms. Those on the ground floor are enormous and adorned with family heirlooms. In the winter, breakfast is served by the fireside in the huge dining room and in a sheltered courtyard in the summer. Pretty garden.

Harmony abounds in all the rooms.

Standing firmly four-square on its arcades, this beautiful, rambling house with an ochre façade is in the heart of the village opposite a 16C hall. The rooms, decorated with tapestries and well-polished antiques, have retained their original parquet or tiled floors. The bathrooms have been renovated. The reading room and walled herb garden are perfect places to relax. Guests have the use of a summer kitchen.

Access : 3km northbound from Mirande on the N 21 route d'Auch

Access : Opposite the covered market

 558 AUBERGE DU BERGERAYRE
Mrs Sarran

 32110 Saint-Martin-d'Armagnac
Tel. : 05 62 09 08 72
Fax : 05 62 09 09 74

Closed in Jan and Feb • 13 rooms located in 2 buildings, all are on the ground floor. Rooms have bath/WC or shower/WC and television • €54; breakfast €7; half board €60 to €77 • Restaurant (closed Tue and Wed) is only for half board guests • Terrace, garden, car park

 559 DOMAINE DE LORAN
Mr and Mrs Nédellec

 32300 Saint-Maur
Tel. : 05 62 66 51 55

Closed from 1 Nov to Easter • 2 rooms and 2 suites with bathrooms • €45, breakfast included • No table d'hôte • Park, car park. Credit cards not accepted, no dogs allowed • Billiards

 Taste a slice of Gascony pastis (pie), flamed with Armagnac!

If words such as foie gras, magret, cèps, Armagnac, tradition, farm or family fail to bring to a gleam to your eye, then read no further. Otherwise make a beeline for this little corner of Gascony where country life still has meaning and take a seat in one of the three rustic dining rooms, or on the terrace overlooking the famous Armagnac vineyards. As for accommodation, you can choose a welcoming rural style or a modern atmosphere and a private terrace.

Access : 8km to the south-west of Nogaro on the D 25, then take a minor road

 Fishing in the lake hidden in the park.

Two towers, a long colonnade of plane trees and parkland graced with huge old trees make this old Gascony farm look more like a castle. A lovely old wooden staircase will take you up to the spacious rooms fitted out with old furniture; the two suites are particularly worth a look. The immense dining room on the ground floor with dark wainscoting is furnished with lovely antiques. Fishing, billiards and table-tennis will keep you amused for hours.

Access : From the N 21 take the long lane that leads to the Domaine de Loran

560 **CHAMBRE D'HÔTE LE SABATHÉ**
Mr and Mrs Barreteau

Le Sabathé
32700 Saint-Mézard
Tel. : 05 62 28 84 26

Open all year • 4 rooms • €37, breakfast included • Table d'hôte €12 • Terrace, car park. Credit cards not accepted

561 **HOSTELLERIE DE L'ARISTOU**
Mr Géraud

Route de Sauveterre
31510 Barbazan
Tel. : 05 61 88 30 67
Fax : 05 61 95 55 66

Closed from 10 Dec to 12 Feb, Sun evening and Mon from 8 Sep to 1 May • 7 rooms, 2 of which are non-smoking, most have bath/WC, all have television • €51; breakfast €7; half board €48 • Menus €17 to €32 • Terrace, garden, private car park. No dogs allowed

Take refuge in this sanctuary of meditation.

Tai Chi sessions are organised every morning in this unaffected, almost monastic abode. The old farm on the doorstep of the town aims to provide sanctuary to those in search of a place for meditation. The rooms, spread throughout the outbuildings, are all fully independent. Depending on the weather, meals are served by the fireside in the dining room or on a tiny walled terrace in front of the main hall, overlooking the chapel of Notre-Dame-d'Esclaux.

The view from the windows is so pretty you will wish you could paint.

This farm, dating from 1832, has been converted into a smartly-kept country inn with apple-green shutters. Painted or antique furniture adorns the rooms, some of which have canopied beds. The dining rooms display the owners' eclectic tastes with 70s-style ornaments alongside classic oil paintings and delightfully outdated floral wallpaper; tables are laid in the inner garden-courtyard when the sun comes out.

Access : 12km northbound on the D 36

Access : To the south-west of Saint-Gaudens, on the outskirts of the village

 562 LE POUJASTOU
Mr Cottereau

Rue du Sabotier
31110 Juzet-de-Luchon
Tel. : 05 61 94 32 88
Fax : 05 61 94 32 88
info @ lepoujastou.com
www.lepoujastou.com

Closed in Nov • 5 rooms upstairs, all have bath/WC or shower/WC • €44, breakfast included • Table d'hôte €13 • Terrace, garden, car park. Credit cards not accepted, no dogs allowed

 563 CHAMBRE D'HÔTE BIGOT
Mr Pinel

Lieu-dit Bigot
31450 Montesquieu-Lauragais
Tel. : 05 61 27 02 83
Fax : 05 61 27 02 83
joseph.pinel @ libertysurf.fr
www.perso.libertysurf.fr/hotebigot

Closed for one week in February • 5 rooms, one of which has a jacuzzi • €45 to €55, breakfast included • No table d'hôte • Sitting room, terrace, car park. Credit cards not accepted, no dogs allowed • Outdoor swimming pool

 Your alpine guide-host organises snowshoe excursions in winter and mountain biking in the summer.

This large south-facing house, which commands fine views of the Luchonnais peaks, began life as the village's concert hall in the 18C. Stylishly renovated, it now offers brand new ochre-coloured bedrooms, some sizeable, others more compact. A warm sitting room lined with works on the region's fauna and flora and a Pyrenean-style dining room are on the ground floor. A terrace, garden and finely-flavoured home cooking round off the picture of an excellent establishment.

 The marriage of old and new.

You won't be disappointed by the comfort of this fully renovated 17C farmhouse. Beautiful old furniture, in the family for donkey's years or picked up in local antique shops, graces the rooms, one of which has a jacuzzi bathtub. The old beams, brick walls and original mangers of the former stables add character to the breakfast room. The huge covered terrace is very pleasant in fine weather.

Access : Near the church

Access : 5km to the north-east on the D 11, take the lane on the left after the A 61, towards Villenouvelle

 564 **LA HALTE DU TEMPS**
Mrs Garcin

72 rue Mage
31310 Montesquieu-Volvestre
Tel. : 05 61 97 56 10
Fax : 05 61 90 49 03

Open all year • 5 rooms with bathrooms • €54, breakfast included • Table d'hôte €18 • Garden. Credit cards not accepted, no dogs allowed • Outdoor swimming pool

 We most liked **Madame's exceptional story-telling talents.**

Cross the charming inner courtyard to reach this elegant 17C mansion in the heart of town: the façade may not seem inspiring but the fully original staircases, floors and furniture make it well worth a stay. Superb, exquisitely decorated bedrooms with alcove bathrooms. The lovely dining room with a huge fireplace is quite the equal of the delicious cuisine.

Access : In the town centre

 565 **AUBERGE DES MAZIÈS**
Mr and Mrs Garnier

Route de Castres
31250 Revel
Tel. : 05 61 27 69 70
Fax : 05 62 18 06 37
bienvenue@mazies.com
www.mazies.com

Closed from 28 Oct to 12 Nov and from 26 Dec to 21 Jan • 7 rooms, 3 of which are air-conditioned, with shower/WC, all have television • €49; breakfast €6; half board €42 • Restaurant closed Sun evening and Mon; menus €12 (lunchtime in the week) to €40 • Terrace, garden, car park. No dogs allowed in rooms

 We most liked **A proper country inn.**

Get back to grass roots in this former farmhouse, now a rustic inn, set in the secluded fields around Revel. Sleep to your heart's content in the comfortable rooms. Exposed beams and a fireplace set the scene of the two rustic dining rooms. In the summer, it is impossible not to linger on the pleasant terrace which lines the manicured garden as you take in the sweeping view. Wonderfully welcoming family.

Access : To the north, 3km on the Castres road

 566 DU COMMINGES
Mrs Alaphilippe

 Place de la Basilique
31510 Saint-Bertrand-de-Comminges
Tel. : 05 61 88 31 43
Fax : 05 61 94 98 22

Open from Apr to Oct and closed on Thu • 14 rooms, most have bath/WC or showers, with or without WC • €64, breakfast • No restaurant • Small car park. No dogs allowed

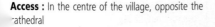 **The peace and quiet of a convent.**

Overlooking the forecourt of the fascinating Cathédrale Ste-Marie, this hotel was once a convent and it cannot be faulted for its peace and quiet, particularly in the summer, when the square is entirely free of cars. The guests' quarters and rooms are all fitted with handsome country furniture. During the long summer months, a pleasant terrace is laid under an arbour behind the main building. Run by the same family for three generations, it is a place you will remember.

Access : In the centre of the village, opposite the cathedral

---

567 HÔTELLERIE DU LAC
Mr and Mrs Maréchal

 Avenue Pierre-Paul Riquet
31250 Saint-Ferréol
Tel. : 05 62 18 70 80
Fax : 05 62 18 71 13

Closed from 23 Dec to 2 Jan (restaurant closed until 15 Jan) • 25 rooms, 4 of which are split-level (with kitchenettes), one has disabled access, all have bath/WC and television • €51 to €56; breakfast €6; half board €48 • Restaurant closed Sun evening except in Jul and Aug; menus €14 (in the week) to €32 • Terrace, garden, car park. No dogs allowed in rooms • Heated outdoor swimming pool

 The view of the lake from the striking terraced swimming pool

If the locals are to be believed, Saint Ferréol, the local patron saint, continues to watch over the tranquillity of this elegant lakeside house surrounded by greenery. A masterful renovation has left the original character of the place intact: most of the rooms share a splendid view of the lake with the exquisite swimming pool. When it comes to relaxing, the warm sitting room-bar, sauna, fitness room and quaint garden are also worthy of mention. Classic dishes on a traditional menu.

Access : Overlooking the lake, 3km to the south-east of Revel on the D 629

568 LAFLÂNERIE
Mr Grobois

Vieille Toulouse Sud
31120 Vieille Toulouse
Tel. : 05 61 73 39 12
Fax : 05 61 73 18 56

Closed from 10 to 21 Feb • 12 rooms, 4 of which are air-conditioned, all have bath/WC or shower/WC and television • €67 to €98; breakfast €8 • No restaurant • Park, car park • Outdoor swimming pool

569 CHÂTEAU DES VARENNES
Mr and Mrs Mericq

31450 Varennes
Tel. : 05 61 81 69 24
Fax : 05 61 81 69 24
j.mericq@wanadoo.fr

Open all year • 5 rooms with bath/WC • €76, breakfast included • Table d'hôte €30 • Terrace, garden, park, car park. Credit cards not accepted • Outdoor swimming pool. Tennis and horse-riding nearby

Lovely view of the Garonne Valley.

Almost hidden by ivy, the carving over the door to this unassuming manor house indicates that it was built in 1790. The somewhat old-fashioned rooms are furnished in a variety of styles – Empire, Louis XVI, etc; those overlooking the main façade are more spacious. A circular fireplace takes pride of place in the sitting room, which overlooks the Garonne, as do the extensive grounds and swimming pool.

The view of the slopes of Lauragais from the swimming pool.

The magic begins from the moment you set foot in the park of this 16C castle next to the church. Push open the iron gate, venture into the wonderful courtyard and through a heavy wooden door into the main pink brick building, where you will find yourself gazing up at a double flight of stairs. Superbly exotic colours adorn the "Bédouin" room on the ground floor and those upstairs are equally elegant and opulent. The sitting rooms and vaulted cellars add the finishing touch.

Access : 9km from Toulouse on the D 4, then take the Lacroix-Falgarde road

Access : 15km westbound from Saint-Félix on the Toulouse road (D 2)

 570 HOSTELLERIE DES CÈDRES
Mr Jaffré

31800 Villeneuve-de-Rivière
Tel. : 05 61 89 36 00
Fax : 05 61 88 31 04
information @ hotel-descedres.com
www.hotel-descedres.com

Open all year. Restaurant closed Sun evening, Tue lunchtime and Mon from Nov to Mar • 20 rooms located in the main building and in a separate wing in the garden, all have bath/WC or shower/WC and television • €61 to €77; breakfast €9; half board €61 to €69 • Menus €22 to €54 • Terrace, garden, car park • Outdoor swimming pool

The white-calf market at St Gaudens.

This 16C monastery, bought by the Montespan family in the 17C, and its old doors, mullioned windows and stone staircases still bear witness to its glorious past. The watchful eye of the Marquise of Montespan and mistress of none other than the Sun King himself, gazes benevolently down as you sit in the recently refurbished dining room. Thick stone walls protect the traditional rooms from the hot summer sun. Magnificent old cedars, the hotel's namesake, stretch their branches in the garden.

Access : 5km westbound from Saint-Gaudens on the N 117

 571 CHAMBRE D'HÔTE MADAME VERMEIL
Mrs Vermeil

3 rue du Château
65400 Arcizans-Avant
Tel. : 05 62 97 55 96
Fax : 05 62 97 55 96

Open all year • 3 rooms • €38, breakfast included • No table d'hôte • Credit cards not accepted, no dogs allowed

A panoramic wide-screen view of the valley.

This handsome 19C house boasts a wealth of attractions. Wood prevails in the attic rooms – walls, floors and furniture – which afford a fine view of the valley or the mountains. Guests have the run of a kitchen, a pleasant garden and a dining room with a relief map of the Pyrenees: plan your next expedition over a coffee and feel free to ask for advice from the owner, a mountain guide who speaks from experience.

Access : 5km southbound from Argelès on the D 101 then the D 13

  572 LE MOULIN D'AVEUX
Mr and Mrs Vayssières

6 avenue de l'Ourse
65370 Aveux
Tel. : 05 62 99 20 68
Fax : 05 62 99 22 27

Closed from 14 to 22 Oct, 25 Nov to 3 Dec, Mon and Tue from Oct to May, Wed from Jun to Sep • 10 rooms with bath/WC or shower/WC • €33 to €42; breakfast €6; half board €36 • Menus €13 (lunchtime in the week) to €37 • Riverside terrace, garden, car park. No dogs allowed • Fishing (lessons available), walks and excursions in the Barousse Valley

We most liked
Fly fishing in the turbulent waters of the Ourse.

This old mill lies in a hamlet in the middle of nowhere in the secluded valley of Barousse. The fast-flowing Ourse alongside the hotel will send you to sleep. You can admire the stonework in the rustic dining room or contemplate the countryside from the lush green terrace poised between millpond and stream. What better place to spend a few relaxing days in the countryside? The owner, a keen angler, delights in sharing his knowledge of the area with other like-minded souls.

Access : 4km southbound from Saint-Bertrand-de-Comminges, on the Mauléon-Barousse road (D 925)

  573 ETH BÉRYÈ PETIT
Mr and Mrs Vielle

15 route de Vielle
65400 Beaucens
Tel. : 05 62 97 90 02
contact@beryepetit.com

Closed from 15 Dec to 15 Jan • 3 rooms with bathrooms • €49, breakfast included • Credit cards not accepted, no dogs allowed

We most liked
The lady of the house's gracious welcome.

This country house, whose name means "little orchard" in Occitan, was built in 1790 in the purest traditions of regional architecture. Tastefully decorated rooms overlook the Lavedan and the Pyrenean peaks, the one upstairs is the most spacious and leads out onto a balcony which runs along the entire length of the façade. There are two others under the eaves. Breakfast is always a delight by the fireside or on the terrace.

Access : 8.5km to the south-east of Argelès on the D 100, then take a minor road

 574 LA COUETTE DE BIÉCOU
Mrs Moreilhon

 65170 Camparan
Tel. : 05 62 39 41 10

Open all year • 3 rooms • €39, breakfast included • No table d'hôte • Car park. Credit cards not accepted, no dogs allowed

 575 CHAMBRE D'HÔTE DORIT WEIMER
Mr Dorit Weimer

 Aries-Espénan
65230 Castelnau-Magnoac
Tel. : 05 62 39 81 85
Fax : 05 62 39 81 85
www.poterie.fr

Open from 15 May to 31 Dec • 5 rooms with bathrooms and separate WC • €52, breakfast included • Table d'hôte €15.50 • Reading room. Credit cards not accepted, no dogs allowed

 Stupendous view of the valley and the Pyrenean peaks.

Right in the heart of town, this attractive stone farm with flower-decked balconies commands a matchless view of the valley and the Pyrenees. Wood sets the tone in the cosy rooms which enjoy exceptional views, one of which overlooks Saint-Lary-Soulan. The hospitable owners are both genial souls and if you're lucky, you'll be able to see how the local "gâteau à la broche" is made, even lending a welcome helping hand in the four hours of spit-roasting in front of the fire.

Access : 4km northbound, on the Arreau road and then turn right

 Open the door and breathe in the perfume of yesteryear.

Time and care have clearly been lavished over the restoration of this 14C mill next door to an attractive manor whose stylish interior reveals original wood floors, an ancient staircase and latched doors. White prevails in the spacious rooms with king-size beds and well-equipped bathrooms. In the mill are a reading and television room and a small bar, all set against the backdrop of the old millstones. Forget about your diet and treat yourself to Gascony's delicacies!

Access : 12km northbound from Castelnau-Magnoac on the D 929, then turn right on the D 166

 576 GRANGE SAINT-JEAN
Mr Igau

Quartier Calypso
65110 Cauterets
Tel. : 05 62 92 58 58

Closed for 2 weeks in May and 2 weeks in November
• 3 rooms • €69, breakfast included • No table d'hôte
• Terrace, garden, car park. Credit cards not accepted,
no dogs allowed

 577 MAISON BURRET
Mr Cazaux

67 place du Cap de la Vielle
65200 Montgaillard
Tel. : 05 62 91 54 29
Fax : 05 62 91 52 42

Open all year • 3 rooms, one of which is a suite • €46,
breakfast included • Table d'hôte €16 • Garden, car park.
Credit cards not accepted

 We most liked
**Stretching out in the warmth after a
day in the open air.**

The blue and yellow walls of this old wood barn never
fail to catch the eye. A mountain flavour has been given
to the beautifully restored interior in the form of
wood-lined walls, occasionally breached by stone, warm
colours and family furniture. The rooms are very
peaceful and one has a private terrace. Children adore
romping about the garden and immense meadow at an
altitude of 900m, in sight of the Pyrenees.

 We most liked
Authentic and anachronistic.

Countless original architectural features are still visible
in this lovely farmhouse, dating from 1791, such as the
dovecote, bakery, stables, cowshed and collection of old
agricultural machinery. The comfortable rooms have
been decorated with some fine antique pieces and in
the winter a fire is lit in the one on the ground floor.
Meals are served in a friendly dining room whose
centrepiece is a handsome carved staircase.

Access : On the Lourdes road

Access : 5km northbound from Pouzac on the D 935

MIDI-PYRÉNÉES

578 **LE RELAIS DU CASTERA**
Mr Latour

65150 Nestier
Tel. : 05 62 39 77 37
Fax : 05 62 39 77 29

Closed from 1 to 8 Jun, from 4 to 26 Jan, Sun evening,
Mon, Tue evening (out of season) • 7 rooms upstairs, all
have shower/WC, some have television • €45 to €49;
breakfast €7; half board €43 to €49 • Menus €17 (lunchtime in the week) to €42 • Terrace

579 **LES ROCAILLES**
Mr Fanlou

65100 Omex
Tel. : 05 62 94 46 19
Fax : 05 62 94 33 35
muriellefanlou @ aol.com

Closed from 1 Nov to late Jan • 3 rooms • €54, breakfast
included • Table d'hôte €17 • Garden, car park. Credit
cards not accepted, no dogs allowed • Outdoor swimming pool

 The delicious cassoulet simmering on the stove

The village in the Comminges region is dominated by
Mount Arès and its unusual calvary of twelve shrines
on the slope. The inn offers recently renovated rooms
in an up-to-date style and a welcoming restaurant
renowned for its generous traditional cooking which
makes the most of local ingredients. The almost
sophisticated rustic interior makes it a pleasant stopping
place near the attractive walled town of Montréjeau.

 The discreet luxury of this snug little nest.

It is impossible not to be won over by the charm of this
small stone house with comfortably modern rooms. One
of the rooms, named "The Seamstress" by the owner
and former wardrobe mistress of the Paris Opera House,
is home to an old sewing machine and a mannequin;
it also has a private terrace. Those under the eaves are
air-conditioned and command a fine view of the valley.
A fireplace and old furniture set the scene in the dining
room and the flowered garden and swimming pool are
most welcome.

Access : Westbound from Montréjeau, take the
D 638 then the D 938 as far as Saint-Laurent-de-Neste
and turn left

Access : 4.5km to the south-west of Lourdes on the
D 13 then the D 213

ORINCLES - 65380 | PINAS - 65300

 580 LE MOULIN D'ORINCLES
Mrs Grimbert

 Passage du Moulin
65380 Orincles
Tel. : 05 62 45 40 65
Fax : 05 62 45 60 50
moulindo @ free.fr

Closed in Nov and Dec • 3 rooms and one gîte • €49, breakfast included • Table d'hôte €17, except Wed • Garden, car park. Credit cards not accepted, no dogs allowed • Spa, jacuzzi

 The murmur of the stream running through the property.

This recently restored cereal mill has nonetheless retained its soul. You can admire the impressive millstones and other mechanical components which are still visible in the sitting and dining rooms. The bedrooms' names – "Corn", "Wheat" and "Barley" – bear proud witness to the mill's past, and exposed beams, hand-stencilled motifs, old furniture and ochre colour-scheme further add to their appeal. The stream running through the courtyard, also home to a kitchen garden, completes the picture.

Access : 3km to the north-west of Loucrup on the D 937 then the D 407

581 DOMAINE DE JEAN-PIERRE
Mrs Colombier

 65300 Pinas
Tel. : 05 62 98 15 08
Fax : 05 62 98 15 08
marie.colombier @ wanadoo.fr
www.domainedejeanpierre.com

Open all year, by reservation only in winter • 3 rooms upstairs • €45, breakfast included • No table d'hôte • Park. Credit cards not accepted, no dogs allowed • Tennis and golf nearby

 Long walks in the country.

This handsome house covered in Virginia creeper stands at an altitude of 600m on the plateau of Lannemezan, looking south towards the Pyrenees. Old furniture and pretty fabrics adorn the spacious, quiet rooms, all of which overlook the beautifully cared-for grounds. The distant notes of a piano being played in the sitting room can sometimes be heard. In the summer, breakfast is served on the terrace. Simple, cordial welcome.

Access : 200m eastbound from the town on the D158

  582 DOMAINE DE VÉGA
Mr and Mrs Mun

65250 Saint-Arroman
Tel. : 05 62 98 96 77
Fax : 05 62 98 96 77

Closed from Nov to Jan • 5 rooms with bath/WC or shower/WC • €40, breakfast included • Table d'hôte €19 • Park, car park. Credit cards not accepted, no dogs allowed • Swimming pool

  583 LE GRAND CÈDRE
Mr Peters

6 rue du Barry
65270 Saint-Pé-de-Bigorre
Tel. : 05 62 41 82 04
Fax : 05 62 41 85 89
chp @ grandcedre.com
www.grandcedre.com

Open all year • 4 rooms with bathrooms • €57, breakfast included • Table d'hôte €21 • Terrace, park, car park. Credit cards not accepted

We most liked
Lovely landscaped garden and grounds.

Originally built in the 16C, this manor house was the property of a Russian prince in the Belle Époque and a Buddhist centre in the 1970s. Now a B&B, it offers pleasant rooms named after flowers, with unusual carved headboards. All overlook the cedars, giant thuja and linden trees in the park and the countryside beyond. In the kitchen, the chef prepares imaginative recipes based on regional produce.

We most liked
Botanical walks in the park.

This 17C country seat owes its name to the three-hundred-year-old cedar planted in the centre of the park, which casts a welcome shade over a few garden chairs. Each of the personalised rooms, linked by an outdoor gallery, is in a different style: Art Deco, Louis-Philippe, Henry II and Louis XV. The music room and piano, the classical dining room, the greenhouse with orchids, geraniums and cacti and the delightful cottage garden are a delight for the eyes.

Access : 11km northbound from Sarrancolin on the D 929 then the D 26

Access : In the village

584 LE BELVÉDÈRE
Mrs Crampe

6 rue de l'Église
65400 Salles
Tel. : 05 62 97 23 65
Fax : 05 62 97 23 68
le-belvedere @ wanadoo.fr

Closed in Nov • 4 rooms and one gîte with shower/WC
• €48, breakfast included • Table d'hôte €15 • Park, car
park. Credit cards not accepted, no dogs allowed
• Excursions to the mountains

585 LA GRANGE AUX MARMOTTES
Mr and Mrs Senac

Dans le village
65120 Viscos
Tel. : 05 62 92 88 88
Fax : 05 62 92 93 75

Closed from 15 Nov to 15 Dec • 6 rooms with bath/WC
or shower/WC and television • €52 to €64; breakfast
€10; half board €49 to €55 • Menus €19 (in the week)
to €34 • Terrace, garden • Outdoor swimming pool

**The enchanting perspective from this
18C abode.**

The sweeping view of the valleys of Luz, Cauterets and
Arrens with the Pyrenean peaks in the distance from this
handsome manor house does full justice to its name.
The rooms under the eaves are modern in flavour while
those on the first floor are decorated with lovely old
furniture and a fireplace; all enjoy the same view. In
the winter, meals are served by the fireside and in the
summer under an arbour.

Heaven for sleepyheads and marmots.

The region is so untamed and rich in spectacular natural
sights that you will spend all your days out exploring
until the mountain cows come home! This old stone
barn, with its cosy rooms and perfect peace and quiet
are just what you need when your head finally does
touch the pillow. The sun will already be high in the
sky before you're ready to get up and feast your eyes
on the sumptuous view of the valley, hemmed in all
sides by peaks and summits.

Access : 12.5km southbound from Lourdes on the
N 21 then the D 102

Access : To the north-west of Luz-Saint-Sauveur
towards Pierrefitte-Nestalas

586 MARLIAC
Mrs Stroobant

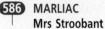

46140 Bélaye
Tel. : 05 65 36 95 50
Fax : 05 65 31 99 04

Closed from late Oct to mid-Apr • 5 rooms • €61, breakfast included • Table d'hôte €12 to €17 • Park, car park. Credit cards not accepted, no dogs allowed

Close your eyes and listen to the sound of silence.

A long, winding lane leads to this 18C farmhouse, a haven of peace and quiet in the midst of over 10 acres of woods and fields. You will want to unpack your cases and spend time in the tastefully decorated utterly calm rooms; two of which are on split levels. The breakfast room has preserved its beams, stonework and the old oven. Engaging welcome.

Access : 15km westbound from Luzech on the D 8 and the D 50

587 CHAMPOLLION
Mrs Pradayrol

3 place Champollion
46100 Figeac
Tel. : 05 65 34 04 37
Fax : 05 65 34 61 69

Open all year • 10 rooms on 2 floors, one of which has disabled access, all have bath/WC and television • €45, breakfast €6 • No restaurant

The Gothic architectural legacy of Figeac which rivals the Champollion Museum.

The Champollion Museum's mummy and sarcophagi and a giant reproduction of the Rosetta Stone in the Place des Écritures leave you in no doubt that you have reached the birthplace of one of France's most famous Egyptologists. The rooms of this medieval house in the historic town of Figeac are modern in flavour with wood floors and practical black lacquered furniture.

Access : Near Place des Écritures, in the heart of the city

 588 **DOMAINE DU BERTHIOL**
Mrs Ribet

Route de Cahors
46300 Gourdon
Tel. : 05 65 41 33 33
Fax : 05 65 41 14 52
le.berthiol @ accesinter.com
hotelperigord.com

Open from Apr to 1 Nov • 29 rooms with bath/WC or
shower/WC and television • €75 (€67 low season);
breakfast €10; half board €71 (€64 low season) • Air-
conditioned restaurant; closed Tue, Wed and Thu lunch;
menus €16 (lunchtime in the week) to €44 • Park, car
park. No dogs allowed in rooms • Outdoor swimming
pool, tennis

 Lush green countryside.

On the outskirts of the town in the middle of a beautifully
maintained park, this impressive country house offers
identical rooms with fully equipped bathrooms. Tennis
courts, swimming pool and children's play area. The
contemporary dining room opens onto the pleasant
greenery. The menu shows a marked preference for local
produce. Immense banquet hall in another wing.

Access : 1km eastbound from Gourdon on the
D 704

 589 **LE LION D'OR**
Mr and Mrs Momméjac

8 place de la République
46500 Gramat
Tel. : 05 65 38 73 18
Fax : 05 65 38 84 50
lion.d.or @ wanadoo.fr
www.liondorhotel.com

Closed from 15 Dec to 15 Jan • 15 rooms, most have
bath/WC, some have shower/WC, all are air-conditioned
and have television • €53 to €76; breakfast €9; half board
€78 (€68 low season) • Air-conditioned restaurant,
closed Thu and Fri from Oct to May; menus €26 to
€54 • Terrace, park, garage

 A real cottage garden.

This stone hostelry built in 1800 lies in the heart of the
small capital of the causse de Gramat. Although the
rooms are a mite old-fashioned and not enormous, the
house is not lacking in appeal: a classical dining room
serving a sophisticated, modern menu, a flowered
terrace shaded by an arbour and 200m away, the park
where you can wander under the branches of cedar and
pine trees.

Access : In the town centre, on the main square

  590 **MOULIN DE FRESQUET**
Mr and Mrs Ramelot

46500 Gramat
Tel. : 05 65 38 70 60
Fax : 05 65 38 70 60

Closed from Nov to Mar • 5 non-smoking rooms with bathrooms • €68, breakfast included • Table d'hôte €19 • Park, car park

 591 **CHÂTEAU DE LA COSTE**
Mr Coppé

46700 Grézels
Tel. : 05 65 21 34 18
Fax : 05 65 21 38 28
gervaiscoppe@wanadoo.fr

Open all year • 5 rooms • €61, breakfast included • No table d'hôte • Credit cards not accepted, no dogs allowed

 Wining and dining by candlelight on Périgord's succulent fare.

The good life at its best! This authentic 17C water mill stands in an idyllic rural spot, just 800m from the centre of Gramat. Lovely furniture and tapestries, exposed stonework and beams and a profusion of good books set the scene for the interior. Most of the comfortable, elegant rooms have a view of the enchanting shaded garden and the stream, much prized by fishermen. Gracious hosts and wonderful food.

 The Cahors Wine Museum within the walls of this fortified castle.

If you're passing through, this medieval fortress dominating the Lot Valley is definitely worth a visit. Character abounds in the rooms which have been given evocative names such as "Study of the setting sun", "Lookout tower" and "Squire's abode" all are furnished with lovely period pieces. In addition, the striking dining room commands an exceptional view. Don't leave without visiting the Wine Museum.

Access : On the way into Gramat

Access : 16km westbound from Luzech on the D 8

592 LA TERRASSE
Mr Amalric

Le Bourg
46120 Lacapelle-Marival
Tel. : 05 65 40 80 07
Fax : 05 65 40 99 45
terrasse2@wanadoo.fr

Closed 2 Jan to early Mar, Sun evening, Mon except evenings in summer, Tue lunchtime out of season • 13 rooms, all have bath/WC or shower/WC and television • €41 to €49; breakfast €7; half board €43 to €46 • Menus €13 to €34 • Garden

593 CHÂTEAU DE GAMOT
Mr and Mrs Belières

46130 Loubressac
Tel. : 05 65 10 92 03

Closed in Oct and Apr • 7 rooms, some have bathrooms • €57, breakfast included • No table d'hôte • Garden, car park. Credit cards not accepted, no dogs allowed

Forty winks in the flower garden.

The hotel is next door to the massive square keep, flanked by the towers of the castle of Lacapelle. Practical, recently renovated rooms and a light, airy veranda-dining room whose bay windows overlook the pretty garden on the banks of a stream, with the Francès Valley in the background. Park and private fishing 2km away.

Conveniently located near Quercy's main tourist attractions.

The allure of this rambling 17C stately home and its pastoral setting opposite the castle of Castelnau never fails to weave its magic spell. The comfortable rooms are well proportioned. Guests who visit in June and September enjoy the run of the owners' private swimming pool. Other leisure activities in the vicinity include a 9-hole golf course, tennis courts and horse-riding.

Access : Near the castle

Access : 5km westbound from St-Céré on the D 673 and the D 30

 594 **LES TILLEULS**
Mrs Ménassol

 46160 Marcilhac-sur-Célé
Tel. : 05 65 40 62 68
 Fax : 05 65 40 74 01

Closed from 16 Nov to 16 Dec • 5 rooms • €40, breakfast included • No table d'hôte • Park, car park. Credit cards not accepted

595 **LA COUR AU TILLEUL**
Mrs Bazin

 Avenue du Capitani
46600 Martel
Tel. : 05 65 37 34 08

Open all year • 3 rooms with shower/WC • €53, breakfast included • No table d'hôte • Credit cards not accepted

We most liked **Meeting the enchanting owner.**

Cradled in the heart of the village, this 18C stately home owes its success to the lady of the house's efforts to make guests feel truly welcome: she is always well informed about life in the region and is happy to suggest local activities. The rooms are comfortable and unfussy and the breakfasts copious to say the least: prepare to delve into a memorable array of up to 24 home-made jams. The garden, complete with barbecue and hammock, is slightly unruly and instantly likeable.

Access : In the village

 We most liked **A bright, well cared-for interior behind very old walls.**

The walls of this enchanting stone house bedecked in flowers date back to the 12C no less! A great deal of time has clearly been lavished on the decoration of the tranquil, spacious rooms which are located to the rear of the house. Depending on the season, breakfast is served in the brightly coloured blue and orange dining room or in the inner courtyard under the shade of a linden tree. The welcome is as friendly as you could wish.

Access : In the village

 596 HOSTELLERIE LE VERT
Mr Philippe

46700 Mauroux
Tel. : 05 65 36 51 36
Fax : 05 65 36 56 84
hotellevert @ aol.com

Open from 14 Feb to 11 Nov; restaurant closed Thu evening • 7 rooms with bath/WC or shower/WC and television • €75 to €85; breakfast €7; half board €62 to €73 • Restaurant only open in the evening; menus €28 to €38 • Terrace, garden, car park. No dogs allowed • Outdoor swimming pool. Bicycle and mountain bike rental in the summer

 597 LE BEAU SITE
Mr Menot

Cité Médiévale
46500 Rocamadour
Tel. : 05 65 33 63 08
Fax : 05 65 33 65 23
hotel @ bw-beausite.com
www.bw.beausite.com

Open from 1 Mar to 12 Nov • 43 rooms located in 2 buildings on each side of the street. Rooms have bath/WC or shower/WC and television, 21 are air-conditioned • €60 to €80 (€48 to €64 low season); breakfast €9; half board €63 (€54 low season) • Res-taurant Jehan de Valon: menus €20 to €45 • Terrace, garage, car park (access by a pedestrianised road)

 Signposted footpaths weaving in and out of vineyards and old farms.

An ideal opportunity to get back to grass roots! This former wine estate, which lies in the remote countryside, is surrounded by a garden planted with cedar trees and a timeless silence. The hotel does its utmost to welcome you in style with its character-filled dining room with exposed beams, stonework and old furniture and personalised rooms in the same vein. The most unusual room is in the converted pantry with a lovely stone vaulted ceiling and tiny windows to keep it cool in the summer.

 The mountain village of Rocamadour – words fail us!

Old beams blackened by the centuries, a massive wooden staircase, stone walls and beautiful worn flagstones: the hall of this 15C bastion in the heart of the city is definitely worth a look. The rooms in the wing, of variable sizes, are more up-to-date and enjoy a fine view. The elegant restaurant-veranda and its flowered terrace overlook the Alzou canyon. 2km from the hotel, a swimming pool has been sunk in a lovely park of oak trees.

Access : In the countryside, 12km to the south-west of Puy-L'Évêque on the D 8 then the D 5

Access : Main road of the medieval city (pedestrian road) between Porte Salmon and Porte du Figuier

598 LES VIEILLES TOURS
Mr and Mrs Caulot

Lieu-dit Lafage
46500 Rocamadour
Tel. : 05 65 33 68 01
Fax : 05 65 33 68 59
les.vieillestours @ wanadoo.fr
www.chateauxhotels.com/vieillestours

Open from 23 Mar to 15 Nov • 16 rooms located in 2 buildings, almost all are on garden level, with bath/WC and television • €56 to €78; breakfast €10; half board €62 to €83 • Restaurant closed lunchtime except Sun and national holidays; menus €21 (in the week) to €38 • Terrace, garden, car park • Outdoor swimming pool

599 LE MANOIR
Mr Klaverstyn

La Forge
46200 Souillac
Tel. : 05 65 32 77 66
Fax : 05 65 32 77 66
m.klaverstyn @ lemanoir.net

Closed from 30 Oct to 15 Apr • 5 rooms and 5 non-smoking gîtes • €48, breakfast included • No table d'hôte • Car park. Credit cards not accepted, no dogs allowed • Outdoor swimming pool

We most liked
Sleeping in a 13C falconry!

The construction of this secluded hunting lodge took place over several centuries from the 13C to the 17C. Most of the rooms in the outhouses open directly onto the garden and enjoy a splendid view of the countryside. Diners can choose between a welcoming country-style restaurant and a quiet, shaded terrace to sample a sophisticated regional repertoire.

We most liked
Countless walking opportunities in the surrounding hillside.

If in dire need of a real break away from it all, this is the place for you! Beautifully decorated and entirely non-smoking, this manor house overlooking meadows and woodland offers B&B rooms and self-catering cottages. At breakfast time, choose between the immense dining room or the shade of a parasol on the sheltered terrace. A barbecue and mountain bikes are available for use by guests.

Access : 4km westbound from Rocamadour on the D 673 towards Payrac, then take a minor road

Access : 5km to the north-west of Souillac on the D 15

 600   **GEORGE V**
Mrs Selles

29 avenue du Maréchal Joffre
81000 Albi
Tel. : 05 63 54 24 16
Fax : 05 63 49 90 78
hotel.georgev @ ilink.fr

 www.hotelgeorgev.com

Open all year • 9 rooms, all have showers with or without WC, television, some have fireplaces • €39 to €42; breakfast €6 • No restaurant • Shaded inner courtyard

 601   **HÔTEL DU PONT**
Mr Saysset

81340 Ambialet
Tel. : 05 63 55 32 07
Fax : 05 63 55 37 21

Closed from 6 Jan to 13 Feb, Sun evening and Mon out of season • 14 rooms in the main building, 6 rooms in 3 bungalows. Most have bath/WC, some have shower/WC, all have television • €47 to €54; breakfast €6; half board €51 • Air-conditioned restaurant; menus €18 to €48 • Terrace, garden, car park • Heated outdoor swimming pool, canoe and mountain bike rental, fishing, hiking

 Basking in the first rays of morning sunshine.

Although not as luxurious as its famous Parisian namesake, this establishment is fully worthy of notice and most definitely less expensive than your average palace! The recently spruced up, spacious rooms are quiet despite the nearby railway station and decorated in pastel shades with good quality furniture; some have fireplaces. In the rear, a small shaded courtyard is perfect for open-air breakfasts.

 Canoeing down the lazy meanders of the River Tarn.

In the same family for two centuries, this solid building has many attractions even though it can't be said to be particularly charming. Its practical rooms command fine views which reach as far as the peninsula of Ambialet topped with a priory. A few bungalows can accommodate whole families. The dining room leads onto a covered terrace whose shade is most welcome in the hot midday sun. The garden extends right down to the banks of the Tarn.

Access : On one of the roads that leads to the railway station

Access : 20km from Albi towards Saint-Juéry, on the right bank of the Tarn, by the bridge

602 LA MÉTAIRIE NEUVE
Mrs Tournier

Bout-du-Pont-de-L'Arn
81660 Pont-de-Larn
Tel. : 05 63 97 73 50
Fax : 05 63 61 94 75
metairieneuve @ aol.com

Closed from 15 Dec to 20 Jan, Sun evening (restaurant) from Oct to Easter and Sat lunchtime • 14 rooms, most have bath/WC, some have shower/WC, all have television • €69 to €76; breakfast €9; half board €54 to €61 (€50 to €58 low season) • Menus €15 to €25 • Terrace, garden, car park • Outdoor swimming pool

603 LE CASTEL DE BURLATS
Mr and Mrs Dauphin

8 place du 8 Mai 1945
81100 Burlats
Tel. : 05 63 35 29 20
Fax : 05 63 51 14 69
le.castel.de.burlats @ wanadoo.fr

Closed from 30 Aug to 3 Sep and from 26 Oct to 3 Nov • 10 rooms, all have bath/WC or shower/WC and television • €61 to €99; breakfast €8 • No restaurant (evening snacks on request) • Park with garden, private car park • Billiard room, reading room, hiking trails nearby

 After a refreshing night's sleep, dig into a delicious breakfast.

We recommend booking one of the rooms recently renovated in a "country chic" style, which are not without character, overlooking the garden of this 18C family farmhouse converted into an inn in the 1980s. There are two pleasantly decorated rustic indoor dining rooms, but most guests prefer the rafters of the old barn which is now a delightful summer terrace.

 Savouring a whisky in the Renaissance salon.

You cannot miss this lovely 14C and 16C "castel" at the entrance to this medieval village in the gorges of the Agout. Spacious rooms, individually decorated with furniture picked up in antique shops, overlook a park where Mother Nature appears to have been given a free rein. Try your hand at billiards or catch up on the region's art and history in the Renaissance room complete with fireplace, wainscoting and beams. Even if it's your first stay, you will be greeted like a friend of the family.

Access : 2km eastbound from Mazamet: leave on the N 112 towards Saint-Pons and turn left at La Richarde

Access : 9km to the north-east of Castres on the D 89, then take the D 58 that runs along the Agout

604 **EUROPE**
Mr Loiseau and Mr Vialarand

5 rue Victor Hugo
81100 Castres
Tel. : 05 63 59 00 33
Fax : 05 63 59 21 38

Hotel open all year; restaurant closed in Aug, from 23 Dec to 2 Jan and Sun • 37 rooms, all have bath/WC or shower/WC and television • €50 to €60; breakfast €7 • Lunchtime: savoury-sweet buffet €10, evening: menus €16 to €19 • Patio • Piano bar on Fri and Sat

605 **LA RENAISSANCE**
Mr Vialar

17 rue Victor Hugo
81100 Castres
Tel. : 05 63 59 30 42
Fax : 05 63 72 11 57

Open all year • 20 rooms with bath/WC and television • €50 to €64; breakfast €7 • No restaurant • No dogs allowed

The unusual interior decoration.

Right in the heart of the historic town of Castres, these three 17C houses linked by a patio have been embellished with a lovely hotchpotch of objets trouvés, sculpture, paintings of cherubs and plants. The owners' originality and flair is also visible in the rooms' brick walls, timbers and open-plan bathrooms. The sitting rooms double as dining rooms and there is live music at the weekends.

Peaceful nights in the heart of the historic town.

This 17C half-timbered brick house offers accommodation in a few rooms whose charm it is impossible to resist. Elegant canopied beds and a beautiful choice of furniture elegantly marrying periods and styles. An inviting bar and sitting rooms adorned with old furniture and objets d'art further contribute to making you feel at home: settle in for the evening and discuss and compare different approaches to interior decoration!

Access : In the town centre, in a quiet street that links Bd des Lices and Place Jean-Jaurès

Access : In the town centre, between Boulevard des Lices and Place Jean Jaurès, in the pedestranised area

606 **AURIFAT**

Mrs Wanklyn

81170 Cordes-sur-Ciel
Tel. : 05 63 56 07 03
Fax : 05 63 56 07 03
aurifat@wanadoo.fr

Closed in Jan and Feb • 4 rooms • €64, breakfast
included • No table d'hôte • Garden, car park. Credit
cards not accepted, no dogs allowed • Outdoor swimming pool

607 **HOSTELLERIE DU VIEUX CORDES**
Mr and Mrs Thuriès

Haut de la Cité
81170 Cordes-sur-Ciel
Tel. : 05 63 53 79 20
Fax : 05 63 56 02 47
vieux.cordes@thuries.fr

Closed in Jan; restaurant closed Sun evening and Mon
out of season • 21 rooms at the Hostellerie, some have
a view over the valley, 8 are in a separate wing: La Cité.
All rooms have bath/WC or shower/WC and television
• €51 to €60 at the Hostellerie, €45 at La Cité; breakfast
€6; half board €50 • Themed food: salmon and duck,
menus €14 to €33 (no restaurant in the separate wing)
• Shaded terrace

 A magical place steeped in history.

The superb restoration of this 13C half-timbered brick
watchtower is most impressive. Its name, which means
"path of gold" was inspired by the Aurosse stream which
runs down below. All the cane-furnished rooms have a
balcony overlooking the fields and valley. Make sure you
have a peep in the suite in the 17C dovecote. The
terraced gardens are also worth exploring. The tower's
situation, just a few minutes walk from the medieval
heart of Cordes, is one of its greatest assets.

**Exploring the countless secrets of the
medieval city of Cordes.**

The tasteful bedrooms might lack the character of the
main building, an old monastery with an original spiral
staircase, but they do allow visitors to explore and enjoy
the heart of this medieval Gothic town, "the city of a
hundred arches". The windows overlook the valley of
Cérou and command picturesque views of the tiny paved
streets or of the old wisteria whose perfume lingers on
the exquisite patio terrace. Salmon and duck take pride
of place on the menu.

Access : 800m from the city on the St-Jean road

Access : In the town centre, between the covered
market and the church

 608 DEMEURE DE FLORE
Mr Di Bari

106 route Nationale
81240 Lacabarède
Tel. : 05 63 98 32 32
Fax : 05 63 98 47 56
demeure.de.flore@hotelrama.com
www.hotelrama.com/flore

Closed from 6 to 21 Jan and Mon out of season
• 11 rooms (3 in a detached house), one of which has
disabled access, with bath/WC and television • €77 to
€84; breakfast €10; half board €79 to €83 • Lunchtime
menu €23, evening menu €30 • Terrace, garden, private
car park. No dogs allowed in restaurant • Outdoor
swimming pool

 609 LE DOMAINE DE RASIGOUS
Mr Pessers

81290 Saint-Affrique-les-Montagnes
Tel. : 05 63 73 30 50
Fax : 05 63 73 30 51
info@domainederasigous.com
www.domainederasigous.com

Open from 15 Mar to 15 Nov; restaurant closed on Wed
• 8 rooms, one of which has disabled access, with
bath/WC and television • €69 to €84; breakfast €9; half
board €85 • Restaurant reserved for hotel guests and
open only for dinner; menu €23 • Terrace, park, car park.
No dogs allowed • Outdoor swimming pool

We most liked **Wandering around the delightfully
unruly garden.**

We most liked **A few lengths in the pool before
apéritifs.**

From the moment you set foot (or wheel) on the drive
lined by majestic linden trees, you will fall under the
spell of this charming manor-villa, built back in 1882.
The rooms are decorated with elegant Louis XVI
furniture and three open directly onto the swimming
pool with the Montagne Noire in the background. The
meals demonstrate a distinctly Italian-Provençal influence but the establishment also serves an excellent cup
of tea – even by British standards!

Nearly five acres of parkland surround this 19C country
home. Although a proper hotel endowed with all the
amenities you would expect, the owners have done their
best to keep all the spirit and the one-off personality
of a guesthouse. The spacious guest-rooms are
decorated with a variety of antique and contemporary
furniture and pretty fabrics, while the dining room is
situated in a study devoted to a collection of modern
art. Perfect for those in search of peace and quiet and
good taste.

Access : In Lacabarède, leave the N 112 and drive
along a lane bordered with lime trees

Access : 10km southbound from Castres, on the
D 85 towards Dourgne

MIDI-PYRÉNÉES

610 L' ARBRE D'OR
Mr Ellard

16 rue Despeyrous
82500 Beaumont-de-Lomagne
Tel. : 05 63 65 32 34
Fax : 05 63 65 29 85

Closed in Jan • 6 rooms, one of which has disabled access, with bathrooms • €50, breakfast included • Table d'hôte €18 • Terrace, garden

611 MAISON DES CHEVALIERS
Mr and Mrs Choux

Place de la Mairie
82700 Escatalens
Tel. : 05 63 68 71 23
Fax : 05 63 68 71 23
claudechoux @ minitel.net

Open all year • 4 rooms with bathrooms • €61, breakfast included • Table d'hôte €15 • Terrace, garden, park, car park. Credit cards not accepted, no dogs allowed • Outdoor swimming pool

We most liked **Lolling on the deck chairs in the delightful garden.**

We most liked **The imaginative cooking of the lady of the house, originally from southern Portugal.**

Although right in the heart of town, this pleasant 17C mansion is surrounded by a vast park. A lovely old staircase leads up to well-proportioned rooms decorated with old furniture; three overlook the garden. A discreetly elegant ambience prevails in the sitting and dining rooms, but as soon as the weather permits, head outside for succulent regional favourites prepared by the lady of the house.

Good taste and a certain daring distinguish the restoration of this lovely 18C manor house. Warm, sunny colours adorn the immense rooms complete with four-poster beds and period furniture, while the bathrooms boast superb old bathtubs and washbasins in Portuguese marble. A games room and a music room have been installed in the outbuildings. Shaded by a two-hundred-year-old chestnut tree, the courtyard is delightful.

Access : Opposite the post office

Access : 14km eastbound from Montauban on the RN 113

612 LE PLATANE
Mrs Hort

Coques-Lunel
82130 Lafrançaise
Tel. : 05 63 65 92 18
Fax : 05 63 65 88 18

Open all year • 3 rooms • €60, breakfast included • Table d'hôte €16 • Garden, car park. Credit cards not accepted • Outdoor swimming pool, horse-riding

613 LE QUERCY
Mr Bacou

Faubourg d'Auriac
82110 Lauzerte
Tel. : 05 63 94 66 36

Closed from 1 to 22 Oct, from 4 to 18 Feb, Sun evening except in Jul and Aug, and Mon • 10 rooms, 4 have a view over the countryside, with bath/WC or shower/WC • €32 to €38; breakfast €6; half board €30 to €35 (€28 to €33 low season) • Menus €10 (lunchtime in the week) to €34 • Small car park

The quintessence of comfort.

This lovely brick country house, flanked by stables and a dovecote, dates from 1904. Comfort was clearly high on the priority list of the restoration and the rooms are spacious and decorated in a modern or Neo-rustic style. Sunbathe around the oval swimming pool or head for the shade of the park's magnificent old planes, lindens and weeping willows. Horse-riding and bicycling available for those in need of more exercise.

Following in the footsteps of the pilgrims on the road to St James of Compostela.

The GR65 footpath runs alongside this late 19C house in the heart of a village, perched high on an outcrop, whose lovely timber framed medieval houses nestle around a pretty covered square. The small rooms have been fully renovated and four, in the rear of the house, overlook the valley of the Barguelonne. The restaurant has also been tastefully and simply redone. Very friendly.

Access : 10km eastbound from Moissac on the D 927, the D 2 and then the D 68

Access : In the heart of the medieval village reached by the D 953, between Montcuq and Valence-d'Agen

 614 LE BARRY
Mr Bankes and Mr Jaross

 Faubourg Saint-Roch
82270 Montpezat-de-Quercy
Tel. : 05 63 02 05 50
Fax : 05 63 02 03 07

Open all year • 5 rooms • €54, breakfast included • Table d'hôte €20 • Garden. Credit cards not accepted, no dogs allowed • Outdoor swimming pool

 615 CHAMBRE D'HÔTE PECH LAFONT
Mrs Perrone

Domaine de Lafon
82270 Montpezat-de-Quercy
Tel. : 05 63 02 05 09
Fax : 05 63 27 60 69
micheline.perrone @ domainedelafon.com

Closed at Christmas • 3 rooms with bathrooms • €64, breakfast included • Table d'hôte €20 • Terrace, garden, car park. Credit cards not accepted

 Forget your worldly cares in this undisturbed setting.

Built on the outskirts of the medieval town close to the collegiate church, this handsome village property commands an exceptional view of the valley and the hillsides. The pleasant rooms are tastefully decorated and one opens directly onto the delightful garden complete with swimming pool. The stylish sitting room is lined with books. A perfect country retreat.

 Taking a course in trompe l'œil painting.

Perched on a green hillside, this 19C square manor house enjoys a sweeping view of the surrounding countryside. Admire the immense rooms decorated by the owner, an artist and a former theatre set designer. The "Indian" is cloaked in oriental fabrics, marble and architectural trompe-l'œil scenes, azulejos tiles adorn the "Parrots" and "Baldaquin" features a pretty yellow and grey foliage pattern. Not to be missed!

Access : In the village

Access : 2km on the D 20 towards Molières, then turn left towards Mirabel for 2km

616 LA RÉSIDENCE
Mr and Mrs Green

37 rue Droite
82140 Saint-Antonin-Noble-Val
Tel. : 05 63 68 21 60
Fax : 05 63 68 21 60

Open all year • 6 non-smoking rooms overlooking the garden or the terrace, all have bath/WC • €69, breakfast included • Table d'hôte €19 to €23 • Garden. Credit cards not accepted, no dogs allowed

Idyllically situated in the heart of the medieval village.

The different cultures and backgrounds of the Franco-British husband and wife team that runs this 18C manor house are reflected in its interior decoration. Most of the spacious, tastefully decorated rooms overlook the Roc d'Anglars; book the one with a private terrace if possible. In the summer, linger in the beautiful garden, unless of course you would prefer the more energetic appeal of the nearby climbing centre.

Access : In the heart of the medieval village

NORD-PAS-DE-CALAIS

This region of northern France has everything to warm the soul of even the most chilly constitution. According to a local saying, "the hearts of the men of the north are warm enough to thaw the coldest climate". Just watch these northerners as they throw themselves body and soul into the traditional "Dance of the Giants", re-enacted everywhere in countless fairs, fêtes and carnivals. Several tons of chips and mussels – and who knows how many litres of beer! – are needed to sustain thousands of stall-holders and over one million visitors to Lille's annual Grande Braderie, just one of many huge street markets. The influence of Flanders can be seen not only in the names of many of the towns and inhabitants and the wealth of Gothic architectural treasures, but also in filling local dishes such as *carbonade* of beef, braised in amber beer, and *potjevleesch*, a chicken or rabbit stew with potatoes. Joyful peals of bells from slender belfries, neat rows of former miners' houses and the distant outline of windmills further remind visitors that they are on the border of Belgium, or, as a glance over the Channel on a sunny day will prove, just a pebble's throw from the white cliffs of Dover!

33 ESTABLISHMENTS
617 to **649**

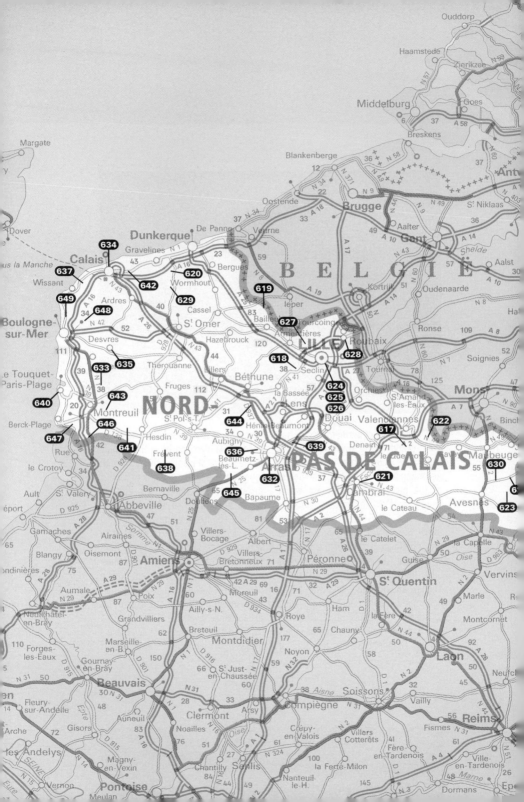

 617 LA GENTILHOMMIÈRE
Mrs Fournier

2 rue de l'Église
59269 Artres
Tel. : 03 27 28 18 80
Fax : 03 27 28 18 81
la.gentilhommiere @ wanadoo.fr
perso.wanadoo.fr/lagentilhommiere

Closed from 12 to 23 Aug • 10 rooms with bath/WC and television • €70; breakfast €8 • Restaurant closed Sun evening; menus €20 (in the week) to €35 • Garden, private car park • Horse-riding treks (by reservation), hiking, mountain biking, horse-drawn carriage rides

 618 CHEZ JULIE
Mr and Mrs Tilmant

59134 Beaucamps-Ligny
Tel. : 03 20 50 33 82
Fax : 03 20 50 34 35

Open all year • 3 rooms with shower/WC and telephone • €42, breakfast included • No table d'hôte • Sitting room, car park. Credit cards not accepted, no dogs allowed

 The Fine Arts Museum of Valenciennes – the "Athens of the North".

This redbrick farmstead on the doorstep of Valenciennes was built in 1746: its surprisingly airy, well-proportioned rooms overlook a quiet inner courtyard or the manicured garden. Sample delicious regional dishes in the light restaurant installed in the converted cow-shed, complete with vaulted ceiling and old mangers. The hotel can arrange horse-riding excursions and outings in a horse-drawn carriage if you book ahead.

Simple and unaffected.

Guests immediately feel at home and welcome in this comfy farmstead, built in Flanders brick on the threshold of a village near Lille. Pastel shades of yellow or beige adorn the immaculate rooms, two of which are upstairs under the eaves. A piano, wood stove and pleasant light wooden furniture adorn the breakfast room. Stretch out in inviting deep armchairs in the sitting room.

Access : Southbound from Valenciennes on the D 958 (towards Le Cateau), take a left on the D 400 after Famars

Access : 12km westbound from Lille on the A 25, exit no 7, then take the road to Radinghem (D 62)

NORD-PAS-DE-CALAIS

 619 AUBERGE DU VERT MONT
Mr and Mrs Zadeyn-Dubrul

 59299 Boeschepe
Tel. : 03 28 49 41 26
Fax : 03 28 49 48 58

Closed Mon and Tue lunchtime • 7 rooms • €58; breakfast €6 • Menus €19 to €28 • Terrace, garden • Children's play area, animal park

 620 LE WITHOF
Mr and Mrs Battais

 Chemin du Château
59630 Bourbourg
Tel. : 03 28 62 32 50
Fax : 03 28 62 38 88

Open all year • 5 non-smoking rooms with bathrooms • €50, breakfast included • Table d'hôte €16 • Garden, car park. No dogs allowed

 We most liked **The pleasant country feel to the dining room.**

 We most liked **The magnificent architecture of this 16C farm.**

This trim redbrick inn perched on the heights of the village is a welcome surprise. Pretty, well-appointed rooms overlook the valley, while those upstairs, the most pleasant, have amusing porthole windows and sloping ceilings. Meals are served in a country dining room adorned with old farm tools and objects such as clogs, kegs and wooden wheels. A children's play area and small animal park will appeal to younger visitors.

This fortified 16C farmhouse seems to float on its moat which, combined with its turrets and an imposing entrance, reminiscent of a drawbridge, gives it the allure of a full-blown castle. This stately atmosphere extends into the parquet floors and lovely doors of the bedrooms, all with immense bathrooms. On sunny days, breakfast is served in the courtyard. Excellent value for money.

Access : 9km northbound from Bailleul on the D 10

Access : 14km to the south-west of Dunkirk on the A 16 towards Calais (exit no 23)

 621 FERME DE BONAVIS
Mrs Delcambre

59400 Cambrai
Tel. : 03 27 78 55 08
Fax : 03 27 78 55 08

Open all year • 3 rooms with bathrooms • €55, breakfast included • No table d'hôte • Credit cards not accepted, no dogs allowed

 622 CHÂTEAU D'EN HAUT
Mr Demarcq

Château d'En Haut
59144 Jenlain
Tel. : 03 27 49 71 80
Fax : 03 27 35 90 17
mdemarcq @ nordnet.fr

Open all year • 6 rooms with bathrooms • €61, breakfast included • No table d'hôte • Park, car park. Credit cards not accepted, no dogs allowed

We most liked **Children adore exploring the ins and outs of this working farm.**

You can't help but be impressed by the handsome scale of this former coaching inn, turned into a farm at the end of the Second World War. High ceilings and parquet floors set the scene for the well-decorated and well-soundproofed rooms. Countless leisure activities on the farm or nearby, including boules, table-tennis, table-football, cycling and walking trails; gliding and aerodrome 9km away.

We most liked **A castle literally crammed with antiques.**

A long paved drive leads up to this magnificent 18C château and dovecote, set in the middle of pleasant parkland. The remarkable interior, rich in marquetry, antiques and period paintings is certainly worthy of the grand approach and is beautifully cared for by the charming hosts. Four-poster beds adorn the comfortable bedrooms and guests have the run of a light, airy breakfast room, library and even a small chapel.

Access : 11km southbound from Cambrai on the N 44

Access : 6km to the south-east of Valenciennes on the D 934 and the D 59

 623 CHÂTEAU DE LA MOTTE
Mrs Plateau

 59740 Liessies
Tel. : 03 27 61 81 94
Fax : 03 27 61 83 57
chateaudelamotte@aol.com

Closed from 20 Dec to 10 Feb and Sun evening • 9 rooms in 2 wings, most have bath/WC, some have shower/WC, all have television • €61; breakfast €7; half board €57 • Menus €19 (in the week) to €33 • Park, car park. No dogs allowed • Mountain bike rental, walking and hiking at Val Joli Lake 5km away

624 LA VIENNALE
Mrs Vienne-Herbert

 31 rue Jean-Jacques-Rousseau
59800 Lille
Tel. : 03 20 51 08 02
Fax : 03 20 42 17 23

Open all year • 12 rooms • €68; breakfast €5 • No table d'hôte • Garden, car park. No dogs allowed

 Sampling a little slice of the local, very, er,... "robust" "Boulette d'Avesnes" cheese.

 The eye-boggling interior decoration.

This delightful pink-brick edifice was built in the 18C on the edge of the forest of l'Abbé Val Joly for the Benedictine brotherhood of Liessies; the monks may have gone, but the peace and quiet remains. The wide bay windows of the restaurant, reminiscent of an orangery, overlook a leafy park and the rooms, furnished with rustic or period pieces, and the bathrooms have just been treated to a new lease of life. Guests can look forward to exploring the paths of the Avesnes Nature Reserve.

Carved woodwork, sumptuous gilded ceilings, period furniture and gigantic Chinese vases may give you an idea of the treasures that await you in the quite astounding interior of this 18C mansion. Each of the generously proportioned and very comfortable rooms has been decorated individually; one boasts a handsome collection of antique plates. Each of the sitting rooms is more remarkable than the last. The garden in the inner courtyard is quite delightful.

Access : Leave Liessies southbound on the D 133 or the D 963 and take the minor road to Motte

Access : On the outskirts of the historic city, in a semi-pedestrian street

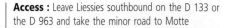

 625 BRUEGHEL
Mrs Lhermie

 3-5 parvis Saint-Maurice
59000 Lille
Tel. : 03 20 06 06 69
Fax : 03 20 63 25 27

Open all year • 66 rooms with bath/WC or shower/WC, all have television • €65 to €74; breakfast €7 • No restaurant • Public car park nearby

 626 PAIX
Mr and Mrs Trénaux

 46 bis rue de Paris
59800 Lille
Tel. : 03 20 54 63 93
Fax : 03 20 63 98 97
hotelpaixlille @ aol.com

Open all year • 35 rooms with bath/WC or shower/WC, all have television • €61 to €84; breakfast €8 • No restaurant • Public car park nearby • Well located: near the Grand'Place, theatre and opera house

 The lively historic centre of Lille and its convivial atmosphere.

This unpretentious establishment is rarely empty and it's not hard to see why. There's the typically Flemish first impression of its redbrick and chalk-white façade, then its pleasing old-fashioned interior with dark wainscoting and a period lift shaft in wood and wrought-iron, not to mention the fresh, pastel-coloured rooms, most of which overlook the Gothic church of St Maurice. Best of all is its practical location in the heart of Lille, just two minutes from the Grand'Place.

 The arty feel to this reasonably priced hotel.

The delightfully askew frontage of the Hôtel de la Paix, which in fact dates back to 1782, hides a collection of 250 reproduction works of art worthy of an art gallery. The rooms, corridors and staircases each has its own "old master", exhibited on yellow, dusty pink or light green walls. This "Who's Who" of fine art is curated by the owner, whose own creations can be admired on the walls of the breakfast room. A friendly establishment which has earned itself a loyal clientele.

Access : Opposite St Maurice Church

Access : In the town centre, near the Grand'Place and the opera house

 627 LA FERME BLANCHE
Mrs Delaval

Rue Pasteur
59840 Lompret
Tel. : 03 20 92 99 12
Fax : 03 20 92 99 12
dadelevad@wanadoo.fr

Closed for a fortnight in August • 3 spacious rooms with
bath/WC • €45, breakfast included • No table d'hôte
• Park, car park. Credit cards not accepted • Outdoor
swimming pool

 628 L'ABRI DU PASSANT
Mr Renart

14 rue de Vauban
59100 Roubaix
Tel. : 03 20 11 07 62

Closed for the first fortnight in August • 5 rooms with
bathrooms • €40, breakfast included • Table d'hôte
€10 • Garden

 Cycling around the countryside.

A stony lane leads to this pretty farm whose
whitewashed buildings form a rectangle behind the large
iron gate, watched over by the vigilant eye of a security
camera. The old barn has been converted into simple,
comfortable rooms; one of which features a lovely
mixture of crimson, pink and white. The exposed beams
and pastel shades in the breakfast room are also very
pleasant. A small swimming pool lies in the inner
courtyard.

**Contemporary works of art adorn the
whole house.**

You will not be disappointed by the restful mood of this
late-19C property next door to Barbieux park. Many
original architectural features, such as the tiled mosaic
floor in the hall, impressive high ceilings and lovely light
wood staircase, still reveal an almost Victorian love of
discreet home comforts. The bedrooms and bathrooms
are all generously proportioned. The sitting and dining
room provide the setting for an exhibition of works of
art by a young local painter.

Access : 7km to the north-west of Lille exit no 6,
then take the lane on the right

Access : To the south-west of town, near the park

629 CHÂTEAU DE SAINT-PIERRE-BROUCK
Mr and Mrs Duvivier

287 route de la Bistade
59630 Saint-Pierre-Brouck
Tel. : 03 28 27 50 05
Fax : 03 28 27 50 05
nduvivier@nordnet.fr
www.lechateau.fr.

Open all year • 5 non-smoking rooms • €54, breakfast included • Table d'hôte €16 • Park, car park. Credit cards not accepted, no dogs allowed

630 HÔTEL DU MARQUAIS
Mrs Carrié and Mrs Guinot

65 rue du Général de Gaulle
59216 Sars-Poterie
Tel. : 03 27 61 62 72
Fax : 03 27 57 47 35

Closed from 15 to 31 Mar • 11 rooms with bath/WC or shower/WC • €41 to €45; breakfast €7 • No restaurant • Garden, car park. No dogs allowed • Tennis

Cosily comfortable.

Nestling in a five-acre park, this impressive château built in 1905 is home to richly furnished rooms, complete with moulded ceilings and marble fireplaces. A lovely winter garden leads off the dining room. Deep, inviting armchairs encourage you to read up on the rich heritage of this tiny corner of Flanders, where Henry V won the day at Agincourt and where Louis XIV's military mastermind, Vauban, built the fortified walls of Gravelines.

Ferreting out a treasure in the stone pottery workshops of Sars, still in working order.

Painted brick walls and old furniture grace the bedrooms of this former farmhouse, converted into a hotel. Depending on the weather, breakfast is served on the large communal table in the hall or on the terrace overlooking the garden. Guests can choose between tennis or a visit to the Museum-Workshop of Glass in the rambling house of the former director of the glassworks.

Access : 8km northbound from Éperlecques National Forest, on the D 1

Access : On the main road through town, on the outskirts

 631 **LA VILLA MARIANI**
Mrs Mariani

 5 Grand' Place
59740 Solre-le-Château
Tel. : 03 27 61 65 30
Fax : 03 27 61 63 38

Open all year • 3 rooms • €46, breakfast included • No table d'hôte • Garden. Credit cards not accepted, no dogs allowed • Bicycles available for guests

 632 **LES 3 LUPPARS**
Mr Libouton

 49 Grand'Place
62000 Arras
Tel. : 03 21 60 02 03
Fax : 03 21 24 24 80

Open all year • 42 rooms, one of which has disabled access, all have shower/WC and television • €46 to €58; breakfast €7 • No restaurant • Sauna

 Regular contemporary art exhibitions.

This impressive 19C mansion built on the ruins of an old fortified castle has charm to spare. Comfortable, elegant rooms survey the peace and quiet of the garden, the shelves in the sitting room are well stocked with books on the region and the walls are frequently adorned with exhibitions of contemporary art, the lady of the house's passion. The house lends bicycles to explore the region.

 Strolling underneath the arcades of the magnificent Grand'Place.

We must admit that the simple, practical accommodation is nothing special in itself and the quieter rooms to the rear don't overlook the square. But surely this is a small price to pay for the luxury of staying in the oldest house in Arras. Built in 1467, its lovely Gothic façade, richly worked with gables, watchtower and ogival windows, fully deserves its place on the meticulously restored Grand'Place, one of the marvels of Flemish architecture.

Access : In the centre of the village

Access : In the town centre, on the Grand'Place

633 LA HAUTE CHAMBRE
Mr Barsby

124 route d'Hucqueliers,
hameau le Ménage
62170 Beussent
Tel. : 03 21 90 91 92
Fax : 03 21 86 38 24

Closed from 1 to 15 Sep and from 15 Dec to 15 Jan
• 5 rooms upstairs • €69, breakfast included • No table
d'hôte • Garden, park, car park. Credit cards not
accepted, no dogs allowed • Visit of the owner's art
studio

634 MEURICE
Mr and Mrs Cossart

5 rue Edmond Roche
62100 Calais
Tel. : 03 21 34 57 03
Fax : 03 21 34 14 71
meuricehotel-meurice.fr
www.hotel-meurice.fr

Open all year; restaurant closed Sat lunchtime • 41 rooms
on 3 floors, most of which have bath/WC, some have
shower/WC, all have television • €70 to €87; breakfast
€12; half board €60 to €68 • At La Diligence: menus
€15 (in the week) to €54 • Garage

 We most liked
**A delightful 19C manor nestling
behind a curtain of greenery.**

Sumptuous! If we only had one word to describe this
mid-19C country house and its idyllic park, that would
be it. A collection of the sculptor-owner's works is dotted
around the grounds. The comfortable, exquisitely
furnished rooms are a feast for the eyes and the
breakfasts generous enough to satisfy the most
demanding appetites. Exploring the park, home to some
300 animals, is always a hit with children.

 We most liked
**The Lace Museum next door to the
hotel.**

Although a coaching inn had stood here since before the
Revolution, its old walls were unable to survive the air
raids of the Second World War. Rebuilt in a style
reminiscent of a miniature palace, this period-piece has
the evocative look of a 1950s film set. Crystal
chandeliers, a fireplace and antique furniture adorn the
vast classical hall, the rooms have a charmingly
old-fashioned feel and the restaurant has kept its
period-style wood panelling.

Access : 10km northbound from Montreuil on the
N 1 then the D 127

Access : Behind the Lace Museum, in a small quiet
street, near Rue Royale and Richelieu Park

635 LA FERME DU MOULIN AUX DRAPS
Mrs Dubret

Route de Crémarest
62240 Desvres
Tel. : 03 21 10 69 59
Fax : 03 21 87 14 56

Open all year • 20 rooms, 5 of which are for non-smokers, 2 have disabled access, all have bath/WC and television • €75 to €81; breakfast €12 • No restaurant • Park, car park • Race-horse stud farm

636 LE CLOS GRINCOURT
Mrs Annie Senlis

18 rue du Château
62161 Duisans
Tel. : 03 21 48 68 33
Fax : 03 21 48 68 33

Closed from Nov to Mar • 3 rooms • €40, breakfast included • No table d'hôte • Park, car park

The inimitable hallmark of Desvres earthenware visible throughout the hotel.

This hotel was rebuilt after the fashion of the old farm next door to the mill that still stands on the banks of the Lène, once renowned for its linen factories. The modern rooms decorated with pine furniture take up the top floor of the building, while part of the ground floor is given over to the loose-boxes of a stud farm of trotters. The breakfast room keeps watch over the peaceful grounds, spread over nearly 20 acres of fields and forest.

The Clos believes in pampering its guests.

As you drive up the paved lane to this delightful manor house, get ready to be coddled and indulged. A lovely white spiral staircase leads up to rooms, more akin to suites, all of which overlook the park, which becomes a carpet of daffodils in the spring. Family photos adorn the walls of this lovely building begun in the reign of Louis XIV but only finished in the Second Empire.

Access : 1.5km on the Crémarest road (D 254 E)

Access : 9km westbound from Arras on the N 39

  637 LA GRAND'MAISON
Mr Boutroy

 Hameau de la Haute-Escalles
62179 Escalles
Tel. : 03 21 85 27 75
Fax : 03 21 85 27 75

Open all year • 6 rooms, 4 of which have bath/WC and television, the other 2 have shower/WC • €49, breakfast included • No table d'hôte • Garden, car park. Credit cards not accepted, no dogs allowed

 638 LE MOULIN
Mr and Mrs Legrand

 16 rue de Saint-Pol
62770 Fillièvres
Tel. : 03 21 41 13 20

Open all year • 4 non-smoking rooms with bathrooms • €49, breakfast included • Table d'hôte €13 to €16 • Garden, park, car park. Credit cards not accepted, no dogs allowed • Fishing, canoeing, mountain bike rental

We most liked

Poised between land and sea.

Wedged between two headlands and just a stone's throw from the white cliffs of Dover, this lovely 18C flower-decked farm has a spacious inner courtyard whose centrepiece is a dovecote. The spacious rooms overflow with antiques, the "prestige" rooms are the most comfortable. Children can romp to their heart's content in their very own play area and in the garden, which is home to a few animals. Walking, mountain biking and windsurfing less than 2km away.

Access : 2km eastbound from Cap-Blanc-Nez on the D 243

We most liked

The idyllic country setting of this mill.

This 18C mill, which boasts its original wheel and mechanism, lies on the road of the Field of the Cloth of Gold, where François I and Henry VIII's diplomatic summit once indulged their shared passion for power politics and full-blown pageantry. The well-restored mill is home to spacious rooms furnished with old pieces, where only the murmur of the Canche flowing beneath the windows will disturb the quiet. Magnificent park with two ponds, one for fishing.

Access : 7km to the south-east of Vieil-Hesdin on the D 340

639 HÔTEL LE MANOIR
Mr Laquette

35 route Nationale
62580 Gavrelle
Tel. : 03 21 58 68 58
Fax : 03 21 55 37 87

Closed for 3 weeks in August, the last week in December and Sun evenings • 19 rooms on 2 levels • €43; breakfast €5 • Menus €17 to €26 • Sitting room, terrace, park, car park

640 LE CHALET
Mr and Mrs Jaunault

15 rue de la Paix
62520 Le-Touquet-Paris-Plage
Tel. : 03 21 05 87 65
Fax : 03 21 05 47 49
jaunault @ wanadoo.fr

Open all year • 15 rooms on 3 floors, all have bathrooms • €54; breakfast €6 • No restaurant • Beach nearby

It is difficult to tell where the park ends and the countryside begins.

If the idea of waking up in the midst of the countryside appeals, book a night or two in this handsome manor house set in a pleasant park. Simple, uncluttered rooms are located in the former stables and those on the ground floor still have their original stone vaults, while the others have sloping ceilings. Traditional cuisine.

An alpine chalet in the heart of northern France's best-known seaside resort.

This Savoyard chalet just 50m from the beach is highly unusual. From the outside it looks like a mountain chalet and the brightly coloured red and yellow breakfast room is adorned with clogs and old wood skis! The pretty rooms are decorated in either a seaside or an alpine theme; all are very comfortable and immaculate.

Access : 11km to the north-east of Arras on the N 50 towards Douai

Access : From Berck-Plage, drive up Bd Dalloz and after the town hall turn left at St Jeanne d'Arc Church

 641 LA COMMANDERIE
Mrs Flament

 Allée des Templiers
62990 Loison-sur-Créquoise
Tel. : 03 21 86 49 87

Open all year • 3 non-smoking rooms • €61, breakfast included • No table d'hôte • Garden, car park. Credit cards not accepted, no dogs allowed

642 LE MANOIR DU MELDICK
Mr and Mrs Houzet

 Avenue du Général-de-Gaulle, le Fort Vert
62730 Marck
Tel. : 03 21 85 74 34
Fax : 03 21 85 74 34

Open all year • 5 rooms • €50, breakfast included • No table d'hôte • Car park. Credit cards not accepted, no dogs allowed

 We most liked **The atmosphere, dripping with character and history.**

The wonderful architecture of this former Knights' Templar command post, said to date back to the 12C, has been beautifully restored. Each of the refined rooms is named after one of the family's ancestors: Alice, Maria, Mancienne and Tantise. An agreeable clutter of old objects adorns the ground floor including pewter pots, a classically-French zinc bar and a set of forge bellows turned into a coffee table. The gurgling waters of the Créquoise add to the appeal of the park.

 We most liked **The owners' attentive care.**

So close to the port of Calais and yet so far, this lovingly restored manor house is a little gem of a find. Each of the spacious, individually decorated rooms is named after a flower: "Daisy", "Cornflower", "Rose" and "Poppy" – "Hyacinth" has a king-sized bed. All are equipped with coffee and tea making facilities and biscuits. Even better than home!

Access : Take the long drive near the river

Access : 6km eastbound from Calais on the D 940 and the D 119

 643 MANOIR FRANCIS
Mrs Leroy

1 rue de l'Église
62170 Marles-sur-Canche
Tel. : 03 21 81 38 80
Fax : 03 21 81 38 56

Open all year • 3 rooms with bath/WC • €46, breakfast included • No table d'hôte • Garden. Credit cards not accepted

  644 LES TOURTERELLES
Mr and Mrs Verbrugge

374 rue Nationale
62290 Noeux-les-Mines
Tel. : 03 21 61 65 65
Fax : 03 21 61 65 75

Open all year • 21 rooms on 3 floors, with bath/WC or shower/WC and television • €38 to €68; breakfast €7; half board €38 to €54 • Restaurant closed Sat lunchtime, Sun evening and national holiday evenings; menus €30 to €42 • Terrace, garden, private car park. No dogs allowed in restaurant • Loisinord Park nearby: year-round skiing, water sports

We most liked **The lady of the house's attention to detail.**

You have to go under the immense porch and through the garden, home to a host of farmyard animals, to reach this 17C fortified farmhouse. We loved the interior, particularly the ground floor with its lovely chalk vaults upheld by diagonal beams. Old furniture, a private sitting room and unusual bathrooms complement the spacious rooms. The terrace under the shade of an apple tree is enchanting.

We most liked **Skiing down the slag heap ski slope of Loisinord!**

This redbrick house was the headquarters a coal mining company over a century ago. The modest rooms are more than compensated for by the elegant restaurant installed in the muted atmosphere of the former boardroom with dark wainscoting, marble fireplace and Louis XVI cane chairs. Terrace in the garden in fine weather.

Access : 5.5km to the south-east of Montreuil-sur-Mer on the D 113

Access : Between Arras and Verbrugge, by the main road going through the town

645 CHÂTEAU DE SAULTY
Mrs Dalle

82 rue de la Gare
62158 Saulty
Tel. : 03 21 48 24 76
Fax : 03 21 48 18 32

Closed in Jan • 5 rooms with bathrooms • €46, breakfast included • No table d'hôte • Park, car park. Credit cards not accepted

646 LE PRIEURÉ
Mr Delbecque

Impasse de l'Église
62180 Tigny-Noyelle
Tel. : 03 21 86 04 38

Open all year • 5 rooms with bath/WC and television • €65, breakfast included • Table d'hôte €22 to €25 • Garden, park

A glass of home-grown apple or pear juice at breakfast time.

This splendid castle, built in 1835, lies opposite a superb park and a fruit orchard. The rooms, of varying sizes, have parquet floors and are decorated with old or pine furniture; all have a decorative marble fireplace. An assortment of home-made jams and fruit juices are served at breakfast in the ancestral dining room. Library and tennis-table table.

Stylish interior decoration.

The owner-antique dealer has lovingly restored his pretty turquoise-shuttered house, set in a small park. The rooms are stylish and feature exposed beams and antiques; the split-level room is most praiseworthy, as is the suite with sitting room and fireplace. The breakfast room and the superb regional fireplace are also worth a look. Golfers will adore the prospect of trying out the 36-hole golf course of Nampont, only 3km away.

Access : 19km to the south-west of Arras towards Doullens on the N 25

Access : Behind the church

647 LA CHAUMIÈRE
Mrs Terrien

19 rue du Bihen
62180 Verton
Tel. : 03 21 84 27 10

Open all year • 4 non-smoking rooms, 2 are on the ground floor and 2 are upstairs • €47, breakfast included • No table d'hôte • Garden, car park. Credit cards not accepted, no dogs allowed

648 LA FERME DU VERT
Mr Bernard

62720 Wierre-Effroy
Tel. : 03 21 87 67 00
Fax : 03 21 83 22 62
ferme.du.vert@wanadoo.fr

Closed from 22 Dec to 31 Jan • 16 rooms with shower/WC • €61; breakfast €8.50 • Menus €20 to €36 • Garden, park, car park

The charm of a doll's house.

Visiting the cheese-makers, also run by your hosts.

This quaint cottage with its thatched roof and flowered garden is just 4km from the sea. An atmosphere of refined elegance and warmth pervades the place. Each of the non-smoking rooms has its own individual personality. Stay for a few days and you'll notice that breakfast is served on different tableware each morning, thanks to the lady of the house's wonderful collection. Golf nearby.

A perfect invitation to get back to grass roots. You won't be disappointed by the comfortable, quiet rooms, decorated simply and tastefully; the largest are full of amusing nooks and crannies. Sample the delicious home cooking made with local produce. Before leaving, make sure you stop by the next door cheese-makers and stock up on fresh and matured cheeses.

Access : 4km eastbound from Berck on the D 303

Access : 10km to the north-east of Boulogne on the N 42 and the D 234

649 **LA GOÉLETTE**
Mrs Avot

13 Digue de Mer
62930 Wimereux
Tel. : 03 21 32 62 44
Fax : 03 21 33 77 54

Open all year • 4 rooms with bath/WC • €76, breakfast
included • No table d'hôte • Credit cards not accepted

Gulping down the fresh sea air when you open your shutters in the morning.

Who could resist the charm of this 1900 villa so well
located on the dike-promenade of Wimereux? The
perfectly restored interior has remained authentic and
the rooms now reveal their original harmonious shades,
moulded ceilings and warm sea-faring pine furniture.
The Blue and Yellow rooms offer a wonderful view of
the sea, while the others overlook the inner garden. Ask
your hosts for walking tips.

Access : On the seafront

NORMANDY

Normandy, the muse of poets and artists from the world over, offers an ever-changing vision of rural pleasures. Take a bracing walk along the miles of coastline and admire her string of elegant seaside resorts. You will be left breathless when you first catch sight of Mont Saint-Michel rising from the sands or look down over Étretat's chalky cliffs into the sea crashing on the rocks below. It is impossible not to be moved by the memory of the men who died on Normandy's beaches in June 1944 or to be captivated by the cottage-garden charm of Guernsey and Jersey. Further inland, acres of neatly tended hedge-lined fields meet the eye, home to thoroughbred horses and herds of dairy cows. Breathe in the scent of the apple orchards in spring and admire the picture-postcard half-timbered cottages and smart manor houses, before wandering down to the Seine, following its meanders past medieval cities, daunting castles and venerable abbeys. No description would be complete, however, without Normandy's culinary classics: fresh fish and seafood, creamy, ivory-white Camembert, cider, fizzing like apple champagne and, last but not least, the famous oak-aged apple brandy, Calvados.

 650 LA MARINE
Mr Verdier

Quai du Canada
14117 Arromanches les Bains
Tel. : 02 31 22 34 19
Fax : 02 31 22 98 80
hotel.de.la.marine@wanadoo.fr
www.hotel-de-la-marine.fr

Open from mid-Feb to mid-Nov • 28 rooms with bath/WC or shower/WC and television • €57 to €65; breakfast €7; half board €60 • Menus €16 (lunchtime in the week) to €48 at the restaurant, and around €22 at Pub Winston • Car park

 651 FERME LE PETIT VAL
Mr Gérard Lesage

24 rue du Camp Romain
14480 Banville
Tel. : 02 31 37 92 18
Fax : 02 31 37 92 18

Closed from Nov 1 until the spring holidays • 5 rooms, 2 of which are on the ground floor and 3 are upstairs, all have bathrooms • €40, breakfast included • No table d'hôte • Garden, car park. Credit cards not accepted

 Imagine the Allied Forces landing on D-Day.

The discreet, practical rooms of this rambling white hotel resemble the cabins of a luxury liner. Taking pride of place on the menu are lobster – choose your own in the tank – fish and shellfish, served in the turquoise dining room and bar-brasserie. All the windows overlook the Channel and the horizon out of which the Allied forces emerged, before landing at dawn on "the longest day", 6th June 1944.

Watch the cows grazing in the meadows.

This characteristic farmhouse, thought to date from the 17C, is ideal to get back to grass roots. Its snug, quietly elegant rooms are spread over two wings around a central courtyard. Family heirlooms adorn the pleasant breakfast room. In the summer, the flowered garden is particularly inviting.

Access : At the port

Access : In the town

 652 AUBERGE DE LA SOURCE
Mr and Mrs Legeay

14600 Barneville-la-Bertran
Tel. : 02 31 89 25 02
Fax : 02 31 89 44 40

Closed from 15 Nov to 15 Feb • 16 rooms with bath/WC
and television • €61 to €104, breakfast included • No
restaurant • Garden, private car park. No dogs allowed

 653 HOSTELLERIE DU MOULIN DU PRÉ
Mrs Holtz

Route de Gonneville-en-Auge
14860 Bavent
Tel. : 02 31 78 83 68
Fax : 02 31 78 21 05

Closed 3 to 18 Mar, Oct, Sun evening, Mon, Tue
lunchtime except from 15 Jul to 15 Aug and holidays
• 10 rooms upstairs. Rooms have showers, with or
without WC • €44 to €56; breakfast €7 • Menus €32 to
€43 • Garage. No dogs allowed in rooms • Park

 Waking to the sound of bird song.

A half-timbered farm and a redbrick house laid out
around a delightful flowered garden with a pool filled
with trout and sturgeon: the perfect picture of a
welcoming country inn. The rooms echo with the sounds
of this country haven and are equipped with modern
bathrooms. Breakfast is served by the fireside in winter
and under the apple trees in the summer.

 Peace and quiet guaranteed.

Just a few kilometres from the sea, this old half-timbered
farmhouse and its outbuildings lie in the middle of the
countryside in grounds complete with a duck pond. The
rooms are modest and a little on the dark side but very
well kept, even though the old hip baths do make
showers something of an acrobatic feat. Lovely rustic
dining room with lace tablecloths, dressers and a huge
fireplace for delicious chargrilled meats.

Access : 6km southbound from Honfleur on the
D 62A, turn right at the entrance to Équemauville
(D 62), then left (D 279)

Access : Leave Cabourg on the D 513 towards Caen,
and after Varaville turn right on the D 95 towards
Gonneville-en-Auge

 654 D'ARGOUGES
Mr and Mrs Ropartz

21 rue Saint-Patrice
14400 Bayeux
Tel. : 02 31 92 88 86
Fax : 02 31 92 69 16
dargouges @ aol.com

Open all year • 25 rooms, most have bath/WC, some have shower/WC, all have television • €62 to €76; breakfast €7 • No restaurant • Garden, garage, car park

655 LE COTTAGE
Mrs Rival

24 avenue du Général Leclerc
14390 Cabourg
Tel. : 02 31 91 65 61
Fax : 02 31 28 78 82

Open all year • 14 rooms on 2 floors, with bath/WC or shower/WC and television • €60 to €86 (€54 to €77 low season); breakfast €7 • No restaurant • Garden • Gym, sauna

 A quiet garden in the heart of the town.

It is more than worthwhile venturing past the rather austere façade of this 18C house to catch a glimpse of the lovely garden in the rear. The house's glorious past can still be seen in the intricate patterns of the parquet floors, old doors and worn beams in some of the rooms. A number of the most spacious bedrooms are perfect for families: new bedding, fabrics and wallpaper are on the agenda for the bedrooms.

 As pretty as a picture.

This lovely 1900 half-timbered cottage lies at the rear of a pretty garden. A staircase winds its way up to snug rooms all of which are individually decorated and regularly smartened up. Those on the upper floor are the least roomy. Family breakfast room, billiards and a small fitness room. Home from home!

Access : In the road running from the town centre to the N 13, Cherbourg road

Access : Opposite the church, on the avenue that extends from the D 514, from Ouistreham

  656 **MANOIR DE CANTEPIE**
Mrs Gherrak

Le Cadran
14340 Cambremer
Tel. : 02 31 62 87 27

Closed from 15 Nov to 1 Mar • 3 rooms upstairs, with bathrooms • €55, breakfast included • No table d'hôte • Sitting room, garden, park, car park. Credit cards not accepted, no dogs allowed

  657 **LES MARRONNIERS**
Mr and Mrs Darondel

Les Marronniers
14340 Cambremer
Tel. : 02 31 63 08 28
Fax : 02 31 63 92 54
chantal.darondel @ wanadoo.fr
www.les-marronniers.com

Open all year • 5 rooms • €52, breakfast included • No table d'hôte • Park. Credit cards not accepted, no dogs allowed

 Normandy at its best!

This splendid early-17C manor house will weave its magic spell the minute you set foot within its elegant, tasteful walls. A superb oak staircase takes you up to immense, well-appointed rooms; the old-fashioned bathrooms are particularly stunning. Family heirlooms grace the sitting room and the flowered grounds are clearly the work of a devoted gardener. Not to be missed!

 Time and care have clearly been lavished over the rooms.

This pleasant 17C edifice set in the middle of a flowered park enjoys a lovely view over the Dive Valley, with the sea in the distance. Each of the personalised rooms has been named after a goddess: "Venus", is full of light, "Diane" is smaller but much more romantic. Tuck into the ample breakfasts served on a pretty patio.

Access : 11km westbound from Lisieux on the N 13 then the D 50

Access : 5km on a by-road

  658 LA FERME DE LA RANÇONNIÈRE
Mrs Vereecke

Route d'Arromanches-les-Bains
14480 Crépon
Tel. : 02 31 22 21 73
Fax : 02 31 22 98 39
ranconniere@wanadoo.com

Open all year • 35 rooms, one of which has disabled access, with bath/WC or shower/WC and television. In the separate wing: La Ferme de Mathan, suites are €120 • €58 to €89; breakfast €10; half board €52 to €120 • Menus €15 to €35 • Garden, car park

  659 LE MANOIR DE CRÉPON
Mrs Poisson

14480 Crépon
Tel. : 02 31 22 21 27
Fax : 02 31 22 88 80

Open all year • 5 rooms with bath/WC • €69, breakfast included • No table d'hôte • Garden, car park • Mountain biking

 A stay in these farms is like reading a page of a history book.

High ceilings upheld by worn beams, vaults, monumental fireplaces, exposed stone walls and flagstones are just some of the original decorative features of this 13C fortified farmhouse. The furniture and ornaments showcased in the rooms were found in local second-hand and antique shops. For a few euros extra, treat yourself to the luxury of added space and calm in the 18C Ferme de Mathan just 800m away.

 A faultlessly decorated home.

Towering trees grace an immense park surrounding this 18C manor house whose blood-red façade is characteristic of the region. Once inside the well-dimensioned, comfortable rooms, the owner-antique dealer's flair is visible in the beautiful choice of furniture. On cold winter days, a log fire burns in the breakfast room, formerly the kitchen. Bicycles rented on the estate.

Access : Westbound from Bayeux, take the D 12 towards Douvres-la-Délivrande for 12km, turn left onto the D 65

Access : In the village

 660 MANOIR DE L'HERMEREL
Mr and Mrs Lemarié

14230 Géfosse-Fontenay
Tel. : 02 31 22 64 12
Fax : 02 31 22 64 12
lemariehermerel @ aol.com

Closed from 11 Nov to 31 Mar • 4 rooms with bathrooms
• €50, breakfast included • No table d'hôte • Car park.
Credit cards not accepted, no dogs allowed

 661 FERME DES GLYCINES
Mr and Mrs Exmelin

14510 Gonneville-sur-Mer
Tel. : 02 31 28 01 15

Closed from Nov to 1 Apr • 3 rooms • €43, breakfast
included • No table d'hôte • Garden, car park. Credit
cards not accepted, no dogs allowed

 A guided visit of the manor and the farm.

Surrounded by meadows, this 17C fortified manor-farm
with its proud aspect, handsome porch, regular lines and
elegant dovecote could easily pass for a castle. The
rooms in the manor are a subtle blend of comfort and
charm. The sitting room in a 15C Gothic chapel is
supremely restful and your hosts' unaffected welcome
quite captivating.

 "Old Macdonald had a farm!"

Children love the horses, sheep, hens and ducks who
live in the grounds of this timber-framed farm which
dates from 1780 and is surrounded by over 40 acres
of orchards and park. The colour schemes render the
rooms most pleasant and one has a private terrace.
Farm produce features prominently on the breakfast
table, served by the fireside in winter. Delightful garden.

Access : 8km northbound from Isigny on the
D 514 then take the D 200 to Osmanville

Access : 7km eastbound from Dives-sur-Mer on the
D 45 and a minor road

NORMANDY

662 LA MAISON NORMANDE
Mrs Menga

Au bourg
14510 Gonneville-sur-Mer
Tel. : 02 31 28 90 33

Open all year • 3 rooms • €40, breakfast included • No table d'hôte • Sitting room, garden, car park. Credit cards not accepted, no dogs allowed

663 L'AUBERGE DU PONT DE BRIE
Mr and Mrs Cottarel

Halte de Grimbosq
14210 Goupillières
Tel. : 02 31 79 37 84
Fax : 02 31 79 87 22

Closed from 16 Dec to 8 Feb, Tue from Sep to May and Mon • 7 rooms with shower/WC, some have television • €42 to €55; breakfast €6; half board €42 to €48 • Menus €15 to €38 • Car park

Within easy reach of Normandy's seaside resorts.

This lovely 16C half-timbered house with slate roof is exactly what you imagine a typical Norman house should look like. The front door takes you straight into an immense country sitting room with fireplace. The rooms are decorated in the same spirit and beautifully furnished. Delicious jams and preserves are served at breakfast, which can be taken outside depending on the weather. The quiet garden is a riot of flowers in the summer.

Switzerland meets Normandy!

This remote family inn in the Orne Valley is ideally located to tour this picturesque region, known as "Swiss Normandy", due to its hilly landscape. The rooms are rustic, well-kept and on the large side, as is the restaurant, and while they may not drip with charm, they are pleasantly countryish. What's more, the youthful owners have their guests' welfare at heart and love recommending walks in the region.

Access : 7km eastbound from Dives on the D 45 towards Lisieux, then take the D 142

Access : Between Caen and Thury-Harcourt, leave the D 562 and drive towards Goupillières (D 171)

 664 1900
Mr and Mrs Lemarie

17 rue des Bains
14510 Houlgate
Tel. : 02 31 28 77 77
Fax : 02 31 28 08 07

Closed from 8 Jan to 1 Feb and from 12 Nov to 7 Dec
• 16 rooms, all have bath/WC or shower/WC and
television • €77 to €90; breakfast €7; half board €64 to
€73 • Menus €16 to €42 • No dogs allowed • Reading
room

 665 MON CASTEL
Mr and Mrs Roger

1 boulevard des Belges
14510 Houlgate
Tel. : 02 31 24 83 47
Fax : 02 31 28 50 36

Closed in Oct and during February holidays. Restaurant
closed Tue evening and Wed evening in season
• 10 rooms on 2 floors, some have shower with or
without WC • €38 to €42; breakfast €6; half board
€37 to €42 • Restaurant closed Sun, Mon and Thu
evenings out of season; menus €12 (in the week) to
€32 • No dogs allowed in rooms

 We most liked
Exploring Houlgate's rich architectural pageant.

Ornate villas, Anglo-Norman manor houses, Alpine
chalets: this adorable resort on the Norman coast is a
delight for anyone intrigued by seaside architecture. The
hotel is located in Houlgate's high street and offers
rooms redecorated in a Belle Époque "chocolate-box"
style; all are well-soundproofed. Painted ceilings, frosted
windows, knick-knacks and a bar found in an antique
shop set the scene for the distinctly "retro" bistro.

 We most liked
Miles and miles of white sandy beach.

"The husband's in the kitchen and the wife at the
reception", the brochure proudly declares. This discreet
house, just off the beach, is two minutes from the casino.
Don't expect a castle, despite the name, but rather, a
simple, well cared-for and reasonably priced establishment. The rooms are tastefully decorated and well
appointed. Straw-bottomed chairs, old wood floors and
copper pots add appeal to the two rustic dining rooms,
where you will be served hearty, traditional dishes.

Access : On the main road of the resort

Access : Coming from Deauville, at the start of the
high street towards the centre

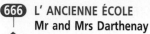 **666** L' ANCIENNE ÉCOLE
Mr and Mrs Darthenay

Route d'Arromanches
14960 Meuvaines
Tel. : 02 31 22 39 59
Fax : 02 31 22 39 11

Open all year • 3 rooms with bath/WC • €39, breakfast included • Table d'hôte €14 • Terrace, car park. No dogs allowed

 667 LE MANOIR DE L'ENGAGISTE
Mrs Dubois

14 rue de Geôle
14290 Orbec
Tel. : 02 31 32 57 22
Fax : 02 31 32 55 58

Open all year • 3 rooms and one split-level • €65, breakfast included • No table d'hôte • Disabled access. Garden

 We most liked
Betwixt land and sea.

As the name suggests, this building which dates from 1741 was formerly the village school. Now a B&B establishment, it offers rustic rooms under the eaves, all of which overlook the countryside. Regional specialities feature prominently on the table, set by the fireside in the pleasant dining room. Nearby are the D-Day Landing beaches and the delightful inland villages of Bessin.

 We most liked
An immaculately decorated half-timbered manor house.

Right in the heart of town, this beautifully restored 16C mansion is definitely worth staying a day or two. You will want to snuggle-up in the thoughtfully decorated bedrooms with terracotta tiled floors, wood panelling and old tapestries. In the winter, a huge fire burns in the exquisite sitting room whose centrepiece is a mezzanine with exhibitions of paintings and sculpture. An old carriage takes pride of place in the vast inner courtyard. Not to be missed!

Access : 8km to the south-east of Arromanches on the D 65

Access : In the heart of the town

NORMANDY

668 LE CLOS FLEURI
Mrs Weidner

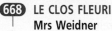

Hameau Lefèvre
14450 Saint-Pierre-du-Mont
Tel. : 02 31 22 96 22
Fax : 02 31 22 96 22

Open all year • 3 rooms with bathrooms • €39, breakfast included • Table d'hôte €14 • Garden, car park. Credit cards not accepted, no dogs allowed

669 LE GRAND FUMICHON
Mr and Mrs Duyck

14400 Vaux-sur-Aure
Tel. : 02 31 21 78 51
Fax : 02 31 21 78 51
duyckja @ wanadoo.fr

Open all year • 4 rooms, one of which is in a separate house • €34, breakfast included • No table d'hôte • Car park. Credit cards not accepted

A garden large enough to accommodate everyone.

No sooner have you settled in than you will feel as if you've always lived in this comfortable house. Old furniture embellishes the spacious, cosy rooms and the family cooking never fails to draw a compliment or two. The enormous garden is big enough to be able to host boisterous children's games, more sedate naps for the less energetic and barbecue lunches for everyone. Even better, you're only two steps from the sea. What more could you want?

An apple a day keeps the doctor away!

A former outbuilding of the abbey of Longues-sur-mer, this fortified farmstead with square courtyard, porch and press is clearly proud of its early 17C origins. Today it is a working dairy and cider farm and also offers simple, rustic rooms overlooking the orchard. The quietest is in a small independent house. Before leaving, stock up on farm-grown cider, Calvados – apple brandy – apple juice and preserves.

Access : 2.5km to the south-east of Pointe du Hoc on the road to Vierville

Access : 3km northbound from Bayeux on the D 104

 670 CHÂTEAU DE VOUILLY
Mr and Mrs Hamel

 14230 Vouilly
Tel. : 02 31 22 08 59
Fax : 02 31 22 90 58

Closed from Dec to Feb • 5 rooms with bathrooms • €62, breakfast included • No table d'hôte • Garden, car park. No dogs allowed

 671 LES SOURCES BLEUES
Mr and Mrs Laurent

 Route du Vieux-Port
27500 Aizier
Tel. : 02 32 57 26 68
Fax : 02 32 57 42 25

Open all year • 4 non-smoking rooms on 2 floors, with baths, showers and separate WC • €45, breakfast included • Table d'hôte €14 • Sitting room, garden, car park. Credit cards not accepted

We most liked **A step back in time.**

This 18C château surrounded by a moat and carefully tended gardens was commandeered as the American press HQ during the landings in June 1944. Beautifully restored by the owner himself, the rooms are spacious and comfortable and some have old furniture. On the ground floor, guests have the run of a string of impressive sitting rooms, one of which doubles as a breakfast room, with lovely old two-tone tiled floors.

We most liked **Exploring the wooded park on the banks of the Seine.**

Nestled in a delightfully untrammelled park, this lovely Norman house built in 1854 enjoys a wonderful view over the Seine and the boats plying their course to and from Le Havre. Wood, old tiles and parquet floors prevail in the welcoming interior. The rooms are comfortably uncluttered and the most pleasant have sloping ceilings. On the leisure side, you can choose from tennis, horse-riding and canoeing.

Access : 8km to the south-east of Isigny on the D 5

Access : 5km northbound from Bourneville on the D 139

 672 LE MOULIN DE BÂLISNE
Mr Gastaldi

 RN 12
27130 Bâlines
Tel. : 02 32 32 03 48
Fax : 02 32 60 11 22

Closed on Mon and Tue except by reservation • 10 rooms • €70; breakfast €8 • Menus €25 to €33 • Terrace, garden, park, car park • Tennis, archery, badminton, canoeing

 The flavour of yesteryear.

This inn, set in grounds which border on wilderness in places, was masterfully built on the ruins of a 17C water mill. Behind the walls, hidden under festoons of ivy, a fine staircase leads up to old-fashioned rooms. A glance at the original beams and tiled floor, fireplace, chandeliers, old furniture, crystal carafes and oil paintings further reinforces the impression that time has stood still in the dining room, and the traditional cooking does nothing to detract from the old-world flavour.

Access : Near the town on the N 12

 673 LE RELAIS DE LA POSTE
Mr and Mrs Bosquer

 60 rue Constant Fouché
27210 Beuzeville
Tel. : 02 32 20 32 32
Fax : 02 32 42 11 01

Open from 1 Apr to 12 Nov • 15 rooms with bath/WC or shower/WC, some have television • €46 to €58; breakfast €6; half board €49 to €57 • Restaurant closed Sun evening from Sep to May and Thu; menus €16 (in the week) to €33 • Terrace, garden, private car park. No dogs allowed in rooms

 You must try the lady of the house's chocolate and potato cake!

A spacious, flowered garden lies hidden behind the stone and brick walls of this coaching inn which first opened in 1854. A wooden staircase climbs up the three floors where the small, simply furnished rooms are located. The appealing dining room is in the former village café which still boasts its original bar. Don't miss the chance to sample the scrumptious result of Madame's highly individual approach to cooking.

Access : On the main road in the centre of the village, opposite the town hall

 674 CHÂTEAU DE BOSCHERVILLE
Mr and Mrs du Plouy

 27520 Bourgtheroulde-Infreville
Tel. : 02 35 87 62 12
Fax : 02 35 87 62 12

Open all year • 5 rooms • €46, breakfast included • No table d'hôte • Sitting room, park, car park. Credit cards not accepted

 "By the work, one knows the workman", Jean de La Fontaine (1621-95)

This delightful 18C château, set in a park of venerable old oaks, was built on the ruins of the one-time home to France's best known writer of fables. Today it houses light, airy rooms which marry comfort and good taste and an elegant sitting room complete with its original decorative woodwork. The breakfast table is piled high with succulent local farm produce and the welcoming owners are a mine of information about the region.

Access : 10km to the north-east of Bec-Hellouin on the N 138, the D 80 and the D 38

 675 L'AUBERGE DU VIEUX DONJON
Mr and Mrs Chauvigny

19 rue de la Soie
27800 Brionne
Tel. : 02 32 44 80 62
Fax : 02 32 45 83 23
auberge.vieuxdonjon @ wanadoo.fr

Closed 9 Feb to 18 Mar, 19 to 26 Aug, 13 Oct to 4 Nov, Sun and Thu evenings (Oct to late Jun) and Mon • 6 rooms with bath/WC or shower/WC and television • €50 to €53; breakfast €6; half board €51 to €56 • Menus €13 (in the week) to €34 • Terrace, private car park

"Trou normand"? a) A hole in Normandy, b) A mid-dinner drink, c) Authentically Norman.

The blue timbers and chequered decoration of this 18C Norman house, its view of the ruined 11C keep and its shady patio terrace make up for the modest comfort of the rooms. Old porcelain, gleaming copper, worn tiles and dark-timbered beams set the scene for the characteristically rustic dining room, which would not seem out of place in a short story by Maupassant! Shaded patio terrace. This is the place to try the famous "trou normand" – a brisk, mid-meal shot of Calvados (apple brandy).

Access : Opposite the market square

676 LE VIEUX PRESSOIR
Mrs Anfrey

Hameau le Clos-Potier
27210 Conteville
Tel. : 02 32 57 60 79
Fax : 02 32 57 60 79

Open all year • 5 rooms with bathrooms • €50, breakfast included • No table d'hôte • Car park. Credit cards not accepted, no dogs allowed

677 LE CLOS DES GASTINES
Mr and Mrs Emiel

Lieu-dit Les Gastines
27330 Épinay
Tel. : 02 32 46 26 34
Fax : 02 32 43 57 89
emiel.e @ club-internet.fr
www.leclosdesgastines.com

Open all year • 3 rooms, 2 of which have a mezzanine • €55, breakfast included • Table d'hôte €20 by reservation only • Terrace, garden, car park. Credit cards not accepted, no dogs allowed • Outdoor swimming pool, sauna

Delightfully old-fashioned.

Lovers of calm and authenticity will immediately fall head over heels for this attractive 18C timber-framed farm set in the midst of Normandy's green fields. The picture-perfect interior features a wealth of 19C and 20C objects and furniture picked up in second-hand and antique shops. Rooms which make up in charm what they lack in size, a garden that can hardly be seen for flowers, ducks paddling on the pond and a three-hundred-year-old press add the finishing touches to this rural landscape.

The "Corneille" family room.

Mr and Mrs Emiel's decorative flair can be admired in the loving restoration of this beautiful old farmhouse surrounded by sleepy countryside. Each of the rooms has been individually decorated and two have sloping ceilings, perfect for sleepy-headed children. Small fitness room, sauna, swimming pool in the garden, animals in the fields, mountain bikes for the taking, pleasant veranda with open fire – we could go on forever!

Access : 13.5km from Honfleur on the Pont-Audemer road (D 580), then take the D 312 on the left

Access : 14km southbound from Bernay on the D 140, Conches road and the D 833

 678 CHAMBRE D'HÔTE M. STEKELORUM
Mr and Mrs Stekelorum

 24 rue du Moulin
27630 Fourges
Tel. : 02 32 52 12 51
Fax : 02 32 52 13 12

Open all year • 3 non-smoking rooms, 2 of which are upstairs • €49, breakfast included • No table d'hôte • Garden, car park. Credit cards not accepted, no dogs allowed

 679 AUBERGE DE L'ABBAYE
Mr Sergent

 27800 Le Bec Hellouin
Tel. : 02 32 44 86 02
Fax : 02 32 46 32 23

Closed Jan, 17 to 30 Nov, Tue lunchtime in summer, every lunchtime in winter (except Sun), and Mon • 9 rooms, all have bath/WC and television • €70 to €75 (€60 to €71 low season); breakfast €8; half board €71 (€64 low season) • Menus €15 (lunchtime in the week) to €33 • Private car park • Shop with local products

We most liked
Less than 10km from Claude Monet's house and gardens in Giverny.

This old farmhouse stands close to the old mill of Fourges, whose picturesque site has prompted more than one budding Monet to reach for palette and canvas. The rooms are located in a separate wing, two are in the former attic and all feature a rustic flavour, which also extends to the raftered breakfast room, old bread oven, family heirlooms and the beautifully landscaped garden. We wished we could stay for ever!

We most liked
Waiting for the cows to come home!

A half-timbered 18C edifice opposite the abbey, creaking floorboards, the sweet scent of beeswax, a choice of sixty varieties of Calvados, home cooking with a distinctly regional accent and herds of peaceful black, white and brown cattle grazing under cider apple trees – could you be anywhere on earth but in Normandy? Even better, the renovated rooms are equally full of character.

Access : In the town

Access : In the centre of the village, near the church

680 LE PRIEURÉ DES FONTAINES
Mr and Mrs Decarsin

Route de Lisieux
27500 Les-Préaux
Tel. : 02 32 56 07 78
Fax : 02 32 57 45 83
jacques.decarsin@wanadoo.fr

Open all year • 5 non-smoking rooms, with bathrooms and telephone • €69, breakfast included • Table d'hôte €25 • Sitting room, garden, car park. Credit cards not accepted, no dogs allowed • Mountain biking, table-tennis

Bicycling in the nearby forest.

This 17C priory cradled in the valley of La Risles has been so well restored, you would be forgiven for thinking that it's new. The well-dimensioned, comfortable rooms are graced with old furniture, beams and tiled floors; all are non-smoking and equipped with telephones. A sitting room with fireplace, hall with piano and lovely garden are perfect to relax in.

Access : 5km to the south-west of Pont-Audemer on the D 139

681 LA HAYE LE COMTE
Mrs Maguet

4 route de la Haye-le-Comte
27400 Louviers
Tel. : 02 32 40 00 40
Fax : 02 32 25 03 85
www.manoir-louviers.com

Closed from 28 Dec to 17 Jan • 16 rooms, 2 of which have disabled access, with bathrooms and television • €80; breakfast €9 • Menus €16 to €39 • Garden, car park • Tennis, hiking and mountain biking

The old-fashioned charm of a French manor house.

Don't be put off by the rather austere walls of this 16C mansion, once inside, you will instantly be captivated by the disarming atmosphere of a bygone era. Each of the rooms is different but they all display a classical flavour. The two small sitting rooms and dining room are models of good taste. Walks, tennis, table-tennis, boules and lawn croquet all take place within the extensive grounds of this country retreat.

Access : 700m southbound from Louviers on the D 113

682 HÔTEL DU SAUMON
Mr Simon

89 place de la Madeleine
27130 Verneuil-sur-Avre
Tel. : 02 32 32 02 36
Fax : 02 32 37 55 80
hotel.saumon @ wanadoo.fr

Closed from 18 Dec to 5 Jan and Sun evenings from 5 Nov to 31 Mar • 29 rooms located in the main building on the street and in 2 separate wings in the courtyard, all have bath/WC or shower/WC and television • €39 to €55; breakfast €7 • Menus €11 (in the week) to €49 • Courtyard

683 HÔTEL D'ÉVREUX
Mr Elbaze

11 place d'Évreux
27200 Vernon
Tel. : 02 32 21 16 12
Fax : 02 32 21 32 73
hotel.devreux @ libertysurf.fr

Open all year; restaurant closed Sun except on national holidays • 12 rooms upstairs with bath/WC or shower/WC and television • €45 to €54; breakfast €6 • Restaurant Le Relais Normand: menus €20 to €26 • Terrace, private car park. No dogs allowed

We most liked **Verneuil's streets lined with half-timbered façades and smart townhouses.**

We most liked **Two kilometres from Claude Monet's lovely house and exquisite garden.**

This elegant late-18C coaching inn stands in the heart of this pretty town, opposite the church of La Madeleine flanked by a 56m-high tower, an ideal starting point for a tour of the countryside which inspired Dorothy Sayers' short story "The Bibulous Business of a Matter of Taste". The rooms of varying sizes are in the main and side wings, around a flower-filled courtyard; ask for one of the renovated rooms and sample the house speciality, salmon, in the tasteful restaurant.

The rooms of this half-timbered 17C house – former home of the Count of Évreux and later a coaching inn – have recently been renovated. Exposed beams, timber-framed walls, hunting trophies and a stone fireplace set the rustic scene for the dining room. In fine weather, tables are laid in the inner courtyard. An excellent wine-list includes a grand cru or two.

Access : On the main square, near the church

Access : In the town centre, opposite the post office

684 VILLAGE GROUCHY
Mr Sebire

11 rue du Vieux-Lavoir
50560 Agon-Coutainville
Tel. : 02 33 47 20 31
Fax : 02 33 47 20 31

Closed from 1 Jan to 1 Mar • 4 rooms • €36, breakfast included • No table d'hôte • Garden, car park. Credit cards not accepted, no dogs allowed

685 LA CROIX D'OR
Mr Bertheaume

83 rue de la Constitution
50300 Avranches
Tel. : 02 33 58 04 88
Fax : 02 33 58 06 95

Closed in Jan and Sun evenings from 15 Oct to 25 Mar • 25 rooms located in several buildings around a courtyard. Rooms have bath/WC or shower/WC and television • €43 to €61; breakfast €7; half board €52 to €60 • Menus €13 (lunchtime in the week) to €46 • Garden, private car park

The rustic modern flavour of this fishermen's house.

Village Grouchy is the name of an old fishing village that formerly stood here. Nowadays the granite walls of this old fishermen's house offer spacious rooms lined in wood from floor to ceiling. In the morning, take a seat on the wooden benches around a large table and toast yourself by the fireside. Summer kitchen in the immense garden in the rear. Warm and welcoming.

Daydreaming in the delightful garden.

This 17C coaching inn stands near the Patton Memorial which commemorates the "Avranches Breakthrough". Its half-timbered façade borders a pretty garden planted with apple trees and hydrangeas. Quiet rooms, some of which have been renovated. A countrified dining room whose collections of gleaming clocks, well-worn wardrobes, porcelain and copper pots, exposed beams and stonework would almost be worthy of a museum.

Access : 2km northbound from Agon-Coutainville on the D 72

Access : From the Mont-Saint-Michel, at Place du Général Patton, turn left onto Rue de la Constitution towards the town centre

686 LE CONQUÉRANT
Mr and Mrs Delomenede

18 rue Saint-Thomas Becket
50760 Barfleur
Tel. : 02 33 54 00 82
Fax : 02 33 54 65 25

Open from 15 Mar to 15 Nov • 13 rooms, some have bath/WC, or shower with or without WC, and television • €49 to €69; breakfast €8 • No restaurant, but there is a crêperie open in the evening for hotel guests • Garden, small private car park. No dogs allowed

 Drinking in the atmosphere of this tiny fishing harbour in a quayside café.

This handsome 17C granite house is just two minutes from the port: back in 1066, its shipyard built the vessel which carried William the Conqueror to the shores of England and victory. Twisting corridors, proof of the house's long past, lead to rustic, immaculate rooms, some of which boast beautiful Norman wardrobes. Breakfasts and supper banquets of sweet and savoury pancakes are served outdoors in the garden.

Access : In the street at right-angles to the seaside, between the harbour and Rue de la Poste

687 BEL AIR
Mr and Mrs Morel

Près du Château
50340 Flamanville
Tel. : 02 33 04 48 00
Fax : 02 33 04 49 56
hotelbelair @ aol.com

Closed from 20 Dec to 4 Jan • 15 rooms, 6 of which are for non-smokers, all have bath/WC or shower/WC and television • €62 to €70 (€50 to €62 low season); breakfast €8 • No restaurant • Garden, car park. No dogs allowed • Piano bar

 The excisemen's cliff path.

The windows of the cosy rooms overlook the neat fields of the Cotentin ("little coast") region of north-western Normandy. The breakfast room is set in a light, airy conservatory, the old-fashioned lounge-bar has a marble fireplace and piano; palm trees adorn the lovely garden. All this awaits you in the thick granite walls of this house, formerly the home of the steward of the castle farms, just a few fields from the beaches overlooking the Atlantic.

Access : By the D 4 that goes through the village, near the château

688 AUBERGE DE LA ROQUE
Mr and Mrs Delisle

50180 Hébécrevon
Tel. : 02 33 57 33 20
Fax : 02 33 57 51 20

Open all year • 16 rooms with bath/WC and television • €77, breakfast included • Menu €17 • Sitting room, park, car park. No dogs allowed • Tennis, fishing, mountain biking. Golf, horse-riding and swimming pool nearby

689 LE LOGIS
Mr and Mrs Fillâtre

50520 Juvigny-le-Tertre
Tel. : 02 33 59 38 20
Fax : 02 33 59 38 20

Open all year • 3 rooms • €37, breakfast included • Table d'hôte €13 • Car park. Credit cards not accepted • Visit the farm and taste local produce. Tennis and lake

Walking, riding or bicycling – the choice is yours.

This 16C and 17C edifice rises up at the end of a handsome drive lined with poplar trees, set in the green hillsides of the Terrette Valley. The rooms, lined in fabric, are decorated with lovely old furniture and the bathrooms are immaculate. Succulent home cooking showcases excellent farm-fresh ingredients. In the grounds, two ponds and a keep-fit track through the woods will keep you busy.

What is so wonderful about France is that you can taste everything!

Old stones and good local produce are the hallmark of this 17C farm. The rooms in the former dovecote are contemporary in style while the one in the main wing, with granite fireplace and beams carved with the royal fleur-de-lys insignia, has more character. Tennis courts and water sports nearby. The farm organises visits and tasting sessions, so save space in the boot to stock up on farm produce, cider and home-made preserves.

Access : 7.5km westbound from Saint-Lô, towards Lessay (D 900)

Access : 12km westbound from Mortain on the D 977 and the D 5, then take the D 55 towards Saint-Hilaire

 690 LE QUESNOT
Mr Germanicus

3 rue du Mont-César
50660 Montchaton
Tel. : 02 33 45 05 88

Closed from late Sep to Easter • 3 rooms • €40, breakfast included • No table d'hôte • Garden, car park. Credit cards not accepted, no dogs allowed

 691 MANOIR DE LA CROIX
Mrs Wagner

50530 Montviron
Tel. : 02 33 60 68 30
Fax : 02 33 60 69 21
contact @ manoirdelacroix.com

Open all year • 4 non-smoking rooms • €71, breakfast included • No table d'hôte • Garden, car park. Credit cards not accepted, no dogs allowed

We most liked
Cradled in a leafy nest of flowers.

Built out of local stone, this 18C house is surrounded by a curtain of foliage and flowers. All the stylish, well-kept rooms are upstairs. On the ground floor is a vast country living-room for the sole use of guests. From the terrace and small garden, you will be able to see the village church perched on an outcrop. Extremely friendly and welcoming.

We most liked **Gulp down the fresh air – inside and out of this non-smoking establishment.**

This 19C Anglo-Norman-style manor house overlooks a lovely garden, home to palms and other rare trees. The Empire and Louis-Philippe suites are immense and adorned with antiques, the other rooms and bathrooms are invariably spotless. The breakfast table is laden with cooked meats, cheeses and home-made jams and preserves. If your lungs have had enough of urban pollution, head for this bubble of atmospheric purity.

Access : 6.5km to the south-west of Coutances on the D 20 then the D 72

Access : 8km to the north-west of Avranches towards Granville (D 973), then the D 41 (1km after Montviron)

OMONVILLE-LA-PETITE - 50440 **RÉVILLE - 50760**

692 LA FOSSARDIÈRE
Mr Fossard

Hameau de la Fosse
50440 Omonville-la-Petite
Tel. : 02 33 52 19 83
Fax : 02 33 52 73 49

Closed from 15 Nov to 15 Mar • 10 rooms located in the hamlet, 9 have bath/WC, one has shower/WC • €47 to €60; breakfast €7 • No restaurant • Car park • Sauna, thalassotherapy, pond with picnic terrace

693 LA FERME DE CABOURG
Mrs Marie

150m de la mer et du Saire
50760 Réville
Tel. : 02 33 54 48 42
Fax : 02 33 54 48 42

Open all year • 3 rooms • €39, breakfast included • No table d'hôte • Garden, car park. Credit cards not accepted

 We most liked **Nothing could be more pastoral than this hamlet.**

This hamlet-cum-hotel is on the doorstep of Omonville, the last resting place of Jacques Prévert, poet-screenwriter and counter-cultural icon. The rooms, which vary in size and comfort, are spread over several sandstone houses. Breakfast is served in the hamlet's former bakery. Young and old always find plenty to do in or around the private pond, 300m away, whether rowing, picnicking or simply making daisy chains.

We most liked **Perfectly located, just 150m from the beach.**

A lovely drive lined in poplar trees leads up to this 15C fortified farm just two minutes from the Saire Valley and the seaside. The white walls of the rooms are dotted with the occasional block of granite and mullioned windows, loopholes and arrow slits, now glazed, you'll be glad to hear. Toast your toes in front of the roaring log fire lit in the sitting room in winter after trekking round the region's countless marvels of Romanesque architecture. Charming welcome.

Access : Near Cap de la Hague, between Saint-Germain-des-Vaux and Omonville-la-Rogue, opposite Anse Saint-Martin

Access : 3.5km northbound from Saint-Vaast on the D 1

  694 **FRANCE ET FUCHSIAS**
Brix family

20 rue du Maréchal Foch
50550 Saint-Vaast-la-Hougue
Tel. : 02 33 54 42 26
Fax : 02 33 43 46 79
France-fuchsias @ wanadoo.fr

Closed from 3 Jan to 1 Mar, Mon from Sep to Apr, Sun evening and Tue lunchtime from Nov to Mar • 33 rooms with bath/WC or shower/WC and television • €36 to €76; breakfast €7; half board €41 to €64 • Air-conditioned restaurant, menus €21 to €52 • Terrace, garden. No dogs allowed in rooms • In August mini recitals of chamber music

  695 **MANOIR DE LA FÉVRERIE**
Mrs Caillet

Village d'Arville
50760 Sainte-Geneviève
Tel. : 02 33 54 33 53
Fax : 02 33 22 12 50

Open all year • 3 rooms • €58, breakfast included • No table d'hôte • Sitting room, car park. No dogs allowed

 That inimitable female touch.

The façade, adorned with magnificent hundred-year-old fuchsias, of this old coaching inn hides the house's masterpiece, an extraordinary walled garden home to palms, mimosa, eucalyptus, banana trees and other exotic specimens. Who said that the Cotentin's "micro-climate" was a myth? In the summer, regional dishes are served on a teak-furnished terrace with the garden in full bloom making an unforgettable backdrop. The rooms in the annex are more spacious than those in the main wing.

 A matchless attention to detail.

The sea and Barfleur's picturesque harbour are only three kilometres from this charming 16C and 17C manor house. The snug bedrooms, reached by a granite staircase, were undoubtedly the work of a romantic at heart, as the pastel wallpaper, old furniture and striped or floral fabrics confirm. Breakfasts, served by the fireside in winter, are a feast for the eyes and the palate. We defy you to resist the temptation to curl up in the soft, inviting sofas and deep armchairs in the sitting room.

Access : In the town centre, not far from the port

Access : 3km westbound from Barfleur on the D 25 and the D 525 Sainte-Geneviève road

 696 FERME MUSÉE DU COTENTIN
Conseil Général de la Manche

Chemin de Beauvais
50480 Sainte-Mère-Église
Tel. : 02 33 95 40 20
Fax : 02 33 95 40 24
musee.sainte-mere @ wanadoo.fr

Closed in Dec and Jan • 4 rooms • €36, breakfast included • No table d'hôte • Car park • Visit to the museum

 697 MANOIR DE BELLAUNAY
Mrs Allix-Desfauteaux

11 route de Quettehou
50700 Tamerville
Tel. : 02 33 40 10 62

Closed from 15 Nov to 15 Mar • 3 rooms upstairs • €54, breakfast included • No table d'hôte • Garden, car park. Credit cards not accepted, no dogs allowed

 Spend a night in a museum!

 History oozes from every crevice of this old manor house.

This farm-museum offers guests the chance to get a real feel for life on the land. The rooms of this 17C and 18C stone farmhouse are an integral part of the museum and their decoration, pastel shades and furniture – including four-poster or alcove beds – is characteristic of the region. Guests can also visit the press, the granite tower where the apples were crushed, the collection of ploughs and the bakery. Highly unusual and well worth a look.

This 16C manor house, flanked by a tower and three handsome Romanesque arches is set in a lovely, tended mature garden. An impressive staircase leads up to the individually decorated rooms, each of which evokes a significant period in the domain's history. "Medieval" on the ground floor, "Louis XV" and "19C Norman" upstairs. The original wainscoting in the breakfast room adds the final touch to this historic abode.

Access : Northbound exit out of Sainte-Mère-Église, on the Valognes road

Access : 3km to the north-east of Valognes towards Quettehou

NORMANDY

698 LA MINOTERIE
Mr Clech

Route de Pontfarcy
50420 Tessy-sur-Vire
Tel. : 02 33 77 21 21
Fax : 02 33 77 21 22
la-minoterie@wanadoo.fr
www.la-minoterie.com

Closed Sun evening, Mon lunchtime and Wed • 7 rooms, one of which has disabled access, all have bath/WC or shower/WC and television • €53 to €69; breakfast €8; half board €39 to €51 • Menus €18 to €28 • Garden, car park

699 MANOIR SAINT-JEAN
Mr and Mrs Guérard

Le hameau Saint-Jean
50110 Tourlaville
Tel. : 02 33 22 00 86

Open all year • 3 non-smoking rooms • €45, breakfast included • No table d'hôte • Car park. Credit cards not accepted, no dogs allowed

 The picturesque Vire Valley.

This impressive stately home built at the end of the Second Empire stands in the heart of Normandy's neat patchwork of hedged fields. The fresh, well-kept rooms are furnished in a variety of styles, some have their original marble fireplaces while others have slightly outrageous bathrooms with Antique columns and frescoes. Red features prominently in the modern dining room. A shaded garden completes the picture of this quiet, secluded establishment.

 It would be difficult to find a more amiable ambassador for the region.

This warm, welcoming 18C manor lies on the edge of the park of the Château des Ravalets. The view from the windows over Trottebec, Cherbourg and the coast is quite superb. The immaculate rooms are adorned with family heirlooms, as are the sitting rooms. Your graceful hostess could talk until the cows come home about her region's immense natural and cultural heritage.

Access : Around 18km southbound from Saint-Lô on the D 28, on the way out of town

Access : 1km past the castle on the D 322, then head for the "centre aéré" (play centre) and the Brix road

700 VERTE CAMPAGNE
Mr and Mrs Bernou

Hameau Chevallier
50660 Trelly
Tel. : 02 33 47 65 33
Fax : 02 33 47 38 03

Closed from 24 Jan to 7 Feb, from 4 to 10 Dec, Sun evening and Wed lunchtime out of season and Mon • 6 rooms upstairs with bath/WC or shower/WC • €40 to €58; breakfast €6; half board €45 to €57 • 2 dining rooms; menus €22 to €55 • Garden, car park • Sitting room

701 GRAND HÔTEL DU LOUVRE
Mr Lehmann

28 rue des Religieuses
50700 Valognes
Tel. : 02 33 40 00 07
Fax : 02 33 40 13 73

Closed from 20 Dec to 21 Jan and Sun from Oct to Apr • 20 rooms, some have shower/WC or bath/WC and television • €42; breakfast €6; half board €39 to €44 • Menus €14 to €25 (dinner only) • Garage, private car park. No dogs allowed

 Wandering over meadow, grove and stream.

It is hard to believe that this authentic Norman farmhouse dates from 1717, so little has it been scarred by the passing of time. Hidden in a remote alcove of green countryside, the ivy-clad house offers modest rooms of matchless peace and quiet. The dining and sitting room have more character with roughly hewn beams, thick stone walls, narrow windows and immense fireplaces. The meals are as tasty as they are sophisticated.

 Valognes: two thousand years of art and history.

This grand residence, built in the early 18C, was converted into a hotel in the 19C. Today's horseless carriages have supplanted the barouches of yesteryear, but you can still see the old tack room in the stables. A superb spiral staircase in the 14C tower leads up to the rooms which are distinctly old-fashioned but nonetheless graced by the memory of a number of famous former occupants. The style of a bygone age still lingers in the restaurant.

Access : Once in Trelly, which is south of Coutances, continue south-east for 1.5km on the D 539, then take a minor road

Access : In the town centre

NORMANDY

 702 MANOIR DE L'ACHERIE
Mr Cahu

L'Archerie
50800 Villedieu-les-Poêles
Tel. : 02 33 51 13 87
Fax : 02 33 51 33 69
bernard.cahu@libertysurf.fr

Closed 24 Feb to 12 Mar, 4 to 20 Nov, Sun from mid-Oct to Easter and Mon, except evenings in summer • 15 rooms located in 3 buildings around a courtyard, one has disabled access, all have bath/WC or shower/WC and television • €40 to €54; breakfast €6; half board €53 to €61 • Menus €15 to €32 • Garden, car park. No dogs allowed • Play area

The peace and quiet of Normandy.

The practical, well-kept rooms have less character than the spot itself, which is comprised of a manor built in 1660, a small 18C chapel and a beautifully manicured flower garden. The restaurant serves copious regional dishes and chargrilled specialities and is extremely popular with locals who come from far and near — always a good sign. Shop selling local produce.

 703 LE GRAND CERF
Mr Bouvet

21 rue Saint-Blaise
61000 Alençon
Tel. : 02 33 26 00 51
Fax : 02 33 26 63 07

Closed from 21 Dec to 5 Jan, Sat lunchtime, Sun and national holidays • 22 rooms, all have bath/WC or shower/WC and television • €47 to €55; breakfast €6; half board €44 to €46 • Menus €16 to €27 • Terrace

Whether made out of wrought-iron or threads as fine as human hair, lace is everywhere.

The ornate wrought-iron adorning the façade of this hotel, built in 1843, has withstood the passing of time and lives up to Alençon's reputation as the capital of lace. The hotel has recently been treated to a facelift, but the hall is still adorned with the establishment's namesake, a stag's head and the restaurant and most of the rooms have retained their original dimensions and moulded ceilings. In the summer, meals are served in a delightful inner walled courtyard.

Access : 3.5km eastbound from Villedieu-les-Poêles on the D 554

Access : From Place du Général de Gaulle, drive towards the town centre, the hotel is on the right past the préfecture

704 HOSTELLERIE LES CHAMPS
Mr Kordalov

Route d'Alençon
61230 Gacé
Tel. : 02 33 39 09 05
Fax : 02 33 36 81 26

Open from Apr to Oct; closed Mon and Tue (except in Jul and Aug) • 14 rooms with bath/WC or shower/WC • €40 to €58; breakfast €8 • Menus €15 (lunchtime only) to €43 • Terrace, garden, private car park • Outdoor swimming pool, tennis

705 L'ORANGERIE
Mr and Mrs Guyard

Lieu-dit Le Pont
61210 La Forêt-d'Auvray
Tel. : 02 33 64 29 48

Open all year • 3 rooms • €39, breakfast included • No table d'hôte • Sitting room, car park. Credit cards not accepted, no dogs allowed

Horse lovers should not miss the chance to visit Le Pin stud farm.

Pick your knowledgeable hosts' brains about the region.

This Second Empire brick manor is home to a comfortable, if a tad out-dated, interior. Wine and dine under the soft lights of crystal chandeliers and sample the region's famous exports, the succulent Camembert and Livarot cheeses. The peaceful, shaded garden is just the place to curl up with a copy of Dumas' "La Dame aux camélias", inspired by the star-studded career of a local girl, Alphonsine Plessis. Tennis courts and a swimming pool await the more energetic.

It takes more than luck to catch a glimpse of this old orangery, at the end of a long drive lined in conifers, and the château it was formerly part of. Rooms full of character furnished with lovely old furniture await you: one even boasts a four-poster bed. The sitting room is crammed with antiques and works on the region. Children are happy playing on the numerous swings and slides in the garden.

Access : As you leave the village towards Alençon, slightly off the N 138

Access : 6km to the south-east of Rouvrou on the D 301 towards Rabodanges

706 L'ORANGERIE
Mr and Mrs Desailly

9 rue des Prés
61290 Longny-au-Perche
Tel. : 02 33 25 11 78

www.lorangerie.free.fr

Open all year • 3 rooms with bath/WC • €39, breakfast included • Table d'hôte (only by reservation) €8 to €12 • Sitting room, garden. Credit cards not accepted, no dogs allowed

707 LA FAÏENCERIE
Mr Dequesne

N 12
61420 Saint-Denis-sur-Sarthon
Tel. : 02 33 27 30 16
Fax : 02 33 27 17 56
la-faiencerie @ wanadoo.fr
www.lafaiencerie.com

Open every day from 15 May to 15 Oct • 16 rooms with bath/WC or shower/WC • €57 to €60; breakfast €8 • No restaurant • Park, private car park

We most liked **Settle down for a quiet evening in front of the fire after a day in the open air.**

We most liked **The authentic character of this old earthenware factory.**

This attractive former orangery is now home to three lovely rooms, each of which is named after a wild flower: Honeysuckle, Buttercup and Bluebell; the last of these is perfect for families. A large sitting room is ideal for long autumn evenings, grilling chestnuts or sizzling mushrooms over a crackling log fire. Ducks and fish have taken up residence in an old wash house hidden in the garden.

A sprawling park enhances the elegance of this former factory, most of whose rooms have been renovated and soundproofed. The comfortably affluent sitting room leads into a large rustic dining room where breakfast is served. The nearby N12, a major route between Brest and Paris, is your link to a host of picturesque landscapes in the area, but doesn't do much for the peace and quiet! Thankfully, the countryside behind the hotel is much more tranquil and relaxing.

Access : In the village

Access : Near the N12 towards Alençon

DUCLAIR - 76480   **EU - 76260**

708 LE PANORAMA
Mr and Mrs Lemercier

282 chemin du Panorama
76480 Duclair
Tel. : 02 35 37 68 84

Open all year • 4 rooms • €46, breakfast included • No table d'hôte • Garden, car park

709 MANOIR DE BEAUMONT
Mrs Demarquet

Route de Beaumont
76260 Eu
Tel. : 02 35 50 91 91

Closed for a fortnight in Nov and a fortnight in Jan • 3 rooms • €45, breakfast included • No table d'hôte • Garden, car park. Credit cards not accepted, no dogs allowed

An exceptional view of the Seine.

This 1930s villa built in the upper part of town lives up to its name, thanks to its idyllic view of the meanders of the Seine down below. The rooms are colourful and attractive; those under the eaves are perhaps the most inviting. The panoramic breakfast room and its tiny sitting room and fireplace are most appreciated, as is the delightful terraced garden.

Access : Take the chemin du Catel and turn left

Guests are offered a welcome drink on arrival.

On the edge of the forest, this former hunting lodge of the château of Eu enjoys a matchless view of the valley. The comfortable, tastefully decorated rooms overlook the park and the countryside; the family room has been thoughtfully equipped with a kitchenette. Relax in the sitting room and library and delve into the numerous books – in French and English – on the area. Bicycles and horse loose-boxes are also available for guests and their four-legged companions.

Access : 2km eastbound from Eu on the D 49 towards Eu forest

 710 **LA FERME DE LA CHAPELLE**
Mr Buchy

Côte de la Vierge
76400 Fécamp
Tel. : 02 35 10 12 12
Fax : 02 35 10 12 13
fermedelachapelle @ wanadoo.fr

Closed from 4 to 24 Nov • 22 rooms around the courtyard, 5 of which are self-contained with kitchenettes, 2 have disabled access, all have bath/WC and television • €64 to €81; breakfast €7; half board €52 (€48 low season) • Restaurant closed on Mon; menu €15 • Garden, car park • Outdoor swimming pool

 711 **AUBERGE DU BEAU LIEU**
Mr and Mrs Ramelet

Route de Paris – Le Fossé
76440 Forges-les-Eaux
Tel. : 02 35 90 50 36
Fax : 02 35 90 35 98
aubeaulieu @ aol.com
www.auberge-beaulieu-cityvox.com

Closed from 20 Jan to 12 Feb, from 2 to 6 Sep, from 9 to 13 Dec, Mon evening and Tue • 3 rooms overlooking the garden, with bath/WC and television • €36 to €53; breakfast €7 • Menus €16 (lunchtime in the week) to €47 • Terrace, garden, car park

 The Museum of Newfoundland Fishermen in Fécamp.

This old farm next door to a fishermen's chapel enjoys a wonderful position on the cliff, surveying the Channel and the port of Fécamp, from where French fishing sloops once set sail for the icy waters of Newfoundland. Inside the hotel can hardly be called luxurious, but it offers simple rooms, decorated with pine furniture and roughcast walls, laid out around a large square courtyard. We'll happily exchange luxury for authenticity any day!

 What could be more symbolic of Normandy than apple trees and dairy cows?

Two minutes from the tiny spa-resort of Forges, this attractive country inn is home to cosy rooms which open directly onto the garden and a snug rustic restaurant complete with beams and a stone fireplace. The tableware is a reminder of the town's illustrious porcelain industry. The warmth of your hosts' welcome is such that you will even forget you're in a hotel.

Access : From the town centre, drive towards Dieppe along the harbour, then left towards Notre-Dame du-Salut

Access : 2km on the D 915, towards Gournay

 712 LE RELAIS DE L'ABBAYE
Mr and Mrs Chatel

 798 rue du Quesney
76480 Jumièges
Tel. : 02 35 37 24 98

Open all year • 4 rooms • €37, breakfast included • No table d'hôte • Garden, car park

 713 VENT D'OUEST
Mr Lassarat

 4 rue Caligny
76600 Le Havre
Tel. : 02 35 42 50 69
Fax : 02 35 42 58 00
contact @ ventdouest.fr
www.ventdouest.fr

Open all year • 35 rooms, all have bath/WC or shower/WC and television • €75 to €80; breakfast €9 • No restaurant (Room service available) • Tea room

 Roman Polanski's "Tess" could well have been shot near here!

Nestling in the shadow of the famous abbey, this pretty Norman slate-roofed house has everything you could wish for in a B&B establishment. A sophisticated rustic interior with beams, timbers, enormous fireplace, ornaments and antique plates. The rooms under the eaves upstairs are the most pleasant and the bathrooms merit a special prize. In the summer, breakfast is served in the garden.

 Visiting the port of Le Havre in a launch.

Betwixt land and sea, the "Westerly" is a haven of charm in the heart of Le Havre's Modern Quarter designed by 20C architect Auguste Perret. A stone's throw from the harbour, the interior decoration has a distinctly briny flavour. The guest-rooms, on the other hand, are more adventurous and guests can choose between "country", "meditation" or "mountain" rooms, among others. Knick-knacks, snug quilts and a host of tiny details make all the difference.

Access : Near the abbey

Access : Drive along Quai Colbert past Vauban docks, turn right at Quai George V (Commerce docks) and continue straight on as far as St Joseph's Church

 714 **GOLF HÔTEL**
Evergreen SARL

 102 route de Dieppe
76470 Le Tréport
Tel. : 02 27 28 01 52
Fax : 02 27 28 01 51
evergreen2 @ wanadoo.fr

Closed in Jan and Feb • 10 non-smoking rooms, all have television • €77; breakfast €6 • No restaurant • Park, car park. No dogs allowed

 715 **LE PRIEURÉ SAINTE-CROIX**
Mr and Mrs Carton

 76470 Le Tréport
Tel. : 02 35 86 14 77

Open all year • 5 rooms with bathrooms • €54, breakfast included • No table d'hôte • Garden, car park. Credit cards not accepted, no dogs allowed

 Extremely well-equipped rooms.

In front of the entrance to Tréport's campsite, turn left onto the tree-lined drive which will take you up to this lovely late-19C half-timbered property set in the grounds of an immense park. All the non-smoking rooms are generously sized, well-equipped and personalised; all have a fridge. Friendly and excellent value for money.

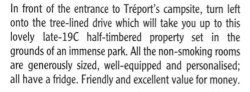 **Listening to the silence all around.**

This farmhouse built in the reign of Louis-Philippe was formerly part of the castle of Eu's estate and is still a working cattle-farm. All the rooms, located in a separate wing, have been decorated in the same spirit with parquet floors, period furniture and recent bathrooms. The breakfast area, although entirely revamped, has retained its rustic appeal. Take a seat under the hundred-year-old flowering cherry trees in the garden.

Access : Near Tréport campsite

Access : 2km eastbound from Le Tréport on the D 925 (Abbeville-Dieppe road)

MARTIN-ÉGLISE - 76370 **QUIBERVILLE - 76860**

716 AUBERGE DU CLOS NORMAND
Mr and Mrs Hauchecorne

22 rue Henri IV
76370 Martin-Église
Tel. : 02 35 04 40 34
Fax : 02 35 04 48 49

Closed from 15 Nov to 15 Dec, Mon evening and Tue
• 8 rooms in a building at the rear of the riverside garden.
Rooms have bath/WC or shower/WC, all have television
• €64 to €79; breakfast €6; half board €61 to
€67 • Menus €27 to €43 • Terrace, garden, car park. No
dogs allowed in restaurant

717 LES VERGERS
Mr Auclert

Rue des Vergers
76860 Quiberville
Tel. : 02 35 83 16 10
Fax : 02 35 83 36 46
chauclert @ aol.com

Open all year • 5 rooms • €55, breakfast included • No
table d'hôte • Garden, car park. No dogs allowed

 A pleasant pause on the edge of the
beech forest of Arques.

This 15C half-timbered brick inn is home to a
characteristically Norman dining room where guests tuck
into tender Dieppe soles or one of the village's famous
trout. All the countrified rooms are located in a quiet
building hidden at the back of a flowered garden on
the banks of the Eaulne. A walk along the forest path
will lead you to an obelisk commemorating Henri IV's
victory here, at the battle of Arques (1589).

 A beautifully decorated period
residence.

Guests can be sure of a pleasant welcome in this early
20C property. The spacious, comfortable rooms show a
distinct preference for a discreetly classical opulence with
pastel shades, floral fabrics and period furniture. Guests
can relax in the lovely landscaped garden. Within easy
reach of the sea, it is ideally situated to explore the
region.

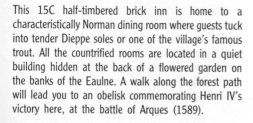

Access : In the village, located 7km to the south-east
of Dieppe

Access : 7km eastbound from Veules-les-Roses on
the D 68 then the D 75

718 DANDY
Mrs Renouard

719 DIEPPE
Mr Guéret

93 rue Cauchoise
76000 Rouen
Tel. : 02 35 07 32 00
Fax : 02 35 15 48 82
contact @ hotels-rouen.net

Place B. Tissot
76000 Rouen
Tel. : 02 35 71 96 00
Fax : 02 35 89 65 21
hotel.dieppe @ wanadoo.fr

Closed from 26 Dec to 2 Jan • 18 rooms with bath/WC and television • €72 to €90; breakfast €8 • No restaurant • Garage • Tea room, piano bar (hotel guests only)

Open all year • 41 rooms, 8 of which are non-smoking, all have bath/WC or shower/WC and television • €72 to €99; breakfast €8 • Air-conditioned restaurant; menus €21 to €36

The lady of the house delights in introducing guests to the many facets of vintage calvados.

Treat yourself to a tipple of well-aged Calvados in the snug bar.

Bathtubs with swan-shaped taps, well-padded beds, Louis XV-style furniture and classical paintings adorn the outrageously dandified rooms that you will either adore or detest! Despite the hotel's position on the doorstep of historic Rouen and in the heart of the busy Rue du Gros Horloge, you will sleep soundly and peacefully. Plans are afoot to open a 100% Norman-flavoured piano bar in the hotel.

The portraits on the walls are a reminder that the Guéret family has been at the reins of the Dieppe Hotel since 1880. The well-soundproofed rooms are regularly refurbished and furnished in cane or in a Louis XVI style. The roasting spit, which takes pride of place in the elegant dining room, sets the tone for the menu, where the local speciality, duckling, features prominently.

Access : Near the town centre in the pedestrian quarter, on the street linking Place Cauchoise to Place du Vieux Marché

Access : Opposite the railway station

 720 HÔTEL DES CARMES
Mr Beaumont

 33 place des Carmes
76000 Rouen
Tel. : 02 35 71 92 31
Fax : 02 35 71 76 96
h.des.carmes@mcom.fr

Open all year • 12 rooms on 4 floors • €45; breakfast
€6 • No restaurant

 721 LE VIEUX CARRÉ
Mr Beaumont

 34 rue Ganterie
76000 Rouen
Tel. : 02 35 71 67 70
Fax : 02 35 71 19 17

Open all year • 13 rooms, one of which has disabled
access, with bath/WC or shower/WC and television
• €51 to €55; breakfast €6 • No restaurant

 Perfectly located for a stay in town.

This 19C hotel, in the heart of Rouen, a stone's throw
from the cathedral and pedestrian streets, is ideally
situated. The refreshingly uncluttered rooms, spread
over four floors, are small but full of charm and
well-appointed; the most attractive overlook the
enchanting Place des Carmes. The breakfast room is
light and airy. Excellent value for money.

 There was nothing we didn't love!

The handsome walls of this house built in 1715, in the
company of other august façades of the same vintage,
line a street which is typical of Rouen and makes an
ideal base camp from which to explore this "museum
town". The interior is equally faultless and the rooms
are decorated with frescoes and old wardrobes straight
out of a boarding school dorm. The sitting room is snug
and welcoming and the hotel boasts a courtyard terrace
where mouth-watering pastries and a few choice dishes
are served.

Access : In the town centre

Access : In the heart of the old town, between the
Palais de Justice and the Musée des Beaux Arts

NORMANDY

 722   **CHAMBRE D'HÔTE MADAME GENTY**
Mrs Genty

Hameau de Ramouville
76740 Saint-Aubin-sur-Mer
Tel. : 02 35 83 47 05

Open all year • 5 rooms, 2 of which are on the ground floor and 3 are in the attic • €41, breakfast included • No table d'hôte • Garden, car park. Credit cards not accepted

 723   **FERME DE BRAY**
Mr and Mrs Perrier

76440 Sommery
Tel. : 02 35 90 57 27
ferme.de.bray @ wanadoo.fr

Open all year • 5 rooms with bathrooms • €40, breakfast included • No table d'hôte • Garden, car park. Credit cards not accepted, no dogs allowed • Farm visits, fishing

We most liked **Waking up to the enticing aroma of oven-fresh bread.**

After a masterful restoration this 18C regional farmstead is back in its prime. The thatched roof may have disappeared, but the lovely half-timbered walls were rescued and well-worn tiles and a fireplace adorn the rustic, warm sitting room. The rooms echo this rustic spirit and three are under the eaves. In the morning, the delicious smell of bread, freshly baked in the old oven, will entice you down to breakfast.

We most liked **The farm continues to uphold local rural traditions.**

The land has been farmed by the same family for 18 generations and their 17C and 18C farmhouse, which doubles as a museum and a B&B, is simply astounding. Rural through and through, the furniture and the simplicity of the interior decoration echo this country spirit: each of the rooms, lightened by striped wallpaper, has its own fireplace. Activities abound on the farm, including a visit to the press, mill, dairy parlour, dovecote, not to mention exhibitions and fishing in the pond.

Access : 4km northbound from Bourg-Dun then drive towards Quiberville

Access : 10km to the north-east of Forges-les-Eaux on the D 915

724 LA TERRASSE
Mr and Mrs Delafontaine

Route de Vasterival
76119 Varengeville-sur-Mer
Tel. : 02 35 85 12 54
Fax : 02 35 85 11 70
FRANCOISDELAFONTAINE @ wanadoo.fr
www.hotel-restaurant-la-terrasse.com

Open from 15 Mar to 15 Oct • 22 rooms with bath/WC or shower/WC • €43 to €49; breakfast €6; half board €43 to €49 • Menus €15 (in the week) to €26 • Garden, car park. No dogs allowed in restaurant • Tennis

725 MANOIR DU PLESSIS
Mr and Mrs Laurent

Le Plessis
76940 Vatteville-la-Rue
Tel. : 02 35 95 79 79
aplvatteville @ free.fr

Open all year • 5 rooms with bathrooms • €48, breakfast included • No table d'hôte • Garden, car park. Credit cards not accepted, no dogs allowed

The family donkey grazing in the field next to the path leading down to the beach.

At the end of a pretty little lane, flanked by fir trees, stands an early-20C brick house, which is the family home of the current owners. Nothing opulent or ostentatious deflects from the establishment's quiet charm: the TV has been thankfully banned from the calm rooms, enhanced by colourful fabrics and tartan carpets. Half of the bedrooms enjoy a sea view. Panoramic restaurant and a shaded garden.

The country flavour of this fine old manor house.

This Napoleonic brick manor-house topped by two high chimney stacks is worth a pause, if only to savour its quiet atmosphere. The rooms with bathrooms boast parquet floors and lovely antique furniture and are full of character; the others are more sober. The rustic dining room, decorated by dark wainscoting and the billiards table in the sitting room further add to the establishment's appeal. If you can tear yourselves away, do you fancy a spot of hunting, or brushing up on your artistic skills?

Access : 3km to the north-west on the D 75, then take the small minor road lined by fir trees

Access : 1km northbound from Vatteville-la-Rue

PAYS-DE-LA-LOIRE

F irst there is the peaceful valley of the Loire, the "Garden of France", renowned for its peaceful ambience, enchanting views, sumptuous manor houses and castles, magnificent floral gardens, lavish orchards, fields of vegetables and acre upon acre of vineyards. Tuck into a slab of rillettes pâté liberally spread on a crunchy baguette, a steaming platter of eels or a slice of goat's cheese while you savour a glass of light Loire wine. Continue westwards towards the sea to Nantes, once a port of entrance for enticing spices brought back from the New World: this is the home of the famous dry Muscadet. Further south, the Vendée still echoes to the cries of the Royalists' tragic last stand. Explore the secrets of its salt marshes, relax in its seaside resorts or head for the spectacular attractions of the Puy du Fou amusement park. Simple, country fare is not lacking, so make sure you taste a delicious dish of *mojettes* (white beans), a piping-hot plate of *chaudrée* (fish stew) or a mouth-watering slice of fresh brioche.

33 ESTABLISHMENTS
726 to **758**

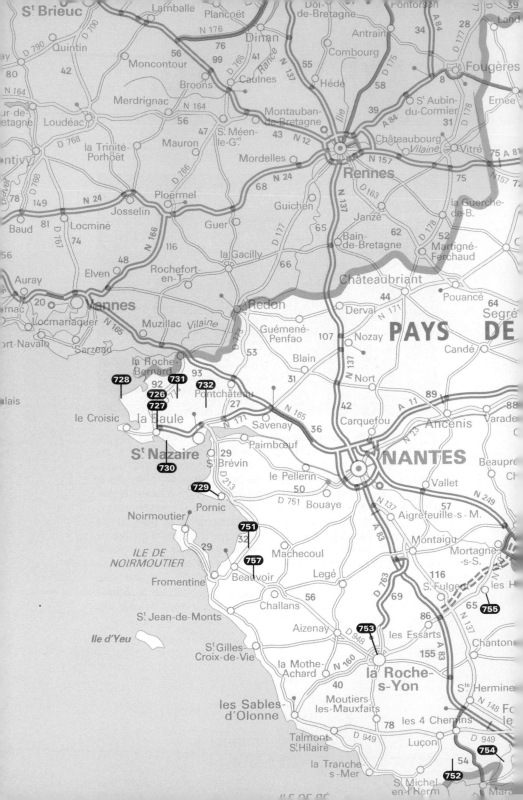

 726 **HOSTELLERIE DU BOIS**
Mr and Mrs Dabouis

65 avenue Lajarrige
44500 La Baule
Tel. : 02 40 60 24 78
Fax : 02 40 42 05 88
hostellerie-du-bois @ wanadoo.fr
www.hostellerie-du-bois.com

Open from 1 Apr to 31 Oct • 15 rooms on 2 floors, overlooking the garden or the street, all have bath/WC or shower/WC and television • €64 to €66 (€55 to €58 low season); breakfast €7 • No restaurant • Terrace, garden

 727 **LE MARINI**
Mr Mélis

22 avenue G. Clémenceau
44500 La Baule
Tel. : 02 40 60 23 29
Fax : 02 40 11 16 98
interhotelmarini @ wanadoo.fr

Open all year • 33 rooms, 29 of which have bath/WC, all have television • €68 to €81; breakfast €7 • Half board guests only, €50 to €56 • Garage • Indoor swimming pool with jacuzzi

 We most liked **La Baule les Pins provides a welcome break from the concrete jungle sadly present along the coast.**

Poised between the ocean and Parc des Dryades, this 1920s seaside hotel has a distinctive green and white half-timbered façade. The well-travelled owners have carefully preserved its pleasantly old-fashioned flavour as a showcase for the countless ornaments and pieces of furniture brought back from their travels in the Far East. The small garden in the back is simply delightful.

 We most liked **The globetrotter spirit of this hotel.**

Whether on a serious excursion throughout France or simply in search of a mooring spot to visit the region, you're bound to warm to the discreet ambience and the well thought-out attention to detail of this hotel. Off the beaten seaside track, it boasts a covered swimming pool and jacuzzi, a welcoming sitting room-bar with cosy armchairs, a reading corner and trim, practical bedrooms equipped with comfortable bedding. Breakfast and dinner are served around the pool.

Access : In the La Baule-les-Pins quarter: at Place des Palmiers head for the railway station

Access : In the town centre

 728 POSTE
Mr Daniel

26 rue de la Plage
44420 Piriac-sur-Mer
Tel. : 02 40 23 50 90
Fax : 02 40 23 68 96

Hotel open from 1 Apr to 11 Nov; restaurant open from Easter to 1 Nov • 15 rooms on 2 floors with bath/WC or showers with or without WC, some have television • €49 to €55; breakfast €6; half board €42 to €51 (€37 to €46 low season) • Restaurant closed Mon and Fri lunchtime; menus €16 to €21

729 RELAIS SAINT-GILLES
Mr and Mrs Robineau

7 rue Fernand de Mun
44210 Pornic
Tel. : 02 40 82 02 25

Open from 29 Mar to 29 Sep • 25 rooms with bath/WC and television • €55 to €61 (€44 to €50 low season); breakfast €7 • No restaurant • Terrace

 We most liked
The footpath to the Pointe du Castelli.

This appealing 1930s villa lies in the heart of a tiny fishing port surrounded by picturesque 17C houses. Its spacious, well-appointed rooms are looked after by the owner, for whom the term "clean enough to eat off the kitchen floor" is clearly not an empty remark! The family dining room is lit by immense arcades and in the summer, tables are laid outdoors.

 We most liked
A castle set in foliage, sandy beaches and a picture-postcard harbour: what more could you wish for?

This mid-19C coaching inn can be found on a quiet side street of this seaside resort. Two wings stand on either side of a terrace shaded by an arbour of climbing vines. Inside are regularly spruced up rooms with fresh wallpaper and paintwork, some with old furniture, and a plush bourgeois dining room. Your host, a former merchant navy officer, can point you towards a whole host of beautiful footpaths.

Access : In the centre of the village, on the main road opposite the chemist

Access : In the upper part of town, on a quiet street above the castle

  VILLA FLORNOY
Mr Rouault

7 avenue Flornoy
44380 Pornichet
Tel. : 02 40 11 60 00
Fax : 02 40 61 86 47
hotflornoy@aol.com
www.villa-flornoy.com

Hotel open from Feb to Nov; restaurant open from Easter to late Sep • 21 rooms with bath/WC or shower/WC and television • €72 to €86 (€61 to €70 low season); breakfast €7; half board €59 to €66 (€54 to €58 low season) • Restaurant closed Mon out of season; menu €20 (dinner only and reserved for hotel guests) • Garden. No dogs allowed in restaurant

 LES CHAUMIÈRES DU LAC
Mr Logodin

Route d'Herbignac
44110 Saint-Lyphard
Tel. : 02 40 91 32 32
Fax : 02 40 91 30 33
les.cinq.chaumières@wanadoo.fr

Closed in Dec and Jan, Mon evening and Tue out of season • 20 rooms, 2 of which have disabled access, all have bath/WC and television • €67 to €88 (€60 to €73 low season); breakfast €9; half board €61 to €72 (€57 to €65 low season) • Auberge Les Typhas: closed Mon and Tue lunchtime in summer; menus €20 (in the week) to €54 • Garden, car park • Swimming in a small lake

 No less than six kilometres of sandy beaches.

 France's best chefs and gourmets only use Guérande's "fleur de sel" – find out why.

The imposing salmon-coloured façade of this 1920s holiday villa is located in a residential area of this appealing southern Brittany seaside town. Inside, floral prints, matching bedspreads and curtains and polished wooden furniture set the scene for the bedrooms. The restaurant and comfortable circular sitting room echo this light, welcoming atmosphere. Hydrangeas and trees line the delightful garden where you can lounge on deck chairs should the beach prove too hectic.

This recently built hamlet of cottages right in the heart of the Brière Nature Reserve may not be the epitome of authenticity, but it is definitely an excellent way of finding out more about the region's salt marshes. The appeal is further enhanced by the tasteful yellow and white restaurant, pretty terrace and stylish bedrooms with canopy beds. All the more so once you've caught a glimpse of what the inside of a local cottage really looked like, at the reconstructed cottages in Kerhinet.

Access : In a residential street that leads into Av du Général de Gaulle at the town hall

Access : Outside the village, by the minor road, opposite the lake

 732 **TY GWENN**
Mr Collard

25 Île d'Errand
44550 Saint-Malo-de-Guersac
Tel. : 02 40 91 15 04

Closed from Oct to Mar • 4 non-smoking rooms, all have shower/WC, television and a small fridge • €46, breakfast included • Table d'hôte €19 • Sitting room, garden, car park. Credit cards not accepted, no dogs allowed • Outdoor swimming pool, billiards. Sailing, golf, horse-riding and fishing nearby

 Barge excursions along the canals of the Brière (on request).

The whitewashed walls, thatched roof and the leaded windows framed with curtains of this adorable cottage may well find you hunting for your camera. Inside, the romantic, snug rooms are equally appealing. In the sitting room you will be met with a sophisticated picture of exposed beams, a fireplace, lovely fabrics and a billiards table. Guests – non-smokers only – have the run of a delightful garden and swimming pool.

Access : 3km from Saint-Malo, straight on after the church

 733 **LE GRAND TALON**
Mrs Guervilly

3 route des Chapelles
49800 Andard
Tel. : 02 41 80 42 85
Fax : 02 41 80 42 85

Open all year • 3 rooms • €57, breakfast included • No table d'hôte • Park, car park. Credit cards not accepted

 Mrs Guervilly does her utmost to make your stay as pleasant as possible.

The graceful façade of this elegant 18C abode, covered in russet-red leaves in autumn, overlooks a square courtyard just two minutes from Angers. The peaceful bedrooms are tastefully decorated. If you're lucky with the weather, you can breakfast and picnic in the garden under a parasol.

Access : 11km eastbound from Angers on the N 147, towards Saumur then take the D 113

PAYS-DE-LA-LOIRE

  734 **HÔTEL DU MAIL**
Mr and Mrs Dupuis

 8 rue des Ursules
49100 Angers
Tel. : 02 41 25 05 25
Fax : 02 41 86 91 20
hoteldumailangers@yahoo.fr

Open all year • 26 rooms on 2 floors, most have bath/WC, the others have shower/WC, all have television • €46 to €59; breakfast €6 • No restaurant • Private car park in the inner courtyard

  735 **DOMAINE DE LA BRÉGELLERIE**
Mr and Mrs Sohn

49490 Auverse
Tel. : 02 41 82 11 69
Fax : 02 41 82 11 87
isabelle.sohn@wanadoo.fr
www.membres.lycos.fr/bregellerie/

Open all year • 5 non-smoking rooms, 4 of which are upstairs, all have bathrooms • €69, breakfast included • No table d'hôte • Garden, car park. Credit cards not accepted • Outdoor swimming pool, fishing in the pond

Angers is famed for its mild climate and a tradition of gracious living.

This discreet hotel standing in a side street of the historic town was an Ursuline convent in the 17C, before becoming a guesthouse and now boutique hotel. It takes a bit of finding but your efforts will be amply rewarded by the personalised, beautifully decorated rooms awaiting you. The breakfast room is decorated in a classic bourgeois style and guests can also venture onto a lovely mini-terrace in the inner courtyard. Definitely worth mailing home about!

"The Loire" bedroom.

After a full-scale renovation this old farmstead has been elevated to the rank of inn. The names of the individually decorated rooms located in a recent wing reveal their one-off themes: "Forest", "Vines", "Fields", "Pond" and "The Loire", whose curious boat-shaped bathtub is worth a special mention. A breakfast room, elegantly understated, a pool table, a large summer swimming pool in the garden and a pond – fishing possible – add the finishing touches.

Access : In a quiet street behind the town hall

Access : 14.5km to the south-west on the D 767, Noyant road and the D 79 on the right

736 **LA CROIX BLANCHE**
Mr and Mrs Thierry

7 place des Plantagenêts
49590 Fontevraud-l'Abbaye
Tel. : 02 41 51 71 11
Fax : 02 41 38 15 38
snc.lacroixblanche @ wanadoo.fr
www-logis-de-france.fr

Closed from 13 Jan to 10 Feb and from 18 to 29 Nov
• 21 rooms with bath/WC or shower/WC, all have
television • €50 to €80; breakfast €7; half board €54 to
€70 • Menus €16 to €39; crêperie as well as a restaurant
• Terrace, private car park. No dogs allowed • Souvenir
shop, boules, table-tennis, bicycles lent

737 **DOMAINE DE MESTRÉ**
Mr and Mrs Dauge

49590 Fontevraud-l'Abbaye
Tel. : 02 41 51 72 32
Fax : 02 41 51 71 90
www.dauge-fontevraud.com

Closed from 24 Dec to 1 Mar and weekends in Mar
• 12 rooms with bathrooms • €53, breakfast included
• Table d'hôte €23 • Park, car park. Credit cards not
accepted

 **Guests can borrow bicycles and
explore the countryside.**

 **Lavender, vetiver, olive oil, thyme,
cinnamon, nutmeg and rose-scented
soaps.**

"It all began in 1696, when Mistress Marie Cohier
wedded Master Mathieux Blochon and they opened the
hostelry." So begins the hotel's brochure and while the
rest is hardly a page-turner, it says a lot for the inn's
devotion to its guests' well-being. For over three
hundred years, its walls have welcomed travellers from
near and far, come to admire the neighbouring
monastery, refresh themselves in its rustic bedrooms and
build up their strength in its traditional restaurant and
crêperie.

This farm and its old tithe barn, dating back to the 13C,
once belonged to the Royal Abbey of Fontevraud:
nowadays, it is home to attractive, individually
decorated rooms in which it is easy to feel at home.
Breakfast and dinner, made with home-grown ingredients, are served in the former chapel. The estate's
woods and gardens are home to ancient cedar and
lime-trees and a visit to the estate's craft soap factory
is always a pleasure.

Access : In the town centre, opposite the entrance
to the Abbaye Royale

Access : 1km northbound from Fontevraud on the
D 947, towards Montsoreau

738 PRIEURÉ-SAINT-LAZARE
Mr Haudebault

Abbaye Royale
49590 Fontevraud-L'Abbaye
Tel. : 02 41 51 73 16
Fax : 02 41 51 75 50
contact @ hotelfp-fontevraud.com
www.hotelfp-fontevraud.com

Open from 29 Mar to 2 Nov • 52 rooms, 6 are for non-smokers, with bath/WC or shower/WC, all have television • €60 to €85; breakfast €10; half board €54 to €74 • Menus €27 to €54 • Garden, private car park. No dogs allowed

739 LE BUSSY
Mrs Roi

4 rue Jeanne d'Arc
49730 Montsoreau
Tel. : 02 41 38 11 11
Fax : 02 41 38 18 10

Closed in Jan, Tue in Mar and from 15 Oct to 28 Feb • 12 rooms, all have bath/WC or shower/WC and television • €53 to €58; breakfast €7 • No restaurant • Private car park

Find sanctuary within the walls of the abbey gardens.

The premises were a leper-house and a priory before being turned into a hotel. Although rich in history, its ancient walls have an eternal quality that appears to withstand the wear and tear of time: the almost monastical bedroom-cells provide a haven of peace and quiet for busy urban dwellers and the vaulted breakfast room and restaurant tables around the cloisters further extend this invitation to meditate and take stock.

What better place to curl up with one of Alexander Dumas' novels of romance and action?

The sign outside this 18C house at the top of the village pays homage to one of Dumas' famous heroes, Bussy d'Amboise, sweetheart of the Dame de Monsoreau. Most of the rooms, furnished in a Louis Philippe style and equipped with brand new bathrooms, survey the castle and the Loire. In the summer, breakfast is served in the flower-decked garden and throughout the rest of the year, in a delightful troglodyte room. Friendly and welcoming.

Access : In the abbey grounds

Access : In the upper part of town behind the castle

 740 DEMEURE DE LA VIGNOLE
Mrs Bartholeyns

3 impasse Marguerite d'Anjou
49730 Turquant
Tel. : 02 41 53 67 00
Fax : 02 41 53 67 09
demeure @ demeure-vignole.com
www.demeure-vignole.com

Open from Apr to Dec • 7 rooms, one of which has disabled access, all have bath/WC and television • €65 to €80; breakfast €8; half board €59 to €66 • Restaurant open only in the evening and only for hotel guests; closed on Wed • Terrace, garden, car park. No dogs allowed in restaurant

 741 CHÂTEAU DE MIRVAULT
Mr d'Ambrières

53200 Château-Gontier
Tel. : 02 43 07 10 82
Fax : 02 43 07 10 82
château.mirvault @ worldonline.fr

Open all year but by reservation only from Nov to Apr
• 5 rooms • €76, breakfast included • No table d'hôte
• Park, car park. Credit cards not accepted, no dogs allowed • Boating

We most liked
The troglodyte chamber where the villagers met in the 12C.

This exquisite estate only opened its doors as a hotel in 2000 following several years of major restoration work under the supervision of the architects of France's Listed Monuments. The 15C manor house and 17C outbuildings perched on the cliff have been turned into individually decorated rooms, where every effort has been taken to retain their historic decorative features such as beams, fireplace and bread oven. A terraced garden commands a wonderful view of the valley. Admirable.

We most liked
Friendly family welcome.

This elegant château on the banks of the Mayenne has been the home of the same family since 1573. The lavish sitting room is furnished with 18C antiques and family portraits, a beautiful tapestry hangs on the wall of the breakfast room and the park is home to warrens of wild rabbits straight out of "Watership Down". The rooms are equally ornate and overlook the river where you can go boating, should you so fancy.

Access : 10km from Saumur on the D 947, in the heart of the village

Access : Northbound on the N 162, on the Laval road on the banks of the Mayenne

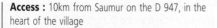

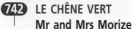

742 LE CHÊNE VERT
Mr and Mrs Morize

53270 Sainte-Suzanne
Tel. : 02 43 01 41 12
Fax : 02 43 01 47 18

Open all year • 10 rooms with shower/WC • €40, breakfast included • Meals €15 • Garden, car park • Outdoor swimming pool, walking, bicycle rental, table-tennis

743 OASIS
Mr Chedor

Route de Javron
53700 Villaines-la-Juhel
Tel. : 02 43 03 28 67
Fax : 02 43 03 35 30

Open all year • 13 rooms with bath/WC and television • €48 to €63; breakfast €6; half board €38 to €48 • No restaurant • Park with an ornamental pond, car park • Gym, mini-golf

We most liked
Sitting down at the large family dining table.

An impressive stone porch stands guard at the entrance to this working cereal farm with 19C origins. The renovated barns are home to light, airy rooms furnished with old Breton and Norman pieces. Breakfast and dinner are served in a pleasant dining room, and when the weather permits, on the terrace. A children's play area in the garden and a swimming pool in the summer keep the youngsters happy for hours.

We most liked
Brand new keep-fit facilities.

The original decorative, half-timbered brick walls, exposed beams and antique wardrobes of this old farm have been carefully preserved. You may be interested to know that two bedrooms have "jacuzzi" bathtubs. The living room is often lit by a roaring log fire at breakfast time. The park is also worthy of mention and although not enormous, boasts an ornamental pool and mini golf.

Access : 6km to the south-west of Sainte-Suzanne towards Sablé-sur-Sarthe, then drive to Chammes on the D 125

Access : Around 1km from the town centre, set back a little from the D 13, towards Javron and Bagnoles-de-l'Orne

744 LA GARENCIÈRE
Mr and Mrs Langlais

72610 Champfleur
Tel. : 02 33 31 75 84
Fax : 02 33 27 42 09

Closed from 25 to 31 Dec • 5 rooms • €42, breakfast included • Table d'hôte €18 • Car park. Credit cards not accepted • Indoor swimming pool

745 CHAMBRE D'HÔTE MADAME BORDEAU
Mrs Bordeau

Le Monet
72190 Coulaines
Tel. : 02 43 82 25 50

Open all year • 4 rooms • €42, breakfast included • No table d'hôte • Garden, car park. Credit cards not accepted, no dogs allowed

Green fields as far as the eye can see.

A country atmosphere on the doorstep of Le Mans.

At the time of the crusades, this hamlet, a former stronghold of the Knights of la Garencière, was a stopover point for pilgrims on the way to St James of Compostela. Nowadays, the large 19C farmhouse, built on the site of the old pilgrims' refuge, offers quiet, tastefully decorated rooms; the one in an independent cottage is ideal for families. Sample a generous spread of local produce, before taking a dip in the covered swimming pool overlooking the countryside.

Saved from ruin in the nick of time, this small country house has made a spectacular recovery. Madame clearly spends many hours in her garden. Inside, the original character has been preserved and enhanced by a generous sprinkling of modern comforts. The rooms are not enormous but beautifully furnished; those on the ground floor have exposed beams and the others are under the eaves. A log fire is lit in the winter to take the chill off the morning in the breakfast room.

Access : 6.5km south-east of Alençon towards Mamers and Champfleur (D 19), then continue towards Bourg-le-Roi

Access : 5km northbound from Le Mans, towards Mamers then Ballon on the D 300

 746 CHAMBRE D'HÔTE MADAME PEAN
Mrs Pean

5 Grande-Rue
72800 Le Lude
Tel. : 02 43 94 63 36

Closed from Oct to Mar • 3 rooms upstairs • €45, breakfast included • No table d'hôte • Garden. Credit cards not accepted

 747 L'AUBERGE DU PORT DES ROCHES
Mr and Mrs Lesiour

Le Port des Roches
72800 Luché-Pringé
Tel. : 02 43 45 44 48
Fax : 02 43 45 39 61

Closed from 28 Jan to 10 Mar, Sun evening, Tue lunchtime and Mon • 12 rooms with bath/WC or shower/WC, half of them have television • €43 to €48; breakfast €6 • Menus €19 to €34 • Terrace and riverside garden, private car park. No dogs allowed

 We most liked **Ideally situated, two minutes from the castle.**

Who could guess that behind the impressive walls of this handsome 17C property lies such a heavenly garden? Spacious, antique-furnished rooms like these, not to mention the delicious breakfasts, are the makings of a good holiday, but it is the atmosphere that will make you want to return: Madame Pean is so genuinely and clearly delighted to meet her guests that visits might well become an annual event.

We most liked **Strolling along the banks of the Loir.**

This smart country inn on the banks of the Loir now enjoys a supremely quiet location: it's hard to imagine that not so long ago, soft local stone was quarried from the surrounding hillsides and loaded onto boats which would be moored in front of the hotel. Light, airy, colourful rooms, a comfortable dining room with a homely feel and a riverside garden-terrace await guests in search of peace and quiet.

Access : In the village

Access : 2.5km eastbound on the D 13 towards Mancigné, then take the D 214

748 LE PETIT PONT
Mrs Brou

3 rue du Petit-Pont
72230 Moncé-en-Belin
Tel. : 02 43 42 03 32

Open all year • One room in the house and 5 others in a separate wing • €40, breakfast included • Table d'hôte €13 to €16 • Garden, car park. No dogs allowed

749 CHÂTEAU DE LA VOLONIÈRE
Mrs Becquelin

49 rue Principale
72340 Poncé-sur-le-Loir
Tel. : 02 43 79 68 16
Fax : 02 43 79 68 18
château-de-la-voloniere @ wanadoo.fr

Closed in Feb • 5 rooms • €76, breakfast included • Table d'hôte €20 to €40 • Park, car park • Visits to castles of the Loire

Your tireless hostess did much of the restoration herself.

Over the years, your energetic hostess has painstakingly restored her lovely house, covered in variegated vine, which is still part of a working farm. Her efforts have resulted in beautifully appointed, individually decorated rooms (non-smokers only). One of the rooms and a self-catering cottage are in the main building, while the others are in an independent wing. Friendly and welcoming.

Bohemian and easy-going.

Guests can depend on a perfect welcome when they arrive in this château, next door to the birthplace of the 16C poet, Pierre Ronsard. A bold colour scheme and antiques set the scene for the bedrooms, each of which is decorated on a the theme of a well-known tale: "Bluebeard", "Arabian Nights", "Merlin" and "Romeo and Juliet". The 15C chapel has been turned into the dining room and exhibitions are held in the former troglodyte kitchen.

Access : 11km southbound from Le Mans on the D 147 towards Arnage, then take the D 307

Access : In the village

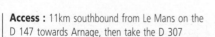

750 LE MOULIN DE LINTHE
Mr and Mrs Rollini

Route de Sougé-le-Ganelon
72130 Saint-Léonard-des-Bois
Tel. : 02 43 33 79 22
Fax : 02 43 33 79 22

Closed in Jan and Feb • 5 rooms • €58, breakfast
included • No table d'hôte • Terrace, garden, car park.
Credit cards not accepted • Fishing in the River Sarthe

751 HÔTEL DU MARTINET
Mrs Huchet

Place du Général Charrette
85230 Bouin
Tel. : 02 51 49 08 94
Fax : 02 51 49 83 08
hotel-martinet@free.fr
www.lemartinet.com

Restaurant closed in Nov, Tue from Apr to Sep, Sun
evening and Mon out of season • 21 rooms, 7 of which
are on the ground floor, with bath/WC or shower/WC
and television • €56 to €71; breakfast €7; half board
€48 to €69 (€48 low season) • Menus €19 (in the week)
to €23 • Garden, car park. No dogs allowed in restaurant
• Outdoor swimming pool, fitness room

Ever visited an ostrich farm?

Get back to grass roots in this three-hundred-year-old
mill surrounded by fields. Anglers can try their luck
tempting the pike in the Sarthe at the bottom of the
garden, others may prefer to visit the nearby ostrich
farm or simply go for long bike rides round the
countryside. Each of the spacious, light rooms is
furnished in a different style: Norman, Louis XVI, 1930s.
The sitting room commands a lovely view of the
millwheel.

Breathe in the scent of fresh flowers and beeswax.

The discreet walls of this 18C house hide a whole host
of assets including a quiet garden, a swimming pool and
spotless rooms – those on the ground floor with tiled
floors and cane furniture are the most pleasant. Come
the evening, take your places in the delightful dining
room with its painted woodwork, parquet floor and
marble fireplace. The owner, ever-active and unfailingly
friendly, will often present you with the catch of the day,
brought home by one of her sons and cooked by the
other!

Access : 400m south of the village towards
Sougé-le-Ganelon

Access : In the centre of the village on the D 758,
from Bourgneuf-en-Retz to Beauvoir-sur-Mer

752 LA CLOSERAIE
SCI de la forteresse

21 rue de la Paix
85450 Champagné-les-Marais
Tel. : 02 51 56 54 54
Fax : 01 69 26 00 07
info @ closeraie.com
www.closeraie.com

Closed from 31 Dec to 15 Feb • 5 rooms • €59, breakfast included • Table d'hôte €15 to €20 • Garden • Outdoor swimming pool, bicycle rentals, regional produce, theme weekends

753 LOGIS DE LA COUPERIE
Mrs Oliveau

85000 La Roche-sur-Yon
Tel. : 02 51 37 21 19
Fax : 02 51 47 71 08

Open all year • 7 rooms, all have bath/WC or shower/WC and television • €64 to €92 (€52 to €68 low season); breakfast €8 • No restaurant • Park with cottage garden and pond, car park. No dogs allowed • Library-sitting room, fishing in pond, bicycles, walking and horse-riding trail

Stocking up on home-made cherry, melon, fig, peach and onion jam.

Your hostess' faultless attention to detail.

It is rumoured that this lovely old mid-19C house was once a convent. Now restored, it offers pretty rooms with terracotta tiled floors, beams, antiques and reproductions of Impressionist paintings. All open onto the garden and one even has a fireplace. Plan on doing full justice to the breakfast table, piled high with a head-spinning array of home-cooked goodies. The establishment rents out bicycles and often organises theme weekends (gastronomy, walking, etc).

As soon as your foot crosses the threshold of this delightful country seat, rebuilt after the Revolution, you know you'll never want to leave. Perhaps it is because the lady of the house is so clearly determined to pamper her guests? Perhaps it is the romantic rooms named after fragrant flowers? Or is it the well-tended garden, vegetable plot or pond where swans and ducks paddle? An unforgettable experience.

Access : 13km southbound from Luçon on the D 50 and the D 949

Access : 5km eastbound: leave on the D 948 towards Niort, then take a left on the D 80

PAYS-DE-LA-LOIRE

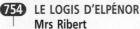 **754** LE LOGIS D'ELPÉNOR
Mrs Ribert

 5 rue de la Rivière
85770 Le Gué-de-Velluire
Tel. : 02 51 52 59 10
Fax : 02 51 52 57 21

Closed from Dec to Jan • 5 spacious rooms with bathrooms • €51, breakfast included • Table d'hôte €19 • Garden

755 LA MÉTAIRIE DU BOURG
Mr and Mrs Retailleau

 85500 Les Herbiers
Tel. : 02 51 67 23 97

Open all year • 3 rooms • €46, breakfast included • No table d'hôte • Garden, car park. Credit cards not accepted • Working farm (cattle breeding)

 Nothing beats delicious home cooking made with high-quality local produce.

What better base camp for exploring the region of the Marais poitevin and this sleepy country town on the banks of the Vendée? This enchanting 18C manor house is surrounded by a walled garden. The exquisite interior decoration reveals terracotta floors, antique furniture and shelves upon shelves of books. Carefully chosen fabrics adorn the light, spacious rooms. Make sure you taste the home-made "brioche" at breakfast time.

 Two minutes from the Puy du Fou Theme Park.

This fine old secluded farmhouse is typical of the region with its stone walls and round tiled roof. Still a working cattle farm, it also offers spotless B&B rooms whose generous dimensions include high raftered ceilings. In the sitting room, a conscious effort has been made to maintain a stylish rustic character with tiled floor, exposed beams, old furniture and a fireplace. Copious breakfasts served by the friendly hosts.

Access : 10km to the south-east of Chaillé-les-Marais on the D 25

Access : 5km to the north-east of Herbiers on the D 755, then the D 11 and a minor road

756 CHAMBRE D'HÔTE MADAME BONNET
Mrs Bonnet

69 rue de l'Abbaye
85420 Maillezais
Tel. : 02 51 87 23 00
Fax : 02 51 00 72 44

Open all year • 5 rooms with bathrooms • €60, breakfast included • No table d'hôte • Garden, park, car park. Credit cards not accepted • Exhibition of antique tools. Boating available

757 LE PAS DE L'ÎLE
Mr Pitaud

Le Pas-de-l'Île
85230 Saint-Gervais
Tel. : 02 51 68 78 51

Closed from Nov 1 to Easter • 3 rooms on the ground floor • €40, breakfast included • No table d'hôte • Garden, car park. Credit cards not accepted, no dogs allowed

Boating on the marsh's meandering, and mercifully mosquito-free, irrigation channels.

Ancient yew trees in the park, an orchard and a cottage garden encircle this 19C manor and its orangery. The stylish rooms are pleasant; the one under the eaves has a four-poster bed and the one in the former hen house opens directly onto the park. Boat-lovers will enjoy exploring the marsh's multitude of canals. Before leaving, make sure you take a peek at the collection of old clogs and farming tools.

Access : Near the abbey

Boating in the salt marshes.

This appealing low house is a fine example of the architectural style favoured in the Breton-Vendée marshes. Laid out around a central lawn, each of the rooms, decorated with lovely regional antiques, has its own private entrance. The most recent, under the exposed rafters, were our favourites. Don't miss the chance to sample the mouth-watering foie gras, made from ducks reared on the premises. Countless bicycling and boating opportunities.

Access : 4km to the south-east of Beauvoir on the D 948, then the D 59 and a minor road

 758 **AUBERGE DE MAÎTRE PANNETIER**
Mr Maillet

 Place du Corps de Garde
85120 Vouvant
Tel. : 02 51 00 80 12
Fax : 02 51 87 89 37

Closed from 15 Feb to 7 Mar, from 19 to 30 Nov, Sun evening and Mon except in Jul and Aug • 7 rooms, all have bath/WC or shower/WC and television • €43 to €49; breakfast €6; half board €53 • Menus €16 to €52 • Terrace • Billiards room, walking in the forest

 The 120 steps up Melusine's tower will have earned you the right to a slice of home-made cake.

This old inn stands in the heart of a picturesque village, built, according to local legend, by a fairy, Melusine who afterwards cast an evil spell over the region. The lady of the house would appear to have little time for such myths and has painstakingly created a warm, cosy atmosphere in the pine-furnished, pastel-coloured rooms. This welcoming spirit spills over into the dining rooms, one of which has a fireplace, the other a vaulted ceiling and the last a sheer rock wall.

Access : Between Fontenay-le-Comte and La Châtaigneraie (D 938), on the main village square

PICARDY

Ready for an action-packed ride over Picardy's fair and historic lands? The birthplace of France itself – the first French king, Clovis, was born in Soissons – Picardy is renowned for its wealthy Cistercian abbeys, splendid Gothic cathedrals, flamboyant town halls, marvellous castles, as well as its poignant reminders of the two World Wars. Those who prefer the pleasures of the countryside can take a boat trip through the floating gardens of Amiens, explore the botanical reserve of Marais de Cessière or observe the thousands of birds in the estuary of the Somme and at the Marquenterre bird sanctuary. Acre upon acre of unspoilt hills, woodland, plateaux, copses, pastures and vineyards welcome you with open arms. Picardy's rich culinary talents have been refined over the centuries and it would be unthinkable to leave without tasting the famous *pré-salé* – lamb fattened on the salt marshes – some smoked eel, duck pâté or a dessert laced with Chantilly cream.

30 ESTABLISHMENTS

759 to **788**

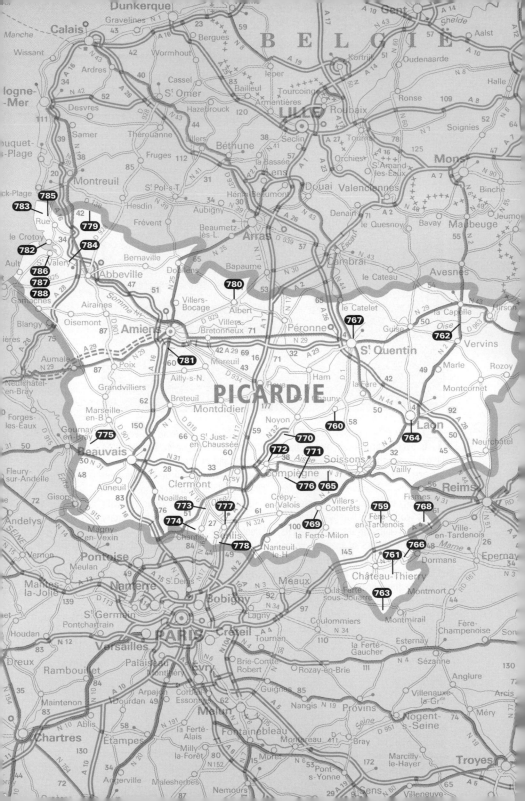

BRUYÈRES-SUR-FÈRE - 02130

CHAUNY - 02300

 759 VAL CHRÉTIEN
Mr and Mrs Sion

Ancienne abbaye du Val Chrétien
02130 Bruyères-sur-Fère
Tel. : 03 23 71 66 71
Fax : 03 23 71 87 35
val.chretien@wanadoo.fr

Open all year • 5 rooms upstairs • €53, breakfast included • Table d'hôte €18 • Park. Credit cards not accepted, no dogs allowed • Tennis

 760 LA TOQUE BLANCHE
Mr and Mrs Legueux

24 avenue Victor Hugo
02300 Chauny
Tel. : 03 23 39 98 98
Fax : 03 23 52 32 79

Closed from 2 to 6 Jan, 17 to 28 Feb, 5 to 25 Aug, Sat lunchtime, Sun evening and Mon • 6 rooms on 2 floors with bath/WC or shower/WC, 3 have television, 2 are for non-smokers • €61 to €83; breakfast €10 • Air-conditioned restaurant; menus €28 (in the week) to €63 • Terrace, park, private car park • Tennis

 Exceptional location in the heart of the legendary site of the Tardenois.

This building on the banks of the Ourcq and in the heart of the 12C ruins of the Abbey of Val Chrétien is quite remarkable. The rooms are soberly decorated with one striking exception, which is lined in red velvet and complete with a four-poster bed. On the ground floor are a breakfast room with exposed beams and a library where a fire is lit in winter. The covered tennis court is in an outbuilding.

Duck foie gras is the house speciality.

The Toque Blanche (Chef's hat), a lovely 1920s bourgeois house, not only provides comfortable personalised rooms but also offers cooking renowned for its subtle blends of flavours in either an Art Deco or a more classically-inspired dining room. Don't worry if your waistline seems to have expanded during the meal, you can walk off the extra calories in the immense shaded park.

Access : 8km westbound from Fère-en-Tardenois on the D 310, towards Bruyères-sur-Fère, on a by-road

Access : Near the town centre

PICARDY

 761 CHAMBRE D'HÔTE M. LECLÈRE
Mr and Mrs Leclère

1 rue de Launay
02330 Connigis
Tel. : 03 23 71 90 51
Fax : 03 23 71 48 57

Closed from 24 Dec to 1 Jan • 5 rooms • €46, breakfast included • Table d'hôte €14 • Park, car park. Credit cards not accepted, no dogs allowed • Bicycle rentals, hiking trails, trout fishing 200m away

762 LE CLOS DU MONTVINAGE
Mr and Mrs Trokay

8 rue Albert Ledent
02580 Étréaupont
Tel. : 03 23 97 91 10
Fax : 03 23 97 48 92
contact @ clos-du-montvinage.fr
www.clos-du-montvinage.fr

Closed Sun evening and Mon lunchtime • 20 rooms, one has disabled access, with bath/WC or shower/WC and television • €60 to €77; breakfast €7; half board €48 to €57 • Auberge du Val de l'Oise: closed in early Jan, 17 to 24 Feb, 12 to 18 Aug; menus €19 to €35 • Terrace, garden, private car park • Billiards room

 Walking or bicycling through vineyards.

This husband and wife team of Champagne producers has been painstakingly restoring this 16C farmhouse, once part of the Château de Connigis estate, for over ten years now. Thanks to their efforts, guests are now welcomed into spacious rooms with original parquet floors overlooking a magnificent park alongside the vineyards; the room in the tower, slightly removed from the main wing and decorated in an attractive Flemish style, is the quietest. Children's play area and bicycle rentals.

 The honeymoon suite and its four-poster bed!

Driving through the village, the eye is drawn to the intricate pattern of the brick walls of this delightful late-19C mansion. A pleasantly old-fashioned atmosphere extends to the well-dimensioned rooms furnished in a Louis Philippe style, while a recently opened wing is home to the establishment's brand new restaurant, pleasantly decorated and serving traditional French favourites.

Access : 12km eastbound from Château-Thierry on the N 3 and the D 4

Access : On the N 2, between Vervins and La Capelle, in the village

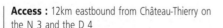

 763 DOMAINE DES PATRUS
Mr and Mrs Royol

02540 L'Épine-aux-Bois
Tel. : 03 23 69 85 85
Fax : 03 23 69 98 49
contact@domainedespatrus.com

Closed from Dec to Feb • 5 rooms, 2 of which are in the attic with a small sitting room • €80, breakfast included • Table d'hôte €28 • Sitting room, library, park, car park. No dogs allowed • Gallery devoted to La Fontaine. Wine and champagne tasting

 764 LA BANNIÈRE DE FRANCE
Mrs Lefèvre

11 rue F. Roosevelt
02000 Laon
Tel. : 03 23 23 21 44
Fax : 03 23 23 31 56
hotel.banniere.de.France@wanadoo.fr
www.hoteldelabannieredefrance.com

Closed from 20 Dec to 19 Jan • 18 rooms, 8 of which have bath/WC, 9 have shower/WC, all have television • €41 to €60; breakfast €6.50; half board €46 to €52 • Menus €20 to €51, children's menu €8 • Garage, public car park nearby. No dogs allowed

 We most liked **The collection of paintings devoted to La Fontaine's fables.**

In addition to the comfort it offers, another reason to stop at this handsome farmhouse is the pleasure of waking up in the morning and gazing out onto the peaceful countryside. The individually decorated rooms are furnished in traditional style; those with sloping ceilings have a little private sitting room. The mezzanine in the library is most attractive. Ask to see the owner's collection of works inspired by La Fontaine's fables; she is a fan and is only too happy to explain them.

 We most liked **A strenuous climb up the 180m-high(!) "Mountain of Laon".**

The central location of this former coaching inn built in 1685 makes it an excellent starting point from which to explore this wonderful Carolingian city in depth. We loved the elegant old-fashioned atmosphere of the establishment and its pleasant rooms; ask for one of the rooms refurbished in cheerful Provençal colours. The chef, head of a dedicated long-serving team, prepares traditional dishes of mouth-watering simplicity.

Access : 8km westbound from Montmirail on the D 933, towards Meaux

Access : In the upper part of town, in the heart of the historic area, opposite the town hall

 FERME DE LA MONTAGNE
Mr Ferté

02290 Ressons-le-Long
Tel. : 03 23 74 23 71
Fax : 03 23 74 24 82

Open all year • 5 rooms with bathrooms • €46, breakfast included • No table d'hôte • Garden, car park. Credit cards not accepted, no dogs allowed • Billiards and piano

 AUBERGE LE RELAIS
Mr and Mrs Berthuit

2 rue de Paris
02850 Reuilly-Sauvigny
Tel. : 03 23 70 35 36
Fax : 03 23 70 27 76
auberge-relais.de.reuilly @ wanadoo.fr

Closed from 10 Feb to 6 Mar, from 18 Aug to 5 Sep, Tue and Wed • 7 rooms with bath/WC or shower/WC, all are air-conditioned and have television • €64 to €82; breakfast €10 • Air-conditioned restaurant; menus €26 (in the week) to €68 • Garden, car park. No dogs allowed in rooms

 The sweeping view of the Aisne Valley.

Built on the edge of the plateau, this old farm of the Abbey of Notre-Dame de Soissons whose foundations date back to the 13C, enjoys a superb view of the Aisne Valley. All the generously-sized rooms have independent access and well-equipped bathrooms. A billiards table and piano adorn the sitting room, which also commands a splendid view of the countryside. Warm and welcoming.

 Limousin veal served with green asparagus in truffle sauce.

The flowered walls of this welcoming roadside-inn invite travellers to pause and stay for a while. The interior decoration reveals a masterful grasp of colour and light: the Provençal or contemporary rooms enjoy a superb view over the Champagne vineyards of the Marne Valley. Not to be outdone, the menu is appetising and up-to-date and served on a terrace-veranda or in the muted atmosphere of the dining room.

Access : 8km westbound from Soissons on the N 31 and the D 1160

Access : In the village by the N 3, between Château-Thierry and Dormans

  767 HÔTEL DES CANONNIERS
Mrs Michel

 15 rue des Canonniers
02100 Saint-Quentin
Tel. : 03 23 62 87 87
Fax : 03 23 62 87 86
www.hotel-canonniers.com

Closed from 4 to 8 Aug and Sun • 9 rooms, 7 of which have equipped kitchenettes, with bath/WC or shower/WC and television • €59 to €73; breakfast €9 • No restaurant • Terrace, garden, private car park • Billiards

  768 FERME DU CHÂTEAU
Mr and Mrs Ferry

02130 Villers-Agron-Aiguizy
Tel. : 03 23 71 60 67
Fax : 03 23 69 36 54
xavferry @ club-internet.fr

Open all year • 4 rooms with bathrooms • €67, breakfast included • Table d'hôte €29 • Park. Credit cards not accepted, no dogs allowed • Golf

 Drop by the Lecuyer Museum and admire the portraits by Quentin de La Tour.

Whether you stay for a night or for two weeks, the Canonniers offers superb personalised suites with a kitchenette at wonderfully reasonable prices. This handsome house, built in 1754, provides the service of a hotel and the charm of a maison d'hôte: guests can play billiards or lounge on the terrace opposite the lush green garden. The establishment also caters to businesses and meetings are held in its handsome old reception rooms.

The luxury of an 18-hole golf course right in the grounds.

Golfers will, of course, not be able to resist the prospect of spending a few days in this 18C mansion, whose park and river are home to an attractive golf course. Each of the spacious, quiet bedrooms is named after and decorated in a different colour: beige, blue, yellow, etc. The bathrooms are large and well-equipped. The table d'hôte has laid the accent on wholesome farm produce. If a round of golf doesn't appeal, perhaps tennis or trout fishing will take your fancy.

Access : Drive past the town hall, take a left on Rue de la Comédie, past the theatre, turn right

Access : 15km to the south-east of Fère-en-Tardenois

PICARDY

769 LE RÉGENT
Mrs Thiébaut

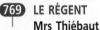

26 rue du Général Mangin
02600 Villers-Cotterets
Tel. : 03 23 96 01 46
Fax : 03 23 96 37 57
hotel.le.regent @ gofornet.com

Open all year, closed Sun evening from Nov to Mar (except during holidays) • 17 rooms on the front or the back, with bath/WC or shower/WC, all have television • €39 to €68; breakfast €8 • No restaurant • Courtyard, car park

770 LA FERME ANCIENNE DE BELLERIVE
Mrs Brunger

492 rue de Bellerive
60170 Cambronne-lès-Ribecourt
Tel. : 03 44 75 02 13
bellerive @ minitel.net

Open all year • 5 rooms • €45, breakfast included • Table d'hôte €14 • Garden, car park. Credit cards not accepted

 We most liked **Remember to bring a copy of "The Three Musketeers", written by local boy, Alexander Dumas.**

The walls of this elegant 18C mansion, just two minutes from the town, are so smart and spruce they could almost be new. Venture past the porch and say hello to the grey cat – the self appointed master of the house – before you cross the romantic paved courtyard. Inside, classically decorated rooms in keeping with the architecture await you, some of which should soon be treated to a facelift.

 We most liked **An authentic two-hundred-year-old farmhouse.**

This wonderful old farm, poised between canal and river, is a must for anyone who loves tranquillity and authenticity. An old barn houses simple, appealing rooms with white walls, net curtains and matching bedspreads, in addition to well-appointed bathrooms. The dining room is decorated in appealing rustic tones and the table d'hôte is open for lunch and dinner, serving appetising farm cooking. Lovely garden.

Access : Drive into Villers-Cotterets, the hotel is not far from the town centre, near the post office

Access : 7.5km to the south-west of Ourscamps on the N 32 and the D 66

CHELLES - 60350

  771 **RELAIS BRUNEHAUT**
Mr and Mrs Frenel

3 rue de l'Église
60350 Chelles
Tel. : 03 44 42 85 05
Fax : 03 44 42 83 30

Closed 15 Jan to 15 Feb and Mon • 7 rooms, one of which has a kitchenette, all have bath/WC or shower/WC and television • €47 to €56; breakfast €8; half board €58 to €60 • Restaurant closed Wed and Thu out of season and Mon and Tue; menus €26 (in the week) to €45 • Inner courtyard, garden, private car park

 Disneyland's Sleeping Beauty Castle was partly inspired by that of Pierrefonds.

A stay in this delightful coaching inn, actually two buildings set round a flowered courtyard, is the perfect opportunity to discover Pierrefonds, home to a splendid reconstruction of a medieval Gothic castle masterminded by Napoleon's talented architect, Viollet-le-Duc. The inn's mill, still in working order, houses most of the appealing, rustic rooms, filled with the sound of the gurgling stream nearby. The restaurant serves tasty, traditional cooking.

Access : In the centre of the village, 5km eastbound from Pierrefonds on the D 85

COMPIÈGNE - 60200

  772 **LE FRANCE ET LA RÔTISSERIE**
Mr Aguzzoli

 17 rue Eugène-Floquet
60200 Compiègne
Tel. : 03 44 40 02 74
Fax : 03 44 40 48 37
contact @ restauranthoteldefrance.fr

Open all year • 20 non-smoking rooms, all have bath/WC or shower/WC and television • €65; breakfast €7 • Menus €18 to €30

The feeling of old world refinement.

After major restoration work, the lovely half-timbered frame of this 17C mansion once again catches the eye of every passer-by. Colourful Jouy tapestries adorn the new bedrooms, antique mirrors and paintings line the walls of the wainscoted restaurant and the old-fashioned bistro is equally inviting. A perfect choice, just two minutes from the town hall with its bancloque (bell) dating from 1303 and three Picantins (automata).

Access : In the town centre

773 LA FERME DE VAUX
Mr and Mrs Joly

11 et 19 route de Vaux
60100 Creil
Tel. : 03 44 64 77 00
Fax : 03 44 26 81 50

Open all year • 29 rooms, 10 of which are upstairs, the others are on garden level, all have bath/WC and television • €57; breakfast €7; half board €53 • Restaurant closed Sat lunchtime and Sun evening; menus €25 to €33 • Car park

The porcelain of Creil is sought after by collectors from all over the world.

The owners of this old farm take great pleasure in sharing their "art de vivre" with guests. Each of the bedrooms is individually decorated, but the medieval chapel and its far-reaching gastronomic reputation are what attracts gourmets from all over the region. Savour the traditional French cuisine served in a Gothic dining room complete with arched windows and tapestries, or in the other more classical but equally sophisticated dining room. Some temptations are definitely worth giving in to!

Access : On leaving Creil after the crossroads of the N 16/D 120 drive towards Verneuil, on the way into the Vaux Industrial Zone

774 HOST. DU PAVILLON SAINT-HUBERT
Mrs Luck

Avenue de Toutevoie
60270 Gouvieux
Tel. : 03 44 57 07 04
Fax : 03 44 57 75 42

Closed in Feb; restaurant closed Sun evening and Mon, except holidays • 19 rooms, all have bath/WC or shower/WC and television • €50 to €65; breakfast €7; half board €55 to €65 • Menus €24 (in the week) to €30 • Riverside terrace, garden, car park

Chocolate lovers should not miss the chance to taste a "Crottin de Chantilly"!

This little gem is hidden at the end of a cul-de-sac, on the banks of the Oise surrounded by acres of peaceful countryside; ask for one of the renovated rooms overlooking the river. In fine weather, let the kids loose in the garden while you linger under the shade of plane trees on the terrace and watch the barges glide gently past. Appetising traditional cuisine.

Access : Leave Chantilly on the D 909 as far as Gouvieux, turn right and at Chaumont take a left into the dead-end road towards the Oise

HANNACHES - 60650

PIERREFONDS - 60350

 775 CHAMBRE D'HÔTE M. BRUANDET
Mr and Mrs Bruandet

13 hameau de Bellefontaine
60650 Hannaches
Tel. : 03 44 82 46 63
bruandet @ club-internet.fr

Closed in Jan • 3 rooms • €39, breakfast included • Table d'hôte €13 • Sitting room, garden. Credit cards not accepted, no dogs allowed

 776 DOMAINE DU BOIS D'AUCOURT
Mr Clément-Bayard

60350 Pierrefonds
Tel. : 03 44 42 80 34
Fax : 03 44 42 80 36

Open all year • 11 rooms with bath/WC • €61, breakfast included • Car park. No dogs allowed • Tennis, walking, mountain biking, horse-riding

 Sign up for an unusual art course with the master of the house.

The interior and exterior decoration of this 19C Picardy farmhouse is entirely the work of the talented sculptor-owner. Modern furniture adorns the relatively sober rooms, one of which has a mezzanine. The garden is strewn with the owner's metal sculptures, made from old materials such as agricultural equipment and everyday household utensils salvaged from tips and farms. Highly original, to say the least...

 A handsome family property surrounded by foliage.

The peaceful silence of the forest of Compiègne has crept into the walls of this large 19C half-timbered manor house. The rooms, all non-smoking, are decorated individually and all have faultless bathrooms. The only problem is deciding between the "Scottish", "Sevillan", "Tuscan", "Zen" or "Tropical" rooms. Breakfast is served in your hosts' warm, welcoming kitchen.

Access : 5km to the south-west of Gerberoy on the D 930, then the D 104 towards Bellefontaine

Access : 1.6km westbound from Pierrefonds on the D 85

  777 HOSTELLERIE DE LA PORTE BELLON
Mr Patenotte

51 rue Bellon
60300 Senlis
Tel. : 03 44 53 03 05
Fax : 03 44 53 29 94

Closed from 21 Dec to 6 Jan • 18 rooms with bathrooms
• €68; breakfast €6 • Menus €23 to €37 • Terrace

 778 CHAMBRE D'HÔTE MME PASSEMIER
Mrs Passemier

2 rue Mortefontaine
60520 Thiers-sur-Thève
Tel. : 03 44 54 98 43
Fax : 03 44 54 14 38

Open all year • 4 rooms • €54, breakfast included • No
table d'hôte • Sitting room, garden, car park. Credit cards
not accepted, no dogs allowed

 **Summer lunches in the delightful
paved courtyard.**

Character is not lacking in this hostelry, an old coaching
inn, just a few steps from the town centre of Senlis. The
well-dimensioned rooms are quiet and beautifully
appointed; those on the second floor have recently been
refurbished. Whenever the weather permits, lunch is
served in the shade of the exquisite paved courtyard
overlooking the garden. Wood prevails in the warm bar
and the vaulted wine cellar is equally attractive.

Snuggle up in a cosy bedroom.

The doors of this 19C hunting lodge, set in a sleepy
village, open onto a beautifully tended garden where
drinks are served on sunny days. The owners, who
clearly have a preference for blue and white, have
tastefully decorated the bedrooms in a pleasant mixture
of periods and styles. One of the rooms under the eaves
is perfect for families. Curl up by the fireside in the
sitting room with a good book or for a quiet chat.

Access : Near the town centre

Access : 9km southbound from Senlis towards Paris,
then take a minor road

ABBAYE DE VALLOIRES - 80120   ALBERT - 80300

 779 ABBAYE DE VALLOIRES
Association de Valloires

 Dans l'abbaye
80120 Abbaye de Valloires
Tel. : 03 22 29 62 33
Fax : 03 22 29 62 24

Open all year • 6 rooms • €71, breakfast included • Table d'hôte €14 • Garden, car park. No dogs allowed

 780 LE ROYAL PICARDIE
Mr and Mrs Altaie

Avenue du Général Leclerc
80300 Albert
Tel. : 03 22 75 37 00
Fax : 03 22 75 60 19
royalpicardie @ wanadoo.fr
www.royalpicardie.com

Closed from 2 to 18 Jan and from 1 to 18 Aug • 23 rooms, 4 of which are for non-smokers, 2 have disabled access and all have bath/WC and television • €75 to €78; breakfast €10 • Air-conditioned restaurant; closed Sun from Nov to Mar; menus €20 (in the week) to €45 • Car park • Tennis

 The historic walls of this abbey still offer sanctuary to travellers.

The Abbey of Valloires, a renowned tourist site, also operates a B&B establishment to help preserve and safeguard its rich architectural heritage. Located in a wing rebuilt in the 18C, the rooms, originally the monks' cells, are surprisingly spacious and attractively furnished: all overlook the superb monastery gardens. Who could resist breakfasting in the refectory of the former Cistercian community?

 The memorial park of Beaumont-Hamel pays homage to the lives lost in the First World War.

On the outskirts of Albert, there's no mistaking the battlements of this impressive modern building in solid stone. The interior is equally grandiose with spacious, attractive rooms, faultlessly soundproofed and perfectly appointed. The elegant dining room's vast dimensions make it a little cold, but the sophisticated traditional fare will soon warm you up.

Access : In the abbey

Access : Leave town on the road to Amiens

781 CHAMBRE D'HÔTE M. SAGUEZ
Mr Saguez

2 rue Grimaux
80480 Dury
Tel. : 03 22 95 29 52
Fax : 03 22 95 29 52

Open all year • 4 non-smoking rooms, one of which is on ground level, all have bathrooms • €49, breakfast included • No table d'hôte • Sitting room, garden, park, car park. Credit cards not accepted, no dogs allowed • Horse-drawn carriage rides

782 LES TOURELLES
Mr and Mrs Ferreira Da Silva

2 rue Pierre Guerlain
80550 Le Crotoy
Tel. : 03 22 27 16 33
Fax : 03 22 27 11 45
lestourelles@nhgroupe.com
www.lestourelles.com

Closed from 17 to 30 Jan • 23 rooms, most have shower/WC, the others have bath/WC, some have television • €38 to €64; breakfast €6; half board €47 to €55 • Menus €20 to €26 • Unusual children's dormitory

The appeal of a countryside setting, just a ten-minute drive from the centre of Amiens.

You will soon forget the nearby road when you see the wonderful country setting of this 19C house and are warmly greeted by the convivial owners. The rooms, non-smoking only, are located in a separate wing and are for the most part spacious, but the smallest of them is also the cosiest. The substantial breakfast, taken in the company of your discreet hosts, will set you up for the day.

The children's "dorm".

The fairy-tale twin turrets of this 19C red and white brick mansion dominate the tiny seaside resort and the "only south-facing beach of the North" (Pierre Guerlain). Most of the rooms, on a contemporary seafaring theme or in a delightfully clean-lined Swedish style, overlook the bay of the Somme. Delicious mounds of fresh fish and seafood will restore the disconsolate spirits of unlucky "shrimpers".

Access : 6km southbound from Amiens on the N 1 towards Beauvais

Access : Overlooking the bay, on the beach road

MONCHAUX - 80120

783 LA FERME DU CHÂTEAU DE LA MOTTE
Mr and Mrs Libert

36 route de la Froise
80120 Monchaux
Tel. : 03 22 23 94 48
Fax : 03 22 23 97 57

Open all year • 5 rooms with bath/WC and television • €55, breakfast included • No table d'hôte • Garden, park, car park. No dogs allowed • Outdoor swimming pool, tennis, table-tennis, fishing, mountain bike rental, clay pigeon shooting

The difficulty is agreeing on what to do!

The perfect "pied-à-terre" to explore the bay of the Somme: the spacious, comfortable rooms have been installed on the first floor of an old farmhouse and all overlook open fields and meadows. Guests have the run of an immense park with pond, tennis courts and table-tennis table. Nearby a vast range of paying activities await those with energy to spare: bicycle and mountain-bike rentals, fishing, clay pigeon shooting and hunting. Riders are also welcome.

Access : 11km to the north-east of Rue on the D 940 then the D 32

PORT-LE-GRAND - 80132

784 CHAMBRE D'HÔTE M. MAILLARD
Mr and Mrs Maillard

Bois-de-Bonance
80132 Port-le-Grand
Tel. : 03 22 24 11 97
Fax : 03 22 31 63 77
maillard.chambrehote@bonance.com

Closed from mid-Nov to mid-Feb • 5 rooms, 2 of which are in a separate wing, with bath/WC • €61, breakfast included • No table d'hôte • Garden. Credit cards not accepted, no dogs allowed • Swimming pool, keep-fit track, table-tennis, children's play area

The charm of a country garden.

You may be amused to learn that the pink walls and narrow Gothic-style windows of this 19C holiday home, in a secluded spot far from the bustle of traffic, are sometimes described as "English"! Whatever, the antique furnished rooms have been decorated with infinite taste; those in the former servants' quarters open directly onto the beautiful garden, brimming with flowers in the summer. In the winter, a cheerful fire adds warmth to the pleasant breakfast room.

Access : 11km eastbound from Saint-Valery-sur-Somme on the D 940, then the D 40 and a minor road

 785 **AUBERGE LE FIACRE**
Mr and Mrs Masmonteil

Route de Fort-Mahon
"Hameau de Routhiauville"
80120 Quend
Tel. : 03 22 23 47 30
Fax : 03 22 27 19 80

Closed in Jan, Tue and Wed lunchtimes • 11 rooms, one
of which has disabled access and 3 are suites. Most
rooms have bath/WC, some have shower/WC and
television • €75 to €80; breakfast €8; half board
€70 • Menus €18 (in the week) to €37 • Garden, car
park. No dogs allowed in rooms • Belle Dune golf course
(18-hole), 1.5km away

 **Fancy a quick two-kilometre-run in
the dunes!**

An old farm has been converted into an appealing inn
surrounded in foliage, where the restful, welcoming
rooms open onto the lovely garden. In addition, three
more modern apartments have recently been created.
The restaurant, for its part, has retained a resolutely
country style with exposed beams and tiled floors, a
perfect setting for its classic repertoire. Character and
quality: what more could you want!

Access : Leave the D 940 at Quend, between
Berck-sur-Mer and Rue, and take the D 32 towards
Fort-Mahon-Plage

 786 **CHAMBRE D'HÔTE MADAME SERVANT**
Mrs Servant

117 rue Au-Feurre
80230 Saint-Valery-sur-Somme
Tel. : 03 22 60 97 56

Open all year • 3 rooms and one suite • €49, breakfast
included • No table d'hôte • Garden. Credit cards not
accepted, no dogs allowed

 **The wonderful view of the unspoilt
bay of the Somme from Porte
Guillaume.**

This country house and neat garden stand in the upper
part of town, just round the corner from the elegant 12C
Porte Guillaume flanked by two towers. Each of the
rooms has been decorated on a different theme: blue
and white for the sea and sailors, old posters in the
cinema room and shades of green and wrought-iron
furniture in the garden room. The breakfast room is light
and airy and your hosts unfailingly friendly and
welcoming.

Access : In the historic town, near the church and
the town hall

  787 LA GRIBANE
Mr and Mrs Douchet

297 quai Jeanne-d'Arc
80230 Saint-Valery-sur-Somme
Tel. : 03 22 60 97 55

Open all year • 4 rooms • €69, breakfast included • No table d'hôte • Park, car park. Credit cards not accepted, no dogs allowed

  788 LE RELAIS GUILLAUME DE NORMANDY
Mr Crimet and Mr Dupré

Quai du Romerel
80230 Saint-Valéry-sur-Somme
Tel. : 03 22 60 82 36
Fax : 03 22 60 81 82
relais-guillaume@wanadoo.fr

Closed from 22 Dec to 31 Jan and Tue apart from 10 Jul to 20 Aug • 14 rooms, all have bath/WC or shower/WC and television • €53 to €63; breakfast €7; half board €53 to €59 • Air-conditioned restaurant; menus €15 to €38 • Terrace, car park

We most liked **The garden has been created in a "polder" opposite the ramparts.**

This 1930 house takes its name from the 18C merchant vessel used to navigate the rivers. The rooms of the main wing, painted in tones of blue, white and beige, overlook the bay; the others are in a pavilion in the middle of the garden. The large bay windows of the breakfast room look out onto the wonderful garden, wedged between the land reclaimed from the sea and the old city walls.

We most liked **A trip across the bay of the Somme aboard a real steam train.**

Take in the lovely Picardy coast from the windows of this elegant manor house facing the bay and on the outskirts of St-Valery-sur-Somme. None of the rooms are enormous, but half face the Channel, where you will sometimes be able to catch a glimpse of seals. The soberly decorated panoramic dining room also enables diners to enjoy the view while sampling the delicious traditional fare rustled up by the chef.

Access : In the historic town, near the beach

Access : On the dike, opposite the bay of the Somme

POITOU-CHARENTES

Illustrious names such as Cognac, Angoulême or La Rochelle all echo through France's history, but there is just as much to appreciate in the here and now. Start your journey lazing on the sandy beaches of its unspoilt coastline where the scent of pine trees mingles with the fresh sea air. A stay in a thalassotherapy resort will revive your flagging spirits, further boosted by a platter of oysters and lightly buttered bread. A bicycle is the best way to discover the region's delightfully unhilly coastal islands as you pedal along quaint little country lanes, lined with tiny blue and white cottages and multicoloured hollyhocks. Back on the mainland, embark on a barge and explore the thousand and one canals of the marshy, and mercifully mosquito-free, "Green Venice". You will have earned yourself a taste of vintage Cognac, or perhaps a glass of the less heady local apéritif, the fruity, ice-cold Pineau. If all this seems just too restful, head for Futuroscope, a theme park devoted to the moving image, and enjoy an action-packed day or two of life in the future.

15 ESTABLISHMENTS
789 to **803**

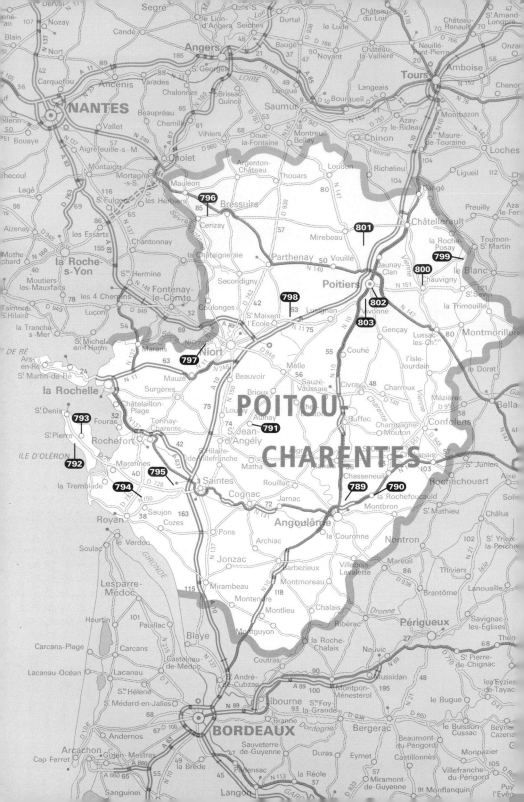

789 LA TEMPLERIE
Mr and Mrs Richon

Denat
16430 Champniers
Tel. : 05 45 68 73 89
Fax : 05 45 68 91 18

Open all year • 5 rooms, 2 of which are on the ground floor, all have bath/WC • €40, breakfast included • No table d'hôte • Disabled access, garden, car park • Outdoor swimming pool

 The windows of this farm have enjoyed the same pastoral view for two hundred years.

Guests are always assured of a warm welcome within this typically regional farmhouse. The rooms, located in the former outbuildings, are colourful and some are furnished with antiques; two open directly onto the garden and the swimming pool. In the winter, a cheerful fire is lit in the immense dining room. The sitting room with a lovely library on a mezzanine particularly caught our fancy.

Access : 9.5km northbound from Angoulême towards Poitiers on the N 10, then Balzac on the D 105

790 LA VIEILLE AUBERGE DE LA CARPE D'OR
Mr Ballanger and Mrs Moreau

1 rue de Vitrac
16110 La Rochefoucauld
Tel. : 05 45 62 02 72
Fax : 05 45 63 01 88

Open all year • 25 rooms, 2 of which have disabled access, all have bath/WC or shower/WC and television • €36 to €45; breakfast €6; half board €31 to €37 • Menus €11 (in the week) to €32 • Private car park 50m away

 The atmosphere is so easy-going, you could almost come down to breakfast in your slippers!

A small watchtower adorns the façade of this well-preserved 16C inn. The sweet scent of beeswax greets you in the dining and sitting rooms and reception, which have all kept a distinctly rustic character. Pristine bedrooms are furnished in a variety of styles; some have canopied beds. Breakfast is served in a wainscoted room with a lovely herringbone parquet floor.

Access : In the town centre, on a street corner

791 LE DONJON
Mr Hervé

4 rue des Hivers
17470 Aulnay
Tel. : 05 46 33 67 67
Fax : 05 46 33 67 64

Open all year • 10 rooms, one of which has disabled access, all have bath/WC or shower/WC and television • €46 to €54; breakfast €6 • No restaurant

792 LES TRÉMIÈRES
Mrs Jenouvrier

5 route de Saint-Pierre
17310 La Cotinière
Tel. : 05 46 47 44 25

Open all year • 5 rooms, 2 of which are suites • €39, breakfast €5 • No table d'hôte • Garden, car park. Credit cards not accepted

Long chats around the fire in the sitting room.

The green shuttered façade of this house stands near the Church of St Pierre, a masterpiece of regional Romanesque architecture. The interior of the house has been carefully restored in order to preserve the lovely old beams and gold-coloured limestone walls. Old furniture graces all the rooms and the bedrooms are further brightened by colourful bedspreads and matching curtains; all have modern bathrooms.

Just two minutes from the port and its brightly-coloured fishing boats.

This early-20C house with sandy-coloured walls and blue shutters is only a short walk from the port of La Cotinière and its shops. All the rooms and suites are personalised and immaculately cared for. Take things easy in the comfortable leather sofas and armchairs by the fireside in the sitting room. In the summertime, breakfast is served under the chestnut tree.

Access : In the heart of the village, near the main square

Access : 600m from the entrance to the village coming from Maisonneuve

793 MADAME MICHELINE DENIEAU
Mrs Denieau

20 rue de la Legère, la Menounière
17310 Saint-Pierre-d'Oléron
Tel. : 05 46 47 14 34
Fax : 05 46 36 03 15
denieau-jean-pierre @ wanadoo.fr

Open all year • 5 rooms • €43, breakfast included • No table d'hôte • Garden, car park. Credit cards not accepted, no dogs allowed

794 LE MOULIN DE CHALONS
Mr and Mrs Bouquet

2 rue du Bassin
17680 Le Gua
Tel. : 05 46 22 82 72
Fax : 05 46 22 91 07
moulin-de-chalons @ wanadoo.fr
www.moulin-de-chalons.com

Closed from 6 to 29 Jan, Sun evening and Mon • 14 rooms, all have bath/WC or shower/WC, some have television • €77 to €86 (€63 to €71 low season); breakfast €11; half board €64 to €79 (€60 to €72 low season) • Restaurant L'Écluse: menus €19 to €60 • Terrace, park with pond, car park • Fishing

Bicycling round the island as you explore its oyster beds and farms.

Oléron wines and the famous fortified Pineau are still produced on the estate of this stone farmhouse which is a fine example of island architecture. The neat and simple rooms are in the outbuildings; the most recent have old furniture and gaily painted green or blue beams; those with a mezzanine are very popular with families. Guests have the run of a kitchen, complete with an old kneading trough and a fireplace.

Boating on the romantically picturesque lake.

The lovely sand-coloured walls of this elegant 18C tidal mill are reflected in the limpid waters of a small lake. The warm, country interior of the mill, built on the estuary of the Seudre, is graced with well-polished regional furniture and lovely old timbers. We preferred the rooms overlooking the idyllic park and its profusion of roses, hydrangeas and geraniums. The country dining room is very pretty.

Access : 3km westbound from Saint-Pierre-d'Oléron

Access : By the D 733 from Rochefort to Royan

 795 CHAMBRE D'HÔTE M. TROUVÉ
Mr and Mrs Trouvé

5 rue de l'Église
17810 Saint-Georges-des-Coteaux
Tel. : 05 46 92 96 66
Fax : 05 46 92 96 66

Closed from 15 Nov to 28 Mar • 4 rooms • €43, breakfast included • No table d'hôte • Garden, car park. Credit cards not accepted, no dogs allowed • Tennis and horse-riding centre in the village

 796 CHÂTEAU DE CIRIÈRES
Mr and Mrs Degast

79140 Cirières
Tel. : 05 49 80 53 08

Closed from Oct to Apr • 3 rooms with bath/WC • €55, breakfast included • No table d'hôte • Garden, park, car park. Credit cards not accepted, no dogs allowed • Fishing, bicycle rental. Tennis, swimming pool and footpaths nearby

 We most liked
Each bedroom pays light-hearted tribute to a famous author.

You will not be disappointed should you decide to spend a night or two in this 18C farmstead, surrounded by a large garden. The cow-shed and barn have been turned into an immense room which serves as a combined lobby, sitting room, library and billiards room. Country furniture adorns the bedrooms, each named after a favourite author – Agatha Christie and Tintin's creator, Hergé are among them. Make sure you take a look at the old wash house or "bujor".

We most liked
Anglers will adore the pond filled with gudgeon.

The granite walls of this château, originally built in 1852, rise up in the midst of nearly 45 acres of parkland. The carved doors, tapestries and prints of hunting scenes, antiques and immense black-and-white tiled vaulted gallery of the stylish interior are fully in keeping with the elegant surroundings, and this sophistication extends to the parquet-floored bedrooms; a canopy bed and old photos in the first, marquetry furniture and rugs in the second and a frieze and park view for the last.

Access : 9km to the north-west of Saintes towards Rochefort on the N 137 then the D 127

Access : 11km westbound from Bressuire on the D 960bis then the D 150 towards Bretignolles

COULON - 79510

SOUDAN - 79800

 797 AU MARAIS
Mrs Nerrière

46 quai Louis Hardy
79510 Coulon
Tel. : 05 49 35 90 43
Fax : 05 49 35 81 98
information @ hotel-aumarais.com
www.hotel-aumarais.com

Closed from 15 Dec to 1 Feb • 18 rooms located in 2 houses, one has disabled access. Rooms have bath/WC or shower/WC, all have television • €52 to €71; breakfast €8 • No restaurant

 798 L'ORANGERIE
Mr and Mrs Drouiteau

N 11
79800 Soudan
Tel. : 05 49 06 56 06
Fax : 05 49 06 56 10
www.lorangerie-hotel.com

Closed from 12 Nov to 12 Dec, Sun evening and Wed • 7 rooms, half of which are at the rear, all have bath/WC or shower/WC and television • €34 to €40; breakfast €6; half board €46 • Menus €14 (in the week) to €38 • Terrace, garden, car park

 Glide over the waters of "Green Venice".

A perfect place to begin exploring the aquatic maze of what is known as "Green Venice". The pale stone walls and blue shutters of this pair of 19C boatmen's houses face the marsh's landing stage. The modern, cheerful rooms are decorated with bold Provençal fabrics and most give onto the toing-and-froing of the boats. In summer, the area is busy during the day but after nightfall, all becomes peaceful and car-free!

 Lina and Alain's enthusiastic greeting.

This 19C orangery was formerly a wrought-iron workshop. The unpretentious rooms are gradually being renovated; we suggest booking one of those to the rear, which are quieter. The breakfast room is on the veranda and the wine-coloured restaurant overlooks the shaded garden. Just down the road, Bougon is home to five prehistoric tumuli, offering a wonderful opportunity for old and young to travel back in time 5 000 years.

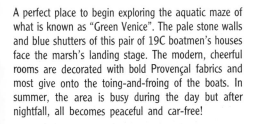

Access : Near the landing stage where boat trips leave

Access : In the centre of the village, on the N 11 from Niort to Poitiers

799 LE RELAIS DU LYON D'OR
Mr Thoreau

4 rue d'Enfer
86260 Angles-sur-l'Anglin
Tel. : 05 49 48 32 53
Fax : 05 49 84 02 28
thoreau@lyondor.com

Closed in Jan and Feb, Tue lunchtime and Mon • 10 rooms, one of which has disabled access and one is split-level, all have bath/WC or shower/WC and television • €75 (€69 low season); breakfast €8; half board €58 to €66 (€55 to €63 low season) • Menus €20 to €30 • Terrace, garden, private car park

800 LA VEAUDEPIERRE
Mr de Giafferi

8 rue du Berry
86300 Chauvigny
Tel. : 05 49 46 30 81
Fax : 05 49 47 64 12
laveaudepierre@club-internet.fr
www.perso.club-internet.fr/laveaudepierre

Closed from Nov 1 to Easter except during school holidays • 5 rooms • €47, breakfast included • No table d'hôte • Garden, car park. Credit cards not accepted, no dogs allowed

We most liked

Relaxing in the idyllic garden.

In a picturesque village, perched on a rocky outcrop, this former 15C coaching inn offers personalised rooms furnished with items picked up in antique shops. The owners clearly have their guests' physical and cultural well-being at heart as is shown by the beauty centre (hammam, massages, etc) and the numerous art courses organised in the spring and autumn (patina, sponge or rag painting, plastering, etc).

We most liked

At the foot of the medieval city.

We were charmed by this superb 18C mansion dominated by the ruins of the baronial castle. The interior is particularly rich in wonderful decoration, including woodwork, period furniture, a lovely stone staircase and a collection of antique musical instruments. Bedrooms in stylish fabrics all overlook the walled garden. The hotel is at the foot of steps which lead to the upper town.

Access : In the centre of the village

Access : From the town hall, take the first left after the church

CHENECHÉ - 86380 **POITIERS - 86000**

801 CHÂTEAU DE LABAROM
Mr Le Gallais

86380 Cheneché
Tel. : 05 49 51 24 22
Fax : 05 49 51 47 38
chateau.de.labarom@wanadoo.fr

Closed from Nov 1 to Mar • 3 rooms • €69, breakfast included • No table d'hôte • Dovecote, park, car park. Credit cards not accepted, no dogs allowed • Outdoor swimming pool

802 CHÂTEAU DE VAUMORET
Vaucamp family

Rue du Breuil-Mingot
86000 Poitiers
Tel. : 05 49 61 32 11
Fax : 05 49 01 04 54

Open all year • 3 rooms with bath/WC • €68, breakfast included • No table d'hôte • Park, car park. Credit cards not accepted

Oh la la! Row upon row of books about the region and all in French!

This 16C and 17C château was built in three hundred acres of parkland. It makes an ideal base camp to explore the region. We loved the well-worn aristocratic feel of the creaky floor boards and old furniture. The spacious rooms are lined in fabric and graced with beautiful antiques: the monumental period fireplace in the breakfast room cannot fail to catch the eye. The owner, who dabbles in art in his spare time, will happily talk you through the rudiments of painting on porcelain.

A countryside setting on the doorstep of Poitiers.

Nearly 45 acres of green meadows and woodland encircle this beautifully restored 17C mansion. The rooms, in the right wing, boast some fine old furniture, prints and paintings and all have immaculate bathrooms. Enjoy breakfast in a light, airy room, then borrow a bike and start exploring.

Access : 15km to the north-west of Futuroscope towards Neuville and Lencloître then the D 15

Access : 10km north-east of Poitiers towards La Roche-Posay on the D 3, then Sèvres-Anxaumont on the D 18

803 **LE CHALET DE VENISE**
Mr and Mrs Mautret

6 rue du Square
86280 Saint-Benoît
Tel. : 05 49 88 45 07
Fax : 05 49 52 95 44

Closed from 6 to 12 Jan, 15 Feb to 4 Mar, 26 Aug to 5 Sep, Sun evening and Mon • 12 rooms, one of which has disabled access, with bath/WC and television • €46 to €58; breakfast €7 • Restaurant closed Tue lunchtime except from Apr to Sep; menus €24 (in the week) to €44 • Terrace, garden, car park

A former Benedictine abbey is the site for this sleepy village.

The austere walls conceal a sumptuous interior. The bay windows of the elegant dining room overlook a riverside garden and some of the modern, practical rooms have a balcony. The riverside terrace is quite idyllic in fine weather, while the meals are imaginative enough to tempt even the most discerning palates. Heaven for gourmets!

Access : In the village, 4km southbound from Poitiers on the D 88, near the town hall

As you listen to the fishmongers hawking their wares under its sunny blue skies, you cannot help but fall in love with the infectious, happy-go-lucky spirit of Marseilles. Elsewhere, the steady chirring of the cicadas is interrupted only by the sheep-bells ringing in the hills as the shepherds bring their flocks home at night. The sun rises early over the ochre walls of hilltop villages which keep a careful watch over the fields of lavender below, shaded only by an occasional line of plane trees. Venture into the multitude of tiny hinterland villages and slow down to the gentle pace of the villagers as they leave the shade of the lime trees for the refreshingly cool walls of the café. However, come 2pm, you will soon begin to wonder where everyone is. On hot summer afternoons, everyone exercises their God-given right to a nap, from the fashionable beaches of Saint Tropez and seaside cabins of the Camargue to medieval walled cities surrounded by cypresses or a tiny fishing boat off the coast of Toulon. As the sun begins to set, life starts up again and the players of pétanque emerge; join them as they down a glass of pastis, then feast on bubbling *bouillabaisse*.

101 ESTABLISHMENTS
804 to **904**

  804 AZTECA
Mr Chabre

3 rue François Arnaud
04400 Barcelonnette
Tel. : 04 92 81 46 36
Fax : 04 92 81 43 92
hotel-azteca @ wanadoo.fr
www.hotel-azteca.fr.st

Closed in Nov • 27 rooms, 5 of which are split-level and one has disabled access. Rooms have bath/WC and television • €65 to €80; breakfast €10 • No restaurant • Private car park, private shuttle bus to the ski resorts • Nearby: swimming pool, tennis, 6-hole golf course, horse-riding, climbing, alpine and white-water sports

  805 MAS DU FIGUIER
Mr Levrault

La Fontaine
04200 Bevons
Tel. : 04 92 62 81 28
Fax : 04 92 62 81 28
mas.du.figuier @ wanadoo.fr

Open all year • 3 rooms with large bathrooms • €49, breakfast included • Table d'hôte €18.29 • Park, car park. Credit cards not accepted

 The fascinating link between this tiny mountain village and Mexico.

A wing has recently been added to this "Mexican" villa built in 1888 by one of the many farmers and craftsmen who left the hills of Ubaye to seek their fortune in the New World, and returned to mark their success in grand style. The hotel's Latin American theme, which may surprise at first but is in fact common throughout the valley, features naive "mural" paintings, an Aztec calendar and arts and crafts from Mexico. We were particularly taken with the three "Mexican" bedrooms.

 Trekking up to the ridge of the Lure – on donkey-back!

A field of lavender stretches in front of this remote 17C mas – or Provençal farm – which stands at an altitude of 650m opposite the Lure Mountain. A proudly southern flavour prevails in the welcoming rooms, decorated in warm colours with tiled ceilings and exposed beams. We particularly liked the large bathrooms and their Moorish influence. In the winter, the fireside in the sitting room is definitely the cosiest spot in the house.

Access : Near the post office

Access : 18km westbound from Sisteron on the N 85, the D 946 and the D 553

806 AUBERGE CHAREMBEAU
Mr Berger

Route de Niozelles
04300 Forcalquier
Tel. : 04 92 70 91 70
Fax : 04 92 70 91 83
charembeau @ provenceweb.fr
www.charembeau.com

Open from 15 Feb to 15 Nov • 22 rooms, one of which has disabled access, with bath/WC or shower/WC, all have television, some have a balcony or terrace • €66 to €81; breakfast €8 • No restaurant • Park, car park. No dogs allowed • Swimming pool (from May to Sep), tennis, bicycles, horse-riding

807 CAMPAGNE "LE PARADIS"
Mr Pourcin

04300 Forcalquier
Tel. : 04 92 75 37 33

Open all year • 4 rooms on ground level and 4 gîtes • €50, breakfast included • No table d'hôte • Garden, terrace, car park. Credit cards not accepted, no dogs allowed

We most liked **What better way to explore the region than by bicycle or on horse-back (on request)!**

We most liked **Horses everywhere – the riding stables are only a horseshoe away!**

This lovely 18C farmhouse, which lies in a secluded landscape of hill and dale, enjoys the patronage of regular, satisfied customers. The lady of the house chose the Provençal fittings and fixtures in the well-proportioned bedrooms herself. The house doesn't have a restaurant but guests are welcome to picnic in the shaded park and perhaps taste the famous local goat's-cheese – banon.

The old horse mangers and photos on the walls of the vaulted breakfast room bear witness to the establishment's long-standing relations with our four-legged friends. The old farmhouse nestles at the foot of a citadel, overlooking the quiet countryside. The immaculate bare walls of the bedrooms in the old barn add a monastical flavour; two have a mezzanine.

Access : Eastbound from Forcalquier, on the N 100 towards Niozelles for 2.5km, then right on a minor road

Access : Villeneuve road on the D 16 and the D 216

 808   **VILLA CASTELLANE**
Mr Coulomb

Avenue des Thermes
04800 Gréoux-les-Bains
Tel. : 04 92 78 00 31
Fax : 04 92 78 09 77
hotelcaste @ ad.com

Closed from Dec to Feb • 16 rooms with bathrooms, all have television • €63; breakfast €8 • No restaurant • Park, terrace, car park • Outdoor swimming pool

 809   **LES MÉANS**
Mrs Millet

Les Méans
04340 Méolans-Revel
Tel. : 04 92 81 03 91
Fax : 04 92 81 03 91
lesmeans @ chez.com

Closed from 15 Oct to 1 May • 5 rooms, all have bath/WC • €58, breakfast included • Table d'hôte €17 • Sitting room, terrace, garden, car park

Right in the heart of this spa-resort.

The former hunting lodge of the Marquis of Castellane was built in a park of ancient cedar trees, now opposite the casino in the centre of the resort. The bedrooms and bathrooms have all been comfortably refurbished: those planning to stay longer will probably opt for one of the apartments. Meals are served on the veranda and when the weather permits, on one of the shaded terraces.

A glimpse of the typical interior of houses in the valley.

Built when this secluded mountain region still swore allegiance to the counts of Savoy, this 16C farmhouse at an altitude of 1 000m is just the place to get away from it all and catch up on your beauty sleep. The spacious, well-appointed rooms all have lovely bathrooms with earthenware tiles; some also have a balcony. In the winter, a roaring log fire takes the chill off the large vaulted room on the ground floor. In the summertime, meals are often served in the garden, near the old bread oven.

Access : In the centre of the village

Access : 4km from Martinet on the D 900, Gap road

  810 LE CLOS DES IRIS
Miss Dorche-Teissier

Le Pavillon Saint-Michel
04360 Moustiers-Sainte-Marie
Tel. : 04 92 74 63 46
closdesiris @ wanadoo.fr
http://perso.wanadoo.fr/soleil2/iris/

Open all year • 8 rooms with shower/WC • €64;
breakfast €8 • No restaurant • Garden, terrace

  811 MONASTÈRE DE SEGRIÈS
Mr and Mrs Allègre

04360 Moustiers-Sainte-Marie
Tel. : 04 92 74 64 32
Fax : 04 92 74 64 22

Closed from Nov to Mar • 5 rooms with bathrooms
• €45, breakfast included • Table d'hôte €14 • Terrace,
park, car park. Credit cards not accepted, no dogs
allowed

 Cat-napping on a deck chair under the trellis.

We fell head over heels for this blue-shuttered mas surrounded by greenery at the foot of the village. All the garden-level rooms and suites have private terraces equipped with garden tables and deck chairs, protected from the sun by a bower of sweet-scented climbing roses. The bathrooms are tiled with the lovely rustic tiles of Salernes, a famous tile village just a short way down the road to Toulon.

 Only tell special friends about this enchanting monastery.

The fragrance of lavender and rosemary is all around you as you make your way up the winding lane to this superb monastery surrounded by oak trees. The spacious rooms, which overlook the cloisters and pool or the valley, are so quiet, you may well wonder if the monastery is still cloaked in its vow of silence. Deep sofas and a billiards table set the scene in the sitting room. It's the sort of place you want to tell everyone about and then worry that it might get overcrowded!

Access : 400m from the village, on the Chemin de Quinson

Access : 6km to the north-west of Moustiers on the D 952

 812 JAS DES NEVIÈRES
Mr Duermael

Route de Saint-Pierre
04300 Pierrerue
Tel. : 04 92 75 24 99
Fax : 04 92 75 03 75
duermael@wanadoo.fr
www.jas-des-nevieres.com

Closed from Nov to Mar • 4 rooms, 2 of which are on the ground floor with shower/WC, the 2 upstairs have bath/WC • €62, breakfast included • No table d'hôte • Terrace, car park. Credit cards not accepted, no dogs allowed • Outdoor swimming pool

 813 LA FERME DU COUVENT
Mr Rieul

Les Molanès
04400 Pra-Loup
Tel. : 04 92 84 05 05
Fax : 04 92 84 05 05

Open all year • 5 rooms • €64, breakfast included • Table d'hôte €15 • Garden • Tennis

The beautifully decorated bedrooms

The thick stone walls of this former sheepfold in the heart of the hamlet hide an undreamt-of haven of style and sophistication. We were unable to find fault with the refined good taste of the lovely bedrooms. Breakfast is served on a delightful inner patio, which echoes to the chirping of cicadas in the summertime. From the pool, you will be able to enjoy an uninterrupted view of mile upon mile of open fields.

A 100% authentic Ubaye farmhouse.

In the heart of the resort, this 14C farm is a welcome surprise among the string of modern chalets. The farm's venerable age is still visible inside, in its low door-frames, floor made out of larch logs, narrow windows and cool rooms. Each of the simple bedrooms has its own terrace overlooking the valley, Barcelonette and the peaks. We particularly liked the fireside dinners.

Access : 6km eastbound from Forcalquier on the D 12 then the D 212

Access : In the resort

814 LE PRIEURÉ DE MOLANES
Mr Paradis

Les Molanes
04400 Pra-Loup
Tel. : 04 92 84 11 43
Fax : 04 92 84 01 88
hotel.leprieure@wanadoo.fr
www.hotel-leprieure.fr

Open from 1 Jun to 16 Sep and from 14 Sep to 15 Apr
• 14 rooms on 2 floors, with bath/WC or shower/WC,
all have television • €60 to 74; breakfast €7; half board
€61 • Menus €20 to €39 • Terrace, garden, car park
• Summer swimming pool

815 LE VIEUX CASTEL
Mr and Mrs Masina

04500 Roumoules
Tel. : 04 92 77 75 42
Fax : 04 92 77 75 42
vieuxcastel@hotmail.com

Closed from Christmas to 1 Apr • 5 non-smoking rooms,
all have bath/WC • €43, breakfast included • No table
d'hôte • Garden, sitting room. Credit cards not accepted,
no dogs allowed

**Did you notice the owner's name?
What more shall we say?**

May the devil take you if don't find happiness in this
17C priory! All the more so, as the chairlift of this alpine
resort overlooking the lovely valley of Ubaye is on the
doorstep of a superb skiing domain which unabashedly
claims to be "a top resort for top people"! If the thrill
of swooping down a powdery slope doesn't appeal, slap
on the sun cream and relax on the south-facing terrace!
A cheerful fire burns in the restaurant where you can
sample a wide range of tasty dishes.

**An afternoon's reading in the family
library.**

Planted over three hundred years ago, the mature
chestnut trees still stand guard in front of this 17C
house, formerly the property of the Clérissy family,
inventors of Moustiers porcelain. The bedrooms have
coffered ceilings and are decorated with hand-painted
stencils; all are non-smoking. Arches, a fireplace and
period furniture in the dining room set-off the ornate
stone patterned floor.

Access : 8.5km to the south-west of Barcelonnette,
on the D 902, then the D 908 and right on the
D 109

Access : 4km to the north-east of Riez,
Moustiers-Ste-Marie road (D 952), on the way into
the village of Roumoules

816 DOMAINE DES RAYES
Mr Masure

04200 Saint-Geniez
Tel. : 04 92 61 22 76
Fax : 04 92 61 06 44
les.rayes@wanadoo.fr

Closed from Oct to May except during school holidays
• 5 rooms • €61, breakfast included • Table d'hôte
€17 • Car park. No dogs allowed • Outdoor swimming
pool, Children's play area

817 LE PETIT PORT
Mr Decaux

Les Ferrières
04500 Sainte-Croix-de-Verdon
Tel. : 04 92 77 77 23
Fax : 04 92 77 77 23
bdx@chez.com

Closed in Jan • 4 rooms, all have bathrooms • €45,
breakfast included • No table d'hôte • Credit cards not
accepted, no dogs allowed • Electric boat rental

We most liked
Blessed with silence.

Exceptional is the only word to describe the location of
this 17C sheepfold perched at an altitude of 1 300m
and surrounded by open heath. Quiet, often immense
bedrooms are decorated in a bold local palette. Wining
and dining in the inviting dining room, reading in the
superb vaulted sitting rooms or daydreaming on the
terrace which commands a stunning view of the Durance
Valley; all offer their own particular pleasure.

We most liked
The sandy beaches of Lake Ste-Croix, just a step away.

This tastefully renovated country villa stands in the heart
of a little village which seems to cling to the
mountainside. Lovely, warm hues adorn the bright
bedrooms, equipped with spanking new bathrooms; two
enjoy a view over the turquoise waters of Lake
Ste-Croix. Don't even attempt to resist the delicious
breakfasts served on the terrace in summer, you'll regret
it!

Access : 17km to the north-east of Sisteron,
Saint-Geniez road on the D 3

Access : In the village

818 CHAMBRE D'HÔTE MADAME FARAUT
Mrs Faraut

14 rue de l'Agachon
06530 Cabris
Tel. : 04 93 60 52 36
Fax : 04 93 60 52 36

Closed from 15 Oct to 1 Apr • 5 rooms • €52, breakfast included • No table d'hôte • Credit cards not accepted

819 LES JARDINS FRAGONARD
Mr Mombeek

12 rue Fragonard
06800 Cagnes-sur-Mer
Tel. : 04 93 20 07 72
Fax : 04 93 20 07 72

Open all year • 3 rooms with bath/WC • €70, breakfast included • No table d'hôte • Sitting room, terraces, garden, car park. Credit cards not accepted, no dogs allowed • Outdoor swimming pool, billiards. Tennis and golf nearby

 Wandering around the lanes of this old village so popular with contemporary artists.

The yellow walls of this tiny village house are bound to catch your eye. The restful rooms are painted a spotless white; some of them enjoy a view of the Esterel massif and St-Cassien Lake, as does the sitting room. A light-hearted atmosphere also prevails in the beams and fireplace in the breakfast room and the countryside almost seems to creep in through the large bay window.

 Conveniently located near the Renoir Museum.

Trees indigenous to the south fill the park of this secluded 1925 villa perched on the heights of Cagnes. An equally authentic Provençal look prevails in the brightly coloured rooms, often furnished in cane; all have brand new bathrooms. Depending on the season, breakfast is served on the terrace or inside, at a large communal table. The shaded garden and swimming pool are ideal for quiet, relaxing afternoons.

Access : In the village

Access : In the upper part of the village

820 LA BASTIDE DU BOSQUET
Mr and Mrs Aussel

14 chemin des Sables
06160 Cap-d'Antibes
Tel. : 04 93 67 32 29
Fax : 04 93 67 32 29
sylvie.aussel @ wanadoo.fr

Closed from Mid-Nov to 20 Dec • 3 rooms with bathrooms • €80, breakfast included • No table d'hôte • Terrace, garden, car park. Credit cards not accepted, no dogs allowed

821 L' AUBERGE DU SOLEIL
Mrs Jacquet

Dans le village
06390 Coaraze
Tel. : 04 93 79 08 11
Fax : 04 93 79 37 79

Closed from Nov to 15 Feb • 8 rooms with bath/WC • €80; breakfast €8 • Menus €19 to €23 • Garden • Outdoor swimming pool

Quiet and yet on the doorstep of the beaches.

We immediately succumbed to the charm of this 18C country house in one of the quietest parts of town. Space, bold southern patterns and colours and lovely antiques set the scene for the bedrooms; the yellow one has to be the pick of the bunch. Scrumptious breakfasts are served on the terrace in the summer. You may feel just too relaxed to leave the peaceful garden and head for the busy beaches.

Access : In a residential area, between Antibes and Juan-les-Pins

Located in what is has been dubbed the "village of sun".

This lovely mansion was built in 1863 and its atmosphere of quiet serenity can only be reached on foot. The immaculate rooms are a happy combination of old and new; four enjoy a view of the valley and the terraced fields: the immense dining room and conservatory also command an impressive vista. Madame uses only fresh produce in her traditional Provençal dishes, whose reputation extends throughout the region. As for relaxation, look no further than the billiard table, garden, orchard and pool.

Access : Between the Turini Pass (D 2566) and l'Escarène (D 21), at La Cabanette take the D 2566 towards Saint-Roch Pass, then the D 15

 822 AUBERGE DE COURMES
Mrs Regad

3 rue des Platanes
06620 Courmes
Tel. : 04 93 77 64 70
Fax : 04 93 77 65 90

Closed from 5 to 29 Jan, Sun evening and Mon • 5 rooms with bathrooms • €49, breakfast included • Menus €18 to €21 • Terrace • Hiking

 823 GRAND HÔTEL DU PARC
Mr and Mrs Lorenian

D 70
06450 La Bollène-Vésubie
Tel. : 04 93 03 01 01
Fax : 04 93 03 01 20
www.legrandhotelduparc.com

Open from 30 Mar to 30 Sep • 42 rooms, most have shower/WC, no television • €43 to €57; breakfast €6; half board €48 to €55 • Menus €18 (in the week) to €25 • Terrace, park, car park. No dogs allowed in rooms • Trout farm, hiking and walking

 Nothing disturbs the peace and quiet.

 Breathe in the revitalising fragrance of this superb forest, only a few miles from the busy Riviera!

Character abounds in this inn at the threshold of a picturesque village overlooking the Loup gorges. Five lovingly-refurbished small bedrooms with whitewashed walls ensure guests hours of peaceful slumber; all have modern bathrooms. The "country chic" dining room on the ground floor serves traditional country dishes and specialities from south-west France.

The park of this grand old centennial hotel commands a superb view of the village of La Bollène and whets your appetite for the maples, chestnuts and pines of the magnificent Turini Forest. The renovated rooms are without doubt comfortable and modern, but we couldn't help falling for the others, which are more "old-fashioned"; all are beautifully kept. We recommend the house speciality, trout, which is served in an immense "guesthouse"-style dining room or on the shaded terrace.

Access : From Gréolières, take the D 3 southbound, then a left on the D 503

Access : Southbound from Saint-Martin-Vésubie, leave the D 2565 before Lantosque to take the D 70, towards the Turini Pass

 824   **LE MIRVAL**
Mr and Mrs Dellepiane

06430 La Brigue
Tel. : 04 93 04 63 71
Fax : 04 93 04 79 81

Open from 1 Apr to 2 Nov • 18 rooms on 2 floors, most have bath/WC, all have television • €45 to €54; breakfast €8; half board €50 (€43 out of season) • Menus €15 to €21 • Terrace, garden, car park. No dogs allowed • Mountain biking, white-water sports, walks and 4-wheel drive excursions

825   **LA BASTIDE DE SAINT-DONAT**
Mr Rosso

Route du pont de Pierre,
parc Saint-Donat
06480 La Colle-sur-Loup
Tel. : 04 93 32 93 41
Fax : 04 93 32 93 41

Open all year • 5 rooms with shower or bath • €61 to €92, breakfast included • No table d'hôte • Terrace, garden. Credit cards not accepted, no dogs allowed

 Anglers will not be able to resist trying to hook a silver trout in the torrents of the Levense.

A late-19C alpine inn in a picturesque medieval village close to the Italian border. Nearly all the modern, practical rooms have been renovated. The restaurant-veranda is nothing special in itself, but does offer a superb view over the tiny stone bridge spanning the village's renowned trout-stream. The owner organises excursions in the Vallée des Merveilles (Marvels) either in a four-wheel drive or on foot.

 Dawdling on the terrace overlooking the river.

The stone walls of this sheepfold built in 1850 hide a wealth of ornate interior decoration. The ground floor has been beautifully restored in keeping with local traditions, including arcades, columns, fireplace and terracotta floor tiles. The pastel shades of the bedrooms are a perfect contrast to the old beams and furniture; some have a balcony. As you sit on the terrace, you will be able to listen to the river babbling gently below.

Access : 6.5km southbound from Tende on the D 204, then at St-Dalmas-de-Tendre take a left on the D 143

Access : 2km southbound from Saint-Paul on the D 6

826 AUBERGE DU BON PUITS
Mr and Mrs Corniglion

06450 Le Suquet
Tel. : 04 93 03 17 65
Fax : 04 93 03 10 48

Open from Easter to late Nov; closed Tue except in Jul and Aug • 8 rooms, 2 of which are non-smoking, with bath/WC, air-conditioning and television • €54 to €58; breakfast €7; half board €53 to €55 • Air-conditioned restaurant; menus €17 to €26 • Terrace, park, car park • Animal park, play area, white-water sports and fishing, scenic-path walks

827 MAS DE CLAIREFONTAINE
Mr and Mrs Lapostat

3196 route de Draguignan
06530 Le Tignet
Tel. : 04 93 66 39 69
Fax : 04 93 66 39 69
lapostattan @ aol.com
http://masdeclairefontaine.online.fr

Open all year • 3 rooms with bathrooms and television • €77, breakfast included • No table d'hôte • Terrace, park, car park. Credit cards not accepted, no dogs allowed • Outdoor swimming pool. Nearby are Provençal villages, fishing or sailing on the lake

We most liked **The joyful shouts of the pony riders in the small animal park.**

We most liked **As you drive up to the mas, wind down your window and listen to the cicadas chirping!**

Children are welcomed with open arms in this old stone coaching inn complete with a play area and a lovely animal park on the banks of the Vésubie. Since 1890, the rooms have been constantly smartened up and embellished by the owners and their forebears. The kitchen is also a family affair and the delicious recipes have been handed down from mother to daughter for generations. Meals are served under the well-polished beams of the gleaming dining room.

The picture of the stone mas and its terraced garden dotted with umbrella pines and clumps of reeds will make you reach for your camera. The Provençal-style bedrooms and bathrooms are strewn with delightful details such as delicately scented Fragonard soaps, postcards and sweets, that make you feel you were expected. The Iris room has its own private terrace. In the summer months, guests are invited to eat outside in the welcome shade of the oak tree.

Access : On the D 2565, between Plan-du-Var and Bollène-Vésubie

Access : 10km to the south-east of Grasse, Draguignan road

828 PIERROT-PIERRETTE
Mr Mitolo

Place de l'Église – Monti
06500 Menton
Tel. : 04 93 35 79 76
Fax : 04 93 35 79 76
pierrotpierrette @ aol.com

Open from 15 Jan to 30 Nov • 7 rooms, 4 of which are in a separate wing, all have shower/WC, no television • €69 to €84; breakfast €6; half board €65 (€62 out of season) • Restaurant closed Mon; menus €25 to €34 • Garden. No dogs allowed • Swimming pool

829 ARMENONVILLE
Mrs Moreilhon

20 avenue des Fleurs
06000 Nice
Tel. : 04 93 96 86 00
Fax : 04 93 96 86 00

Open all year • 13 rooms with bath or shower, 4 do not have WC in the rooms, all have television • €57 to €92; breakfast €6 • No restaurant • Garden, private car park

We most liked **Your northern pallor will soon turn a lovely golden brown under Menton's bright sun.**

This delightful little inn perched in the upper reaches of a peaceful hamlet lies just outside Menton. Most of the family-sized simply-furnished rooms have balconies. The rustic dining room has its charm, but guests generally come back for the luxurious garden, full of exotic southern plants and sweet-scented roses, and the swimming pool overlooking the valley of Carei.

We most liked **The old "Russian" district of Nice and its Orthodox cathedral.**

This 1900 villa stands at the end of a cul-de-sac in the old Russian immigrant district. A faded charm emanates from the high-ceilinged rooms of varied sizes decorated with "old-fashioned" furniture from the opulent Negresco Hotel. Some overlook the flowers and palm trees in the garden where breakfast is served on sunny days, i.e. almost every day of the year. A pretty iron stove takes pride of place in the sitting room.

Access : 5km northbound from Menton, on the D 2566 towards Sospel

Access : From the Promenade des Anglais, take Boulevard Gambetta, then turn left

 830   **DURANTE**
Mr Stramigioli

 16 avenue Durante
06000 Nice
Tel. : 04 93 88 84 40
Fax : 04 93 87 77 76
info @ hotel-durante.com
www.hotel-durante.com

Open all year • 24 rooms, 19 of which have kitchenettes, all are air-conditioned with bath/WC or shower/WC and television • €73 to €84 (€68 to €73 low season); breakfast €9 • No restaurant • Garden, car park

 831   **HOSTELLERIE LA VALLIÈRE**
Mr Hug

 06470 Saint-Martin-d'Entraunes
Tel. : 04 93 05 59 59
Fax : 04 93 05 59 60

Open from 1 May to 1 Nov; closed Sun evening and Thu except in Jul and Aug • 10 rooms with shower/WC • €43 to €49; breakfast €7; half board €43 to €49 • Restaurant only for hotel guests; menus €19 to €25 • Terrace, car park

 Breakfast on the terrace amid the tangy perfume of citrus fruit trees.

The pink façade and mascarons (carved caricatures) over the windows of this elegant abode, in a quiet cul-de-sac near the railway station are a reminder that Italy is just down the road. It is a pleasure to sleep with the window wide open, because all the rooms, recently refurbished in a Mediterranean flavour, overlook a terracotta tiled terrace-garden lined with rows of palm, orange and lemon trees.

 The unspoilt setting of this hostelry.

The high, yellow walls of this impressive house stand out for miles around. All the spacious, well cared-for and modern rooms have good bedding. A cool, comfortable dining room is the scene for mealtimes. The owners greet guests as if they were long-awaited friends.

Access : From the railway station, take Av Durante and turn left in the cul-de-sac after Rue Alsace-Lorraine

Access : Leave the N 202 between Annot and Entrevaux: towards Guillaume, then Saint-Martin-d'Entraunes

 832 **HOSTELLERIE LES REMPARTS**
Mr Tibaud

 72 rue Grande
06570 Saint-Paul
Tel. : 04 93 32 09 88
Fax : 04 93 32 06 91
h.remparts@wanadoo.fr

Open all year • 9 rooms with bath/WC or shower/WC
• €80; breakfast €7 • Menu €25 • Car park

 833 **MAS DES CIGALES**
Mr and Mrs Montegnies

 1673 route des Quenières
06140 Tourrettes-sur-Loup
Tel. : 04 93 59 25 73
Fax : 04 93 59 25 78
macigales@aol.com
www.le-mas-des-cigales.com

Closed from 30 Oct to 1 Mar • 6 rooms • €77, breakfast
included • No table d'hôte • Garden, car park. Credit
cards not accepted, no dogs allowed • Outdoor swimming pool, tennis

 **Saint Paul and this old hotel are
everything you expect Provence to be.**

Beautifully preserved stone walls, antique furniture,
rustic earthenware tiles, bright colours and a faultless
welcome paint the picture of this delightful hotel, hidden
in a narrow street in historic St Paul. Each of the
personalised rooms is named after a flower and the
largest offer a fine view of the countryside. It is hard
to leave the shade of the lovely covered terrace.

 **The "cigale" (cicada) is the emblem of
Provence, as you will soon realise.**

This pleasant villa perched on a hillside of pine trees
commands a wonderful view of the Riviera coastline and
the Mediterranean. Hand-painted furniture adorns the
personalised rooms named after local fauna and flora:
Nasturtium, Peony, Butterfly, Violet and Olive. You can
choose between a covered veranda overlooking the
garden or a poolside table for breakfast. If you lean
slightly over the terrace, you will catch sight of a small
waterfall and the property's tennis courts.

Access : In the part of Rue Grande situated between
Rue de l'Étoile and Rue des Pontis

Access : 2km from Tourrettes, Saint-Jean road

 834 **BLANCHE NEIGE**
Mr and Mrs Kretchmann

06470 Valberg
Tel. : 04 93 02 50 04
Fax : 04 93 02 61 90

Closed in Nov • 17 rooms with shower/WC, some have bath/WC, all have television • €71; breakfast €8; half board €52 (low season) to €63 (high season) • Restaurant closed out of season; menu €22 • Terrace, garage, car park. No dogs allowed • Skiing, hiking

 835 **AUBERGE DES SEIGNEURS**
Mrs Rodi

Place du Frêne
06140 Vence
Tel. : 04 93 58 04 24
Fax : 04 93 24 08 01

Open from 15 Mar to 1 Nov • 6 rooms with shower/WC • €61 to €70; breakfast €10 • Restaurant closed Tue, Wed and Thu lunchtime, and Mon; menus €28 to €40

 Hey Ho, Hey Ho, it's out to play we go!

Once upon a time there was a chalet whose green and yellow shutters looked onto a forest of larch trees. Legend has it that these small rooms decorated with hand-quilted bedspreads and painted furniture were formerly the home of seven cheerful dwarves and their guest, Snow White – the hotel's namesake. Nowadays the region's white gold – 50km of slopes between 1 500 and 2 000m – has stolen the limelight from the princesses of yesteryear. Snug restaurant and spacious terrace overlooking the road.

 Ladies are offered a flower after the meal.

This historic 17C inn next door to the Château de Villeneuve is said to have enjoyed the patronage of famous people such as François 1st, who died in 1547! "But, but", you stammer as you quickly compare dates. However the original decoration of this house has been so skilfully preserved that you would be forgiven for falling into the trap! Whatever the case, a taste of the superb spit-roasted lamb from the open fire is bound to reconcile you with the hotel's miraculous past.

Access : At the entrance to the resort

Access : In the grounds of the old town, near the castle

836 **MIRAMAR**
Mr Varlet

167 avenue Bougearel – Plateau Saint-Michel
06140 Vence
Tel. : 04 93 58 01 32
Fax : 04 93 58 20 22
resa @ hotel-miramar-vence
www.hotel-miramar-vence.com

Closed from 15 Nov to 15 Dec • 18 rooms with bath/WC or shower/WC and television • €68 to €95 (€45 to €60 low season); breakfast €10 • No restaurant • Terrace, car park • Outdoor swimming pool, table-tennis, pétanque

The magnificent view of the Baous mountain range and St Jeannet.

The interior of this pleasant pale-pink villa, built in 1927 on the doorstep of Vence, has just been renovated from top to bottom. Its pretty rooms, named after the region's flowers, are decorated with friezes and frescoes. A pleasant Mediterranean lounge-bar equipped with a large-screen TV is perfect for a drink before dinner. Outside, the breakfast terrace, garden and swimming pool all command the same lovely view of the Baous and the Riviera.

Access : On the plateau overlooking the road: from the centre, on Avenue du Général Leclerc (Cagnes road) then turn right

837 **LE PRIEURÉ**
Mrs Le Hir

Route des Alpes
13100 Aix-en-Provence
Tel. : 04 42 21 05 23
Fax : 04 42 21 60 56

Open all year • 22 rooms with bath/WC and television • €53 to €61; breakfast €6 • No restaurant • Car park. No dogs allowed

The quiet atmosphere after the bustle of the town.

The rooms of this 17C priory overlook a delightful period house, now home to the Law Faculty, and formal French gardens, designed by none other than Le Nôtre, creator of the gardens of Versailles. The restful and delicately romantic, chocolate-box style with floral fabrics, artificial flowers and chandelier lamps is in perfect keeping with the setting. A terrace lined with superb hydrangeas is where breakfast is served in the summertime.

Access : Leave Aix-en-Provence north-eastbound on Bd É Zola, the hotel is 2km away, on the right on the N 96, Sisteron road

 838 QUATRE DAUPHINS
Mr Darricau

54 rue Roux-Alphéran
13100 Aix-en-Provence
Tel. : 04 42 38 16 39
Fax : 04 42 38 60 19

Closed from 9 Feb to 3 Mar • 12 rooms with bath/WC or shower/WC, all have television • €55 to €70; breakfast €7 • No restaurant

 839 SAINT-CHRISTOPHE
Mr Bonnet

2 avenue Victor Hugo
13100 Aix-en-Provence
Tel. : 04 42 26 01 24
Fax : 04 42 38 53 17
saintchristophe @ francemarket.com
www.hotel-saintchristophe.com

Open all year • 52 air-conditioned rooms, 6 are split-level and one has disabled access. Rooms have bath/WC and television • €70 to €85; breakfast €8; half board €71 • Brasserie Léopold: closed in Aug and Mon; air-conditioning; menu €19 • Garage. No dogs allowed in restaurant

 You won't regret opting for the romantic rooms under the eaves, however stifling in summer!

The tiny lanes lined with lovely old 17C and 18C mansions, the busy café terraces of the Cours Mirabeau, a multitude of tiny restaurants and colourful street markets – it could only be Aix en Provence! Turn a deaf ear to the noise, steel yourself to the heat and immerse yourself from head to toe in the charm of this hotel's tiled floors and painted furniture, only a step from the graceful little square of the Quatre Dauphins.

 Admire the paintings by a local artist on the walls of the comfortable lounge-bar.

The smart pink walls of this small building were home to a garage before the Bonnet family bought the premises in 1936 and turned them into a hotel-restaurant. Most of the rooms echo the establishment's Art Deco origins, but several are more Provençal in inspiration. The restaurant and conservatory-terrace have adopted the spirit of a Parisian brasserie, serving a somewhat eclectic range of dishes, including the house special of choucroute!

Access : In a quiet, small street in the Mazarin area

Access : In the town centre, near the tourist office and the Cours Mirabeau

 840 L'AMPHITHÉATRE
Mr Coumet and Mr Piras

5 rue Diderot
13200 Arles
Tel. : 04 90 96 10 30
Fax : 04 90 93 98 69
contact @ hotelamphitheatre.fr
www.hotelamphitheatre.fr

Open all year • 15 rooms on 3 levels, most have shower/WC, all have television • €48 to €63; breakfast €6 • No restaurant

 841 CALENDAL
Mrs Jacquemin

5 rue Porte de Laure
13200 Arles
Tel. : 04 90 96 11 89
Fax : 04 90 96 05 84
vontact @ lecalendal.com

Closed from 6 to 26 Jan • 38 rooms, all have bath/WC or shower/WC and television • €60 to €75 (€55 to €60 low season); breakfast €7 • Restaurant only open at lunchtime in season; buffet €12 • Garden. No dogs allowed

 Breakfasting on fresh fruit juice, crusty croissants and home-made fruit preserves.

 Proof that France also drinks tea!

A line of plane trees masks this small 17C house whose façade is adorned with a statue of the Virgin Mary. All the airy, tasteful and well cared-for rooms have just been treated to a facelift with painted and wrought-iron furniture and lovely draperies. The sitting and breakfast room feature the same happy blend of old walls, modern décor and bright southern colours. The hotel is ideally situated to explore Arles' countless treasures.

Teatime, something of an institution in this establishment, means tasty pastries and a wonderful selection of teas from one of France's most famous tea houses, served in a light, airy room with veranda, which also doubles as a breakfast room when the weather is not fine enough to enjoy the shade of the palms on the terrace. The rooms overlook either the garden, the Antique theatre, or, for a lucky few, the Arena; ask for one with a view when booking. All are decorated in bright, warm colours.

Access : In the historical centre, near the Antique theatre and arena

Access : Between the Antique theatre and arena

842 LA MUETTE
Mr Deplancke

15 rue des Suisses
13200 Arles
Tel. : 04 90 96 15 39
Fax : 04 90 49 73 16
hotel.muette @ wanadoo.fr

Closed during Feb school holidays • 18 rooms on 2 floors, with shower/WC, some have bath/WC, all have television • €53 to €61; breakfast €6 • No restaurant • Garage. No dogs allowed

843 LE CLOS DES ARÔMES
Mr and Mrs Bonnet

10 rue Paul Mouton
13260 Cassis
Tel. : 04 42 01 71 84
Fax : 04 42 01 31 76

Open from early Mar to 1 Nov • 14 rooms, most have shower/WC, some have bath/WC, all have television • €60 to €70; breakfast €7; half board €60 to €63 • Restaurant closed Tue and Wed lunchtimes and Mon; menus €19 to €25 • Terrace, garden, garage

 The friendly, unaffected greeting.

This rather austere edifice, on a little square in the historic town, dates from the 12C and 15C; exposed stonework, regimental lines of beams and narrow bay windows bear witness to its age. A handsome spiral staircase leads up to the rooms, most of which are on the old-fashioned side, some do, however, sport Provençal prints and period furniture. Breakfast is served in a delightful rustic room, under the somewhat unnerving glare of a stuffed bull's head.

 Epitome of the best of life in Provence.

The doors of this pretty blue-shuttered house lead into a cheerful, flowered garden. Provençal prints and colours adorn the tasteful, well-soundproofed rooms, one of which is perfect for families. The meals, equally southern in flavour, are served in the bright dining room or, in the summer, under the shade of plane trees on the terrace.

Access : On a small square in the heart of the historic centre

Access : From the town centre: on Place de la République, take Rue A Thiers then continue straight on past the church

 844 **LA GALINIÈRE**
Mr and Mrs Gagnières

 N 7
13790 Châteauneuf-le-Rouge
Tel. : 04 42 53 32 55
Fax : 04 42 53 33 80
www.lagaliniere.com

Open all year • 17 rooms overlooking the courtyard or the garden, most have bath/WC, all have television • €52 to €74; breakfast €9; half board €68 to 77 • Menus €22 to €46 • Terrace, garden, 2 car parks one of which is private • Swimming pool, stud farm, horse-riding

 45 acres of grounds and a riding centre with horses and ponies for the kids.

Built in the 17C on the ruins of a Templar chicken farm, La Galinière was initially a coaching inn and Pope Pius VII slept here on two occasions, in 1809 and 1814. At the foothills of the Ste-Victoire mountain range, immortalised by Cézanne, the estate's elegant wrought-iron gate, still flanked by the stones designed to protect it from the carriage wheels, leads into the inn, which now offers rooms decorated in a rustic style and a characterful restaurant in an old outhouse with a carriage door.

Access : By the N 7, 2km from Châteauneuf-le-Rouge, towards St-Maximin-la-Sainte-Baume

 845 **VAL MAJOUR**
Mr Güell

Avenue d'Arles
13990 Fontvieille
Tel. : 04 90 54 62 33
Fax : 04 90 54 61 67
contact @ hotel-valmajour.com
www.hotel-valmajour.com

Open all year • 32 rooms with bath/WC or shower/WC and television • €61 to €91 (€48 to €58 low season); breakfast €9 • No restaurant • Park, garage, private car park • Outdoor swimming pool, tennis, table-tennis, pétanque

 The trees in the park are home to dozens of busy squirrels.

A stay in this regional house built on the doorstep of Alphonse Daudet's village is always a pleasant prospect. The spacious, rustic rooms are decorated with cheerful Provençal patterns; some have a terrace, while others have a balcony overlooking the park's many trees. On the leisure side, you can choose between a dip in the superb swimming pool or a friendly tennis match in the cool of the evening.

Access : On leaving the town, by the Arles road

 846 PARC
Mrs Uguen

Vallée de Saint-Pons
13420 Gémenos
Tel. : 04 42 32 20 38
Fax : 04 42 32 10 26

Open all year • 12 rooms with bath/WC and television • €48 to €80; breakfast €7; half board €48 to €58 • Menus €15 to €31, children's menu €11 • Garden, terrace, private car park

 847 DOMAINE DU BOIS VERT
Mr and Mrs Richard

Quartier Montauban
13450 Grans
Tel. : 04 90 55 82 98
Fax : 04 90 55 82 98
leboisvert @ hotmail.com
www.multimania.com/leboisvert

Closed from 5 Jan to 15 Mar • 3 rooms • €64, breakfast included • No table d'hôte • Terrace, park, car park. Credit cards not accepted, no dogs allowed • Outdoor swimming pool, table-tennis

 Cool down in the refreshing shade of Saint Pons Park in the summer.

This enchanting Provençal home stands in a haven of greenery just as you leave town. The rooms are modern and appealing; some enjoy a view of the park. The large bay windows of the dining room-conservatory open onto a cheerful flowered garden. The shade of the plane trees is most welcome in the summer. Friendly and unaffected.

 The award-winning friendly owners.

This dry-stone mas is surrounded by a riverside park of oak and pine trees. All the ground floor rooms share a typical local style with terracotta tiles, exposed beams and old furniture; one has a canopied bed. Depending on the season and your inclination, breakfast is served in a large dining-sitting room or on the terrace overlooking the garden. Guests have the use of a library and a refrigerator.

Access : 1km on the Sainte-Baume road (D 2)

Access : 7km southbound from Salon on the D 16 and then towards Lançon (D 19)

 848 LE CADRAN SOLAIRE
Mrs Guilmet

 Rue du Cabaret Neuf
13690 Graveson
Tel. : 04 90 95 71 79
Fax : 04 90 90 55 04
cadransolaire@wanadoo.fr
www.hotel-en-provence.com

Open all year, but by reservation only from Nov to 15 Mar
• 12 rooms with bath/WC or shower/WC • €49 to €71;
breakfast €6 • No restaurant • Breakfast terrace, garden,
private car park. No dogs allowed

 849 LE MAS DES RIÈGES
Mr Ducarre

 Route de Cacharel
13460 Les Saintes-Maries-de-la-Mer
Tel. : 04 90 97 85 07
Fax : 04 90 97 72 26
hoteldesrieges@wanadoo.fr

Closed from 15 Nov to 15 Dec and from 5 Jan to 5 Feb
• 20 rooms on the ground floor with bath/WC or
shower/WC, all have television • €63 to €81; breakfast
€7 • No restaurant (snacks available around the pool on
sunny days) • Garden, car park • Swimming pool,
horse-riding centre offering treks, beauty centre with
hammam and balneotherapy

 **The lady of the house treats her
guests like friends of the family.**

A glance at the sundial on the façade of this
three-hundred-year-old post house will explain the
establishment's name. Not content merely to represent
the timeless charm of Provence, the energetic lady of
the house was determined to breathe a new lease of
life into her property, and the result is impressive!
Enchanting small rooms are decorated with taste and
a profusion of delicate details, the bathrooms have been
redone and the wrought-iron terrace surrounded by
plants is a joy to behold.

 **Step out of your ground floor room
and straight into the Camargue.**

Just a few minutes from the tourist bustle of the town
centre and already surrounded by marshes, you won't
be able to miss this hacienda-style house set in a large
garden full of flowers and trees. The lovely rustic-
inspired rooms are adorned with Provençal fabrics and
all have a private terrace. Treat yourself to a session
in the beauty institute, complete with hammam,
balneotherapy and a sun bed. Horse-riding possible.

Access : In a residential area, on the way into the
village

Access : In the heart of the marshes, 1km from
Saintes-Maries-de-la-Mer, on the Cacharel road, then a
minor road

 VILLA MARIE-JEANNE
Mrs de Montmirail

4 rue Chicot
13012 Marseille
Tel. : 04 91 85 51 31

Open all year • 3 rooms, one of which has a terrace
• €54, breakfast included • No table d'hôte • Garden,
car park. Credit cards not accepted, no dogs allowed
• Outdoor swimming pool

 LE BERGER DES ABEILLES
Mrs Grenier

Route de Cabanes
13670 Saint-Andiol
Tel. : 04 90 95 01 91
Fax : 04 90 95 48 26
abeilles13 @ aol.com

Closed from 15 Nov to 15 Mar • 9 rooms upstairs, with
bath/WC or shower/WC, all have television • €65 to €84;
breakfast €12; half board €63 to €73 • Restaurant closed
Mon and Tue lunchtime; menus €23 to €40 • Terrace,
garden, car park

 **Just a kick away from the
Stade-Vélodrome, home of Olympique
Marseille football club!**

A rare pearl in the heart of a residential district that has
gradually merged with the village of Saint Barnabé. The
interior of this tasteful 19C house features a pleasant
blend of traditional Provençal colours, old furniture,
wrought-iron and contemporary works of art. The rooms
are in the outbuildings and overlook the plane trees in
the garden; one has a private terrace. Not to be missed!

 **Ask the lady of the house why the
house is named "The bee shepherd"?**

The authenticity of this peacefully situated mas, off the
busy N7, cannot be doubted. The charm is enhanced
by a wonderful flowered terrace, shaded by a majestic
plane tree. The rooms, some of which are furnished with
old pieces, are comfortable and well looked after; three
open directly into the garden. The rustic dining room
is equally appealing, as is the lady of the house's
pleasant welcome.

Access : From Marseille, take Boulevard de la
Blancarde eastbound

Access : 2km to the north-west of Saint-Andiol,
towards Avignon, leave the N 7 and take the D 74 E
towards Cabanes

852 CASTELET DES ALPILLES
Mrs Canac-Roux

6 place Mireille
13210 Saint-Rémy-de-Provence
Tel. : 04 90 92 07 21
Fax : 04 90 92 52 03
hotel.castel.alpilles @ wanadoo.fr
www.castelet-alpilles.com

Open from late Mar to early Nov • 19 rooms in 2 buildings. Most rooms have bath/WC, all have television • €68 to €83; breakfast €8 • No restaurant • Garden, private car park

853 ANGLETERRE
Mr Ferrandino

98 cours Carnot
13300 Salon-de-Provence
Tel. : 04 90 56 01 10
Fax : 04 90 56 71 75

Closed from 20 Dec to 6 Jan • 25 rooms on 3 levels, 15 of which are air-conditioned, with bath/WC or shower/WC, all have television • €42 to €51; breakfast €6 • No restaurant • No dogs allowed

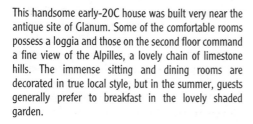

We most liked
Just a five minute walk from St Rémy, home to Nostradamus and Van Gogh.

This handsome early-20C house was built very near the antique site of Glanum. Some of the comfortable rooms possess a loggia and those on the second floor command a fine view of the Alpilles, a lovely chain of limestone hills. The immense sitting and dining rooms are decorated in true local style, but in the summer, guests generally prefer to breakfast in the lovely shaded garden.

We most liked
The "Château de l'Empéri": former residence of the archbishops of Arles.

This former convent dates back to the early years of the 20C and enjoys a matchless location in the heart of the old town and close to the museums. The simple, but comfortable rooms, with double-glazing and air-conditioning, lie behind well-restored walls. Breakfasting under a glazed dome has a distinctly "Empire" feel. Attentive, friendly service.

Access : On leaving the town drive towards the site of Villa Glanum

Access : In the town centre, near the pedestrian area

854 DU CHÂTEAU
Mr and Mrs Laraison

24 rue du Château
13150 Tarascon
Tel. : 04 90 91 09 99
Fax : 04 90 91 10 33
ylaraison @ wanadoo.fr

Closed from Nov to 20 Dec • 5 rooms • €76, breakfast included • No table d'hôte • Credit cards not accepted, no dogs allowed

855 LA GIRANDOLE
Mr Morel

À Brunissard
05350 Arvieux
Tel. : 04 92 46 84 12
Fax : 04 92 46 86 59

Closed from 15 Oct to 20 Dec • 5 non-smoking chambres d'hôte with shower/WC and bath/WC and 2 gîtes • €55, breakfast included • No table d'hôte • Garden, car park. No dogs allowed • Outdoor swimming pool

Faultless, down to the tiniest detail.

A porch and heavy door guard the entrance to this 18C edifice in a quiet side street leading up to the castle of King René. The beautifully restored rooms are of an extremely high standard; two are reached via a lovely medieval-style staircase. As soon as the sun is warm enough, breakfast is served on a lovely flowered patio with ochre-red walls.

Well-situated on the "Sundial Route" – a themed tour of the villages of Haute-Provence.

Both the architecture and the sundial which adorns the façade of this old farmhouse are typical of the valley of Arvieux. The interior has been tastefully refurbished with old furniture and objects, colourful prints and fabrics, a piano and soft sofas in the sitting room. The rooms display a more uncluttered style with plain white walls and have balconies with a variety of views over the pleasant hilly landscape. Guests have the use of a kitchen.

Access : Near the castle

Access : Northbound, 3km on the D 902

 856 **LES PEUPLIERS**
Mr Bellot

Chemin de Lesdier
05200 Baratier
Tel. : 04 92 43 03 47
Fax : 04 92 43 41 49
info @ hotel-les-peupliers.com
www.hotel-les-peupliers.com

Closed from 2 to 25 Apr and from 30 Sep to 24 Oct
• 24 rooms, 6 of which are non-smoking, with bath/WC
or shower/WC and television • €45 to €48 (€38 to
€43 low season); breakfast €6; half board €41 to
€43 • Restaurant closed Tue and Wed; menus €14 to
€21 • Terrace, car park. No dogs allowed in restaurant
• Outdoor swimming pool, pétanque

 857 **LES CHEMINS VERTS**
Mrs Dubois

05500 Buissard
Tel. : 04 92 50 57 57

Open all year • 4 rooms and one gîte • €43, breakfast
included • Table d'hôte €13 • Terrace, car park. Credit
cards not accepted, no dogs allowed

 We most liked

As welcoming in winter as in summer.

This alpine chalet enjoys a wonderful position surrounded by mountains and overlooking the lake of Serre
Ponçon. The rooms are a cheerful mixture of sturdy,
hand-painted furniture and bold regional fabrics; those
on the second floor with a lake-view balcony were our
favourite. Stone and wood feature prominently in the
alpine dining room. Put your feet up on the shaded,
south-facing terrace after a couple of hours energetic
hiking, mountain biking or cross-country skiing, depending on the season!

  We most liked

Fill your lungs with fresh mountain air.

At an altitude of 1 200m, this pretty 18C farmhouse,
run by amiable, helpful hosts, surveys the Drac valley
and the rocky bastion of Dévoluy massif. The tasteful
rooms are comfortable; the one called "Fleurette" has
the best view. A brand new apartment is also available
and the sitting room and panoramic terrace are worthy
of note.

Access : Leave the N 94 towards Les Orres, then
Baratier, in the village, take the second turning on the
right

Access : 1km eastbound from
Saint-Julien-en-Champsaur on the D 15

 858 LES BARTAVELLES
Mrs Pernin

05200 Embrun
Tel. : 04 92 43 20 69
Fax : 04 92 43 11 92
info @ bartavelles.com
www.bartavelles.com

Closed for 10 days in January and Sun evening out of season • 43 rooms, 12 of which are in a separate wing, with bath/WC or shower/WC, all have television • €74 to €80; breakfast €9; half board €64 to €71 • Menus €15 to €33, children's menu €10 • Garden, car park, garage • Swimming pool, tennis

 859 LA FERME BLANCHE
Mr Catier

Route de Romette
05000 Gap
Tel. : 04 92 51 03 41
Fax : 04 92 51 35 39
la.ferme.blanche @ wanadoo.fr

Open all year • 23 rooms with bath/WC or shower/WC, all have television • €49 to €69; breakfast €7; half board €40 to €56 • Menus €23 to €39 • Terrace, garden, car park. No dogs allowed in restaurant

 In the air, on the water, up a mountain or down on the ground, the list of activities is endless.

Even though the impressive outline of this 1970s "cottage" may lack character, the rooms, decorated in a rustic style, combine tranquillity with comfort and there are three bungalows for families dotted about the immense garden. In the summer you can choose between a quick snack on the terrace or dining indoors in the more traditional restaurant.

 A country ambience two minutes from busy Gap, the gateway to the Alps.

This farmhouse overlooking Gap has been owned by the same family since the 18C. Brick vaults, old farm furniture, such as a kneading-machine and the cow shed-turned-restaurant bear witness to the establishment's agricultural origins. As a result of some serious renovation work, mainly in the bedrooms, those overlooking the rear are particularly tasteful and benefit from the cool breeze of the nearby woodland; the other rooms face the town.

Access : 3km to the south-west on the D 94, on the Gap road

Access : Leave Gap on the N 86 (Grenoble road), then turn right on the D 92 towards Romette

 860 LE PARLEMENT
Mr and Mrs Drouillard

 Charance
05000 Gap
Tel. : 04 92 53 94 20
Fax : 04 92 53 94 20

Open all year • 5 rooms • €77, breakfast included • No table d'hôte • Car park. No dogs allowed • Swimming pool, sauna, billiards, play area and climbing wall for children

 861 LES BARNIÈRES
Garcin family

 05600 Guillestre
Tel. : 04 92 45 04 87
Fax : 04 92 45 28 74
hotel-lesbarnieres @ wanadoo.fr
www-hotel-lesbarnieres.com

Closed from 15 Oct to 20 Dec • 40 rooms with bath/WC and television • €77; breakfast €10 • Menus €17 to €32 • Garden, car park • Swimming pool, tennis, sauna, jacuzzi, table-tennis, pétanque, mini-golf

 This establishment democratically offers something for everyone!

This appealing 18C house surrounded by greenery was formerly an outbuilding of the castle of Charance. Although only a few minutes from Gap, it is quiet and peaceful. The rooms are spacious, sophisticated and quite spotless; some command a view of the town. The basement has been fitted out with a wide range of activities including billiards, games room with a climbing wall for children and a sauna. The owner, an alpine and mountain-bike guide, will happily give you ideas for outings.

 The sweeping view over the Durance Valley and the Alps.

In the upper reaches of Guillestre, this hotel is comprised of two chalets facing the mountains in the distance. The main wing is currently being tastefully renovated, but the summer wing has already been finished. Make the most of the garden and its leisure activities: swimming pool, tennis courts and pétanque and we can guarantee that you won't need to count the sheep at night.

Access : From Gap, 4km towards Orange and Valence (D 994), at the Rond Point des 3 Cascades, drive towards the Charance domain

Access : On the way out of the village, by the road

 862 **LE COGNAREL**
Mr and Mrs Catala

 Le Coin de Molines
05350 Molines-en-Queyras
Tel. : 04 92 45 81 03
Fax : 04 92 45 81 17
cognarel @ imaginet.fr

Open from 1 Jun to 15 Sep and from 21 Dec to 14 Apr
• 21 rooms located in 2 chalets and 4 gîtes, most rooms
have bath/WC, no television • €62 to €65; breakfast €7;
half board €61 (€52 low season) • Lunchtime menu only
(by reservation) €21 • Terrace, garden • In summer:
hiking. In winter: snowshoe walking, cross-country skiing, nordic skiing

 863 **LE CHALET D'EN HÔ**
Mr Baudoux

Hameau des Chazals – Le Roubion
05100 Névache
Tel. : 04 92 20 12 29
Fax : 04 92 20 59 70
chaletdenho @ ad.com
www.chaletdenho.com

Open from 15 Jun to 15 Sep, 1 Nov and from 20 Dec to
15 Apr • 13 non-smoking rooms with bath/WC or
shower/WC and television, most have a balcony • €68 to
€80; breakfast €9; half board €66 to €78 (€58 low
season) • Non-smoking restaurant; menu €18 (dinner
only) • Car park • Singing courses, cross-country skiing,
hiking, sauna

 **In the heart of the Queyras Regional
Park and a stone's throw from Italy.**

Perched above a hamlet on the road leading up to the
Agnel Pass, two modern chalets make up this hotel
which offers a variety of accommodation and activity
packages including skiing, Nordic hiking, mountain-
biking, etc. The quiet rooms, decorated in an alpine
style, afford fine views of the valley. In the kitchen, the
chef subtly blends classic Provençal flavours with those
of nearby Dauphiné.

 **Breakfast on the terrace overlooking
the valley's multitude of wild flowers.**

The climb up to this larchwood chalet will reward you
with lovely bedrooms named after the mountains and
lakes you can see from the balconies. A tasteful marriage
of walls lined in pine and local draperies and the dining
room is adorned with tools which recall the local
tradition of woodworking. The nature-loving owners are
always happy to pass on tips and expert advice on
exploring the lovely Clarée Valley.

Access : Leave Molines-en-Queyras on the D 205,
and after 3km turn left

Access : Northbound from Briançon, leave the
N 94 for the D 994G that follows the Clarée, turn
right at Roubion

 864 AUBERGE LA NEYRETTE
Mr and Mrs Muzard

05250 Saint-Disdier
Tel. : 04 92 58 81 17
Fax : 04 92 58 89 95
info@la-neyrette.com
www.la-neyrette.com

Closed in Apr and from mid-Nov to mid-Dec • 12 rooms with bath/WC or shower/WC, all have television • €49 to €63; breakfast €7; half board €50 to €54 • Menus €18 to €34 • Terrace, garden, car park • Pond with trout fishing, play area

 865 LA CORDELINE
Mr Dyens

14 rue des Cordeliers
83170 Brignoles
Tel. : 04 94 59 18 66
Fax : 04 94 59 00 29
lacordeline@ifrance.com

Closed in Jan and Feb • 5 rooms with bathrooms • €61 to €77, breakfast included • Table d'hôte €23 • Terrace, garden. No dogs allowed

 Fancy a nap under a tree in the company of the local marmots?

This inn lies in a secluded spot on Dévoluy's high plateau at the foot of an arid crest of peaks. The recently renovated rooms are decorated in keeping with their wild flower names. The peaceful garden boasts a pond where you can fish for your own trout, the house speciality. In the summer, meals are served on the terrace overlooking the solitary stone fortress. In the winter, the ski slopes of Superdévoluy are just a short drive away.

 Listen to the birds singing and the fountain murmuring in the garden.

A haven of well-being right in the heart of town. This splendid 17C mansion offers immense rooms furnished with family heirlooms; all have new bathrooms and a small private sitting room. As soon as the sun begins to shine, breakfasts are served outside on the terrace under the trellis.

Access : On leaving the village, on the Superdévoluy road

Access : In the town centre

CARQUEIRANNE - 83320

COTIGNAC - 83570

866 **L'AUMÔNERIE**
Mr and Mrs Menard

620 avenue de Fontbrun
83320 Carqueiranne
Tel. : 04 94 58 53 56
www.bbfrance.com/menard.html

Open all year • 4 rooms • €61 to €77, breakfast included • No table d'hôte • Garden, car park. Credit cards not accepted, no dogs allowed • Direct access to the beach

867 **DOMAINE DE NESTUBY**
Mr and Mrs Roubaud

83570 Cotignac
Tel. : 04 94 04 60 02
Fax : 04 94 04 79 22
nestuby @ wanadoo.fr
www.sejour-en-provence.com

Closed from 15 Nov to 1 Mar • 5 rooms • €61, breakfast included • Table d'hôte €18 • Car park. Credit cards not accepted • Wine tasting on the estate

 Take a seat in the garden and dangle your feet in the Mediterranean!

The total lack of signposts, in fact signs of any kind, bears witness to this establishment's desire to preserve the quiet tranquillity that reigns within its walls. The rooms are tastefully appointed and breakfast will be served either in your room or, whenever the weather permits, under the shade of the terrace's tall pine trees. The garden which has a tiny staircase down to the sea, was what we liked best, however. All that now remains is to enjoy the luxury of your very own private beach.

 Nathalie and Jean-François love introducing guests to their estate's red, white and rosé wines.

You know you're in for a treat as soon as you catch sight of this lovely 19C property surrounded by vineyards. The pastel coloured rooms, furnished with items picked up in second-hand and antique shops, are named after the region's grape varieties. The large country dining table is in the old cow-shed, surrounded by mangers and a fireplace. In the summer, you will appreciate the shade of the plane trees and the cool spring water of the large pond.

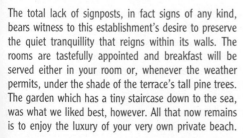

Access : In a park by the seaside, 5km from Hyères

Access : 5km southbound from Cotignac towards Brignoles

868 LES CANCADES
Mr and Mrs Zerbib

1195 chemin de la Fontaine de Cinq-Sous
83330 Le-Beausset
Tel. : 04 94 98 76 93
Fax : 04 94 90 24 63
charlotte.zerbib @ wanadoo.fr

Open all year • 4 rooms • €61, breakfast included • No table d'hôte • Garden, car park. Credit cards not accepted, no dogs allowed • Outdoor swimming pool

869 MAS LEÏ BANCAU
Mr Buyse

Chemin de Maran
83330 Le Beausset
Tel. : 04 94 90 27 78
Fax : 04 94 90 29 00

Closed from 5 Jan to 5 Feb • 8 rooms, one of which has disabled access, most have shower/WC, all have television • €76 to €90; breakfast €7 • No restaurant • Terrace, park, private car park. No dogs allowed • Swimming pool

 We most liked **Breathe in the scent of pine, olive and cypress trees.**

A steep, narrow lane takes you up to this Provençal villa surrounded by pine and olive trees in a quiet, wooded residential district. Designed by the owner, a retired architect, the tasteful rooms are of varying sizes; two have a terrace overlooking the sumptuous swimming pool. The summer kitchen is in a cabin in the pleasant garden.

We most liked **Dark green cypress trees stand guard over the swimming pool.**

The Provençal mas with sky-blue shutters stands at the end of a steep lane on a hillside, home to the Chapel of Our Lady of Beausset-Vieux. A walk among the olive and fruit trees of the lovely park will fill your nostrils with the sweet scent of lavender and rosemary. The view of the vineyards of Bandol and the beautiful interior decoration – oak furniture and beams in the rooms and terracotta tiles and colourful paintings in the breakfast room – all add to the appeal.

Access : 3km eastbound from Castellet, then opposite the Casino supermarket take chemin de la Fontaine de Cinq-Sous

Access : As you approach Beausset, leave the N 8 Toulon-Aubagne road and turn left towards "Beausset-Vieux"

LE CANNET-DES-MAURES - 83340   **LE CASTELLET - 83330**

 870 LA HAUTE VERRERIE
Mr Brun

Route de Saint-Tropez
83340 Le Cannet-des-Maures
Tel. : 04 94 47 95 51

Open all year • 4 rooms • €45, breakfast included • No table d'hôte • Garden, car park. Credit cards not accepted, no dogs allowed • Outdoor swimming pool

 871 LE CASTEL LUMIÈRE
Mr Laffargue

Le Portail
83330 Le Castellet
Tel. : 04 94 32 62 20
Fax : 04 94 32 70 33

Closed from 4 Jan to 9 Feb, Sun evening and Mon • 6 rooms upstairs with bath/WC or shower/WC, all have television • €65 to €89; breakfast €10; half board €58 to €89 • Menus €29 to €43 • Terrace

Right on the edge of the Forest of Maures.

A stream runs at the foot of this delightful mid-18C house, originally built as a glass-blowing workshop. The outbuildings are now home to individually decorated rooms. We loved the one under the eaves of the old attic, which has its own sun-deck, and the tiny stone cottage in the garden. A fireside adds character to the sitting room and the swimming pool in the small garden is also very welcome.

Access : 6km eastbound from Luc on the D 558, towards Saint-Tropez

A must for film buffs!

The beauty of this high-perched village has earned it the patronage of several well-known film directors over the years, including Pagnol for starters. The establishment itself is in the former home of none other than the inventors of cinema, the Lumière brothers. The rooms are being refurbished and personalised with four-poster beds and an African theme; the restaurant gives out onto the vines of Bandol and the Vars landscape. The verdant terrace is also very pleasant.

Access : At the entrance to the medieval village

 872 LA GÎTHOMIÈRE
Mr Fauvet

Route de Saint-Tropez
83340 Le Luc
Tel. : 04 94 60 81 50
Fax : 04 94 60 81 50

Closed in Jan • 4 rooms with bathrooms • €61, breakfast included • No table d'hôte • Terrace, park, car park. Credit cards not accepted • Outdoor swimming pool

 873 LE MAS DES OLIVIERS
Mr Leroy

83390 Puget-Ville
Tel. : 04 94 48 30 89
sapori @ club-internet.fr

Closed from late Oct to late Mar • 3 rooms • €57, breakfast included • No table d'hôte • Terrace, garden, car park. Credit cards not accepted, no dogs allowed • Outdoor swimming pool, horse-riding, cycling

A perfect spot opposite the Maures massif.

The fragrant scent of pine, cypress and eucalyptus trees lingers in this lovely stone house clinging to the hillside. All the rooms are different and furnished tastefully and all enjoy a view over the forests of cork-oak trees of the Maures massif; the spacious, comfortable bathrooms are also worth a special mention. Depending on the season, breakfast is served in a large sitting room complete with a billiards table or on the terrace facing the park.

The unmistakable stamp of Provence.

Situated in the heart of the Vars countryside and in the midst of nearly 10 acres of vineyards and olive groves, this mas will delight travellers in search of peace and quiet. Good-sized, well-kept rooms sport the colours of southern France and the bathrooms are very pleasant. The distinctive flavour of Provence can also be tasted in the ochre colours and terracotta decoration of the sitting rooms. Bicycling and horse-riding can be organised on request.

Access : 7km eastbound from Luc on the D 558, towards Saint-Tropez

Access : 2.5km on the N 97 Cuers road

 VILLA LOU GARDIAN
Mr and Mrs Castellano

 646 route de Bandol
83110 Sanary-sur-Mer
Tel. : 04 94 88 05 73
Fax : 04 94 88 24 13

Open all year • 4 rooms, 2 of which are in the garden • €69, breakfast included • Table d'hôte €23 to €46 • Garden, car park. Credit cards not accepted, no dogs allowed • Outdoor swimming pool, tennis

 CHÂTEAU DE VINS
Mr Bonnet

 83170 Vins-sur-Caramy
Tel. : 04 94 72 50 40
Fax : 04 94 72 50 88
château.devins @ free.fr

Closed from Nov to Apr • 5 rooms with bathrooms • €70, breakfast included • Table d'hôte • Garden, car park. Credit cards not accepted • Cultural events organised, music courses and summer concerts

 Conveniently located near the sandy beach of La Gorguette.

Despite the nearby road, this recent villa surrounded by palm trees and a pleasant garden is quiet and peaceful. The bedrooms are colourful and well-soundproofed and all have lovely bathrooms; we preferred those near the large swimming pool. Meals are served on the patio. Tennis courts and table-tennis available in the grounds.

 A listed historic castle with an emphasis on culture, music in particular.

Saved from ruin and lovingly restored by its owner, this 16C château, complete with towers on all four corners, now offers moderately sized, but beautifully appointed and utterly peaceful rooms, each of which is named after a musician. The former hunting room is now the dining room. Art exhibitions, concerts and music courses take place throughout the year in the other elegantly restored rooms.

Access : On the Bandol road

Access : 9km from Brignoles on the D 24, Thoronet road

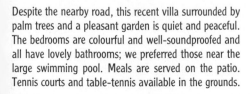

876 RELAIS DE ROQUEFURE
Mr and Mrs Rousset

84400 Apt
Tel. : 04 90 04 88 88
Fax : 04 90 74 14 86
www.relaisderoquefure.com

Closed from 15 Dec to 31 Jan • 15 rooms with shower/WC • €58 to €76; breakfast €8; half board €50 to €61 • Restaurant closed Tue in winter; dinner only: €18 (except Sun lunchtime €19) • Terrace, park, car park • Outdoor swimming pool, horse-riding, bicycles lent

877 DE BLAUVAC
Mrs Flavi

11 rue de la Bancasse
84000 Avignon
Tel. : 04 90 86 34 11
Fax : 04 90 86 27 41
blauvac @ aol.com
www.hotel-blauvac.com

Closed from 6 to 26 Jan and from 11 to 24 Nov • 16 rooms, most have bath/WC and a mezzanine, some have shower/WC, all have television • €58 to €74; breakfast €8 • No restaurant

 Long horse-back rides along the paths around the hotel.

This old farm was threatened with ruin before being bought and entirely restored by the current owners, who undertook much of the work themselves. The old stables were turned into an excellent riding school and the hotel rapidly attracted horse-lovers from far and wide. The personalised rooms have just been refurbished and individually styled. All overlook the mighty Mont Ventoux or a cedar forest. Meals are generally served outdoors. The swimming pool was sunk directly in the rock.

 A stay in the heart of Avignon without the fuss of a busy town.

The Marquis de Blauvac built this 17C house in a quiet street near the Palais des Papes, from where Avignon's medieval "antipopes" defied Rome for almost 70 years. Its elegant wrought-iron balustrade and thick stone walls are typical of the period: the breakfast room is decorated in a Louis XV style. Most of the rooms, simply furnished but full of character, have a mezzanine with an extra bed.

Access : 6km westbound on the N 100 towards Avignon, then a minor road on the left

Access : In the town centre, in a side street leading to Place de l'Horloge (town hall)

 **878** LA FERME
Mrs Wawrzyniak

Chemin des Bois – Ile de la Barthelasse
84000 Avignon
Tel. : 04 90 82 57 53
Fax : 04 90 27 15 47
info @ hotel-laferme.com
www.hotel-laferme.com

Open from 19 Mar to 1 Nov • 20 rooms, 3 of which are non-smoking, with bath/WC or shower/WC, air-conditioning and television • €67 to €77; breakfast €9; half board €64 (€59 low season) • Restaurant closed Mon and Wed; menus €20 to €42 • Terrace, private car park. No dogs allowed in rooms • Swimming pool

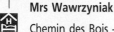 **If you come here, you will have to learn the nursery rhyme "Sur le pont d'Avignon…"**

This handsome farm is located near to the Papal City on the Island of Barthelasse, one of the largest in Europe and a haven of greenery in Avignon. The tastefully decorated rooms ensure that the only sounds you will hear are those of the dawn chorus. The dining room features enormous beams, thick stone walls and a huge fireplace, while out on the terrace you can relax in the shade of the ancient plane tree.

Access : 5km northbound, on the Ile de la Barthelasse, by the D 228 then a minor road

879 LE MÉDIÉVAL
Mr and Mrs Mauriès-Belou

15 rue Petite Saunerie
84000 Avignon
Tel. : 04 90 86 11 06
Fax : 04 90 82 08 64
hotel.medieval @ wanadoo.fr
www.avignon-et-provence.com/hotels

Closed from 5 to 28 Jan • 34 rooms, all have bath/WC or shower/WC and television, most have a kitchenette • €42 to €55; breakfast €6 • No restaurant • No dogs allowed • Patio

 The kitchenettes in the rooms come in handy for a long stay during the festival.

This late-17C mansion built for a cardinal was formerly linked to the Papal Palace by an underground passage. A statue of the Virgin Mary stands in an alcove of its beautiful stone façade. A period staircase leads up to the rooms, a touch outdated but furnished in a rustic style. We recommend booking one of those overlooking the flowered patio, particularly during the summer. Multilingual staff.

Access : In a side street in the heart of the town, from the Porte St-Lazare, take Rue Carreterie and turn right

880 LA MAISON
Mrs Laurelut

84340 Beaumont-du-Ventoux
Tel. : 04 90 65 15 50
Fax : 04 90 65 23 29

Open from 20 Apr to 10 Nov; restaurant closed Mon and Tue out of season • 3 rooms with separate entrances, on the courtyard, with bath/WC or shower/WC • €54 to €64; breakfast €8; half board €58 to €65 • Restaurant closed lunchtime in Jul and Aug (except Sun); menu €26 • Terrace

881 LA GARANCE
Mr and Mrs Breuton

Hameau de Sainte-Colombe
84410 Bédoin
Tel. : 04 90 12 81 00
Fax : 04 90 65 93 05

Open all year • 13 rooms located upstairs and on the ground floor, with bath/WC or shower/WC, all have television • €50 to €55; breakfast €7 • No restaurant • Car park. No dogs allowed • Swimming pool, hiking

 You won't find a warmer welcome anywhere.

This old farm in the region of Malaucène has been transformed into an attractive Provençal house with blue shutters. Each of the three tastefully decorated rooms has its own independent access. The smart dining room is proudly decorated in bright southern colours, but it is the exquisite terrace that will remain in our memory. Dining by candlelight or lunching under the shade of a wonderful lime tree was sheer bliss.

 Take on the ascent of Mont Ventoux on foot... or by car!

It is a pleasure to drive into this pretty hamlet surrounded by vines and orchards and up to the front door of the farmhouse. Inside, the rooms' furnishings are modern and the tiles are old. You will be able to wake up and feast your eyes on Mont Ventoux, before tripping down to breakfast on the terrace or in the brightly-coloured dining room. Afterwards embark on the assault of this "giant of Provence" along signposted footpaths. Well worth writing home about.

Access : 4km to the north-east of Malaucène on the D 153

Access : Head for Bédoin on the D 19 from Malaucène or the D 974 from Carpentras, then drive towards Mont-Ventoux

882 BASTIDE DE SAINTE-AGNÈS
Mr Pinbouen

1043 chemin de la Fourtrouse
84200 Carpentras
Tel. : 04 90 60 03 01
Fax : 04 90 60 02 53

Open all year • 5 rooms with bathrooms • €65 to €81, breakfast included • No table d'hôte • Sitting room, garden, car park. No dogs allowed • Outdoor swimming pool, pétanque, mountain biking

883 LE COMTADIN
Mr Van Orshoven

65 boulevard Albin Durand
84200 Carpentras
Tel. : 04 90 67 75 00
Fax : 04 90 67 75 01
le.comtadin @ wanadoo.fr
www.le-comtadin.com

Closed from 27 Dec to 20 Jan and Sun from Oct to Feb • 19 rooms, 2 of which are non-smoking, one has disabled access. Rooms have bath/WC or shower/WC, all have air-conditioning and television • €74; breakfast €9 • No restaurant • Patio, garage

We most liked
Conveniently located on the doorstep of Carpentras to explore the region.

Lovely old trees from the tropics and the Midi surround the dry-stone walls of this grand old house. The interior reflects the outer flavour with ochre tones, old tiles and regional patterns; all in a distinctly tranquil atmosphere. You can breakfast in a lovely dining room shaded by a trellis or around the unusual swimming pool which used to be a water tank!

We most liked
Breakfasting on the patio.

This late-18C mansion stands on the ring road round the busy capital of the Comtat region. Recently refurbished, it proudly sports wrought-iron furniture, high-quality materials and a contemporary decorative style. Most of the rooms overlook the peaceful patio which echoes to the murmur of the fountain in the centre. The reception is home to orchids, the owners' pride and joy.

Access : 3km to the north-east on the D 974 towards Bédoin and D 13 towards Caromb

Access : On the ring-road

 884   **LA BADELLE**
Mrs Cortasse

84220 Gordes
Tel. : 04 90 72 33 19
Fax : 04 90 72 48 74
badelle @ club-internet.fr
www.guideweb.com/provence/bb/badelle

Closed in Jan • 5 rooms • €74, breakfast included • No table d'hôte • Garden, car park. Credit cards not accepted, no dogs allowed • Outdoor swimming pool

 885   **AUBERGE DU CHEVAL BLANC**
Mr and Mrs Moullet

84240 La Bastide-des-Jourdans
Tel. : 04 90 77 81 08
Fax : 04 90 77 86 51
provence.luberon @ wanadoo.fr

Closed from mid-Jan to mid-Feb; hotel closed Thu except in summer • 4 rooms with bath/WC, air-conditioning and television • €77; breakfast €10; half board €65 to €70 • Restaurant closed Wed evening and Thu (low season), Thu lunch and Fri lunch (in sumumer). Menus €25 to €33 • Terrace, private car park, air-conditioned restaurant

 A beautiful combination of old and new.

A tiny country road leads to this ancient farmhouse. The rooms in the outbuildings have been entirely redone and all feature the same whitewashed walls, rustic earthenware tiles, old furniture and excellent bathrooms. Four open onto the swimming pool. In the summer guests are offered the use of a practical kitchen.

 The Luberon Regional Park is riddled with paths.

In just a few years, this former post house has been elegantly transformed into an up-to-date country inn. Exposed beams, thick stone walls and tiled floors set the scene for the spacious, welcoming rooms, some of which have a small cane-furnished sitting room. Warm, sunny colours adorn the elegant dining room which leads into the dappled shade of a quiet terrace.

Access : 7km southbound from Gordes on the D 104 towards Goult

Access : On the main road of the village

886 LES FENOUILLETS
Mr Courrege

Quartier Revol
84240 La Tour-d'Aigues
Tel. : 04 90 07 48 22
Fax : 04 90 07 34 26
mail @ lesfenouillets.com
www.lesfenouillets.com

Open from 30 Mar to 31 Oct • 15 rooms, one of which
has disabled access, most have bath/WC, some have
shower/WC, all have television • €55; breakfast €10; half
board €52 • Menu (dinner only) €21 • Terrace, garden,
private car park. No dogs allowed in restaurant

887 LA MAISON DES SOURCES
Mrs Collart

Chemin des Fraisses
84360 Lauris
Tel. : 04 90 08 22 19
Fax : 04 90 08 22 19

Open all year • 4 rooms with bathrooms • €69, breakfast
included • No table d'hôte • Sitting room, garden, car
park. Credit cards not accepted, no dogs allowed
• Hiking, horse-riding, mountain biking

 **Relax in the shade of a mulberry tree
on the terrace.**

Wherever you turn, the eye is greeted with the distinctive
charm of hand-printed cotton fabrics, reminiscent of the
work of the Souleïado workshop, reputed for its designer
Provençal-prints and cotton. These fabrics adorn the
rooms, restaurant and terrace, adding a lovely hint of
gaiety to the modern and unusual architecture. The
garden is as well-tended as the rest of the establishment, which welcomes growing numbers of regulars who
appreciate the care and attention.

 **Breakfast in the welcome shade of
acacia trees.**

This old farmhouse, built against a cliff face riddled with
caves, is hidden in the midst of vineyards, orchards and
olive groves in the Luberon foothills. After some major
restoration work it was saved from ruin and now offers
brightly coloured rooms, the most curious of which
features no less than four four-poster beds. The sitting
and dining rooms have fine old vaulted ceilings and the
somewhat unruly garden only adds to the appeal.

Access : At Pertuis, leave the D 973 for the D 956:
after 5km the hotel is on the bend before the Tour
d'Aigues

Access : 4.5km to the south-west of Lourmarin on
the D 27

 888 LES GÉRANIUMS
Mr and Mrs Roux

84330 Le Barroux
Tel. : 04 90 62 41 08
Fax : 04 90 62 56 48

Open from 16 Mar to 12 Nov • 22 rooms located in
2 buildings, with bath/WC or shower/WC, no television
• €47; breakfast €7; half board €40 to €43 • Menus
€16 (in the week) to €46 • Terrace, garden, private car
park. No dogs allowed • Llama farm in the village

 Hiking through vineyards and olive groves in the foothills of the Montmirail.

This impressive stone house stands in the heart of a
fortified village overlooking the Comtat plain. The
spotless rooms are furnished in a rustic style; some have
balconies facing the valley. The chef's delicious recipes,
made with local produce, are definitely worth sampling,
either on the spacious terrace which overflows with
geraniums or in the dining room decorated with
paintings left by an artist and regular to the
establishment.

Access : In the centre of the village

 889 HOSTELLERIE FRANÇOIS JOSEPH
Mr Pochat

Chemin des Rabassières
84330 Le Barroux
Tel. : 04 90 62 52 78
Fax : 04 90 62 33 54
hôtel.f.joseph @ wanadoo.fr
www.hotel-francois-joseph.com

Open from late Mar to early Nov • 18 rooms, 6 are
apartments, 5 are studios and one has disabled access.
All have bath/WC or shower/WC and television • €62 to
€80; breakfast €11 • No restaurant • Park, car park. No
dogs allowed • Outdoor swimming pool

 Snoozing under the umbrella pines.

In the heart of the countryside, this group of modern
buildings has remained true to local architectural
tradition. The modern rooms are brightened up by
cheerful fabrics; half have loggias or ground floor
terraces and families can book one of two cottages. A
happy mixture of unruly bushes cohabit peacefully with
perfect lawns in the garden and from the swimming
pool, you can admire the view of Mont Ventoux.

Access : 2km from Barrous on the Monastères
Ste-Madeleine road

LE BARROUX - 84330   **LE CRESTET - 84110**

890 **MAS DE LA LAUSE**
Mr and Mrs Lonjon

Chemin de Geysset
84330 Le Barroux
Tel. : 04 90 62 33 33
Fax : 04 90 62 36 36
www.provence-gites.com

Closed from Nov 1 to Mar • 5 rooms with shower/WC
• €68, breakfast included • Table d'hôte €15 • Garden,
car park. Credit cards not accepted

891 **LE MAS DE MAGALI**
Mr and Mrs Bodewes

Quartier Chante Coucou
84110 Le Crestet
Tel. : 04 90 36 39 91
Fax : 04 90 28 73 40
www.guideweb.com/provence/hotel/magali

Open from late Mar to 20 Oct • 11 rooms with bath/WC
and television • Half board only €76 (€61 low season)
• Restaurant closed Wed, guests only in the evening
• Terrace, garden, car park. No dogs allowed in rooms
• Outdoor swimming pool

We most liked **Apricot rooms, apricot trees, apricot
jam and nectar of apricot.**

Nestled among vineyards and apricot trees, this mas
built in 1883 has been renovated in true Provençal
fashion. The bright sunny rooms, recently repainted,
echo their evocative names. Sunflower and Iris overlook
the castle of Barroux and the Comtat plain, while Apricot
faces the orchards. How about a quick game of pétanque
before sampling the tasty regional cooking under the
shade of an arbour?

We most liked **The heady perfume of Provence's
vegetation.**

The utter peace and quiet, magnificent view of Mont
Ventoux and the remote Vaucluse landscape, colourful
blue and yellow dining room and spacious rooms, some
with terraces: this modern mas captures all that is best
in Provence. Magali, the lady of the house, oversees
every aspect of your stay from pétanque and pastis to
a quiet afternoon nap.

Access : 800m towards Suzette

Access : Leave Vaison-la-Romaine on the
D 938 (towards Malaucène) and after 3.5km, turn
right (D 76)

 LE MAS DU SOULÉOU
Mr and Mrs Lepaul

5 chemin St-Pierre-des-Essieux
84300 Les Vignères
Tel. : 04 90 71 43 22
Fax : 04 90 71 43 22
www.souleou.com

Closed in Feb • 4 rooms with bath/WC • €74, breakfast included • Table d'hôte €20 • Garden, car park. Credit cards not accepted, no dogs allowed • Outdoor swimming pool

 LE DOMAINE DES TILLEULS
Mr Chastel

Route du Mont-Ventoux
84340 Malaucène
Tel. : 04 90 65 22 31
Fax : 04 90 65 16 77

Open all year • 10 rooms, half of which overlook the park, all have bath/WC or shower/WC and television • €69 to €84; breakfast €6 • No restaurant • Park, private car park • Outdoor swimming pool, numerous footpaths nearby

Sunset over the Durance Valley.

Elegance and good taste abound in this lovely 19C mas set in secluded countryside. It is difficult to choose between the spacious, well-furnished rooms: "Papaline" is the largest and has a mezzanine, but "Cannelle" has a private terrace. On lazy afternoons, you can curl up with a good read in the immense book-lined sitting room or stretch out in the sun by the swimming pool. Let yourself be tempted by Nadine's excellent cooking, served under the trellis.

The lovely swimming pool surrounded by foliage.

The enormous rooms of this former Templar stronghold are now adorned with bold fabrics, pastel colours and earthenware tiles. The thick stone 18C walls make air-conditioning thankfully unnecessary even during heat waves. Ask for a room facing the lime, plane and chestnut trees in the enormous park. Walkers will be happy to learn that the young owners can indicate endless paths between Mont Ventoux, the "Giant of Provence" and the ragged crests of the Dentelles de Montmirail.

Access : 7km northbound from Cavaillon on the D 938 towards Carpentras, take the D 22 then Les Vignères

Access : At Malaucène drive towards Mont-Ventoux, the hotel is on the left

MORNAS - 84550   **MURS - 84220**

894 **LE MANOIR**
Mr and Mrs Caillet

Route Nationale 7
84550 Mornas
Tel. : 04 90 37 00 79
Fax : 04 90 37 10 34
lemanoir@ifrance.com

Closed in Jan, Feb, and Sun evening and Mon from Sep
to Jun (hotel and restaurant) • 25 rooms located in
2 wings with bath/WC or shower/WC, some have
air-conditioning and television • €46 to €54; breakfast
€7; half board €49 to €55 • Restaurant closed Mon and
Tue lunchtimes from Jun to late Aug; menus €22 to
€39 • Terrace, car park, garage

895 **LES HAUTS DE VÉRONCLE**
Mr and Mrs Del Corso

84220 Murs
Tel. : 04 90 72 60 91
Fax : 04 90 72 62 07
hauts.de.veroncle@wanadoo.fr

Closed from 1 Jan to 29 Mar and from 4 Nov to 31 Dec
• 3 rooms • €48, breakfast included • Table d'hôte
€20 • Sitting room, terrace, garden, car park. Credit
cards not accepted

We most liked **Wining and dining by candlelight on**
the patio.

This impressive 18C mansion stands at the foot of a
steep cliff, dominated by the outline of Mornas fortress.
The new owners have so far concentrated their
restoration efforts on the restaurant, but they plan to
redo the rooms shortly. That said, beautiful old
wardrobes and marble fireplaces add a great deal of
old-fashioned charm to the rooms. The verdant patio
and flowered terrace echo to the light-hearted, sunny
disposition of Provence.

We most liked **Ever longed to be somewhere no-one**
could find you?

In the middle of nowhere – there is no other way to
describe the peaceful tranquillity of this blue-shuttered
mas with its dry stone walls, fragrant garrigue and
chirping cicadas. A sophisticated cuisine is served by the
fireside in winter or under the wisteria in the summer.
If you feel like a walk, ask Mr or Mrs Del Corso to point
you towards the path of the seven mills which runs
alongside the gorges of the Véroncle.

Access : Beside the N 7 through the village

Access : 8km to the north-east of Sénanque on the
D 177, the D 244 then the D 15

 896   **MAS DES AIGRAS**
Mr and Mrs Davi

Chemin des Aigras
84100 Orange
Tel. : 04 90 34 81 01
Fax : 04 90 34 05 66

Closed from 24 Dec to 24 Jan, Tue evening and Wed (except evenings from Apr to Sep) • 12 rooms, 8 of which are air-conditioned, all have bath/WC or shower/WC and television • €65 to €71; breakfast €10; half board €66 to €84 • Menus €16 (lunchtime in the week) to €43 • Terrace, garden, private car park • Outdoor swimming pool

 897   **L'HERMITAGE**
Mrs Oury

Route de Carpentras
84210 Pernes-les-Fontaines
Tel. : 04 90 66 51 41
Fax : 04 90 61 36 41
hotel.lhermitage @ libertysurf
www.ifrance.com/lhermitage

Closed in Dec, Jan and Feb • 20 rooms upstairs, most have bath/WC, all have television • €72 to €80; breakfast €9 • No restaurant • Park, private car park • Swimming pool

 The amazing botanical garden of a leading 19C entomologist, J-H Fabre.

The stone walls of this mas are hidden amid vineyards and fields on the outskirts of Orange. The cheerful young owners have thrown themselves into the task of rejuvenating their property, adding colourful cotton fabrics and hand-painted walls. Little by little, the rooms are regaining their rightful Provençal colours and are also being treated to air-conditioning. Organic produce figures prominently on the up-to-date menu, served in a dining room or on a teak and wrought-iron furnished terrace.

Access : 4km northbound from Orange on the N 7, then take a minor road (100m from the bypass)

 A refreshing drink from one of the 36 fountains of the "pearl of the Comtat".

Once the property of a relative of the famous Captain Dreyfus, whose court-martial divided public opinion in 1890s France and inspired Emile Zola's famous counterblast "J'accuse", this 19C house has retained a characteristically Provençal atmosphere. Majestic trees, statues and fountains abound in the immense park, together with a host of shaded corners, perfect for a quiet pastis. The colourful rooms are gradually being refurbished. The sitting rooms are decorated with period furniture.

Access : Set back from the road, 2km northbound from Pernes-les-Fontaines, towards Carpentras on the D 938

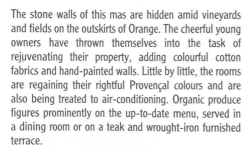

  898 MAS LA BONOTY
Mr Ryan and Mr Cuff

Chemin de la Bonoty
84210 Pernes-les-Fontaines
Tel. : 04 90 61 61 09
Fax : 04 90 61 35 14
bonoty @ aol.com
www.bonoty.com

Closed in Jan and Nov; restaurant closed Mon and Tue
from Oct to Mar • 8 rooms, 6 of which have shower/WC,
2 have bath/WC, all have television • €77, breakfast
included; half board €59 to €62 • Menus €28 to
€38 • Terrace, garden, private car park • Swimming pool

  899 LES AUZIÈRES
Mr Cuer

84110 Roaix
Tel. : 04 90 46 15 54
Fax : 04 90 46 12 75

Closed from Nov to Mar • 5 rooms bathrooms and
television • €69, breakfast included • Table d'hôte
€23 • Sitting room, car park. Credit cards not accepted
• Outdoor swimming pool, pétanque, table-tennis,
billiards

 **Your English hosts have, naturally,
equipped all the rooms with
tea-making facilities.**

A few cypress trees stand guard over this 17C stone
farmhouse. Sturdy, country furniture and terracotta tiles
set the scene in the rooms, which overlook a romantic
garden of fruit trees, olive groves and lavender. An old
sheepfold has become a rustic dining room. On fine
days, lunch is served under the shade of pine trees on
the terrace and dinner by the swimming pool.
Up-to-date Provençal cuisine.

 A sweeping view of the valley.

It would be hard to find a more secluded spot than this
Provençal farm perched on a hillside in the midst of
vineyards, olive groves and lavender fields. The
spacious, cool bedrooms are spotless and utterly
tranquil. Sample the traditional cooking at a huge
wooden table in the dining room or on the terrace, facing
Mont Ventoux and the jagged peaks of the Dentelles
de Montmirail.

Access : 5km to the north-east of
Pernes-les-Fontaines on the D 1, then take a minor
road

Access : 6km westbound from Vaison on the
D 975 towards Orange

 900 LES SABLES D'OCRE
Mr Hilario

 Les Sablières
84220 Roussillon
Tel. : 04 90 05 55 55
Fax : 04 90 05 55 50
sabledocre @ free.fr
www.roussillon-hotel.com

Closed in Feb and from 10 Nov to 15 Dec • 22 rooms with balcony, or terrace on the ground floor, 2 have disabled access, all have bath/WC or shower/WC, air-conditioning and television • €61 to €72; breakfast €8 • No restaurant • Garden, car park. No dogs allowed • Outdoor swimming pool

 Walk along the "ochre footpath" to the breathtaking Giants' Causeway.

The colourful walls of this modern hotel pay homage to the "red villages" of Roussillon and their picturesque houses. The mas built in 1998 on the outskirts of the village offers rooms which are handsomely equipped and have a balcony or garden-level terrace, even though they do rather lack character; some have brass beds. 400m away, the old Mathieu factory has been turned into a pigment conservatory – tours and courses.

 901 MONTMIRAIL
Mr Nicolet

 Montmirail
84190 Gigondas
Tel. : 04 90 65 84 01
Fax : 04 90 65 81 50
hotel-montmirail @ wanadoo.fr
www.hotelmontmirail.com

Open from 15 Mar to 15 Oct • 39 rooms, one of which has disabled access, with bath/WC or shower/WC and television • €66 to €88; breakfast €9; half board €66 to €77 • Restaurant closed Thu and Sat lunchtimes; menus €26 (in the week) to €32 • Terrace, garden, car park • Swimming pool

Villages which set the taste buds tingling: Gigondas, Vacqueyras, Beaumes-de-Venise...

Until the First World War, this 19C building accommodated visitors who came to take the waters at the foot of the famous Montmirail range of mountains. The rooms, although practical and modern in style, have retained a certain indefinable "resort" flavour, ditto the restaurant. Who cares though when Provence is on the doorstep? Indeed the establishment's outdoor facilities include a spacious garden, enormous swimming pool, inviting deck chairs and the pleasant shade of tall plane trees on the terrace.

Access : Around 10km from Apt, towards Avignon, leave the N 100 and turn right onto the D 149 for 4.5km

Access : 2km eastbound from Vacqueyras on a minor road

902 L'ÉVÊCHÉ
Mr and Mrs Verdier

Rue de l'Évêché
84110 Vaison-la-Romaine
Tel. : 04 90 36 13 46
Fax : 04 90 36 32 43
eveche @ aol.com

Closed from 15 Nov to 15 Dec • 4 rooms • €73, breakfast included • No table d'hôte • Sitting room, terrace. Credit cards not accepted, no dogs allowed

903 MAS DE BOUVAU
Mr Hertzog

Route de Cairanne
84150 Violès
Tel. : 04 90 70 94 08
Fax : 04 90 70 95 99
www.provenceguide.com

Closed from 2 to 31 Jan, 20 to 30 Dec and evenings except Sat and Mon from Nov to Feb • 6 rooms with bath/WC or shower/WC and television • €65; breakfast €8; half board €54 to €58 • Menus €21 (in the week) to €40 • Terrace, garden, car park. No dogs allowed in rooms

A warm country welcome after a hard day's sightseeing.

This former Episcopal palace, dating from the 16C, stands in the medieval part of town. Most of its countless rooms, on a variety of levels, overlook a tiny terrace. The breakfast room is the largest and it offers a wonderful view of the lower town. A lovely spiral staircase winds up to the well-furnished and tasteful rooms. Don't forget to take a look at the interesting collection of prints originally from a treatise on lockmaking.

Daydreaming as you gaze on the jagged peaks of the Dentelles de Montmirail.

This old farmhouse is surrounded by the vineyards of the Plan de Dieu plateau which have been cultivated since the Middle Ages. The sober rooms are furnished with sturdy country pieces. Sample the traditional menu in one of the Provençal dining rooms or on the terraces – our favourite is in the old barn. The wine-list is a credit to the region.

Access : In the old town

Access : Northbound from Violès, leave the D 977 and turn left towards Cairanne

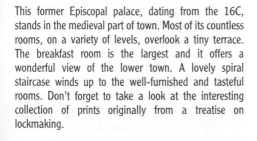

904 **LA FARIGOULE**
Mrs Cornaz

Le Plan-de Dieu
84150 Violès
Tel. : 04 90 70 91 78
Fax : 04 90 70 91 78

Closed from Nov to Mar • 5 rooms with shower/WC
• €51, breakfast included • No table d'hôte • Sitting
room, garden, car park. No dogs allowed • Play area,
table-tennis

**The erudite atmosphere of this
characterful house.**

This 18C wine-growers' house has lost none of its
authenticity over the years. A fine staircase leads up to
antique furnished rooms, each of which is named after
a local writer, including Frédéric Mistral, Alphonse
Daudet and Marie Mauron; you won't be surprised to
discover that your hosts used to own a book shop.
Breakfasts are served in a lovely vaulted room. As for
free time, there is a play area for children and the hotel
rents out bicycles (including tandems).

Access : 10km westbound from Gigondas on the
D 80 towards Orange, then the D 8 and the D 977
towards Violès

RHÔNE-ALPES

A land of contrasts and a veritable crossroads of culture, the Rhône-Alpes region offers visitors a thousand different faces. Its lofty peaks are heaven on earth to skiers, climbers and hikers attracted by the sublime beauty of its immaculate summits, glittering glaciers, torrential streams and tranquil lakes, while its fashionable resorts, like Chamonix and Courchevel, set the tone in alpine chic. If you can tear yourself away from the roof of Europe, venture down past the herds of cattle grazing on the rich mountain grass and into the intense bustle of the Rhône valley, symbolised by its fast-flowing waters. From Antique Roman roads to high-speed inter-city trains, the main artery between north and south has forged the reputation of this region's economic drive. Rhône-Alpes lies on the route taken by hordes of holidaymakers every summer, and those in the know always make a point of stopping in the region to taste its culinary specialities. The area abounds in restaurants, from three-star trend-setters to Lyon's legendary neighbourhood *bouchons*, whose unparalleled standards and traditions have made the region the kingdom of cuisine.

96 ESTABLISHMENTS
905 to **1000**

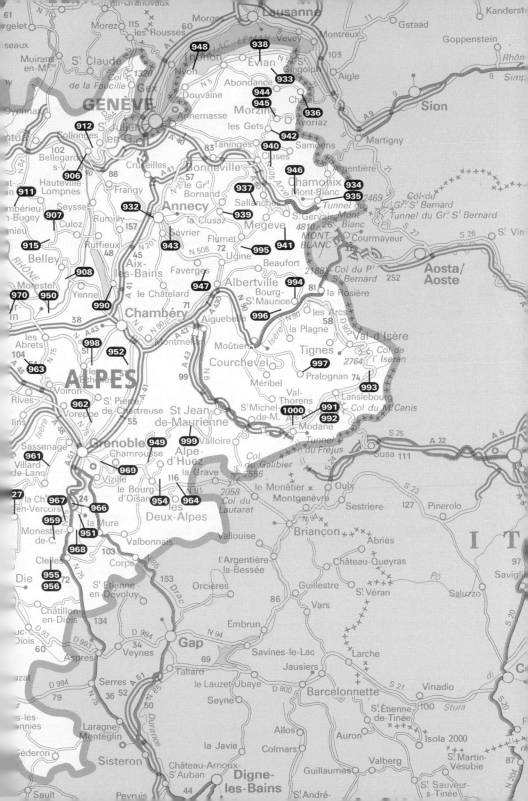

 905 AUBERGE DES BICHONNIÈRES
Mr Sauvage

Route de Savigneux
01330 Ambérieux-en-Dombes
Tel. : 04 74 00 82 07
Fax : 04 74 00 89 61
bichonnieres@aol.com
www.aubergedesbichonnieres.com

Closed 15 Dec to 15 Jan, Sun (except in Jul and Aug), Mon except summer evenings and Tue lunchtime • 9 rooms with bath/WC or shower/WC and television • €40 to €54; breakfast €7; half board €47 to €55 • Menus €21 to €31 • Terrace, garden, private car park

 906 AUBERGE LE CATRAY
Mr Chappuis

Plateau de Retord
01200 Bellegarde-sur-Valserine
Tel. : 04 50 56 56 25

Closed from 11 to 15 Mar, 3 to 7 Jun, 9 to 20 Sep, 12 to 22 Nov, Mon evening and Tue • 7 rooms, all have showers, some have WC • €36 to €43; breakfast €5; half board €34 to €38 • Menus €15 to €22 • Terrace, garden, car park • Hiking and mountain biking, mini-golf, children's games, cross-country skiing, snowshoe hiking (in winter)

 The charm of the "Route des étangs" (Pond Route).

 On a fine day you can see as far as Mont Blanc.

Guests are pampered within the cob walls of this old farm, typical of the Dombes region. The rooms overlooking the courtyard, although a little on the small side, are refreshingly quiet. The cuisine draws on local traditions and ingredients and is served in a rustic dining room near an old stove or under a canopy on the terrace. Rows of crimson geraniums brighten up the peaceful garden.

This hilltop chalet is lost amid the remote countryside of high mountain pastures. Only the bells of solitary cows grazing nearby pierce the silence of the wood-lined, simply decorated rooms. Wood furniture and a fireside set the scene for the alpine restaurant which specialises in traditional cheese dishes such as raclette and fondue. In the winter, the establishment rents snowshoes and cross-country skis.

Access : On leaving the town, on the Ars-sur-Formans road

Access : 12km westbound from Bellgarde on the D 101: cross Vouvray then continue towards the Plateau de Retord

 907 AU VIEUX TILLEUL
Mr Guyon and Mr Tournier

01260 Belmont-Luthézieu
Tel. : 04 79 87 64 51
Fax : 04 79 87 54 50

Closed Sun evening and Mon from Oct to Apr • 15 rooms with bathrooms and television • €46; breakfast €6 • Menus €17 to €30 • Terrace, car park

 908 FERME DES GRANDS HAUTAINS
Mr and Mrs Veyron

Le Petit Brens
01300 Brens
Tel. : 04 79 81 90 95
 Fax : 04 79 81 90 95

Closed from 15 Nov to 20 Dec and Sun • 4 non-smoking rooms • €37, breakfast included • Table d'hôte €10 to €13 • Terrace, car park. Credit cards not accepted, no dogs allowed

 A panoramic view of the Grand Colombier from the terrace and most of the rooms.

It is hard to resist the peaceful entreaty of this establishment surrounded by unspoilt countryside. A palette of contrasting blues and yellows has been applied to the interior, even down to the matching fabric, that would not be out of place in a painting by Van Gogh. Most of the very comfortable rooms overlook the 1 534m-high Grand Colombier mountain or the forest. The round tables on the pleasant terrace are rarely empty.

Lively meals of beautifully cooked garden-fresh vegetables.

The farmhouse and pergola are delightful. The rooms under the eaves are snugly welcoming, furnished with family heirlooms and decorated in an old-fashioned style; all are non-smoking. The dining table, which shows the chef's preference for home-grown produce, is located in a welcoming room, or when the weather allows, around a stone table in the garden under the shade of an oak and birch trees.

Access : 10.5km westbound from Virieu-le-Petit on the D 69F then the D 54C

Access : 3km southbound from Belley on the D 31A

 909 AUBERGE DE CAMPAGNE DU MOLLARD
Mr Decre Frères

 01320 Châtillon-la-Palud
Tel. : 04 74 35 66 09

Open all year by reservation • 4 rooms • €46, breakfast included • Menus €16 to €35 • Car park

 910 CHAMBRE D'HÔTE M. SALMON
Mr and Mrs Salmon

 150 place du Champ-de-Foire
01400 Châtillon-sur-Chalaronne
Tel. : 04 74 55 06 86
Fax : 04 74 55 42 56
alsalmon @ club-internet.fr

Closed from Christmas to Jan 1 • 5 rooms • €45, breakfast included • No table d'hôte • Garden, car park. Credit cards not accepted, no dogs allowed

We most liked **The religiously preserved rustic appeal.**

A tiny country lane will take you up to this attractive farmhouse and courtyard-garden bedecked with flowers – a sight to behold in the spring. The four rooms in an outbuilding have wonderful carved wooden beds, but have a shared bathroom. Meals are served in a country-style dining room with a fireplace and a huge cauldron. The tasty family cooking focuses on local produce.

We most liked **A breakfast worth getting up for!**

Old wardrobes, a wooden staircase, huge beams and floral wallpaper: the stage is set and the curtain can rise on this welcoming home. Bunches of fresh flowers and well-polished wooden furniture greet you in the rooms. Make sure you get up early and have had time to work up an appetite, if you want to do justice to the substantial mounds of croissants, walnut bread, pancakes and no less than thirty home-made jams!

Access : 14km north-east of Pérouges on the D 984 and the D 904, towards Chalamont, then a lane on the left

Access : In the town centre

911 L' AUBERGE CAMPAGNARDE
Mrs Merloz and Mrs Mano

01230 Évosges
Tel. : 04 74 38 55 55
Fax : 04 74 38 55 62
mano-merloz@wanadoo.fr

Closed from 7 Jan to 6 Feb, from 12 Nov to 5 Dec, Tue evening and Wed out of season • 14 rooms with bath/WC or shower/WC, all have television • €39 to €62; breakfast €6; half board €40 to €54 • Menus €21 (in the week) to €43 • Terrace, garden, car park • Outdoor swimming pool, mini-golf, table-tennis, play area, fishing

912 LE SORGIA
Mr Marion

01200 Lancrans
Tel. : 04 50 48 15 81
Fax : 04 50 48 44 72

Closed from 23 Aug to 17 Sep, 21 Dec to 7 Jan, Sat lunchtime, Sun evening and Mon • 17 rooms upstairs, all have bath/WC or shower/WC and television • €39 to €41; breakfast €6; half board €36 to €38 • Menus €12 (in the week) to €28 • Terrace, garden, car park

 Ideal for nature lovers with energetic children.

This old family farmstead in a remote village of Bugey has been turned into a lovely country inn with rustic or modern-style rooms and an inviting restaurant with stone walls and a fireplace. Children however generally prefer the shaded garden with play area, mini-golf and swimming pool.

 The Valserine River which "disappears" into deep crevices, near the hotel.

For five generations and a century or so, this family has been entertaining guests in their chalet-inn in the heart of the village. All the compact, simple rooms display the same rustic decoration and well cared-for feel; one or two have recently been renovated. The old rustic dining room opens onto the country garden, where tables are laid in the summer.

Access : Leave the N 504 (Ambérieu-Belley) between St Rambert-en-Bugey and Argis and follow the D 34

Access : On the road through the village, 3km northbound from Bellegarde-sur-Valserine

 913 LA VILLA DU RHÔNE
Mrs Beauvois-Cabardi

Chemin de la Lune
01700 Miribel
Tel. : 04 78 55 54 16
Fax : 04 78 55 54 16
christine.beauvois @ laposte.net

Open all year • 3 rooms • €60, breakfast €5 • Table
d'hôte €15 • Garden, car park. Credit cards not accepted
• Outdoor swimming pool

 914 CHAMBRES D'HÔTES DE BOSSERON
Mrs Rivoire

325 route de Genève
01160 Neuville-sur-Ain
Tel. : 04 74 37 77 06
Fax : 04 74 37 77 06
arivoire @ free.fr
http://arivoire.free.fr

Open all year • 4 rooms with bathrooms • €50, breakfast
included • No table d'hôte • Park, car park. Credit cards
not accepted, no dogs allowed • Fitness room, billiards

We most liked **Peace and quiet on the threshold of
Lyons.**

This modern villa on the heights of Miribel commands
a superb view of the Rhône and the valley. Two of the
three rooms overlooking the swimming pool have their
own private terrace with a view of the landscape. The
redbrick walls of the sitting room beneath the veranda,
complete with indoor garden and fireplace, are full of
appeal. Breakfast on the terrace in the summer is a pure
joy.

We most liked **Immaculately decorated.**

You won't regret your decision to stay here when you
see the impressive manor house and the five acres of
parkland on the banks of the Ain. Good taste and a flair
for interior decoration have resulted in comfortable,
well-soundproofed rooms. A fitness room and billiards
table in the outbuildings are for the sole use of guests.
Your gracious hostess certainly knows how to make
visitors feel welcome.

Access : 12km to the north-east of Lyon, A 42
towards Geneva, leave Miribel-Jonage Park, then D 71
towards the Mas Rillier and the Madone Campanile

Access : 8km to the north-east of Pont-d'Ain on the
N 84

915 LES CHARMETTES
Mrs Vincent

La Vellaz, Saint-Martin-de-Bavel
01510 Virieu-le-Grand
Tel. : 04 79 87 32 18
Fax : 04 79 87 34 51

Open all year • 3 rooms, one of which has disabled access
• €37, breakfast included • No table d'hôte • Car park.
Credit cards not accepted • Hiking and mountain biking

916 LE JEU DU MAIL
Mr and Mrs Arlaud

07400 Alba-la-Romaine
Tel. : 04 75 52 41 59
Fax : 04 75 52 41 59
lejeudumail @ free.fr

Closed from 1 Nov to 1 Mar • 5 rooms • €58, breakfast
included • No table d'hôte • Garden, terrace, car park.
Credit cards not accepted, no dogs allowed • Outdoor
swimming pool

Mother Nature at her best.

Why not treat yourself to a stay in this lovely farmhouse
and enjoy the superb surrounding countryside? The
snug, comfortable rooms are in the beautifully restored
stables and one is equipped for disabled guests. Visitors
have the use of a fitted kitchen and dining and sitting
rooms in a separate wing. The owner is extremely
knowledgeable about his region's tourist attractions.

**A lengthy lunch under the trellis or in
the shade of the plane tree.**

The owners of this former 19C Templar stronghold were
among the precursors of the Ardèches chambre d'hôte
phenomenon in the 1970s. Since then, they have never
stopped taking great pleasure in entertaining guests. All
the rooms are very pleasant and each has been given
a name which relates to the property's history, including
Émilie, Jesuit's suite and Servants Quarters. In the
summer, breakfast and lunch, served under a shaded
trellis or plane tree, are sheer delight.

Access : 11km northbound from Belley on the
N 504 as far as Chazey-Bons, then take the D 31C

Access : In the village

917 LA SANTOLINE
Mr and Mrs Espenel

07460 Beaulieu
Tel. : 04 75 39 01 91
Fax : 04 75 39 38 79
contacts@lasantoline.com
http://perso.wanadoo.fr/santoline/

Open from 1 May to 30 Sep • 8 rooms (some have a balcony), one of which is a suite, all have bath/WC, some have air-conditioning • €69 to €95; breakfast €10; half board €60 to €84 • Restaurant for hotel guests and open evenings only • Terrace, garden, car park. No dogs allowed in restaurant • Outdoor swimming pool

 The lovely view of the Ardèche countryside and the Cévennes foothills.

Farm? Stronghold? Hunting lodge? Whatever the case, these 16C walls now house a hotel in a remote spot of garrigue that will appeal to urbanites in search of authenticity and tranquillity. The cheerful Provençal rooms would be quite at home in a glossy home-decoration magazine. Some have air-conditioning, but to our mind the thick dry-stone walls are more than sufficient to keep the scorching heat firmly outside. Vaulted restaurant, pretty terrace and a swimming pool surrounded by greenery.

Access : To the south-east, 1km on a small graveled lane

918 LE MAS DE MAZAN
Mr Croze

07200 Mercuer
Tel. : 04 75 35 41 88
Fax : 04 75 35 41 88

Open all year • 5 rooms • €38, breakfast included • No table d'hôte • Car park. Credit cards not accepted, no dogs allowed

 The owner takes guests round his pride and joy, a silk-worm farm.

This typical Cévennes farm has been lovingly restored by a farming couple, who enthusiastically greet all new guests. The spot is stunningly tranquil and the view of the valley, wooded hills and the village is matchless. The rooms are inviting and well restored but all, sadly, do not enjoy the wonderful view. The owner breeds silk worms and loves explaining the finer points of his "hobby".

Access : 5km to the north-west of Aubenas on the D 104 and the D 435

 919 **DOMAINE DE RILHAC**
Mr and Mrs Sinz

 07320 Saint-Agrève
Tel. : 04 75 30 20 20
Fax : 04 75 30 20 00

Closed in Jan, Tue evening, Thu lunchtime and Wed
• 7 rooms with bath/WC and television • €79; breakfast
€10; half board €73 to €82 • Menus €21 (lunchtime in
the week) to €66 • Garden, car park

920 **LA DÉSIRADE**
Mr and Mrs Mennier

 07340 Saint-Désirat
Tel. : 04 75 34 21 88

Closed Christmas and 1 Jan. Bookings only • 6 rooms
• €43, breakfast included • Table d'hôte €16 • Terrace,
garden, car park. Credit cards not accepted

 We most liked
"Oyez, oyez, Epicureans pay heed!"

Stick a bookmark in this page, because the vision of
this lovely 19C Ardèche farm lost in the countryside is
definitely worth the trek. The individually decorated
rooms afford great views, some of which extend as far
as the Gerbier de Jonc. Even better, the chef, a proud
Michelin star recipient since 1998, masterfully rustles up
tasty, inventive recipes based on local produce. Meals
are served in an elegant Provençal dining room and
guests can relax peacefully in the shaded garden
afterwards.

 We most liked
The lady of the house's talented culinary skills.

This fully renovated 19C mansion among Saint Joseph's
trees and vineyards is a feast for the eyes. The simple,
light and airy rooms overlook the magnolia tree in the
courtyard, or the park and vineyard. Your cordon-bleu
hostess loves surprising her guests with tasty regional
recipes. A perfect base camp from which to explore the
Ardèche.

Access : 2km to the south-east: leave Saint-Agrève
on the D 120, then take a sharp left onto the D 21

Access : 15km eastbound from Annonay on the
D 82, towards Andance, then take a minor road

 921 CHAMBRE D'HÔTE BOURLENC
Mr and Mrs Ventalon

 Route de Saint-Andéol
07200 Saint-Julien-du-Serre
Tel. : 04 75 37 69 95
Fax : 04 75 37 69 95

Open all year, booking necessary • 5 rooms • €49, breakfast included • Table d'hôte €19 to €23 • Garden. Credit cards not accepted, no dogs allowed

 922 LA PASSIFLORE
Mrs Luypaerts

07460 Saint-Paul-le-Jeune
Tel. : 04 75 39 80 74
Fax : 04 75 39 80 74

Open all year • 3 rooms • €42, breakfast included • No table d'hôte • Garden, car park. Credit cards not accepted, no dogs allowed

A chance to taste forgotten varieties of fruit and vegetables.

It is impossible not to wind down during a stay at this house perched on a rock and surrounded by acacias. Colourful wardrobes, whitewashed walls and earthenware tiles add a delightful southern accent to the interior. The Pass of Lescrinet can be seen from the light, airy and generously proportioned rooms. Farm-grown fruit and vegetables take pride of place on the appetising dining table.

The owners bend over backwards to make their guests feel at home.

This Flemish couple clearly care about their guests and want to make sure their stay in the Vans region is memorable. Despite the nearby road, the well-isolated house is a haven of peace. The agreeable rooms are extremely well-soundproofed and guests can choose from countless delightful sitting rooms. As to the breakfasts, served under an arbour near the mulberry tree and aviary, you'll certainly pass your plate for more...

Access : 3.5km from Saint-Julien-du-Serre on the D 218 towards Saint-Andéol-de-Vals

Access : 13km southbound from Vans on the D 901, then the D 104 towards Alès

 923 HOSTELLERIE "MÈRE BIQUETTE"
Mr and Mrs Bossy

 07580 Saint-Pons
Tel. : 04 75 36 72 61
Fax : 04 75 36 76 25
merebiquette @ europost.org
www.logis-d-ardeche.com/merebiquette/

Closed from 1 Dec to 5 Feb, Sun and Mon lunchtime from Oct to Mar • 9 rooms in a separate wing, with bath/WC and television • €54 to €71; breakfast €7; half board €64 (€57 low season) • Menus €16 to €38 • Terrace, garden, car park • Outdoor swimming pool, tennis

 924 VIVARAIS
Mrs Brioude

 Avenue Claude Expilly
07600 Vals-les-Bains
Tel. : 04 75 94 65 85
Fax : 04 75 37 65 47

Closed in Feb • 47 rooms on 5 floors, with bath/WC or shower/WC, all have television • €54 to €77; breakfast €9; half board €58 to €94 • Menus €28 to €43 • Terrace, private car park. No dogs allowed in rooms • Outdoor swimming pool

 Tucking into the appetising breakfast buffet.

 Lounging on the balcony overlooking the fast-flowing Volane.

This old country farm is named after a goat's cheese formerly produced here: "la mère biquette" (a biquette is a kid goat) was sold by the current owners' parents in the local markets. It's a perfect hideaway to build up your strength in well-appointed rooms overlooking the chestnut trees or vineyards, a stone and wood rustic-styled restaurant, a shaded terrace overlooking the valley and a superb swimming pool.

Near the casino, this old pink building is adorned with a frieze and terraces decked in flowers. The delightfully old-fashioned floral wallpaper and mahogany furniture in the bedrooms, the original bathrooms and elegantly dated atmosphere of the restaurant all add to the appeal. The mistress of the house's love of her region and its culinary traditions makes cooking with local produce, such as mushrooms, chestnuts and goat's cheese, a point of honour.

Access : Leave the N 102 between Villeneuve-de-Berg and Le Teil, take the D 293, through Saint-Pons and on for 4km

Access : Next to the casino

925 **LA TREILLE MUSCATE**
Mr Delaitre

26270 Cliousclat
Tel. : 04 75 63 13 10
Fax : 04 75 63 10 79
latreillemuscate @ wanadoo.fr
www.latreillemuscate.com

Open from 1 Mar to 15 Dec • 14 rooms, 6 of which overlook the countryside. Rooms have bath/WC or shower/WC, most have television • €54 to €85; breakfast €8; half board €67 to €98 • Menu €24 • Terrace, small garden, private car park

926 **LA MARE**
Chaix family

Route de Montmeyran
26800 Étoile-sur-Rhône
Tel. : 04 75 59 33 79
Fax : 04 75 59 33 79

Open all year • 6 rooms • €40, breakfast included • Table d'hôte €14 • Garden, car park. Credit cards not accepted

 The fruit trees in blossom in the spring.

Midway between Valence and Montélimar just off the A 7 motorway, this village lying in the hills of the Drôme valley is home to an inn, made up of two old stone houses with lilac shutters. Terracotta tiled floors and second-hand furniture adorn the uncluttered, individually styled bedrooms. Sunny Provence can be felt in the dining room and the lovely terrace is hidden in a secret garden. However, if you are unable to resist the temptation of a motorway hotel, then have it your own way...

 The warm-hearted hospitality of this farming family.

On the threshold of the south of France, this lovely stone house run by a farming family is a unique chance to taste the legendary "savoir-vivre" of the region first-hand. The comfortable, appealing rooms are fitted with home-made furniture. Garden-produce features prominently in the delicious, generous helpings of home cooking. We also appreciated the friendly greeting and the modest prices.

Access : Leave the Valence-Montélimard road (N 7) between Loriol-sur-Drôme and Saulce-sur-Rhône for a minor road eastbound

Access : 15km to the south-east of Valence on the D 111 and the D 111B

 BELLIER
Mrs Bellier

 26420 La Chapelle-en-Vercors
Tel. : 04 75 48 20 03
Fax : 04 75 48 25 31

Closed Tue evening and Wed except Jul and Aug (from Oct to Apr, by reservation only) • 13 rooms with bath/WC and television • €58 to €69 (€46 to €55 low season); breakfast €6; half board €53 to €58 (€44 to €49 low season) • Menus €14 to €30 • Terrace, garden, car park • Outdoor swimming pool. In winter, cross-country skiing, snowshoe hiking

 DOMAINE DE MAGNE
Mr and Mrs Andruejol

Val des Nymphes
26700 La Garde-Adhémar
Tel. : 04 75 04 44 54

Open all year • 3 rooms • €43, breakfast included • Table d'hôte €16 to €24 • Terrace, garden. Credit cards not accepted • Outdoor swimming pool

 Right in the heart of the Vercors, in nearly 450 000 acres of Regional Park.

Air raids and fires took their toll on the village in 1944, which explains why the spruce chalet on a rocky outcrop over the road only dates from 1946. The majority of the spacious, welcoming rooms have a balcony. A mountain flavour adds warmth to the dining room and the fireplace in the sitting room is very welcome after a long day's skiing. In the summer, tables are laid round the swimming pool.

 Filling a basket with fruit from the estate.

This mouth-watering fruit farm is built on a hillside in immense grounds which formerly included the Chapelle des Nymphes. The rooms are located in a small independent house overlooking the orchards. Meals are served in a vaulted dining room where old farm tools and family photos hang on the walls. Music lovers can try the family piano, while others may prefer to lounge in the garden. Before leaving, fill your basket with freshly picked peaches and apricots.

Access : In the village, on a rocky outcrop overlooking the road

Access : 1km on the Chapelle du Val des Nymphes road

 929 LA CAPITELLE
Mr Dunaud

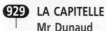

Le Rempart
26270 Mirmande
Tel. : 04 75 63 02 72
Fax : 04 75 63 02 50
capitelle @ wanadoo.fr

Closed from Dec to Feb, Tue lunchtime and Mon (except in Jun, Jul and Aug) • 11 rooms, all have bath/WC or shower/WC and television • €69; breakfast €10; half board €69 • Menus €22 to €33 • Terrace

 930 SPHINX-HÔTEL
Mr and Mrs Harnichard

19 boulevard Desmarais
26200 Montélimar
Tel. : 04 75 01 86 64
Fax : 04 75 52 34 21
reception @ sphinx-hotel.fr
www.sphinx-hotel.fr

Closed from 20 Dec to 6 Jan • 24 rooms on 2 floors, all have bath/WC, air-conditioning and television • €40 to €55; breakfast €6 • No restaurant • Inner courtyard, private car park

 Breakfast on the ramparts.

 Mornings in the lovely inner courtyard.

This Renaissance house was a Templar stronghold before it became the home of Cubist artist, André Lhote, thereby attracting a whole host of other painters and rescuing from certain ruin the rest of this superb hilltop village. Furniture picked up in local antique shops adorns the rooms which gaze down on the tiny narrow streets or across the landscape of orchards; some have mullioned windows. Vaulted dining room and pleasant terrace.

This 17C mansion stands on Montélimar's tree-lined Allées Provençales, now a busy pedestrianised shopping area. Lofty ceilings, parquet floors, wainscoting and huge beams bear witness to the home's stately origins, while individual air-conditioning, greatly appreciated in the summer, is a small concession to modernity. All the rooms will soon have been refurbished.

Access : Leave the N 7 southbound from Saulce-sur-Rhône for the D 204

Access : In the town centre, alongside the Allées Provençales

931 LA CARAVELLE
Mr and Mrs Pedrazzini

8 rue des Antignans
26110 Nyons
Tel. : 04 75 26 07 44
Fax : 04 75 26 23 79

Closed from Nov to Jan • 11 non-smoking rooms with bath/WC or shower/WC and television • €66 to €80; breakfast €8 • No restaurant • Garden, private car park

932 PALAIS DE L'ISLE
Mr Mamet

13 rue Perrière
74000 Annecy
Tel. : 04 50 45 86 87
Fax : 04 50 51 87 15
palisle @ wanadoo.fr
www.hoteldupalaisdelisle.com

Open all year • 26 rooms with bath/WC (2 have shower/WC) and television • €65 to €88 (€57 to €75 low season); breakfast €9 • No restaurant

We most liked
A quiet read in the unusual garden.

The sign outside and a series of portholes from the Jean-Bart battleship are the legacy of the former hotel owner who had a reputation as something of an old seadog. If you then add the unusual architecture of this 1900 villa and its curious garden full of Indian bean trees, you will be prepared for a stay in the earthly paradise of the olive kingdom but minus the traditional Provençal style. Quiet, well-cared for rooms.

Access : On the Promenade de la Digue

We most liked
A stroll down the canal banks of the "Venice of the Alps".

This charming building in the heart of historic Annecy dates from the 18C. The rooms are decorated in black and white and furnished with pieces designed by Philippe Starck; some command a view of the castle, while others survey the palace, a former prison encircled by canals which has become the city's emblem. The hotel is in a pedestrian district, but guests are allowed to drop-off suitcases by car. Discount for the neighbouring public car park.

Access : In the centre of the old town, near the lake, between Rue Sainte-Claire and Place Saint-François-de-Sales

 933 L' ÉCHELLE ET HÔTEL GRAND CHÉNAY
Mr and Mrs Mercier

74500 Bernex
Tel. : 04 50 73 60 42
Fax : 04 50 73 69 21

Closed from 15 Nov to 15 Dec • 6 rooms upstairs and 6 studios with kitchenettes. Rooms have bath/WC or shower/WC • €50 to €60; breakfast €7; half board €52 (€47 out of season) • Restaurant closed Mon and Tue; menus €23 (in the week) to €30 • Garden, car park • Ideal for summer and winter mountain sports

 934 L' AIGUILLE DU MIDI
Mr and Mrs Farini

479 chemin Napoléon – Les Bossons
74400 Chamonix-Mont-Blanc
Tel. : 04 50 53 00 65
Fax : 04 50 55 93 69
hotel.aiguille @ telepost.fr
www.hotel-aiguilledumidi.com

Open from 12 May to 20 Sep and from 20 Dec to 20 Apr • 40 rooms with bath/WC and television • €69 to €75 (€54 to €72 low season); breakfast €10; half board €64 to €72 (€61 to €68 low season) • Menus €21 to €29 • Terrace, garden, car park. No dogs allowed in restaurant • Outdoor swimming pool, tennis, fitness room, sauna, jacuzzi

 The owner-chef's cooking.

The fish on your plate comes from a nearby lake and the cured meats are prepared in the hotel kitchen. People come from far and wide to enjoy the warm hospitality of the dining room whose decoration reflects the owner's other passion, the mountains. The rooms and flatlets are simple, well cared-for and ideal for long stays in the unspoilt countryside. The Dent d'Oche (2 222m) attracts rock-climbers and mountaineers from all over France, while the migratory birds keep "twitchers" happy.

 The view of the Bossons glacier from the shade of the park.

This impressive old country chalet has been a hotel since 1908. Behind the Tyrolean-style frescoes are wood panelled rooms, most a little faded, but all overlooking the wonderful Mont Blanc range. The circular dining room and the terraces in the well cared-for park are lovely places to linger for a minute or two. Make sure you look up and admire the lovely carved ceiling in the sitting room. Numerous leisure activities.

Access : In the centre of the village, 50m from the church

Access : 3km southbound from Chamonix-Mont-Blanc

 935 CHALET CHANTEL
Mr Schmid

391 route de Pècles
74400 Chamonix-Mont-Blanc
Tel. : 04 50 53 02 54
Fax : 04 50 53 54 52
chantel@chamonixleguide.com

Closed from 4 to 19 Apr and from 29 Oct to 10 Nov
• 7 rooms on 2 floors, with bath/WC or shower/WC
• €52 to €66; breakfast €5 • No restaurant • Garden, car
park. No dogs allowed

 936 LE KANDAHAR
Mrs Vuarand

Route du Linga
74390 Châtel
Tel. : 04 50 73 30 60
Fax : 04 50 73 25 17
lekandahar@wanadoo.fr
 www.lekandahar.com

Open in May, from 16 Jun to Oct and from Christmas to
Easter • 20 rooms, 13 of which are in a separate wing
with kitchenettes, all have bath/WC and television
• €31 to €58; breakfast €8; half board €45 to €58 (€43 to
€51 low season) • Restaurant closed Sun evening and
Mon out of season, menus €13 (except Sun) to €26 • Terrace, garden, car park • Fitness room, sauna

 **Cuddle up in this snug mountain
chalet.**

A spread of delicacies at breakfast time, a sitting room
strewn with furniture picked up in antique shops and
a flight of stairs leading up to cosy rooms adorned with
flowers and frills; those on the second floor have sloping
ceilings. These are among the appeals of this enchanting
hotel-chalet run by an Englishman in a residential
district of Chamonix. The pleasant garden commands a
splendid view of the Mont Blanc range.

 **The family atmosphere of this alpine
chalet.**

This hotel on the border of Switzerland is renowned for
the hospitable, welcoming aspect of its rooms. Within
easy reach of the ski slopes thanks to frequent, free
shuttles to the Linga, it is also surrounded by gentler
hillsides for the less energetic, but the breathtaking
viewpoints over the Chablais definitely require the efforts
of serious walkers. In the kitchen, the chef sets-to with
a will, to restore and revive body and soul with delicious
local specialities.

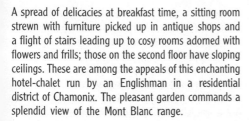

Access : In a quiet district on a road out of the
centre

Access : 1.5km to the south-west, on the Bechigne
road, then left on the Linga road

 937 LE CORDONANT
Mr and Mrs Pugnat

Les Darbaillets
74700 Cordon
Tel. : 04 50 58 34 56
Fax : 04 50 47 95 57

Open from 18 May to 20 Sep and from 20 Dec to 15 Apr
• 16 rooms with balconies, bath/WC (2 have shower/WC) and television • €57 to €68 (€50 to €58 low season); breakfast €7; half board €61 to €68 (€57 to €63 low season) • Menus €20 (in the week) to €28 • Terrace, car park. No dogs allowed in restaurant • Fitness room, sauna, jacuzzi

 938 LE BOIS JOLI
Mr and Mrs Birraux

74500 La Beunaz
Tel. : 04 50 73 60 11
Fax : 04 50 73 65 28
hboisjoli@aol.com
www.hotel-bois-joli.com

Open from 2 May to 15 Oct and from 20 Dec to 2 Apr
• 27 rooms, 8 of which are in a separate wing, all have bath/WC or shower/WC and television • €69 (€48 to €54 low season); breakfast €7; half board €56 (€49 low season) • Restaurant closed Sun evening and Wed; menus €15 (in the week) to €38 • Terrace, garden, car park • Outdoor swimming pool, tennis, sauna, table-tennis, billiards

 We most liked
The ear-splitting silence and stunning view from the valley windows.

We most liked
The country appeal of this panoramic chalet.

The pink roughcast walls and creamy coloured wood-work of this smart chalet stand on the heights of the "Mont Blanc balcony". The rooms have been refurbished in a contemporary Savoyard style with wood-lined walls, painted furniture and pretty fabrics. From the dining room, you will be able to enjoy a breathtaking view of the "rooftops of Europe" as you sample the appetising, generous cooking, before settling down for a nap in the sun in the flowered garden.

The bedrooms, dining room and terrace all enjoy a view of the Dent d'Oche, Mount Billiat and the summits of the Chablais. In the summer, activities include a swimming pool surrounded by foliage and a tennis court, in the winter the ski slopes are nearby while year-round activities include a children's play area and billiards room with Lake Léman and its prestigious spa-resorts just a few kilometres away. Idyllic in any season.

Access : 4km to the south-west of Sallanches on the D 113

Access : Below the road, 1.5km from Bernex on the D 52

939 **FLORALP**
Mrs Pollet

74220 La Clusaz
Tel. : 04 50 02 41 46
Fax : 04 50 02 63 94
info @ hotel-floralp74.com
www.hotel-floralp74.com

Open from 28 Jun to 15 Sep and from 20 Dec to 14 Apr
• 22 rooms, all have bath/WC or shower/WC and
television • €58 (€43 to €46 low season); breakfast €7;
half board €59 to €69 (€49 to €58 low season) • Menus
€19 (in the week) to €23 • Car park. No dogs allowed
in restaurant • Billiards room

940 **LA CROIX DE SAVOIE**
Mr and Mrs Tiret

768 route du Pernand
74300 Les Carroz-d'Araches
Tel. : 04 50 90 00 26
Fax : 04 50 90 00 63
jean-marc.tiret @ wanadoo.fr
www.perso.wanadoo.fr/lacroixdesavoie/

Open all year • 19 rooms with shower/WC, most have
a balcony • €42 to €44; breakfast €6; half board €47 to
€49 (€33 to €36 low season) • Menus €11 to €20 • Terrace, garden, car park

A traditional mountain chalet.

The simple rooms at the front have an east-facing
balcony and are much sought after by all the chalet's
numerous regular guests. The region is riddled with
beautiful, immaculate peaks, dales covered in rhodo-
dendron bushes and high rocky ranges. Tangy Tomme
and Reblochon cheeses tempt the palate at lunchtime
and dinners enable your hostesses to show off the full
scope of their culinary skills. The sitting room with bar,
billiard table and fireside is the perfect place for a
nightcap.

**Savour the tranquillity and the view
of the Aravis and lose track of time.**

This lovely little establishment, ideally located in the ski
resort, is a haven of friendliness. The rooms, nearly all
of which have a balcony, are an excellent combination
of simple comfort and warm wood-panelling. In the
winter, the immense skiing domain offers nearly 400km
of pristine slopes and in the summer, walkers set off
to conquer the mineral kingdom of Platé. If you're lucky,
you may catch a glimpse of a wild ibex following your
climb.

Access : At the entrance to the resort, coming from
Annecy on the D 909, take a right

Access : In the upper part of the resort, 1km from
the centre, towards Flaine

 941 GAI SOLEIL
Mrs Mermoud

 288 chemin des Loyers
74170 Les Contamines-Montjoie
Tel. : 04 50 47 02 94
Fax : 04 50 47 18 43
gaisoleil2@wanadoo.fr
www.gaisoleil.com

Open from 15 Jun to 15 Sep and from 20 Dec to 20 Apr
• 19 rooms with bath/WC or shower/WC, no television
• €55 to €67; breakfast €7; half board €58 (€55 low
season) • Menus €16 to €24 • Garden, car park. No dogs
allowed in restaurant • Fondue evenings and films on
mountain life

 942 RÉGINA
Mrs Barras

 74260 Les Gets
Tel. : 04 50 75 80 44
Fax : 04 50 79 87 29

Open from 10 Jul to 31 Aug (hotel only) and from 22 Dec
to 15 Apr • 21 rooms, all have bath/WC or shower/WC
and television • €57 to €75 (€49 to €54 low season);
breakfast €7; half board €71 to €73 (€45 to €65 low
season) • Menus €14 (in the week) to €30 • Car park.
No dogs allowed in restaurant

 We most liked **Mount Joly and the snowy peaks of the Miage greet you in the morning.**

The painting on one of the beams bearing the date
1823, was the work of the chalet's original owner. The
Gai Soleil's website joyfully relates this family farm's
intriguing history – an English version is in the pipeline,
we're told. Ask for one of the rooms refurbished in a
mountain style with wood walls and pine furniture. The
south-facing terrace is popular in winter and summer
alike. Attractive garden.

 We most liked **A skiing domain which is particularly suitable for children.**

A wooden façade, carved balconies, a pine frieze, thick
planks of pine on the walls, carved ceilings, solid
furniture and a well-worn wooden mantelpiece over the
fireplace. Wood reigns throughout the inner and outer
decoration of this family-run hotel-chalet in the heart
of a small ski resort, within easy reach of the ski lifts.
The warm, welcoming interior is brightened up by
cheerful, multicoloured fabrics and friendly staff.

Access : In the upper part of the resort

Access : On the main road of the resort

943 BEAU SEJOUR
Mr and Mrs Blanc

Allée des Tennis
74000 Menthon-Saint-Bernard
Tel. : 04 50 60 12 04
Fax : 04 50 60 05 56

Open from 15 Apr to late Sep • 18 rooms, 14 of which have shower/WC, 4 have bath/WC • €69; breakfast €7 • No restaurant • Garden, private car park • Table-tennis, reading room. Tennis, golf and water sports nearby

Visit the fairy-tale castle of Menthon.

One hundred metres from Lake Annecy, this early-20C villa stands in an enormous park. The bedrooms with balcony, the most spacious, have recently been renovated, doing away with the distinctive hallmarks of the seventies. The bay windows of the breakfast room overlook the flowered garden where meals are served whenever the weather is warm enough. Friendly, family service.

Access : 100m from the lake

944 LA BERGERIE
Mr and Mrs Marullaz

Route du Téléphérique
74110 Morzine
Tel. : 04 50 79 13 69
Fax : 04 50 75 95 71
info @ hotel-bergerie.com
www.hotel-bergerie.com

Open from 28 Jun to 15 Sep and from 18 Dec to 25 Apr • 5 rooms facing the road and 22 studios with balconies and kitchenettes on the garden side. All have bath/WC and television • €79 to €84 (€61 to €79 low season); breakfast €10 • No restaurant • Terrace, garden • Heated outdoor swimming pool, fitness room, sauna, play area

The lively "children's table d'hôte".

The "cribs" of this sheepfold, an immense dark wooden chalet in the heart of Morzine, are of varying sizes. You will be able to choose from bedrooms, studios and apartments with balconies, most of which overlook the shaded garden, with the sumptuous panorama of the Chablais range in the distance. Kitchenettes, a warm mountain decoration and a youthful, friendly, atmosphere make it feel a bit like a "home from home".

Access : Arriving on the D 902, near the centre of the resort, turn right past the tourist office

RHÔNE-ALPES

 945 **FLEUR DES NEIGES**
Mr Archambault

74110 Morzine
Tel. : 04 50 79 01 23
Fax : 04 50 75 95 75
fleurneiges @ aol.com
www.fleurdesneiges.com

Open from 1 Jul to 15 Sep and from 15 Dec to 30 Apr
• 34 rooms, all have bath/WC or shower/WC and
television • €60 to €85 (€48 to €65 low season);
breakfast €8; half board €65 to €70 (€55 to €60 low
season) • Menu €20 • Terrace, garden, car park. No dogs
allowed • Indoor swimming pool, tennis, fitness room,
sauna, table-tennis, boules

 946 **GORGES DE LA DIOSAZ**
Mr Vandenkoornhuyse

"Sous le Roc"
74310 Servoz
Tel. : 04 50 47 20 97
Fax : 04 50 47 21 08
info @ hoteldesgorges.com
www.hoteldesgorges.com

Closed from 6 to 17 May and from 16 Oct to 9 Nov
• 9 rooms with bath/WC or shower/WC and television
• €49 to €68 (€40 to €60 low season); breakfast €6; half
board €52 (€45 low season) • Menus €16 (lunchtime in
the week) to €30 • Terrace. No dogs allowed

 **Soothing your aching muscles in the
pool after a day on the slopes.**

This chalet-style building is a little out of the centre of
Chablais' tourist capital, Morzine. When booking, ask for
one of the renovated rooms with wood-lined walls, pine
furniture and matching fabrics; plans are afoot to
redecorate the rather dour dining room in the near
future. The hotel's facilities – fitness room, sauna, tennis
court, swimming pool (indoor in winter) – reflect the
resort's combination of sport and leisure activities.

 **Francine and Sébastien greet guests
energetically and warmly.**

This traditional mountain chalet decked in flowers stands
on the edge of the gorges of the Diosaz. The restful
rooms have been refurbished in a sober, contemporary
alpine style and the windows of the inviting rustic dining
room overlook the Mont Blanc range. Wood prevails in
the sitting room and bar, where you can gratefully relax
with a glass of mulled wine after a hard day on the
slopes.

Access : Slightly out of the centre, on the
Thonon-les-Bains road

Access : In the centre of the village, near the post
office

947   AU GAY SÉJOUR
Mr and Mrs Gay

 74210 Tertenoz
Tel. : 04 50 44 52 52
Fax : 04 50 44 49 52
hotel-gay-sejour @ wanadoo.fr
www.hotel-gay-sejour.com

Closed from 17 Nov to 19 Dec, Sun evening and Mon from Sep to Jun (except holidays) • 11 rooms with bath/WC and television • €60 to €78; breakfast €10; half board €75 to €83 • Menus €24 to €68 • Terrace, car park. No dogs allowed in rooms • Snowshoe hiking. Annecy Lake and ski slopes nearby

 We most liked **A summer vista of lush mountain pastures or a winter picture of fields of snow.**

This 17C farm, nestling in a peaceful medium-altitude hamlet, has been turned into a pleasant family inn where you can be sure of a lung-full of pure mountain air. Though hardly stylish, the rooms are nonetheless wonderfully peaceful and some enjoy a lovely view of the valley. In the restaurant, the focus is on immaculate service and well-judged traditional cooking.

Access : 4km to the south-east of Faverges

948   LE VIEUX LOGIS
Mr Jacquier

 Rue des Remparts
74140 Yvoire
Tel. : 04 50 72 80 24
Fax : 04 50 72 90 76
contact @ levieuxlogis.com
www.levieuxlogis.com

Open from 1 Mar to 30 Nov • 11 rooms, all have bath/WC and television • €58; breakfast €7 • Restaurant closed Sun evening and Mon; menus €23 to €33 • Terrace, private car park

We most liked **The Maze-Garden of the Five Senses in the medieval village.**

This "old abode" of character, run by the same family for four generations, is set right in the ramparts. The rooms are practical and those on the first floor have a balcony; thick 14C walls keep the interior cool, even during the hot summer months. Under the vaulted ceiling and well-worn beams of the dining room, you will be invited to sample the house speciality of fillets of perch. In the summer, meals are also served on the lovely shaded terrace.

Access : On the way into the old town, set in the ramparts

949 GINIÈS
Mr and Mrs Giniès

38114 Allemont
Tel. : 04 76 80 70 03
Fax : 04 76 80 73 13
hotel-ginies @ wanadoo.fr

Closed in Apr and from 1 Nov to 15 Dec • 15 rooms, one of which has disabled access, all have bath/WC or shower/WC and television • €48; breakfast €7; half board €48 • Menu €18 (Sun lunchtime €21) • Terrace, garden, car park • Mini-golf

950 AU COQ EN VELOURS
Mr and Mrs Bellet

1800 route de Saint-Genis
38490 Aoste
Tel. : 04 76 31 60 04
Fax : 04 76 31 77 55

Closed from 1 to 22 Jan, Sun evening and Mon • 7 rooms with bath/WC or shower/WC, all have television • €55; breakfast €7 • Restaurant closed Thu evening; menus €19 (lunchtime except Sun) to €52 • Terrace, garden, car park

Ideally located near some of the best skiing domains in the Alps.

A sleepy village in the valley of the Eau d'Olle is home to this inn and its recent wing. The rooms are spacious, practical and well looked-after and some have balconies. You will have a choice of dining rooms, ranging from stones and beams in a rustic room to two more modern rooms with a view of the garden. A recently redone mini-golf completes the picture.

Ever tasted "rooster in velvet breeches"?

This smart village inn run by the same family since 1900 receives its guests in style. The bedrooms, named after different species of the hotel's namesake (rooster), all overlook the rear; those with a bathtub are the most spacious. Fowl take pride of place in the dining room, as a glance at the menu, paintings and ornaments will quickly confirm: unsurprisingly perhaps, the house speciality is "cockerel"! Pleasant terrace under the tall trees in the garden and near a refreshing ornamental pool.

Access : In the village, 9km northbound from Bourg-d'Oisans on the N 91 then right on the D 526

Access : 2km to the north-east of Aoste on the N 516, at the Gare de l'Est

951 CHÂTEAU DES MARCEAUX
Mr and Mrs Rocca

38650 Avignonet
Tel. : 04 76 34 18 94
Fax : 04 76 34 18 94

Open all year • 3 rooms • €56, breakfast included • No table d'hôte • Park, car park. Credit cards not accepted, no dogs allowed

952 AUBERGE AU PAS DE L'ALPETTE
Mr Letellier

Bellecombe
38530 Chapareillan
Tel. : 04 76 45 22 65

Fax : 04 76 45 25 90

Closed from 10 Oct to 10 Nov, Tue and Sun evenings, Wed except in season • 13 rooms with shower/WC • €34; breakfast €6 • Menus €15 to €32 • Garden, car park • Outdoor swimming pool

Superbly original rooms.

The diversity of architectural styles in this 18C château is such that the ensuing variety of bedroom styles seems perfectly natural. The first room, in the old dovecote, is most spectacular with a superb staircase and walls adorned with hundreds of roosting places. Original parquet floors and high ceilings set the tone for the second in the square tower, while the third in an independent cottage is simply enormous. Look out for the fresco in the dining room, painted by the owner-artist himself.

Access : From the road, take the lane to the castle gates

A sumptuous view of Mont Blanc.

This isolated alpine inn in a remote corner of the Chartreuse massif enjoys a stunning view of the "rooftops of Europe". Wood prevails inside lending it a warm, welcoming air. The rooms have sloping ceilings and are neat and spotless. Local delicacies, such as cheese specialities including wild goat's cheese in mushrooms, feature prominently on the menu. Depending on the weather, diners can choose between a wood-lined dining room or the terrace around the swimming pool.

Access : Between Montmélian and Pontcharra (N 90)

RHÔNE-ALPES

 AUBERGE DU VERNAY
Mr and Mrs Raoul

Route d'Optevoz
38390 Charrette
Tel. : 04 74 88 57 57
Fax : 04 74 88 58 57
aub.vernay @ litertysurf.fr

Closed from 11 to 21 Jan, from 14 Jun to 2 July, from
9 to 17 Sep, Sun evening and Mon • 7 rooms, one of
which has disabled access, all have shower/WC and
television • €47; breakfast €6; half board €41 • Menus
€15 to €23 • Terrace, car park

 LA FORÊT DE MARONNE
Mr Ougier

Châtelard
38520 La Garde
Tel. : 04 76 80 00 06
Fax : 04 76 79 14 61

Open from 10 Jun to 20 Sep and from 20 Dec to 20 Apr
• 12 rooms, most have shower/WC • €38 to €49 (€37 to
€46 low season); breakfast €6; half board €42 to
€50 (€40 to €45 low season) • Menus €14 (in the week)
to €28 • Terrace, garden, car park. No dogs allowed in
restaurant • Outdoor swimming pool. In winter, skiing
nearby

 Halcyon days in the countryside.

The spruce white stone walls of this 18C farmstead have
been given a new lease of life. All the delightful rooms
are decorated individually. In the restaurant, old
flagstones, a huge fireplace large enough to roast a
whole cow, sandblasted beams, cheerful paintings and
multicoloured modern chairs provide an amusing and
appealing mixture of tastes and styles. Outside, the old
bread oven can still be seen on the shaded terrace.

 **There is no end to the stunning views
on the nearby GR54 footpath.**

Come winter, the hairpin bends of this mountain road
seem endless; it takes a certain perseverance to reach
this tranquil hamlet at an altitude of 1 500m and
connected by ski lifts to the 220km of signposted slopes
of the Alpe-d'Huez domain. The modest rooms of this
1950s chalet are well looked-after and all are as
peaceful as the surrounding countryside. The rustic
dining room and terrace enjoy sweeping views of the
mountains and the Maronne pine forest.

Access : After the town hall drive towards Optevoz

Access : 12km to the north-east of Bourg-d'Oisans,
on the D 211 (towards Alpe-d'Huez), then right on
the D 211A

955 CHÂTEAU DE PASSIÈRES
Mr Perli

38930 Chichilianne
Tel. : 04 76 34 45 48
Fax : 04 76 34 46 25

Closed in Nov, Dec and Jan, Sun and Mon out of season
• 23 rooms, all have bath/WC or shower/WC, half have
television • €57 to €65; breakfast €7; half board €51 to
€66 • Menus €18 to €34 • Terrace, garden, car park. No
dogs allowed • Outdoor swimming pool, tennis

956 FERME DE RUTHIÈRES
Mr Sauze

Lieu-dit Ruthières
38930 Chichilianne
Tel. : 04 76 34 45 98

Closed at Christmas • 4 rooms upstairs • €39 • Table
d'hôte €13 • Garden, car park. Credit cards not accepted
• Outdoor swimming pool

 **Watch a climbing party make the
ascent of Mont Aiguille (3842m) from
the comfort of your deck-chair!**

The turrets of this small 14C manor house look out onto
a hamlet in the shadow of Mount Aiguille. Most of the
23 bedrooms are contemporary in style, but three
furnished with old pieces and lined in dark wood have
more character. The owner, a professional footballer in
his day, is a fan of 19C art as the numerous oils on
the restaurant and sitting room walls illustrate.

 **A strong focus on farm-grown
produce.**

This young farming couple extends a warm, unaffected
welcome to guests to their farmhouse. The cow-shed has
been turned into enormous guest bedrooms furnished
in a country style; two enjoy a view of the Vercors.
Regional art exhibitions are regularly held in the vaulted
dining room complete with fireplace and columns: try
the delicious home-grown produce.

Access : Leave the N 75 after 12km southbound
from Monestier-de-Clermont, at "La Gare" take the
D 7

Access : 4km to the north-west of Chichilianne on a
minor road

957 LE DOMAINE DE CLAIREFONTAINE
Mr and Mrs Girardon

Chemin des Fontanettes
38121 Chonas-L'Amballan
Tel. : 04 74 58 81 52
Fax : 04 74 58 80 93
domaine.de.clairefontaine @ gofornet.com
www.domaine-de-clairefontaine.fr

Closed from 18 to 23 Aug and from 16 Dec to 17 Jan
• 9 rooms, 2 of which have disabled access, with
bath/WC and television • €38 to €61; breakfast €10; half
board €68 to €82 • Air-conditioned restaurant; menus
€28 (lunchtime in the week) to €84 • Terrace, park with
aviaries, private car park. No dogs allowed in restaurant
• Tennis

We most liked **A ten-acre park surrounds this elegant manor house, two minutes from the A 7.**

Formerly a convalescent home for the bishops of Lyons,
these walls have been standing since 1766. Perhaps it
is no surprise that the rooms look a little old-fashioned,
but the sophisticated cuisine and the dining room more
than compensate. A blend of contemporary and plush
19C styles, the dining room leads onto a terrace
overlooking mature parkland. For just a few euros extra,
you may be interested to know, there is an exquisitely-
decorated room which has been built in the old
walnut-drying room.

Access : 9km southbound from Vienne on the N 7

958 LA GABETIÈRE
Mrs Lentillon

D 502
38780 Estrablin
Tel. : 04 74 58 01 31
Fax : 04 74 58 08 98

Open all year • 12 rooms with bath/WC or shower/WC
and television • €45; breakfast €7 • No restaurant • Park,
private car park • Outdoor swimming pool

We most liked **An easy-going 16C manor.**

On the outskirts of Vienne, trees and parkland surround
this little 16C manor. A stone staircase in the tiny tower
leads up to individually decorated boudoir bedrooms,
recently equipped with double-glazing which cuts out
the noise of the nearby road. Character also abounds
in the exposed beams and late-17C fireplace in the
breakfast room.

Access : 8km eastbound from Vienne on the D 41,
then the D 502

959 LE CHALET
Mr Prayer

38650 Gresse-en-Vercors
Tel. : 04 76 34 32 08
Fax : 04 76 34 31 06
lechalet @ free.fr
http://lechalet.free.fr/

Open from 4 May to 13 Oct, from 21 Dec to 17 Mar.
Closed Wed except school holidays • 26 rooms, 16 of
which are in a separate wing, all have bath/WC or
shower/WC and television • €52 to €68; breakfast €8;
half board €57 to €64 • Menus €16 (in the week) to
€46 • Terrace, garage, car park. No dogs allowed
• Outdoor swimming pool, boules

960 LE RELAIS DU ÇATAY
Mr Ducretet

10 rue du Didier – Le Bourg
38080 L'Isle-d'Abeau
Tel. : 04 74 18 26 50
Fax : 04 74 18 26 59
www.le-relais-du-catay.com

Closed from 3 to 9 Mar, from 4 to 26 Aug, Mon
lunchtime and Sun • 7 rooms with bath/WC or
shower/WC and television • €57; breakfast €6; half
board €44 to €47 • Menus €18 (lunchtime in the week)
to €39 • Terrace, garden, car park

We most liked **Botanical walks in the high mountain pastures.**

We most liked **Sample the chef's creative recipes on the terrace.**

Despite its name and warm atmosphere, this hotel bears
more resemblance to a prosperous farm than a chalet.
The bedrooms are being progressively renovated and all
have a view of the village and the mountains. Take a
seat in one of the comfortable dining rooms and tuck
into large helpings of traditional cuisine. A glance at the
visitors' book reveals a number of famous patrons,
including actor Gérard Dépardieu and HRH Albert II of
Belgium.

This elegant Louis XV house surrounded by trees and
flowers lies in a residential district, only 10min from the
international airport of Lyons. The cosy comfort of the
bedrooms has recently been enhanced following
high-quality renovation work. Wrought-iron and tasteful
paintings adorn the contemporary restaurant, further set
off by the original flagstones. Lime and Indian bean
trees shade the pleasant terrace. Excellent, imaginative
cuisine.

Access : In the centre of the village

Access : North-west of Bourgoin-Jallieu

 961 LE VAL FLEURI
Mr Bonnard

730 avenue Léopold Fabre
38250 Lans-en-Vercors
Tel. : 04 76 95 41 09
Fax : 04 76 94 34 69

Open from Jun to 20 Sep and from 20 Dec to 20 Mar
• 16 rooms, all have bath/WC and television • €33 to
€63; breakfast €7; half board €38 to €50 • Menus €18 in
the week, €28 on Sun • Terrace, garden, garage, car
park. No dogs allowed in restaurant

 **An action-packed resort perfect for
energetic children!**

The old belfry of the church stands guard over the blue
shutters of the Val Fleuri Hotel, built in the 1920s.
Almost as if defying time to take its toll of the delightfully
old-fashioned interior, the decoration of the dining room
is exactly as it was when the establishment opened and
some of the beautifully-kept bedrooms still boast their
original Art Deco furniture or lamps. The fresh mountain
air on the terrace, under the lime trees in the flowered
garden, will whet your appetite.

Access : In the main road, behind the church

 962 LES SKIEURS
Mr and Mrs Jail

38700 Le Sappey-en-Chartreuse
Tel. : 04 76 88 82 76
Fax : 04 76 88 85 76
hotelskieurs@wanadoo.fr
www.lesskieurs.com

Open from May to Oct and from 31 Dec to 30 Mar
• 18 rooms with bath/WC or shower/WC and television
• €49; breakfast €6; half board €52 • Menus €21 (in the
week) to €32 • Terrace, garden, car park. No dogs
allowed • Outdoor swimming pool

 **Save room for the tempting cheese
and home-made desserts.**

A curtain of fir trees conceals this house, lost in the
remote high pastures of the Chartreuse. The wood-lined
walls inside lend that unmistakable alpine touch. The
rooms are cosy as opposed to enormous, but the
welcoming restaurant has a huge stone fireplace for
spit-roasting and chargrilling: the chef's regional recipes
attracts gourmets from far and wide. A balcony-terrace
overlooks the valley.

Access : On leaving the village drive towards the
Porte Pass

 963 | CHAMBRE D'HÔTE MADAME FERRARD
Mrs Ferrard

145 chemin de Béluran, lieu-dit Vers-Ars,
route de Billieu
38730 Le Pin
Tel. : 04 76 06 68 82

Open all year • 5 rooms with bathrooms • €34, breakfast
included • Table d'hôte €13 • Credit cards not accepted,
no dogs allowed

 964 | LE PANORAMIQUE
 Mr Keesman

38142 Mizoen
Tel. : 04 76 80 06 25
Fax : 04 76 80 25 12
info @ hotel-panoramique.com
www.hotel-panoramique.com

Open from 1 Jun to 1 Oct and from 20 Dec to 1 May
• 9 rooms, 5 of which are non-smoking, all have bath/WC
or shower/WC and television • €59 to €63; breakfast €7;
half board €44 to €54 (€43 to €51 low season) • Menus
€20 to €30 • Terrace, garden, car park. No dogs allowed
in restaurant • Sauna

 **Watch Lake Paladru change colour
throughout the day.**

Half the windows of this gradually restored old
farmhouse face Lake Paladru, while the other half gaze
out over fields and woods. The majority of the snug,
simple bedrooms enjoy a view of the lake's deep waters;
three have a kitchenette and all have spanking-new
bathrooms. In the morning, you will breakfast in an
enormous living room, in the centre of which stands a
pyramidal fireplace. Warm and friendly.

 **If you're lucky, you may catch a
glimpse of the chamois who live in
the mountains.**

In the summer, window boxes laden with geraniums
adorn the balconies of this hillside chalet. Recently
purchased by a young couple from the Netherlands who
speak Dutch, French, English, German and Spanish, the
atmosphere is decidedly polyglot. Among the establishment's numerous appeals are the warm mountain-
style adopted in the bedrooms, a south-facing terrace,
sauna and a superb panoramic view of the town, Oisans
Valley and surrounding mountains.

Access : 1km to the south-west of Paladru Lake on
the D 17

Access : Between Le Freney-d'Oisans and the
Barrage du Chambon tunnel, leave the N 91 and take
the D 25

965 LES BASSES PORTES
Mr and Mrs Giroud-Ducaroy

Torjonas
38118 Saint-Baudille-de-la-Tour
Tel. : 04 74 95 18 23
mirvine @ wanadoo.fr

Closed from mid-Nov to late Jan • 3 rooms • €45, breakfast included • Table d'hôte €16 • Terrace, park, car park. Credit cards not accepted, no dogs allowed

A happy marriage of past and present.

Extensive renovation work has restored this old farmhouse without removing any of its rustic charm. Whenever possible, the old stones, beams and parquet floors have been preserved. The somewhat surprising style of the bedrooms features a happy blend of old and new, in addition to brand-new bathrooms. A perfect base camp to explore the Île Crémieu.

Access : 2km northbound on the D 52B

966 LE CHÂTEAU DE PÂQUIER
Mr Rossi

38650 Saint-Martin-de-la-Cluze
Tel. : 04 76 72 77 33
hrossi @ club-internet.fr
http://chateau.de.paquier.free.fr

Open all year • 5 rooms • €52, breakfast included • Table d'hôte €17 • Garden, car park

Unaffected and welcoming.

The owners have clearly put their body and soul into the restoration of the Renaissance castle and pretty garden and the result happily does justice to their efforts. Countless decorative features have been preserved, such as the exposed beams, wooden ceiling, spiral staircase and mullioned windows. The spacious rooms are beautifully decorated and furnished; one affords you a rare opportunity of sleeping in an old chapel. Garden produce and meat chargrilled on the open fire.

Access : 12km northbound from Monestier-de-Clermont on the N 75 and a minor road

 967 AU SANS-SOUCI
Mr Maurice

 38650 Saint-Paul-lès-Monestier
Tel. : 04 76 34 03 60
Fax : 04 76 34 17 38
au.sans.souci @ wanadoo.fr
www.sudisere.com/ausanssouci/

Closed from 20 Dec to late Jan, Sun evening and Mon except in Jul and Aug • 16 rooms, all have bath/WC or shower/WC and television • €49 to €53; breakfast €6; half board €49 • Menus €15 (in the week) to €36 • Terrace, garden, private car park • Outdoor swimming pool, tennis

 968 LE CHÂTEAU D'HERBELON
Mr Castillan

 au bord du Lac de Monteynard
38650 Treffort
Tel. : 04 76 34 02 03
Fax : 04 76 34 05 44
chateaudherbelon @ wanadoo.fr
www.chateau-herbelon.fr

Closed half-term Nov holidays, 20 Dec to 7 Mar, Mon eve, Tue and Wed except Jul-Aug • 9 rooms, all have bath/WC and television • €60 to €71; breakfast €7; half board €50 to €71 • Menus €17 to €32 • Terrace, garden, car park. No dogs allowed in rooms • Ideally located for wind-surfing

 We most liked **Alpine, cross-country and water-skiing: depending on the season, take your pick!**

This former sawmill in a quiet hamlet was turned into a hotel-restaurant in 1934 by the grandfather of the current owners. Whether you prefer contemporary or alpine-style, book one of the renovated rooms, which are the largest. Tasty dishes made with fresh local produce are served in the rustic dining room, decorated with farming implements and old wooden skis from the early days. Mount Aiguille looms down over the shaded terrace, garden, tennis court and swimming pool.

We most liked **The 20km-long lake is renowned for its windsurfing.**

This traditional country house covered in Virginia creeper and climbing roses stands on the banks of the Monteynard reservoir lake. A great deal of care and attention has clearly been lavished on the sizeable, usefully equipped rooms. An old stone fireplace adds character to the restaurant, while a lovely vaulted room in the basement is regularly rented out for weddings, communions and other family banquets. Children's play area in the walled garden.

Access : On leaving Monestier-de-Clermont (towards Grenoble), leave the N 75 and turn left on the D 8

Access : By the lake, 3km on the D 110e

 969 LES MÉSANGES
Mr Prince

 Route de Bouloud
38410 Uriage-les-Bains
Tel. : 04 76 89 70 69
Fax : 04 76 89 56 97
prince@hotel-les-mesanges.com
www.hotel-les-mesanges.com

Open from 1 May to 20 Oct, February holidays and weekends in Mar • 33 rooms with bath/WC or shower/WC and television • €50 to €58; breakfast €7; half board €45 to €51 • Restaurant closed Tue; menus €18 to €42 • Terrace, garden, car park • Outdoor swimming pool, table-tennis, boules, play area

 970 CHÂTEAU DE CHAPEAU CORNU
Mr Regnier

 38890 Vignieu
Tel. : 04 74 27 79 00
Fax : 04 74 92 49 31
chapeau.cornu@wanadoo.fr
www.chateau-chapeau-cornu.fr

Closed from 22 Dec to 13 Jan and Sun evening except in Jul and Aug • 18 rooms (and 2 suites) with bath/WC or shower/WC and television • €68; breakfast €11; half board €55 • Menus €16 (in the week) to €45 • Terrace, park, private car park. No dogs allowed in rooms • Outdoor swimming pool

We most liked **Special hotel and golf packages.**

The villa overlooks the spa-resort and castle. Ask for one of the renovated, practical rooms with balcony and enjoy the view over the Chamrousse range. A light, airy dining room in a modern style, pleasant terrace shaded by plane trees, peaceful garden with a play area and swimming pool complete the facilities of this family-run establishment, on the doorstep of two golf courses.

We most liked **If only a night in this fairy-tale castle could turn our fortunes from rags to riches!**

The names of the former owners of this 13C fortified castle, Capella and Cornutti, explain the origins of the castle's amusing name which translates as Battered Hat. The rooms, which are gradually being treated to a new coat of paint, tasteful fabrics and wrought-iron furniture all have antique wardrobes; some also boast a four-poster bed. A stone-vaulted dining room, attractive inner courtyard terrace and a 10-acre park with ornamental pools and tree-lined paths complete the picture.

Access : Avenue des Thermes, drive alongside the park, turn left onto the Chamrousse road, then at the spa hospital, turn right on Bouloud road

Access : From Bourgoin-Jallieu take the N 6 (towards Lyon), then right on the D 522 as far as Flosaille, then the D 19 and 5km after Saint-Clef, turn right

 971 CHÂTEAU BLANCHARD
Mr Bonnidal

 36 route de Saint-Galmier
42140 Chazelles-sur-Lyon
Tel. : 04 77 54 28 88
Fax : 04 77 54 36 03

Closed from 12 to 26 Aug • 12 rooms, all have bath/WC
and television • €69; breakfast €6; half board €50 to
€58 • Restaurant closed Fri and Sun evening, and Mon;
menus €19 to €41 • Garden, car park

 972 LA BUSSINIÈRE
Mrs Perrin

 Route de Lyon
42110 Feurs
Tel. : 04 77 27 06 36

Open all year • 3 rooms • €39, breakfast included • Table
d'hôte €13 • Garden, car park. Credit cards not accepted

 **The Hat Museum's collection shows
off hats and caps of the rich and
famous!**

This rambling, elegant period house built in a shaded
park once belonged to a family of milliners and after
extensive renovation, it once again shines with the glow
of its former youth. Inside, a marble staircase will take
you up to comfortable bedrooms decorated individually
in a contemporary flavour. The restaurant has opted for
a traditional repertoire.

 **The lady of the house's ceaseless
quest for perfection.**

The comfort of this renovated farmhouse leaves nothing
to be desired: everything has been designed with the
welfare of the guest in mind, from the digicode-access
on the main gate and the excellent soundproofing to the
high quality bedding. Huge beams and tasteful colours
adorn the stylish bedrooms, which have immaculate
bathrooms. Meals are taken around the large table in
the dining room.

Access : On the way into the village, on the
Saint-Galmier road

Access : 3km eastbound from Feurs on the D 89,
towards Lyon

 973   **DOMAINE DE CHAMPFLEURY**
Mrs Gaume

Le Bourg
42155 Lentigny
Tel. : 04 77 63 31 43
Fax : 04 77 63 31 43

Closed from 15 Nov to 15 Mar. Booking advisable in winter • 3 rooms • €63, breakfast included • No table d'hôte • Park, car park. Credit cards not accepted, no dogs allowed

 974   **LA CHARPINIÈRE**
Mrs Mazenod

42330 Saint-Galmier
Tel. : 04 77 52 75 00
Fax : 04 77 54 18 79
charpiniere.hot.rest @ wanadoo.fr

Open all year • 46 rooms, 14 of which are air-conditioned, all have bath/WC and television • €74 to €92; breakfast €9; half board €62 to €70 (€59 to €65 low season) • Restaurant La Closerie de la Tour: menus €20 to €39 • Terrace, park, car park. No dogs allowed in rooms • Outdoor swimming pool, tennis, fitness room, sauna, hammam, games room, billiards

 Explore the secrets of the park.

This 19C country house stands proudly in a luxurious park planted with a wide range of trees. The guest rooms are light and airy; two can be turned into a family suite. Tennis courts and a large games room await guests and whenever the weather is fine enough, you can picnic in the park and lounge on the deck-chairs.

 Find out more about Badoit, one of France's most famous springs.

Everything about this country retreat seems to have been designed for the sole convenience of its modern-day guests, whether they have come for business or pleasure: 10 acres of ancient trees, fitness room, outdoor swimming pool, tennis courts, private sitting rooms and countless conference rooms. The practical, rather compact rooms are decorated identically. The restaurant serves delicious meals in a light, airy dining room-conservatory.

Access : 8km to the south-west of Roanne on the D 53

Access : Set back from the town centre, towards the Badoit springs

 975 CASTEL-GUÉRET
Mr Coulaud

 42220 Saint-Julien-Molin-Molette
Tel. : 04 77 51 56 04
Fax : 04 77 51 59 13
contact @ domaine.com
www.domaine-castelgueret.com

Open all year • 5 non-smoking rooms • €65, breakfast included • Table d'hôte €19, only by reservation • Park, car park. Credit cards not accepted • Outdoor swimming pool

976 LA RIVOIRE
Mr and Mrs Thiollière

 42220 Saint-Julien-Molin-Molette
Tel. : 04 77 39 65 44
Fax : 04 77 39 67 86
larivoire @ chez.com

Closed in Jan • 5 rooms • €46, breakfast included • Table d'hôte €14 • Terrace, garden, car park. Credit cards not accepted, no dogs allowed

 We most liked **Lording it for a weekend.**

Nearly five acres of ancient trees surround this 19C château, painstakingly restored in keeping with the spirit of the period. Original parquet floors, marquetry work and antiques set the scene for the refined interior. All the Louis XV or Louis XVI-style rooms have their own private sitting room; the quality of the bedding and bathrooms deserves a special mention. When it comes to relaxing in the open air, the surrounding countryside offers numerous opportunities for long walks.

We most liked **Cottage-garden vegetables and local cooked meats on the menu.**

A circular stone tower and enormous kitchen garden contribute to the appeal of this lovely stately home, thought to date from the 15C. It enjoys a lovely position in the Nature Park of Pilat, overlooking the fir trees of the Ardèche hillsides, which is the view you will have from the cheerful rooms. Three sitting rooms, complete with piano, board games and a television, are reserved for the use of guests.

Access : 1km northbound from Saint-Julien-Molin-Molette on the D 8 towards Le Besset

Access : 5km eastbound from Bourg-Argental on the N 82

 977 L'ÉCHAUGUETTE
Mr and Mrs Alex

 Ruelle Guy-de-la-Mûre
42155 Saint-Maurice-sur-Loire
Tel. : 04 77 63 15 89

Open all year • 4 rooms • €53, breakfast included • No
table d'hôte • Credit cards not accepted

 978 SAINT-ROMAIN
Mr and Mrs Levet

 Route de Graves
69480 Anse
Tel. : 04 74 60 24 46
Fax : 04 74 67 12 85
hotel-saint-romain @ wanadoo.fr
www.hotel-saint-romain.fr

Closed from 25 Nov to 5 Dec and Sun evening from early
Nov to late Apr • 23 rooms, most have bath/WC, all have
television • €41 to €51; breakfast €6; half board €40 to
€85 • Menus €16 (except Sunday lunchtime) to
€44 • Terrace, garden, private car park

 Watch the pleasure boats on the lake.

It is difficult to resist the charm of these three houses
hidden in a medieval village opposite the peaceful
waters of Lake Villerest. All the tastefully decorated
rooms are different: one has a fireplace, the other enjoys
a view of the lake encircled by hills, while the last
overlooks the keep and church. Breakfasts are served
on the terrace or behind the kitchen's bay windows: a
feast for the palate, and the eyes.

 **Make sure you don't get lost in the
labyrinthine passages of the village's
13C castle.**

Don't pass up the chance of a visit to this lovely stone
farmhouse in the heart of the Beaujolais region, where
only the wind whispering through the foliage disturbs
the silence. The somewhat faded air of the rooms is
balanced by their spotless upkeep, while a welcoming
rustic dining room leads onto a summer terrace, always
packed in the high season. Your taste-buds may already
be salivating at the prospect of sampling the inspired
meals rustled up by your owner-chef.

Access : 12km to the south-west of Roanne on the
D 53 and the D 203

Access : Set back from the village, near the
gendarmerie (police station)

BRULLIOLES - 69690

LANCIÉ - 69220

979 **LA MAISON DE NOÉMI**
Mrs Noëlle Pierre

Le Pothu
69690 Brullioles
Tel. : 04 74 26 58 08
Fax : 04 74 26 58 08

Open all year • 3 rooms with bathrooms • €37, breakfast included • No table d'hôte • Garden. Credit cards not accepted

980 **LES PASQUIERS**
Mr and Mrs Gandilhon

69220 Lancié
Tel. : 04 74 69 86 33
Fax : 04 74 69 86 57
ganpasq @ aol.com

Open all year • 4 rooms with disabled access • €65, breakfast included • Table d'hôte €20 • Sitting room, garden, car park. Credit cards not accepted • Outdoor swimming pool

We most liked **Druids were said to dwell in the neighbouring wood.**

At a height of 750m in the upper part of the village, this 17C farmstead commands a superb view of the Lyonnais mountains. The spotless and soberly decorated rooms lie in a separate wing and all have bathrooms. A communal living room is equipped with practical cooking facilities. The mistress of the house, who used to work for the Tourist Board, is a treasure-trove of information about the region.

We most liked **A step back in time to Second Empire France.**

High walls protect this lovely old house and garden from prying eyes. Many of the decorative features inside are original, such as the moulded ceilings, fireplace, carpets, library and grand piano in the sitting room. The rooms in the main house are furnished with 19C antiques, while those in the outbuilding have been reworked to a more modern design with coconut matting, bathrooms hidden by Japanese screens and children's drawings. The terrace is laid next to the swimming pool.

Access : 10km westbound from La Brevenne on the N 89 and the D 81

Access : 2km southbound from Romanèche-Thorins

  981 DOMAINE DES QUARANTE ÉCUS
Mr and Mrs Nesme

 Les Vergers
69430 Lantigné
Tel. : 04 74 04 85 80
Fax : 04 74 69 27 79

Open all year • 5 rooms with bathrooms • €42, breakfast included • No table d'hôte • Garden, car park. Credit cards not accepted, no dogs allowed • Outdoor swimming pool. Wine cellars, sales and tasting of the domain's wine

  982 L'ARDIÈRES
Mr and Mrs Bonnot

 Le Bourg
69430 Les Ardillats
Tel. : 04 74 04 80 20

Closed in Jan • 5 rooms • €39, breakfast included • Table d'hôte €15 • Garden, car park. Credit cards not accepted

We most liked **Sipping a glass of the estate's red or white Beaujolais.**

The French common name of the ginkgo biloba tree – known as Maidenhair in English – in front of the house gave the estate its name. The bedrooms, furnished with old and new pieces and hung with reproductions of works by Van Gogh, overlook the vineyards or the garden and orchards of peach, cherry, apricot and plum trees. Breakfast is served in a rustic dining room, embellished by a dresser. The owners happily invite guests to look around the cellars and sample and purchase the estate's wine.

We most liked **Pamper your taste-buds in this lovely Beaujolais home.**

This handsome farm on the doorstep of a sleepy country village is the sort of place you dream of. Its thick stone walls and natural wooden shutters immediately catch the eye, which is further treated to the vision of a lovely country interior. Bright colours and thick beams paint the juicy picture of the rooms, each of which is named after a fruit – raspberry, pineapple, plum, grapefruit and mandarin. Sample the delicious home cooking, washed down with a fruity glass of Beaujolais.

Access : 4km eastbound from Beaujeu on the D 78

Access : 5km to the north-west of Beaujeu on the D 37

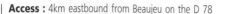

983 ARTISTES
Mrs Lameloise

8 rue Gaspard André
69002 Lyon
Tel. : 04 78 42 04 88
Fax : 04 78 42 93 76
hartiste @ club-internet.fr

Open all year • 45 rooms, all have bath/WC or shower/WC and television • €66 to €99; breakfast €9 • No restaurant

984 LE MONTJOYEUX
Mr Mollard

avenue Victor Hugo
(près du Lac du Grand Large)
69330 Mézieu - Le Carreau
Tel. : 04 78 04 21 32
Fax : 04 72 02 85 72
monjoyeux @ club.internet.fr

Open all year • 20 rooms, one of which has disabled access, all have bath/WC and television • €70 to €87; breakfast €10; half board €69 • Menus €20 (in the week) to €43 • Terrace, garden, car park • Outdoor swimming pool

Old Lyons' giant maze of "traboules" – covered pedestrian passages.

This delightful hotel is located right in the heart of Lyons, on the peninsula opposite Fourvière Hill. The rooms are light and airy and make up in practicality what they lack in luxury; some overlook the Célestins Theatre, hence the hotel's name. The breakfast room is adorned with a fresco inspired by Cocteau. A nearby public car park is also most appreciated.

A moonlit stroll along the banks of Lac du Grand Large.

Although only a few minutes from the centre of Lyons, it feels light years away. Imagine paddling in the turquoise blue waters of the swimming pool or admiring those of Lac du Grand Large next to the villa. Accommodation-wise, you can choose between pretty rooms with balconies or terraces overlooking the garden or treat yourself to the luxury of one of four pavilions. The lakeside dining room and terrace offer the chance to taste the chef's tasty fish recipes.

Access : Near Place Bellecour (and Bellecour car park), opposite the theatre

Access : Leave the suburbs of Lyon on the D 517 (towards Crémieu), at the centre of Mézieu, take a left towards Le Carreau

985 CHAMBRE D'HÔTE GÉRARD LAGNEAU
Mr and Mrs Lagneau

Huire
69430 Quincié-en-Beaujolais
Tel. : 04 74 69 20 70
Fax : 04 74 04 89 44
lagneau-gerard @ wanadoo.fr

Open all year • 4 non-smoking rooms upstairs, all have bathrooms • €50, breakfast included • Table d'hôte €19 • Garden, car park

986 DOMAINE DE ROMARAND
Mr and Mrs Berthelot

69430 Quincié-en-Beaujolais
Tel. : 04 74 04 34 49
Fax : 04 74 04 35 92

Open all year • 3 rooms • €51, breakfast included • Table d'hôte €16 to €19 • Garden, car park. Credit cards not accepted, no dogs allowed • Outdoor swimming pool. Wine tasting and sales

A genuine wine-growing atmosphere.

A hamlet encircled by vineyards is the scene for the pleasant stone-built home of this wine-growing family who bend over backwards to make you feel at home with them. The rooms upstairs are simply decorated and spotlessly clean. You will breakfast under the beams of a rustic room. The icing on the cake is, however, the 16C cellar. Where better to sample the house vintages?

The overwhelming bouquet of fine wines.

This lovely stone house run by a wine-growing couple is set in a U-shaped courtyard overlooking a flowered rock garden and the vineyards: all the modern, comfortable rooms enjoy this same rural view. The rafters, fireplace, huge wooden table and maps of the Beaujolais region add character to the dining room. A profusion of home-made pastries and jams adds that little extra to breakfast time.

Access : In the middle of the vineyards

Access : 9km to the south-east of Beaujeu on the D 37 and the D 9, then drive towards Varennes

987 LE SAINT-LAURENT
Mr Lavault

8 rue Croix Blanche
69720 Saint-Laurent-de-Mure
Tel. : 04 78 40 91 44
Fax : 04 78 40 45 41

Closed from 2 to 7 Jan, from 3 to 25 Aug, Fri and Sun evenings, and Sat • 29 rooms located in 2 buildings, with bath/WC or shower/WC, all have television • €57; breakfast €6 • Menus €16 (in the week) to €46 • Terrace, park, 2 car parks one of which is private. No dogs allowed

 Entirely devoted to guests' welfare.

This 18C mansion and its flowered park make an ideal stopover for weary travellers. It offers small, comfortable rooms – those in a separate wing are more modern. At mealtimes, you can choose between the warmth of maple wood or immense bay windows overlooking the greenery. In fine weather, the shade of the three-hundred-year-old lime tree is sheer bliss.

Access : 15km from Lyon, set back from the N 6

988 LA TERRASSE
Mr and Mrs Arnette

Le Bourg – Marnand
69240 Thizy
Tel. : 04 74 64 19 22
Fax : 04 74 64 25 95

Closed during Feb and Nov half-terms, Mon (except the hotel) and Sun evening • 10 rooms, one of which has disabled access, with bath/WC and television • €42; breakfast €6; half board €39 • Menus €12 (in the week) to €43 • Terrace, car park • Children's games room

 Just six kilometres from the water-sports of Lake Sapins.

This old textile factory, typical of the Beaujolais region, has been turned into a hotel. The agreeable rooms with terraces open directly onto the garden; each is named after a flower or aromatic plant and the decoration, even the fragrance, matches the theme. Two modern, soberly decorated dining rooms and a spacious terrace overlooking the mountains of the Lyonnais complete the picture: their modern menu features regionally inspired recipes.

Access : 2km to the north-east on the D 94, on the way into Bourg-Marnand, opposite the town hall

RHÔNE-ALPES

989 LA FERME DU POULET
Mr and Mrs Rongeat

180 rue Georges Mangin
69400 Villefranche-sur-Saône
Tel. : 04 74 62 19 07
Fax : 04 74 09 01 89

Closed from 5 to 20 Aug, from 23 Dec to 2 Jan, Sun evening and Mon • 10 rooms, all have bath/WC and television • €80; breakfast €10 • Menus €31 to €55 • Terrace, car park

990 LA CROIX DU SUD
Mrs Collot

3 rue du Docteur Duvernay
73100 Aix-les-Bains
Tel. : 04 79 35 05 87
Fax : 04 79 35 72 71

Open from early Apr to early Nov • 16 rooms, some have bath/WC or shower/WC and television • €25 to €37; breakfast €5 • No restaurant • Small courtyard-garden • Television room with a small library

 A cheerful blend of rustic and contemporary flavours.

A sanctuary of greenery in the heart of an industrial estate, this beautifully-restored 17C fortified farm is protected from the bustle of urban life by a wall. All the spacious, functional rooms have excellent bedding. Multicoloured tableware livens up the magnificent old beams of the dining room. Pleasant inner courtyard terrace.

 The faded charm of the early 20C.

Could it be to conjure up memories of his trips to distant lands that the former owner built up this collection of hats from the world over? Equally popular with tourists and "patients" come to take the waters, this hotel is renowned for its faultless hospitality. The generously-dimensioned and rather faded bedrooms are most stylish.

Access : North-east of Villefranche, in the Industrial Zone (ZI) near the exhibition park

Access : In the town centre, in a small, quiet street

991 LES MOTTETS
Mr Montaz

6 rue Les Mottets
73500 Aussois
Tel. : 04 79 20 30 86
Fax : 04 79 20 34 22
infos@hotel-les-mottets.com
www.hotel-lesmottets.com

Closed in May and from 1 Nov to 15 Dec • 25 rooms with bath/WC or shower/WC and television • €35 to €56 (€33 to €51 low season); breakfast €7; half board €54 (€46 low season) • Menus €15 to €28 • Car park • Sauna, jacuzzi, gym

Bask on the balcony as you enjoy a vista worthy of a postcard.

Most of the simple yet practical rooms command views of the surrounding peaks, summits and pinnacles that invite the energetic walker and climber to pull on boots and explore their hidden secrets. In the summer, you may encounter herds grazing on the rich mountain pastures, while in the winter, fasten up your skis and swoop along vertiginous mountain crests. The fitness room and copious Savoyard cuisine further contribute to getting you back into peak condition.

Access : In the centre of the village

992 SOLEIL
Mr Montaz

73500 Aussois
Tel. : 04 79 20 32 42
Fax : 04 79 20 37 78
www.hotel-du-soleil.com

Open from 16 Jun to 15 Sep and from 17 Dec to 20 Apr • 22 rooms, one of which has disabled access, with bath/WC or shower/WC, all have television • €54 to €80; breakfast €12; half board €75 (€67 low season) • Menus €20 to €27, children's menu €12 • Terrace, car park. No dogs allowed in rooms • Cinema room, sauna, hammam, jacuzzi, souvenir shop, billiards, skiing in season

Discover the thrill of the 2 560m Via Ferrata rock-climbing course – the longest in France.

Next door to the church, whose bells are considerate enough to remain silent after nightfall, the walls of this austere chalet hide a warm interior. The rooms enjoy superb views of the village and the Vanoise range; ask for one of the renovated chalet-style rooms with light wood and pretty fabrics. There is no lack of outdoor activities from the roof terrace sun deck, open air jacuzzi, giant chess board and skittles, while indoors, you can sample the sauna, hammam and home cinema facilities.

Access : Near the church

 993 **À LA PASTOURELLE**
Mr Blanc

73480 Bonneval-sur-Arc
Tel. : 04 79 05 81 56
Fax : 04 79 05 85 44
www.pastourelle.com

Closed in May and on Nov 1 • 12 rooms with bath/WC
• €45 to €53; breakfast €6; half board only in season
€42 to €46 • Restaurant closed out of season; menus
€11 to €15, children's menu €7 • Library-sitting room. No
dogs allowed • Skiing and hiking nearby

 994 **L'AUTANTIC**
Mrs Bourgeois

69 route d'Hauteville
73700 Bourg-Saint-Maurice
Tel. : 04 79 07 01 70
Fax : 04 79 07 51 55
hotel.autantic@wanadoo.fr
www.hotel-autantic.com

Open all year • 23 rooms, 2 of which have disabled
access, with bath/WC (2 have shower/WC) and television • €60 to €70; breakfast €7 • No restaurant • Car
park • Sauna

 **On the doorstep of one of France's
most beautiful skiing domains.**

The roof of schist tiles and the name, which means
cowgirl, both bear witness to the house's dedication to
local traditions. Whether a one-night stopover on your
journey through the French Alps or a base camp for
breathtaking races down the slopes of La Vanoise, it will
provide that little extra to make each day just perfect.
The rooms are snug and cosy and the dining room is
rich with the perfume of savoury cheese raclettes,
fondues and sweet pancakes.

 **Tasting the thrills of white-water
rafting on the Bourg.**

The stone walls and narrow windows of this sturdy
house, in the style of a traditional mountain chalet, were
built recently in a quiet district of Bourg St Maurice, near
the futuristic funicular railway up to the Arcs resort. The
rooms, decorated with roughcast walls and pine
furniture, overlook the peaceful valley and four have a
balcony. Friendly staff and breakfast on the terrace are
among the other perks of this modern chalet.

Access : In the upper part of the resort

Access : On the way into the village, a little set back
from the road

995 CAPRICE DES NEIGES
Marin-Lamellet family

 Les Reys
73590 Crest-Voland
Tel. : 04 79 31 62 95
Fax : 04 79 31 79 30
lecapricedes-neiges @ wanadoo.fr
www.caprice-des-neiges.com

Open from 20 Jun to 15 Sep and from 15 Dec to 20 Apr
• 16 rooms with bath/WC, some have television • €59 to
€69; breakfast €7; half board €58 to €68 • Menus €15 to
€20 • Terrace, garden, car park. No dogs allowed in
restaurant • In summer: tennis, fly fishing, mini-golf; in
winter: skiing and snowshoe hiking

996 CHALET LE PARADOU
Mr Hanrard

 Pré Bérard
73210 La Côte-d'Aime
Tel. : 04 79 55 67 79
hanrard @ aol.com

Closed in May and Jun and from 10 Sep to 15 Dec
• 5 rooms, 4 of which overlook a large terrace • €52,
breakfast included • Table d'hôte €17 • Garden, terrace,
car park. Credit cards not accepted, no dogs allowed

 Little teddy bears adorn some of the rooms of this friendly, family establishment.

The soft warm hues of wood greet the eye wherever you look in this exquisite chalet, just outside the village but at the foot of the slopes. Step into its welcoming doll's house interior and feast your eyes on the lovely fabrics, ornaments and Savoyard furniture. The rooms on the second floor have been renovated and it is planned to refurbish the others in the near future. All offer spectacular views of the Aravis and the mountain pastures. Regional delicacies.

 An impeccably-run mountain chalet.

This superb wooden chalet perched at an altitude of 1 000m commands a stunning view of the Tarentaise Valley and Mount Pourri. The spotlessly clean, comfortable rooms open onto a large terrace. The wood-lined sitting room, complete with piano, matches the alpine spirit that prevails throughout the establishment. Skiing packages are available in the winter, and in the summer, you can laze about in the flowered garden.

Access : On the road from Col des Saisies, 1km from the resort and 50m from the ski lift

Access : 3km to the north-east of Aime on the D 86

 997 **LES AIRELLES**
Mr Boyer

Rue des Darbelays
73710 Pralognan-la-Vanoise
Tel. : 04 79 08 70 32
Fax : 04 79 08 73 51

Open from 1 Jun to 21 Sep and from 20 Dec to 19 Apr
• 22 rooms with bath/WC or shower/WC and television
• €56 to €73 (€50 low season); breakfast €8; half board
€51 to €64 (€48 to €54 low season) • Menus €16 to
€22 • Terrace, garage, car park. No dogs allowed in
restaurant • Outdoor swimming pool, billiards, table-
tennis, shuttle to the ski lifts

 **Pralognan combines the charm of a
village with the facilities of a
top-class ski resort.**

This chalet, built on the outskirts of the resort, is
encircled by the ridges and crests of the Vanoise massif.
The mountain view from the rooms and balconies never
fails to bring gasps of admiration. In the kitchen, the
talented young chef's recipes provoke further cries of
approval. On the leisure side, the swimming pool is
heated, and the owner, an enthusiastic hiker, never tires
of indicating paths and trails to eager guests.

Access : In the upper part of the resort, next to the
Granges forest

 998 **LA FERME BONNE DE LA GROTTE**
Mr Amayenc

73360 Saint-Christophe-la-Grotte
Tel. : 04 79 36 59 05
Fax : 04 79 36 59 31
fermebonne @ wanadoo.fr

Open all year • 4 rooms, some have mezzanines • €54,
breakfast included • Table d'hôte €16 • Terrace, park, car
park. Credit cards not accepted, no dogs allowed

 **Irresistibly Savoyard in spirit and
flavour.**

In the space of a year, this three-century-old farm at
the foot of the Échelles caves has become a must in
the region. The renowned cuisine has remained true to
its Savoyard roots and the gourmet chef takes great
pleasure in watching his guests devour his tasty home
cooking. The immense but still cosy rooms are all graced
with painted furniture; some also boast a mezzanine.

Access : 4km to the north-east of Échelles on the
N 6, Chambéry road

 999 BEAUSOLEIL
Mr and Mrs Vermeulen

73530 Saint-Sorlin-d'Arves
Tel. : 04 79 59 71 42
Fax : 04 79 59 75 25
beausoleil @ club-internet.fr
www.hotel-beausoleil.com

Open in Jul and Aug and from 15 Dec to 13 Apr
• 23 rooms on 3 floors, 2 of which have balconies. All
have bath/WC or shower/WC and television • €54;
breakfast €7; half board €70 to €80 (€58 to €70 low
season) • Menus €15 to €20 • Terrace, garden, car park.
No dogs allowed in the restaurant • Walks in the Croix
de Fer Pass and mountain sports

 1000 CHÉ CATRINE
Mrs Finas

88 rue Saint-Antoine
73500 Villarodin-Bourget
Tel. : 04 79 20 49 32
Fax : 04 79 20 48 67
checatri @ club-internet.fr

Open all year • 3 rooms, all have bath/WC • €61,
breakfast included • Table d'hôte €16 • Garden. Credit
cards not accepted, no dogs allowed

 Sunshine and powdery snow: what more could you want?

You know you're in for a treat right from the moment you begin to climb the road by the Combe Genin or the Croix de Fer Pass, driving past snowy peaks or pastures of wild mountain flowers up to this remote mountain chalet. Families are welcome in the practical, attractively furnished rooms. After a long day out in the open air, you will be ready to feast on the delicacies rustled up by your cheerful host.

Savour the good things of life in this superb mansion.

This country house, built in 1524, and restored in keeping with Savoyard traditions, is a gem of a find. You will immediately feel at home in the rooms and suites, decorated with solid pine furniture. Meals are served in the vaulted stables and the lounge-bar – hewn out of solid rock – is a delight for the eyes. The chef makes it a point of honour to use only garden vegetables and meat from the Maurienne Valley. Definitely worth writing home about, unless you'd rather keep it to yourself!

Access : Away from the centre of the resort, towards the Col de la Croix-de-Fer

Access : Motorway A 43, exit Modane, then after Modane 2km on the RN 6 towards the Haute Maurienne

€€ So that you can treat yourself without having to break open your piggy bank, we have selected hotels and chambres d'hôte which offer a warm welcome, pleasant setting and character combined with affordable prices. The coin symbol next to an establishment indicates that it is a hotel or maison d'hôte with rooms at a maximum price of €40 per night for two (breakfast included in the maions d'hôte, but extra in hotels).

Good food is of course an essential prerequisite for a successful holiday and we should know! We have therefore decided to point out all the hotels and maisons d'hôte whose cuisine is in some way outstanding. The hotels have all been awarded either one or more "Stars" for excellent cooking or a "Bib Gourmand" for good food at moderate prices by the Michelin Red Guide. In the maisons d'hôte, you will tuck into delicious home cooking, often prepared using home-grown produce.

Feel like getting away from it all? Ready for a change of scenery? Want to get out into the countryside and work off some stress or extra pounds? The hotels and maisons d'hôte listed below all have a swimming pool at the very least and generally one or several other sports facilities or activities, either on site or very nearby. These include themed or signposted walks, fishing, tennis, golf, a fitness room/mini-gym, or riding, so check out each establishment to discover what is on offer.

ALPHABETICAL INDEX OF HOTELS AND MAISONS D'HÔTE

INTRO : *Food:* Saint-Nectaire cheese and a glass of wine (63). J. Damase/MICHELIN
Place: Doëlan harbour (29). G. Targat/MICHELIN

REGIONS

ALSACE : *Vertical photo:* House of Heads, Colmar (67). R. Mattes/MICHELIN
Horizontal photo: Éguisheim village (68). R. Mattes/MICHELIN

AQUITAINE : *Horizontal photo:* Arcachon Bassin (33). A. Thuillier/MICHELIN

AUVERGNE : *Horizontal photo:* Turlurons, Billom (63). J. Damase/MICHELIN

BURGUNDY : *Vertical photo:* Beaune Hospices (21). Ph. Gajic/MICHELIN
Horizontal photo: Briare Canal Bridge (45). Ph. Gajic/MICHELIN

BRITTANY : *Vertical photo:* Rood-screen of St Fiacre, Le Faouët (56). H. Le Gac/MICHELIN
Horizontal photo: Port du Palais, Belle-Île (56). C. Guégan/MICHELIN

CENTRE AND UPPER LOIRE VALLEY : *Vertical photo:* Stained-glass window, Bourges Cathedral (18). S. Sauvignier/MICHELIN
Horizontal photo: Château of Chambord (41). H. Le Gac/MICHELIN

CHAMPAGNE-ARDENNE : *Vertical photo:* Angel of the Annunciation, Reims Cathedral (51). S. Sauvignier/MICHELIN
Horizontal photo: Côte des Blancs champagne vineyard (51). S. Sauvignier/MICHELIN

CORSICA : *Vertical photo:* Genoese bridge, Pianella (2A). G. Magnin/MICHELIN
Horizontal photo: Bonifacio (2A). G. Magnin/MICHELIN

FRANCHE-COMTÉ : *Vertical photo:* St Claude's pipe (39). G. Magnin/MICHELIN
Horizontal photo: Château of Joux (25). G. Benôit à La Guillaume/MICHELIN

ÎLE-DE-FRANCE AND PARIS : *Horizontal photo:* Overground métro line (75). S. Sauvignier/MICHELIN

LANGUEDOC-ROUSSILLON : *Horizontal photo:* Oyster beds, Thau (34). D. Pazery/MICHELIN

LIMOUSIN : *Vertical photo:* Benedictine clock tower, Limoges (87). S. Sauvignier/MICHELIN
Horizontal photo: Sénoueix bridge (23). S. Sauvignier/MICHELIN

LORRAINE : *Vertical photo:* Place Stanislas, Nancy (54). R. Mattes/MICHELIN
Horizontal photo: Bitche (57). R. Mattes/MICHELIN

MIDI-PYRÉNÉES : *Horizontal photo:* Ambialet (81). B. Kaufmann/MICHELIN

NORD-PAS-DE-CALAIS : *Vertical photo:* Lille Belfry (59). Y. Tierny/MICHELIN
Horizontal photo: International Kite Meeting, Berck (62). Y. Tierny/MICHELIN

NORMANDY : *Vertical photo:* Mont-St-Michel (50). B. Kaufmann/MICHELIN
Horizontal photo: Cows grazing under an apple tree, Auge (14). G. Targat/MICHELIN

PAYS-DE-LA-LOIRE : *Vertical photo:* Meule port, Island of Yeu (85). M. Thiery/MICHELIN
Horizontal photo: Harvesting salt, Noirmoutier (85). M. Thiery/MICHELIN

PICARDY : *Horizontal photo:* Marquenterre Nature Reserve (80). S. Sauvignier/MICHELIN

POITOU-CHARENTES : *Vertical photo:* Hollyhocks, Island of Aix (17). M. Thiery/MICHELIN
Horizontal photo: Arçais port, Marais poitevin (79). D. Mar/MICHELIN

PROVENCE-ALPS AND FRENCH RIVIERA : *Horizontal photo:* Calanque, Sormiou (13). G. Magnin/MICHELIN

RHÔNE-ALPES : *Horizontal photo:* Gorges of the Ardèche, Pont d'Arc (07). J. Damase/MICHELIN

Manufacture française de pneumatiques Michelin
Société en commandite par actions au capital de 304 000 000 EUR
Place des Carmes-Déchaux, 63 Clermont-Ferrand (France) - R.C.S. Clermont-Fd B 855 200 507
Michelin et Cie, Propriétaires-Editeurs, 2003 - Dépôt légal Février 2003 – ISBN 2-06-710004-1
No part of this publication may be reproduced in any form without the prior permission of the publisher
Printed in France 01-2003/1.1

Typesetting : Maury Malesherbes (France)
Printing and binding : Aubin, Ligugé (France)

Layout : Studio Maogani
4, rue du Fer à Moulin, 75005 Paris - Tel : 01 47 07 00 06

Photography : Stéphane Sauvignier/MICHELIN : Regional introductions

Photographs of hotels and maisons d'hôte :
Project manager – Production photos Alain LEPRINCE
Agence ACSI – A CHACUN SON IMAGE
2, rue Aristide Maillol, 75015 Paris - Tel. : 01 43 27 95 55
Photo credits : Philippe GUERSAN, Lawrence BANAHAN, Romain AIX, Annick MEGRET

YOUR OPINION MATTERS!

To help us constantly improve this guide, please fill in this questionnaire and return to:

**Michelin Travel Publications – Hannay House 39 Clarendon Road
WATFORD Herts WD17 1JA – U.K.**

> **1- Have you ever bought other Michelin guides?**

Yes .... ❏   No .... ❏

If yes, which one(s)?

Red Guide (hotels and restaurants) .... ❏

Green Guide (tourism) .... ❏

Other (please specify) .... ❏

> **2- Did you buy this guide:**

For holidays .... ❏

For short breaks or weekends .... ❏

For business purposes .... ❏

As a gift .... ❏

> **3- Will you be travelling:**

In a couple ... ❏   With family .... ❏

Alone .... ❏   With friends ... ❏

Other .... ❏

> **4- You are a:**

Man .... ❏   Woman .... ❏

< 25 years old .... ❏   25 – 34 years old .. ❏

35 – 50 years old .. ❏   > 50 years old ..... ❏

Profession: ....

> **5-How would you rate the following aspects of the guide?**

1 = Very good   *2* = Good   *3* = Acceptable   *4* = Poor   *5* = Very poor

	1	2	3	4	5
Selection of establishments ...	❏	❏	❏	❏	❏
Number of establishments	❏	❏	❏	❏	❏
Hotel/Maison d'hôte mix	❏	❏	❏	❏	❏
Prices of rooms	❏	❏	❏	❏	❏
Practical Information (prices, etc.)	❏	❏	❏	❏	❏
Description of the establishment	❏	❏	❏	❏	❏
Photos	❏	❏	❏	❏	❏
General presentation	❏	❏	❏	❏	❏
Distribution of establishments across France ..	❏	❏	❏	❏	❏
Themed indexes	❏	❏	❏	❏	❏
Cover	❏	❏	❏	❏	❏
Other (please specify)	❏	❏	❏	❏	❏

> **6-Please rate the guide out of 20:**   / 20

> **7- Which aspects could we improve?**

....
....
....
....
....
....
....
....
....
....
....
....
....
....
....
....
....

YOUR OPINION MATTERS!

> **8**-Was there an establishment you particularly liked or a choice you didn't agree with? Perhaps you have a favourite address of your own that you would like to tell us about? Please send us your remarks and suggestions: